D0622503

Business and Government in Canada

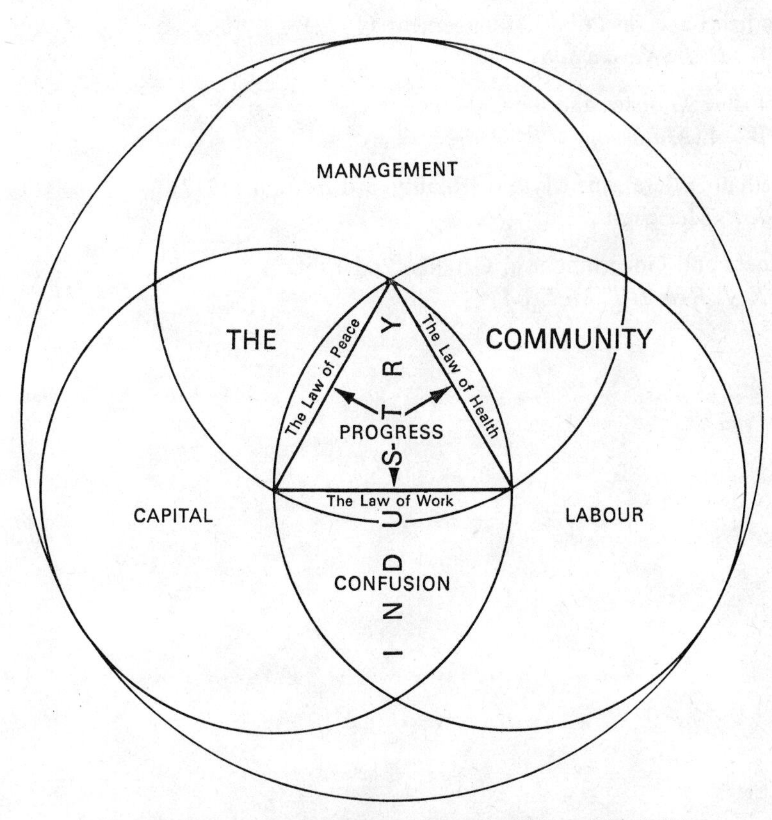

Mackenzie King, W. L., *Industry and Humanity* (First published 1918. New edition reprinted by the University of Toronto Press, 1973.), p. 343. Reproduced by permission of the University of Toronto Press, © University of Toronto Press, 1973.

Methuen: Canadian Politics and Government

The Provincial Political Systems: Comparative Essays
D. Bellamy J. H. Pammett, D. C. Rowat

Politics and Government of Urban Canada: Selected Readings, 3rd Edition
L. D. Feldman, M. D. Goldrick

Public Administration in Canada: Selected Readings, 3rd Edition (1977)
W. D. K. Kernaghan

Canadian Cases in Public Management (1977)
W. D. K. Kernaghan

The Prime Minister and the Cabinet
W. A. Matheson

Canadian Federalism: Myth or Reality, 3rd Edition (1977)
J. P. Meekison

Business and Government in Canada, 2nd Edition
K. J. Rea, J. T. McLeod

Business and Government in Canada

selected readings

second edition

edited by

K. J. Rea
University of Toronto

and

J. T. McLeod
University of Toronto

Methuen
Toronto • London • Sydney • Wellington

Canadian Cataloguing in Publication Data

Main entry under title:

Business and Government in Canada

ISBN 0-458-91400-2 bd.
ISBN 0-458-91890-3 pa.

1. Industry and state – Canada –
Addresses, essays, lectures.
I. Rea, Kenneth J., 1932-
II. McLeod, John T., 1932-

HD3616.C22B88 1976 322'.3'0971 C76-017021-5

Printed and bound in Canada

1 2 3 4 5 BP 80 79 78 77 76

Table of Contents

Preface

This is a book about capitalism. In most Western nations in the twentieth century, government not only directs the "public" sector but also plays an important and growing role in the "private" sector of the economy. Under contemporary capitalism it is scarcely possible to understand the operation of the economic system if the role of the state as a regulator of industry is ignored.

There may have been a time when it was possible to study "capitalism" as an economic system that had a relatively limited relationship to the state and politics. It was once argued that if the state kept its hands off business activity, all would turn out for the best: productivity and the public welfare would be maximized. But the slogan "That government is best which governs least" has slipped very far from fashion, and it is now clear that completely laissez-faire arrangements do not exist and never have existed in Canada or in any other Western nation. Still, the economic institutions and political ideology that we call "capitalistic" have by no means passed from the contemporary scene.

The expanding role of the state in economic life has shifted our assumptions and altered our practices, but the debate continues as to what are the proper or "best" relationships between business and government. Probably no issue of political life during the past two centuries has sparked more controversy than the relationship of the state to economic affairs. That is the subject of this volume; capitalism is now closely interrelated with the state, and that is where the cut and thrust of public policy is sharpest in political economy of today.

Our interest lies in the role of the state in economic life, but in a special and particular way. We are not primarily concerned with the more orthodox "macro" considerations of monetary and fiscal policies designed to stabilize the business cycle. The focus of this book, while not entirely "micro," is on the particular patterns of state intervention in the private sector; the way in which government influences or determines specific prices and regulates the conduct of many industries.

Students and the general public may be relatively less familiar with the logic underlying the massive and comprehensive collection of policies by which our governments seek to influence the internal operations of our economic system. To what extent and for what reasons do governments deliberately influence the functioning of markets and the behavior of individual producers, consumers, and resource owners?

Strangely enough, these are questions that have been neglected by Canadian social scientists. Our economists have tended to concentrate on evaluating specific policies in the light of highly abstract theoretical models of doubtful relevance, while our political scientists are increasingly preoccupied with "value free" behavioral and quantitative studies. The two academic disciplines have drifted apart and left the central question of what kind of system we have evolved almost untended. That central question, we believe, is precisely the point at which the two disciplines intersect and should be most practically and socially useful. That central question is the focus of this book.

It is undeniably true that the economic system we call capitalism has been altered almost beyond recognition in recent decades. As state regulation of industry steadily advanced in the Western world, the free enterprise system has been transformed into a "welfare state" in which governments broadly assume that they know not only what is "best" for the economy but what is "best" for business. At present in Canada it is impossible to discover a single industry that has not come under deliberate government regulation, either directly or indirectly.

And yet most of us continue to discuss the system in terms of "theory of capitalism," a theory with both economic and political implications. Contemporary society still recognizes and pays lip service to this theory. It is a powerful and often persuasive set of interrelated principles by which advocates of capitalism explain and interpret the operation of a market society as it is, or ought to be. Although the theory of capitalism for the most part may be neglected in practice, the capitalist ideology abides and is constantly invoked by politicians as well as businessmen. It remains an important part of the intellectual underpinning of the Western world. Emphatically there is a general philosophy of capitalism.

But that philosophy has undergone substantial modification in the twentieth century. It has been altered and adapted into the more nebulous and inadequately articulated concept of "collectivism." The capitalist beliefs remain; but the invisible hand of the market society has become the visible hand of state regulation.

The theory of capitalism becomes very much confused by the assumption introduced by some of its defenders that society is "naturally" organized on the basis of private property and competitive markets. They fail to see that, far from being "natural," capitalism may just as reasonably be regarded as an intellectual construct and an artificial order invented to explain the emerging industrial society of the nineteenth century. In other words, capitalism is more of a theory than it is a fact, more of a myth than a reality. It is extremely difficult, if not impossible, to make the realities of the market conform to the theory of the competitive model, even when the state with all its power strives deliberately to do so.

Moreover, when we look at the actual policies pursued by the state in Western nations, we find in many segments of the economy that the policies do not reflect much or any of the orthodox capitalist theory. As we will show in Section 3, public policy in Canada, as in more Western countries, is not even strongly committed to the maintenance of competition, the basic self-regulatory aspect of commercial enterprise under the capitalist theory.

How is it possible to reconcile the conflict between theory and practice, and the lofty generalizations of Sections 1 and 4 with the somewhat more pedestrian descriptive material in Sections 2 and 3? The actual practice of today's capitalism is difficult to explain in abstract theoretical terms, and still more difficult to relate to the body of theory that is supposed to explain how the system works. An orthodox "liberal" reconciliation of our practical policies with our traditional ideology is to say that we depart from the theoretical model of the system in discrete and more or less "knowable" ways, and that our public policies are means merely of offsetting these departures. This view is not so easy to accept after we have examined the vast array of often contradictory policies that the state actually implements. Therefore, we have included a wide selection of descriptive material in Sections 2 and 3 to illustrate the real degrees of divergence between traditional capitalist theory and our present practices.

Although our selections cannot be comprehensive, they may suffice to show how most of these policies have a logic of their own, a logic that bears no relation whatever to the traditional theory of a capitalist market economy. How then are we to understand the nature of our system? Might it be possible to move toward a new political economy that could encompass these disparate elements? It is our impression that the existing system now departs so much from the capitalist norm that we can no longer hope to understand contemporary issues in terms of obsolete ideas, ideas that probably even at their inception were no more than marginally descriptive. Many of the particular public policies now being pursued may be misguided and perverse because politicians, and the public they serve, may not comprehend the consequences of what they are doing.

We are in serious danger of ending up with political policies that make no sense economically and economic policies that make no sense politically—policies which might seriously distort our traditions of individual freedom and liberal democracy.

We hope this volume will not be read merely as one more eclectic anthology, but rather as a book with a thesis. Facts, without a context of ideas, are meaningless. Therefore, although we have tried to assemble a useful collection of information on our theme, our main purpose has been to provoke the reader into asking what it all means. In our erratic world, meanings are less than clear or certain, but we are persuaded that the relations between business and government in Canada have been seriously misunderstood. We believe, as Section 4 will illustrate, that this country is drifting toward a particular kind of relationship between business and government which may have serious repercussions for our whole political system, repercussions which may pose a growing threat to liberty.

Section 1

Canadian Business — The Political Context

Introduction

Capitalism is a very tricky word. Certainly it is one of the most controversial and elusive terms in political economy. A capitalist or "individual enterprise" system of economic relations emerged gradually in Western Europe as medieval forms of economic organization faded away. In 1776, Adam Smith coined the phrase the "invisible hand" to describe the system of individual initiative that he advocated and that we have come to know as free enterprise. The word capitalism did not come into widespread common usage until the end of the nineteenth century, and people have been arguing about its meaning and virtues ever since.

In large measure, the history of the last two or three centuries is the history of capitalism. There is, however, no single time or place in history to which we can point and say, "that was when pure capitalism flourished," or "that was when capitalism reached its peak." The phenomenon known as capitalism has undergone constant change, and it continues to evolve today in response to changing social circumstances. The nature and direction of its change in the future can only be guessed at. What we must first concern ourselves with is a definition of capitalism so that we may at least be clear on our terminology before we grapple with the content of the subject.

There are almost as many definitions of capitalism as there are writers on the subject. Usually, capitalism is defined in some broad way as an economic institution characterized by private ownership and private property, the profit motive, consumer sovereignty or consumer choice, competition, and a market system in which prices allocate economic resources. The capitalist ideology maintains that these characteristics of the 'free enterprise" system are good and desirable.

Not everyone would agree with so simple and general a definition of capitalism, and it is easy to raise objections to it. Many of these characteristics of capitalism may be found in other economic systems. For example, in the medieval economy and in the ancient slave economies of classical Greece and the Roman Empire, many merchants and traders sought profits, but we do not call those economic systems capitalistic. Similarly, it can be argued that not all capitalist corporations seek to maximize profit: they seek instead to achieve relatively modest and stable returns on investment and aim at maximizing control of a market. At least some degree of consumer sovereignty or consumer choice exists in both socialist and communist economies. Then too, contemporary writers such as J. K. Galbraith have suggested that the manipulation of the consumer by advertising techniques severely limits consumer sovereignty under capitalism. Moreover, many kinds of economic competition existed in various precapitalist economies, and certain forms of competition may be found between state-owned enterprises in communist countries. Furthermore, both communist and socialist countries often use a system of market prices to measure efficiency and allocate resources; markets are not found exclusively in capitalist countries.

Because these characteristics of capitalism may also be found in other economic systems, we are driven back to the essence or basis of contemporary capitalism in the first characteristic that was mentioned in our definition: private ownership and private property. Thus it cannot be too strongly emphasized that the core of the system and the fundamental characteristic of twentieth century capitalism is private economic decision-making, private ownership, and private property.

The capitalist insistence upon private ownership of the means of production is based upon two principal considerations. First, because ownership of productive property involves power over the lives of other individuals, it is preferable that such power be diffused among as many property owners as possible rather than being held by any one owner or institution such as the state. Second, it is argued that economic innovation and technological progress will be facilitated when each individual minds his own business and strives to increase his own profit, and has a profound personal incentive to do so. Many people believe, or assume, that man's desire to acquire, protect and expand his property is "natural" or "instinctive," and that man is both happier and more productive when he possesses property of his own.

But there exists an extremely wide variety of arguments in support of the capitalist ideology. Innumerable writers have extolled the virtues of capitalism and presented a wide range of arguments urging the superiority of capitalism to any alternative economic system. The best known advocacy of free enterprise, and a major landmark in economic literature, is Adam Smith's *The Wealth of Nations*. Since the publication of that classic work, the capitalist ideology has spread, flourished and become one of the most astonishingly successful ideologies ever known to man. As many observers have remarked, however, it is surprising that, since 1776, there has been no book published in defence of capitalism that has been universally acknowledged as "great" or regarded as "basic" to an understanding of the system. In modern times the capitalist ideology has penetrated Western society as rapidly and persuasively as any other social doctrine, but there is no one particular apology for or interpretation of capitalism that has captured the popular imagination. Fascism has its *Mein Kampf*; communism has its *Manifesto* and *Das Kapital*. To what single volume can we point as providing the core of capitalist doctrine?

If no one such sovereign volume exists, advocates of capitalism can at least point to the whole body of normative theory in contemporary economics, plus the long tradition of "liberal" political philosophy from Hobbes and John Locke to John Stuart Mill and beyond. This state of affairs makes the case for capitalism extensive and sophisticated, but it does not simplify our task of distilling the arguments in favour of the free enterprise system. Still, we must make the attempt, even at considerable risk of oversimplification.

The ideology of capitalism proceeds from assumptions of individualism and individual enterprise. Both classical and neoclassical economics, the familiar tools which we use for the explanation, analysis or apologia of the capitalist system, are rooted in assumptions of individuals competing within the institution of a market. Thus, capitalism reflects or partakes of the liberal paradigm of politics. The liberal paradigm posits that the claims of free individuals take precedence over any other claims and, therefore, the ultimate value for liberalism is the individual and his pursuit of self-fulfillment. This is in contrast with both the Marxist paradigm which emphasizes the primacy of class and the class struggle, and the precapitalist "Old Tory" view which stresses the primacy of society over the individual and proceeds from the assumption of an hierarchic, organic community. Essentially, then, liberal capitalism is rooted in assumptions of what C. B. Macpherson has called "possessive individualism." From the fountainhead of individualism, everything else flows.

Essentially the case for capitalism boils down to two main propositions: an economic argument and a political argument. If we take capitalism to be a system principally characterized by private decision-making about privately owned property, the economic argument for it is mainly in terms of incentives. Individuals will act rationally in the market to maximize their own production and profit, and hence to maximize total productivity. Individuals will work harder because they are working for themselves. It is suggested that without private property and the search for profits, the major economic incentive would be removed; individual initiative would be lessened and the processes of invention and the application of inventions would be inhibited, thereby tending to decrease total productivity.

It is argued further that leaving individual entrepreneurs free to compete in a market will result automatically in an optimum allocation of resources, thereby maximizing consumer satisfaction or total economic "welfare." This point is fundamental to the thesis advanced by most defenders of capitalism, but it need not be laboured here because it is an implicit or explicit assumption that pervades many of the readings in Section 1.

The main political argument for capitalism is that it provides a firmer basis for individual liberty and individual freedom than any other system. Historically, democracy and individual liberty have flourished side by side with the rise of capitalism. Private property is regarded not only as the basis of capitalism but also as the basis of individual liberty: if an individual has private property, it is more difficult for the state or for society to deprive him of his liberty. Capitalism is said to emphasize both individualism and rationality, and both are extremely important to the maintenance of democracy and of political liberty. Thus the political dimension of capitalism is extremely important. Democracy and capitalism are held to be mutually reinforcing.

On the other hand, it is obvious that capitalism does not *guarantee* liberty. In many countries today, private property and capitalism go hand in hand with fascism, authoritarianism or dictatorship. Capitalism and private property are to be found, for example, in Spain, and in many countries of South America that live under systems of political dictatorship. Indeed, Hitler's Germany and Mussolini's Italy were no strangers to capitalism and private property. Similarly, a high degree of both consumer choice and political freedom are to be found in socialist countries such as Britain and Sweden. Capitalism and democracy may be interrelated, but they are by no means synonymous or identical. Capitalism is an economic institution, whereas democracy is a political institution. In the Western world, both are liberal because they stress individualism, but the one does not necessarily depend upon, or preclude, the other. It is possible to point to nations and periods of history in which we find capitalism without political liberty, and political liberty without capitalism. We will return to this issue in Section 4, where it will be suggested that trends hostile to liberal democracy may already be present in Canada, even though no overt attack on private property is evident.

Serious students of capitalism will want to read Adam Smith's *The Wealth of Nations*; our present volume is confined to Canadian sources which are relatively contemporary. The case for capitalism is put effectively in Readings 1 and 2 taken from publications of the Canadian Chamber of Commerce, plus Readings 3 and 4 selected from a recent booklet issued by the Investors Syndicate. These selections emphasize the importance of individual initiative, the profit motive, and free enterprise untrammelled by state intervention. For comparative purposes, students should consult the more elaborate arguments for capitalist enterprise to be found in American literature such as E. V. Rostow's *Planning for Freedom* (1959), Chapter 3 and Milton Friedman's *Capitalism and Freedom* (1962), particularly Chapter 2. Students desirous of amplifying their knowledge of liberal-capitalism will also consult F. von Hayek's *Road to Serfdom* (1944) and his more challenging *The Constitution of Liberty* (1960). Hayek, an Austrian economist of the Chicago school, argues that the substitution of the state for the free market in the allocation of resources infringes not only upon efficiency and individual freedom, but also upon the rule of law.

A book which has influenced many Canadian scholars is Karl Polanyi's *The Great Transformation* (1944). In a work which many economists regard as seminal, Polanyi deals with the broad historical sweep of the rise of capitalism. He argues that until the nineteenth century, all economies were contained within and shaped by the societies in which they existed. He contends that nineteenth century laissez-faire in Britain was a short-lived and "utopian" departure from the historical norm of communal control of the economy and, thus, was a brief historical aberration. Polanyi agrees with Marx that capitalist markets were extraordinarily efficient and raised standards of living, but he also contends that free markets were socially disruptive, and that markets destroy "community" as individualism becomes dominant.

How competitive have individualist entrepreneurs been in Canada? The considerable disinclination of Canadian businessmen to engage in free competition is reflected in two recent works on business history that students will find useful: *The History of Canadian Business, 1867-1914* (two volumes, 1975) by Tom Naylor, and *A Living Profit* (1973) by Michael Bliss. If market competition is a norm or necessity of capitalism, these two authors provide abundant evidence that Canadian capitalists have been wary at best in their practice of competition.

In fact, Professor Alexander Brady, in Reading 5, suggests that market competition is not at all the most prevalent or common structure of economic activity in this country, and that the state has traditionally played a strong, if not dominant, role in Canadian economic activity. In Brady's view our economy has always been as much "collective" as purely capitalist. He insists that the Canadian business environment has always been characterized by the strong presence of the state as a director of, and a major participant in, our economic development. The "staples approach" of Harold Innis always emphasized the creative effects of the state in fostering the growth of Canada's economy, an economy which Brady styles "collectivist." This collectivism is not peculiar to Canada, but is reflected in the economic experience of Britain and to some extent the United States as well.

Certainly one of the most striking general characteristics of Western civilization in the twentieth century has been the rise of the welfare state, or Big Government. In almost all industrialized countries in this century there has been a rapid expansion in the functions of the state in economic life and a shift from the passive or "negative" state toward the "positive" state. What has emerged in this century is a general acceptance of the view that the government should play an active role in regulating the capitalist economy. This view has eroded and substantially altered the orthodox concept of laissez-faire.

Even in Britain in the middle of the nineteenth century, where doctrines of laissez-faire found most favour, some considerable degree of government intervention in the market always existed. As early as the 1820s, laws were passed in Britain to regulate the labour market and control the number of hours worked by women and children in mines and factories. By the middle of the nineteenth century, Britain and many other countries had passed innumerable acts to limit child labour, regulate conditions of work and provide for one day's rest in seven. Eventually, after much conflict and even bloodshed, legislation was passed to legalize the formation of unions, collective bargaining and the right to strike.

As collectivism spread, the movement away from laissez-faire and the expansion of government economic regulation took many forms. Many countries maintained or raised tariff barriers and experimented with public subsidies to particular industries. The state took an active role in establishing public education throughout most of the Western world. Public health acts and pure-food and drug acts were passed in most jurisdictions. Britain was only one of several nations to experiment with public ownership in such public utilities as gas, electric power and urban transportation facilities. Railroads, for example, came under public ownership in Australia by the end of the nineteenth century; in Canada the Canadian National Railway was established as a crown corporation under public ownership by a Conservative government in 1917. Similarly, it was a Conservative government in the Province of Ontario that brought hydroelectric facilities under public ownership as early as 1906. In the twentieth century, most industrialized Western countries implemented various welfare schemes and social insurance plans. Canada, for example, introduced old-age pensions in 1927, unemployment insurance in 1940, family allowances in 1944 and health insurance or "medicare" in 1968.

Further examples of such collectivistic interventions in the market could be piled up almost endlessly, but the important point to be emphasized here is that all of these developments were particular rather than general. They involved no widespread or fundamental rejection of capitalism; instead, they were qualifications or adaptations of the market economy. The capitalist system based upon private property continued to flourish, but state intervention in the economy or state regulation of business became increasingly accepted as "normal." Many of these collectivistic acts, or techniques, were introduced by liberal or conservative governments of a procapitalist 'stripe' in an attempt to improve upon, and compensate for, some of the weaknesses and shortcomings of the unregulated market. It cannot be overemphasized that these actions were mainly pragmatic and *ad hoc*. Such government intervention was not usually based upon any particular doctrine or ideology. Certainly it did not represent any deliberate attempt to abolish the capitalist system. The movement toward collectivism was piecemeal, slow and gradual. It reflected empirical and generally nondoctrinaire attempts by governments to respond to particular and practical problems with particular and practical solutions involving state intervention. For the most part, the growth of collectivism has been pragmatic rather than ideological.

Thus, collectivism should be regarded as a general retreat from the doctrine of laissez-faire. In most countries, collectivism has been marked by a high degree of government intervention in the capitalist market without destroying private property or the market mechanism. Collectivism is a somewhat vague term generally used in contrast to the extreme individualism of nineteenth century laissez-faire doctrines. It is, broadly, a term for a trend in social and political development and a program for economic reform to supplement or offset the excesses and shortcomings of the market. The general goal of collectivism is the "welfare" of society and the greatest happiness for the greatest number, a familiar Benthamite or Utilitarian notion. Collectivism involves deliberate and positive action by the state for the purpose of furthering certain broad objectives of social welfare, particularly the social welfare of the working poor rather than the capitalist middle class.

In his chapter on "Empirical Collectivism" in *Recent Political Thought*, F. W. Coker observes that collectivists usually aim at the reform and improvement of the capitalist system, although they reject the extreme dogmas of both the socialists and the advocates of extreme laissez-faire. Coker says that the collectivist seeks to understand the economic interdependence of all members of society and to find the proper adjustment of their economic and political relations to one another through the active use of the mechanism of the state. He suggests that democratic collectivists typically share the following views on certain basic social issues. *On property*: the collectivist believes that neither private ownership nor public ownership should become a fetish. The collectivist believes in general that private ownership is to be preferred, but that there may be cogent arguments for public ownership of certain productive resources, particularly when monopolies or public utilities are involved. *On labour legislation*: he believes that state legislation is necessary and desirable to protect the interests of the workers in the industrial system through such means as minimum wage legislation and laws relating to the conditions of work. *On regulation of prices*: he takes the view that the state must intervene to regulate and set limits to profits and prices in certain industries that may be regarded as public utilities, such as electric power and transportation. *On taxation*: the collectivist tends to believe that state fiscal powers should be used to redistribute income in the interests of social justice, generally taxing the rich more heavily than the poor, and providing for certain welfare payments from the public treasury to the socially disadvantaged. *On land and natural resources*: he believes that there is a legitimate role for the state to play in conservation policy, policies to assist farmers, provision of low rental or public housing, and the provision of parks and public recreational facilities.

If Bentham was the nineteenth century source of most collectivist thought, a major wellspring of mid-twentieth century collectivist thinking has been John Maynard Keynes. Certainly Keynes was the most influential English-speaking economist of this century and, equally certainly, he was no socialist; yet his ideas have been an enormous force in the expansion of state economic activity and the reform of the market economy. Although Keynesian and post-Keynesian monetary and fiscal policy lie beyond the scope of these readings, it would be difficult to exaggerate the degree to which his ideas have permeated Western economic and political thought in recent decades. In an essay titled "The End of Laissez-Faire," written in 1926, Keynes laid bare the political assumptions that underlie his economic analysis of capitalism's ills, stated fully ten years later in his book *The General Theory*. He was particularly insistent that many of the old assumptions imbedded in traditional economic thinking had to be swept away.

> Let us clear from the ground the metaphysical or general principles upon which, from time to time, *laissez-faire* has been founded. It is *not* true that individuals possess a prescriptive "natural liberty" in their economic activities. There is *no* "compact" conferring perpetual rights on those who Have or on those who Acquire. The world is *not* so governed from above that private and social interest always coincide. It is *not* so managed here below that in practice they coincide. It is *not* a correct deduction from the Principles of Economics that enlightened self-interest always operates in the public interest. Nor is it true that self-interest generally *is* enlightened; more often individuals acting separately to promote their own ends are too ignorant or too weak to attain even these. Experience does *not* show that individuals, when they make up a social unit, are always less clear sighted than when they act separately.

This statement illustrates the early rejection of purely market assumptions by many moderate liberals who wanted to reform capitalism, not to abolish it. In a frequently quoted paragraph from that same esssay of 1926, Keynes argued for an empirical redefinition of the functions of government and an expanded economic role for the state.

> We cannot, therefore, settle on abstract grounds, but must handle on its merits and in detail, what Burke termed "one of the finest problems of legislation," namely, to determine what the State ought to take upon itself to direct by the public wisdom, and what it ought to leave with as little interference as possible, to individual exertion. We have to discriminate between what Bentham, in his forgotten but useful nomenclature, used to term *Agenda* and *Non-Agenda*, and to do this without Bentham's prior presumption that interference is, at the same time, "generally needless and generally pernicious." Perhaps the chief task of economists at this hour is to distinguish afresh the *Agenda* of Government from the *Non-Agenda*; and the companion task of Politics is to devise forms which shall be capable of accomplishing the *Agenda*.

The seed of Keynesian doctrine fell on very fertile soil in Canada because we had never known a period of total laissez-faire in this country, and because our state had always assumed a very considerable Agenda since the days of Sir John A. Macdonald's national policy. Ours was always a peculiarly state-directed and state-created economy in which the role of private enterprise was in large measure sheltered under the umbrella of government initiatives. This truism will be apparent to any reader of Harold Innis and is underlined by John Hutcheson in Reading 6. Hutcheson argues from a Marxist perspective that the role of the Canadian state has always been to augment the power of the owning classes and to serve the interests of private property, even if this meant a sellout to foreign (American) capitalist interests. Students who wish to pursue this line of inquiry should read Robert Laxer, ed., [*Canada*], *Ltd.* (1973) and Gary Teeple, ed., *Capitalism and the National*

Question in Canada (1972), particularly the articles by Tom Naylor.

The strong role of the state in Canadian economic development is also reflected in two recent works by non-Marxist writers which deserve the reader's attention, but which space does not permit us to reprint here. Herschel Hardin's book, *A Nation Unaware* (1974), puts the case that our economic experience reveals a national penchant for public enterprise rather than private enterprise. American-style individualist capitalism, he argues, has never been the backbone of our economy. "The American ideology-in-Canada, with all its phantasmagoric potency, stands Canadian reality on its head." Similarly, D. V. Smiley's admirably synoptic article, "Canada and the Quest for a National Policy" (*Canadian Journal of Political Science*, March, 1975), examines our national policies old and new as foils or counterpoints to economic liberalism. The clear implication is that the state has played and must still play a major creative role for our national economy to persist in juxtaposition to the American giant.

R. S. Ritchie, who has served as the Research Director of the Conservative Party of Canada, reveals in Reading 7 how businessmen have responded to social and political pressures and have become more socially aware or socially responsible in the conduct of commercial enterprise. It is evident that the "social responsibility" of businessmen looms more and more important in the attitudes (if not always the behaviour) of contemporary entrepreneurs. Ritchie shows how Canadian capitalists remain mindful of public reactions to commerce and to the interrelations of companies and the community. Ritchie demonstrates that the policies and determinations of government and the society influence business decision-making in various important ways.

The three selections that follow elaborate this theme and illustrate the rather surprising degree of agreement among Canada's three main political parties on the amount of state intervention that is necessary under a "mixed" economy. A Liberal view is put by Senator Maurice Lamontagne, a former cabinet minister and an influential Liberal brain-truster. The late George Hogan, a former secretary and national vice president of the Progressive Conservative Association of Canada, urges that public and private enterprise must be complementary, and the former Premier of Saskatchewan and NDP leader, T. C. Douglas, argues for an expanded role for government in the marketplace. There are differences between these three Canadian party spokesmen, but none suggests that the role of the state in the economy is, or should be, unimportant. In fact, these three readings underline the point that all major political parties in Canada recognize (or assume) the primacy of the state over individual commercial enterprise. It is noteworthy that no major political party in Canada insists upon pure free enterprise or laissez-faire as a desirable goal or norm of the Canadian economy. All parties seem to assume that ours is a highly political economy, and that the state has a major role to play in directing economic activity.

The reaction of many businessmen is illustrated in Reading 11 by D. R. Huggett. It is apparent that many Canadian capitalists see themselves on the defensive against the onslaught of government intervention. Huggett recognizes the "role of the state" in the modern economy but urges consideration of the needs of business, which "makes all possible" in the contemporary mixed economy. Without freedom for commercial initiatives, he argues, the heavy-handed state may slay the goose that lays the essential golden egg.

Many of the readings in this Section might well dispose the reader to the view that Canadian individualist entrepreneurs are less ruggedly capitalist, or independent of government, than is sometimes supposed. Business and government have been more interrelated than much contemporary rhetoric would lead us to assume. Public policy has always been important in the determination of private decision-making concerning the allocation of our economic resources. The liberal-capitalist model of the market which we have borrowed from our American neighbours may not be appropriate to Canadian circumstances because our economy has been conditioned by the needs of our nation, or shaped by the interrelatedness of business and government in the peculiar environment of our northern society. Our governments have always been concerned with the promotion of business enterprise, as we will demonstrate in Section 2, but they have also been concerned with the shaping and regulation of that type of enterprise, as we will describe in Section 3. Section 4 of this book will focus on the unique Canadian response, different from that of the United States, to the problems of capitalism in the environment of a northern hinterland.

The Canadian business environment has never been identical to that of the United States. The roots of collectivism and the interrelationships of government and business go much deeper on this part of the continent than they do to the south. Before Canadians can achieve a proper perspective on their own economic history and development, they will have to come to grips with the fact that our economy is not a replica of the British, or of the American economies, but is a reflection of our needs, our geography, our cultural heritage and our uniqueness in North America. The story of business and government in Canada is a complex one, reflecting the distinctive Canadian environment, but it does not reflect nineteenth century British norms of laissez-faire or American norms of the relative separation of the state and commerce. In Canada, the history of the state and economic life are inextricably interwoven and inseparable. Sections 2 and 3 of this book will illustrate that interrelatedness.

1 Freedom in Canada *

Canadian Chamber of Commerce

The Canadian Chamber of Commerce as a movement believes in and supports the economic system of private competitive enterprise based on individual freedom of choice and personal initiative and responsibility. We also believe that one of the basic aims of public policy should be the maintenance of personal freedom and an atmosphere in which individuals are free to make their own choice as to how or when they will spend their incomes. These individual choices, we believe, collectively provide the great stimulating and controlling force governing the provision of goods and services.

Canada can be great and prosperous only if all individuals have the incentive of adequate reward for risk, energy, initiative and enterprise, along with the right to enjoy the fruits thereof.

We recognize the responsibility of society to help those individuals incapable of providing for themselves, but do not believe that it is the business of the State to provide those services which the individual can supply for himself. Social security must not become an end in itself and Canadians must beware of looking to the State to provide security to such an extent that the individual loses incentive to provide for himself.

If ever business, or the people in general, come to believe that they can turn to government in every difficulty, the springs of initiative and self-reliance will run dry. We put our faith in the responsibility and the resourcefulness of individuals operating under the private competitive enterprise system, believing that these factors will ensure the highest possible standard of living for the whole Canadian people. . . .

In conclusion our feelings on the subject of freedom were well expressed by a Standing Committee on Finance of the Senate:[1]

> Above all, it is important to keep alive in the minds of the people of the nation an understanding of what freedom means. People may clamour for security—many are doing that today—but it should never be forgotten that if personal freedom is sacrificed for personal security provided by Governments, the individual can have no guarantee that in the end he will have either freedom or security.

Notes

*Canadian Chamber of Commerce, *Submission to the Royal Commission on Health Services* (March, 1962), pp. 27-28 (reproduced by permission).

[1]*Report of the Proceedings of the Standing Committee on Finance of the Senate, No. 5, Thursday, June 16, 1955.*

2 Competitive Enterprise: Canada's Economic System *

Canadian Chamber of Commerce

Canada's economic system is based upon competitive enterprise. This system, which permits maximum individual freedom, encourages the exercise of individual initiative, broad dispersal of decision making, and the most economic allocation of human and material resources. It promotes dynamic economic growth and a steady rise in living standards. One of the major roles of government in such a system is to maintain an equitable and favourable climate for private action.

The operation in Canada of the competitive market economy, motivated by opportunities of profit and the dangers of loss, is responsible in large measure for the improvements in social and living standards which have been achieved over the years. The competitive enterprise system develops maximum managerial capabilities, technical knowledge, operating skills and competitive attitudes required for sound growth. The profit motive exercises a determining influence upon the use of resources, the level of savings, the volume of investment, and it compels private enterprise to operate efficiently.

The role of government is: (a) to establish, promote and enforce the rule of law in all relations between individuals and between groups in the economy including the government; (b) to foster an equitable and favourable climate for the private sector, enabling it to utilize its resources, both human and material, with the utmost efficiency; the greater the efficiency in this respect, the better able is this sector of the economy to contribute to the improvement of the nation's social environment; and (c) to give appropriate encouragement and financial support to the provision of social capital, consistent with the growth of the economy.

Sustainable social betterment depends on healthy competitive enterprise. The responsibility of business includes proposing and promoting sound solutions to social and public problems.

Competitive markets function best when the public is well informed and understands the principles of our economic system. To this end, the Chamber is committed to further the public understanding of our economic system and the essential role played by the profit motive.

The Annual Reviews of the Economic Council of Canada have depicted great potential for long term economic growth in Canada. If Canada is to realize this potential, however, and attain the goals outlined by the Council, rational and consistent policies must be developed and followed by business and by government at all levels. Sustained, well balanced economic growth cannot be based on a succession of opportunistic decisions as the needed policies, for the most part, can be effective only in the longer term, particularly where they are concerned with such basic questions as education and training, research and patterns of investment and trade.

As the Council points out, the attainment of maximum growth for the future rests on sound national economic and industrial policies, as well as on the efforts of individual businessmen. Thus, the goals, and the means of reaching them, are a matter of prime concern to all Canadians.

Recommendations:

1. that each Canadian business carefully examine the Goals for 1970 suggested by the Economic Council of Canada, translate them into individual objectives and then enlist its resources, human and material, to attain these objectives.

2. that business promote a greater appreciation and understanding of our economic system, and take advantage of every opportunity to bring to Canadians, and particularly employees, the story of the role of business in the economy, and to speak out on related matters of public interest.

3. that community and provincial Chambers of Commerce and Boards of Trade urge local and provincial authorities to emphasize teaching in the schools the principles of democracy, of our economic system, and of freedom of the individual, and that maintaining these heritages depends on each individual's acceptance of social and civic responsibility.

4. that member Boards and Chambers establish active Public Affairs Committees with a view to developing at the community level programs of study and action with respect to community, provincial and national problems.

5. that member Boards and Chambers place emphasis on liaison with educational authorities and teachers and that organized efforts be encouraged to assist young Canadians to gain a better understanding of economics and how our competitive enterprise system operates, to the end that students may better understand the economic as well as the cultural and political principles of freedom.

6. that the Federal Government, in consultation with other levels of government and various segments of the economy, concern itself with fostering an economic climate conducive to optimum economic growth.

7. that government confine its activities to areas which are not being or cannot be served adequately by private enterprise.

Notes

*Canadian Chamber of Commerce, *1967-68 Statement of Policy* (Montreal, 1968), pp. 12-14 (reproduced by permission).

3 Attacks on Business and the Response *

Investors Syndicate

In the mid-1970s thoughtful Canadians began to worry. Complaints and accusations about business and corporations were seeping through the community. Some were valid; many were not. While recognizing that skepticism is valuable in any free society, these thinking Canadians worried that unreasonable criticism, unanswered complaints, might blind many—especially the young—to the real strengths and values of our competitive system.

Winnipeg businessman Robert Jones, president of The Investors Group, decided to do something about it. He cancelled a week of appointments, bought a sheaf of airline tickets, and set out to visit the chief executives of a dozen major corporations, inviting and challenging them to help answer the criticisms.

Nine agreed to try. They hired freelance writer Dean Walker to confront them with North Americans' main concerns about business, as revealed by research, then sponsored newspaper advertisements to publish their responses.

In the first interview, Walker asked Bob Jones why he bothered to set all this in motion.

We were getting concerned about the outlook for the private enterprise system.

Through Investors' companies, more than half a million Canadians have a direct stake in that system. On their behalf, as well as our own, it seemed time to speak up.

Another aspect, too, is *very* important. As we looked ahead to the potential for growth, and the need for growth in Canada, we were disturbed that it will not be realized if the private sector is enfeebled by attacks. If corporations are discouraged from making the very large capital investments required to assure Canada's economic growth, the future of smaller enterprises and, indeed, the prosperity of a great majority of Canadians will be in question.

Many businessmen told me they were especially worried about attacks on profits and the profit motive. It seemed to them that people somehow fail to understand what profits are and what they do. Again, it seemed time to speak up.

Three main groups have been complaining about business: intellectuals and academics; activists and union leaders; and governments. They're concerned, involved people and I don't question their motives nor their right to be heard. There always have been some citizens who distrust private enterprise and that's ok; their criticisms and suspicions help keep us all on our toes. But suddenly, because of inflation, they were getting more support than usual. A disturbing amount of support.

During periods of inflation, everybody looks for a scapegoat. This time, many had settled on business and profits.

On the surface, they have a point. They see a rise in prices and then newspaper reports of higher profits, and they think they see a cause and effect. But it's a misunderstanding.

Where do these attacks occur?
In the news media. And through the political system.

Amongst politicians, now it's not only the New Democrats who are attacking business. Representatives of the other parties are doing it, too.

It's understandable. But it's misguided. And it's happening because many politicians and civil servants, like so many of us, don't fully understand the workings of our economic system. I think it is unfortunate today that too many politicians neglect any leadership role and see their prime responsibility as being to respond to what they presume to be public opinion. Often, when you suggest solutions to economic problems to them, you run into the stone-wall statement, "That's not politically acceptable." And that's what indicated to me that, if business is now going to speak up, our first communications target must be the people themselves. The politicians are responsible—and responsive—to the public.

I soon learned something else. Like politicians, very few businessmen, including me, really understand the system. Businessmen have been content to go on doing their thing, supplying goods and services, hopefully at a profit, to the general benefit of the community, without really understanding how business fits in with the other institutions of our society.

So a double education job is needed.

You're saying that executives of million-dollar corporations can work successfully within the system without fully understanding how it works!
I now believe that to be true. You have to consider the milieu in which so many businessmen grew up. Most of us are products of the depression, and saw the shortcomings of the private enterprise system then. A critic can still stop us in our tracks by saying, "Do you want to go back to the 1930s? Do you want to go back to having unemployed people on the street? Do you want to throw away the social benefits introduced over the last thirty years?" They imply that somehow you're unconcerned with the well-being of your fellow citizens, and that everything you're doing is selfish. The businessman, exposed to this on all sides, becomes very defensive and often sounds like a terrible reactionary, because usually he doesn't have enough grounding in the theoretical or philosophical justification of the system. Of course, nobody wants to go back to the 1930s. But nor do we want the government interfering at every level of the marketplace.

When I realized our difficulties in saying some of these things, I pulled out textbooks and looked again at why the system operates the way it does. And I found that many attitudes which, on the surface, seem to go against the interests of the average man, are really to his benefit in the long run.

Take the proposal to create a guaranteed annual income. The federal Minister of Health and Welfare justifies it by pointing out that, in the last thirty years, income distribution in this country has not changed—the same shares still go to the people at the top, the middle, and the bottom. They say this unequal distribution is wrong.

Yet, to me, the very success of the system justifies that distribution. Today, people at the base of the pyramid enjoy a much higher standard of living than they did thirty years ago. Their share has not changed, but the pie has grown. Better, I say, to share a bigger pie than to put your efforts into rearranging distribution of a smaller one.

Then the Minister says he will build in *incentives*, so that people will be encouraged to work. They will distinguish between the poor and the working poor. But who are they kidding? Human nature being what it is, some people will respond well to incentives and will better their lot, and others will not. And you'll end up with just the same income distribution as before.

Now, take it one step further. To improve the lot of the people at the base of the pyramid, you have to pay for it from the output of the whole country. You may take away from someone elsewhere on the pyramid. If you reduce the incentive to work of the people who normally create the jobs and boost production, that pie will not continue to grow as fast. In the long run, everyone will be worse off, not better.

It's already happening in some areas. Many doctors and dentists now say to themselves, "I could see 120 patients a week, and earn extra income. But since I keep only 30 or 35 cents of every extra dollar I earn, I might as well cut down on my work load and see only ninety people." A guaranteed annual income could repeat that process further down the scale. Then costs will go up as output goes down.

Only a handful of people publicly attacked businessmen. What do you think the attitude of the rest of us is? Are we suspicious of you? Jealous? Do we hate you?

I think people feel confusion as much as anything. I don't mean that condescendingly, because there's a legitimate reason for the confusion. It is very difficult to look at the problems currently facing the economy and the political system in Canada without looking for a convenient object to blame. It's natural to transfer one's frustration and discomfort about inflation, recession and unemployment to the private sector.

The politician then responds to the trend of public opinion. He says to himself, "Whatever the reason, the public are not very happy with business. I must follow the public trend." And there, the dangers become very great.

It's an over-simplification to imply that, because the people who attack business are a small minority, the problem isn't deep. The problem is extremely serious and, if the trends that have been unleashed in this country are followed for any length of time, they will, in the first analysis, destroy the competitive enterprise system.

You're trying to scare me. Business is invulnerable!
I'm not trying to scare you. The idea that business is invulnerable was, until recently, held by many people in the private sector. When these attacks first became noticeable, five years ago, most businessmen perceived them as transitory. But with inflation, the intensity increased.

A lot of people still think that business is so big, and such an important part of the constituency, that it is invulnerable. They're wrong.

If the attacks continue, will business crumble?
It's possible. Consider this: The basis of capitalism is gathering together the savings of individuals who are prepared to forgo current consumption in order to build production facilities for future increased consumption. To do that, they have to be assured of some future reward for what they give up today.

If business continues to be attacked by activists and undermined by government trends, the rate of return to the individual who is willing to forgo current consumption will become less and less. Eventually his incentive will disappear. Then business will not be able to finance itself, and there will be no capital spending, no growth of productive facilities. But Canada must have that growth for jobs and output. The government will step into the breach and start doing these things. And then, willy nilly, without conscious political choice by the electorate, we will have changed our whole economic system.

Our best warning comes from the United Kingdom. The private sector there has been under terrific pressure from high taxation and wage demands; many businesses cannot maintain their profit margins. The way it works is diabolical. Companies are forced to price themselves out of the market. They run into a cash bind, and then the government says, "We won't give you a cash transfusion unless we get ownership." The state buys the equity, and the company becomes another government-owned socialist enterprise.

Further steps follow. What has become apparent to me lately is the failure of myself, and others, to appreciate the link between the economic system and the social and political systems, our whole way of life. Because when you tear down the business sector, the competitive private enterprise capitalist sector of society, you have to put something else in its place. And what you put there will inevitably infringe on the individual's freedom of choice.

This outcome is vastly more important than what happens to the business community, as such.

Our economic system, with all its faults, all its warts, all its convolutions, remains what it has long been: an effective way of increasing the standard of living of the population as a whole, while maintaining a high degree of individual liberty. Breaking down this system and substituting an inferior one will be very costly to the people in the long run.

Why is the alternative necessarily inferior?
Because it impedes the energies, motivations, desires, and freedoms of the individual. That is the principal reason why state-run economic systems have not been as successful as ours in improving the lot of the population.

Doesn't the citizen have more control as a voter over government than as a shopper over private corporations?
The marketplace has more control over even the largest corporation than voters have over the government. If you don't like your Ford, you can go to General Motors. Ford knows that; therefore it's going to do its damnedest to make sure you're satisfied. On the other hand, a number of provincial governments have entered the automobile insurance field. As a condition of obtaining a license, car owners must be insured under the government plan. If they're unsatisfied with the plan, they have no alternative; freedom of choice is lost.

Couldn't a socialist government combine public ownership and competition by setting up parallel competitive enterprises?
The answer to that is obvious. Look at the record of government endeavors in competition with the private sector. They're always a miserable failure.

Government enterprises cannot compete. Because of their lack of incentives, and because of their unavoidable rigidities, they can only function under monopoly situations.

It sounds as if your aim is to make sure that if changes are going to be made in our basic economic/political system, they will be made by conscious choice by the electorate and not snuck in through the back door?
That is correct. And I hope that many other initiatives will be pursued by other segments of our society, so the electorate can make an intelligent choice.

Notes

*Investors Syndicate (reproduced by permission).

4 The Enterprise System: Best in Many Ways *

Dean Walker

The system has many names. Free enterprise, business, capitalism, competition, private enterprise, responsible enterprise, competitive enterprise. Call it what you will, it's the productive engine of our society, and it's the most effective that man has ever known.

It's strong, tough, resilient, adaptable. But not indestructible.

Attitudes and beliefs that put the system in jeopardy are on the increase in Canada today.

This publication, created by ten men who work at the heart of private enterprise, is presented as counterweight to those growing beliefs. It reminds us all of six special values of The Enterprise System: best in many ways.

Best Because:

1. IT PRODUCES MORE FOR EVERYONE.

The main motive power in the enterprise system is that special human characteristic, the urge to grow, to progress, to get ahead. The system encourages this drive in people by rewarding those who work the hardest, produce most, apply most ingenuity. These unleashed energies then help create wealth, both for the energetic, and for society in general. North America's envied material standard of living is a product of natural resources, capital accumulation, and the release of those energies.

In a competitive, reward-oriented system, different people inevitably reach different levels. Everyone has a chance to win the top prizes—or to miss by a mile. Even for losers, however, there's enough wealth generated that, if the society is run decently, they can be looked after well, too.

A goal of every enlightened society, capitalist or socialist, is to make the poor richer, and there are two basic ways of trying to achieve this—by redistributing existing wealth, or by increasing total wealth.

Socialists in North America put their emphasis on redistributing existing wealth. Enterprisers believe the poor could get richer faster if the same effort went into increasing total wealth, and that's something that the enterprise system does best. Redistribution, they argue, achieves almost nothing. If every Canadian received exactly the same income, the average would hardly alter, yet the incentive to get ahead would have been removed, so growth and progress would dwindle.

Best Because:

2. IT RESPONDS TO THE DEMOCRACY OF THE MARKETPLACE.

Competitive enterprise is ruled by the marketplace, its prices established by supply and demand. It's in the marketplace that business learns what people truly want, by what they're prepared to pay. In the marketplace, every decision to buy or not to buy is a democratic vote for or against a product or service at a certain price.

The marketplace is a computer bigger than man could ever create, control, or copy. No state planning mechanism can ever provide the depth and accuracy of the information offered routinely by the market which, every hour, throughout Canada, processes millions of individual buying decisions.

Supply and demand in the marketplace establish the price for consumer products such as cars, cameras, cartons of milk, and for industrial supplies such as factory sites or typewriter ribbons or legal services. And supply and demand establish what you are paid in your job and how fast you'll move in your career.

The marketplace is so complex that it cannot be duplicated or purposefully manipulated by elected or self-appointed experts, no matter how well-trained or well-intentioned. Efforts to regulate what will be bought and how much will be paid only distort the delicate balance between supply and demand. Such efforts are like trying to suppress the steam in boiling water; pressure eventually builds to the exploding point.

Some people dislike the marketplace. They blame it for selling "useless" stuff. When they see lower income people buying candies instead of nutritional foods, they blame the marketplace for making the candy available. When they see rush hour commuters driving large, empty cars downtown at snail's pace, they'd like to stop them because it seems so illogical. They believe that people need to be protected against the apparent absurdity of some of their desires, and that "experts" should decide just what is really worth putting on sale.

Such people don't truly believe in democracy. They don't fully accept that, in the long run, given a proper chance, the so-called "common man" exhibits unfailing common sense.

In the competitive marketplace, companies live or die by their ability to decide, correctly, what people want. It's comforting to visualize all those eager enterprisers competing to anticipate what we want, so they can supply it to us first or best.

The marketplace can seem, at times, over responsive, and success often leads to excess. If a flavored toothpaste sells well, a dozen imitators will appear. Yet, even there, the marketplace eventually sorts things out in the best interests of the most people. The surge of imitators stops the originator of the idea from making unreasonable profits for long; their competition forces him to set his price as low as he economically can.

Best Because:

3. IT FOSTERS FREEDOM.

When parents buy "empty calorie" cereals, it's often because they'd rather do that than hassle with their kids. The choice is theirs; the enterprise system and the marketplace make the choice possible.

Few people need protection against their inadequacies (and society offers protection to that special few). We live in a free society because we want freedom to make our own choices, even "wrong" ones. The more real choice we have, the more freedom we have.

We grant legislators limited right to reduce our freedom. If they reduce it more than we want them to, we wait four years, then throw them out. Our control over them can be exercised only at election time.

Our control in the marketplace, on the other hand, is immediate, frequent, and very specific. Every buying decision adds a message to a supplier about his particular product or service. There's a nationwide daily referendum on everything that's offered for sale.

The marketplace is, thus, a better public control and communications device than the ballot box. It follows, then, that every time a decision is taken out of the marketplace and put into the hands of government, our control over it deteriorates and we lose a bit more of our freedom.

The enterprise system fosters freedom in other ways, too.

A modern society needs, for example, huge amounts of investment capital. It raises capital in the marketplace, by paying people for the use of their savings. Everyone has the choice, whether to spend every nickel he earns, or to save some and lend it to others at a profit.

That's not the only way to accumulate capital. An alternative is for governments to collect it in taxes, then allocate it. That *forces* everyone to save and further reduces our freedom.

Freedom and the enterprise system reinforce each other wherever they touch. Some people, for example, like to work as hard as they can, to earn as much as they can. Some prefer to work less, and find their pleasure in leisure. The enterprise system, virtually by definition, gives them that freedom of choice.

Best Because:

4. IT PUTS PROFIT TO WORK.

The chicken-or-the-egg question in modern business is does a corporation exist to make a profit, or make profits to exist? Perhaps, unexpectedly, it's the latter.

If profits were not necessary, they would disappear; the competitiveness of our system guarantees that. The corporate businessman who could steal a march on his competitors by dropping prices the ten percent or so represented by pre-tax "profit" would be delighted to do so. He cannot, because, without profits, his corporation would soon splutter and die.

Profits—the difference between what a thing costs to create and what it is worth to its buyers—are essential for many reasons. Profits pay to replace equipment as it wears out. Profits reward investors for providing the extra funds needed for expansion and innovation.

Profits are essential to business, but are also a problem, because many people just don't understand them and associate them with greed rather than need. Most North Americans think that companies make after-tax profits of close to thirty percent, whereas five percent is nearer the average. During inflation, profit levels appear to climb. That's because the inflation has increased the bookkeeping value of the company's inventory of completed, but unsold goods. As those inventories have to be replaced with goods manufactured at the new cost, there is no real boost in profits at all.

Profits create growth and, our growing concern for "quality of life" notwithstanding, growth is good.

Growth does not necessarily mean more factories flowing over former fields, or increases in the industrial uglies. Growth occurs when an improved process replaces an inferior one, when a product line is diversified to offer more meaningful choice, when additional investment in machinery or people helps cut costs or improves value.

Improved productivity is a form of growth, and improved productivity raises the standards of living, and of opportunity, for everyone.

Best Because:

5. IT LEADS TO THE INSTITUTIONALIZATION OF BUSINESS.

Bigness in business these days is inevitable, because of the size of the tasks to be tackled. Small organizations cannot build world-scale manufacturing plants or transcontinental pipelines or communications networks. Companies with only a hundred employees cannot extract resources, smelt ore, provide the industrial base on which a hundred thousand independent enterprises can grow. It takes huge organizations to handle such jobs.

The corporation—which is essentially an organizational means of letting people pool their energies, skills, and/or dollars for productive ends—has proven itself capable of coordinating men and money in staggering numbers. In 1970, in Canada, a hundred enterprises accounted for 47 percent of all manufacturing output. Of the hundred biggest money powers in the *world*, 51 are corporations and only 49 are countries.

Can a corporation grow *too big* for the good of society? No one knows, so a Royal Commission is about to study the question. At least one *advantage* of bigness will, presumably, be noted by that Commission; that is, it brings "institutionalization", which welds new ethical safeguards to the enterprise system.

Institutionalization forces corporations to be more interested in longterm considerations than shortterm, because an institution plans to *endure*. Fast-buck schemes are useless to it.

Institutions cannot fly in the face of the public interest, because their activities are subject to public scrutiny at almost every level.

Institutions have to be seen to be fair to employees because they rely on the trust, energy, and enthusiasm of so many. Major Canadian corporations offer better staff benefits and pension plans than perhaps any socialist enterprise ever found possible.

Most important, the institutionalization of business lets us all share in corporate profits. We share through taxation, which extracts tens and hundreds of millions of dollars from each corporation each year. And we share through ownership. A few hundred thousand of us have bought corporate shares on the stock exchange. Most of the rest of us own shares indirectly, through pension funds, mutual funds, and life insurance policies.

Non-government pension funds in Canada now total $20 billion, and a lot of that money is invested in shares of large corporations. Life insurance totals nearly $29,000 per Canadian household, and much of that, too, is invested in corporations. The mutual fund industry has billions of dollars invested in corporate shares. Part of your bank savings are invested in company bonds or are lent to corporations, and the proceeds filter back to you, too.

Each large corporate institution is the sum of years—it may be fifty or sixty or more—of the slogging process of creating profit, ploughing it back in, building a bigger enterprise, creating more profit, ploughing that back in. Laboriously, these productive enterprises—machines, in effect—worth millions and billions of dollars, have been shaped and built. They are truly community assets, not only because most of us indirectly own part of them, but also because only machines of this size can economically provide goods and services to fill many of our needs. Whenever any large corporation is destroyed, by bad management or undue government interference, the laborious process of building up that great economic asset has to start all over again.

The size of corporate institutions does not necesssarily confer undue power. (Again, the Royal Commission will have interesting areas to explore.) While the proprietor of a smaller enterprise has considerable leeway to exercise his will, no one within the corporate institution has much immediate freedom. Senior executives are all responsible to the chief executive who, in turn, is responsible to the board of directors. The directors are responsible to the shareholders and, these days, with increasing numbers of shares held by pension and mutual funds, that responsibility is more than just nominal. The alert and knowing eyes of sophisticated fund managers assess their performance continually.

And managers and directors and shareholders alike can make decisions and judgments only within the framework of the needs of the corporation, which is, in turn, controlled by the marketplace, within a framework of increasing government regulation.

The men and women who head these corporate institutions are more like public servants or diplomats than entrepreneurs. The instincts and style of a hustler hardly help the chief executive who must run a corporation with 10,000 employees, meet with government leaders, deal with heads of other corporations, inspire and coordinate bright, aggressive and ambitious vice-presidents, report to a board of powerful directors, represent the company in the mass media, and keep in steady focus the aims and social contributions of a huge and complex enterprise.

Best Because:

6. IT LETS US GET THE BEST OF BOTH WORLDS.

Few corporate businessmen, today, believe that the marketplace alone can set the rules. They listen to other voices: the mass media, politicians, consultants and staff specialists who advise on social well-being and expectations. They accept that, without some government involvement, the marketplace can be a fiercer, more primitive environment than affluent twentieth century Canadians need to inhabit.

Today's corporate leaders aren't rednecks, they're pragmatists. In a political-philosophical spectrum ranging from left to right, they're closer to the center than the right. They accept the need for many types of government involvement and regulation, but they are alarmed that such involvement might increase until there's no room left for productive enterprise. They don't want Canada to back into socialism without the electorate having made a decision.

The backdoor approach is of real concern. Governments already spend forty cents of every dollar in Canada and that share grows every year. Government restrictions make it more difficult to operate many parts of the enterprise system. Every time that private enterprise can no longer provide a needed product or service, government steps in to fill the need. And every time *that* happens, the efficiency of the Canadian economic machine slips another notch and the proper allocation of resources is further impaired.

Corporate leaders aren't Pollyannas who insist that everything about the business world is perfect. That world is so big and diverse that almost any accusation thrown at it is bound to be true somewhere. They simply claim that, warts and all, the enterprise system of production, and the marketplace system of communication, are better than any known alternatives.

Canada has long been a mixed enterprise economy. We've always been less reluctant than the United States to set up state enterprises to compete with private enterprise. CBC, National Film Board, Canadian National, Air Canada, Polysar, Petrocan, many others, are public enterprises. It's a Canadian strength that we have countenanced public as well as private enterprises. It indicates a willingness to compromise in an attempt to get the best of all possible worlds.

It's inevitable, and probably even healthy, that there should be continuing tension between those who want the government to take care of things and those who want to leave as much as possible to private enterprise. Modern society must offer assistance to citizens who cannot keep up with the rest; that's a government role. The trick is to maintain a balance. If government does not offer enough assistance, or make enough effort to reduce inequalities in society, it invites revolution. If it devotes too much of everyone's wealth to this, it creates a "welfare state", eliminates incentives, and thus reduces the enterprise system's capacity to perform.

Some Canadians think that business wields immense influence with legislators. Businessmen don't think so. They are very concerned that their voice is not being heard at all. They hear no politicians speaking out on their behalf. To say, today, that a politician "favors big business" is not a statement, but an accusation.

If a politician won't, then someone else should stress the following points to the Canadian public:

(i) Critics of business should be careful that they are not tilting at windmills. The strength of the enterprise system is its flexibility. Business has continued to change as the social, political and marketplace demands on it have changed. Yesterday's abuses have been corrected, and today's are being identified so that they, too, will be corrected.

(ii) Corporate businessmen do not suggest that Canadians accept the enterprise system lock, stock and barrel. But they do plead that Canadians analyze the system carefully, nurture what's best in it, help it continue to evolve into new and better versions, and make sure that it is not accidentally wiped out.

Canadians sometimes smile at their own inclination to compromise. Compromise is at the heart of Canada's mixed enterprise system. To borrow a phrase used elsewhere: "There are no simple solutions. Only intelligent choices."

Notes

*Investors Syndicate (reproduced by permission).

5 The State and Economic Life in Canada *

Alexander Brady

In modern Canada the activity of the state has hitherto been shaped by the pioneer nature of the country, the physical structure of the half-continent, the imperial sweep of settlement after 1867, the influence of the interacting ideas and institutions of Britain and the United States, and the quick response of the whole society to the advance of western industrialism. State action is similar to that in the other Dominions or indeed to that of other northern countries with moving frontiers of settlement. The special distinctions that exist are rooted in differences of geographic position, physical environment, and cultural quality. Here there is space for only a brief sketch of the general theme. The role of the state in the economic life of Canada is really the modern history of Canada. . . .

Notable is the presence in numerous forms of protective or neo-mercantilist policies with both political and economic ends. From the establishment of the federal state in the 'sixties of the last century, the commercial, financial, manufacturing, labour, and even agrarian groups have exerted persistent pressure to transform a simple colonial economy into one integrated and national. This national aspiration has involved not merely protective tariffs, adopted in the 1870's and ever since maintained, but also bounties for struggling industries, prohibitions on the export of raw materials in order to stimulate domestic processing, the building and administration of canals, state aid to or direct participation in the construction of railways in order to exploit soils and forests and mines, the public generation and distribution of hydro-electric power, and the fostering of agriculture. Most of these state policies were concerned with creating and maintaining a continental economy wherein trade would flow east and west across the continent within the political boundaries of a growing nation.

Here we witness the familiar process whereby national economic policies are shaped in any modern democratic state, whether of Europe or of the New World. Special interests, conscious of their disadvantages and anxious for succour, argue their case before the public or directly exert upon governments such pressure as they can command. The organized groups of Canada are anxious to protect their economic identity against the formidable competition of rival groups in the United States. They are always conscious of a hard and unremitting struggle for survival in a continental environment wherein American industrialism, fed by rich natural resources, is an imperial and ever-expanding power. The concept of Canadian nationality has lent coherence to the numerous claims of these interests for protection, and in public debate has given such claims a more attractive complexion.

Protection, however, has extended beyond the sphere of material interests. The establishment of the Canadian Broadcasting Corporation (1936), patterned in the main upon the British, was designed to afford protection and encouragement to many elements of cultural life. It has ambitiously but quietly sought to foster in the populace some sense of a national community and a national culture, both of which have seemed menaced by the power and success of the private broadcasting companies in the neighbouring country. While the proximity of the United States is only one of many influences, it is a major one, written clearly not merely in the fiscal but in all phases of state activity.

Varied circumstances have tempered the policy of fiscal protection. The agrarian interest, although weakened by regional fissures, has always had considerable weight in politics, and has been prompt to withdraw support from parties that seek what it regards as an extravagant protection of secondary industry. It has not been reticent in demanding protective duties for its own products, but large sectors of the rural community concerned with production for export have always supported freer trade, if not free trade. The growing political power of the wheat areas in the West during the early decades of the twentieth century strengthened such views in Ottawa, and in particular helped to revive interest in the idea of trade reciprocity with the United States.

The division of Canada into geographic and economic regions has also helped to modify the protectionist impulse, for rarely do all the regions obtain a similar benefit from a specific form of protection, and some regions disclaim ever receiving a major benefit from protective tariffs. A cautious policy that will appease as many sections as possible becomes politically imperative in order to ease the strains of the federation and save it from disruption. Such a policy has been dictated no less by the kindred need of maintaining a balance between Canada's commercial relations with the United States and those with Great Britain. Imperial preference, introduced in the 'nineties, was motivated not merely by sentiment for the motherland, or special economic interests shared with Great Britain, but by the necessity of exerting a bargaining influence upon the United States. From the 'seventies of the last century to the present, tariffs as an instrument in nation-building have been used with opportunism in performing a difficult task.

In Canada public ownership is closely related to protection in that most of it was undertaken in connexion with public utilities, such as railways and electric power, in order to quicken development in primary and secondary industry and to create an economy more integrated and diversified, able to stand on its own feet alongside the young, powerful economy of the neighbouring Republic. The factor of competition between American and Canadian transport routes has always been present, and helps to explain the fostering solicitude of government. Nation-building through the tying together of scattered settlements and the opening up of fresh territories has been the primary motive for railway subsidies or direct state construction. The unity of Canada has required railway lines no less than the Roman Empire required roads; they have been the main agency of colonization and industrial diversification. To the men who established federation in 1867, they were imperative to bind the Maritime Provinces to the St. Lawrence Valley and the western lands to the urban areas of the East, creating a continental market within which a national economy could be built.

But, in a new country, lines had to be pushed ahead of available traffic, involving hazards of heavy capital investment from which private enterprise shrank without state support. The Intercolonial Railway, completed in 1876 and built directly by the Government to connect Halifax with Quebec and Montreal, illustrates that combination of political and economic design which is implicit in all state-sponsored railways. Judged by the yard-stick of private business, it was never a commercial success. But it is almost irrelevant to assess it by the criterion of deficits or surpluses, since it was primarily a political achievement that served well the ends of a national government seeking to create an integrated community. Its administration was never brilliant and was always handicapped by competition with water-transport and shorter rail-routes through the United States, and by political interference, especially political patronage and the insistence of the Government on low rates in order to lessen the hostility of the Maritime Provinces towards other federal policies.

The transcontinental Canadian Pacific line was begun by the Government, but it was soon transformed into a private enterprise, much aided by public land-grants and capital. The land-grants were intended to make the railway no less responsible for colonization than the Government itself. The later transcontinental lines, the Canadian Northern and the Grand Trunk Pacific, were similarly assisted by the federal and provincial governments. The eastern branch of the Grand Trunk Pacific was built directly by the Government, and its route and terminus were in part determined by political considerations and regional claims. Generous public aid through land-grants, cash subsidies, and bond guaranties helped to double railway mileage between 1900 and 1915, an increase which resulted in excessive capacity and created heavy overhead costs that could not be met from current revenues. The financial plight of these railways during the First World War brought them under the Government as the guarantor of their bonds, and between 1918 and 1923 the present Canadian National Railways took form, incorporating the Intercolonial with other lines. In this instance public ownership was virtually predetermined by the former lavish aid to private corporations, which in turn was derived from the perennial pressure exerted on the Government by commercial, industrial, and agrarian interests determined upon an expanding and continental economy. Historical cause and effect have here a singular lucidity.

What has been the record of the Canadian National Railways? It is obvious that the system suffers from serious disadvantages when compared over the last quarter of a century with the great private road, the Canadian Pacific: it had a larger mileage of light traffic lines; its equipment and property were at the outset in wretched physical condition; it faced throughout vast territories the task of creating goodwill among shippers and the public; as a government-owned railway it was subject to embarrassing pressures from various organized groups, which hampered effective management; and finally, in 1922 it was simply a collection of different lines, built for competition, which had to be welded into a genuine unity. Inevitably, the Dominion was compelled annually to pay millions of dollars in deficits. But the Canadian National Railways are not to be judged merely by the test of profitable returns on investment, since, like other lines, they have been an instrument of nation-building, drawing together widely-scattered communities and making possible the exploitation of natural resources remote from the industrial heart of Canada. Credit, moreover, must be given for a notable improvement in their character. They became a distinguished railway system.

What happened within the national sphere happened also within the regions, especially in Ontario and Quebec. In Ontario the province constructed and operated the Temiskaming and Northern Railway, which was planned to quicken and integrate the development of a provincial economy and to bind the growth of the northern region, with its forests and mines, to the financial and industrial metropolis of Toronto. By 1913 the railway was extended to tide-water at Moosonee on an estuary of James Bay, and since then it has helped to open up the resources of the northland and to consolidate Ontario's industrialism.

Despite periodic flurries of opinion on the issue, the state-owned railway operates across the continent virtually side by side with the Canadian Pacific, accepting the same system of rates but in some degree competing in the quality of service. Thereby a giant railway monopoly is avoided. In times of economic adversity an amalgamation of the railways is advocated under either public or private management, but the powerful railway unions have hitherto resisted such a solution, fearing a reduction in staff. Other regional and group interests would also be sharply affected by amalgamation, and hence private enterprise and public policy continue to be mixed in the railway operations of Canada.

In the administrative organization of state railways Canadian experience may not afford so rich a variety as that found in Australia, but it has interest. Canada, on the whole, has discarded the direct operation of the lines by a department of the Government, a system which had exhibited the ills of political patronage in the days of the Intercolonial Railway. When the Canadian National Railways were established, provision was made for a public and independent board, appointed by the Government, resembling the organized directors in a private corporation, and fully answerable for administration. But while the Government did not attempt to control the day-to-day operations, it could not avoid a perennial interest in the performance of the management because of the profound importance of the railway to the public and because it paid the deficits. In 1932 the Duff Commission condemned the large board on the ground that it provided too much opportunity for regional pressures to assert themselves, and recommended instead a small body of three trustees. This institution in turn worked ill, and was replaced by a larger body, whose performance is under the annual scrutiny of a standing committee of Parliament.

State provision of electricity has a developmental role somewhat similar to that of railways, and the hydro-electric power system of Ontario easily holds pride of place. It represents the most impressive experiment in public ownership and is influential in other like ventures not merely within Canada but in the United States. Collectivism in the hydro-power of Ontario, in contrast to private enterprise in the hydro-power of the neighbouring state of New York, is a provincial complement to that national policy pursued by governments at Ottawa since the 'seventies: the public construction of canals, the building or subsidizing of railways, and the provision of protective tariffs and bonuses for secondary industry. It received its initial impulse from the small manufacturers, merchants, and municipal councillors of southern Ontario, who, in a province without coal, were zealous to exploit the sole major source of power in order to further a sturdy industrialism and a robust urban life. The insecurity of relying solely on American coal, periodically accentuated by stoppages and strikes in the mines of Pennsylvania, alarmed the public and influenced its action. In the early years of the century there was a prevalent fear that private companies financed in the United States might exploit the spectacular waters of Niagara and create a local aggregation of industry beneficial principally to American interests.

During the first decade of the century the urgent need of cheap power for industrial expansion was decisive in creating a drive for public ownership. The expanding market for goods on the new agrarian frontiers of Saskatchewan and Alberta impelled manufacturers in Ontario to support any measures that enabled them to lessen their costs and enlarge their output in the face of American competition. Heavy investment of capital in transmission lines was necessary in order to utilize in Toronto and other urban centres the water resource of Niagara; under government guaranty such capital was obtainable at relatively low rates. The chief creator of the public hydro-system, Adam Beck, always emphasized that cheap power was not to be had if private companies were permitted to command the situation and extract profit on watered stock. To be cheap, power must be sold at cost, and from the outset sale at cost has been the cardinal trait of the Ontario system. Public ownership was designed to eliminate profit-taking from the distribution of electricity. Such has been the interpretation placed upon the popular slogan that did such doughty service on many a political platform—"The water-powers of the province for the people of the province." In their more ebullient moods, politicians even spoke of making electric power as free as air, but this language was merely the customary hyperbole of a popular appeal.

The administrative instrument for this collective ownership of power is the Hydro-Electric Power Commission of Ontario, which since 1906 has existed as a body corporate of three members, appointed by the Lieutenant-Governor in Council and holding office during pleasure. From the outset the tie with the provincial government has been intimate. . . . Up to 1935 the capital used was advanced by the Government. After 1935 the Commission began to raise its own financial requirements. Adam Beck, the remarkable chairman of the Commission from its inception in 1906 till his death nineteen years later, was for part of the period a Minister of the Crown as well as chairman of the Commission. But Beck was always determined to make "the Hydro" as autonomous as possible in order to protect it from a political interference fatal to efficiency. Hence he emphasized that it was strictly a co-operative enterprise of the numerous municipalities in the province, existing only because these municipalities freely contracted to buy power from the Commission at prices fixed to cover the costs of generation and transmission. Through their payments for power the municipalities liquidated the borrowings made by the province for generating plants and transmission lines.

Yet in only a limited way is the actual administration of the system operated as a co-operative enterprise. The provincial Commission, under the authority of a provincial statute, exercises a decisive jurisdiction over the councils and commissions engaged in distributing electricity within their local areas. It controls wherever necessary the rates of municipalities which purchase power from the Commission, directs the use of profits in reducing rates, and insists on a uniform system of book-keeping. At every turn it makes them cling to its interpretation of the principle of power at cost, and more than once in the exercise of its authority it has clashed with the City of Toronto.

As a result of its essential nature the hydro-system was never remote from miscellaneous pressures, on the one hand from the provincial government and on the other from the municipalities. Adam Beck, through the weight of his personality and the skill of his leadership, created in all parties a strong following which shielded the administration and policies of the hydro-system from becoming a political football. Indeed he was one of those men, rarely met with in political life, who, fortunately for Canada, was able to make his cause transcend the bounds of party. But soon after his death the management of the system came under intense political fire. The expanding consumption of electricity in the 'twenties, quickened by the growing industrialization in southern Ontario, began to strain the existing generating capacity, and a continued growth in the demand threatened to create an acute shortage of power. This threat drove the Commission to make contracts with private corporations in Quebec for the purchase of current generated in the Ottawa and St. Lawrence valleys. . . .

But on the whole no serious political interferences with the administration of the hydro-system have been revealed. Certainly, although mistakes have been made, no political corruption has reduced the quality of its performance. The engineer has generally been left with adequate freedom to perform his technical task. The Commission has been fortunate in securing distinguished engineers, whose utilization of the provincial water resources has made possible a steady industrial advance. The municipal distribution of the system increased from 2,500 horse-power in 1910 to 2,608,000 in 1945, and the number of co-operating municipalities from ten to more than nine hundred. Isolated generating stations have been linked by a vast network of transmission lines, and from hydro-power in country and town the economy of Ontario has received a remarkable stimulus.

Although the experiment of Ontario in public ownership profoundly influenced other provinces, the character and the pace of public policy in each province have varied greatly in accordance with physical, industrial, and cultural circumstances. Quebec for some decades shrank from entrusting the state with the electrical industry. In this province, industry was less diversified and there were fewer small manufacturers, merchants, and workers scattered in many towns and eager for cheap power. In Quebec, moreover, hydro-electric power at widely-distributed sites was developed incidentally by large companies concerned with other industries such as pulp and paper, asbestos, cement, and mining. Once firmly established in the production of electricity, these giant corporations were not easy to dislodge, and in any event the French electorate was not greatly stirred by the evangel of public ownership that was prevalent in the English-speaking community. In the early years of the century, public ownership was considered to be closely akin to socialism, and socialism was frowned upon by most of the Roman Catholic hierarchy as something sinister.

Yet in the 'thirties, under the sharp spur of new social discontents and a fresh upsurge of French-Canadian nationalism, a movement was launched for greater provincial control and ownership of water-power. In 1935 a commission of three members was appointed to co-ordinate the activity of power companies in the province and to supply electricity to the largest possible number of citizens. This was the first of a series of measures which culminated in 1944, in the creation of the Quebec Hydro-Electric Commission and the expropriation of the wealthy Montreal Light, Heat and Power Company, a supplier of electricity and gas in metropolitan Montreal. Behind such action was the mounting influence of a national and popular creed which declared that the humble French-speaking people of the province were being exploited by the wily English-speaking capitalists dominating the board-rooms of the power companies. Provincial autonomy and self-assertion, as well as the prospect of cheaper power, thus seemed to dictate the need of public ownership. Drifting away from old loyalties, Quebec tardily began to emulate the example of Ontario [and by 1963 Quebec Hydro had absorbed almost all of the private electric companies].

In some of the other provinces, notably in Manitoba and Nova Scotia, public and private ownership of power exist side by side, but in the last twenty-five years the trend has been towards a wider jurisdiction by public bodies. [For example, British Columbia brought all of its hydro facilities under public ownership in 1961.]

The heavy taxation by the federal government of private power companies during the Second World War sometimes strengthened the case of the advocates for public ownership, since it was assumed that under provincial management the revenue which flowed to Ottawa could instead be used to extend the local consumption of electricity. The specious simplicity of this argument made it popular, and it harmonized well with the sentiments of those who were anxious to build up provincial institutions. But more important in the long run was the growing necessity in all provinces to integrate and simplify the generation and distribution of electricity and to extend its use to as many citizens as possible. In Manitoba and Nova Scotia, for example, the pressure for wide-spread rural electrification has tended to enlarge the activity of the public commissions, because they are best able to build lines into areas of low population density, where the development of an adequate load is inevitably slow. In this situation a public authority with public capital can meet the costs of service better than a private company.

Early in the present century public ownership in utilities other than electric power had already begun. The properties of the Bell Telephone Company in the three Prairie Provinces were purchased and administered by the governments. Here the special pressure came from farmers. Their amenities of life could be greatly enlarged by the telephone, but they were prompt to realize that a private company would shrink from providing service to a thinly-scattered rural population. Hence the risks of telephone service were made a collective responsibility. Within the same region other forms of assistance were offered: public elevators, credit facilities, debt-adjustment boards, the encouragement of co-operatives, and experimental farms.

Despite the individual organization of production on the typical prairie farm, successful growing of wheat on the great plains has always been peculiarly dependent on numerous aids from provincial and federal governments, including the provision of railways, the regulation of railway rates, the grading of grains, the supervision of marketing, and in the last generation the stabilizing and bolstering of prices for the product. It is little wonder that the western farmer is much more of a conscious and zealous collectivist than his fellow-agrarians of Ontario and Quebec. He opened up a hard frontier, which has remained hard. Through the state he has endeavoured to lessen or even to pool the risks of his highly commercialized and precarious agriculture. In this endeavour he has often been encouraged by industrialists in eastern Canada, for to them a prosperous agrarian frontier in the West has been crucial. Significant, in addition to other forms of government aid, is the prairie farm rehabilitation programme, inaugurated under federal legislation in 1935 to rehabilitate farm lands in the dry and soil-drifting districts of the West; it constitutes one of the first attempts on a major scale to conserve agrarian resources by direct public action.

Labour leglislation has been moulded by the peculiar influences of the social environment and the federal system. Until the last decade the growth of the Canadian labour movement, unlike that in its sister Dominions of Australia and New Zealand, has been delayed by regional fissures, racial divisions, the mobility of labour in the hopeful era of the open and accessible frontier, and perhaps most of all the agrarian nature of the economy for many decades after 1867, wherein the rural labour force has felt no urge to seek organization. Farm labour has been provided mainly by the farmer and his family. The hired man who may supplement the toil of the proprietary family has never been a suitable recruit for the ranks of organized labour. Where he is anything more than a temporary labourer on the land, his homely ambition is to possess a farm of his own, and hence his concern is less with his fellow-labourers than with the class of producers which he is anxious to join. In the Canadian country-side there has been nothing equivalent to that dynamic agent of pressure, the Australian Workers' Union; indeed, there has been no organization worthy of mention because no large units exist like the sheep-stations of the Australian outback, employing a rural proletariat.

Consequently, strong labour organizations have come only with the progress of urban industrialization, a progress much stimulated by the two world wars of the twentieth century, especially the second. Thus in 1937 the number of organized workers in Canada was 383,000, which was the largest figure of any year up to that date. By 1944 the number had almost doubled. [It increased to 1.7 million in 1968.]

Yet the ranks of urban labour are always weakened by the dispersal of the population in towns and cities across a continent, rendering organization difficult and exposing the movement to regional cleavages. The division into English-speaking and French-speaking groups impairs co-operation in central Canada, where the great metropolitan centres exist and where most of the industrial population is concentrated. The Roman Catholic unions of Quebec often have a different view of the goals sought through the state by the unions of the neighbouring Ontario. They are much less state-conscious, much less inspired by the secular philosophies of labour in North America, and, because of their Catholic leadership, much less militant. They are disposed to emphasize social collaboration rather than class struggle. But here again a fast-growing industrialism is introducing significant changes. The position of the Catholic unions is being challenged by the aggressive invasion of unions from English-speaking Canada and the United States, and the French workman in the industrial town is responding to social stimuli that differ from those traditional in rural Quebec.

The boundary between Canada and the United States is rarely a barrier to the migration of ideas, least of all in matters of labour organization and social pressures. The international unions of North America have created funnels whereby influences from the United States easily flow into the Canadian labour camp, sometimes with the effect of checking its national cohesion. British influence has always been present and often potent, owing to the fact that hitherto British immigrants provided much of the union leadership; but varied and pervasive influences from the United States are evident in the present active lobbying by labour and in its past tendency to avoid direct political action, a tendency now clearly on the wane.

Such circumstances, combined with the divisions of jurisdiction explicit in the federal system, determine the character of labour law. Most of the legislative power dwells with the provinces in virtue of their control over property and civil rights. Laws have been passed on the employment of women and children, minimum hours of work, wages, factory inspection, workmen's compensation in accidents, and conditions under which a stoppage in industrial work is legal. In brief, the Canadian labour code is mainly a complicated structure of provincial codes, but in substance it is similar to that found in other countries of the English-speaking world. The security of trade unions under the law came more slowly than in Great Britain; but the enactments, when made, tended to follow British models, with the most significant variations in Quebec, which through its Civil Code has a distinct legal tradition. The broad trend, most evident in the 'thirties and 'forties of the present century, is clearly towards protecting the unions as free associations, enabling them to exert their maximum power in industry and the state. Provincial legislation, much influenced by the National Industrial Recovery Act of the United States (1933) and by the Wagner National Labor Relations Act (1935), has been reasonably effective in protecting the right of workers to join unions and in compelling employers to negotiate with them.

Besides the provincial enactments, there were the Dominion amendments to the Criminal Code in 1939, making it illegal for an employer to dismiss or threaten to dismiss a workman simply because of his membership in a lawful trade union. With its increased powers during the emergency of the Second World War and under pressure of labour, the Dominion Government sought to strengthen trade-unionism and protect its personnel, notably in the War-Time Labour Relations Regulations of 1944, which proclaimed the rights of employees and employers, formulated rules for collective bargaining, and provided machinery for conciliation in industrial disputes. These Regulations set the pattern for post-war legislation in the Dominion and the provinces.

The most significant early federal legislation, which influenced all subsequent enactments, even when these go beyond it in scope, was the Industrial Disputes Investigation Act of 1907. This provided for compulsory investigation of disputes in industries in which stoppages of work diminish the welfare of citizens in general. But no attempt was made to compel parties to a dispute to accept the recommendations of the conciliation boards. Canada did not follow the precedents of Australia and New Zealand in providing for compulsory arbitration under the state. Underlying Canadian legislation was the assumption that conciliation would adequately serve the public interest by advancing a settlement. The statute was circumscribed by the limited jurisdiction of the Dominion Parliament in labour matters, but over the years it has had an important ameliorative effect on industrial struggles, and its essential elements are still retained in Dominion and provincial legislation.

Social services in their evolution have been affected by the same basic forces that shape the character of labour law. Only a few general observations are needed here. In Canada, as in the other democracies of the English-speaking world, notable spurts occurred in the rise of public social services as a consequence of three related events in the twentieth century: the First World War, the depression in the 'thirties, and the struggle against Nazi Germany. Of these, the depression was notable because it greatly enlarged the range of state action and made imperative heavy levies upon the Dominion treasury in Ottawa to aid the provinces and municipalities in providing relief payments.

Attempts in the national sphere to follow the example of the United States in its generous social-security measures and industrial regulation were, however, frustrated by the rigidity of the federal constitution. The draftsmen of the British North America Act had not envisaged national social services, which consequently remain limited by the letter of the law. In 1937 the enactments sponsored by the Bennett Government, the nearest equivalent in Canada to Roosevelt's New Deal, were in the main declared to be *ultra vires* of the federal Parliament. Nothing, therefore, was achieved comparable to the contemporary revolution in the social services of the United States or to the sweeping innovations embodied in the social-security legislation of New Zealand. Apart from any restraining influences within the community itself, the federal system of Canada was a barrier to drastic national change.

Yet expenditures on social services inclusive of education were steadily on the increase, costing the nation by 1939 more than a quarter of all public spending. The annual expenditures of Dominion, provincial, and municipal governments on public welfare and relief, excluding education, were in 1913 some $15,000,000; in 1930 they were $83,000,000; by 1937, $236,000,000. This increased public spending inevitably came to be reflected in taxation. In 1925 federal, provincial, and municipal governments were raising in taxes some 14.7 per cent of the national income. By 1938 that percentage had increased to 19.7 per cent [and by 1963 had reached 25 per cent].

The Second World War, through its economic and social consequences, created much public debate on the necessity for social reform, aroused public sentiment, and deepened the pressure for national action. Extensive publicity was given to the Beveridge Report and its implications. Democratic strategy, it was argued, required more effective social services. But more important than such general debate was the rapid emergence of a war economy which speeded the process of industrialization, still further enlarged the chief cities, and created a more powerful labour movement clamorous for social-security measures. The Rowell-Sirois Commission, whose monumental report was completed in 1940, prescribed a realignment of constitutional powers and financial responsibilities in order to place social services on a sounder basis; but attempts both during and after the war to implement its recommendations encountered stubborn opposition in the central provinces and some of the outlying provinces. Two important steps were, however, taken during the war in the establishment of unemployment insurance (1940), patterned in the main upon the British system, and in the provision (1944) for the payment of monthly family allowances out of the Dominion treasury. [More recently two further developments in the field of health have been significant. The C.C.F. government of Saskatchewan established public hospital insurance in 1947 and medical insurance in 1962. As similar schemes were adopted in other provinces, national cost-sharing arrangements were instituted for hospital insurance in 1958 and "medicare" in 1968.]

The problem of state action in the sphere of social services inevitably becomes a constitutional issue, and that, in turn, a problem of achieving sufficiently wide agreement in a federal community. The major jurisdiction still dwells with the provinces, but most provinces are experiencing a decrease in their financial power to implement the far-reaching schemes of social amelioration demanded by advancing industrialism. While no province, least of all a province on the lean federal periphery, seeks to get sharply out of step with its fellows, there is an obvious lack of uniformity in the range and quality of services from province to province. The wealthy can afford to be generous, but the poor must be parsimonious. Ontario and to some extent Quebec, enriched by their industrial diversity, are strong enough to enact such social legislation as they deem suitable for their needs. [Since 1950, increased federal grants to the provinces and shared-cost programmes have eased the situation somewhat.]

In social services, as in public utilities, Quebec in particular has its own distinctive views and peculiar procedures, determined by Roman Catholicism, its Civil Code, and its nationalist traditions. Here a well-established practice of activity by the religious orders in providing many services [at least prior to 1960] weakened the political impulse to look to the state and especially to Ottawa for assistance. Charity, inspired and organized by the religious communities, is regarded as a more desirable dynamic than the philosophy of state collectivism, and it provides hospitals, orphanages, and asylums. In the smallest social cell, the parish, the *curé* directs the application of local charity, and in the larger social units the bishops provide appropriate organization for social amelioration. The Church, an indefatigable upholder of private property as an agency for developing personality, looks suspiciously on the enlargement of state functions, especially those which threaten to draw away influence and responsibility from itself. It readily sponsors co-operative enterprise among all portions of the population, but it fears the growth of the secular Leviathan. Nevertheless, even in Quebec the role of the state grows ever larger, for with the march of industrialism private charity is inadequate to cope with the modern problems of social service, particularly during periods of depression. [In the 1960's, Quebec's expenditures on welfare and education increased dramatically.]

The conclusions are self-evident. Since 1867 Canada as a state has become more collectivist in character, owing mainly to those economic and social forces which explain collectivism throughout the Western world. There is nothing singular in this phase of her evolution, nothing in the role of her government that cannot be paralleled elsewhere, especially in countries, like the Dominions, with moving frontiers of settlement and development. She accepts as a matter of course that the state must become "the universal intervener", the chief instrument of economic co-ordination and direction, particularly in adverse times. She also responds to the urges of an industrial society, the incitements of nationalism, and the claims of democracy, but she responds with those subtle variations that derive from the quality of her community and the influence of geography. Much of her state intervention has been concerned directly with the building of a national economy over half a continent, alongside the United States, and with the aspiration to maintain independence and balance within that economy.

In recent decades the most distinctive and important trend pertains to welfare legislation and social services. Here as elsewhere in the Western world there has been a widening concept of welfare, an ever-growing sense of public responsibility for the ill-favoured individual or for the ordinary individual as a citizen. The change is profound from the simple colonial economy of 1867, with its reliance upon the capacity of the rural family to provide a livelihood and shelter for its members, to the complex economy of the present, with its accelerated tendencies to devolve upon the state the responsibility for personal security. Regions as well as individuals expect and demand security, and are subsidized by the national government through transfers of income from more affluent regions.

This collectivism is throughout empirical, shaped by the thinking of those who are concerned with the practical problem of the moment and the exigency of given situations. Hence all political parties in turn have furthered it, and in this matter the labels of Liberal and Conservative are almost irrelevant. Political leaders have responded to concrete necessities, mass pressures, and the inevitable reorientation in public sentiment with the expansion of an industrial civilization.

The rise since the 'thirties of the Co-operative Commonwealth Federation [since 1961 known as the N.D.P.], inspired by a socialist sentiment and determined to reduce private profit-making, has introduced more ideological discussion on the role of the state, but it is only a symptom of the new social forces that are beginning to change the programmes and actions of the older parties. The C.C.F.-N.D.P. has been nourished by intellectual food of mixed origin—the ideas of British liberal socialism, the aspirations of American reformers associated with some of the Protestant churches, and the traditions of agrarian democrats and trade unionists anxious to curb big business. Whatever its own future as a third party, its ideas and feelings will have an influence in this generation in helping to reshape the functions of the state into a more collectivist mould.

Finally, it is to be emphasized that, owing to the federal structure of the state and the bi-national character of the community, Canadian state collectivism is not highly centralized. The federal government at all times exercises powerful controls over the economy through the currency, tariff, and taxation, but, so long as the federal system survives, it is forbidden to operate directly in some spheres except in periods of national emergency and war [although this tradition has been altered by numerous precedents and by judicial interpretation of the constitution since 1949]. Significant differences exist among the policies of the provinces. Each provincial government is held accountable to its electorate for the development of local natural resources and the provision of most social services, a circumstance which prevents a highly centralized and top-heavy state.

But any growing trend towards collectivism in the next generation will increasingly be related to the strains of the federation. As the provinces, especially those on the periphery, enlarge the functions of their governments, they will inevitably look to the national treasury for financial assistance. Conversely, as the central Parliament endeavours to hold the national economy in balance, it will seek more controls over local policies and provincial incomes. What government does and how the federation works will continue to be two inseparable issues in the Canadian state.

Notes

*Brady, A., "The State and Economic Life in Canada", in G. W. Brown (ed.), *Canada* (Los Angeles: United Nations Series, University of California Press, 1950) Chapter 15 (reproduced by permission of author and publisher). With the author's permission, some post-1950 material has been added by the editors.

6 The Capitalist State in Canada *

John Hutcheson

Many people in Canada are ready to believe that politicians are self-serving even to the point of corruption. But it is more difficult for them to see that governments serve specific class interests and thus systematically act against the interests of the overwhelming majority of the population. Canada's energy policy is clearly in the interest of U.S. corporations. In spite of rising public indignation, the government continues to pursue a policy which results in non-renewable resources, along with the profits from these ventures, flowing out of Canada at an increasing rate. In return for this few jobs are created and energy costs for Canadians are driven up; moreover, these resource exports set in motion de-industrializing effects which undermine the manufacturing sector of the economy.

Why does the Canadian government pursue a policy so clearly in violation of the interests of Canadians? In order to answer this question it is necessary to look at the nature of political power in this country.

There is a widely-held view of political power which suggests that the government is merely a focal point for pressures from all parts of the society, and that the government, as a neutral force, merely reflects, adjudicates and resolves the competing pressures. Those who hold this view may also believe that some interest groups are better organized and more articulate and thus get their way more often than others. But in the long run, the argument goes, all the competing interests have to be taken into account. This can be called the "pluralist" view of politics. Pluralism starts from an assumption that society is an aggregate of individuals who come together in many different kinds of groupings to pursue their individual interests.

There is a variety of this view that can be called "radical pluralism." Radical pluralists believe that the disadvantaged and the poor in our society have no say in our society and they thus call for "participatory democracy," that is, for a real voice for the poor. While such a concept complains that not all the interests in society receive equal treatment, it holds that there is a harmony of interests which will be realized if all groups of people are able to have a say in decision-making.

There are also some people who believe that, while capitalism may have been marked by gross injustices in the past, the growth of the government has offset the unequal distribution of power which results from ownership of property. These people are encouraged in this view by unrealistic conservatives who mutter about "creeping socialism," and who complain that Canadians are being mollycoddled by the welfare system. Also many Canadians no doubt believe that the capitalist economy has been replaced by a modern, "mixed economy."

It is of course true that from World War I, though more obviously from the second half of the 1930s, the direct economic role of the government has increased markedly. It is equally true, however, that any close analysis of this development will show that the nature of the mix in the mixed economy is of a very particular kind. In fact, what the Canadian government is doing is continuing a policy of creating the conditions for the maintenance of capitalism, but under changing conditions in the forces of production and the social relations of production. The achievement of a high rate of profit is the driving force of capitalism. What has happened in the twentieth century is that the direct use of the government has become necessary for the maintenance of a high rate of profit.

Much of the ideological justification of the "new" economic role for capitalist governments was provided by the economist John Maynard Keynes. In concluding his analysis of twentieth century capitalism, Keynes wrote:

> I conceive, therefore, that a somewhat comprehensive socialisation of investment will prove the only means of securing an approximation to full employment; though this need not exclude all manner of compromises and of devices by which public authority will co-operate with private initiative. But beyond this no obvious case is made out for a system of State Socialism which would embrace most of the economic life of the community. It is not the ownership of the instruments of production which it is important for the State to assume. If the State is able to determine the aggregate amount of resources devoted to augmenting the instruments and the basic rate of reward to those who own them, it will have accomplished all that is necessary. Moreover, the necessary measure of socialisation can be introduced gradually and without a break in the general traditions of society.[1]

Another ideologue of the "welfare state", William Beveridge, spoke of the desirability of the "socialization of demand without the socialization of production."

In Canada the Department of Regional Economic Expansion has eagerly taken up the role of "augmenting the instruments [of production] and the basic rate of reward to those who own them." A recent study[2] shows how much public finance is used to support such social enterprises as I.B.M., I.T.T., Westinghouse, and Procter and Gamble. And DREE is not the only agency for this type of activity. Recently the Canadian Export Development Corporation loaned "Brazil" $26.5 million for the purpose of buying electrical equipment. That this is not altogether charitable aid to a struggling bastion of democracy can be seen from a closer analysis of the terms.[3] The money, rather than being loaned to the people of Brazil, who are represented neither by those who rule in Brazil nor by the companies concerned, was loaned to a "private Brazilian utility company" (Light-serviços), which is 83 per cent owned by Brascan, one of Canada's very own multi-national corporations. Also the equipment was to be purchased from a specified group of corporations operating branch plants in Canada.

The situation is well summarized in the Quebec Federation of Labour's Manifesto, "The State is Our Exploiter":

> . . . under the liberal state, public financing injected into the economy is given outright to private capital, or supports it so as to raise profit ratios. This strengthens the private sector at the expense of the public sector.[4]

The government in Canada has always been essential to the development strategy of capitalism and it continues to act in the interests of a capitalist class.

The Marxist analysis of political power in fact recognizes that the government is merely one aspect of a wider political framework which can be called the "state." Ralph Miliband, in his study of the contemporary capitalist state, defines the state as "a number of particular institutions which, together, constitute its reality, and which interact as parts of what may be called the state system."[5] Thus, apart from governments at various levels, there is the administrative element of the state, which is not just the government bureaucracy but also public corporations, central banks, regulatory commissions, etc. There are also the military and police forces, the coercive apparatus of the state. There is also the judiciary which in constitutional theory is independent of the government. In practice, the legislature, too, is distinct from the government, and thus parliamentary assemblies form part of the wider sphere of the state.

There is a further aspect of power in capitalist societies which cannot be neglected. This is the power that results from what the Italian Marxist Antonio Gramsci called the "hegemony" of the dominant class, that is, its ideological predominance over subordinate classes. This hegemony is exercised through a variety of institutions; political, cultural and social. These institutions include political parties, churches, radio, television, newspapers, cinema, theatre, schools and universities, and the family. (I do not mean to imply that the existence of these institutions *inevitably* serves the capitalist state, but at present most manifestations of them do reinforce the capitalist state.) Not all of these institutions are normally reckoned to be part of the state, but it is important to see how they are used to buttress the capitalist state.

Any discussion of class in Canada and of the class conflict that is inevitably part of the capitalist mode of production shows that the nature of the state grows out of this fundamental aspect of capitalist society. As Miliband puts it:

> The economic and political life of capitalist societies is *primarily* determined by the relationship, born of the capitalist mode of production between . . . two classes—the class which on the one hand owns and controls, and the working class on the other. Here are still the social forces whose confrontation most powerfully shapes the social climate and the political system of advanced capitalism. In fact, the political process in these societies is mainly

> *about* the confrontation of those forces, and is intended to sanction the terms of the relationship between them.[6]

That is to say, the power of the capitalist class does not arise simply from its control of the state. One can identify *three levels* at which the power of the capitalists is exercised: through control of the means of production, through control of the dominant ideological institutions of society, and through control of the state. Within each of these three levels there is a spectrum of control from leadership (or "hegemony" in Gramsci's terminology) to overt domination. Obviously control within any one of these three levels reinforces control within the others. For example, when control is effective within the first two, there is little need to resort to overt domination in the third. But should a serious challenge arise at any one level, power is quickly mobilized at the other levels. Workers in a factory know that they are "under control" once they have passed the steel fence that typically surrounds factories, but should they challenge that everyday control, the forces of the state in the form of the police and the courts are soon brought into action. It is in fact through the state that the power at the other levels is guaranteed and co-ordinated, though it is the control of the means of production that makes possible control at the other two levels. (This type of analysis, incidentally, suggests that it is dangerous to make too sharp a distinction between "base" and "superstructure" when analysing capitalist society.)

The importance of an analysis of power which takes into account all three levels is shown by the history of attempts to transform capitalist societies. Challenges to the capitalists' control which have not been effective throughout the three levels have always met with defeat.

Sometimes even where the government has fallen into the hands of "outsiders," capitalist states have managed to survive. It is a question of the nature of the "outsiders," specifically of their willingness and ability to permanently change capitalist social relations of production. For example, as Miliband argues, the fascists of the 1930s advanced a "rhetoric of total transformation and renewal" with "anti-bourgeois resonances,"[7] but neither Mussolini nor Hitler dislodged big business, because neither sought to transform capitalist social relations. As Miliband says:

> The most telling fact of all about the real nature of the Fascist systems is surely that, when they came to an end, twenty years after Mussolini's "March on Rome" and twelve years after Hitler's assumption of the chancellorship, the economic and social structures of both countries had not been significantly changed.[8]

Perhaps more surprising to many have been the results in countries where social democratic and labour parties have formed governments on programmes which expressed an intention to transcend the capitalist system by means of the use of state power in the service of reform. They have not done so. This is not to say that the presence of such parties has not contributed to important reforms, or to say that it makes no difference which party is in power. The point is that social democratic parties have been unable to control the power of the capitalists and to change capitalist social relations. They have not faced up to the realities of the class conflict which grows out of the capitalist mode of production and which produces the class nature of the bourgeois state.

In the 1890s Rosa Luxemburg clearly indicated the limitations of what are now called social democratic parties. In her essay *Social Reform or Revolution,* she outlines the petty-bourgeois basis of the tendency which refused to acknowledge the real nature of the development of capitalist society:

> The theory of the gradual introduction of socialism proposes a progressive reform of capitalist property and the capitalist state in the direction of socialism. However, in consequence of the objective facts of existing society, one and the other develop in a precisely opposed direction. The process of production will be increasingly socialized and state intervention, the control of the state over the process of production, will be extended. But at the same time, private property will take on more and more the form of open capitalist exploitation of the labour of others, and state control will be more and more penetrated with the exclusive interests of the ruling class. Inasmuch as the state is the *political* organization of capitalism, and property relations, that is, the *juridical* organization of capitalism, become more *capitalist* as they develop, and not more socialist, they oppose to the theory of the progressive introduction of socialism two insurmountable difficulties.[9]

The development of capitalist property and the capitalist state is not leading in the direction of socialism.

For anyone concerned about the future of this country, it is extremely important to arrive at a clear understanding of this point. Many Canadians believe that there is an inherently progressive tendency at work that is increasing the well-being of the people of this country by substantial modifications of the capitalist system. Many Canadians, for example, support the NDP because they believe that a series of such modifications can remove the undesirable features of capitalism. In that way many hope that capitalism can be controlled without a fundamental challenge to the power of capitalists which results from their control of the means of production. But that is to hope that the capitalists will not use all the power at their disposal to maintain their domination. One weapon that the capitalists have at their disposal is control of the state.

We have already seen some examples of the way in which capitalists are using their control of the state to maintain capitalism. But there are other examples of this which show clearly the economic role of the government. And it is important to realize that these policies affect the lives of all of us and our prospects for the future.

Since the 1950s capitalist governments have attempted to avoid crises by supporting profit rates through control of wage levels, deflationary policies and direct controls. In Canada only the first of these has been used on a comprehensive scale. In the late 1960s, for example, the government decided that it could run the risk of creating high levels of unemployment. Of course this was not explained in terms of income redistribution. Rather, the policy was justified by reference to a creature of some economists' imaginations, the Phillips curve. Essentially the argument was that "society" had to choose between unemployment and inflation. The importance of being able to find such technical arguments to justify unpopular actions was well appreciated by Keynes. In 1925 Keynes had written the following advice to a government:

> We ought to warn you . . . that it will not be safe politically that you are intensifying unemployment deliberately in order to reduce wages. Thus you will have to ascribe what is happening to every conceivable cause except the true one.[10]

It is possible that the grain of truth in the Phillips curve argument lies in a connection between inflation and "unproductive" labour. What may be happening is that the growing size of the unproductive labour force, which is necessary for the maintenance of profit rates, is also creating a level of inflation which threatens the stability of the system. It has certainly been the experience of several countries, however, that inflation was not reduced by creating general unemployment. The resort to income policies suggests that, in some countries at least, high levels of unemployment have not proved to be satisfactory to the capitalists with respect to income distribution, though the costs of the policy have been very high for the hundreds of thousands of unemployed.

It is worth discussing, briefly, the use of incomes policies since, although they have not been used here, they have been used elsewhere and some have thought that they might be useful in Canada. The first point to notice is that an incomes policy is in reality a wage freeze. The policy is made to appear to demand equality of sacrifice since the reality must not appear to be too seriously at variance with the ruling ideology of pluralism in which the state is the arbiter of competing pressures. But the point of the policy is to reduce wages in order to maintain the rate of surplus-value.

The policy has been introduced in some countries when it was found that deflationary policies did not reduce inflation, thus leaving problems for foreign trade, but did create problems for productivity growth as a result of demand fluctuations. The disadvantages of the incomes policy, from the capitalists' point of view, is that the class nature of income distribution is made clear to all, except presumably to some economists who remain lost in the fogs of their own creation.[11] The class nature of the incomes policy becoming clear, the chances of the policy actually redistributing income are obviously dependent on the balance of political forces.

What we now have to consider is the question of the stability of the capitalist economy under the "new" economic policies. The capitalists have expanded the direct economic role of the government in order to achieve a higher rate of profit and to maintain their domination. But they cannot do this without causing important structural changes in the economy. Many economists have argued that these structural changes promote stability. But many capitalist governments are now finding that they are facing a growing "fiscal crisis."

In Canada the government is now responsible for about 18 per cent of all investment and the proportion of investment coming from the public sector has increased by about 21 per cent from 1950 to 1970. Correspondingly the rate of business investment has been decreasing. Government expenditure, without including transfer payments, is about 20 per cent of GNP. The government directly employs about 12 per cent of the labour force, this figure increasing to about 18 per cent if you include hospitals, education and other indirect government employment.[12] The fiscal crisis is a consequence of the tendency to a declining rate of profit. It is the tendency for the profit rate to decline, which necessitates the high level of government expenditure and creates problems for the financing of that expenditure.

The problem of financing this level of government expenditure is becoming acute and yet it is politically necessary. Government expenditure must be supported out of either surplus-value or out of wages. An important debate is developing on the correct analysis of this expenditure. One side tends to argue that unproductive expenditure, particularly military budgets, maintain rates of profit through providing markets for capitalist production. The other side stresses the problem of the production of surplus-value and argues that unproductive government and private expenditure must be paid for out of increased productivity in some parts of the private sector. Obviously the argument turns on an adequate delineation of productive and unproductive labour, and also on the extent to which taxes redistribute income from wages to surplus-value.

To the extent that government expenditure is supported out of surplus-value and does not contribute to increasing total surplus-value, the output of productive workers must increase correspondingly to maintain rates of profit. This means job speed-up and deteriorating conditions of work. Of course much government expenditure is supported by taxes on wages and in fact the fiscal policy of the government is increasingly redistributing income to the benefit of corporations. The ability to do this, however, is limited by the resistance of the working class to decreased standards of living, and the limits of the process have been indicated by increased militancy of large sections of the working class in recent years.

In Canada, as in other capitalist countries, the contradictions of capitalist growth are becoming increasingly impossible to hide. In Canada, however, these contradictions are heightened by the dependency of the country. As the U.S. attempts to resolve some of its own structural problems, the development of Canada is likely to be further jeopardized.

This latter point is a reminder that one cannot discuss the capitalist state in Canada without taking into account the specific aspects of the state which arise from the dependency of Canadian capitalism. There are features of the Canadian state, some of which have been discussed, which are similar to those in other capitalist states. But the present state in Canada is also the result of a specific historical development of the forces of production and the social relations of production. We must consider that history if we are to understand the way in which the state has both been used to create a dependent capitalist economy and has also been the result of a dependent capitalist development. That history will also help us to understand why the Canadian bourgeoisie has increasingly lost control of the state.

In Canada we live in a society that can be described as "liberal-democratic." There is a political competition amongst several parties, there is the right of opposition, there are regular elections, representative assemblies, civic guarantees and various restrictions on the use of state power. But we should recognize, as Professor C. B. Macpherson reminded us,[13] that the democratic aspect of our society was added on to a solidly established liberal capitalist society and, as we have already seen, this particular kind of democratic government exists to uphold and enforce capitalist society. That is, the democratic element was granted by the ruling class in order to contain popular pressures, but it has been granted in such a way as to maintain the capitalist economy.

It is easy to see that this country was not founded on democratic principles when one considers how recently the franchise was granted to all adults. It was well into the twentieth century before that limited form of democracy was achieved. And it is easy to see how little it was a matter of principle for the ruling class in this country, by considering the two bills introduced by Arthur Meighen and passed by Parliament in 1917.[14] One of the bills denied the vote to conscientious objectors, to those of enemy alien birth, and to those of European birth speaking an enemy alien language and naturalized since 1902. The second, to show that some principles were a fine thing, gave the franchise to all on active service and to wives, widows and other female relatives of servicemen overseas. Thus were women first admitted to this democratic society.

It is necessary to note here that, although liberal-democracy has been associated with capitalism, it does not follow that capitalism requires liberal-democratic politics. As Marx noted:

> Confronted by the working class, the still ruling class—whatever the specific form in which it appropriates the labour of the masses—has but one and the same economic interest: to maintain the enslavement of labour and to appropriate the fruit.[15]

Perhaps because the overtly oppressive state tends to be unstable, there is a tendency towards the apparently "classless" state. For those who believe in the security of liberal democracy, however, it is worth considering the frightening ease with which the War Measures Act was brought into action in 1970.

In order to understand the present liberal-democratic state we have to look at the history of liberal society in Canada and the specific nature of that liberal society. First it is necessary to understand how a liberal capitalist society was created, since it is not a common feature of dependent societies.

The emergence of liberal society in Europe was the result of a long struggle between two social systems—capitalism and seigneurialism. (The latter term is better than the more commonly used "feudalism," since feudalism designates a particular political system within seigneurialism.) It is impossible to summarize the history of this struggle which was carried on for many centuries and with varying intensity at different times in different countries. It is important, however, to note several points:

1. The triumph of liberal society was achieved after long years of class conflict between bourgeoisie and nobility, and in each country the new liberal society was marked by the particular national form of this class conflict. This is particularly true of the "superstructural" aspects of each society.
2. The method of transforming agrarian society was at the centre of the conflict.
3. The history of the modern working class (or proletariat) begins with the triumph of liberal society.[16]

The first two of these points are not of major importance in Canada. There was no entrenched seigneurial society of lords and peasants (see further comments on this below) and the only significant non-bourgeois rural population, the sparsely settled Indians, was evicted and to a considerable extent destroyed. There were of course conflicts over land policy once the Indians had been evicted, but these were conflicts within the framework of an emerging capitalist society. The third point is of major importance, and the emergence of a working class defined by capitalist production is a major feature of Canada's development.

In addition to this, in discussing the development of liberal society in Canada, we have to take into account the factor of its dependent status. That is we need to see the link between the development of the metropolis and the hinterland, and the way in which the development of both social relations of production and forces of production in the metropolis have influenced the development of both social relations of production and forces of production in the hinterland.[17]

The basic relationship between metropolis and hinterland is elementary and was stated clearly as long ago as the eighteenth century by a contributor to the great document of the Enlightenment, the *Encyclopedia*:

> These colonies being established solely for the utility of the metropolis, it follows that . . . the colonies would be of no more use, if they were able to do without the metropolis; thus it is a very law of nature that the arts and cultiva-

> tion in a colony must be confined to such and such objects, according to the convenience of the country of domination.[18]

The prospects for development, *under capitalism*, of countries placed in such colonial relationships have not been very good. This problem has been discussed by, among others, Paul Baran.[19] As Baran points out, European expansion has been responsible for the destruction of self-sufficient rural societies and, by the seizure of land for production of export crops and by the exposure of rural handicrafts to the competition of industrial exports, has in most places created only vast pools of pauperized labour. Only one Asian country, for example, has escaped its neighbours' fate and developed under capitalism, and that is Japan. As Baran noted, it is perhaps not coincidental that Japan was never part of the capitalist colonial world.

There are, however, a few areas of the world where European expansion has resulted in the development of prosperous capitalist economies. One area is North America. For the U.S. the only obstacle to accumulation and capitalist expansion was foreign domination. The bourgeoisie in that country was strong enough to overthrow that domination and to create a political framework conducive to the growth of capitalism. In fact, as William Appleman Williams has shown,[20] the achievement of capitalist development in the U.S. was not merely the result of independence, but (as with Japan and the major European powers) entailed the creation of a new empire, starting from the date of independence. And the development of the U.S. empire has had profound implications for the other parts of the Americas.

Obviously, then, we have to look at the specific nature of any colonial relationship. The role of the metropolis-hinterland relationship in the distortion of the structure of the hinterland has recently been emphasized by André Gunder Frank.[21] Frank's argument, which has been formulated for Latin America but has been generalized to other situations (in fact "Latin America" is already a generalization), can be summarized as follows: first, Latin America has had a market economy from the beginning of colonialism; secondly, it has been capitalist from the beginning; and, thirdly, the dependent nature of its insertion into the capitalist world market is the cause of its under-development.

Gunder Frank is right to insist that from the beginning of their colonial period American societies, and this holds for Canada, have been tied to a capitalist world market; but, as several of his critics have observed,[22] it does not follow that the American colonies of Europe developed capitalist relations of production from the beginning of their colonial history. As Marx showed:

> Capital can spring into life only when the owner of the means of production and subsistence meets in the market with the free labourer selling his labour-power. And this one historical condition comprises a world's history.[23]

In fact, in a comparative analysis of dependent societies it is of particular importance to investigate the extent to which capitalist integration has been achieved. That is the extent to which the population is involved in the capitalist mode of production in each dependent country. The degree of capitalist integration is undoubtedly *one* factor in the prosperity of the dependent society. The peculiarly destructive consequences of a non-capitalist society being drawn into an international market dominated by the capitalist mode of production are summarized by Marx's comment: "The civilized horrors of over-work are grafted on to the barbaric horrors of slavery, serfdom, etc."[24]

In Canada an almost fully-integrated capitalist social structure *did* grow out of a colonial society which was already integrated into a capitalist empire. Though the key factor in Canada's development has been the extraction of a series of staple products by a series of imperial powers, Canada has never been *merely* a resource colony. Canada is unlike other colonies in which capitalism promoted plantation production, using slavery or indentured labour, or perpetuated various forms of non-capitalist production based on peasant labour. Canada has become a fully integrated capitalist society, that is a society with capitalist property relations, and a society in which the overwhelming proportion of the population is engaged in capitalist production. It is perhaps for this reason that Canada, despite its colonial aspects, has developed into a rich country. This development is now threatened. The succession of capitalist development by under-development has been a common fate for many regions of capitalist countries, as the history of the Maritimes testifies. In fact, as the example of Argentina may show, this is a fate that can be visited upon whole countries.

As I have argued above, capitalist social relations in Canada did not arise, as in Europe, out of a prolonged conflict between capitalist society and seigneurial society. The fur trade was long the dominant economic activity in Canada and, after fishing, was the means by which Canada was joined to the European economy. The fur trade, however, was based neither on capitalist nor on seigneurial relations of production, but on mercantile exploitation of Indian production. It is true that in New France a form of seigneurial society had been established, though it is important to see that this was not a simple reproduction of European society and it had little of its tenacity.[25]

That there were some barriers to capitalist development, however, can be seen from an article that appeared in *Le Canadien* about 1810. The article defended bourgeois society, contrasting the U.S.A. with Lower Canada. It is interesting as an example of more than one kind of chauvinism:

> First we have an overwhelming aversion towards feudal tenure . . . Since our revolution all our actions are geared towards commerce . . . all our institutions tend to favour its operations. For example, suppose you wish to speculate and you do not have enough money. You can go to a banker who knows something of the value of your property and you will soon have the sum you need, for a small discount . . . But if your property is held under feudal law its value cannot be so easily determined and it may be subject to [obligations]. But there is a more important consideration in favour of [freehold]. In our

> country the husband is the sole controller of all goods, we do not have laws which protect wives and children; so that the husband can use as security all his property without his wife being able to prevent him. . . . Thus a respectable man can always find credit, while with your Canadian laws a man who appears to have property will find difficulty in raising loans because his wife always retains some rights [over other creditors;] and it is precisely that which we do not like. These laws are all very well for a rural population, but they are insupportable for a people who devote themselves entirely to commerce.[26]

The survival of seigneurial property combined with the dominance of the new colonial merchants and government led to the unstable political situation of the 1830s.[27] Though the struggle was led by pre-industrial social classes, as were many of the democratic struggles in Europe between the 1790s and the 1840s, it was essentially a struggle for a democratic control of the capitalist society that was emerging rather than a struggle against capitalist society. The defeat of the 1837 rebellions meant that in Canada, as in Europe, democracy would be granted later as an appendage to liberal society. But in Canada the particular nature of the bourgeoisie and its colonial situation had the additional result that the defeat of the national and democratic struggles of the 1830s doomed the possibility of the development of an *independent* capitalism. There is an essay by Tom Naylor[28] which is of fundamental importance since it shows the mechanism by which Canada could emerge as a capitalist and yet dependent state. The commercial bourgeoisie in Canada used their position of dominance to bring about precisely this situation. Following the suppression of the rebellion the Canadian mercantile bourgeoisie could settle down to creating a dependent society with capitalist social relations of production.

A main role of the state in Canada has always been the maintenance of "peace, order, and good government," which means ensuring an expanding market economy, allowing for capital accumulation and maintaining the necessary labour supply. Control of the state by the bourgeoisie has been crucial in carrying out this form of development.

First let us look at the provision of the necessary labour supply, that is the creation of a modern working class. As Pentland put it:

> The capitalistic labour market . . . is the one so well supplied with labour that employers feel free to hire workers as desired, on a short term basis without assuming any responsibility for their overhead costs. There is not much sign of such a market in Canada before 1830. In the next two decades there is evidence of transition towards it. . . . The essential structure of a capitalistic market existed in the 1850's, and the market had attained some sophistication by the 1870's.[29]

In bringing about this situation the role of the government was crucial, both in controlling land policy and in maintaining an appropriate immigration policy, and in controlling the conditions of work of those immigrants when they had arrived. Of course this type of government activity is not particular to any one period in Canadian history. The way in which the government has always controlled conditions of work can be seen from a reading of Charles Lipton's *The Trade Union Movement of Canada, 1827-1959.*[30]

It was not until 1872, and then as the result of considerable demonstrations, that a Trade Union Act was introduced to legislate that the mere fact of combining to increase wages or to reduce hours of work was not a conspiracy and did not violate the common law. Even then, along with the Trade Union Act, the government passed the Criminal Law Amendment Act. This Act, by providing penalties for violence or intimidation during organizing campaigns and strikes, left plenty of room for anti-union interpretation and convictions of conspiracy by anti-union courts.[31] In 1947, following the textile strike at Lachute, at a mill where one woman could work 108 hours for $11.17, two union organizers (Madeleine Parent and Azéluz Beaucage) were convicted of seditious conspiracy.

The state has also, from early times, been able to rely on the use of court injunctions to prohibit organization and to end strikes. In Quebec recently the government has gone from the use of injunctions to jail striking workers to the introduction of legislation (Bill 89) to eliminate the right to strike in the public sector and in transport and communications.[32] This is only an echo of the Industrial Disputes Act of 1907 dealing with strikes in public utilities, mining and railroads. And the Federal Government has also used direct legislation to end specific strikes. Consider the National Railway Strike of August, 1950. This strike led the Ottawa correspondent of the Montreal *Gazette* to remind the government of its powers under the War Measures Act (a useful item as we have recently seen). A special session of Parliament was summoned and the Prime Minister stated that the strike was harming the United States, a country which depended on "effective co-operation from Canada." Having heard that, Parliament passed an Act to require workers to return to work within 48 hours.[33] In 1954 a strike vote by 90 per cent of the membership of the unions of non-operating railway employees was met by a federal government announcement that if the strike took place, another parliamentary act would be brought in to ban the strike.[34]

Let us turn now to the particular form of the state in Canada. We have seen that by the mid-nineteenth century Canada had emerged as a liberal capitalist society with a clearly defined dominant commercial bourgeoisie and a growing working class. We have seen that the state performed the classical functions of any capitalist state in suppressing any opposition to this development and the human costs of this type of society. But we have to consider the particular nature of the Canadian state as an instrument of both the ruling class of the imperial country and the ruling class of Canada. The Canadian state has been a critical link between the domestic and foreign ruling classes.

In the days of the British Empire the Canadian state served as a guarantor of the loans of British investors and banking houses and at the same time served their partners, the Canadian bourgeoisie. Both the Act of Union of

1840 and Confederation were identified by Harold Innis[35] as instruments to secure low interest rates for the transportation system. Donald Creighton went even further. In discussing the British government's decision to support the proposals made at Quebec for confederation, he said:

> This British assistance might be interpreted as an effort to assist in the creation of a great holding company in which could be amalgamated all those divided and vulnerable North American interests whose protection was a burden to the British state and whose financial weakness was a grievance of British capital.[36]

And in the same study Creighton explains the true meaning of Canada for the capitalist class:

> Railways were not mere adjuncts to Confederation, they were of its essence; and the *moral bases* of a transcontinental union were the two solemn engagements to provide railway communications from the St. Lawrence valley to the oceans. . . . Political union would at once provide a basis upon which [past obligations resulting from the construction of a transportation system] could be more easily borne, and a fund of resources out of which the transport system could be completed and the existing investments made more profitable.[37]

In fact the constitution of 1867, which was designed for one particular economic strategy, has been a problem ever since as the result of the emergence of an economic reality unlike that imagined by the Fathers of Confederation.[38] The economic goal of Confederation was the creation of a continent-wide trading system. The 1867 Act assumes growth based on the development of the new Western agricultural regions, the emergence of a national industry, large-scale immigration, and a continuation of the commercial system of the British Empire. The powers necessary to guide such development were conferred upon the Ottawa government. Macdonald's National Policy of 1879 showed how the state was to be used in the interest of the Canadian bourgeoisie. The National Policy provided government backing for the building of the railway; it established a tariff which would provide business for the CPR, shipping manufactured goods from the east to the prairies and wheat east towards Montreal and thence to Europe. The government in Ottawa showed that it was determined to bring the west under the control of Canada. In 1885 troops were sent to put down the second Riel rebellion, showing that Métis and Indians would not be allowed to interfere with the "sub-imperial" interests of Canada's merchant capitalists.

As things turned out, however, the major bases for development in much of Canada in the years after Confederation were mining, newsprint and hydroelectric power, and later urbanization and road transportation. This has meant that the provincial governments, which were given control over the public domain have emerged as critical institutions within the Canadian state. In addition, the U.S. branch plants began to appear in Canada in large numbers. And the fact that much of this post-Confederation industrial development has been directed from the U.S. has added a further and profoundly important facet to the role of the state in Canada. Harold Innis pointed to this when he noted that the achievement of "independence" in Canada was connected with the decline of Canada's economic role in the British Empire:

> The end of the period of expansion based on the St. Lawrence and trade with Great Britain coincided roughly with the achievement of Dominion status which followed the Great War and which was marked by the Statute of Westminster. ... The extension of the American empire, the decline of its natural resources, and the emergence of metropolitan areas, supported capitalist expansion in Canada and reinforced the trend of regionalism. The pull to the north and south has tended to become stronger in contrast with the pull of east and west. The British North America Act and later decisions of the Privy Council have strengthened the control of the provinces over natural resources such as minerals, hydro-electric power, and pulpwood on Crown lands, resources which have provided the basis for trade with the U.S. and for investment of American capital.[39]

The changing pattern of dominion-provincial relations has thus echoed the transition from formal colonial status within the British Empire to informal dependent status within the U.S. empire. Informal empire has a long history of which the variety known as neo-colonialism is only one type. It was in 1824 that the British foreign-secretary, Canning, said "Spanish-America is free and, if we do not mismanage our affairs sadly, she is English."[40] U.S. capitalists had long understood the meaning of this statement, although they had not waited for some Spanish colonies to liberate themselves. It was during the period following World War I that Canada was subjected to the decisive shifts towards the economic structure which we now know. The flow of resources to the south was increased and U.S. branch plants established complete domination in the automotive, electrical and chemical industries in Canada.

It should not be thought that the transition from one empire to another has occasioned much conflict within the capitalist class. The majority of the Canadian bourgeoisie was quick to discover the benefits of continentalism. For them it has paid. For the rest of the country the long-run price has been high, as Harold Innis observed in the concluding pages of *The Fur Trade in Canada*:

> The economic history of Canada has been dominated by the discrepancy between the centre and margin of western civilization. Energy has been directed toward the exploitation of staple products and the tendency has been cumulative. ... Agriculture, industry, transportation, trade, finance, and governmental activities tend to become subordinate to the production of the staple for a more highly specialized manufacturing community.[41]

In fact, even a few members of the Canadian bourgeoisie have worried that too high a price would eventually be paid for development within the U.S. empire. Until the 1940s the Canadian bourgeoisie, through their control of a state within the British Empire, were a valuable asset to the U.S. capitalists. The "North Atlantic Triangle" was then a reality, though the interests of the U.S. capitalists extended well beyond the North Atlantic portion of the British Empire. From the early twentieth century to the 1940s the Canadian bourgeoisie was in a relatively favourable situation as it balanced on the base created by the other two corners of the triangle. With the decline of the British Empire the base for this balance was destroyed though, like a sleepwalker, the Canadian bourgeoisie appeared not to notice. Some voices tried to waken them gently. It was no accident that this gentle alarm was sounded by figures both associated with the financial bourgeoisie and with an active role in the Canadian state. James Coyne and Walter Gordon both realized that, with the rapid take-over of Canadian resources and productive facilities, the Canadian bourgeoisie would be left with an increasingly insignificant role in the U.S. empire. Even the role of the state would pass from that of an intermediary between the U.S. and Canadian bourgeoisie to becoming increasingly a direct creature of the U.S. imperialists.

The loss of sovereignty by the Canadian government can be seen in many ways. In fact the term "special status" is only a euphemism for the sale of sovereignty. The process began in earnest in 1940 with the creation of the Permanent Joint Board of Defence. The process was carried further by Canada's participation in NATO and NORAD. The events of the "Cuban missile crisis" of 1962 revealed that the Canadian government had virtually lost ultimate authority over its own military forces. Pressure to mobilize the Canadian forces from NORAD and the U.S. government was stronger than the misgivings of the Prime Minister and the unwillingness of the Minister for External Affairs. It was in vain that the latter pleaded "if we go along with the Americans now we'll be their vassals forever."[42] The delay in jumping to the bidding of the U.S. by Diefenbaker and Howard Green split the Conservative government. Since the Liberal party has been the agency of "special status," it is doubtful that a Liberal government would have even noticed that a fundamental issue of Canada's sovereignty was in the balance.

The defence of U.S. "security" was also an issue in the death of a high-ranking Canadian diplomat in 1957. Herbert Norman, Canadian Ambassador to Egypt, was hounded to his death by accusations from the U.S. Senate Internal Security Subcommittee. This witch-hunting was abetted by the supply of confidential information from the Canadian government.[43] (In May, 1973, in response to an allegation that the Nixon administration had planned to break into the Canadian Embassy in Washington, an external affairs spokesman stated that "all the Americans would have had to do was ask for any information they wished."[44])

In 1965 it became apparent that the Canadian government could not even control its own taxation policy. Walter Gordon's budget proposed to disallow tax deductions for advertising in foreign-owned newspapers and periodicals. Bowing to pressure from the U.S. State Department, the government exempted *Time* and *Reader's Digest* from this legislation. It appeared that the U.S. government used both the quota on oil exports and the auto-pact as levers in the "negotiations."[45] The auto-pact itself is a mechanism by which the Canadian government has ceded control of a critical industry to the U.S. government and foreign corporations.

From resource sell-outs to low taxation for U.S. corporations, from Defence Sharing Agreements to the auto-pact, Canadian governments have surrendered the Canadian economy to U.S. control. The loss of sovereignty has been an inevitable consequence. It is ironic that "special status" has been ended, not by the anger of the Canadian people, but by the measures taken by the U.S. empire to help it digest its other intended victims.

The Canadian state is now in the control of the dominant section of the ruling class in Canada—the U.S. corporations. The Canadian state furthers the interests of U.S. capitalists and by so doing contributes to Canada's further integration into the U.S. empire. This is leading to the disintegration of Canada. But the fact that a Canadian state still exists is of great significance. For the Canadian people to demand the right to control that state would be a profoundly anti-imperialist action. This would not mean the defence of the present state which daily works in opposition to the interests of the people of this country. It would mean the political possibility of creating a Canadian state controlled by the working people which would serve as an instrument of national liberation. The demand for an independent state would itself be a demand for a state in the hands of the people. The capitalists in Canada are well aware of this danger and for this reason work assiduously to undermine the concept of Canadian sovereignty. That is why it is essential for Canadians to defend Canadian sovereignty and to assert their right to their own independent state at the same time as they struggle against the policies of the capitalist state in Canada.

Notes

*Hutcheson, J., "The Capitalist State in Canada", in R. Laxer (ed.), *Canada Ltd.* (Toronto: McClelland and Stewart, 1973), pp. 153-177 (reproduced by permission of author and publisher).

[1]J. M. Keynes, *The General Theory of Employment, Interest, and Money*. Macmillan, London, 1961, p. 378.

[2]R. Chodos, "The Great Canadian DREE machine", reprinted in the Last Post Special, *Corporate Canada*. ed. M. Starowicz and R. Murphy, James Lewis and Samuel, Toronto 1972.

[3]See *The Last Post*, March, 1973.

[4]In D. Drache (ed.) *Quebec—Only the Beginning*, New Press, Toronto, 1972, p. 210.

[5]R. Miliband, *The State in Capitalist Society*, Weidenfeld and Nicholson, London, 1969, p. 49. This is an important study for an understanding of the class nature of the capitalist state. One of the difficulties with Miliband's analysis, however, is that he does not show the way in which the nature of the state is linked to a theory of social change resulting from class conflict. That is, he provides an essentially static analysis, influenced by the fact that he is refuting the pluralist argument, which does not specify the structures by

which movements at the different levels of capitalist society are linked together and determined by one another. He emphasizes the cohesion of the capitalist state but not the way in which the state adjusts to make certain of the *reproduction* of the conditions of production under changing conditions of forces of production and social relations of production.

Miliband in fact notes that the Marxist theory of the state has lagged behind other aspects of Marxist analysis. (A summary of its development can be found in Miliband's article "Marx and the State" in *Socialist Register*, 1965.) It could be argued that a Marxist theory of *the* capitalist state is impossible since analysis of elements of the superstructure must take into account the historical specificity of class structures in each capitalist state. Of course a theoretical problematic is necessary and an important contribution to this has been made by Nicos Poulantzas in his *Pouvoir Politique et Classes Sociales*, Maspero, Paris, 1970. An English edition of this book has just been published by New Left Books, London, 1973. There is an interesting exchange between Poulantzas and Miliband which first appeared in *New Left Review*, nos. 58 and 59, and is reprinted in R. Blackburn (ed.) *Ideology in Social Science* (Fontana), London, 1972.

[6]Miliband, *The State in Capitalist Society*, p. 16.

[7]*Ibid.*, p. 88.

[8]*Ibid.*, p. 92.

[9]This passage from *Social Reform and Revolution* can be found on p. 84 of *Selected Political Writings of Rosa Luxemburg*, Monthly Review Press, 1971. On the general nature of social democracy see the essay by Lucio Colletti, "Bernstein and the Marxism of the Second International" in L. Colletti, *From Rousseau to Lenin*, New Left Books, London, 1972.

[10]J. M. Keynes, *Essays in Persuasion*, Norton, N.Y., 1963, p. 253.

[11]For a discussion of some of the strange inhabitants of the mystical world of the "neo-classical" economists, see E. K. Hunt and Jesse Schwartz, *A Critique of Economic Theory*, Penguin Modern Economics Readings, 1972.

[12]R. Deaton, "The Fiscal Crisis of the State", *Our Generation*, v. 8, no. 4 and also available as a reprint. This is an important article with the exception of the last section which is curiously unrelated to what has gone before. The nature of the "fiscal crisis" should be seen as an issue in the debate referred to below.

[13]C. B. Macpherson, *The Real World of Democracy*, CBC Publication, Toronto, 1965.

[14]They are mentioned in A. R. M. Lower, *Colony to Nation*, Longmans, Toronto, 1957, p. 465.

[15]K. Marx, *The Civil War in France*.

[16]There is of course an outline of the conflict between capitalism and seigneurialism by Marx in the *Communist Manifesto*. Some detailed discussion can be found in the important work of E. J. Hobsbawm. See, for example, his essay "The Crisis of the 17th Century", reprinted in T. Aston (ed.), *Crisis in Europe, 1560-1660*, Anchor, Garden City, 1967, and also his book *The Age of Revolution, 1798-1848*, Mentor, N.Y., 1964. The importance of the type of agrarian revolution has been stressed by Barrington Moore in *Social Origins of Dictatorship and Democracy*, Beacon, Boston, 1966. For the history of the early years of the English working class and an example of the kind of history we need, see E. P. Thompson, *The Making of the English Working Class*, Penguin, Harmondsworth, 1969. The continuing importance of all these points was stressed by Antonio Gramsci. See, for example, his essay "The Southern Question" in Gramsci, *The Modern Prince and Other Writings*, International Publishers, N.Y., 1957.

[17]See E. Genovese, *The World the Slaveholders Made*, Vintage Books, N.Y., 1971, Part I.

[18]Article "Colonies" by Véron de Forbonnais in *L'Encyclopédie*. Quoted by S. B. Ryerson in the *Founding of Canada*, Progress Books. Toronto, 1972, p. 178.

[19]P. Baran, *The Political Economy of Growth*, Monthly Review Press, N.Y., 1957, Ch. 5.

[20]W. A. Williams, *The Contours of American History*, Quadrangle Books, Chicago, 1966. For a brief review see his article in *Canadian Dimension*, Vol. IV, 1967.

[21]See, for example, his *Capitalism and Under-development in Latin America*, Monthly Review Press, N.Y., 1969.

[22]For example, Ernesto Laclau, *New Left Review*, 67, 1971 and also the argument in Genovese's book cited in n. 19.
[23]K. Marx, *Capital*, v. 1, ch. 6.
[24]*Ibid.*, ch. 10.
[25]On this see Phillipe Garigue, "Sociological Interpretations of the Social Evolution of French Canada", in M. Rioux and Y. Martin, *French-Canadian Society*, McClelland and Stewart, Toronto, 1964.
[26]Translated from Gilles Bourque, *Classes Sociales et Question Nationale au Québec*, 1760-1840, Parti Pris, Montreal, 1970, p. 196-8.
[27]For an understanding of the events of 1837 and their significance for the emergence of the capitalist state in Canada the studies of S. B. Ryerson, *Unequal Union*, International Publishers, N.Y., 1968, and Giles Bourque (cited above) are of major importance. For an understanding of the democratic struggles in Europe from the 1790s to the 1840s, with which the events in Canada should be compared, see the important work of George Rudé. One example is *The Crowd in the French Revolution*, Oxford U.P., 1959.
[28]Tom Naylor, "The Rise and Fall of the 3rd Commercial Empire of the St. Lawrence" in G. Teeple (ed.) *Capitalism and the National Question*, University of Toronto Press, Toronto, 1972. An understanding of the nature of the Canadian bourgeoisie is essential for an understanding of the Canadian state. See also Gustavus Myers, *A History of Canadian Wealth*; Libbie and Frank Park, *Anatomy of Big Business.* The last two are published by James Lewis and Samuel, Toronto, 1972 and 1973. The books by Stanley Ryerson and Gilles Bourque, cited in n. 27, are both important for an understanding of the development of the class structure in Canada.
[29]H. C. Pentland, "The Development of a Capitalistic Labour Market in Canada," *Canadian Journal of Economic and Political Science*, v. 25, 1959, p. 455.
[30]C. Lipton, *The Trade Union Movement of Canada*, 1827-1959, Canadian Social Publications Ltd., Montreal, 1968.
[31]*Ibid.*, p. 32.
[32]See *Last Post*, March, 1973.
[33]Lipton, op. cit., p. 285-6.
[34]*Ibid.*, p. 308.
[35]H. A. Innis, *Essays in Canadian Economic History*, Vol. 8, Toronto, 1956, p. 174.
[36]D. Creighton, *British North America at Confederation*, Queen's Printer, Ottawa, 1963, p. 10. This was Creighton's submission to the Royal Commission on Dominion-Provincial Relations (Rowell-Sirois Commission).
[37]*Ibid.*, p. 59 (My emphasis).
[38]On this see A. Dubuc, "The Decline of Confederation and the New Nationalism" in P. Russell (ed.) *Nationalism in Canada*, McGraw Hill-Ryerson, Toronto, 1966.
[39]H. A. Innis, *Essays in Canadian Economic History*, p. 209.
[40]Quoted in F. Clairmonte, *Economic Liberalism and Under-development*, Asia Publishing House, Bombay, 1960, p. 14.
[41]H. A. Innis, *The Fur Trade in Canada*, University of Toronto Press, Toronto, 1962, p. 385.
[42]Quoted in Peter C. Newman, *Renegade in Power: The Diefenbaker Years*, McClelland and Stewart, Toronto, 1963, p. 337.
[43]W. L. Morton, *The Canadian Identity*, University of Toronto Press, Toronto, 1964, p. 81.
[44]*Toronto Star*, May 30, 1973.
[45]See Peter C. Newman, *The Distemper of Our Times*, McClelland and Stewart, Toronto, 1968, pp. 224-26.

7 Analysing Competitive Enterprise *

Ronald S. Ritchie

Central to the whole process of the competitive enterprise system are competition and the forces of the marketplace. Where they are effective they discipline the actors concerned, direct enterprise and productive effort, and induce adjustments needed to meet new situations. Within this fluid and changing situation, the profit test is both compass and measure of performance in the basic task of meeting consumer wants in an acceptable and economic manner.

What are the strengths of this competitive enterprise system? First, it has shown throughout the western world and Japan that it is a powerful engine for growth, growth of the kind which is based upon productivity improvement and, as a result, the creation of rising incomes along with the goods and services to satisfy them. It induces innovation which is central to the whole process. When allowed to function effectively, the forces of the market demonstrate their value in allocating resources, balancing supply and demand, and making the economy responsive to new factors of all kinds, whether changes in costs, supply sources and technologies, or shifts in consumer demands, including the appearance of wholly new wants.

There is also, however, another central element in the system: government. It is government which determines by law and regulation the powers of corporations, the rules of the marketplace, and inducements or deterrents to various courses of action. On the constraint side, we have such things as minimum wage laws, workmen's compensation boards, combines legislation, truth in advertising regulations. On the inducement side, there are tariffs, tax incentives, and capital and other payments to encourage job creation in disadvantaged areas.

The market mechanism, then, is vital to our economic system. If the stage is properly set, it will work in suitable harmony with our social objectives and help us to achieve them. Constraints such as the prohibition of child labor during the last century, or air pollution controls in this, are entirely compatible with the market mechanism. It can, indeed, be used to induce development of better means for achieving agreed-upon social objectives.

We can and should use the strengths and the flexibility of the competitive enterprise system to handle many problems which are new to our society, and to handle some traditionally considered outside its province. What we cannot afford is to let the market mechanism be interfered with in ways which undermine it to the point where we could wake up some years hence to find out that it no longer existed, that we had unwittingly given up a social tool of great adaptability and proved power.

None of the long array of current apparent threats to the competitive enterprise system can be disregarded by thoughtful businessmen. We need to know their implications, to know which are in the nuisance category, which would strike seriously at the heart and strength of the system, that is, at the market mechanism itself. We need to know too which are those which should call forth a constructive response from businessmen. In every case, we need to know the real nature of the threat — if it is one — and what we should be saying to employees, customers, shareholders, governments, and the public at large.

Threats to the System

Let us consider briefly first two criticisms which I feel need not really be serious, and then two which do seem to be serious because they threaten the effectiveness of the market mechanism itself.

First, consumerism. Some of its current phenomena are undoubtedly annoying, frustrating, costly, and even unfair. Some consumerism spokesmen sound as if a combination of absolute wisdom and perfect performance would not satisfy them. Others espouse reforms which may not be in the general interest. Still, it is a fact that the purpose of our system is to supply the consumer with what he wants and is willing to pay for. Consumerism which genuinely seeks better performance from the consumer's point of view is, therefore, aimed directly in line with the justification for the whole system. One does not have to go all the way with extremists to agree that there are examples of the consumer being misled, confused, or inadequately served. None of us should be unwilling to see such failures of the system corrected if they can be.

Next, environmentalism. Here we have serious questions to face as a society. Partly, they are questions of cost. How much will protection or improvement of the quality of our air and our water, for instance, cost us in prices, incomes, or employment, and how much as a society do we wish to pay in these forms? Such costs are no threat in themselves to the competitive enterprise system. The market mechanism is at its best in accepting costs, devising ingenious ways to minimize them, and then passing them onto the consumer. Any actual situation is, of course, always complicated by the fact of existing plants and jobs which may not be able to bear costs acceptable in new installations.

Then, of course, there is always the question of the extent to which our economy can move ahead of others with which it must compete in world markets, and what price we are prepared to pay for doing so. None of these questions is easy and most likely they will have to be put and answered again and again over many future decades. However, our social choices can be made in ways which will capitalize upon the innovative and cost management abilities of the market mechanism and the competitive enterprise system to ensure that the best cost-benefit balance is achieved.

Unlike consumerism or environmentalism, however, the possibility that we shall for some time have to live with chronic inflation does seem to me to pose a serious threat to the competitive enterprise system.

Factors which make inflation a chronic risk are complex. Some of them relate, I suspect, to the common commitment of most industrialized societies to full employment and more income security. Neither of these objectives is one we can afford to jettison. Yet when Lord Keynes, against the backdrop of the great depression and World War II, persuaded his fellow economists and governments that there were means for making these objectives feasible, he set in train a variety of new forces, expectations, and ways of behaving which affected all the actors in our type of economy.

As a result, governments seeking to promote full employment and greater income security must now do so in a different context from that originally foreseen. Businessmen, labour, and consumers have become sophisticated about the objectives of governments, the pressures upon them, and the methods by which they strive to keep the economy operating somewhere near its potential and on a growth trajectory.

Inflation, if long continued, strikes a drastic blow at the effective functioning of the market mechanism and competitive enterprise in resource allocation, price and cost constraint, and responsiveness to consumer wants. We are in something of a cleft stick because the alternate of price control on anything but the most temporary basis destroys a great part of the benefits of the market mechanism even more directly.

Social Responsibility

It can be argued that we can afford a certain amount of inflation, particularly if we protect our competitive position in world markets by avoiding inflating at rates greater than those prevailing in the rest of the world. With a floating exchange rate, it can even be argued that we can inflate faster than some of our competitors and customers in world markets, protecting our competitive position through a declining value of the dollar. The dilemma is not really escaped, however. Inflation does not hit all areas and all sectors of our economy evenly. Moreover, there is serious doubt as to whether it can really be contained if we accept even a modest rate of inflation as a goal. If it does become extreme, the certainty of injustice makes internal dissension and conflict likely. So long, then, as inflation threatens, the market mechanism is in danger either from inflation itself or from controls designed to cure it.

A second area of potential major threat to the competitive enterprise system and the market mechanism, in my view, is centred in the phrase "the social responsibilities of business." Certainly, I feel that corporations and businessmen should be socially responsible. But I do not believe they should turn away from the responsibilities of their basic social role, neglect the guidelines which the system provides for them in that area, and begin to assume responsibility for social choice in a variety of areas where they have no legitimacy and little to guide them beyond their individual inclinations and individual judgments about the social good.

Corporations and businessmen command enormous resources. A basic assumption is that, in general, they will direct the use of these resources for the production of goods and services desired by consumers, combining scarce economic resources efficiently in such a way as to be able to do so at prices which consumers will pay. Within this general context, and without any special directives from society via governments, they can use some of these resources in ways sanctioned by social custom for things not strictly dictated by the market, such as support of a variety of community projects and welfare, health, educational, and cultural undertakings. In such matters, custom and the expectation of society can be as satisfactory a guide as legislation or the market mechanism in other activities. In general, however, when the businessman and the corporation, acting as such, step far out from their economic roles, and particularly when for socially conceived purposes they undertake to deny or seriously challenge the directions suggested by the marketplace, they undermine the role for which their function, and the institutions of which they are a part, were set up in the first place. If the marketplace appears to give the wrong answers, its rules should not be defied in favour of unchecked personal inclination. Rather, they should be changed by proper processes so that they give right answers in terms of new situations and a new consensus.

It is undoubtedly true that the corporation and the businessman acting as such have, or could have, very large roles in many of the areas in which we are being challenged to become "socially responsible." This is true in fields such as quality of environment; or income and job security in relation to new technology, changing costs, and the changing demands of consumers; or the rate at which money incomes should rise in relation to general productivity growth. How should the businessman make his choices when he is told on all sides that if he simply follows the direction of the market he is socially irresponsible? A key element in the answer is that in matters of consequential change for which the market gives him no guidance, or guidance which seems to be contrary to what society appears to want, the businessman is dealing with social choices of kinds not delegated to him to make.

Probably, these choices should be made by the institution which society has devised for arriving at social choices for which the market mechanism is an inappropriate vehicle. In general, the institution we have devised for these purposes is government.

Businessmen can play a very important role in helping governments and the societies they represent to make such choices on an informed basis. They can help ensure that once made, the choices are implemented so as to take full advantage of the strengths of the competitive enterprise system and the market to achieve desired answers. In the field of environmental protection, for instance, businessmen can bring to bear technical expertise and knowledge of costs and benefits which can be of great value to the social decision-making process. They can help devise rules which will ensure that the marketplace goes to work to produce the desired results in the most effective way. They can also alert society to questions which should be asked, choices which should be made. In all these ways they can play valuable and socially responsible roles.

If the social responsibility is interpreted in this fashion, businessmen and corporations can rise to the challenge and can bring to bear both their knowledge and their vision in the interests of a steadily improving society. If they have a more diffused concept of their role, the challenge to social responsibility can become a swamp in which the competitive enterprise system and the market mechanism, along with the businessman, will lose their way and become mired down.

The competitive enterprise system, then, does face substantial threats and challenges. The threats will be less and the challenges better met in proportion as businessmen understand their basic role, understand what conflicts with it and what reinforces it, understand how the institutions of competitive enterprise and the market can be used effectively by society to achieve a wide range of purposes, and ensure that others who are not businessmen understand these things as well. Given such understanding and the action for which it calls, the prospects for the continued survival and continued usefulness of the competitive enterprise system are excellent indeed. As the tasks of government expand because of the need to make many more social decisions, or, as some might put it, to make more public policy, we could even conceive an expanded role for the competitive enterprise system. Perhaps it can take off the shoulders of governments many of the operating functions they have assumed over the years, functions they probably handle less effectively than would the private competitive enterprise system guided by market forces.

Notes

*Ritchie, R. S., "Analysing Competitive Enterprise," *Canadian Business*, November, 1972, pp. 28-32 (reproduced by permission of author and publisher).

8 The Role of Government *

Maurice Lamontagne

. . . We are now in a position to set out the main conclusions concerning the evolution of the role of government in Canada since Confederation. Past experience shows that the striking fact in that respect has not been so much the extension of government responsibilities as their changing character.

Up to the twenties, government played an active role in the field of a long-term economic development through its programme of direct public investments and of encouragement to private initiative. It was the real dynamic factor in industrial progress during that period. On the other hand, because of its long-term influence over the Canadian economy and because of other features of the industrial structure, short-term economic instability was not so much a problem; to a certain extent, this explains why the responsibilities of the public authority in that respect as well as in the field of social security were almost negligible.

Since the twenties, however, the role of government has followed a different pattern. Long-term economic development has been taken over by private initiative, while public authorities have assumed new and increasing responsibilities first in the field of welfare and social security and later, especially since the forties, in respect to short-term economic instability.

It is highly important to note the Canadian past experience, because it shows that there is no basic general trend pointing toward an increasing role of government in the same direction. It also reveals that political ideologies have not played a decisive influence in determining State responsibilities. On the contrary, the role of government has been primarily functional in character; it has been adapted, with certain lags, to changing economic and social circumstances, which, in the last resort, were determined by the recurrence and the impact of industrial revolutions. . . .

The recognition of the complementary relationship between private initiative and government action has been the dominant feature of our political history at least since 1867, and there is no evidence at present to show that this long-established tradition will be broken. On the contrary, all the facts indicate that it will be strengthened.

First, the attitude of a Canadian Liberal government in that regard is clear and has been re-stated on several occasions since the publication of the White Paper on employment and income. Only recently, the Prime Minister, the Right Honourable Louis St. Laurent, declared:

> I think all of us recognize the fact that there are some things which it is more appropriate to have done by public authorities than by free enterprise. But I think we are all most happy when free enterprise does what is required to be done and public authorities do not have to intervene.[1]

On another occasion, he said:

> I don't think that free enterprise requires that governments do nothing about economic conditions. Governments can—and I believe governments should—pursue fiscal and commercial policies which will encourage and stimulate enterprise and wise government policies can do a lot to maintain the right kind of economic climate.[2]

Secondly, the major political parties recognize this fundamental complementarity existing between private initiative and government action, although they differ slightly, especially during electoral campaigns, on the emphasis to be put on either of these forces. Basically, those parties, once in power, behave according to the same functional principles.

Finally, it is evident that there are differences of opinion among the various sectors of the Canadian population as to what government should or should not do. However, these divergent preferences have not developed into opposite ideologies. Slogans denouncing the Welfare State or creeping socialism or government controlled by wicked capitalists had to be imported from other countries and were soon found to be unfit for Canadian consumption.

Thus, it may be inferred that the Canadian situation in the future will continue to reflect the equilibrium position and that the basic complementarity between private initiative and government action will be recognized in fact as it is described by our functional theory. . . .

The normal implication to be drawn from this outlook is that private initiative will continue to play the dynamic and dominant role in the field of long-term industrial development in Canada during the next decades. The role of government will be auxiliary and conditioning. It will consist mainly in maintaining a favourable climate for private initiative and in adopting policies designed to ensure that the natural resources will be rationally utilized to the advantage of the Canadian population.

Notes

*Lamontagne, M., "The Role of Government," in E. P. Gilmour (ed.), *Canada's Tomorrow* (Toronto: Macmillan, 1954), pp. 132-33 and 143-46, reproduced by permission of The Macmillan Company of Canada Limited and Canadian Westinghouse Co. Ltd.).

[1]*Debates,* Commons (Monday, May 4, 1953), p. 4764.

[2]Statement by the Prime Minister at the Annual Convention of the Canadian Lumbermen's Association (Montreal, February 9, 1953), pp. 9 and 10.

9 Free Enterprise *

George Hogan

We have said that Conservatism's main purpose is to preserve our national heritage. What is the Canadian heritage? In my view, the Canadian heritage is one of progress based on individual freedom and national independence. . . .

The second component of the Canadian heritage Conservatives uphold is our economic system based upon free enterprise. Like our Constitution, this system is not perfect; but it has one great proven advantage: it works. In terms of the individual standard of living of our citizens, in terms of the aggregate wealth of our country, and in terms of the position it holds in the world because of its material progress and strength, our economic system has shown itself at least as successful as that to be found in any other country.

An economy genuinely based upon free enterprise is characterized by three main features: private ownership, individual economic decision, and competition. When any one of these features is seriously weakened, the system cannot honestly be called "free." Naturally, in the complex conditions of a modern economy, no system can be applied or defended as a theoretical absolute. All parties today believe in some form of what is commonly called a "mixed economy." Any return to the uncontrolled economics of *laissez-faire* capitalism is a practical impossibility. Conservatives believe in an economic system based upon free enterprise, but this is as far as it can be taken. The differences among our parties today are not differences as to whether there should be a privately or publicly controlled economy, but rather as to the extent and manner in which both private and public enterprise should participate in a mixed economy.

Fifteen years ago, free enterprise seemed the chief Canadian institution to be defended, because it was the most openly under attack. At the end of the Second World War, socialism, as expounded by what was then known as the CCF, was a vociferous and growing philosophy in this country. Its avowed aim, as proclaimed in the CCF's Regina Manifesto, was to eradicate capitalism. In those years, there was a real public issue about the very existence of an economy based on free enterprise, and at least in Ontario, Saskatchewan, and British Columbia, some serious doubt about the outcome.

Conservatives defended free enterprise against this open frontal attack, on the grounds that it was the system which best gave expression to the two foundations of the Canadian heritage, progress and freedom. For the adoption of a socialist society would do violence to both concepts. The socialists claimed that they stood for a policy of "democratic socialism." But they forgot that you can maintain democracy and still lose freedom. The whole concept of socialism requires the replacement of individual decisions and individual initiatives by government decisions and government initiatives. It seems obvious that the more we surrender to government of our right to make decisions concerning our individual daily lives, the less freedom we retain to make such decisions for ourselves. And even if we retain the democratic right to elect the people who will make those decisions for us, this does not alter the loss of the freedom to make the decisions themselves. On the other hand, Conservatives pointed out, an economic system that removed the incentive provided by competition for improvement in prices and products would greatly retard our rate of economic progress; and a system that, in addition, superimposed upon the economy a dead weight of restrictions and controls might well end up in a total throttling of all progress.

Today such issues sound as quaintly dated as a Second World War propaganda movie. The fact that these socialist theories, like the economic difficulties that gave rise to them, have now been left far behind in the wake of Canada's economic progress, is in itself an impressive example of that progress. The heirs to this socialist tradition now call themselves the NDP. They retain its old enmity to free enterprise, but they have lost both its reason for it and its alternative to it. The socialists don't talk much about socialism now; but they have certainly not espoused free enterprise. In this posture of baffled obsolescence, they remain a minor threat to the progress and freedom that result from free enterprise, and a major obstacle to the effective working of parliamentary democracy.

In their defence of free enterprise against socialism, Conservatives are careful not to equate socialism with social security, or social justice, as they usually call it. It is a common mistake, made by both the friends and enemies of socialism, to describe social welfare measures as socialistic. To do so is to give the socialists an easy patent on a vital field of public policy. Socialism requires a preference, in principle, of public ownership over private ownership; of a "planned economy" over individual economic decision; of state monopoly over competition. An acceptance, in principle (there will always be detailed exceptions), of any of these preferences is incompatible with a belief in free enterprise. But the acceptance of social justice measures is in no way incompatible with free enterprise. Indeed, free enterprise (and by this we still mean a mixed economy based upon free enterprise) is probably more compatible with social justice than any other system. For it is from the growth and progress free enterprise makes possible, and the revenues which flow from the profits of free enterprise, that the means to pay for social justice principally come.

. . . In purely economic terms, social justice measures such as old age pensions and unemployment insurance provide a constant element of purchasing power which help to level out the peaks and valleys of the business cycle. It does not provide equality, but it does help to provide equality of opportunity, by making sure that no Canadian family need fall below a basic standard of health and education. Conservatives have made major contributions to the growth of social justice in Canada. In so doing they have helped to strengthen the economic basis of free enterprise itself, and to make sure that its benefits were in some measure shared by all Canadians. . . .

The modern Conservative approach to free enterprise is based on the very old Conservative principle that free enterprise and government should be partners, not rivals, in economic progress. It was not *laissez-faire* capitalism that built the early St. Lawrence canals, or the Canadian Pacific Railway, but free enterprise in partnership with government. This same relationship can be, and must be, maintained if Canadians are to get the maximum benefit from their resources and their efforts.

Conservatives today believe, and I think unitedly believe, in an economic system in which free enterprise and government will work together for the economic betterment of Canada. They believe that wherever possible free enterprise should be left alone because progress and freedom are best ensured by its natural workings. But they also believe that government should create the environment in which free enterprise can be most productive; that government should establish conditions under which all Canadians will have a share in its benefits; and that government should, where necessary, take economic measures of its own for the general good where it can do so more effectively than can free enterprise. In this spirit of partnership, free enterprise and government will achieve the economic growth and national prosperity which Canada's natural wealth makes possible.

Notes

*Hogan, G., *The Conservative in Canada* (Toronto: McClelland and Stewart Ltd., 1963), reproduced by permission of The Canadian Publishers, McClelland and Stewart Ltd.

10 The Government and the Economy *

T. C. Douglas

In my view there is a clear and positive case today documenting the need for an expanded government role in the overall direction of the Canadian economy. The case rests upon the evidence of the long sweep in our social evolution, upon the contemporary experience and evident failure of our economy to measure up to its potentials, and upon the political and social goals which we set for ourselves as a Canadian people. Contrary to what is often asserted, the expansion of government need not at all imply a growth of restriction, an erosion of freedom, or a loss of initiative and enterprise. Rather, the people of this country, acting through democratically elected governments, can broaden our freedom and opportunity, assure higher standards of living for ourselves, and impart a new dimension to national growth. But to do so we must have governments prepared to accept an enlarging role, inspired to meet new challenges and organized to carry out creative new responsibilities....

It is clear, for example, that maintaining a rapid growth in employment, given the accelerating pace of labour-saving technology and automation, has become a very complex process. An indispensable adjunct to normal market forces is an array of labour market services embracing adequate information and forecasting of employment change, aids for geographic and occupational mobility on the part of workers, long-range manpower training and retraining, and effective adjustment programmes to meet technological and economic shifts in employment. The improvement in productivity advance calls for expanded investment in many forms of human capital and human skills, a great extension in public social capital, particularly in meeting the mushrooming needs of our cities, and a rapid expansion of industrial construction, machinery and equipment. A far greater effort in research and development, in the application of new technology, and in basic scientific investigation must be launched. We need to explore methods for increasing specialization in Canadian industry, for expanding foreign trade on a truly multi-lateral basis, and for effecting a sweeping rationalization of our industrial structure to make our economy more fully competitive in the international league. An important lift to growth in real production and consumption should be sought, on one hand, by the expansion of long-standing public services and the introduction of new public programmes. On the other hand, there is a pressing urgency to provide adequate consumer protection and information and to curtail wasteful production processes and inflated selling costs. These latter add nothing to the real level of output, and in fact impose a burden upon our economy equal in cost to many of our basic social services.

In all of these economic areas there is urgent need and wide scope for extending the role of government. But little will be gained if this extension takes place only on a makeshift, haphazard basis, with response to this pressure and that, usually at the last moment. The obvious result of the traditional sticking-plaster approach to the problems of a complex, integrated economic system has been confusion, inconsistency and conflict in public policy. Rather, as I have stressed, the expansion of the government's role must proceed in a planned, co-ordinated way, with a firm but flexible integration and consistency among strategic economic goals, specific operational targets, and applied action programmes.

In this planned approach it is essential to adopt new vigour, imagination, and a willingness to experiment and innovate in the whole range of traditional techniques of government intervention; for example, in fiscal, monetary and commercial policies, in the use of legislation and statutory regulation, in new forms of grants, subsidies and incentives to private enterprise, and in the broad revenue and spending powers of all levels of government. In the same way, if government is to effectively carry out its larger and more complex responsibilities in the period ahead, it must also be prepared to intervene directly in the economy. This includes recognizing the need for an expanded role for government enterprise whenever it is appropriate to the circumstances, the need for new vehicles to mobilize private savings for industrial investment, the possibilities for a productive partnership with private industry, and the long-range importance of direct participation in research and development. . . .

Notes

*Douglas, T. C., "The Government and the Economy," in I. A. Litvak (ed.), *The Nation Keepers: Canadian Business Perspectives* (Toronto: McGraw-Hill, 1967), pp. 45-50 (reprinted with the permission of author and publisher).

11 Businessmen, Wake Up! *

Donald R. Huggett

We are all aware of inflation. We are equally aware that there are no simple answers or solutions, but businessmen have a responsibility—and a heavy one at that—to point out the consequences of rampant inflation and to inform both the the public and government. And yet businessmen have failed!

For example, corporations—except for a modest few—are reporting to their shareholders on the basis of historical costs. We all know—and say—that such inflation-induced profits are illusory and do not represent increased ability to pay wages or dividends, but must be husbanded to replace goods and equipment which now cost more. While we say this in private, annual reports and other published results are still based on historical costs and do not indicate how waterlogged the profits are. Such information falls far short of meeting the requirements of the financial community. What can we expect the public to believe other than that the profits are unconscionably high and that business is ripping-off the public. The situation is so unreal that we have proposals for anti-profiteering legislation at a time when the overpowering judgment of the stock markets is that true corporate profits are too low.

Does business use the LIFO method of accounting for inventory costs? No, it does not, even though this method provides a more accurate picture of real profits and eliminates illusory gains resulting from holding inventories in an inflationary period. Why don't we use it? Is it because management is remunerated on the basis of profits? Is it because the LIFO method has not been allowed for income tax purposes? If it is the latter, why hasn't someone challenged Revenue's position which is based upon a Privy Council decision in a 20-year-old suit. Times and fashions change. Surely the Supreme Court of Canada would stick by its original decision and allow LIFO. But nobody has tried it.

I have been told by my partners not to flog old tax horses, but I cannot resist suggesting that the business community was somewhat mulish about tax reform. As a consequence, we lost the opportunity of avoiding double taxation of corporate profits. What we gained was a half-rate capital gains tax that cannot be adjusted for inflation. The result is that Canadian business, entrepreneurs and investors are now facing a tax on notional gains which, in many cases, are not real at all and hence result in a confiscation of capital.

If we had had the foresight and an attunement with the times, we would have accepted the inevitable conclusion that real capital gains are as fit a subject for tax as any other source of income. If this philosophy had been accepted, we would now be in a position to demand that gains based upon historical costs must be discounted for inflation. This would be so much fairer than what we have today that it seems incredible that we missed the boat by such a wide mark.

These are but examples of the malaise and problems we are presently facing as a consequence of inflation. While there are no panaceas, it seems to me that if business is to survive it must:

1. Find a way to separate inflationary—and hence illusory—profits from real profits or gains;
2. Find a way to explain the role of profits to government, labor and the public;
3. Find a way of ensuring that illusory gains are not confiscated and capital not eroded through a tax system that cannot cope with real values.

There is one solution, but the problems cannot be resolved until such time as the business community

1. Reports more accurate profits,
2. Reappraises the tax system, and
3. Finds a way of dealing with unrealistic demands from labor.

While there are no perfect solutions, I am reminded of the statement of Lord Keynes that "It is better to be imprecisely right than precisely wrong."

It has been said in jest that we are indeed fortunate that we do not get as much government as we pay for. Yet, one of the largest problems faced by business today is the multitude of regulations and constrictions governing the conduct of business. The escalation of governmental controls during the last decade is indeed frightening and costly.

Tax reform, foreign investment controls, consumer protection mechanisms, employee benefit requirements, security issue regulations, labelling requirements, price scrutiny or regulation, language requirements, public disclosure rules, liabilities of directors and officers, professional regulation—all these, and more, are ample evidence that if the government does not have a place in the bedrooms of the nation, it certainly feels that it belongs in the boardrooms.

Taken individually, each of these laws, regulations or controls, is well-intentioned. Taken collectively, they represent a haemorrhage of legislation that can easily choke any business that is not in a position to cope with and adapt to them.

Why must we have such a torrent of constricting legislation? Is it because business has not lived up to its social responsibilities? Is it because contemporary society requires more and more complex laws? Is it because governments and their servants seek growth as the measure of success? Is it because our society has abandoned all morals and ethics?

Situation Almost Intolerable

One suspects that no single reason is the cause, but that all of them together have conspired to bring about a situation that is becoming almost intolerable. I say intolerable because in many cases they are adding more to the cost of production than any benefits derived. They are intolerable because they are a threat to a free enterprise society as we know it. And I say intolerable because no one can be expected to understand and digest such a massive infusion of new rules, regulations and procedures.

The cure of course is not simple. One suggestion which appeals to me is to point out in no uncertain terms to our governments the principle that "the law is not an instrument for guaranteeing exact justice, but rather one for preventing the grosser kinds of injustice." This principle was enunciated by J. A. Corry, former law professor and principal of Queen's University, and deserves a lot of support. It is worth thinking about.

Another suggestion is to call a halt to new regulations until the rest of society can catch up with what we already have.

Perhaps the best idea is to impose "cost-benefit" measurements to our existing programs. President Ford of the United States has recognized this problem, promising to curb the powers of regulatory agencies. If labor can be fired and management dismissed because of a lack of markets, I see no reason why civil servants cannot be dispensed with because of ineffective programs.

At one time, it was thought that civil servants and public administrators should have tenure of office. As a *quid pro quo*, they usually received lower remuneration and were denied the right to strike. They now receive comparable remuneration, some of the best pensions in the land and seem to strike at will. I cannot help but suggest that if they want the perquisites of business, they should also accept the risks—that is the possibility of being laid off because they cannot contribute effectively to our society.

But as long as business is lined up against government, business will lose. If our beliefs in hard work and compensation for effort and ability are to survive, we must communicate the virtues of this system. It is not done by means of the adversary process. It can be done by cooperating with governments, by taking the broad view of society's demands and by being realistic enough to appreciate that we cannot leave our children money—only a society and system which has proven to be superior to any other. Governments are elected to do this very thing and business must help them perform their duty. We are partners in more ways than one and it is time that we acted as such.

At the moment there appear to be three separate and distinct factions in our society—business, government and labor—each intent on receiving the largest slice of the pie. Surely the proper way, and the only way to beat inflation, is to work together for a larger pie. It sounds quite trite, but I have been amazed to find so many adversary positions, to find such a lack of communication, to find that neither side really appreciates the problems and pressures of the other. We must correct this situation, but how?

Icing on the Cake

As is well known in the business area formal contracts are merely the icing on the cake. The cake itself is baked by informal contracts, by discussions, by kneading and needling and all the other goings on involved in informal dialogue. As businessmen we must get to know our government. We must do it at higher levels, but perhaps more importantly, at lower levels too. The isolation of civil servants must be broken. We must find a way of bridging the gap between the factions and realize that our goals and objectives are, in many ways, common.

By way of illustration, in an area familiar to me, recall the violent opposition of the mining and oil industries to the threatened loss of their depletion allowances at the time of tax reform. The resource sector was quite effective in its communications with government that such a dastardly thing would ruin the industry and would make the country an economic backwater. Unfortunately, the industry could not see the handwriting on the wall and did not accurately assess the mood of the public nor the practical or theoretical arguments against unlimited depletion allowances. They were, of course, successful in their campaign, but they forgot that governments and the public have a long memory.

When the world prices of minerals and oil escalated a few years ago, governments seized the opportunity and hit the industry so hard that they are still reeling from the blows. In the short space of several years they went from one of the lowest taxed segments of our economy to one of the highest taxed—to the point almost of marginal rates exceeding 100%.

There is a lesson here: communication is simply not screaming and shouting, but should be based upon sound theoretical principles, taking into account not only the prime interests of the business itself, but also melding these interests with those of the public and the governments elected to represent the varied interests of the country. Without this broad view, communication may gain only a short-term advantage at, perhaps, a greater cost in the long run.

This is a most difficult thing for businessmen to understand, but understand it they must. We are but a part of the society in which we live and we must be able to prove that our objectives and desires are good for the country as a whole.

Deal with Problems

We have problems and we must develop new philosophies and mechanisms to deal with them. It will not be easy, but in brief,

1. Inflation cannot be dealt with until all factions in society determine

to create a larger pie rather than battle over their individual slices.

2. Business cannot hope to receive its fair share until it can explain more believably the role and quality of profits. It must now, as never before, be able to convince government, labor and the great unwashed public of the importance of business and its role in our society.

3. Government intervention and regulation—even joint ventures—are now a cloying part of the business scene and must be appreciated, understood and dealt with.

4. Business cannot hope to cope with this new environment unless it finds new ways of communicating with government—at all levels—on a two-way basis involving mutual respect, trust and understanding.

5. Social responsibility will be an increasingly important element of business and may be exceedingly important in dealing with labor and the public.

6. The interests of both business and government are really, in the long run, parallel. The interests of business and labor may also be parallel, but only to the extent that each understands the other and a greater degree of responsibility (and less militancy) is achieved.

7. Our society is not completely washed-up, but to save it from drastic decline we must develop new mechanisms of information and communication, a new awareness of the demands and power of the various segments of society, and a new appreciation of the role of business in a society where it no longer controls all, but nevertheless makes all possible.

These are the challenges.

Notes

*Huggett, D. R., "Businessmen, wake up!" *Canadian Business*, July, 1975, pp. 19-22 (reproduced by permission of author and publisher).

Section 2

Government Promotion of Business

Introduction

We have seen in Section 1 that there has been a long tradition in this country of governments aiding and assisting private business firms while, at the same time, pursuing policies which were intended to control and restrict their activities. It is not immediately evident why either of these kinds of measures have been necessary in a so-called "free market, private enterprise" economy. Nor is it easy to understand what the effects of such government involvement in the activities of private business firms have been, either in terms of their economic or their political consequences. In this, and the following section, material is presented which indicates something of the range and characteristics of various government policies affecting business in this country today. We look first at policies apparently intended to promote business activities and then, in Section 3, at those which seem to be aimed at controlling such activities.

Part 1
Commercial Policies

Introduction

The most conspicuous and time-honored policies to restrict competition are the tariff and other measures to protect domestic producers from foreign competition in home markets.

The logic of the free market private enterprise model upon which the Canadian economy is commonly held to be based makes no provision for tariffs or other impediments to free international trade. David Ricardo, one of the nineteenth-century architects of the system, wrote: "The sole effect of high duties on the importation, either of manufactures or of corn or of a bounty on their exportation, is to divert a portion of capital to an employment which it would not naturally seek. It causes a pernicious distribution of the general funds of the society—it bribes a manufacturer to commence or continue in a comparatively less profitable employment." (*The Principles of Political Economy and Taxation*, London, Everyman's Library Edition, 1911, p. 210.)

This view was attacked by a number of writers, most notably, perhaps, by Frederich List in his book *The National System of Political Economy.* Classical economists such as Smith and Ricardo, he argued, quite neglected the causes of national wealth, the process by which the "productive forces" for the state came to be developed. In order to get established, he contended, the state should protect newly created industries from foreign competition. Such a policy of protection had much to commend it in the eyes of manufacturers operating in a country such as Canada, struggling to industrialize under difficult conditions in the late nineteenth century.

The "National Policy" implemented by Sir John A. Macdonald's Conservative government in 1879 marked the official declaration of Canada's rejection of free trade and the adoption of protectionism as part of the grand strategy for Canadian development. The Liberal Party, the Opposition, vigorously denounced the principle of protection.

At the Liberal Convention in 1893, Sir Wilfrid Laurier eloquently denounced the Canadian tariff as "a servile copy of the American system of protection," and as a "fraud and robbery under which Canadians suffer." He depicted it further as a means of "levying tribute upon the people . . . for the benefit of a private and privileged class." "Let it be well understood," he declared, "that from this moment we have a distinct issue with the party in power. Their ideal is protection; our ideal is free trade." Anticipating some difficulties in implementing reform, he observed: "Nothing is more difficult . . . than to wipe away protection, because under it interests have been established which every man who has at heart the interests of all classes must take into consideration." [See: E. Porritt, *Sixty Years of Protection in Canada, 1846-1912*, 2nd edition (Winnipeg Grain Growers' Guide, 1913), pp. 311-14, from which these and the following quotations are taken.] Another prominent speaker at the same convention elaborated: "You can have no true liberty under a system the function of which is to create a privileged class, and to concentrate an undue proportion of the wealth of the community in the hands of a few individuals." Note was taken of the political power such beneficiaries of protection could wield by contributing to "corruption funds . . . sharing with their masters the plunder which they have been enabled to take from the people."

Once in power, however, the Liberal Party appeared to develop more sympathy with the protectionist point of view, and the student of subsequent Canadian tariff history is hard pressed to correlate changes in tariff policy with changes in governments. Much of the subsequent debate on free trade versus protectionism in this country has been between Canadian manufacturers in central Canada and spokesmen for the Western and Maritimes hinterlands, with the latter finding allies in the ranks of academic economists.

The most recent discussion of this perennial issue has been initiated by the Economic Council of Canada which, in 1975, produced a "consensus document" entitled *Looking Outward: A New Trade Strategy for Canada.* The overall position adopted by the Council on the subject is remarkably close to that advocated by most Canadian academic economists over the years and is quite at odds with the popular and "business" views on the subject. The Council quite bluntly advises the Government of Canada to do everything it can "to eliminate its own and other countries' trade barriers" (p. 188). Reading 12 traces the historical background of Canadian tariff policy and indicates something of its effects on the Canadian economy. These effects, it is argued, have been generally adverse. The following extracts from the Economic Council of Canada's report deal with the question that everyone faced with the prospect of free-trade must ask: What would happen to the levels and distribution of employment and income in Canada if we abandoned our tariff protection? Reading 13 surveys the probable impact of trade liberalization on the Canadian economy. This is followed by the Council's assessment of the probable benefits we would reap from such a policy.

While the tariff has been Canada's major instrument for protecting producers operating in this country from foreign competition, a large number of other policies of government have had a similar purpose or effect. These "nontariff barriers to trade" include quantitative restrictions on imports of particular goods, government purchasing policies and subsidies to Canadian producers of goods which might otherwise be imported. Klaus Stegemann, in Reading 14, considers how extensive this kind of protection has been in Canada and what measures might be adopted to eliminate or reduce the ill effects of these policies.

12 Legacy of Protection *

Economic Council of Canada

Canada's economy has long been dependent on foreign trade, foreign investment, and immigration to an extent almost unequalled among nations. And, while there are differences of opinion about some aspects of this openness to the outside world, Canadians by and large recognize that they have prospered from this interchange of goods, money, population, and ideas. Given this position, the importance of global economic developments for Canada is undeniable, and recent profound changes in the international context should be examined with care. Some of these events, in the view of the Economic Council, call into question the validity of a long-standing feature of this country's economic arrangements: the use of a protective commercial policy to promote Canada's national development.

One of the most significant recent trends in world affairs is the emergence of an integrated international economic system. Whereas twenty years ago there were more than twenty economically advanced noncommunist countries, each with an essentially separate economy, today there are three economic superpowers—the United States, the European Economic Community (EEC), and Japan. Other economic units appear very small in comparison with these giants. The thrust of development in these affluent economies is, on the whole, towards industrial activities that are technologically advanced or in other ways skill-intensive. The key to efficiency, at least in the goods-producing sector, is a highly sophisticated organization of output, usually involving large scale and elaborate industrial plant and product specialization.

Equally significant is the emergence of a number of "new Japans"—that is, countries displaying an extensive capability for production of a range of "standard-technology" manufactured goods, such as were made in Japan in the years before the Second World War. As was the case in that country, wages paid in these industries are very low, labour is diligent, and in consequence the goods produced are extremely cheap. A large proportion of these goods is exported to the advanced countries, where they easily undersell comparable products made locally.

These developments are of particular significance to a country like Canada, which is an advanced industrial nation but a relatively small economic unit lacking the domestic scope for enhanced efficiency through large scale and specialization in the manufacturing sector. This situation limits Canada's ability to compete effectively with both the major developed countries and the newly industrializing areas of the developing world, not only in export markets but even at home. Moreover, these characteristics tend to inhibit technological and other initiatives in Canada that could offset the disadvantages of high unit costs.The competitive weakness of Canadian enterprises in turn encourages their takeover by foreign concerns more fortunately placed. Then, as subsidiaries of companies headquartered abroad, firms in Canada are operated in most cases as satellite activities outside the main areas of industrial innovation and growth. At the same time, the comparative advantage that Canada could gain through the production of those commodities that it is potentially capable of producing most efficiently is lost because of its lack of free access to larger markets.

The problems associated with this train of events can already be observed in the rather slow rate of expansion in output per person employed in Canada. Although the overall level of Canadian output has risen quite rapidly, much of this performance can be attributed to the unusually high rate of labour force growth, derived from a high birth rate in the 1950s and a large influx of immigrants. Growth in output per person employed, which is a convenient proxy for productivity or efficiency, has compared poorly with that of other countries, and the evidence is that, unless strong policy measures are taken, it may not improve very much in the future, despite the many advantages that Canada possesses.

One of the basic causes of our poor productivity performance is the type and organization of manufacturing fostered by the commercial policies adopted by Canada and other countries over the years. Such measures were aimed directly at influencing the terms under which goods and services could be imported and exported and included the use of import duties (tariffs) and nontariff barriers to trade, such as subsidies to domestic firms, export and import licensing, and various quantitative restrictions.

Canadian governments have long employed the tariff as one of the main ways of furthering the attainment of national economic and political goals. This approach was embodied in the National Policy, which was introduced in 1879. The National Policy was a combination of protective tariffs and immigration and transportation policies that were all designed to foster the development of manufacturing, mainly in central Canada, and to stimulate the growth of population and resource-based industries in western Canada. It was a response to changing events in the external world—to the dynamic westward expansion of the United States and to Canada's failure to regain a preferential position for trade in either Britain or the highly protected U.S. market of the 1870s. Indeed, much of Canada's tariff history has been influenced by the level of tariffs in the United States.

The initial emphasis of the National Policy was on stimulation of east-west trade within Canada and between Canada and Europe, in order to balance the growing continental economic dominance of the United States. Around the turn of the century, for example, Canada extended unilateral tariff preferences to the United Kingdom primarily to strengthen the European orientation of Canadian trade. The east-west approach, however, did not always enjoy unequivocal support. Efforts to abandon the National Policy in favour of free trade with the United States gained a considerable following at various times, and the case for "reciprocity" was a major focus of the general elections of 1891 and 1911. These initiatives reflected the fact that, in the pre-Confederation period, a treaty for limited Canada-U.S. free trade was actually operative from 1854 to 1866, when it was abrogated by the United States. But, despite periodic interest in free-trade arrangements, the concepts originated by the National Policy survived as the basis of Canadian commercial policy for more than fifty years.

In the early 1930s, Canadian protection was increased substantially, primarily in response to the violent swing towards protectionism throughout the world and especially in the United States, which had become a major market for Canadian products. While the exchange of tariff preferences with Britain and other Commonwealth countries in 1932 followed the traditional east-west approach to international trade, the major Canadian motivations were defensive. Canada sought to maintain employment and to find export markets in an otherwise depressed and protectionist world economy. Canadian tariffs had in the past stimulated foreign investment in this country's industry, but the depressed state of the economy led to an actual outflow of capital after 1932. It was not until after the Second World War, in a climate of greater prosperity, that the net inflow of capital resumed on a large scale.

Even in the 1930s, the efforts of the industrial countries to promote employment through increased protection were recognized as self-defeating, but there was no effective machinery for promoting international economic co-operation or domestic stabilization. However, some attempts were made to retreat from the costly impasse to which national measures of high protection had led. The U.S. Reciprocal Trade Agreements Program was initiated in 1934 by Secretary of State Cordell Hull, and in the latter part of the decade both Canada and the United Kingdom reduced their tariff levels and Commonwealth tariff preferences in order to bring about a reduction of U.S. tariffs.

The end of the Second World War was a turning point in Canadian international economic relations. To offset U.S. influence, strong support emerged in Canada for multilateral action to reduce world trade barriers; this was preferred over the narrower concept of a trade relationship focusing on Europe and particularly Britain. In practice, however, the United States was increasingly becoming Canada's most important trade partner and source of capital.

The multilateral approach to reduction of trade barriers came to centre around the General Agreement on Tariffs and Trade (GATT), negotiated in 1947. As one of the main initiators of GATT, Canada accepted the principle that no new preferential arrangements would be exchanged between countries, and recognized implicitly that the existing Commonwealth preference would wither away as most-favoured-nation tariff rates were reduced through GATT negotiations.[1] In common with the other members, Canada also agreed that national commercial policy measures should be used to promote the growth of world trade, international specialization, and efficiency of national production and *not* primarily to achieve high levels of employment in protected industries—the "beggar-my-neighbour" policies of the 1930s. All of the industrial countries developed increasingly comprehensive domestic instruments designed to maintain growth and employment.

Meanwhile, world economic conditions tended to increase the interdependence of the Canadian and U.S. economies. Canada provided a stable and attractive location for a growing volume of U.S. investment. The U.S. share of Canadian direct investment abroad also increased rapidly until the early 1950s and, although it has declined in relative importance since then, it still accounts for more than half of the total.

With respect to trade, both the Canadian and U.S. markets were relatively open in the 1950s when most other countries controlled imports—particularly those from the "dollar" countries—to conserve foreign exchange. And, in comparison with the war-shattered economies of the other industrial nations, both countries were in a good position to supply products that the other required. The European Economic Community and Japan grew faster than the United States in the 1960s, but their trade with Canada was modest and their investment in Canadian industry small. Moreover, Canada's competitive position in the European market deteriorated with the establishment of the EEC, and it was impaired even more by British entry into the Community in 1973.

Canada-U.S. economic integration was also reinforced through bilateral policy measures. The defence production sharing program with the United States was renewed in 1959, and the Canada-U.S. Automotive Agreement, which resulted in a major expansion of north-south trade and much closer integration of a major industry in the two countries, was signed in 1965.

More recently the interdependence of the two countries has become a matter of increasing political concern in Canada. A widely quoted statement on this issue, released in 1972 by the Secretary of State for External Affairs, suggested a number of alternatives for Canadian policy with respect to the United States:

> In practice, three broad options are open to us:
> (a) we can seek to maintain more or less our present relationship with the United States with a minimum of policy adjustments;
> (b) we can move deliberately toward closer integration with the United States:
> (c) we can pursue a comprehensive, long-term strategy to develop and strengthen the Canadian economy and other aspects of our national life and in the process to reduce the present Canadian vulnerability.[2]

The Minister chose the third option as the one most likely to ensure Canadian sovereignty, independence, and distinctness. Thus in effect he reaffirmed his attachment to a policy of national consolidation along the east-west axis as opposed to an acceptance of the forces tending to bring Canada into a north-south "continental" economic system.

According to one interpretation of this option, Canada must, and in fact does, strongly support the multilateral approach to the reduction of trade barriers. Indeed, Canada participated in the six GATT negotiating rounds held from 1947 to 1967. Substantial progress was made in the dismantling of Canadian import barriers in this process, so that our economy—like those of our trading partners—is much less protected now than it was in 1945. Even so, there remains a hard core of what might be described as "lingering protectionism" in this country and elsewhere. There is no adequate system of regulating the widespread use of nontariff barriers, and there is a residue of national tariffs that still discriminate against the import of manufactured goods.

These difficult problems must be tackled in the round of GATT negotiations that began in 1975. Comprehensive and constructive negotiations on all trade barriers will be required to consolidate the gains from earlier negotiations and to prevent the world from slipping into a costly new spate of protectionism. Such backsliding would be disastrous for Canada. Without free access to foreign markets, this country cannot evolve in the direction of large-scale specialized production in the manufacturing industries, and will not be able to overcome its productivity or innovation difficulties in areas of high technology and "knowledge-intensive" endeavour.

Commercial policy is thus of paramount importance if Canada is to achieve the sort of economic growth and dynamism that will provide its population with the wealth, security, and well-being that they desire for the future. This report is devoted to an analysis of Canadian commercial policy requirements on the basis of contemporary national goals. Of these goals, the most fundamental are the same basic political imperatives that were recognized a hundred years ago when the National Policy was established: national unity and independence. Today, however, they take a different form from that underlying the development strategy of the late nineteenth century. The need for unity, which then led governments to foster the construction of railways and the settlement of land, now encourages a search for greater regional representation in national decision-making and for means of reducing the disparities in levels of wealth among various parts of the country. Similarly, the preoccupation with independence, which in earlier times was expressed in action to prevent physical occupation of Canada's empty spaces by Americans, is today manifested in a concern to limit U.S. investment and cultural penetration.

Commercial policy must also clearly be related to a number of economic goals, the most significant of which have been subject to widespread discussion and study in recent years.[3] These include substantial increases in real living standards over time; full employment, including productive jobs for an increasingly educated labour force; reasonable stability of prices; a more equitable distribution of income among different groups and regions; and steady growth in the world economy, with accelerated progress for the developing countries.

Notes

*Economic Council of Canada, *Looking Outward: A New Trade Strategy for Canada* (Ottawa: Information Canada, 1975, reproduced by permission of Information Canada).

[1]New preferential tariffs are prohibited by GATT, save for arrangements substantially freeing trade among countries, as in a customs union (common market) or free trade area.

[2]Honourable Mitchell Sharp, "Canada-U.S. Relations: Options for the Future," *International Perspectives* (Fall 1972).

[3]Canada's economic goals have been set out in Canada, Department of External Affairs, *Foreign Policy for Canadians* (Ottawa: Information Canada, 1970); and various Annual Reviews of the Economic Council of Canada.

13 The Case for Trade Liberalization *

Economic Council of Canada

The Impact of Trade Liberalization

In analysing the potential of Canadian industry under liberalized trade, one very important point should be noted at the outset. This is the elementary economic principle of comparative advantage expressed in this simplified form by David Ricardo:

> Two men can both make shoes and hats, and one is superior to the other in both employments; but in making hats he can only exceed his competitor by one-fifth or 20 per cent and in making shoes he can exceed him by one-third or 33 per cent; will it not be for the interest of both that the superior man should employ himself exclusively in making shoes and the inferior man in making hats?[1]

What this principle implies is that this country's ability to prosper in a liberalized trading environment does not depend on whether certain industries enjoy *absolute* cost advantages over those in other nations. Even if Canadian factor costs were found to be generally out of line with those of our trading partners, the corrective forces of international trade and payments would eventually exert pressures leading to a shift in the exchange rate and/or internal prices and costs; such a shift, or shifts, would tend to bring about a new equilibrium position in which Canada would specialize in those goods in which its *comparative* efficiency was greatest. But just which goods it would export and which it would import at a given rate of exchange would depend upon the relative domestic factor and output prices. In brief, the levels of absolute costs and prices are important in determining how the economy would adjust to freer trade, but they do not determine the long-run pattern of trade.

With this broad proposition in mind, we can go on to consider how benefits would accrue from freer trade. They would derive from several sources. Economies would result from increased specialization; that is, industries would concentrate their production on goods in which Canada had a comparative advantage internationally. These gains would accrue even if there were no economies of scale in production, but such economies would also come into play. This means that, over and above the benefits from specialization as such, costs would fall as production runs were lengthened to meet expanded domestic and foreign demand. There could also be other economies of market size, including increased efficiency in selling, servicing, and distribution, as well as other scale-related factors such as opportunities for development of entrepreneurial skills and capacity to bear risks.

The achievement of these benefits would quite clearly imply a considerable reorganization of Canadian manufacturing. For this reason, it is useful to think of the effects of trade liberalization in three parts: the initial impact, assuming no change in the structure of production with its protection-induced inefficiencies; a period of reorganization to meet international competition; and the long run—the period after reorganization has been completed. The first two of these comprise what we frequently refer to as the transition period.

We have already pointed out that, because of protective policies, present costs and prices in many Canadian industries—particularly in the secondary manufacturing sector—are higher than those of their counterparts in the United States and other countries. Consequently, it should come as no surprise that if markedly freer trade were introduced before affected industries and firms had a chance to adjust to the new situation, the impact on output and employment would be adverse in many cases. The rationale for a rather lengthy tariff-reduction period is that reorganization would go hand in hand with liberalization. The initial effects could also be mitigated by appropriate complementary policies, and the temporary costs associated with shifting Canada's productive resources into new activities could quite properly be considered as an investment in new long-term economic viability. We now look at how these long-range gains would be achieved.

REORGANIZATION OF INDUSTRY

The impact of freer trade would be confined largely to secondary manufacturing. Canada's primary and related processing industries are already export-oriented and internationally competitive. They might benefit somewhat from cheaper imports, and they would be able to increase production of some processed products that have had to contend with higher tariffs than the primary forms. However, in this sector there would be no more than a modest increase in production and employment without, in most cases, the necessity of any large-scale reorganization.

The service industries are only slightly affected by existing trade barriers because their output consists largely of nontraded products and because many of their inputs come from within the sector itself.[2] They could benefit slightly from cheaper imports, and they would tend to expand as real income rose through increased efficiency of the economy. But the direct impact of a marked liberalization of trade would be minor in this sector too.

Deep cuts in Canadian and foreign trade barriers would, on the other hand, have complex effects on this country's secondary manufacturing sector. Some industries would expand and new ones would appear; others—or at least parts of them—would decline relatively or absolutely. Responses would vary depending upon the particular trade option followed and the ability of particular firms to exploit the advantages that they might have under free trade.

Some Canadian manufacturing industries are, of course, already well able to compete internationally. There are others—the manufacture of fertilizers is a good example—where a higher present Canadian price may reflect negative effective protection. With the adoption of much freer trade, their average costs would fall more than the prices of their products because of lower prices for inputs that are currently protected. Of more general importance, however, is the now extensive evidence suggesting that only rarely would the dropping of import barriers result in the displacement of whole industries by import competition. In the great majority of instances, what could be expected is a shift to more specialized lines of production *within* industries. This type of reorganization would not necessarily be a painful or costly process.

Intra-Industry versus Inter-Industry Specialization

On the basis of experience in free trade areas, it is hard to understand how the idea is perpetuated that Canada would be incapable of adjusting to much freer trade. In Europe, small nations like the Netherlands, Belgium, Denmark, Norway, and Ireland have joined the freely trading communities of the EEC and EFTA, and their adaptation to these new environments is one of the greatest economic success stories of the past quarter century. How is it that Canada is thought to be unable to reorganize its industrial system for competition under liberalized trade conditions with larger countries, including the United States, when Belgium, for example, is evidently thriving in a customs union with much stronger powers like West Germany and France?

The fact is that trade liberalization in the EEC, EFTA, and such other free trade arrangements as the Central American Common Market (CACM) and the Australia–New Zealand trading scheme have resulted in far greater trade expansion and fewer adjustment problems than had been anticipated.[3] The reason for this is that much of the adjustment took place not in terms of expansion or contraction of whole industries but by virtue of increased specialization within individual industries, resulting in expansion of both exports and imports of the items they could produce. This kind of intra-industry specialization and trade has occurred elsewhere too, partly at least as a result of the general lowering of trade barriers.

Table 1 illustrates the growth in intra-industry trade in a number of industrial countries in the 1959-67 period. For Australia, the increase in the total was very small, but detailed examination reveals that intra-industry trade with New Zealand was much larger than that with any other country.

The Canada-U.S. Automotive Agreement played an important role in the very large increase in Canada's intra-industry trade. Prior to the Agreement, Canadian automotive subsidiaries produced a full range of cars to serve the small domestic market. After the Agreement came into effect, they specialized in a smaller number of models for the whole North American

Table 1

Intra-Industry Trade,[1] Selected Countries, 1959-67

	Percentage of total trade			*Change*	
	1959	*1964*	*1967*	*1959-64*	*1959-67*
			(Per cent)		
Canada	28	35	48	25.0	71.4
United States	40	40	49	0.0	22.5
Japan	17	21	21	23.5	23.5
Belgium–Luxemburg	53	60	63	13.0	18.9
Netherlands	55	58	56	5.5	1.9
Germany	39	42	46	7.9	17.9
France	45	60	65	11.1	44.4
Italy	35	44	42	25.7	20.0
United Kingdom	32	40	69	25.0	115.6
Australia	14	17	17	21.4	21.4
Mean	36	42	48	16.7	33.3

1. Intra-industry trade is defined as the value of exports of an industry that is exactly matched by imports of the same industry. For comparing various industries, this value can be expressed as a percentage of each industry's total trade (exports + imports). For comparisons among countries, as in the table above, total intra-industry trade is expressed as a proportion of a country's total commodity export plus import trade adjusted for any trade imbalance.

Source: Herbert G. Grubel and P. J. Lloyd, *Intra-Industry Trade* (London: Macmillan, 1975), p. 42.

market. The increase in specialization was most marked in automobile assembly, in which productive efficiency rapidly approached U.S. levels. Increased specialization and efficiency gains also occurred in automotive parts, though on a lesser scale.[4] Evidence of increased intra-industry trade and specialization in Canada is not, however, confined to the automobile industry. Intra-industry trade increased from 1961 to 1971 in other manufacturing industries, notably machinery and chemicals, and this has been attributed to the effect of Kennedy Round tariff reductions.[5]

This type of adjustment to the lowering of trade barriers reflects the characteristics of modern industry. Most groups of production establishments that are classified as "industries," particularly in manufacturing, do not produce only a single commodity, each unit of which is a perfect substitute for the others; rather, they make a range of products, under varying cost conditions, that are commonly differentiated from those of their competitors either by style (for example, in packaging or brand identification) or quality (with different performance characteristics, such as durability). Typically, manufacturers within a given industry in one country will be more competitive, relative to other countries, in some of the goods they can produce than in others. This is reflected, for instance, in the wide range of effective protection applying to products of the same industries, as well as in the simultaneous export and import of goods produced by the same industries in different countries. International competitiveness must, therefore, be considered in terms of both production costs and product differentiation and in terms of specific commodities rather than whole industries.

Product differentiation is, of course, apparent in both investment and consumer goods. Wherever it occurs, the possibilities for specialization in production and trade are broadened in two ways. First, the more distinctive the product, the less the producer will have to compete on price alone. Second, specialization in differentiated products increases the possibility of cost savings from longer production runs, albeit perhaps in narrower lines of specialization. Even with a relatively small domestic market for a particular item, longer runs may be possible under a liberalized trade situation if the product appeals to enough buyers in other countries.

Opportunities for Specialization

Lowering Canadian trade barriers would reduce the costs of inputs and spur Canadian industry on to reorganize in order to become internationally competitive. Substantial cuts in other countries' trade barriers would open possibilities of much larger production runs with consequent cost reductions. In brief, protection-induced costs would decline or disappear.

The possibility of product differentiation greatly strengthens the argument that, under a liberalized trading regime, industrial reorganization would be feasible and could be accomplished without great difficulty. But just which product lines are suited for specialization by Canadian manufacturers, and how great the gains from this process would be, depends not only upon their ability to offer distinctive items but on a variety of other factors affecting the location of industry in Canada—factors that would remain in effect even after the reduction of trade barriers. Considerable analysis of this subject has been undertaken over the last decade, primarily in terms of the removal of trade barriers between Canada and the United States. However, since 70 per cent of our trade is already with that country, not too much modification would be required for the conclusions to apply to wider liberalized trading schemes.

Perhaps the most important feature of this recent analysis is that examination of Canada's position in an open trading environment centres on comparisons of regions rather than on national aggregates. The locational advantages of Canadian regions relative to their competing U.S. counterparts were set out in some detail in a study of free trade between Canada and the United States by Ronald and Paul Wonnacott.[6] Their comparison was based on two main elements: first, on the readily measurable costs of the various productive factors, including labour, resources, transportation, and capital; and, second, on a group of intangible factors whose effects are difficult to measure in quantitative terms, such as proximity to markets and manufactured supplies, as well as other benefits that industrial concentration may provide.

Factor-cost advantages are, of course, likely to shift over time; in addition, they are interrelated with movements in the foreign exchange value of the Canadian dollar. This implies that the range of products in which Canadian manufacturers would be likely to specialize would also shift, which means that continuous, extensive, and up-to-date analysis would be needed to identify the best possibilities for specialization under freer trade at any given time.

Since the mid-1960s a number of studies have been devoted to this question. Although they do not answer all of our needs, they nevertheless illustrate the feasibility of specialization by Canadian industries in a free trade arrangement. Assessing tangible factor-cost advantages for particular industries in different regions of North America, the Wonnacotts found that in the late 1950s Canadian locations were as attractive as those in the United States for the manufacture of a broad range of goods for an integrated market, including food and beverages, machinery, transportation equipment, apparel, and books and other printed material.[7] This was primarily because lower labour costs outweighed any disadvantages with respect to capital and transportation costs. The industrial belt between Windsor and Quebec City appeared especially well placed, comparing favourably with the Chicago-Boston-Baltimore triangle—the major U.S. industrial area. In only a handful of industries were southern Ontario and western Quebec clearly inferior to the prime U.S. location.

The position of the Canadian industrial belt was less advantageous than the Chicago-Boston-Baltimore triangle in the Wonnacotts' evaluation of proximity to markets and other "intangible" factors. But, in comparison with U.S. regions outside the industrial triangle, southern Ontario and western Quebec had an advantage in terms of both factor costs and nonquantifiable factors. Given that the level of industrialization and the rate of economic growth in the U.S. South, the Midwest, and the Far West approximated those of central Canada, the Wonnacotts concluded that the latter's potential for manufacturing activity under free trade would be strong. For many industries specialization would be the only additional element required for effective competition with their U.S. counterparts. The Wonnacotts' work also confirmed that the gains from specialization would be very high in some industries.

Canadian regions outside the Windsor–Quebec City corridor—areas in which production tends to be resource-based—were judged to have every prospect of continued prosperity where it already existed; some gain was expected where economic standards were low. To the extent that Canada-U.S. wage parity was not fully realized or that wage and salary cost increases in these regions were more modest than elsewhere in North America, a greater proportion of the industrial expansion resulting from free trade might be expected to occur there. In the absence of such special advantages, however, the opportunities for agriculture, resource exploitation, and other primary activities would be enhanced anyway, and benefits from lower import prices would accrue to all consumers.

The Wonnacotts' 1967 book was followed by detailed assessments[8] of the free trade potential of several Canadian industries. The steel industry was found to be already internationally competitive, although it has been concerned with dumping from overseas sources. Its existing level of specialization implies that it would be able to prosper in a free trading world without the necessity of any large-scale reorganization. Pulp and paper are also being produced in Canada under internationally competitive conditions. Other parts of the paper industry are now protected, but research indicates that they have prospects for effective operation in a liberalized trade environment, notably in the specialized production of items whose costs would be affected by such things as the availability of low-cost electricity. Even the furniture industry, which was chosen for analysis in trade studies because of its import vulnerability, was considered to have potential in a number of specialty items and to be protected by transport costs in the case of bulky goods like upholstery and bedding.

Recent Changes in Factor Costs and Real Incomes

Since these analyses were undertaken, some of the cost comparisons underlying them have changed (Table 2). Average hourly *money* wages of production workers in Canadian manufacturing were more than 20 per cent below the U.S. level in the early 1960s, but by 1974 that gap had disappeared. The gap also narrowed in real terms (that is, after allowance for price changes in both countries); in 1974, real hourly wages of production workers in Canadian manufacturing were only about 4 per cent below the U.S. level.[9] These changes do not mean that Canada would no longer benefit from a further freeing of trade. They do imply, however, that the process of adjustment to a free trade situation would be somewhat different from that envisaged earlier by the Wonnacotts.

Real wage gains in Canadian manufacturing are likely to be sustainable over the long run only to the extent that they are matched by increases in productivity relative to our trading partners. Part of the closing of the gap in money and real earnings from the early 1960s to the early 1970s was associated with a narrowing of the Canada-U.S. productivity difference. Increases in output per man-hour were indeed greater in Canada than in the United States over this period (Table 3). The "catch-up" in productivity occurred largely in the late 1960s, however, and it resulted, partly at least, from trade liberalization. The largest gain in Canadian productivity, for example, was in transportation equipment, reflecting greater specialization under the Automotive Agreement. But, despite the gain, the productivity gap was still over 20 per cent in 1972 (Table 4), and preliminary evidence suggests that it had closed little further by 1974. And Canada's rate of productivity growth still remained below that recorded in a number of advanced European countries and Japan.

Table 2

Average Hourly Earnings[1] of Production Workers in Manufacturing, in Current and Constant (1961) Dollars, Canada and the United States, 1960-74

	Current dollars			*Constant 1961 dollars*[2]	
	Canada	*Canada*	*U.S.*	*Canada*	*U.S.*
	($ Can.)	($ U.S.)	($ U.S.)		
1960	1.79	1.85	2.26	1.80	2.28
1961	1.83	1.80	2.32	1.82	2.32
1962	1.88	1.76	2.39	1.81	2.36
1963	1.95	1.81	2.46	1.88	2.40
1964	2.02	1.87	2.53	1.92	2.44
1965	2.12	1.96	2.61	1.96	2.47
1966	2.25	2.09	2.72	2.00	2.51
1967	2.40	2.23	2.83	2.07	2.54
1968	2.58	2.39	3.01	2.14	2.59
1969	2.79	2.59	3.19	2.20	2.60
1970	3.01	2.87	3.36	2.30	2.59
1971	3.28	3.24	3.56	2.44	2.63
1972	3.54	3.57	3.81	2.51	2.73
1973	3.85	3.85	4.07	2.54	2.74
1974	4.39	4.49	4.40	2.61	2.73

1. Earnings figures do not include fringe benefits.
2. These are the current-dollar figures deflated by the consumer price index for each country. The Canadian figures have also been adjusted to allow for a slight difference in the average level of consumer goods and services in each country for a benchmark year (1965). See Appendix by E. C. West in Dorothy Walters, *Canadian Income Levels and Growth: An International Perspective,* Economic Council of Canada Staff Study 23 (Ottawa: Queen's Printer, 1968).

Source: Based on data from Statistics Canada; the U.S. Bureau of Labor Statistics; and the U.S. Department of Commerce.

The fact that the Canada-U.S. wage differential has narrowed more rapidly than the productivity gap, particularly in the 1970s, is explained in part by the significant improvement in Canada's terms of trade. This has permitted a given quantity of exports to be exchanged for a larger quantity of imports, with favourable effects on real income. Furthermore, the appreciation of the Canadian dollar limited price increase for both export and import items, while domestic wages and other factor costs were increasing—supporting larger gains in real incomes in Canada than might have been anticipated from the gains in manufacturing productivity.

It seems unlikely that these rather special circumstances will continue. The competitive position of Canadian manufacturing has been eroded, particularly in the last several years (Table 3). Unit labour costs—a measure that combines the effects of wages and productivity changes—have risen more rapidly than in the United States, and average increases for some non-labour costs per unit have been slightly higher still. In terms of U.S. dollars, Canadian cost increases have been even greater, because of the appreciation of our dollar after mid-1970. Part of the recent deterioration in Canada's balance of trade on manufactured goods may be attributed to these costs, although cylical factors have also been important. In any event, the effects of such changes on Canada's balance of payments on current account are less likely to be offset in the period ahead, since gains from sales of our resource products are already declining.

Thus measures to stimulate productivity in Canadian manufacturing are all the more important, and further substantial gains from specialization and longer runs must be sought. Indeed, wage parity makes the need for such gains even more immediate, although it also implies that initially there will be greater problems of adjustment to freer trade.

Despite the closing of the wage gap at the national level, Canadian regions may, of course, still retain some labour-cost advantage relative to

Table 3

Indexes of Labour Productivity, Average Hourly Earnings, and Unit Labour Cost in Manufacturing, Canada and the United States, 1963-74

	Real output per man-hour		*Compensation per man-hour*[1]		*Unit labour cost*[1]	
	Canada	*U.S.*	*Canada*	*U.S.*	*Canada*	*U.S.*
			(1961 = 100)			
1963	109.4	110.1	106.7	109.0	97.6	97.8
1972[2]	159.7	149.7	195.1	175.0	122.2	117.3
1974 (est.)	169.6	157.9	242.5	202.0	143.1	128.4
Percentage increase, 1963-74	55.0	43.4	127.3	85.3	46.6	31.3

1. The original data are in terms of each country's national currency; that is, the series do not reflect exchange rate changes. Compensation figures do not include fringe benefits, and they cover production workers only.
2. Subject to revision.

Source: Based on data from Statistics Canada and estimates by the Economic Council of Canada.

competing U.S. areas. In April 1974 the difference in average hourly money wages in manufacturing between Ontario and the Great Lakes states (Wisconsin, Michigan, Illinois, Indiana, and Ohio) stood at about 9 per cent, even after allowance for the higher value of the Canadian dollar. Quebec's manufacturing wages were about 6 per cent below those in the New England states (Maine, Massachusetts, New Hampshire, Rhode Island, Connecticut, and Vermont) and 16 per cent below those in the mid-Atlantic states (New York, Pennsylvania, and New Jersey), again after allowance for the exchange rate. Even if productivity gaps were eliminated, of course, some such differences might be required for particular Canadian industries to be able to offset the

Table 4

Indexes of Real Net Output per Man-Hour in Manufacturing, Canada and the United States, 1963-74

	1963	*1972*[1]	*Estimated 1974*
	(U.S. data for 1963 = 100)		
United States	100.0	136.0	143.5
Canada	72.8	106.3	112.9
Canada as percentage of United States	72.8	78.2	78.7

1. Subject to revision.

Source: E. C. West, *Canada–United States Price and Productivity Differences in Manufacturing Industries, 1963,* Economics Council of Canada Staff Study 32 (Ottawa: Information Canada, 1971), adjusted to a man-hour basis. The data were updated to 1972 for the Economic Council of Canada and the Ontario Economic Council, using data from Statistics Canada. The 1974 figures are estimates by the Economic Council of Canada.

transport and other disadvantages entailed in slightly greater distances from the main industrial and market centres of the United States. The same could, of course, be said for U.S. locations outside the prime industrial area, such as Minneapolis or Atlanta.

As noted earlier, regional comparisons are the relevant ones for the assessment of locational advantages. Since they too have changed greatly since the early 1960s, however, the Council has made some evaluations of its own, based on more recent data. These studies were carried out in two stages, the first involving a recalculation of relevant costs in selected Canadian and U.S. manufacturing industries as of 1969, and the second, an updating of these results to early 1974 in the light of more recent wage changes.[10]

Despite the shrinking of the wage gap, the 1969 calculation revealed substantial competitive advantages for many Canadian industries in a free trading situation with the United States alone. Ontario producers of electrical industrial equipment, for example, were well placed to compete with manufacturers of comparable products in the Great Lakes states, and Quebec-based knitting mills and clothing factories had a potential cost advantage in the New York market compared with competitors in the U.S. South. The same general results held for other central Canadian industries, such as those producing tires and tubes, communications equipment, and cutlery, hand tools, and hardware. In contrast, it appeared that the metal fabricating industries would be at a disadvantage in U.S. markets, even with increased specialization under free trade, because the lower labour costs in Canada would not be sufficient to offset the high transport charges incurred in shipping over substantial distances.[11] When these findings were updated to early 1974, the results were still broadly the same, although the competitive advantages for Canadian locations were all somewhat reduced, and in one case—electrical industrial equipment—the advantage had turned into a disadvantage.

So far we have focused on absolute cost advantages at particular wage and exchange rate levels. However, as we pointed out earlier, under free trade a country will tend to specialize, in the long run, in those goods in which its comparative efficiency is greatest and import those goods in which it is least. Particularly because of the widespread wage advantages that existed for Canadian industry, the Wonnacotts concluded that adjustment to free trade with the United States would bring an expansion of Canadian manufacturing output, an appreciation of the Canadian dollar, and general increases in money wages. At present wage levels relative to the United States, the achievement under liberalized trade of competitive cost levels by Canadian manufacturers could be most easily brought about by a depreciation of the Canadian dollar. Such depreciation could provide more of the initial incentive required to induce reorganization of Canadian industry.

As industry reorganizes to attain greater productivity, benefits again could be realized because lower prices and higher money incomes would combine to raise real income. In present circumstances, however, it would be important that further narrowing of the productivity gap be reflected in lower prices to consumers. This would facilitate greater restraint on prices, a major public concern of recent years, and reduce the risks both of adjustment problems during the transition period and of adverse balance-of-payments developments.

Reorganization of Industry under Wider Free Trade Arrangements

We have emphasized that a good deal of the specialization that would follow a Canadian move to more liberalized trade would occur within, rather than between, industries, thus reducing the adjustment costs. Adjustment would be somewhat different, to the extent that free trade arrangements included overseas countries—especially if they involved the low-wage developing nations. In those circumstances more extensive adjustment problems could be expected to arise in the production of such items as textiles, clothing, footwear, toys, household utensils, and bicycles—all industries in which overseas sources, particularly developing countries, are highly competitive. Difficulties have already arisen in some industries, such as the automotive parts industry, because of the general preferential arrangements granted to countries classified as developing. Much of the ability of Canadian industries to prosper under these conditions would relate to their potential for taking advantage of special skills, distinctive styling, and new technology so as to affect cost differences through product differentiation and superior quality.

The experience of the textile industry is illuminating in this respect. Although most of the restructuring that has taken place in that industry in recent years has been designed to increase the share of the domestic market rather than to expand exports, some substantial improvements in efficiency and scale have in fact been achieved as a result. In synthetic textiles, for example, increased effectiveness in the face of foreign competition enabled producers to expand markedly and to hold employment constant between 1965 and 1971, despite a 9 per cent decline in jobs in the textile industry as a whole. There is scope for further developments along the same lines in other textile items.

Nevertheless, in a liberalized trading world including the low-wage countries, more extensive adjustment would be required in some vulnerable sectors. Parts of these sectors would contract further, and this would pose problems in cases such as textiles, where a high proportion of production is centred in small communities like some of those in the Eastern Townships of Quebec and where many of the workers are relatively unskilled and lack mobility. These difficulties could, however, be dealt with by other measures. We should not allow the legitimate concerns over particular cases to obscure the main findings of our analysis—that trade liberalization would, with rather few exceptions, be readily accommodated by Canadian industry through increased specialization of operations, largely within individual industries.

THE DISTRIBUTION OF INCOME AMONG REGIONS AND GROUPS

Given time for industry to reorganize, real income in Canada would rise with the elimination of Canadian and foreign trade barriers.[12] But, as the previous section suggests, this does not mean that the various regions or income and occupational groups would necessarily share equally in the increase. The most obvious effect of removing the Canadian tariff would be to reduce the prices all consumers pay for internationally traded goods. Removal of our own tariff—and even more so, foreign tariffs—would also involve net gains for producers. But, since industry is not evenly distributed across the country, the prospective gains could differ substantially among the various regions.

The Atlantic and western provinces could expect substantial gains with relatively little adjustment and reorganization.[13] They are considerably more dependent upon primary industries than the central provinces, and such industries could expect moderate expansion without any restructuring. There would be opportunities for secondary industry to increase modestly in these provinces, too, mainly because of improved access to neighbouring foreign markets, particularly in the United States. The need for reorganization would, at least for the present, be confined mainly to a small group of industries, such as manufacturers of clothing in Manitoba and textiles in Nova Scotia.

Ontario would face a good deal of industrial reorganization because of its greater dependence upon manufacturing, but by the same token it would have opportunities for much greater gains than the Atlantic and western provinces. Ontario manufacturing is already considerably more export-oriented than its Quebec counterpart, partly because of the increase in automotive exports in recent years. Moreover, it is less dependent upon manufacturing industries that are highly protected and, in particular, upon industries that are subject to competition from "low-cost" imports. The removal of trade barriers, particularly between Canada and the United States, could be expected to result in much greater manufacturing specialization, especially through reorganization of individual firms. Extension of free trade arrangements to other countries would involve less additional reorganization in Ontario than Quebec. Ontario would also gain by virtue of its position as a primary producer.

Quebec would be in a somewhat different position, since its industrial structure is not the same as that of Ontario. The primary sector, which is considerably more important in Quebec, would experience greater growth under free trade conditions, and the province's strong resource base would supply large opportunities for further processing. In addition, Quebec has a number of manufacturing industries— transportation equipment, some paper products, and chemicals, for example—whose profitability would be greatly enhanced by access to large nearby markets. Such sectors would undergo reorganization like their counterparts in Ontario. And the rapid increase in industrial skills in the province, as well as its stronger orientation in recent years towards technological and entrepreneurial activity, would favour these industries and the development of firms in new lines.

On the other hand, a large share of Canadian production of textiles, shoes, and other labour-intensive manufactures is located in Quebec. Under free trade with the United States, they could deliver their output to the major U.S. markets at prices relatively competitive with similar industries in the southern United States. However, if they had to face competition from low-wage economies in the developing world, they would experience much more severe adjustment problems. But this competition will increase in any event. The real question is whether adjustment will be carried out in a planned and orderly manner or through a series of ad hoc responses to a worldwide trend.

In brief, for Quebec as for Ontario. the elimination of Canadian and foreign trade barriers offers the possibility of greater ultimate gains than would accrue to the Atlantic and western provinces. However, achievement of these gains would involve greater adjustment costs in Quebec than it would elsewhere.

The question of the effects of free trade on the distribution of income among income and occupational groups is even more complicated, and we cannot claim to have examined it intensively. Nevertheless, our work does provide some indication as to how distribution might be affected.

Although all Canadians would gain as consumers, we have not been able to determine which groups of consumers spend the largest proportion of their income on tariff-protected goods. However, it may be interesting to note that, in the United States where the tariff structure is roughly similar to that in Canada, there is evidence to suggest that tariff reduction would provide the greatest benefit to low-income consumers.[14]

The effect on incomes would be much more complex. Removal of Canadian tariffs alone might provide larger income increases in resource industries, but it could involve lower returns for some manufacturing industries, particularly those that are now most highly protected. Removal of foreign tariffs would, however, tend to raise incomes in the Canadian manufacturing industries that could become internationally competitive. On balance, there would be an overall gain.

At present, labour-intensive industries that employ many workers with elementary and high school education receive the highest protection from the Canadian tariff.[15] Those industries that are heavy users of university-trained labour receive relatively little protection. Removal of the Canadian tariff alone would mean that a somewhat greater-than-average share of the overall gain would probably accrue to the more highly educated groups, particularly those employed in the natural resource intensive industries. Even greater premiums for educated workers would result from removal of foreign tariffs, since that would stimulate expansion of the specialized manufacturing industries that are relatively heavy users of their skills.

These same effects would hold for management skills. The Canadian tariff can provide protection for inefficient or poorly trained management. Its removal would tend to favour highly trained, efficient managers, and the scope for such people would be further enhanced if removal of foreign trade barriers gave their firms access to much larger markets.

Clearly, changes in commercial policy could of themselves have a significant impact on the distribution of income among various regions and groups in Canada. Far more important, however, is the fact that income distribution can be even more readily affected by changes in the fiscal system. Shifts in income could be offset, if necessary, by changes in government taxes and expenditures, so that the overall gains from free trade could be retained without unfavourable effects on particular groups or regions. It is worth recalling that Canada already has a number of programs for improving regional balance, upgrading manpower skills, and redistributing income to disadvantaged groups. Free trade could provide increased resources for these and other programs.

The Gains from Free Trade

Under free trade with the United States, Canadian manufacturing productivity could move up to U.S. levels. Given manufacturing's present share in GNP, elimination of the gap shown in Table 4 would imply an increase in this country's GNP of about 5.7 per cent. But this would be due in considerable part to the lengthening of production runs. Even apart from scale economies, however, some gains could accrue from Canada's greater specialization in items in which this country has a comparative advantage. These have been estimated at 4 per cent of consumer expenditure, or about 2.3 per cent of GNP.[16] Wider industrial free trade arrangements would not likely result in further substantial gains from scale economies, although they could lead to further benefits from specialization in accordance with Canada's comparative advantage. Small additional gains of this nature might also accrue from the inclusion of agriculture in a free trade arrangement. Thus we conclude that total gains from free trade would amount to at least 5 per cent of GNP and perhaps somewhat more.[17]

Such estimates are necessarily imprecise, but it seems clear that substantial results could be achieved from a freeing of trade. In a single step our living standards would be raised permanently to a new level, which would become the base on which future increases could be developed. And the prospect of future increases would be enhanced, because industrial free trade would have increased the efficiency of an important sector of the Canadian economy partly by opening up fresh opportunities for effective development and innovation, thereby improving our growth performance. Multilateral free trade would provide the most remarkable improvement in the economic well-being of Canadians that could result from a single step by a government today —or at any time since the Great Depression.

However, gains of this magnitude would hold only if trade were completely freed. It must be emphasized that the extent of the benefits from any trade liberalization would depend on the size of the cuts in import barriers at home and abroad and on the range of countries included in the arrangement. Post-war experience has shown that the results of the gradual reduction of obstacles to trade have not been very satisfactory from Canada's point of view; by and large, productivity growth has not been rapid enough. The gradual approach has also resulted in a very uneven application of trade barriers—measured in terms of effective protection—to various Canadian industries. Indeed, it is difficult to perceive a continuing and consistent economic philosophy that has shaped this outcome. Rather, the evidence may be interpreted as implying that, once an industry has come into existence, the government has been concerned to provide it with sufficient protection to keep it in operation.[18] Although efficiency has sometimes been a consideration, this rationale could well be pushed far enough to perpetuate uneconomic methods of production, especially since it is applicable industry by industry. Also the effects on other industries are often obscure and are not easy to take into account.

In addition, for a country like Canada, small tariff cuts have unequal effects on exports and imports. Canadian goods manufactured behind protective barriers in a relatively narrow market tend to be high-cost, and minor reductions in foreign trade barriers may not provide our manufacturers with sufficient scope for lowering costs through specialization and longer runs. On the other hand, a similar reduction in our own trade barriers allows foreign manufacturers who already have advantages of scale and specialization to become more competitive here. This is the dilemma of a too-gradual approach. What is required is a reciprocal reduction in import restraints deep enough to promote a basic reorganization of manufacturing in Canada, so as to eliminate the gap between production costs here and in competing countries. If Canadian businessmen feel that remaining barriers are significant and likely to remain in effect for some time, they have little incentive to undertake the thorough reorganization required to compete internationally.

Thus it is that a totally free trade situation has to be seen as the best answer to Canada's industrial concerns. While practical necessities may require that we look for more limited short-term measures, multilateral free trade alone has the capacity to remove completely the constraints on our manufacturing sector and induce the type of reorganization of production that will make Canada truly competitive. This is the policy that must be our ultimate goal in all discussions of this subject and the fundamental basis of any initiative we may contemplate to improve this country's economic performance through changes in commercial policy.

Notes

*Economic Council of Canada, *Looking Outward: A New Trade Strategy for Canada* (Ottawa: Information Canada, 1975, reproduced by permission of Information Canada).

[1]David Ricardo, *The Principles of Political Economy and Taxation* (Homewood, Ill.: Richard D. Irwin, 1963), p. 72.

[2]Bruce W. Wilkinson and Ken Norrie, *Effective Protection and the Return to Capital*, Economic Council of Canada (forthcoming).

[3]Herbert G. Grubel and P. J. Lloyd, *Intra-Industry Trade* (London: Macmillan, 1975), pp. 9-10 and Chapter 9.

[4]Despite the very considerable reorganization that took place, government assistance to the industry was not large: loans to producers of automotive parts amounted to only $115 million from 1965 to mid-1973. It has been estimated also that the Automotive

Agreement resulted in Canadian GNP being 5.3 per cent higher in 1971 than it would otherwise have been. See David A. Wilton, *An Econometric Analysis of the Effects of the Canada–United States Automotive Agreement*, Economic Council of Canada (forthcoming).

[5]George Lermer, "Evidence from Trade Data Regarding the Rationalizing of Canadian Industry," *Canadian Journal of Economics* 6, no. 2 (May 1973): 248-56.

[6]Ronald J. and Paul Wonnacott, *Free Trade between the United States and Canada* (Cambridge, Mass.: Harvard University Press, 1967).

[7]These comparisons were based on the assumption of parity between U.S. and Canadian dollars.

[8]Jacques Singer, *Trade Liberalization and the Canadian Steel Industry* (Toronto: University of Toronto Press, 1969); W. E. Haviland, N. S. Takacsy, and E. M. Cape, *Trade Liberalization and the Canadian Pulp and Paper Industry* (Toronto: University of Toronto Press, 1968); and David E. Bond and Ronald J. Wonnacott, *Trade Liberalization and the Canadian Furniture Industry* (Toronto: University of Toronto Press, 1968). These studies were published as part of its "Canada in the Atlantic Economy" series by the Private Planning Association of Canada (now the C. D. Howe Research Institute).

[9]The gap would be somewhat greater if nonproduction workers were included in the comparison and if allowance were made for the higher fringe benefits of U.S. workers.

[10]This work, like that of the Wonnacotts, assumed parity of the U.S. and Canadian dollars.

[11]The same high transport costs would, of course, provide some protection from U.S. products in local markets.

[12]The impact of unilateral removal of Canadian trade barriers is discussed in Chapter 8.

[13]It has been estimated that North Atlantic free trade involving both Europe and the United States would have resulted in a gain of 5.5 per cent of personal income for British Columbia in 1963. See Ronald A. Shearer, John H. Young, and Gordon R. Munro, *Trade Liberalization and a Regional Economy: Studies of the Impact of Free Trade on British Columbia*, Private Planning Association, Canada in the Atlantic Economy series (Toronto: University of Toronto Press, 1971), p. 202.

[14]See Norman S. Fieleke, "The Cost of Tariffs to Consumers," *New England Economic Review* (September-October 1971): 13-18.

[15]Postner and Gilfix, *The Factor Content of Canadian International Trade*, Chapter 7.

[16]James R. Williams, "The Canadian-U.S. Tariff and Canadian Industry," 1974 (mimeo.) Chapter 1, p. 46.

[17]By way of illustration, using the assumptions about population and GNP growth incorporated in our *Eleventh Annual Review*, an increase of 7 per cent in per capita incomes would give the average Canadian nearly $650 more income in 1985 (in terms of 1974 prices). Of course, not all of this would really be more disposable income in the hands of individuals since, for one thing, some part of the increment would presumably accrue to governments to spend on public consumption and investment. There would, nevertheless, be 7 per cent more real income for the country as a whole. In this same sense, there would, on average, be extra income of $1,950 per family of three (in terms of 1974 prices) in 1985.

[18]This hypothesis would at least partly explain the dispersion of effective rates of protection. See James R. Melvin and Bruce W. Wilkinson, *Effective Protection in the Canadian Economy*, Economic Council of Canada Special Study 9 (Ottawa: Queen's Printer, 1968). Also Wilkinson and Norrie, *Effective Protection and the Return to Capital*.

14 Canadian Non–Tariff Barriers to Trade*

Klaus Stegemann

Standards of Comparison

... This chapter deals explicitly with the questions, How bad is Canada's NTB protectionism? What should (could) be done about it?

Asking the question, How bad?, inevitably raises the response, Bad compared to what? The answer would seem to depend largely on a person's background. A hardened free-trader might argue that any obstacle to international trade is bad and must be abolished for the sake of the most efficient allocation of resources. A reformed free-trader might admit that not all obstacles to free trade are necessarily bad for the efficiency of allocation if other obstacles exist that cannot be removed; or he might concede that some NTBs are better than other obstacles, if one wants to achieve policy objectives other than efficiency alone. A lawyer might use the rules of the GATT and similar international codes as his standard—after giving due consideration to the current interpretation and enforcement of such rules. Businessmen or employees who are favourably (or adversely) affected might point out that the policies of other countries are worse (or better) than Canadian policies. Others will judge the merits of certain NTBs on the grounds of equity between different industries or regions within the country which receive protection in some other form or are fortunate enough not to require protection at the present time.

There should be no pretense that a political economist could juggle all these considerations at once and strike some balance that would not reflect his personal predilections. It is hoped that the approach employed in the following summary sections keeps the influence of the author's value judgments at a minimum, while still giving guidance for the reader's evaluation. The general line of the argument that applies to all species of NTBs discussed can be described by the following three statements:

(i) In many respects Canada's NTB protectionism has not been as "bad" as the policies pursued by other developed countries, particularly the United States, Japan, and a number of European countries.

(ii) Over the past few years Canada's NTB protectionism has tended to get "worse" in most areas analyzed, and strong pressures are pushing the government further in this direction.[1]

(iii) Alternative policies that might achieve the objectives pursued with NTBs in a more rational fashion have not been developed sufficiently in Canada. An international initiative that would restrict the use of NTBs could be the impetus needed to set in motion the substitution of superior alternative measures for actual and potential NTBS.

With respect to the first point, there is some published evidence that in the late 1960s NTB protection was less pervasive in Canada than in other developed countries.[2]

With respect to the second of the three points listed above... one can distinguish between demand and supply factors leading to more NTB protectionism. On the demand side there may be a greater "need" for protection owing to increased international competition; there certainly are growing expectations as to what governments should do to avoid serious upheavals in their people's lives, to reduce regional and other disparities in income, and generally to intervene in economic affairs on a micro level. The objective need for protection may have increased in recent years, mainly because of the rapid expansion of industrial output in developing or "low-cost" countries, which is challenging traditional producers to an extent that is often regarded as "disruptive" or "unfair." Roy Matthews put this problem succinctly in the introduction to another volume in this series:

> The problem of market disruption is seen as arising principally in advanced-country industries that continue to manufacture goods that are at the mature phase of the product cycle—that is, where the comparative advantage has moved to less highly developed economies. In many cases—though by no means all—the relevant industries and firms in the developed countries concerned are not very dynamic, their workers are not as mobile or adaptable as they might be, and their corporate organization is highly specific to the threatened activity.[3]

One might add that in Canada, as in other countries, the difficulties of a threatened industry—such as textiles or shipbuilding—are frequently compounded by the fact that these industries are regionally concentrated in areas which suffer from a disparity of income and of employment opportunities anyway.

The unusually high levels of Canadian unemployment in recent years appear to have contributed to the more widespread use of NTB protectionism, since this general unemployment problem has accentuated sectoral and regional difficulties so that cases of "market disruption" have taken on the appearance of crises requiring the use of emergency measures. However, even if the level of general unemployment could be reduced significantly, the demand for NTB protection would not disappear, since the factors spawning non-tariff protection are essentially related to the interests of particular groups and regions affected by import competition. While it is often argued that balance of payments difficulties are an important motive for the use of NTB protection,[4] this certainly has not been the case in the recent history of Canadian commercial policy.

On the supply side, the increasing willingness of the Canadian government to provide NTB protection reflects, in a way, the changing attitude towards government intervention in economic affairs; it may also be a reflection of factors that restrain the use of traditional tariff barriers. As for the changing mood, it is quite plausible that a government would welcome the opportunity to force new domestic policy tools as soon as it became politically feasible to employ them. Objective needs, personal characteristics of leading politicians, and the example of other countries may have played a role when it was decided that Canada needed a regional development policy, an "industrial strategy," or a "science policy." However, the fact remains that governments regard policy tools as an opportunity to exert power and to improve their chances of re-election.[5] Once they have established a program that results in a net gain of power and votes, they have acquired a vested interest. This is one of the major reasons why we have to search for alternative policies to *replace* undesirable NTBS and cannot just aim at an international code that simply *prohibits* the use of certain domestic policy tools.

The other important factor on the supply side is related to the increasing restraint placed on the use of tariff barriers by international commitments and to the realization that NTBS are a more flexible and selective way of dealing with domestic problems than tariffs would be in any event. The substitution of one kind of protection for another can, of course, be carried out in an enlightened spirit that tries to minimize the cost of domestic adjustment and to limit the adverse effects on international trade. We are thus coming back to our third general consideration cited above, which will be explored in the following sections.

Mandatory Quotas Versus Voluntary Restraint

In the case of quantitative restrictions, the three general observations of the previous section are borne out quite clearly: Canada has not resorted to quotas as frequently as some other developed countries; there seems a trend towards increased use of quotas; and alternative policies have not been developed beyond a rudimentary stage. When Canadian textile and footwear manufacturers and the corresponding unions urge the government to employ quantitative import restrictions, they can confidently point to countries that have moved much further in this direction. The same applies for the coasting trade and similar shipping interests. (The Darling report[6] time and again refers to legislation in countries such as the United States and Australia that must be a Canadian shipping lobby's dream.) And one should not forget that other countries also employ quantitative restrictions for industries that are not even mentioned in this study because the Canadian counterparts have not had a serious chance to succeed with requests for quotas or import licensing.[7] If Canada is "behind" other countries in this respect, it does not follow, of course, that Canada could afford to (or ought to) be as "bad" as the others.

Since about 1971, Canada has been catching up with other countries. The government first tried to expand the system of Voluntary Export Restraint

(VER) agreements, but this apparently resulted in little relief for domestic producers and many administrative headaches.[8] Finally, a big new defence was put in place: the *Textile and Clothing Board Act* of 1971. While it is too early for an evaluation of the actual effects of this legislation, we can apply a brief general analysis to epitomize the potential implications of the new tools and procedures.

There are certain reasons why economists generally regard quantitative restrictions as more damaging to international trade than tariffs. It is for related reasons that countries often prefer to employ quantitative restrictions rather than tariffs in dealing with "serious injury" to domestic producers that is caused by rapidly growing imports. Quotas are regarded as a "safer" way of restricting the quantity of imports, because the foreign supplies frequently respond very little to a tariff-induced decrease in the exporters' net revenue (price-inelastic supply), or imported quantities respond more slowly to higher tariffs than to a quantitative limit. Quotas are also more flexible from an administrative point of view, and they lend themselves more easily than tariffs to discrimination between exporting countries.

Assuming for the moment that quotas are the appropriate instrument to deal with market disruption, what difference does it make that Canada has the new legislation and is no longer solely dependent on VER arrangements? It will be possible to employ mandatory quotas effectively to keep out all imports that are regarded as disruptive. It will be possible to enforce VER arrangements. It will be possible to use the threat of mandatory quotas to arrange for VERs more speedily, and thus to discriminate between countries without much embarrassing publicity or danger of retaliation. And all this can be done for any kind of manufactured product, although the main purpose of the legislation was to aid the Canadian textile and clothing industries. Thus the new legislation clearly points towards more severe quantitative restrictions than Canada has had in the past. This result can hardly be surprising if one considers the economic and political factors that led to the adoption of the legislation. And there will be more pressure on the government to use the tools it now has in its kit.

However, it would seem unduly pessimistic to conclude that the results of this Act will be all negative in terms of trade liberalization. The legislation introduced certain procedural improvements that might, if properly developed, come closer to resolving the market disruption issue than would have been possible with the previous procedures. The stipulation that "serious injury" has to be determined by the Textile and Clothing Board (or the Anti-dumping Tribunal under section 16A of the *Anti-dumping Act*) might have a restraining influence and will also make the use of the emergency measures more acceptable in an international context. To a great extent, the outcome will depend on the views of the members of the Board. But there will now be an opportunity for public scrutiny. The Board will have to justify its recommendations, it will have to develop criteria for the determination of serious injury, and it will have to balance explicitly the interests of different groups. Even if the criteria were the same as under the previous system, there will be more opportunity for a public debate and criticism of the Board's recommendations.[9]

Furthermore, the new procedures contain various elements that could potentially reinforce the professed intention of employing the emergency measures under the new legislation only as a form of *temporary* relief to provide threatened manufacturers with an opportunity to reorganize or to phase out certain lines of production completely. The *Textile and Clothing Board Act*, in section 18(d), clearly states the principle

> that special measures of protection are not to be implemented for the purpose of encouraging the maintenance of lines of production that have no prospects of becoming competitive with foreign goods in the market in Canada if the only protection to be provided is that provided at any time by rates of duty of customs.

Forecasting future prospects, of course, will include many elements of judgment. And the submission of adjustment plans as stipulated in the Act might only be of cosmetic value if the policy-makers wish to provide increased protection for non-viable producers or lines of production.

The extent of abuse of the temporary emergency measures will depend on two factors: the vigilance of the people who pay the cost of protecting grossly non-competitive production, and the employment of alternative measures that actively aid threatened industries in restructuring, transferring of workers, etc. The vigilance of consumers, expressed by their representatives and the press, need not exert much influence at the time when quantitative restrictions are first introduced for certain products. However, these measures have to be reviewed periodically. And if it turns out that prospects were repeatedly evaluated with too much optimism, or that adjustment plans were not carried out effectively, at some point enough countervailing power may build up to prevent the Board from recommending a prolongation of alleged emergency protection. It is essential for this purpose that the Board's proceedings and reports should be made public to the greatest degree possible.[10] An internationally acknowledged Code of Good Conduct concerning the use of emergency measures would help to stiffen the government's back.[11]

In summary, it can be said that the new procedures may turn out to be a means of securing certain domestic goals through the temporary use of quantitative import restrictions while not impeding the adjustment to changing patterns of international trade. However, the procedural safeguards against an excessive use of quantitative restrictions would seem much more reliable if temporary import restrictions were supplemented by positive measures to speed up the transition process and make it less painful for the workers involved.

One other concern derives from the continuing reliance on VER agreements. It has been mentioned that the government can now use the imposition of mandatory quotas as an arm-twisting device to make trade partners more amenable to speedy acceptance of VERs. The Textile and Clothing Board has even openly suggested this procedure in its report on cotton and polyester/cotton yarns. It seems that the Canadian government should be urged to discontinue the use of VER agreements completely. These agreements are as "voluntary" as mandatory quotas. And they are worse than mandatory quotas for three reasons:

(i) The negotiating process and the criteria used, as well as some of the terms of VER agreements, are subject to diplomatic secrecy. This is incompatible with the corrective functions of public scrutiny discussed above. All quantitative import restrictions should be subject to the same public procedures.

(ii) VER agreements are used to discriminate against individual exporting countries to a greater extent than would be opportune under a global quota system—and clearly to a greater extent than is permissible under GATT rules.[12] By restricting "low-cost" imports, Canada also protects its "normal" sources of imports—and thus sacrifices possible improvements in its terms of trade.

(iii) Whatever quantities of "low-cost" goods are admitted tend to be supplied at higher prices, because the allocation of quotas under VER agreements may be organized by the exporting countries in such a fashion that the quota profits largely accrue to foreign rather than to Canadian traders. Under a global quota, foreign suppliers of various countries would compete with each other in offering Canadian importers the most favourable terms. When the quota is fragmented on a country-by-country basis, the exporters are more likely to organize exports to Canada on a national monopoly basis (with government assistance), leaving a margin for importers that is just sufficient for them to compete in the Canadian market.[13]

It seems quite obvious that, *ceteris paribus*, there will be greater reliance on quantitative import restrictions, the less conspicuous these measures are to the public, the easier it is to avoid antagonizing "normal" sources by discriminating against "low-cost" imports, and the better the discriminated suppliers can be appeased by leaving the quota profits to them.

Procurement: A Poor All-Purpose Tool

The Canadian government is clearly willing to make a substantial sacrifice in terms of tax funds by not generally procuring its material needs from the lowest-price sources. The objectives to be achieved with this sacrifice are less clear. Only a minority of the objectives that have been pursued by government purchasing were legally required under an Act of Parliament or an Order in Council. This minority includes the aim of general protection for Canadian labour and the maintenance of a viable national defence industry. Other goals must be inferred from administrative practices. Such practices have tended to broaden the scope of protectionism by favouring all Canadian inputs, not just labour, and by trying to develop all Canadian manufacturing industries, not just the defence industries. On the other hand, administrative practices have introduced elements of differentiation in addition to the division between Canadian and foreign sources. Some foreign suppliers enjoy a preferential treatment for the purpose of re-enforcing international trade-preference systems and defence agreements. Some Canadian firms or regions are favoured over others in an attempt to employ government purchasing as a means for pursuing such diverse objectives as reduction of regional economic disparities, technological advancement, support for small business, and (potentially) Canadian ownership of industry.

It is hard to tell whether the protectionist aspects of government purchasing are becoming worse. Like most government policies, Canada's procurement policy has been influenced by shifting and frequently conflicting considerations and pressures. It seems impossible even for insiders to establish the priorities and the trade-offs between different objectives at any point in time. In a rough way, one can conclude that the goal of maintaining a viable defence industry has gradually lost its importance since the Korean War and has been superseded by the goals of more economical procurement, international integration of defence efforts, regional balance, and technological advancement. Things may get worse in the sense that it will be harder to find any room for offshore procurement, the stronger the domestic claims concerning a multitude of objectives that, in the minds of many people, should be achieved through government purchasing. The stronger the domestic claims, the less hope there is for an international agreement on less protectionist procurement, because one has to persuade so many policy-makers and interest groups that procurement should be replaced by other tools more suitable for the particular purpose.

Public procurement, unfortunately, is regarded as an all-purpose tool. During the first six months of 1972 alone, three important documents were released in Ottawa that more or less confidently claimed government purchasing for three different goals which conflict with economical procurement —and possibly conflict with each other. The first document was the "Herb Gray Report" which cautiously recommends the use of procurement as a tool to increase Canadian ownership in selected industries. The second document was Volume 2 of the "Lamontagne Report," which—less cautiously—suggested that it was "a pity" that government procurement is not yet "really taking into account the important contribution it could make to an overall industrial and technological strategy."[14]

The third document was a statement on new regional directives for DSS which the Minister of Supply and Services announced during the budget debate on June 12, 1972. The new policy has three main parts: DSS plans to establish four regions—Canada East, Quebec, Ontario, and Canada West—with the objective that federal buying in each of these four regions should approach in percentage terms the population of these regions; DSS also plans to decentralize its activities and to purchase more through regional offices; finally, DSS plans "the establishment of a policy under which any Canadian who wishes to sell to his national government can bid on the basis of his cost at his plant—that is, his bid will be judged f.o.b. plant rather than c.i.f. destination."[15]

The new purchasing policy, which is proposed under the appealing label "equality of opportunity for Canadians in all parts of Canada," might not make much difference to the opportunity of foreign suppliers because DSS in any event resorts to offshore procurement only if there is absolutely no Canadian source that could supply the required product. However, the new policy would make it still more difficult to achieve any liberalization of Canadian procurement through a negotiated agreement. When each region has its quota, and when Ontario and Quebec, now attracting 85 percent of all federal purchasing, have to share with Canada East and Canada West, it is hard to believe that the government would be willing to make them share their quotas with foreign suppliers. The suggested waiver of transportation cost is a monstrosity to an economist. Again, it would only be relevant for offshore procurement if DSS would allow mixed bidding.

One could point out in detail why purchasing policies are a poor all-purpose tool. There are administrative aspects to this question: purchasing agents have to be qualified to take into account the various objectives in their decisions; it is more difficult to audit their decisions; the user departments require budgetary compensation for the extra cost of multiple-purpose procurement of their needs; the responsibility for the achievement of the various policy goals is fragmented; etc. Procurement also is a poor all-purpose tool in the sense that more efficient alternative measures are available that have a less uneven incidence than procurement, are more specialized, and achieve the objectives with a lower cost. Examples for alternative policy tools are employment policies, regional development policies, industrial development programs, subsidies for R & D, etc. For details, we can, fortunately, refer to an up-to-date discussion of these matters.[16]

There appear to be two reasons why procurement is still being used as an all-purpose tool: for one, the alternative policies are often of recent origin and/or are not really well developed; second, the interested parties, politicians, and administrators try to use whatever tools they can lay their hands on. It is the function of independent observers and of such international bodies as the GATT and the OECD to press for a rational discussion.

As far as GATT rules are concerned, a distinction must be made between state trading and public procurement. For state trading, the GATT stipulates in Article XVII that it should be conducted solely in accordance with commercial considerations and without discrimination between sources of supply. Thus there is a clear rule covering the provincial sale of alcoholic beverages. How this rule might be enforced seems less clear, given that the practical aspects of liquor control are a matter of provincial jurisdiction.

Surprisingly, protectionist procurement policies do not contravene any GATT rules. Article III(8b) explicitly permits "the payment of subsidies exclusively to domestic producers, including . . . subsidies effected through governmental purchases of domestic products." Nevertheless, protectionist procurement policies have attracted a great deal of attention during international trade negotiations under the GATT, and the OECD has been working on a government purchasing convention for about ten years.[17] Although the twenty-three members of the OECD agree, in principle, that government purchasing policies should not discriminate between national and foreign sources of supply, there seems little reason for optimism concerning the feasibility of a practical solution.

One relatively promising route might be to gradually expand the reciprocal purchasing agreements that have been tried within the framework of the EEC, EFTA, and NATO. Canada, of course, has had some limited experience in this respect under the defence production sharing agreement with the United States. Since Canadians have become more interested in a diversification of their foreign-policy connections, the government might aim at broadening the production sharing agreement by including other countries and possibly also products other than defence goods. However, any international agreement intended to give (almost) equal opportunity for offshore suppliers would require a much larger degree of transparency, possibly public—and certainly "mixed"—tendering, and many other changes that would amount to a virtual upheaval in present procurement procedures.

As a postscript, it should be pointed out that preferential procurement in certain circumstances can be shown to have very little protective impact or none at all. If the government is not the only purchaser of certain domestic goods, the adoption of preferential domestic procurement will tend to result in increased private imports. This shift comes about because the government absorbs a larger share of domestic output and potentially drives up the price of domestic goods, whereas import prices potentially fall when a large government purchases less abroad.[18] Under certain supply conditions, the intended protectionist effect may thus not materialize because the reduction of government imports is compensated for by the exactly opposite result in the private sector. In other circumstances, preferential procurement may result in a subsidy effect, lowering the domestic price and increasing domestic sales to the private sector at the expense of imports. It would take a separate paper to sort out the factors that make Canada's procurement policy effective or ineffective as a protectionist tool.

Aid to Facilitate Adjustment

Our general conclusion that over the past few years Canada has stepped up its use of non-tariff measures appears to be borne out most clearly in the area of federal aid programs. Both the proliferation of industrial and regional aid programs and the growing magnitude of funds allocated to these programs demonstrate that Canada is following the international trend of increasing reliance on government activity to improve the structure of the economy and to stimulate growth in depressed regions. On closer inspection, one finds that it is difficult to conclude that the increasing incidence of aid programs actually has led to more protection for Canadian industries. One reason is that the protective effects of many of the programs seem trivial and/or incidental. A second reason is that government aid programs, even if they involve import substitution or export promotion, might be regarded as better (or less bad) than alternative means of protectionism.

That means we have to face a dilemma. On the one hand, government aid programs may involve distortions of international trade, and there is a danger that they might spawn further protectionism because countries emulate each other's measures or resort to retaliation—in the form of countervailing duties, for example. On the other hand, economists more or less agree that subsidies do less harm than tariffs if one takes as given that governments desire to assist particular activities, groups, or regions.[19] And it is now also a generally accepted idea that temporary adjustment assistance programs may be a prerequisite for—or at least an effective means of—reducing the need for more permanent protection.

R. E. Baldwin clearly hits the nail on its head when he states that

> domestic subsidies must be judged individually. No simple, precise rule or enumeration of specific types of subsidies can be formulated to differentiate between "good" and "bad" subsidies.[20]

For this reason, the long list of Canadian aid programs has been examined in some detail and the need for further research has been emphasized. For the purpose of providing a tentative generalized evaluation we will briefly evaluate Canada's use of

(i) production subsidies for particular industries;
(ii) short-run employment support programs;
(iii) temporary adjustment assistance programs;
(iv) industrial incentives programs aimed at innovation and increased productivity of manufacturing industries; and
(v) regional development programs aimed at manufacturing industries.

The only Canadian manufacturing industry that receives a production subsidy is shipbuilding. At the present time subsidies are granted both for domestic orders (SCSR) and for export sales (STAP). The initial purpose of the subsidy was to equalize building costs between Canadian and U.K. shipyards in order to encourage Canadian shipbuilding at a time when the opening of the St. Lawrence Seaway created new opportunities for Canadian coastal shipping.[21] The *Customs Tariff* does not provide for any tariff protection vis-à-vis British-built, British-registered vessels, whereas "foreign-built" (i.e., non-Commonwealth-built) vessels have to pay 25 percent import duty to engage in the Canadian coasting trade even if they fly the right flag. Apparently Canada chose a production subsidy rather than an import duty on Commonwealth-built ships in order not to violate the terms of the British Commonwealth Shipping Agreement of 1931. There is little evidence that the subsidy was chosen on the grounds that it is a "better" form of protection than a corresponding import duty.[22] The prices of Canadian shipping services presumably were lower than they would have been with a tariff on British ships. The cost of protection has been more visible. Still, there seems to be a little public concern about the magnitude of this cost, and the rate of 17 percent at which SCSR grants are supposed to level out in 1973 must realistically be regarded as a lower limit. The use of non-tariff barriers to protect national shipbuilding is a worldwide chronic affliction, and no remedy seems to be in sight.[23]

With respect to the second category of aid programs, the 1971 Employment Support Program largely had a psychological impact by demonstrating that the Canadian government was determined to deal quickly with the threatening effects of the U.S. surtax. Potential protectionist effects of an extended use of ESA would seem mostly incidental rather than intentional. Still, it would be safer for the harmonious development of international trade if countries could agree on a code of conduct that would regulate the terms under which temporary employment support programs are permissible as a reaction to another country's import-restricting measures. Such a code might help to avoid beggar-my-neighbour policies and escalating protectionism during periods of cyclical unemployment.

Adjustment assistance programs, narrowly defined, are aimed at facilitating adjustment of ailing domestic industries to the effects of a removal or reduction of tariffs and other import restrictions. As the Curzons put it:

> Under such programmes, inefficient industries would be gently phased out or re-converted with a minimum of social strain, to the benefit of all concerned: consumers would have access to cheaper goods; labour and capital would be freed to seek more dynamic and profitable occupations; and wider market access for developing countries.[24]

Part of the philosophy behind these programs is that an "orderly adjustment process" is a more efficient form of restructuring than the turmoil that might result in a case of unmitigated "market disruption." At least equally important, however, is the consideration that adjustment assistance often is a political prerequisite for a reduction of import restrictions because increased efficiency and specialization can be achieved only if the potential resistance of politically influential groups is bought off and/or because policymakers and legislators would regard it as inequitable if overall gains from trade were achieved at the expense of serious injury to particular groups.

On the basis of this narrow definition, Canada's AAA and GAAP hardly deserve the name adjustment assistance, because these programs have not been employed as a means of softening potential injury resulting from a reduction of Canadian import restrictions: nor do they provide for grants that could be used to buy off anybody's resistance. It remains to be seen to what extent the "new" GAAP as amended in 1971 will be used to substitute adjustment loans to textile and clothing manufacturers for "special measures of protection"—as quantitative restrictions are bashfully referred to in the legislation.

These special measures are regarded as a form of adjustment assistance, and in some cases temporary quotas might well achieve the same end result as would adjustment grants. However, most economists would prefer adjustment grants to quotas, chiefly on the grounds that grants can be aimed more selectively at those producers and activities that ought to be supported to achieve a speedy adjustment process, and also on the grounds that the cost of the temporary protection is more visible than it is in the case of special import restrictions. The need for fresh appropriations for subsidies would continually remind policy-makers to keep the objectives of the program clearly in mind and to keep comparing costs with expected benefits. The latter fact should hopefully help to prevent an unwarranted prolongation of the adjustment aid.[25]

It follows from these considerations that Canada's policy with respect to "market disruption" resulting from severe import competition could be improved by a staged approach that should rely on quantitative import restrictions only in the short run when an emergency arises that cannot be dealt with quickly enough by other means. In the second phase—or preferably even before an emergency arises—the policy should resort to the selective use of grants to assist potentially competitive producers with specified adjustment tasks. When it is apparent that all efforts at restructuring are unlikely to result in a competitive domestic production, the firms in question might still be offered grants on the condition that they abandon the inefficient activities. Such "abandonment compensation" will often be cheaper for the economy than a continuing drain resulting from high-cost production.[26] Several adjustment schemes are already in existence for workers affected by restructuring or abandonment of production. The *Textile and Clothing Board Act* specifically provides in section 21 for adjustment assistance benefits for employees suffering from lay-offs directly attributable to reduced protection or to cases of serious injury without increased protection.[27] The Cape Breton development program (DEVCO) also contains an element of direct adjustment and abandonment aid.

There would appear to be two main reasons why adjustment grants are not widely applied as an alternative to import restrictions. One is that industries in need of adjustment suspect—with some justification—that the grants they could possibly receive would be only a fraction of the income they are able to earn in a more highly protected market. The other reason is that governments fear the strain on their budgets of a subsidy scheme.[28] An alternative version of this second reason would be to say that governments seem to prefer spending money on more "positive" aid programs. Developing new products, supporting R & D, expanding exports, improving the infrastructure of a depressed region—such activities would seem more attractive to a politician than putting tax funds into a losing industry.

In a critical vein, one might argue that there is a tendency for governments to seek the glamour of building monuments and to neglect the menial cleanup operations that potentially could do more good for a larger number of people. But then it must be recognized that the expansionary programs are also aimed at improving the structure of the economy and that, to a certain extent, they must be regarded as alternatives to the implementation of adjustment programs in the narrower sense. When the government succeeds in stimulating new activities and in developing depressed regions, it becomes possible to absorb resources that are employed in non-competitive production. The start-up aid for new activities might thus reduce the need for protection for traditional industries that are losing their markets to new products or to new producers in developing countries. It is impossible to prescribe an optimal strategy for the improvement of Canadian industrial structure. However, it should be reiterated that there appears to be a gap in Canada's policy mix in that the government has not yet seriously employed adjustment aid to reduce the resistance of groups that ought to give way to the forces of structural change.

Incentive Programs and Countervailing Duties: A Matter of Current Concern for Canada

The conclusion, reached towards the end of the previous section, that in a broader sense all kinds of industrial development schemes might be regarded as forms of adjustment assistance should not be read to imply that all kinds of subsidies are innocuous—or even beneficial—for the harmonious development of international trade as long as they are aimed at improving the structure of the national economy.

One has to be careful to define structural improvement in such a way that long-run adjustment to competitive conditions is eased rather than impeded. Simply increasing the efficiency of a non-viable industry by aiding investment could be counter-productive, since the combined vested interest of people in the industry and government officials might make it more difficult for desirable structural change to take its course.

While it would seem alarmist to conclude that the present levels of aid pose any great problem and utopian to expect that governments could ever be persuaded to give up completely those economic policy tools that nowadays significantly affect their chances of being re-elected, there are several good reasons for having an international code of conduct that puts certain constraints on the use of industrial aid programs. And, fortunately, there is also at least some justification for hoping that self-interest might motivate national governments to agree to limitations on aid programs that can be enforced in an international context.[29]

An international code of conduct concerning industrial aid programs is needed to reduce the three principal dangers that can arise from the increasing reliance on such programs:

(i) the danger of hardening that turns temporary start-up or adjustment assistance into more or less permanent production subsidies;
(ii) the danger of emulation that defeats the development efforts of individual countries and might lead to worldwide excess capacity in certain sectors;
(iii) the danger of excessive retaliation, especially in the form of countervailing duties, that creates protectionist threats and effects in excess of the compensative protection necessary to rectify export-promoting measures of other countries.

The motivation for governments to negotiate and enforce an international code of good conduct would seem to be closely related to the three dangers listed. The self-interest of national governments in rules that limit their sovereignty in administering aid programs might be less obvious with respect to the first point—especially since governments might be reluctant to admit failure if temporary aid did not achieve the hoped-for results. However, previous rounds of trade negotiations seem to provide at least some evidence that enlightened governments might be interested in such rules because the reference to an international commitment is a relatively convincing way of fending off insatiable demands of a protectionist constituency.

As regards the second point, the self-interest of national governments in slowing down the "aid race" is more obvious—although it is difficult to see just how emulation could be prevented. A meaningful code of conduct should be much easier to negotiate when most countries are becoming aware that intergovernmental competition for "footloose" industries is a costly game to play and that they must find ways of limiting this kind of competition.

The danger of excessive retaliation, finally, would appear to provide the strongest motivation for agreeing on a code of conduct. For most countries there are at least two important aspects to this. One is that under the GATT system, retaliation is, for all practical purposes, the only means of enforcing rules of conduct.[30] The contracting parties thus have certain rights to defend their markets against misconduct. The other aspect is that the participating countries agree to circumscribe the conditions under which retaliation may be applied. Governments would thus be able to anticipate more correctly the forms of industrial assistance that will be tolerated by trading partners, and any sanctions, if warranted, would have to be instituted in accordance with an agreed procedure and subject to certain limitations. In practice, any code of conduct covering the use of aid programs would have to be closely intertwined with a code for the use of countervailing measures.[31]

Broadly speaking, a code of conduct should thus ensure that national aid programs will be limited in three essential ways:

(i) they should provide only temporary assistance in the form of adjustment aid or start-up aid;
(ii) they should be administered as selective incentives for certain types of activities, firms, or locations, rather than as production subsidies;
(iii) they should not cause "material injury" to competing industries of other countries.

There is no point trying to spell out operational definitions and procedures for these general criteria. GATT, OECD, EEC, EFTA, and other international institutions have demonstrated that workable codes of conduct—albeit imperfect ones—are possible even if the initial approach seemed impossibly vague.

The requirement that aid programs should not cause material injury to competing industries of other countries has been—and will remain—an important issue in the debate on the proper use of countervailing duties. Countervailing duties are governed by Article VI of the GATT. Paragraph 6(a) of that article stipulates that the contracting parties may not levy any countervailing duty unless the effect of a trade partner's subsidy program "is such as to cause or threaten material injury to an established domestic industry, or is such as to retard materially the establishment of a domestic industry." This provision has been of limited practical importance because, under the Protocol of Provisional Application, existing legislation conflicting with this provision (or any other provisions in Part II of the GATT) does not constitute a violation of the General Agreement.[32] It happens to be the case that the U.S. Countervailing Duty Law, dating back to 1897, does not contain any injury criterion. Apparently this was one reason why a countervailing duty code—which, unlike the GATT Anti-Dumping Code, would require amendment of the relevant U.S. statute—could not be achieved during the Kennedy Round of negotiations.

The European Community has long advocated the adoption of a countervailing duty code, with a view to getting the United States to accept material injury as a criterion for imposing countervailing duties. "This would be useful to members of the Common Market which operate large-scale regional development policies, and which fear that the United States might use these schemes as a trigger for countervailing action."[33] Canada recently had reason to join the Europeans in their fear, when the U.S. Treasury Department on May 12, 1972, initiated countervailing duty proceedings against imports of X-radial steel belted tires produced by the Michelin tire company in Canada.[34] For the first time, federal and provincial regional incentives programs have been challenged under the U.S. Countervailing Duty Law, and even if this particular case is dismissed, considerable doubt might be cast on the future of Canadian industrial and regional assistance programs.

Under present U.S. legislation, the critical question is whether various forms of start-up assistance provided to Michelin by various levels of government in Canada constitute a bounty or grant upon the manufacture, production, or exportation of Michelin tires.[35] Without going into the particulars of the Michelin case, it can be said that there would be a larger safety margin against invocation of the U.S. Countervailing Duty Law if the act contained a material-injury criterion—provided that "material injury" means just that and is not merely assumed to exist as soon as any negative effects on domestic industries can be established. A serious-injury test would presumably save most of Canada's incentive programs even if it were found that the financial incentives constitute "bounties or grants" within the meaning of the U.S. statute.

Conversely, as long as the degree of injury to U.S. industries is irrelevant, actual or potential application of the U.S. Countervailing Duty Law could effectively threaten the more important of Canada's efforts to improve its industrial structure or to develop depressed regions. If the United States imposes a countervailing duty which attempts to nullify the effect of Canadian government aid, this would generally make exportation of the products in question to the United States unprofitable, assuming that the investment in the particular venture or region would not be undertaken without government assistance. If it is anticipated that exports to the United States will be unprofitable because of countervailing measures, many a venture would be completely unfeasible despite government incentives. Canada could certainly no longer rely on industrial (and even regional) aid programs that emphasize export-orientation of new industries as much as the present programs do.

The Canadian government firmly denies that export orientation of the Michelin tire plant in Nova Scotia was a factor in the decision to provide start-up assistance;[36] this denial is generalized for all assistance under the RDIA program, and it is pointed out that, owing to traditionally strong trade links between Canada and the United States, "some of the output of almost any plant established in Canada must be exported to the United States."[37] However, it seems plausible that for political reasons . . . governments will try to avoid assisting firms that compete with established domestic producers.

And one can think of several economic reasons why Canada in particular should aim its industrial and regional incentives at industries that promise to be strong exporters. The most prominent reason, of course, is that Canadian manufacturing industries must increase their penetration of foreign markets in order to increase their productivity. This is the familiar argument that the size of the Canadian market, in relation to a given number of firms in it, does not permit the use of most efficient technology and/or optimal production runs. Academic writings,[38] as well as public documents,[39] have recommended that Canadian industry should be geared towards increased specialization—and this implies increased export activity of the specializing industries. The Minister of Industry, Trade and Commerce recently confirmed that these ideas are still very much at the basis of Canada's "industrial strategy."[40] To achieve specialization, however, economic policy cannot rely on import restrictions. On the contrary, import restrictions have to be reduced, and the emphasis of industrial policy shifted to various forms of start-up aid and export-market development for industries that potentially are competitive in international markets.

Foreign producers who feel the impact of new Canadian competition may ask, Why should we suffer if Canada helps its producers to lower their cost? This may be a legitimate question from the point of view of the individual foreign industry, and to the extent that it might suffer material injury, there would be a case for protecting such an industry by countervailing measures. However, Canada should not be forced to give up efforts at improving its industrial structure simply for the reason that the new industries compete internationally. To avoid a concentrated impact on U.S. producers, Canada should try to diversify its export markets regionally.[41] However, it should not diversify production unless it is efficient to do so in a competitive world market. The Canadian government should point out to its trade partners that the alternative to an expansion of its exports lies in the development of less efficient protected manufacturing industries substituting for imports. The government may be able to offer concessions as regards Canadian import restrictions in exchange for more freedom with respect to providing industrial aids. It may also be able to persuade international companies with subsidiaries in Canada that they stand to benefit from an increased trend towards international specialization.

Notes

*Stegemann, K., *Canadian Non-Tariff Barriers to Trade* (Montreal: Canadian Economic Policy Committee of the C. D. Howe Research Institute, 1973, reproduced by permission of author and publisher).

[1]The wording implies, of course, that the author generally regards protectionism as an evil. One might substitute "widespread" for "bad" and "more prevalent" for "worse."

[2]See Ingo Walter, "Non-Tariff Barriers and the Free-Trade Area Option," *Banca Nazionale del Lavoro Quarterly Review*, No. 88 (March, 1969), pp. 33-38; H. H. Glismann and A. Neu, "Towards New Agreement on International Trade Liberalization: Methods and Examples of Measuring Non-Tariff Trade Barriers," *Weltwirtschaftliches*

Archiv, Vol. 107 (1971 II), pp. 238-39; Caroline Pestieau and Jacques Henry, *Non-Tariff Trade Barriers as a Problem in International Development* (Montreal: Canadian Economic Policy Committee, 1972), pp. 84-89; and various documents published by the Secretariat of the United Nations Conference on Trade and Development (UNCTAD), cited in the above publications.

[3]Introduction to Roy A. Matthews to Pestieau-Henry, *op. cit.*, p. xiii.

[4]See, for example, R. E. Baldwin, *Non-Tariff Distortions of International Trade* (Washington, D.C.: The Brookings Institution, 1970), pp. 14-17 and 171-73.

[5]Similar ideas were expressed, in a Canadian context, by Albert Breton in *Discriminatory Government Policies in Federal Countries* (Montreal: Canadian Trade Committee, 1967), Chap. VI.

[6]H. J. Darling, "Report of Inquiry on the Coasting Trade of Canada and Related Marine Activity," mimeographed (Ottawa: Canadian Transport Commission, October, 1970).

[7]The United States, for example, is using a much more extensive system of "voluntary export restraint agreements" than Canada to limit Japanese imports. In July, 1971, the number of Japanese items under export restraint with regard to the United States was close to 100, including a large number of cotton and other textile products, 17 items in steel, and 18 other items such as wall tiles, baseball gloves, umbrellas, bicycles, and dry cells. See United States-Japan Trade Council, "U.S.-Japan Bilateral Non-Tariff Barriers, Part I: U.S. Barriers," Fact Sheet No. 5, mimeographed (Washington, D.C., June, 1971).

[8]See also Jacques Henry in Pestieau and Henry, *op. cit.*, Chap. 6 and Appendix B.

[9]The government does not have to accept the Board's recommendations. However, it seems safe to assume that in most cases the measures adopted will not be less restrictive than the measures "awarded" to domestic producers by the Board.

[10]The Consumers' Association of Canada has not been noted for its vigilance and aggressiveness on the import front. However, recently the Association demanded the immediate removal of the import quota on men's and boys' shirts, in effect since November 1971. See "Consumers Ask for End to Quota on Import Shirts," *Globe and Mail* (Toronto), October 24, 1972.

[11]See, for example, the proposal by Bela Balassa discussed in J. Henry, *op. cit.*, pp. 175-76.

[12]Discrimination, of course, is permissible under the LTA. [Ed. Note: see the appendix to Chapter 2 of *Canadian Non-Tariff Barriers to Trade.*]

[13]See W. M. Corden, *The Theory of Protection* (London: Oxford University Press, 1971), pp. 206-208.

[14]*A Science Policy for Canada*, Report of the Senate Special Committee on Science Policy, Vol. 2, *Targets and Strategies for the Seventies* (Ottawa: Information Canada, 1972), p. 549.

[15]Quoted from the Minister's statement, *House of Commons Debates*, Monday, June 12, 1972 (Ottawa: Information Canada, 1972), p. 3040.

[16]See K. Stegemann and K. Acheson, "Canadian Government Purchasing Policy," *Journal of World Trade Law*, Vol. 6, No. 4 (July/August, 1972), pp. 442-78.

[17]See Gerard and Victoria Curzon, *Global Assault on Non-Tariff Trade Barriers* (London: Trade Policy Research Centre, 1972), pp. 22-27.

[18]See J. David Richardson, "The Subsidy Aspects of a 'Buy American' Policy in Government Purchasing," *The Economics of Federal Subsidy Programs* (A Compendium of Papers Submitted to the Joint Economic Committee, Congress of the United States), Part 2, *International Subsidies* (Washington, D.C.: U.S. Government Printing Office, June, 1972), pp. 220-42.

[19]For a technical discussion see Harry G. Johnson, "Optimal Trade Intervention in the Presence of Domestic Distortions," *Trade, Growth, and the Balance of Payments* (Haberler Festschrift) (Chicago: Rand McNally, 1965); a less technical treatment is given by Kenneth W. Dam, *The GATT: Law and International Economic Organization* (Chicago: University of Chicago Press, 1970), Chap. 8; and R. A. Matthews, *Industrial Viability in a Free Trade Economy: A Program of Adjustment Policies for Canada* (Toronto: University of Toronto Press, 1971), pp. 10-14.

[20]R. E. Baldwin, *op. cit.*, p. 130.

[21]See the Robertson Report (Report of the Committee on Shipbuilding in Canada [Ottawa: Queen's Printer, 1970]), pp. 13-14.

[22]For foreign-built ships, tariff and subsidy protection are cumulative. It has been estimated that in 1967 this cumulative rate of effective protection was between 80 and 90 percent on Canadian value added in shipbuilding. See James R. Melvin and Bruce W. Wilkinson, *Effective Protection in the Canadian Economy*, Economic Council Special Study No. 9 (Ottawa: Queen's Printer, 1968), p. 71.

[23]See Gerard and Victoria Curzon, *Hidden Barriers . . .*, *op. cit.*, pp. 18-21. There may be some basis for a less pessimistic appraisal, since recently eleven main shipbuilding nations committed themselves to reducing trade-distorting assistance to shipyards with the goal of eliminating it by late 1975. The new arrangement was worked out by the OECD Council's working party on shipbuilding under the chairmanship of the former Canadian ambassador to the OECD, Russell McKinney. See "Shipbuilders Agree to New Policy," *Globe and Mail* (Toronto), October 28, 1972.

[24]Gerard and Victoria Curzon, *Global Assault . . .*, *op. cit.*, p. 12.

[25]A more subtle "welfare" argument for subsidies as opposed to import restrictions is discussed in the article by H. G. Johnson, *op. cit.*, especially pp. 9-10. See also Yeong-Her Yeh, "On Subsidies Vs. Tariffs," *Southern Economic Journal*, Vol. 38, No. 1 (July, 1971), pp. 89-92); and W. M. Corden, *op. cit.*, Chap. 2.

[26]On the problems of abandonment compensation see R. A. Matthews, *op. cit.*, Chap. 7.

[27]See also Adjustment Assistance Benefit Regulations, P.C. 1971-558, SOR/71-129, *Canada Gazette*, Part II, Vol. 105, No. 7 (April 14, 1971), pp. 623-31.

[28]If the alternative to a subsidy is a tariff, rather than a quota, there would be a loss of tariff revenue in addition to the extra expenditure.

[29]For a more detailed discussion of this point, in a European context, see Klaus Stegemann, *Wettbewerb und Harmonisierung im Gemeinsamen Markt* (Cologne: Carl Heymanns, 1966), especially pp. 92-105 and 114-17.

[30]For a discussion of an alternative means of enforcement, see Gerard and Victoria Curzon, *Global Assault . . .*, *op. cit.*, pp. 9-10.

[31]*Ibid.*, pp. 19-21.

[32]See Kenneth W. Dam, *op. cit.*, pp. 178-79 and 341-42.

[33]Gerard and Victoria Curzon, *Global Assault . . .*, *op. cit.*, p. 21.

[34]For a brief summary of the relevant facts and opinions, see "X Radial Steel Belted Tires from Canada—Countervailing Duty Proceeding," preliminary memorandum submitted on behalf of the Government of Canada by Bruce E. Clubb, Walter A. Slowinski, and J. P. Janetatos of the law firm Baker & McKenzie, Washington, D.C., mimeographed (Washington, July 12, 1972).

[35]*Ibid.*, pp. 4-6 and 17-18.

[36]*Ibid.*, pp. 14-15 and 17-18.

[37]*Ibid.*, p. 14.

[38]The standard references are H. Edward English, *Industrial Structure in Canada's International Competitive Position* (Montreal: Canadian Trade Committee, 1964); and H. C. Eastman and S. Stykolt, *The Tariff and Competition in Canada* (Toronto: Macmillan Company of Canada, 1967).

[39]For example, the report of the Task Force on the Structure of Canadian Industry, *Foreign Ownership and the Structure of Canadian Industry* (Ottawa: Queen's Printer, 1968), and the Economic Council of Canada in its *Fourth Annual Review* (1967), Chap. 6; *Fifth Annual Review* (1968), Chap. 7; and in its *Interim Report on Competition Policy*, Chap. 5 (1969) (Ottawa: Queen's Printer).

[40]See notes for a speech "Industrial Strategy," by the Honourable Jean-Luc Pepin to the Annual General Meeting of the Canadian Manufacturers' Association in Edmonton on June 5, 1972, mimeographed, especially pp. 7-10.

[41]This is already being done, to some extent, under the DITC Program for Export Market Development. See DITC *News Release*, No. 89/71 of December 16, 1971, and Stephen Duncan, "Ottawa Sweetens Incentives to Export beyond the U.S.," *Financial Post* (Toronto), February 19, 1972.

Part 2
Industrial Incentives

Introduction

The tariff, and the various non-tariff measures described in the preceding part of this section, have provided incentives to private firms to undertake manufacturing and a number of secondary processing activities in Canada. They have consequently served to redirect labour and capital resources to uses other than those which might have been determined by the free operation of market forces; the object of this redirection of resources being, it would seem, to promote the industrialization of the Canadian economy.

In recent years there have been further efforts to shape the structure of Canadian industry at both the federal and provincial levels. These have had two main objectives: to get a "better" geographic distribution of industry throughout the country and to promote the growth of new kinds of industries in accordance with some overall "industrial strategy" for the country as a whole. These efforts to get more of the desired kinds of industries, and to get them in the desired locations, all appear to represent a deliberate rejection of the "free market" as a device for achieving such ends. The federal government's location policies are mainly the responsibility of the Department of Regional Economic Expansion. DREE's efforts have been directed largely towards increasing employment opportunities in those parts of Canada that have been more afflicted with unemployment than others. How difficult it is to manipulate resource allocation to achieve desired outcomes is demonstrated by Professor Woodward in Reading 15, which shows that DREE's subsidies to firms locating in specified areas appear to have encouraged these firms to substitute capital for labour in their operations, thereby minimizing the employment-creating effects of the subsidies! The efforts of provincial governments and even local municipal governments to attract certain kinds of industries to their jurisdictions are epitomized in the Nova Scotia government's widely copied Industrial Estates Limited undertaking. R. E. George, in Reading 16, analyzes the activities of this organization and identifies a number of interesting interactions between the political and economic forces with which it has had to contend.

Many provincial governments have also attempted to get new, often quite large-scale, industrial operations started up in their jurisdictions by entering into special "deals" with large, outside private firms. Despite the secrecy that typically surrounds such arrangements, Phillip Mathias has pieced together the story of five such undertakings in his book, *Forced Growth*, from which Reading 17 has been extracted. Again, the interaction of economic and political forces is highlighted in this selection, which also draws into focus some of the possible connections between the issues of foreign investment, public ownership and Canadian development strategy.

Recent world experience, as shown in the Economic Council of Canada readings in Part 1 above, has indicated that a country's ability to remain "progressive" and competitive in world markets depends increasingly on its access to technological knowledge and the capacity of its business enterprises to effectively utilize new technological knowledge. Recognizing this, national governments, including the Canadian, have added to their "promotion activities" a number of measures intended to strengthen the technological resources (and resourcefulness) of their producers. The relevance of these to the problems faced by certain Canadian business firms is studied in Reading 18 which, by drawing attention to the difficulties faced by small entrepreneurs attempting to develop new businesses in this country, also introduces a number of issues which are further considered in Section 3. In particular, the question of whether the"bigness" of business should be thought of as a virtue, rather than a fault, is presented.

15 The Effectiveness of DREE's New Location Subsidies *

Robert S. Woodward

Background

... That increased employment in depressed areas is the primary objective of the DREE incentives is clear from the original RDIA and the DREE staff papers. The Act was intended "to provide incentives for the development of productive employment opportunities in regions of Canada determined to require special measures ..." (Canada, 1970, 6543). Furthermore, regions were designated as eligible for DREE incentives if 'existing opportunities for productive employment in the region were exceptionally inadequate' (*ibid.*, 6544). Francis and Pillai (1972, 44-5) confirm the department's *raison d'être* as 'the provision of appropriate programs to stimulate new productive employment opportunities.'

A slight change in the presentation of DREE's goals occurred in a more recently published staff paper which affirms that employment is the primary objective but implicitly (and incorrectly) suggests that no inconsistency exists between investment subsidies and increased employment as the primary goal. In this staff paper DREE's primary goal is given as increasing manufacturing job opportunities in designated regions 'by stimulating private investment' (Canada, DREE, 1973, 3). Goals which would be consistent with subsidies which stimulate private investment are listed as secondary.

DREE argues (1973, 38) that it achieves these employment objectives by affecting manufacturing investment and location decisions in four ways. The subsidies may induce a firm to locate a plant in a designated region, to construct a larger facility, or to undertake a project now rather than some time in the future. Or, the subsidies may make a marginal project viable. DREE calls these four effects 'incrementality' factors.

Regardless of which incrementality factor is being affected, the difficulty with seeking any employment goal using capital (or capital biased) subsidies follows from the flexibility each firm has in choosing the amount and quality of machinery and equipment used by each employee. This flexibility has been documented in Canada by Kotowitz (1968), who used to cross-section data to estimate that many firms are sufficiently flexible so that each 10 per cent change in the relative prices of capital and labour would lead to approximately a 5 per cent change in the ratio of capital to labour used in production.[1] For example, if the price of machinery was reduced by 20 per cent relative to the price of labour, a firm with this degree of flexibility would increase the value of machinery used per employee by 10 per cent.

As a result of this flexibility, each single manufacturing firm accepting a capital-location subsidy will adjust its factor intensity, as well as one or more of the incrementalities. For example, firms which already plan to locate in a designated region and which respond to the DREE subsidies by increasing their size will both expand their output and use more capital relative to all other inputs (including labour). While the increased output causes additional employment, the greater capital intensity reduces employment. The indeterminant net change in number of jobs is the sum of the positive output and the negative substitution effects.

If the DREE subsidy affects a firm's location, but not any of the other incrementality factors, and if the designated region has lower wages than the firm's initial location, the designated region's employment will be increased by the firm's responding to a capital-location subsidy. However, the firm, and thus the region, would not experience as much additional employment as would be possible from a neutral or a labour-biased subsidy (Woodward, 1974b).

In short, flexibility in the production process allows each firm to respond to every aspect of a subsidy. For capital-location grants, a firm will 1) either increase its output, change its location, speed up its timing or proceed with an otherwise unviable project, and 2) increase its use of capital relative to other inputs. Additional employment at the firm's location may, or may not, follow.

Despite their recognition that in each firm employment subsidies will create the most jobs per subsidy dollar, some scholars nevertheless suggest that capital subsidies will create more regional jobs in the long run. A greater long-run employment effectiveness of capital subsidies is possible only if at least one of the following arguments is valid: 1) the capital subsidy attracts a sufficiently greater number of firms; 2) the indirect employment effect—the number of regional jobs created in firms supplying a) intermediate goods to the subsidized firm, and b) consumption goods to the employees of the subsidized firm—is greater for firms attracted by the capital subsidy, or 3) the agglomeration economies occur more quickly among firms attracted by capital subsidies. Additionally, the capital subsidies might have a superior employment effect in the long run if firms attracted caused fewer employment reductions in the unsubsidized firms already existing in the depressed region.

In fact, evidence for all these propositions is extremely weak, especially when compared to the importance of the capital bias for each firm. First, there is no reason why labour and capital grants of an equal size would have different impacts on a firm's profits. Thus, there is no reason to suspect that capital, or capital biased, grants are more likely to attract more firms than labour grants of equal size.

Second, the indirect employment effects of subsidized firms are often much smaller than anticipated. In their in-depth study of the employment impacts of the ADA incentives in the Southern Georgian Bay region of Ontario,

Yeates and Lloyd (1970) discovered that the additional 2222 workers in ADA plants were likely to induce only 7 additional jobs in firms supplying intermediate products. Additionally, the net employment multiplier (including intermediate manufacturing goods and consumption effects) was only 1.083. Since each 12 direct new jobs caused only 1 additional job, it is hard to argue that directly created jobs produce much additional employment. And since many of these ADA plants were capital intensive, it is harder to argue that capital subsidies which attract capital intensive firms will create a sufficient amount of additional indirect employment to offset their smaller direct employment impact.

Since available empirical evidence about agglomeration economies is extremely limited,[2] it is difficult to determine whether the self-sustained employment growth associated with the realization of agglomeration economies will occur more rapidly with capital intensive or with labour intensive firms. Therefore, it is impossible to attribute stronger agglomeration economies to capital, rather than labour, subsidies. In particular, there is no evidence to indicate that agglomeration economies will reduce the superiority of employment subsidies in creating additional employment in depressed regions.

A final determinant of the long-run employment impact of labour and capital subsidies is the degree to which subsidized firms use their grant money to push out existing firms from competitive product markets (by selling the same product at a lower price) or from their input markets (by buying limited resources at higher prices). For grants of a given size, there is no evidence that either capital or labour subsidies are more likely to attract firms which will use the subsidy to put existing unsubsidized firms at a competitive disadvantage.

Since employment subsidies must create more jobs in each firm per subsidy dollar; since there is no evidence to suggest that capital subsidies attract more firms, induce more indirect jobs, stimulate agglomeration economies more quickly, or reduce unsubsidized employment less; and since its goal is to create additional job opportunities in depressed regions, DREE should recognize the overall superiority of employment subsidies.

Although insufficient evidence exists to evaluate the recently accepted offers to large firms, the capital bias in all other aspects of the DREE subsidies clearly remains. First, all modernization and expansion grants are pure capital-location subsidies. Second, the new plant and new product standard formulas for small firms reduce labour costs by far less than 25 per cent—the percentage reduction in the approved capital costs. Third, the bias in the unchanged maximum grants for large firms was documented in an earlier paper on capital bias (Woodward, 1974a). Fourth, the two capital constraints act to transform the small and large firm new plant and product formulas into pure capital subsidies for average firms in a surprising proportion of industries. Finally, taxation continues to reduce the size of the grants without changing the direction of the bias.

Policy

Here and elsewhere, DREE has been criticized for subsidies which are inconsistent with their policy goals. After clarifying the difference between appropriate public policy objectives and regional economic problems, this section reviews several alternative subsidies and policy objectives which satisfy some of the objections to the current RDIA grants.

Because of the positive (yet limited) corporate flexibility in production, each specific subsidy (or combination of subsidies) can be entirely consistent with only one ordering of policy goals.[3] For example, job-location subsidies are consistent only with policy objectives which give the highest priority to *jobs* in depressed regions. Additional regional production, wages, income, capital investments or technology all depend critically upon the degree of flexibility (or lack of it) demonstrated by the firms receiving the subsidies.

Because each set of subsidies corresponds to only one set of policies, choosing the appropriate subsidy is largely an exercise in selecting policy objectives. While substantial agreement may be found about the broadly defined goal of increasing the spatial equality of economic opportunities, there is a notable lack of agreement about specific goal definitions. For example, there is wide disagreement about whether employment, investment, or income should take priority in policy objectives.

The lack of agreement about the priorities among policy goals is compounded by a confusion over whether the subsidies should be directed towards overcoming the cause of inadequate regional growth or towards achieving the policy objectives directly. Suppose employment is the policy objective and the lack of entrepreneurship actually causes high unemployment. Profit or investment subsidies might be directed at stimulating entrepreneurship and thus creating employment. Or job subsidies might be directed at creating additional employment directly.

Since subsidies can only be consistent with one ranking of policy objectives, and since firms exhibit significant flexibility in the amount of machinery and equipment used per employee, the most effective subsidy can only be directed at achieving the publicly accepted goal. Subsidies which seek to achieve policy objectives indirectly, even those which correctly identify and attack the roots of the depressed region's economic problems, can only achieve the objectives at a higher cost or with less success.

In the current situation, the publicly-recognized RDIA goal is employment in certain depressed regions. In contrast, the DREE capital (or capital biased) subsidies are consistent only with an objective ranking which gives additional plant, machinery and equipment the highest priority. Even if the lack of plant, machinery and equipment is the cause of the designated regions' high unemployment (which is disputable), DREE fails to achieve the greatest number of new jobs, and incurs a higher cost per new job created, by continuing with the subsidies which are inconsistent with their goals.

DREE could resolve the current inconsistencies attributable to the capital bias by modifying the subsidies or modifying the goals to be consistent with existing subsidies or to be sufficiently vague to be consistent with any location incentive. Possible subsidy modifications include increasing the per cent of wages and salaries, increasing the dollars paid per job, reducing the capital subsidy, and/or removing the capital constraints.

DREE could make the RDIA goals consistent with existing subsidies by indicating that private investment is a more important goal than additional jobs. Alternatively, DREE could back away from its admirable policy of publicly stating its specific objectives and subsidy formulas. One justification for such a regression would be the possible existence of important regional variations in specific policy objectives. Were such regional differences to exist, the newly created DREE regional offices could be assigned the responsibility of selecting the mix of policy objectives and subsidies appropriate for their jurisdictions. This last alternative seems more consistent with the present DREE trend towards regional decentralization and might avoid the current academic criticism of the national program.

References

Canada (1970) *Revised Statutes of Canada* VI, Chapter R-3 (Ottawa)

Canada. Department of Regional Economic Expansion (1972-3) 'Report on Regional Development Incentives,' Table 3: Offers Accepted.

Canada. Department of Regional Economic Expansion (1973) 'Assessment of the Regional Development Incentives Program,' one of a series of *Staff Papers* prepared by the Federal Department of Regional Economic Expansion.

Canada. Department of Regional Economic Expansion (1974 'Regional Development Incentives 1974: Questions and Answers.'

Canada. Department of National Revenue, Taxation (1971) 'Income Tax Act: Government Grants to Industry,' *Interpretation Bulletin*, Serial No. IT-49.

Canada. Dominion Bureau of Statistics (1965-9a) *Census of Manufacturing* (Ottawa)

Canada. Dominion Bureau of Statistics (1965-9b) *Corporation Financial Statistics* (Ottawa)

Canada. Statistics Canada (1970) *Corporation Financial Statistics* (Ottawa)

Canada. Statistics Canada (1972) *Canada Yearbook* (Ottawa)

Dudley, C. L. (1973) 'Adjusted Average Financial Statistics: Canadian Manufacturing Industries, 1965-1969,' part of a Ph.D. dissertation, University of California at Berkeley.

Francis, J. P. and N. G. Pillai (1972) 'Regional Development and Regional Policy: Some Issues and Recent Canadian Experience,' Department of Regional Economic Expansion, mimeographed.

Kotowitz, Y. (1968) 'Capital-Labour Substitution in Canadian Manufacturing 1925-39 and 1946-61,' *Canadian Journal of Economics* 1, pp. 619-32.

Usher, D. (no date) 'A Critique of the Canadian Program of Subsidizing Investment in the Less-Developed Regions,' mimeographed.

Wolkowitz, B. (1973) 'Estimation of a Set of Homothetic Production Functions:

A Time Series Analysis of American Postwar Manufacturing,' *Southern Economic Journal* 39, April, pp. 626-637.

Woodward, R. (1974a) 'The Capital Bias of DREE Incentives,' *Canadian Journal of Economics* 7, pp. 161-73.

Woodward, R. (1974b) 'Effective Location Subsidies: An Evaluation of DREE Location Subsidies,' *Canadian Journal of Economics* 7, pp. 501-510.

Woodward, R. (1974c) 'The Effectiveness of Intra-Island Industrial Incentives in Puerto Rico,' *National Tax Journal* 27, pp. 261-273.

Yeates, M., and P. Lloyd (1970) 'Impact of Industrial Incentives: Southern Georgian Bay Region, Ontario.' Geographical Paper No. 44, Department of Energy, Mines and Resources.

Notes

*Woodward, R. S., "The Effectiveness of DREE's New Location Subsidies," *Canadian Public Policy*, 1:2, Spring, 1975 (reproduced by permission of author and publisher). This research was financed in part by a grant from Canada Council. The author wishes to thank Mark Frankena, Gordon Davies, Kevin Collins and the Journal reviewers for their helpful comments. However, none of these necessarily agrees with the text.

[1]Estimates of the elasticity of substitution are sensitive to the production function specification and to the industry being examined. While the parameter incorporated in our text is roughly at the mid-point of the ranges indicated by Kotowitz for all manufacturing and for each two-digit industry, it is meant as an example rather than an accurate estimate of any particular case. More recent and more sophisticated estimates of the elasticity of substitution for US manufacturing data roughly confirm the Kotowitz elasticity values. For example, see Wolkowitz (1973).

[2]For the purposes of this paper, it is sufficient to define agglomeration economies as the cause of a spontaneous and continuous employment growth which occurs as regional employment or population is large. For example, see Woodward (1974c) in which intra-island employment growth in Puerto Rico is significantly explained by population only in regressions which include municipalities with over 40,000 people.

[3]A rigorous proof of this proposition is beyond the scope of this paper. Nevertheless, in a manner similar to Woodward (1974b), it is possible to prove for a single firm in a competitive environment that each subsidy or group of subsidies can be consistent with only one ranking of policy priorities. The argument would continue by demonstrating, as done in Section II above, that effects outside the single firm competitive model are unlikely to be sufficiently strong to cause an ordering of subsidy impacts on a region's economy which is different from the subsidy's effect on the single firm.

16 The Life and Times of Industrial Estates Limited *

R. E. George

Though judged on ordinary business criteria IEL has proved a fiasco, it has been beneficial to Nova Scotia. The province's material standard of life is higher for IEL having been born. If probable future benefits are taken into account, there seems no doubt that IEL's efforts have paid off more than if the money it poured into industrial promotion had instead been doled out in welfare payments or left in the public's hands by reducing taxation. It is possible that, if the money had gone instead into tourist development, public works, education, health services and the like, the results would have been better still—but this we do not know.

There is, however, no indication that IEL has succeeded in reducing Nova Scotia's lag in the development of its manufacturing sector. The best that can be said is that it may have prevented further deterioration. But even if the results of this study are viewed in the most favourable light, there still is no reason to conclude that IEL's performance could not have been better. Nova Scotians have a right to expect IEL to heed any lessons which can be learned from the past, since it has disposed of, and presumably will continue to dispose of, significant amounts of the resources of a relatively poor province.

Directors and Officers

One may first consider the composition of IEL itself. In the past, the directors have been drawn from the local business community, and there are indications that attempts have been made to ensure representation from the various parts of the province; and a director has been able to count on indefinite tenure if he did not get at loggerheads with his colleagues or the government. The arguments in favour of such a system are obvious—one thereby procures people who know the problems and characteristics of the province and are likely to have a loyalty to it which assures their devotion to their task; and there is stability and continuity. The disadvantages, however, are at least equally compelling. Nova Scotia is a small province and its pool of persons with appropriate qualities who are willing to serve as IEL directors is very limited. Consequently, though some very competent men have served on the board at various times, there have been some serious gaps. In particular, there have been only two directors who could claim any connection with manufacturing—though IEL is concerned solely with manufacturing industries. While there is no need for all directors to be drawn from manufacturing (clearly that would be undesirable), there should be significant manufacturing expertise on the board. In order to secure this expertise, it seems inevitable that some directors should be drawn from outside the province, since the manufacturing sector in Nova Scotia is not highly developed.

Appointment exclusively from within the province also carries another disadvantage. Because Nova Scotia is a small and, by North American standards, an old society, its business community is closely connected by intermarriage and long-standing friendships. It is therefore inevitable that IEL directors drawn from within the province will be involved in deciding on proposals for business deals which involve themselves, or their relatives or friends. At best, this makes their positions difficult, leaving them open to suspicions that they are using their offices to feather their own nests or the nests of others with whom they have connections. In the past, there has certainly been a good deal of gossip in this connection. No improprieties have ever been demonstrated but this does not still the rumours, and it is almost impossible for a director upon whom suspicion has fallen to establish his innocence.

The stability of the board has almost certainly not helped matters. A group of persons inevitably invite suspicion if they allow themselves to appear to become a semi-permanent self-perpetuating clique. This was recognised in 1970, when IEL's principal agreement was amended to limit the terms of office of all directors other than the chairman, president, and executive vice-president to four years and permit re-election only after at least a year's absence from the board. Though the first retirement under this rule will not take place until 1974, it promises to help the situation in time.

Everything said above about directors in general applies with special force to the president, since he personifies IEL to a considerable extent and it is largely upon him that the effectiveness of IEL depends. Apart from being a good leader and administrator, he should be able to command public respect by dint of his ability, honesty, and personality. When a new president has to be found, the task is likely to be very difficult, since the number of competent Nova Scotians who would find such a position acceptable and happen to be available just when needed will always be small—even zero at some times. And it seems undesirable to entrust the leadership of an organization like IEL to someone's part-time attention; steering the IEL organization and projecting its image to the business community and the public, both in the province and outside, is surely a full-time job for anyone.

When the choice of a president is also influenced by political considerations, and an incumbent's position becomes insecure when a new government takes power, then the task of procuring and keeping good presidents becomes well-nigh impossible.

Selection of its presidents from the best people available, whether native Nova Scotians or not and without regard to political allegiance, seems the only way IEL is likely to attract good chief executives. And appointment for limited periods (three years, for instance) also has much to recommend it.

Under such a system, a president who does not fulfil his promise is much easier to dispose of, a fresh personality often revitalizes an organization, and the "inbred clique" situation is largely avoided.

Even a good board and a good president will not achieve much without a good staff. The right of IEL's directors to appoint their own staff and fix their salaries is important and should be preserved. The people IEL needs would not be attracted if their appointments were to be made the subject of political manoeuvre and controversy. Even IEL's autonomy in this matter does not appear to have been used well since, at certain times in its history, it has tried to recruit and hold professional people at patently unrealistic salaries. And the board seems deliberately to have kept its staff too small to undertake industrial promotion, exercise the scrutiny and control which is necessary, and extend help to clients in need of it. In 1968, with assets approaching $100 million and over fifty clients, there were only twelve staff, of which half were secretaries! An aversion to empire-building is commendable, but should not be carried to absurdity.

Objectives

Even if IEL obtains the best possible board of directors, president and staff, it will never perform to the optimum unless it knows precisely what it is supposed to be doing. In the past, its objectives have been repeated year after year in the notes to its financial statements as "the creation of employment opportunities through the development of industry in the province of Nova Scotia." Elsewhere a slightly more refined version expressing the aim as jobs at lowest cost has been stated, and IEL seems to have judged the extent to which it has achieved this aim by dividing employment in its clients' plants into its total investment (after forgetting Deuterium and Clairtone since 1970). Using this basis, a computation from IEL's press release dated 5 January 1971 but including its input into Deuterium and Clairtone produces a figure of about $40,000 per job (about $140 million for 3,500 jobs). This is considered very high by those who choose to measure performance of industrial promotion schemes in this way. But, as was argued earlier, cost per job is a silly criterion. Since IEL was obviously intended to raise the standard of living of the inhabitants of the province, surely the obvious objective is to take that action in the area designated to it (manufacturing industry) which will result in the highest possible increase in the provincial income for any given input of funds. This implies a public cost-benefit approach to all decisions. Before any decision is taken by IEL, it should consider (a) whether the public benefits arising from the proposed action, in the form of increased provincial income, are likely to be greater than the public costs of that action in the form of servicing the borrowing entailed,[1] and (b) whether there is any alternative action which is likely to produce better results judged on a cost-benefit basis.

It should be recognised that this objective is quite different from that followed by a private enterprise. IEL must not, therefore, think like a private lending institution concerned primarily with security for its loans. It is a public institution created for a public purpose: it should therefore "think public."

Operating Techniques

For most of its life, IEL has tried to achieve its objectives (nebulous though they were) by 'shot-gun' tactics—blanket publicity and continuous travel in the hope of finding profitable leads. While this is expensive and hit-or-miss, one or two big successes can justify it in the end. And so it has been with IEL, since both Michelin and Anil arose from chance encounters and may well justify the many years of time and money devoted to the endeavours of those concerned. But reliance on this approach alone seems highly undesirable, since a further ten years might pass without any further success, and it overlooks the more sophisticated methods available which would allow IEL's promotion to be directed more accurately to industries which are best suited to the province and will bring it most benefit.

The limitation of IEL to "secondary manufacturing industry" seems to have been an unnecessary restriction. Though it is sufficiently nebulous to have allowed IEL to become involved in such different industries as heavy water, fish products, cement, and animal feed, it seems to have effectively restricted IEL's area of interest. IEL was obviously chafing at the bit in 1971, and shortly afterwards played a part in the creation of an autoport in Dartmouth (a non-manufacturing activity and, incidentally, a very successful one). It seems desirable that if industry requires services that are not being provided, IEL should be empowered to stimulate the establishment of such services, even if they are not classifiable as manufacturing.

The incentives used by IEL to attract new activity to the province are similar to those used elsewhere and seem sensible. Loans at lower rates of interest or (what boils down to much the same thing) for greater amounts than can be obtained commercially are attractive to industry, and the favourable repayment arrangements are also welcome to prospective clients. Factories built to clients' specification and let at relatively low rents achieve a similar effect.

The absence of one incentive, however, calls for special comment. Although IEL was set up primarily to establish industrial estates or parks in the province, it has done so only in a very small way. The Stellarton estate was badly chosen, was very expensive to service, and has evidently proved unattractive, presumably because of its location. The Woodside estate in Dartmouth has little in the way of services and, in its present state, could probably not accommodate much more than the four plants it now holds (including one which was established in 1972). In all other cases, IEL has built factories, or financed their building, wherever the client wanted them.

Industrial estates afford firms very distinct advantages. They are likely to offer serviced land cheaper than can be obtained privately. Facilities such as canteens, public transportation, and professional offices may be made available on the estate or nearby. And "linkages" may be established between plants on the same estate, the output of one becoming the input of another. Perhaps most important, the delay and uncertainty which face a firm when it comes to a strange region seeking to establish a plant are largely avoided if serviced lots are available on industrial estates. Delay and uncertainty are further greatly reduced if standard factories are built for rent or sale on estates in advance of demand (something IEL was empowered to do but never did). The ability to be able to move equipment into an existing factory, rather than first having to go through the tedium of negotiating with landowners, architects, local authorities and contractors, is very valuable to an industrial firm. And standard factories are easier to re-let or resell than custom-built ones if the original occupants vacate them for any reason.

Industrial estates have become widespread in the world and almost every country which is seeking to develop industrially has established them, generally with advance factories, and they appear to have been almost universally successful, so long as political or other non-economic considerations have not caused them to be badly sited or constructed. It is important that they should be built only in areas which can offer the facilities that firms need. Transportation for materials and products should be easy and the existence of a nearby airport to facilitate the travel of executives and salesmen is of great importance. Full and adequate services must be available quickly—including not only electricity, telephone, water and sewer, but also central services such as canteens, fire-fighting equipment, security services and the like. In order to achieve this economically, to provide the linkage and attract auxiliary industries, estates must be reasonably large. Three hundred acres should be the minimum.

Although the case for well-designed, well-located industrial estates with advance factories seems to have been established beyond reasonable doubt by international experience, it is not surprising that an organization like IEL should be reluctant to become involved in them. They would have to be built in a very few selected locations in the province and political pressures would immediately be exerted by those areas which felt neglected. Also, should an estate including advance factories lie idle for any length of time, political scorn will be heaped upon the developer, and taking such a risk requires more political courage than politicians and their offspring often possess. It is easier to sit back and wait until a client commits himself than to prepare in advance, even if such advance preparation is beneficial to the development of the province.

Another incentive which IEL has been reluctant to offer is equity capital. For small new firms in particular, the raising of equity is a serious barrier; and if they cannot raise it in sufficient quantities, they are shut out from some government incentives and from private financing. With government permission, IEL has been empowered to supply equity, but has chosen to do so on only a few occasions (Deuterium, Clairtone, Pyrominerals, and perhaps a few little firms under the Small Loans Programme) and even then with reluctance. Partly this reluctance may be due to political philosophy (governments keeping hands off private business) and partly to the lack of personnel through whom IEL might have played its part as a substantial shareholder. But partly it may derive from IEL having no funds of its own. All its investment money has to come from the government, and making special cases to justify IEL going into business partly on its own account requires special effort which its officers have been reluctant to make. If IEL had had investment funds of its own, it might have been more enterprising. It is true that, since IEL debentures sold to the government are not secured, IEL could legally raise its own funds by borrowing on the security of some of its better properties and loans; but this might cause adverse government reaction, and has not been tried except for short-term borrowing from banks and trust companies.

Relationships

IEL's relations with governments appear to have been excellent. This is just as well, since otherwise it could not have functioned because the restrictions placed upon it by the Principal Agreement and the budgetary system make it unable to carry out its agreements with its clients without tacit government approval of its actions (unless it borrowed on the security of its properties and mortgages, which it has not tried to do except for short-term moneys).

Relations with the public have been a very different story. Nowadays, private business recognises the importance of establishing good public relations, and, for public bodies, a good public image is essential to success. Yet, except for a short time while Finlay MacDonald was president, IEL seems to have been completely oblivious of this fact, imagining that it could operate quietly behind a veil of secrecy. No details of any dealings with clients were willingly made public, even after a client was dead and buried and could not possibly be harmed by anything that was said. A few scraps of information leaked out in 1967 and a few more were squeezed out by the opposition during the inquests on Deuterium and Clairtone. While MacDonald was president, a much more open policy was followed, he being prepared to disclose and defend what IEL was doing. This period ended with MacDonald's departure and the door again shut, to the extent that not even the identities of many recipients of IEL loans (the small borrowers) are disclosed.

The result has been predictable. Rumours have been widespread about business deals taking place between certain IEL directors and IEL or its clients on undisclosed terms, about large amounts of public money being poured into ill-fated projects, of company promoters from outside the province coming in and eventually leaving behind their worthless projects on which they themselves did not appear to have lost very much, and about local well-heeled businessmen apparently being able to obtain public funds on secret terms to expand their businesses. Hearing these rumours, the public has tended to assume the worst.

... None of the arguments advanced to justify IEL's secretive way of life holds water. The initiated (which presumably includes other firms of any sophistication with which IEL clients might trade or compete or with which IEL might have dealings) can easily obtain all details of IEL loans to particular firms. Consequently, the only object in avoiding frankness must be to try to keep the public in the dark, thereby avoiding possible criticism.

IEL and the government would do well to reconsider their positions on this matter. They should remember the uniformly disastrous results of concealment of the details of government industrial promotion projects in Manitoba, Prince Edward Island, and Newfoundland.[2] In the end, though frankness may attract short-term criticism, it avoids the more damaging effects of public suspicion and loss of confidence. After all, the public has the right to know that its money is being honestly and sensibly handled.

Notes

*George, R. E., *The Life and Times of Industrial Estates Limited* (Halifax: Institute of Public Affairs, Dalhousie University, 1974), No. 93 (reproduced by permission of author and publisher).

[1]The importance of public costs such as pollution should not be forgotten.

[2]See Philip Mathias, *Forced Growth: Five Studies of Government Involvement in the Development of Canada*, Toronto: James Lewis and Samuel, 1971.

17 Forced Growth: Government Involvement in Industrial Development *

P. Mathias

Forcing: *the process of hastening growth of a plant by an artificial environment and the application of growth-promoting substances obtained from external sources. A forced plant tends to be less robust.*

In the late 1950s, there appeared in Canada a strong "development psychology" among both federal and provincial governments, and lots of hard cash was set aside for programs of assistance to companies prepared to build manufacturing plants in areas of high unemployment or low wages.

At the provincial level, new lending agencies like the Manitoba Development Fund and Nova Scotia's Industrial Estates Ltd. were born, and endowed with the power to borrow large sums of money for assistance programs.

At the federal level, the 1960s brought many major assistance programs such as the Agricultural Rehabilitation and Development Act (ARDA), the Fund for Regional Economic Development (FRED), the Area Development Incentives Act (ADA) and the Atlantic Development Board (ADB).

During the decade, billions of dollars of capital was spent by federal and provincial governments to persuade anyone, from major international corporations to penniless promoters, to build large industrial plants in places in which they would not normally locate. Fish plants were built in the Maritimes and pulp and paper plants in the northern Prairies. A chemical plant in underdeveloped Manitoba established a struggling subsidiary in underdeveloped New Brunswick. An electronics firm uprooted its plant in Ontario to qualify for assistance in Nova Scotia. A small money-losing shipyard moved from New Brunswick, one region of high unemployment, to another, Prince Edward Island. The assistance programs were undoubtedly a success in that much valuable industry did settle in the underdeveloped parts of Canada. But they were only a partial success. A large number of the major manufacturing plants that were built with the help of government money gave rise to widespread contention that the money had not been wisely used.

Many important issues intrude into the development question: foreign ownership, public ownership, the justifiable cost of creating a job, the adequacy of the province as a political unit responsible for resource development, and even the validity of spending large sums of money on development at all. A few of these projects of the 1960s have brought out some of the most crucial dilemmas Canada faces in her economic and social life today.

Before these dilemmas can be examined, the question must first be asked: Why bother to develop the remote parts of Canada at all?

From an economic point of view, the importance of development varies from region to region. In the unpopulated parts of the Northwest Territories, for instance, development simply brings into use the local resources and generates revenue for the several levels of government. There may be no society in the region for it to affect. The same is true of vast regions of Labrador and the northern parts of the Prairie Provinces. But in the more populated southern Prairies, in Quebec and in the Maritimes, industrial development is needed to end poverty and redress social disorders created by sweeping changes in the economic patterns of the country. Many of the places that need industrial development in Canada are old centres of industry or commerce that have been bypassed by new technology or changes in the economy.

In the 1800s, the Maritimes were busy centres of shipbuilding, immigration and transportation. With the development of the steam-driven vessel and the emergence of Ontario as the industrial heart of Canada, the Maritimes started an economic slide from which they have never recovered.

Like the Maritimes in miniature, the city of The Pas in northern Manitoba grew as a railway distribution centre for trappers and the smaller towns of northern Manitoba. It was bypassed when an air service was started to Thompson, an important mining centre farther north. The same sort of thing has happened to Winnipeg, which used to be an important distribution centre for western Canada. This role has diminished, though Winnipeg has managed to build other economic functions in its place.

The regions that have fallen into decline after a commercial heyday suffer special forms of social distress. One of the most serious is the constant drain of the young and the educated away into southern Ontario and British Columbia, where they have better chances of employment. In the period 1946-66, 30% of all the migration that occurred in Canada consisted of movement away from Saskatchewan and 20% consisted of net migration away from Nova Scotia. The only regions enjoying a net gain in population were Ontario, Alberta, and British Columbia. The net result of the population movements is to improve the labor forces of Ontario and British Columbia and to reduce their quality in such provinces as Saskatchewan and Newfoundland. According to the 1966 census, men between the ages of 20 and 44 comprised 17% of the total population in Ontario, whereas in industry-poor Prince Edward Island they comprised only 14% of the population.

Such depletion of the labor force has two effects. It becomes more difficult for industry to find suitable labor in a depleted region, and the market for locally produced consumer products diminishes, making it even less attractive for certain industries to locate there.

Many people in these regions can leave and seek their fortunes elsewhere, but there are some that cannot, such as the Indians, who often have special problems related to discrimination and an inability to understand the demands of an industrial society. The highest populations of Indians are in the two underdeveloped Prairie Provinces of Manitoba and Saskatchewan, where they represent more than 3% of the population. In Ontario and Quebec, Indian people comprise less than 1% of the population. Emigration of part of the working force from provinces like Saskatchewan increases the proportion of the less fortunate within the population, and these become a greater responsibility to the underdeveloped provinces. Industry has to be brought to these people who cannot move away to Ontario and British Columbia.

As well as high unemployment in the underdeveloped regions of Canada, there is also a markedly lower level of wages in the jobs that are available in these places. The personal disposable income per capita in Ontario in 1968 was $2,520 a year, 13% above the national average, and the highest in Canada. In Newfoundland, on the other hand, personal disposable income was $1,280 per capita, about half of Ontario's. Weekly earnings in Newfoundland averaged $99.15, considerably lower than the Ontario average of $113.52.

These disparities of income and opportunity in the underdeveloped regions tend to disturb national harmony. The people of the Prairies believe their economic misfortunes are partly due to discrimination against them by Ottawa and the Canadian business establishment in Ontario. The election of the Liberal Government of Robert Bourassa in Quebec in the turbulent times of 1970 on a platform of economic progress demonstrates that even cultural troubles can be partly soothed by economic remedies.

As well as economic, humanitarian and political reasons for industrial development, there may be important cultural reasons. In many, many things Canadian, there appears to be a powerful centrifugal force at work. The population hugs the border with the United States, and the eastern and western sea coasts. Industry is even less well distributed. Most of it is in the "golden horseshoe" around international Lake Ontario and in the Pacific rim provinces of Alberta and British Columbia. This centrifugal tendency is also evident in culture. Many Canadians of even second and third generation like to preserve their identity by remaining partly British, French, Ukrainian or perhaps Mennonite.

The result is a "cultural mosaic," which many Canadians proudly distinguish from the "melting-pot." But there seems to be little Canadian cultural cement between the ethnic tiles of the mosaic, and so it might perhaps be reasonable to look for the cement in such places as Vermilion, Alberta, and St. Jones Without, Newfoundland, which are not subject to the same international influences as Toronto and Winnipeg. Industrial development in these places might help Canada to become a more homogeneous nation with the distinct personality so many Canadians seek.

The first major development program instituted by the federal government in the 1960s was the Agricultural Rehabilitation and Development Act (ARDA). Its primary purpose, initially, was to help impoverished farmers by improving their land, relocating them off marginal land, and increasing output. ARDA later turned its attention to basic deficiencies in farm structure and organization, and from there to a "total approach" to resource development, involving the expenditure of several hundreds of millions of dollars on mining, fishing and industry, to help rural areas break out of poverty.

Other federal programs were subject to the same continual change as the ARDA program, and some confusion and lack of enthusiasm developed among the civil servants administering these programs in Ottawa.

In 1962, the Atlantic Development Board (ADB) was created to advise the Atlantic Provinces on the best ways to attract development. In 1963, the Board was provided with funds totalling $100 million to implement an overall plan for the Atlantic Provinces and to build up the region's infrastructure: roads, electric power, services at industrial sites, etc. The Atlantic Provinces have the lowest incomes in Canada and the highest unemployment. In 1968, the average personal income in Newfoundland was only 55% of the Canadian average. In Prince Edward Island, it was 63% of the average, in Nova Scotia 78%, and in New Brunswick 71%. On the Prairies, average personal income in 1968 was closer to the Canadian average, the lowest being Saskatchewan's at 90% of the national average. Unemployment in Newfoundland often runs at two or three times the national average and the seasonal swings in employment are extreme. When the Atlantic Development Board had spent all of its $200 million, it resumed the role of an advisory body.

In 1963, the federal government formed the Area Development Agency (ADA) to "encourage industrial development in areas of chronic unemployment on a planned basis." In July 1965, ADA was provided with what became its main development instrument—generous incentive grants provided by the Area Development Incentives Act. Under a program that lasted until March 31, 1971, ADA offered cash grants to secondary industry establishing in designated areas, which contained most of Canada's chronic unemployment and low-income regions. The program provided for cash grants of up to $5 million to be made to any company building new manufacturing or processing facilities in these areas or to firms that were engaged in expansion.

In late 1967, doubts were raised about the effectiveness of some of the federal government's programs. An Economic Council of Canada study prepared by research economists of the Canadian Centre for Community Studies declared that the hundreds of millions of dollars being paid out under ARDA, the Prairie Farm Rehabilitation Act (PFRA), and the Maritimes Marshland Rehabilitation Act (MMRA) were not producing a net benefit to the economy. The PFRA alone had spent about $300 million in the previous 30 years on soil and water conservation and projects to stabilize the Prairie economy. The Economic Council study said: "From the hundreds of projects listed in the ARDA catalogue, it would not be difficult to pick out many in which the taxpayer pays one dollar so that the farmer somewhere in the fringe area can make 50¢." Talks between Ottawa and the provinces got under way within a few months of the report to change the thrust of the ARDA agreement.

As well as grants, the federal government has used tax relief incentives to encourage development. In the budget of 1963, Finance Minister Walter Gordon introduced generous tax incentives for companies locating in the designated areas of ADA. Initially these incentives were to expire in December 1965. They consisted of a three-year tax holiday and provision for write-off of up to 50% of the depreciable value of machinery in any one year and of 20% of the depreciable value of buildings. Normal rates of depreciating machinery and buildings for tax purposes are 20% and 5% or 10%. The benefit of rapid write-off is that it heavily reduces taxes in the early years so that an early, high return on investment can be achieved. The quick profits can be reinvested and made productive in other plants.

These generous write-off and tax incentives had a powerful effect, and undoubtedly contributed to the capital expansion boom of 1966-67. Large numbers of pulp and paper mills were built in remote places like Lac Quévillon and Portage du Fort, Quebec, in order to qualify for the incentives, though these mills were also built as a competitive reaction to expansion triggered in British Columbia by provincial policies of the time.

The most flexible and probably the most valuable federal assistance plan was launched in mid-1969, when the federal government introduced a new incentive grant scheme to combat regional disparity, under which the maximum grant to an individual applicant was raised from the $5 million stipulated by the ADA program to $12 million. The regions in which these grants were available included most of the Maritime Provinces, eastern Quebec, a broad region stretching across Ontario at the same latitude as Winnipeg, the southern quarter of Manitoba, strips of Alberta and Saskatchewan to the south of Regina and Calgary, and the southeastern corner of British Columbia. The regions designated by the Department of Regional Economic Expansion have been fixed for three years to July 1, 1972. Before that date, there is to be a review after consultation with the provinces.

The amount of assistance dispensed by Ottawa under the new scheme has been doubled to $100 million a year, and the amounts available to individual companies have also been increased. There are two qualifications: the amount paid on any plant may not be more than $30,000 per new job created nor more than 50% of the capital employed in the operation. The new program has also been streamlined and made much more flexible than the old.

In the late 1950s and early 1960s, many provincial agencies for attracting industry were created. The most controversial have been the Manitoba Development Fund (MDF) and Nova Scotia's Industrial Estates Ltd. (IEL). Both IEL and MDF were made responsible to a board of directors which, though appointed by the Government, was not directly responsible to the Government for the activities of the corporation. The directors were all members of the business establishment. Both corporations were headed by drum-beating promoters, Rex Grose and Bob Manuge, tough, hard-working salesmen who would travel around the world to personally persuade business tycoons to come to Nova Scotia or Manitoba. The style was the same; some critics called it "twanging the old-boy network," an activity facilitated by having leaders of the business community on the board of directors. Manuge and Grose would both work out "deals" with companies they felt they could persuade to come to their province, offering incentives that were often not made fully public.

The more secretive of these two Crown corporations was the Manitoba Development Fund, which was enjoined by law not to make public the details of loans made to companies settling in the province. This provision gave the Fund considerable freedom to offer loans of magnitude that might have raised controversy had the details been made public. Under the Development Corporation Act passed in 1970, the NDP government of Premier Ed Schreyer changed the name of the MDF to the Manitoba Development Corporation (MDC). MDC now makes details of its loans public and is empowered to take equity in a corporation to which it grants assistance. The taking of equity will enable the MDC to share in the management and the profits of the assisted company. In some cases, the old MDF lent 80% of a plant's cost without participating in the ownership or profits of the company through its equity. In 1971, in a move suggesting a similar restructuring, Nova Scotia's Industrial Estates Ltd. was subjected to a searching investigation by the new Liberal Government of Premier Gerald Regan, who wanted a detached cost benefit analysis of its 13-year record.

Unlike the Manitoba Development Fund, which borrowed money on the market against MDF bonds guaranteed by the Government, the Saskatchewan Economic Development Corp. (Sedco), another provincial lending agency, borrows from the Saskatchewan treasury against Sedco securities. Sedco also keeps the details of its loans secret, but there has been no major controversy over Sedco, which has always been much less in the limelight than the Manitoba Development Fund. In Saskatchewan, under the Liberal government of Premier Ross Thatcher, development decisions have been taken openly by the Premier. In Manitoba, the previous Progressive Conservative governments claimed the MDF made its decisions independent of Cabinet control.

The provincial lending agencies make it much easier for local companies to borrow development capital. As the agency is on the spot, the borrower can call at the head office and present his case much more convincingly in person. The agency can also appraise an enterprise in terms of local conditions and can call on the expertise of government officials who are well acquainted with the local economy. Managerial ability of a prospective borrower can be more easily gauged by a face-to-face interview. Some government agencies also say that they can make a loan much more quickly than most commercial institutions. These factors tend to overcome the disadvantage felt by Prairie or Maritime companies trying to deal with the local branches of a bank that has its head office in remote Ontario.

But the greatest service the provincial lending agencies provide is that they act as lenders of last resort and will usually take a greater risk than a commercial lender.

On the other hand, there are indications that the provincial lending agencies suffer from parochialism and a very limiting form of penny-pinching. In several of the controversial projects that went ahead in Manitoba, Nova Scotia and Prince Edward Island in the 1960s, there is evidence that few people on the staff of the provincial lending agency or in the civil service had the expertise to really assess whether a given project was a valid economic proposition or contained a reasonable financing agreement. In Manitoba, a provincial civil servant with a little paper mill expertise would have been able to tell very quickly that the capital cost figures quoted for the "$100 million" paper and lumber complex at The Pas were too high according to ordinary standards. Shocked by the quantity of money absorbed by the Churchill Forest Industries paper complex at The Pas, Premier Schreyer's government has appointed a pulp and paper engineer to the staff of the Manitoba Development Corporation.

Another clear case where provincial authorities were not able to handle the technical side of a project is the heavy water plant in Glace Bay, Nova Scotia.

The financing of the Prince Albert pulp mill in Saskatchewan, financed with the help of the Saskatchewan government and controlled by the New York based firm of Parsons & Whittemore, involves a finely calculated distribution of risks and profits between the Government and its entrepreneur partner and contains many precautions for protecting the Government's interest. But some of the misleading information that has found its way into the press suggests that few officials of the Saskatchewan Government understand the complicated financing of the Prince Albert mill. The agreement appears to have been designed by Parsons & Whittemore, a company which has accumulated much expertise in paper industry matters and world markets. What sort of agreement, though, might have been drawn up if Saskatchewan had entered into partnership with a company less scrupulous and less expert than Parsons & Whittemore?

The lack of the proper experts in provincial governments is attributable to a misguided search for economy and the few occasions in the past when an expert on, say, heavy water production might be needed by a provincial government. But it is also partly due to the ease with which a government can call upon the services of independent consultants for a particular project without incurring the expense of employing them permanently. However, this involves another set of problems, as Manitoba has discovered in its experience with the pulp and paper mill at The Pas. It is generally admitted that an independent consultant may be subject to pressure to provide its client with the sort of advice he would like to hear, rather than the sort of advice he should get.

The drift of Canada's poorer provinces towards larger units may tend to remove some of these shortcomings. In late 1970, a report was published recommending that the Maritime Provinces join to form a single regional government. The Prairie Premiers, in the same period, were also developing joint policies on universities and other regional matters. Bigger "provinces" would be able to hire more experts and economists to evaluate proposals from companies asking assistance and to work out more of the sophisticated and imaginative deals that are needed to attract industry and make it viable.

Another advantage of the larger units would be a reduction in competition between the provinces for development industries.

Such competition has tended to increase the price that is ultimately paid for the prize by the winner. Before it settled in Manitoba, the Churchill Forest Industries group was holding talks with the government of Quebec over the possibility of building a paper mill there. Undoubtedly, the price Manitoba paid for the Churchill Forest Industries complex was affected by the need to attract it away from Quebec. In early 1970, the Michelin tire group of France decided to build three plants costing $100 million in Nova Scotia, but only after a period of fierce competition between Nova Scotia and Quebec to capture them. The intrigue behind the scenes even involved pressure by Charles de Gaulle on the Michelin company in favour of a Quebec location. Michelin stubbornly stuck to its decision to locate the plants in Nova Scotia, and is receiving $50 million assistance.

Competition for development also taxes the facilities and patience of Canada's commercial counsellors in the embassies abroad. Some say there is a continual stream of industrial commissioners from the cities and the provinces through the embassies. They ask that thousands of leaflets be distributed and that the special advantages of their particular city or region be extolled to local industrialists who might be interested in expansion in North America.

A provincial government that has decided to offer assistance to promote local industry would appear to have a choice of three partners in development—a Canadian company, a Crown corporation or a foreign-owned company. But in reality the province is often left with little alternative but to go along with a foreign-owned company, distressing though the implications may be for long-term control of the Canadian economy. Canadian companies may not have the resources or the imagination or even sometimes the inclination to build a major plant where an underdeveloped province needs it. Before Saskatchewan entered into an agreement with Parsons & Whittemore Inc. of

New York for a pulp mill at Meadow Lake, it asked for proposals from major Canadian pulp and paper companies and received none.

Crown corporations are usually not acceptable—even to a New Democratic party government. Manitoba's NDP government, elected in 1969, had to tread cautiously over the use of Crown corporations for development for fear of frightening away businesses that might have been thinking of coming to Manitoba. Besides, a Crown-owned paper company, for example, would find it difficult to compete in the North American market, where all other companies are in the private sector.

At first glance there would appear to be many Canadian precedents for the creation of Crown-owned development corporations. But in fact, few of Canada's Crown corporations are inspired by the need to create jobs for the unemployed or to help the unfortunate. Provincial ownership of Canada's power generation and distribution facilities is as much for the benefit of free-enterprise industry which needs a reliable power source as it is for the domestic user. Other Crown corporations have been set up for special historical reasons. Canadian National Railway Co. was formed by the merger of several private railroads in northern Canada that were unable to operate profitably but were needed for development of such places as Sudbury and Timmins. Air Canada was created because there was not sufficient private capital to set up a Canadian-owned airline. Polymer Corp., the rubber producer in Sarnia, was formed during World War II because Canada needed a rubber producer in a hurry. From time to time, there have been movements to have these companies transferred back into the realm of private enterprise and out of the hands of government ownership, rather than to make more Crown corporations.

But there are precedents for province-owned development corporations even in non-socialist governments. Liberal Premier Jean Lesage's Quebec government (1960-66) set up, in 1964, Sidbec, the province-owned steel mill, after unsuccessfully talking to big steel companies in the private sector.

The shunning of "socialism" has driven several provincial governments into arrangements in which they have paid all or most of the expenses of establishing a plant, using a promoter or a company as a "private enterprise" front that gave the project political respectability. In the Churchill Forest Industries forest-products complex at The Pas, Manitoba, and in the Gulf Garden Foods fish plant in Prince Edward Island, the provincial governments put up almost all the money, and the profits—if any had been generated—would have gone entirely to the promoters.

If neither a Canadian partner nor a Crown corporation is available to develop a particular resource, a province is left with the choice of not developing and leaving its people unemployed or taking a foreign partner. The passage into US hands of an established Canadian company like Ryerson Press, Toronto, in late 1970 may be deplorable, but different standards of judgment must surely be applied to concessions made to foreign interests in underdeveloped regions. The five case studies in this book seem to prove the point. Two heavy water plants give a pungent commentary. Near the provincially owned heavy water plant at Glace Bay—a $120 million disaster—is a smart new heavy water plant being operated efficiently by the Canadian subsidiary of a major US company, General Electric Co. For its fish plant, Prince Edward Island would have done better to bring in a competent US company like the food, chemicals and packaging conglomerate W. R. Grace & Co., rather than to pour $10 million into the hands of a virtually unknown Canadian promoter. The pulp mills built in Saskatchewan by Parsons & Whittemore may be financed in a way that is favourable to the American company, but what real alternative was available to the Government of Saskatchewan to diversify its wheat and potash economy?

Each of the five cases chosen for this book represents the single biggest development in the recent history of the province. The most successful is the development of the mighty Churchill Falls in Labrador by a largely British-owned consortium. Newfoundland will reap nothing but profit from Churchill Falls, though its development was agonizing at times. The creation of Saskatchewan's two pulp mills will also probably prove a success, though the assumption by the province of a risk of about $150 million has been necessary and the deal is rather generous to the private partner. But the other three cases are disasters. Into Prince Edward Island's fish plant, Manitoba's forest-products complex, and Nova Scotia's heavy-water plant, about $220 million of precious public funds have been poured. Only one of the plants—the fish plant—is close to proving it can operate normally and at full capacity.

Notes

*Mathias, P., *Forced Growth* (Toronto: James Lorimer & Co., 1971, reproduced by permission of author and publisher).

18 Government–Business Interface: the Case of the Small Technology-based Firm *

Isaiah A. Litvak and Christopher J. Maule

The Study

In 1971, the authors conducted an empirical study of successful Canadian technical entrepreneurs in secondary manufacturing industry.[1] One major objective of this study was to ascertain the entrepreneurs' perception of the environment for entrepreneurship in Canada, with a view to determining the form that Canadian government assistance might take.

The population examined in this study consists of 39 entrepreneurs involved in the establishment of one or more technologically-based enterprises in the secondary manufacturing sector. Most of these enterprises are small, with a present annual sales volume of less than $1 million. Over 75 per cent of the entrepreneurs considered their first venture to be successful. Thus, our observations with respect to innovation and entrepreneurship in Canada relate mainly to this group of firms. 'A technologically-based firm is defined as a company which emphasizes research and development or which places major emphasis on exploiting new technical knowledge. It is often founded by scientists or engineers and usually includes a substantial percentage of professional, technically-trained personnel.'[2]

The term 'successful' in the context of this study is seen as the survival of the entrepreneurial operation during its initial years. Professor E. B. Roberts notes that 'the first several years are the tough ones and that those surviving the first five years are likely to survive thereafter.'[3] Approximately 90 per cent of the respondents in our sample satisfied this criterion. Professor Roberts also notes that,

> Survival is not the same as success, of course, although for many entrepreneurs survival may in fact be sufficient success. We typically define enterprise success in such businessmen's terms as growth, sales, profitability, and the like. But entrepreneurs do not necessarily have those objectives in going into new enterprises; for some, simply producing an organization that has survivability is a sufficient reward—even if it yields no greater income to the entrepreneur than he made in his previous employment.[4]

In the remainder of this article we present the major findings of our study and put forward policy recommendations for consideration.

The Environment for Entrepreneurship: Findings

As previously noted, a primary objective of our study was to gain an appreciation of the entrepreneurs' perception of the problems affecting their activities, as well as to elicit their views on the type of policies that should be introduced to promote a healthy entrepreneurial climate. Our interpretation of the entrepreneurs' comments recognizes that they reflect the abilities and characteristics of the entrepreneurs, as well as the environment in which the entrepreneurs operate.

VENTURE CAPITAL

A major finding is that the respondents share a condensed image of the problems which afflict the fledgling entrepreneur in Canada. In brief, they believe that the cards are stacked against them in terms of limited access to capital and markets, coupled with government policies which blatantly favour the large well-established firm. For example, on the question of the availability of venture capital, the majority of the respondents felt that such capital was hard to come by. They viewed this lack of venture capital as being responsible for limiting their business opportunities, and, for having prevented the commercialization of potentially profitable projects in Canada.

This perception of the venture capital problem is in contrast with that of the venture capital firms which maintain that capital is available, but that proposals put forward by many Canadian entrepreneurs are so poorly researched, documented and presented that, even if the project idea is a viable one, it is seldom communicated adequately, and for this reason is turned down. Moreover, it is found that many of the prospective entrepreneurs, who are themselves deficient in management skills, seldom employ the kind of supporting staff necessary to instill confidence on the part of the venture capital firm.[5] This point may help to explain why Canadian venture capital firms are investing heavily in entrepreneurial undertakings based in the United States. In some instances, more than fifty per cent of their capital is invested in US projects. It is the contention of these Canadian venture capital firms that the management sophistication of US entrepreneurs is markedly superior to their Canadian counterparts, and that this determines their investment pattern.[6]

Some of the respondents complained that the venture capital firms insist on too great an equity position. In part this is a defensive measure by the venture capital firm, because the equity position allows it to influence the management direction, and thus increase the probability of bringing the project to commercial fruition.

Another major complaint voiced by the respondents is that Canadian banks are too conservative in their approach to assessing entrepreneurial projects, and that along with other financial institutions they lack confidence in Canadian entrepreneurs. There is little doubt that this lack of confidence and conservatism is partly due to the management weaknesses exhibited by Canadian entrepreneurs. However, the nature of the Canadian banking system also militates against the promotion of Canadian entrepreneurship.

Unlike the US unit banking system, the Canadian branch banking system tends to depersonalize the working relationship between the entrepreneur and the bank manager. This is particularly so in smaller urban centres away from Toronto and Montreal, because loans above a certain size have to be approved by head office. The geographical and decision-making distance between the bank manager and his head office does not lend itself to the kind of symbiosis that one detects in the relaionships of many U.S. banks and entrepreneurs. In the US, because the bank official and entrepreneur usually reside in the same community, their economic objectives are much more interdependent through closer social and working relationships, with the banker having greater lending authority.

GOVERNMENT POLICIES AND THE FORMATION OF NEW ENTERPRISES

Taxes are too high for new ventures, the government is too conservative in its support of Canadian entrepreneurs, and ends up supporting firms which do not require assistance. These were the three major criticisms directed by the respondents against the government for its failure to promote the formation of more new firms in Canada. Complaints against high taxes is an accepted fact of life, and is particularly evident on the part of owner-managers of small and medium-sized firms. Nonetheless, this is not a sufficient reason for dismissing this complaint.

The critical feature of the tax complaint is that there is little tax incentive for the prospective inventor/entrepreneur to invest his time and capital in the pursuit of a product concept or market opportunity. This is particularly so for those who are employees of other firms. Most of these respondents also maintain that there should be a lower corporate tax assessment made on new firms for an extended period, thus encouraging more Canadians to establish ventures of their own. It is the contention of these respondents that the foregoing measure would increase the number of prospective Canadian inventors and entrepreneurs, as well as making more risk capital available to the entrepreneur through his own business efforts, as opposed to 'standing in line for government hand-outs' (grants).

The point about the Canadian government being too conservative raises the question of what role the government should play in promoting entrepreneurship. While this question was not tackled *per se,* a number of respondents maintained that the government should invest in worthwhile projects. What is worthwhile was not defined, but the point to note is that many of the respondents had difficulty in attracting funds from venture capital firms for reasons already discussed. This leaves one with the question of how a civil servant can justify 'gambling' public funds on projects deemed too risky, in many instances, for venture capital firms. In other words, should the government act as a venture capital firm of last resort?

An examination of government grants to business shows that the larger, more established firm is often in the major recipient category. This has not gone unnoticed by the respondents who equate this phenomenon with the argument that 'the rich get richer and the poor get poorer.' Although the government can justify their grants by some set of criteria, the fact that they have not done so effectively explains this attitude of smaller firms. Moreover, the communication linkages between government and entrepreneurs are poor, inasmuch as this group of businessmen is least knowledgeable about the availability of government programs designed to encourage technological advancement and industrial activity.

Distortion of facts and lack of information, often communicated through rumours of grants and their recipients in corridor gossip among entrepreneurs, has generated a sense of hostility towards the government, and a lack of confidence in its ability to assist the entrepreneur in his commercial efforts.

MARKETING OF NEW PRODUCTS

Most of the respondents argued that the Canadian market is too small and that Canadian customers—consumers and industrial users—are unwilling to purchase goods which have not received the prior seal of approval through customer acceptance in the U.S. The foregoing criticism was viewed as the major marketing obstacle to the introduction of new products by entrepreneurs in Canada. While this observation may be valid, it also signals a major shortcoming on the part of Canadian entrepreneurs. Few of them conduct any marketing research before making the decision to commercialize their product idea. Market assessment in terms of size and customer acceptance is virtually absent in their 'technical' feasibility studies. This is one of the chief reasons underlying the fact that sales performance of their 'new' products seldom achieves their initial sales projections.

In addition, it is well known that heavy promotional outlay at the time of product introduction is a prerequisite to achieving desired market penetration, especially in the consumer field. Many of the entrepreneurs lacked the funds to engage in such activity and, thus, were disadvantaged vis-à-vis the market, and their competitors. Some of the respondents stated that they found themselves in a subordinate bargaining position with their distributors, because of their total dependence on middlemen. In short, they lacked the power to influence the marketing direction of their product.

One way of obviating the limited market size constraint is to export. The entrepreneurs were cognizant of this fact and many of them included potential export sales in their market calculations. Regrettably, the marketing shortcomings exhibited by small and medium-sized firms often become accentuated when they engage in export business. This fact may help to explain why a number of the respondents recommended that incentives, in the form of subsidies, be introduced to promote export sales.

RESEARCH AND DEVELOPMENT POLICIES

It was noted earlier that most of the respondents were largely critical of government policies. Not enough, too late and for the wrong people was an oft quoted statement in the study. However, on the question of specific government support for research and development through such programs as Program for the Advancement of Industrial Technology (PAIT), the consensus was extremely favourable. The fact that most of the respondents were recipients of such grants may help to account for their praise. Nonetheless, it is probably true that the receipt of government grants by business is not necessarily a pre-condition for eliciting business support for government programs in general.

ENTREPRENEURS' PROPOSALS

In the light of their experiences, the respondents were asked to comment on the measures which should be taken to promote the environment for entrepreneurship. It was noted earlier that the respondents regarded lack of venture capital and high taxes as the two major obstacles to the formation of new enterprises. It is therefore not surprising that most of the respondents centred their recommendations on increasing the supply of venture capital, and on the need for lowering the tax base for new ventures. Two other key recommendations were included, albeit a distant third and fourth, namely improving the screening procedure for government assistance, and the use of procurement policies, as well as the provision of greater incentives for investing in Canadian-owned firms. In short, the recommendations focused on things external to the entrepreneur, and little mention was made of self-improvement as a means of affecting change.

Notes

*Litvak, I. A., and C. J. Maule, "Government-business interface: the case of the small technology-based firm," *Canadian Public Administration*, 16:1, Spring, 1973 (reproduced by permission of author and publisher). The authors gratefully acknowledge the financial assistance given by the Department of Industry, Trade and Commerce in support of their research.

[1]Litvak, I. A., and C. J. Maule, *A Study of Successful Technical Entrepreneurs in Canada*, Ottawa, Office of Science and Technology, Department of Industry, Trade and Commerce, 1972.

[2]Cooper, A. C., "Incubator Organizations, Spin-offs, and Technical Entrepreneurship," *Proceedings of the Indiana Academy of the Social Sciences, 1969*, 3rd series, vol. 4, April 1970, p. 33.

[3]Roberts, E. B., "How to Succeed in a new Technology Enterprise," *Technology Review* (Dec. 1970), p. 22.

[4]*Ibid.*, p. 22.

[5]See I. H. McLeod, "Can Canadians be Successful Entrepreneurs," and A. Grieve, "Venture Capital Sources and the Canadian Entrepreneur," both in *Business Quarterly*, vol. 37, no. 1 (spring 1972), pp. 28-36 and pp. 54-9 respectively.

[6]Based on interviews with Canadian venture capital firms.

Part 3
Natural Resource Policies

Introduction

Most of the material discussed so far in this section has been concerned with the promotion of manufacturing and other activities which we associate with the phenomenon of "industrialization." Canada remains, however, a major raw material producing country. It is appropriate, therefore, to consider the extent and nature of government interaction with business firms engaged in the "primary", or natural resource, industries. This interaction might be expected, by anyone unfamiliar with Canada, to take the form mainly of attempts by government to divert labour and capital away from primary industries into the manufacturing sector: this is, after all, what most of us understand by "industrialization". Indeed, Canadian tariff policy, and other measures designed to favor Canadian manufacturers, have usually been seen by farmers, lumbermen, miners and other resource-exporting groups to be harmful to their particular interests.

Yet there appears to be no such general plan to restrict primary production. As will be seen from the selections in this part, the primary industries too have been protected and subsidized by Canadian governments. In seeking the reasons for this, one may not want to go any further than to note that farmers and other land-based producers also have votes, and some of them are well organized for the purpose of exerting political pressure. Are there reasons to believe that competitive market controls would not work well as regulators of these industries? Must government intervene to protect primary producers from exploitation by uncompetitive oligopolistic suppliers of credit, machinery and other inputs required by farmers and other resource-based businessmen?

It will be noted that many of the problems of the resource-based industries arise from the fact that they are inherently highly competitive in the economist's sense of the term. Many producers contribute to the total output of these industries, with the result that individually they find it difficult to influence the market price of their output. Such producers feel they are at the mercy of erratic market forces over which they have little control. They are unlikely to find much solace in the economist's assurance that this is exactly how things should be in a free-market economy, especially when they see that the bankers who lend them money, and the manufacturers who sell them machinery and consumer goods, are not only conspicuously able to exert an influence on the prices of their products, but also are enabled to keep their prices high by virtue of tariff protection from foreign competitors.

Consequently, we find that the declared purposes of agricultural policy in Canada are to establish a stable agricultural industry in the interests of the national economy and to provide farmers with a fair share of the national income. The spectrum of policies applied to these ends is surveyed in Reading 19. Note the implication that agriculture, like manufacturing, is an essential national industry and that it would not be adequately sustained if exposed to unregulated market forces. Yet Canadian agriculture operates under conditions quite different from those surrounding our manufacturing industry. Most Canadian agriculture is relatively efficient and would seem to possess certain natural advantages that should enable it to compete effectively in world markets. Unlike manufacturing, it can hardly be thought of as a struggling infant industry trying to break into world markets. As its spokesmen would be quick to point out, however, these world markets are not freely competitive, being dominated as they are by state purchasing agencies and by foreign selling agencies acting on behalf of farmers who are much more heavily and conspicuously subsidized than their Canadian counterparts.

Must we, in the light of this, tax ourselves for the doubtful privilege of maintaining an agricultural industry of a given size? To Adam Smith and his followers who sought to refute such "mercantilistic" positions, the answer was, emphatically, "No." It is perhaps a measure of the political relevance of classical market theory today that most Canadians would accept the mercantilist's point of view and answer "Yes," going on to cite national independence, strategic considerations and the maintenance of employment as justifications for manipulating our agricultural as well as our manufacturing activities.

The same arguments, presumably, must apply to our other natural resource-based industries as well. Of these, the mining and forest industries are the most important in terms of value of output and, perhaps, in terms of the subjective importance attached to them as sources of employment and national strength. (The fisheries and fur-trapping industries are of mainly regional importance as sources of employment and income and, because of this, aid to them is likely to be regarded as a matter of regional rather than national importance.)

An important difference separating agriculture from the mineral and forest industries is that the latter are based on resources that in Canada are usually publicly rather than privately owned. Because of this, private firms exploiting mineral and forest resources are entrusted with the utilization of a national resource in a legal as well as an economic sense. This gives governments the ability not only to regulate these industries effectively, but to directly influence the prices of their output by charging more or less for the right to exploit the publicly owned resources involved. Whether or not our traditional policies in this respect have resulted in Canadians getting as much from their natural resource endowment as they might, has become a major public issue, particularly in the western provinces. An important, and certainly highly controversial, contribution to the whole subject of natural resource policy has been made by Professor Kierans in a report prepared in 1973 for the government of Manitoba. In Reading 20 Professor Kierans briefly reviews both federal and provincial approaches to natural resource policy and then specifies four major policy options open to a province; options which include public ownership and operation of resource industries, public participation with private investors in such ventures and several variations on the conventional systems of regulation and taxation.

A different perspective on the appropriate public policy for resource development is provided in Reading 21, by R. S. Ritchie, a former Senior Vice President and Director of Imperial Oil Limited. After tracing the background of government intervention in the Canadian petroleum industry, Mr. Ritchie notes that today governments "are appearing as competitors, self-invited partners, and monopoly purchasers and sellers with unilateral power to fix prices and terms." He blames this for discouraging further development of Canada's petroleum resources at a time when activity in this area should be promoted.

19 The Role of Government in the Organizational Structure of Agriculture *

Canada, Task Force on Agriculture

One of the most basic questions in Canadian agriculture relates to the extent, nature and effectiveness of government involvement. It is obvious that action—perhaps drastic and far-reaching—must be taken by many individuals and organizations to help define the problems of agriculture and formulate and implement the policies and programs necessary to bring about improvement. Few exercises are as pointless as recommending objectives, policies and programs without agreement as to who has responsibility and authority to implement. The Federal and provincial governments have become deeply involved—many argue primarily responsible—for the overall well-being of agriculture. Government power over agriculture includes the right to decide and/or influence objectives and policy, legislate and implement programs and through the distribution of tax revenue, allocate funds to agriculture and from one province to another.

Such extensive political power is offset by checks and balances that tend not only to guard against its abuse but also sometimes to obstruct its purposes. Nevertheless, no organization exercising this kind of power can absolve itself of responsibility for results.

In view of the deep seated problems and sombre prospects of Canadian agriculture, we must attempt to resolve several basic issues in regard to the roles of the Federal and provincial governments. Some of these are as follows:

What ideally should be the roles of government in agriculture?

What is the nature and extent of the involvement of Federal and provincial governments in agriculture?

What criteria should be used to evaluate the performance of governments in agriculture?

How well have governments performed their roles in agriculture?

Who ultimately is responsible for diagnosing the problems of agriculture and taking the action to solve them?

What kind of overall structure and relationship for the key groups in agriculture would be best?

How should governments, farmers, farm organizations and agribusiness fit into this ideal organization?

Until these issues have been researched, communicated and debated, at least to the point of a workable consensus, Canadian agriculture will probably continue in its present state. No one will be able effectively to assign responsibility for the problems relating to unsatisfactory income performance on any individual and/or organization, nor will any one have a mandate to bring about needed improvement.

Current Issues

Study of research reports, press comments and statements by farmers and farm leaders make it clear that there are many issues being raised in regard to government participation in agriculture. We present a number of quotations to highlight four main issues and to show the diversity of opinion on these.

1. Extent and Nature of Government Involvement

In regard to government involvement, farmers seem divided: Some western cattle and grain farmers are vocal supporters of less government involvement. As one western cattleman put it:

> There is nothing much wrong with agriculture that wouldn't be improved if the government moved out.

The opposing point of view was stated by a turkey grower:

> Let's face it, the only way out of this mess is for the government to take complete control. They have to say what to produce, how much to plant, when and how it will be sold and what the price will be. Otherwise you have farmers fighting each other.

EFFECTIVENESS OF GOVERNMENT INVOLVEMENT

Consideration of the issue of the effectiveness of government involvement leads to questioning whether the government is doing the right thing. For example, one well known authority on agriculture has written about poverty as follows:

> The rural poverty problem has been around a long time and it remains a hard-core, unsolved problem in the 1960's . . . There have been policies and there have been programs for combating rural poverty. But it is a sad story of ineffective policies and programs; it is a record of *too little, too late.* (Cochrane, Willard W., *The City Man's Guide to the Farm Problem*, p. 194.)

An allegation of lack of effectiveness in government policy related to research was:

> For some years now, attention has been drawn to the lack of co-ordination between research in the field of physical and biological sciences and in the socio-economic field. Very often, research is not at all oriented toward the solution of problems of competition that face the country of a given region. It even seems that too many resources are used on certain projects which are not economically viable, either on a short-term, middle-term or long-term basis. (M. Daneau and Y. Dube, Federal Provincial Relations in Agriculture in Canada, Ch. V. A study for the Task Force.)

EFFICIENCY OF GOVERNMENT INVOLVEMENT

Many farmers are sceptical that good dollar value is derived from government agricultural expenditures. One provincial official stated that there could be considerable waste and graft in his province's production subsidy program.

There have been few known and publicized in-depth reviews of existing programs and their results. Programs like PFAA, PFRA, MMRA etc. have been in existence for years; they may have good results or bad results or (more likely) both but the point is that adequate reviews of these good or bad results have never been made and publicized.

It is, of course, impossible to poll all the stakeholders in agriculture to find out what all the issues are and what the consensus is on each. Comments such as those above are, however, frequently repeated. In spite of the fact that it is impossible to judge whether they are truly representative or not they represent the attitudes and conclusions of many farmers, government officials and responsible observers of government agricultural policy. As such, they deserve consideration. If they are wrong the reasons why should be spelled out publicly; if they are not wrong the underlying problems should be diagnosed and corrected.

2. Lack of Integrated Objectives

> For many years governments have been following a haphazard approach to agricultural problems. The general policy has been to attack individual problems as they appear. Many programs end up conflicting with each other. Worse yet, they often conflict with the ultimate objective of increasing farm incomes. (Report of the Special Committee on Farm Income in Ontario, p. 27.)
>
> The basic conflict in Canadian agricultural policy has been an *implicit* cheap food policy and an *explicit* small farm maintenance policy. The developmental policies of research, extension, subsidized credit, settlement expansion and resource development, actually contribute to and constitute the so-called 'implicit' cheap food policy.
>
> The provisions of various acts favoring small farms, such as the Homestead provisions, Agricultural Stabilization Act provisions, PFAA provisions, credit ceilings and cash grants, are evidence of the existence of an explicit farm maintenance policy.
>
> Not only have the two policies been pursued simultaneously in Canada but are in direct conflict with each other. This is the heart of the basic conflict in agricultural policy, a cheap food policy together with a small farm maintenance policy. (Philip J. Thair, *Goals for Agricultural Policy*, a study undertaken for the Task Force.)
>
> As for the programs connected with the development of resources, irrigation and drainage programs, community programs relating to pastureland, conservation programs, these have double objectives: (1) to increase the efficiency and yield of the farming sector by an intelligent use of soil and water; (2) to protect, if not increase, the national heritage in these areas. None will doubt the validity of these objectives. But there can be no doubt that they may conflict with the objectives of other agricultural programs. For example, certain farm programs aim at increasing both prices and the earnings of farmers. How are these objectives consistent with those aimed at increasing production, at developing resources? (M. Daneau and Y. Dube, Federal Provincial and Interprovincial Relations in Agriculture in Canada, Ch. 8) op. cit.

3. Expediency in Decision Making

> Canadian farm policy since 1930 . . . has been largely one of providing expedient measures to meet crises of depression, drought, war, inflation and surpluses . . . There is little evidence that Canada has had any overall national policy based on clear thinking and economic and sociological research facts. (Lorne Hurd, *Policy Research is Agriculture's Greatest Need*, Agricultural Institute Review, Jan.-Feb. 1960.)

4. The Issue of Independence

Some people have argued that government involvement in agriculture has become so pervasive that it has reduced, perhaps considerably, the will and ability of the farmer to stand on his own. Government responses to farm problems have, for better or worse, resulted in a system where many farmers hold the government responsible for solving their problems. A major difficulty arises, of course, when individuals or organizations in the government justifiably or not, have a very different view of their role and do not accept such a responsibility.

As a result of the political reality that Canadian voters are divided 92% non-farmer and 8% farmer and as the government increases its influence in agriculture it must give primary attention to the views of the urban population.[1] This political reality applies, of course, to all minority groups.

It is also perhaps worthwhile to speculate about the effect of government involvement on farm organizations. It is noticeable that farm organizations often place their fate in the hands of the government to a much greater extent than business and unions, the other major countervailing powers in our society.

Government Involvement in Agriculture

While it is practically impossible to describe accurately the total government involvement in agriculture ranging over the Federal, provincial and local levels and from formal, direct, open and legal control to informal, indirect and subtle influences, a short summary of the more obvious aspects has been stated by Garland and Hudson:[2]

> The traditional structure of agriculture, consisting of a large number of independent, small-scale, family-operated farm units, plagued by variable yields and variable prices and under pressure to make continual adjustments to keep pace with technological and economic development, has invited a much greater degree of governmental involvement than is the case with other industries.
>
> Land settlement programs providing for grants and sales of land to prospective settlers during the first 60 years following Confederation were the first form of government involvement in agriculture in Canada. During those early years of settlement government assistance to increase the production of crops and livestock was provided through grants to agricultural societies whose aim was to improve production and marketing efficiency.[3]

The Health of Animals Act of 1879 involved the federal government in the control and prevention of livestock diseases. The establishment of the federal experimental farms system in 1886 was the beginning of the experimental and scientific research work which has played such a large part in the development of the agriculture industry in Canada. It was during the last decade of the 19th century,[4] when financial assistance was provided for the establishment and operation of dairy plants and equipment that the federal government introduced its first real program to improve the quality of farm products.

The expansion of agriculture on the Prairies in the early 1900's brought grain marketing problems, with resultant pressure from producers to improve marketing facilities and the subsequent involvement of both the federal and provincial governments in marketing. The Manitoba Government operated country elevators in 1909 and 1910, and in 1913 the federal government undertook the operation of terminal elevator facilities.

The 1920's saw an expansion of the research work begun with the establishment of the experimental farm system. Inspection and grading which had previously been largely confined to products for export were extended to many agricultural products sold for domestic use.

The depression of the 1930's with the accompanying drought in the Prairie Provinces gave rise to various forms of relief assistance and thus involved governments in income maintenance payments as well as in conservation and rehabilitation programs. The Canadian Wheat Board, the Prairie Farm Rehabilitation Administration and the Prairie Farm Assistance Administration which were established by the federal government during that period are still operative.

Price controls and programs to stimulate production as part of the overall war effort were introduced in the early 1940's by the federal government. Cash payments were made to farmers to supplement their incomes in lieu of price increases and to encourage shifts in production from one product to another and quality premiums were introduced to obtain the type of product required. Public funds were also used to subsidize the purchase of a wide range of agricultural production inputs including feed, seed, fertilizer, limestone and machinery.

During the early post-war years, price controls were relaxed and eventually eliminated. Subsidies were reduced and most were eventually discontinued. However, agricultural limestone subsidies, freight assistance on feed grain shipped to eastern Canada and British Columbia and hog quality premiums are war-time programs that became a permanent part of the post-war agricultural assistance program. Legislation passed in 1944 to provide for the support of prices of agricultural products during the transition from war to peace was given continuing status in 1950. The Farm Improvement Loans Act of 1944 provided a federal government guarantee for short and intermediate term loans to farmers. Financial assistance was provided for veterans of the armed forces for land settlement, under terms of the Veterans' Land Act. Provincial governments assisted by making new lands available for settlement, often with special provisions for financing clearing and breaking. The rapidly changing technology in agriculture brought increased requirements for capital to finance farm operations in the 1950's. To assist in meeting this demand the federal government and almost all provincial governments introduced new farm credit programs. During this decade the provincial governments intensified their extension activities with increased emphasis on conservation, quality improvement, eradication of disease, increased production and farm management.

The Agricultural Prices Support Act of the federal government was replaced by the Agricultural Stabilization Act of 1958, making price support mandatory for nine key commodities. The Crop Insurance Act, Farm Machinery Syndicates Credit Act, Agricultural and Rural Development Act and the Canadian Dairy Commission Act have been enacted by the federal government during the past decade as part of the effort to improve the economic welfare of the agriculture industry.

An indication of the extent and rate of growth of government involvement in agriculture can be obtained from a comparison of federal and provincial government expenditures on agriculture during the three years 1964-65 to 1966-67 with government expenditures on agriculture during the 1930's. Total government expenditures on agriculture amounted to $442 million in 1966-67, $387 million in 1965-66 and $323 million in 1964-65 compared with $22 million in 1933-34, $62 million in 1937-38 and $66 million in 1943-44.

The factors responsible for the phenomenal growth may be determined by dividing expenditures into *three broad groups based on the nature of the individual program.* These groups are (1) those intended to facilitate the production and marketing of farm products; (2) those concerned with producer price and income maintenance; and (3) programs of research, education and extension. Production and marketing programs accounted for 60 per cent of government assistance in 1933-34 as compared with 35 per cent in 1966-67. At the same time expenditures for price and income maintenance increased from 16 per cent in 1933-34 to 41 per cent in 1966-67. Large relief expenditures in rural areas of western Canada during the 1930's and wartime expenditures in connection with agricultural production caused the percentage distribution for 1937-38 and 1943-44 to depart somewhat from the overall trend. Expenditures on education, research and extension accounted for 19 per cent of expenditures in 1933-34, essentially the same proportion as in the years 1964-65 to 1966-67.

Table 1 helps put government expenditures on agriculture in perspective. The total of $442 million in 1966-67 does not include expenditures for the benefit of agriculture in a variety of other federal or provincial departments such as Industry Trade and Commerce, Post Office, Forestry, Energy Mines and Resources and the like.

This total represents an expenditure of about $20 per capita for the total Canadian population. To see this figure in perspective it can be compared to per capita expenditures of roughly $8 on the C.B.C. and $90 on National Defence.

Another way of viewing this situation is to see government as a collector and allocator of revenues and resources. Although it is not necessary for us to evaluate the rationale of the collection method—this was presumably covered by the Carter Commission—we should assess the effectiveness and efficiency of the government as an allocator of resources (a) from the rest of the economy to agriculture and (b) among competing projects in agriculture.

Table 1

Distribution of Government Expenditures on Agriculture by Major Category, Selected Years, 1933-34 to 1966-67

Year	*Production and marketing*		*Price and income support*		*Education, research extension*		*Administration*		*Wartime*		*Total amount*
	Amount	*Per cent*	*Amount*	*Per cent*	*Amount*	*Per cent*	*Amount*	*Per cent*	*Amount*	*Per cent*	
	(thousand dollars)		(thousand dollars)		(thousand dollars)		(thousand dollars)		(thousand dollars)		(thousand dollars)
1933-34	13,040	60.3	3,414	15.8	4,140	19.1	1,039	4.8			21,633
1937-38	20,631	33.3	33,814	54.5	6,482	10.4	1,115	1.8			62,042
1943-44[1]	24,788	15.9	34,358	22.0	5,630	3.6	1,487	1.0	89,813	57.5	156,076
1943-44[2]	24,788	37.4	34,358	51.9	5,630	8.5	1,487	2.2			66,263
1964-65	130,713	40.4	116,069	35.9	67,831	21.0	8,720	2.7			323,362
1965-66	136,613	35.3	162,178	41.8	76,237	19.7	12,314	3.2			387,342
1966-67	156,339	35.4	180,329	40.8	89,190	20.2	16,197	3.6			442,054

1. Including wartime expenditure.
2. Excluding wartime expenditure.

Source: Expenditure data for 1933-34, 1937-38 and 1943-44 from *Agriculture*, Reference Book for Dominion-Provincial Conference on Reconstruction, 1945, Tables 1 and 5, pp. 82 and 84.

Reprinted from Garland, S. W. and Hudson, S. C. *Government Involvement in Agriculture*, a study for the Task Force.

Some of the other chapters in this Report indicate that a considerable number of programs are of dubious value. Many programs are apparently being carried on without the tough minded, systematic procedures desirable for evaluation of total costs, benefits and return on investment. There does not seem to be enough pressure to cancel programs that have either served their purpose or proven unsatisfactory. Lacking tight criteria and practical routines for evaluation, programs tend to be carried on from year to year.

Perhaps the most difficult aspect of government involvement in agriculture is that it has become so extensive and complex that it is impossible to describe and assess it. Due to the complexity and fragmentation of Federal Government departments and agencies concerned with agriculture, as well as the problems of federal-provincial co-ordination, no structure of authority and responsibility exists for integrating and co-ordinating government activities.

The Political Bargaining Arena of Canadian Agriculture

In order to understand the role of government, it is necessary to begin with an overview of the organizational system which constitutes "Canadian Agriculture".

Although there are literally hundreds of significant groups involved, Canadian agricultural policy is governed primarily by the interplay of the following interests and points of view:

—farmers and farm population divided into sub-groups relating to commodities, regions, income classes and political-economic biases.

—agribusiness divided into sub-groups relate primarily to commodities and functions.

—provincial governments standing both individually and combining in groups related to regions and common problems.

—consumers whose desires are made known through independent consumer associations and the Federal Government Department of Consumer and Corporate Affairs.

—Federal government departments and agencies who present and defend points of view related to various functions, departments, programs and policies.

In addition there are many jurisdictional questions associated with the federal-provincial division of responsibilities in agriculture.

The constitutional division of jurisdictions in agriculture sets up a joint assignment of authority with priority to Federal legislation. The pertinent legislation, section 95 of the B.N.A. Act, describes the relationship as follows:

> In each Province the Legislature may make laws in relations to Agriculture in the Province . . . and it is hereby declared that the Parliament of Canada may . . . make laws in relation to agriculture in all or any of the Provinces . . . and any law of the Legislature of a Province relative to Agriculture . . . shall

Table 2

Five Stages of Government Involvement in Farming
Degree of Government Planning and Control

Stage One	*Two*	*Three*	*Four*	*Five*
Minimum	*Medium*	*High*	*Public Utility*	*Nationalization*
		General characteristics		
—Laissez-faire —free markets —little if any direct government involvement.	—Government involvement in research special problems and in emergency situations —no continuing support programs —selective international tariffs.	Continuous government involvement in subsidies, regulation of supply and marketing becomes taken for granted.	Private ownership but state control of marketing (products, prices, service, etc.) and profits.	—Government ownership —state monopoly of output —state control of all input and output.

Scale and extent of Government planning and control

0	20	40	60	80	100%

General Position of Selected Countries on Spectrum

U.S. and Canada, late 1800's.

E.E.C. ⟶
France ⟶
Britain ⟶
⟵Yugoslavia
⟵Russia
China
Czechoslovakia
Canada⟶
U.S. ⟶
Sweden

> have effect in and for the Province as long and as far only as it is not repugnant to any Act of the Parliament of Canada.

Despite the apparent clarity of this text, many legal issues have arisen, especially in regard to the scope and nature of activities that constitute "agriculture", and what constitutes legislation that is "repugnant" to a Federal Act. As agricultural affairs have worked out in practice a complex mix of joint Provincial-Federal responsibilities has evolved. It is important to note that all eleven governments co-operate with cordiality and a real degree of success in attempting to work out mutually acceptable policies and solutions.

Philosophy—the Role of Government

There never has been and there never will be full agreement about the proper role of government in relation to an economy or a sector of an economy. Obviously a great deal depends upon the political philosophy of the people, the social structure, the distribution of wealth, the capacity and honesty of the civil service and even seemingly non-political events like droughts and inventions. In a country like Canada, governments provide certain services exclusively (post office), control partly public, partly private enterprises (airline franchises), support some prices (butter), leave other enterprises almost completely free (beef) and operate monetary, fiscal and commercial policies. In a pluralistic[5] society, it is natural that the role of government will be conceived quite differently by different groups and in regard to different sectors. Yet some generalization is necessary if the question of the role of government is to be seen in perspective and general guidelines developed for action.

Table 2 presents a rough spectrum of government involvement in agriculture, varying from the minimum in Stage One to the maximum in Stage Five. Table 3 spells out some of the major characteristics of these five stages especially as they relate to farmers. Obviously these two tables are entirely arbitrary in their numbers and description of stages but they help to put the extent of government involvement into perspective.

It is instructive to attempt to place different countries in the various stages of Table 2 and to attempt to determine whether they are moving in the direction of more planning or less. However, any attempt to make such a generalization runs into problems because of the complexities involved and a lack of the hard research data necessary to make judgments that are more than rough approximations. Countries such as Mainland China and the U.S.S.R. are in Stage Five, with almost total government planning and control. In a mixed economy in which ownership and control are divided between the government and private owners it is difficult to generalize with confidence because the type and extent of government involvement varies so much among different sectors of the economy.

The most important controversy in regard to government involvement—

Table 3

Major Characteristics of Farming Systems in the Five Stages of Government Involvement

Stage	*One*	*Two*	*Three*	*Four*	*Five*
Major characteristic	*laissez-faire free enterprise*	*medium government involvement*	*heavy government involvement*	*public utility*	*complete government control*
Role of farmer	on his own with almost complete freedom and risk	on his own but looks to government for limited help	runs farm in context of government planning and welfare	owns farm but works for government with output, marketing wages and return on investments regulated	farmer and employee of government
Role of government	no involvement except for basics such as favourable environment, statistics, import regulations and the like	government gets involved in research, special problems, welfare on a discontinuous basis	government becomes responsible for supply-demand, welfare, continuous government involvement taken for granted	control of production, prices, quality	complete ownership and control
Supply management	none	suasion but no control	government control	government control and plan	government control and plan
Input control	none directly	suasion but no control	government plans resource inputs but no control unless necessary	human inputs controlled in number and education; non human inputs planned	all resource inputs (including labour) government planned and controlled

Marketing	farmers compete on open market, no marketing boards	marketing boards optional	national marketing boards for all commodities	government control of prices	total government control of allocations, prices, etc.
Structure	result of free enterprise	government suasion but no control	some regulations regarding size and integration	comprehensive planning and control of structure	total government plan
Farm prices	determined on open market	some supports in case of emergencies	complex structure of government supports nearly in all commodities	government regulation of all farm prices	government regulation of all farm prices
Income	farmer on his own in free market	government assists in income problems	government supports income at definite level	government regulates income	government pays wages

the basic issue between the approaches of communist and western countries—relates primarily to the ideal model to be sought in the organization of a political-economic-social system. The western assumption is that a democratic political system ensuring the highest practical degree of individual freedom is of primary importance and that government economic planning must be conditioned by this supreme principle. The guiding principle in communist countries, opposing this western concept, holds that rationalization of the socio-economic system is of primary importance and that the form of government should be the one that is best suited to implement the ideal (socialized) economic system. Although there are many other basic economic, social, cultural and technological differences between communist and western countries, this fundamental difference in ideological commitment is the most important and is reflected in the extent and nature of economic planning and control by government.

The Task Force opts for a position between Stage Two and Stage Three—but closer to Stage Two than Three.

Stage One—the free enterprise option—has great attraction for those who desire maximum individual freedom and have little confidence in the effectiveness and efficiency of bureaucracy, government or otherwise. It is also attractive to those who retain a simplistic Adam Smith concept of economics. It obviously appeals to farmers who are doing well as they see it, stand only to lose, in one way or another, if government planning and control are increased.

The problems of this approach are also obvious. It is not feasible. To reach this system farmers would have to go through the wringer in adjusting to a free market. This would almost certainly invite crisis and disaster. It is out of tune with the realities of government-business-union interactions circa 1970.

Stages Four and Five, at the other extreme, also stand out in black and white. Their major attraction is for those who favour a planned, socialistic, utopian, 1984 approach to solving the problems of society including agriculture. Whatever its merits in other sectors, it is clear that socialism has not worked well in agriculture. Complete planning and control assume a kind of human nature and motivation which have been generally rejected in North America. Moreover, it is clearly out of tune with the environmental systems in which Canadian agriculture exists.

An advantage of Stages Two and Three is that they so closely resemble the status quo in Canadian agriculture that they do not imply drastic change in the system. In spite of the many problems involved, they have been proven to work after a fashion. However, their main disadvantages are that they are not working satisfactorily and there are few responsible observers of Canadian agriculture who advocate continuance of the status quo.

Thus not only does the Task Force opt for a stance of medium government involvement (Stage Two plus a small amount of Three) but it also opts for vastly improved performance in these stages. Ways in which performance may be improved appear in most chapters of this Report. In summary then, the general role of government should be to produce a favourable economic climate for farmers and agribusiness but not to attempt to "manage" or "direct" agriculture. Many basic decisions must still be made by hundreds of agribusiness firms and by thousands of individual farmers and their families but governments must do a better job of ensuring a higher degree of knowledge and possible co-ordination among agribusiness, farmers and government.

Notes

*Canada, Task Force on Agriculture, *Canadian Agriculture in the Seventies* (Ottawa: Queen's Printer, 1970), pp. 270-285 (reproduced by permission of Information Canada).

[1]The 92:8 ratio gives an erroneous impression. Rural-urban representation in the House of Commons is of the order of one-third *versus* two-thirds. In a free vote on an issue involving a clear conflict between farm and urban interests almost all of the members from the Prairie provinces and large numbers from other provinces would vote rural. (David L. MacFarlane.)

[2]Garland, S. W. and Hudson, S.C., *Government Involvement in Agriculture*, a study for the Task Force, pp. 314-318.

[3]W. M. Drummond, et al., *A Review of Agricultural Policy in Canada*, The Agricultural Economics Research Council of Canada, June 1966.

[4]*Ibid.*, p. 21.

[5]A pluralistic society is one in which there are many groups and organizations serving many different purposes. A typical Canadian belongs to many bodies—political, social, religious, financial—all competing for his support and sometimes in conflict with one another.

20 The Options *

E. Kierans

Resource policy has been dictated by the federal government. Canadian economic policy has always been based primarily on the sale and export of our resources. We have never grown out of the patterns of investment and growth established in our colonial past by the two mother countries, England and France. Of course there has been industrialization but the real changes in the Canadian economy can be traced in "the major shifts over the long period through fish, fur, forest products, wheat, base and precious metals, hydroelectric power development and so on."[1] Current federal policy adds oil and gas to the long list of basic resources that we are determined to export.

No area of the Canadian economy has received more fiscal encouragement in the form of tax incentives, exemptions and privileges than the mining and mineral fuels sectors. By comparison, all other sectors have been discriminated against and discouraged.[2] Since growth of the Canadian economy had always been assured by a national policy in the colonial tradition, we have continued to define ourselves and act as colonies long after Confederation. The national product has increased but resource growth does not place great demands on the knowledge, skills and development, both human and technological, of a people. Both brain drains and heavy secular rates of unemployment have been a feature of the Canadian economy, especially since the Second World War. At the very moment when Canada might have capitalized on its industrial performance during that war and reached for industrial maturity, our policymakers turned their back on or feared the consequences of change and reverted to our traditional policies of encouraging the exploitation and export of resources. These policies were consecrated in Canadian tax legislation on April 15, 1955, when the Hon. Walter Harris stated in his budget address, "these special tax provisions (for the petroleum and mining industries) have clearly established their value in promoting expansion and I now propose to make them a permanent part of our law." The special features were depletion, a three-year mining tax holiday, the writing off of exploration and development investments and accelerated depreciation. Prior to 1955, they had been renewed annually in each budget address on a three-year basis. Thus a temporary policy to encourage resource development became a permanent feature of Canadian tax law.

Table 1 illustrates the differing impact of our corporate income tax on the sectors of the Canadian economy.

Nearly half a billion dollars of the profits of metal mining companies and nearly $400 million of the profits of oil and gas producers were untouched by the federal income tax in 1969. This was not an unusual year for these two sectors. For the four years, 1965-68, the corporations paid taxes on 13% and

Table 1

Comparison of Book Profit to Taxable Income by Major Industry Group, 1969

	Number of corporations	Book profit before taxes	Taxable income	Taxable income / Book profit
		thousands of dollars		%
Agriculture, fishing, forestry	5,792	51,364	29,060	57
Metal mining	268	610,882	113,936	19
Mineral fuels	718	415,538	23,643	6
Manufacturing	20,955	3,437,937	2,702,478	79
Construction	19,202	293,659	230,060	78
Transportation, utilities	7,821	843,362	498,636	59
Services	26,721	331,282	276,688	84
Wholesale trade	22,985	666,716	586,000	88
Retail trade	30,435	480,223	435,601	90

Source: Corporation Taxation Statistics, 1969, Statistics Canada, 61-208, March, 1972.

5.7% of their profits respectively, leaving approximately $1,500 million of mining profits and $750 million of oil and gas profits free from corporate income tax. By contrast, the heavily competitive construction, manufacturing and service industries were taxed at full corporate rates on 78% to 90% of their book profits. If Canada cannot break out of its developing nation status, i.e., heavy reliance on staple exports, it is because our federal policy makers have so decided. They cling to the image of a Canada whose growth depends on the export of its wealth. They fail to see that their policies work against the real development that comes from the transformation of raw materials by human skills into final products. How else can one explain the taxation of the chemical industry on 91% of its profits or the pulp and paper manufacturer on 68% of its book profits when compared with the concessions to the resource industries?

Within the framework of overall federal resource policy, each province carries out its own policies. The objective is the same, growth as measured by the additional number of jobs. Each province vies with its neighbor to attract the large corporation that will employ a few hundred more workers in the process of extracting its wealth. In this contest, the initiative and the flexibility lies with the corporation. They can pick and choose between the offers, compare the tax exemptions and the subsidies and prolong the bidding until the last concession has been gained. By then, little of the surplus remains to the owners. The provinces, competing with each other, have given away their right to the super-profits, i.e., profits in excess of the returns needed to attract capital and which economists call "economic rent."

If additional jobs are the only benefit, the province has given away the surplus between the costs of production, including normal profits, and the selling value in return for that employment. Does a province have to bid so high for such growth? Can a province obtain the employment and a greater share of the surpluses in its negotiations?

There are four major options open to a provincial government in its consideration of policies that will determine the future development of its resource base. A fifth option, nationalism, applicable in other nations where land is held in freehold, is not relevant in Canada where the public lands, except for the alienated portion (CPR, etc.), are owned by the provincial governments. A province can choose among the following alternatives.

1. Establishing crown corporations to explore and develop its resources through the mining and milling stages at least. There is a mythology surrounding government effort in the "private" sector that condemns such activity as inherently inefficient. In the first place we are not dealing with the private sector but with the public domain. It is surely as incumbent upon the owner of public resources to reach for as great a return as possible as it is for any private investor. Secondly, it is held that crown corporations know little of markets, technology or the financing of commercial operations. Whatever validity the criticism may have in highly specialized or differentiated product markets, it has none in the homogeneous and uniform nature of raw materials. In these markets, control is exercised by the supplier and entry is a matter of costs and price. The technology is a matter of public knowledge, not monopoly patents. The financing is not nearly the obstacle that is put forward, as we shall see. In fact, public planning of resource developments can take account of returns over time in a manner that the operator, uncertain of his tenure rights, political changes in climate, tax privileges and new discoveries, can never do. Precisely because of these uncertainties, the private corporation will be inclined to forego greater future returns for the immediate but lower surpluses from current production. Finally, it may be said that the extension of the principle of government enterprise to the development of public resources is not different from that accepted in the fields of hydro-electric power or telephone systems.

2. Investing in existing resource corporations. The continuation of existing leases could be made contingent upon the provincial government obtaining a substantial percentage of the equity. This would be neither new nor an unfair weapon. Holders of leases, usually obtained at nominal registration fees from governments, have been able to transfer their rights for substantial capital sums or percentages of the equity in newly formed operating units. The "depletable asset" accounts of metal mining firms in Canada were valued in 1969 at $749 million, the bulk of which accounts covered payments to licensees who held the rights to exploration and development. Transferability and the traffic in licenses yielded enormous capital gains to the holders of rights but

not to the ultimate owners, governments. Renewals of such rights could be bargained against equity participation. Failure to reach agreement would not result in a shutdown of operations but their continuance by the government. A policy along these lines could do much to reduce the loss of revenues arising from past policies without abrogating the law of acquired rights. For new development, mixed enterprises would be a second-best solution since a share of the surpluses (rents) above a normal return to capital (profits) would be given away for no functional purpose. There would also be a clear conflict between the public interest and the objectives of the private sector. The former would be interested in maximizing the returns from its fixed supply of resources over time while the latter would be concerned with immediate returns and using profits to force the pace of exploration and development outside the province to increase total reserves and control over supply.

3. Continuing the policy of granting licenses for exploration and development to all applicants but insisting on greater revenues by increasing royalties, taxing reserves, raising licensing fees and rentals and imposing heavier provincial income tax rates. There is little doubt that this can be done and that the revenues from present mining operations can be expanded enormously without forcing shutdowns, despite the probable threats. For the present it may be sufficient to observe that the imposition of higher taxes must be supported by a convincing demonstration by the government that it was prepared to take over and operate any facilities that did in fact close down. It must be remembered that existing mines will have an incentive to continue operations even if all existing surpluses (rents) were absorbed by increased taxation and only normal profits on investment remained in the hands of the firm. That incentive will be the retention of control of the output of the mine to maintain existing market conditions and to avoid the effect of a new source of supply, a new entrant, into the market; to the extent that reserves exist and are known, they must be controlled and administered by members of the association to preserve their monopoly position.

4. Closing the open access to the resources of the province. This open access now exists in all provinces and in federal territories. The adoption of such a policy requires that the province assume full and complete responsibility for the discovery and development of the people's endowment in the most efficient manner possible. No other policy will assure the maximum benefits to the province as a whole. An unlimited freedom of access to the resources of Manitoba will result either in a large number of operators competing away all the rents and surpluses of Manitoba's wealth or in the gradual ascendancy of giant firms who will buy out the smaller competitors and impose their own barriers to entry. The process has been called "the tragedy of the commons."

> "The tragedy of the commons" develops in this way. Picture a pasture open to all. It is to be expected that each herdsman will try to keep as many

cattle as possible on the commons. Such an arrangement may work reasonably satisfactorily for centuries because tribal wars, poaching and disease keep the numbers of both man and beast well below the carrying capacity of the land. Finally, however, comes the day of reckoning, that is, the day when the long-desired goal of social stability becomes a reality. At this point, the inherent logic of the commons remorselessly generates tragedy.

As a rational being, each herdsman seeks to maximize his gain. Explicitly or implicitly, more or less consciously, he asks, "What is the utility to me of adding one more animal to my herd?" This utility has one negative and one positive component.

1. The positive component is a function of the increment of one animal. Since the herdsman receives all the proceeds from the sale of the additional animal, the positive utility is nearly +1.

2. The negative component is a function of the additional over-grazing created by one more animal. Since, however, the effects of over-grazing are shared by all the herdsmen, the negative utility for any particular decision-making herdsman is only a fraction of −1.

Adding together the component partial utilities, the rational herdsman concludes that the only sensible course for him to pursue is to add another animal to his herd. And another; and another . . . But this is the conclusion reached by each and every rational herdsman sharing a commons. Therein is the tragedy. Each man is locked into a system that compels him to increase his herd without limit—in a world that is limited. Ruin is the destination toward which all men rush, each pursuing his own best interest in a society that believes in the freedom of the commons. Freedom in a commons brings ruin to all.[3]

In fact, while there is public ownership of resources throughout Canada there is anything but free access. Effective entry is confined to the very rich and the very large corporations who are unwilling, given alternative possibilities in other countries, to offer reasonable returns to the people whose resources have been enclosed. They propose increased activity and employment and little more. The provinces fail to realize that they could provide this by developing the resources themselves and without giving up the ownership or the returns from the liquidation and transformation of existing wealth into new forms. In private hands, the activity and employment will last until the resources and wealth have disappeared. In public hands the activity and employment will last just as long and, in addition, the new wealth will remain as the capital thus generated finances other economic and social objectives. Provinces settle for too little and give too much. Closing of access means, then, the development of resources by the people who own them through their governments and an end to the neo-colonialism that sends trade missions to the financial centers of the world offering all the privileges that an older colonialism once imposed on subject peoples.

"Few economists today would dispute the eighteenth-century voice of Arthur Young, renowned observer of the English enclosure movement, that 'the magic of property turns sand into gold'. The English enclosure movement of the eighteenth and early nineteenth centuries was a classic case of transition from open range to private tenure."[4] Closing down the "open range" of natural resources to private tenure would be a return to the original foundations of provincial ownership of the land, i.e., public tenure, as the means of financing the development and self-realization of a community. When the surpluses and profits from their wealth are torn away, the provinces are left only with the daily wage. In 1969, book profits of the metal mining industry in Canada totalled $611 million while total salaries and wages amounted to $494 million. In the three years 1968-9-70, the book profits of the three largest mining companies in Manitoba exceeded their total wage and salary bill by a considerable margin.

When Manitoba loses the surpluses arising from the marketing of its resources, then it must rely, to finance its development and growth, on savings out of wage income plus what it can borrow in Montreal, Toronto and New York. The book profits of the three largest mining companies operating in Manitoba in 1970 may be estimated at $86 million approximately before corporate income taxes. Wages and salaries paid by them amounted to $68 million. If one estimates the savings out of wage income at a generous 5%, then savings would have amounted to $3.4 million compared with the foregone book profits of $86 million less Manitoba mining and income taxes of approximately $7 million. The surpluses which are drained away to finance growth and development elsewhere are 22 times as great as the savings from wage income that remain in Manitoba. These surpluses, the economic rent arising from the scarcity of resources such as nickel, copper, etc., would be, if retained in Manitoba, the cornerstone of the province's effort to break away from continued reliance on resource growth and to move into more dynamic development patterns. While much is made of the original investment as a boon to the province, it is conveniently forgotten that much more than the initial sums pour out. Otherwise, the investments would not have been made. Such investments can claim the normal return to capital. They cannot claim super-returns or super-profits which is the meaning of the term, economic rent. It is vital to the growth and development of a province or nation that it retain these super-returns as a means of ensuring its growth and lessening its dependence on others.

As with Manitoba, so with the other provinces and Canada. We lessen our dependence on foreign capital in the measure that we keep our own surpluses at home. The Mackenzie delta is a case in point. Spreading industrialization and rapid population growth have created an assured market for our oil and gas. But we have leased these resources, at 5-10%, to the oil giants who will reap the super-returns. Long after they have recovered their investment, they will still be gathering in the surplus harvest. Did we have to turn over our petroleum wealth to these corporations? In a world of scarcity, one does not need middlemen to reach the markets. Whoever has the resource will sell it. We are big enough and rich enough to do it ourselves, especially when the surpluses are so large and the pay back period so short. When others develop our wealth, we lose the economic rents that would strengthen us and make us less dependent on the savings and capital markets of foreign countries.

A new resource policy must recommend an effective method of provincial appropriation of the returns from its own wealth. Without such self-appropriation, the province will continue to be overly dependent on new injections of capital by giant corporations in return for grants of still more land and resources and increasingly dependent on yearly equalization payments from the federal government to meet its annual expenditures.

Nor can the provinces look to the federal government for leadership in devising new policies. The Canadian government is still committed to a policy of growth by expansion of the resource industries. While some tax privileges were taken away in the recent tax review, new concessions were introduced which will not materially change the tax burden on the primary sector until the middle eighties. Thus, the surpluses for financing a breakout from our resource growth pattern into an industrial and development structure will not be available for at least a decade. The provinces, therefore, must provide this leadership.

Notes

*Kierans, E., *Report on Natural Resources Policy in Manitoba* (Prepared for the Secretariat for the Planning and Priorities Committee of Cabinet, Government of Manitoba, February, 1973, reproduced by permission of the author and publisher).

[1]Resources and Growth in the Canadian Economy. W. T. Easterbrook, Proceedings of the Resources for Tomorrow Conference, Vol. 3, p. 17, Queen's Printer, Ottawa, 1962.

[2]This is not to deny that secondary industry has received tax concessions but they have been much less. The service sector receives very little. See Table 1. Capital flows into the tax favored sectors leading to under-investment elsewhere.

[3]The Tragedy of the Commons. Garrett Hardin, Science Vol. 162, pp. 1243-1248, 13 December, 1968.

[4]Extractive Resources and Taxation. Mason Gaffney, editor, p. 112, The University of Wisconsin Press, 1967.

21 Public Policies Affecting Petroleum Development in Canada *

Ronald S. Ritchie

Twenty-seven years ago the discovery of oil at Leduc in Alberta opened the door to a new status for Canada as a petroleum and natural gas producer. The history of the Canadian industry goes much further back, of course. In fact, Canada lays claim to the first oil well drilled in the world, citing evidence that a well at Petrolia, Ontario, in the '50's of the last century was at least some months ahead of the first United States oil well drilled in Pennsylvania. It was not until the 1947 discoveries, however, that Canada's petroleum production potential could be regarded as having significance on a world scale.

Since 1947, the industry has spent more than $25 billion on exploration and development in Canada, drilled some 300 million feet in some 65,000 oil and gas wells, produced as a result of this effort some 7 billion barrels of liquid petroleum and 25 trillion cubic feet of natural gas, and ended the year 1972 with 9.7 billion barrels of crude oil and 52.9 trillion cubic feet of natural gas in remaining proved reserves. Public and private incomes have been multiplied in Alberta and have been given a substantial fillip in Manitoba, Saskatchewan, and British Columbia. At the same time, income flows generated have stimulated the industrial and commercial sectors in central Canada and have added to federal government revenues. The contribution to Canada's balance of payments on current account has been substantial, although, if all related income and expenditure flows were properly traced and netted the effects would not be as large as might be suggested by a simple summing of indicated import displacement and export revenue.

Throughout this 27-year period, government had never been far from the scene. Most of the mineral rights involved have been owned by provincial governments. Their policies as owners have had much to do with the pace and the costs of exploration and development. In the past 3 years new and substantially different elements have been introduced into these policies, partly because of changed circumstances in the world petroleum situation, partly because of changes in public opinion and political philosophy. These changes are bound to have important consequences in the future.

The federal government, too, has been a principal actor, particularly since the late '50's. Through most of the intervening period its primary concern has been the building of markets for Canadian crude oil production, partly by protecting important segments of Canadian demand against imports from abroad, partly by supporting industry efforts to enlarge Canadian access to United States markets. In the case of natural gas, it has combined support for the export effort of Canadian producers with concern for the adequacy of established reserves to meet future Canadian requirements. More recently, it has been concerned to ensure the adequacy of export prices for both oil and gas, and has enforced its views by direct action. In light of the new world energy situation, it has also shown intensified concern for the adequacy currently and in the future of petroleum energy supplies to meet future domestic demands.

Private initiative and government policies have created a substantial industry with important current and future significance for the Canadian economy. Recently, however, both public opinion and government policies have reflected what to the industry participants must appear as an unnerving degree of confusion about objectives and the means for achieving them. With overlapping powers and jurisdiction, confrontation seems for the moment to have displaced co-operation between the federal government and the mineral owning provincial governments. It is timely then to make some assessment of the effects of government policy to date and to consider what might be guideposts to wisdom for the future.

To be of much value, an appraisal of the policies and practices of governments must be based on critical assessment of both objectives and methods. If the means for achieving a public objective are effective, but the goal itself is misguided in terms of the public's interest, judgment should be negative. Equally, if the goal is constructive, but the means adopted for moving towards it prove relatively ineffective or unduly costly in terms of other goals, then the judgment must again be negative. On such tests, the writer believes that the past record suggests a mixture of good and of faulty goals and a mixture of effective and ineffective methods on the part of both the federal government and the provincial governments involved in the development of petroleum energy resources in Canada since 1947. On balance, he would register more of a positive than a negative judgment. On the current scene, however, he would find it necessary to be more critical and to voice some apprehension about medium and longer term costs to the economy if some government policies and practices are not soon modified and clarified.

As a first step in assessment, it may be useful to identify some of the stated or apparent objectives of the governments involved in the development of crude oil and natural gas production in Canada. The first major actor, of course, and, with the federal government, still one of the two principals, was the province of Alberta. A 'have not' province at the time of the Leduc discovery, Alberta's interest was to use its ownership of most of the mineral rights within its borders to attract exploration and development effort while ensuring the best revenue results for the province.

In support of these objectives and on broader grounds of long-term public interest, Alberta has also been concerned from the beginning with conservation, with the enhancement of recovery of oil and gas from their reservoirs. These objectives have shaped Alberta's land regulations (i.e. its conditions for granting rights to explore and to produce), its prorationing formulae,[1] its royalty rates, and its conservation requirements for gas brought to the surface in association with crude oil.

Alberta's approach took account originally of American experience and practice in some areas, for instance, prorationing. It was an innovative approach as well, one which made imaginative use of the province's large ownership position in mineral rights. It was a competitive approach, one which seldom lost sight of the essential fact that Alberta had to compete for risk capital and scarce skills. It was an adaptive approach, one which was modified from time to time as a result of experience and changing circumstances. Measured both by the revenues it succeeded in obtaining for the provincial coffers and by the growth of the industry in exploration, production and reserves, Alberta's policies for the first quarter of a century after Leduc have to be rated as generally pretty successful.

Some critics give a more negative judgment on some scores. For instance, some deplore the relatively non-discriminating welcome given to foreign capital through most of the period since 1947. Others are critical of what they consider to have been an excessive pace of development and an overcommitment, particularly in the case of natural gas, to export markets. On both of these counts, the federal government must presumably share any indictment levelled.

The three chief tools of Alberta policy have been its land regulations, its royalty rates, and prorationing. The basic pattern of the land regulations has been to grant exploration rights under sufficiently attractive conditions to bring many oil searchers into the prospective areas. Work obligations were stressed more than revenue from rental payments. After a discovery the operator has had to move from exploration status to a lease which would permit development and production. He could, however, go to lease on no more than 50 per cent of his exploration area and that 50 per cent had to be selected under specified checkerboard constraints which usually meant that the surrendered land must be considered valuable. The latter was then available for auction and, depending on its attractiveness, could produce substantial bonuses for the Crown, usually in the form of cash payments. This system meant that the Crown as mineral owner shared in the benefits of success beyond the royalty benefits accruing to it from production. It also multiplied the number of entrants, because one could come in via the auction route without assuming the greater risks of initial exploration efforts.

The prorationing regulations also tended to encourage a large number of entrants. Instead of production allowables[2] being tied simply to the ratio between purchaser nominations and the produceability of existing wells, a modified approach was adopted which established an 'economic' allowable for each well. The economic allowable ensured that less prolific wells had what in some sense might be called a floor allowable designed to allow operators to recover their investment more quickly. One result was, of course, to reduce production from the better wells. Besides encouraging the drilling of wells in areas of low reserve per acre, this approach reduced the pressure for premature abandonment of wells. On the other hand, it also for a time provided an incentive for over-drilling, thereby tending to increase the real economic cost of production.

Prior to 1972, the royalty policies of the Alberta government were reasonably stable and, from the standpoint of participants in the industry, reliable. They provided for a maximum royalty of 16⅔ per cent of well head values for oil, with a scale of lesser rates applying for wells producing below a certain rate. For leases issued after 1962 the maximum royalty rate applied to both oil and natural gas for the initial ten years of a lease and lesser royalties applied for oil wells producing below specified limits. The industry assumed that these royalty rates would continue to apply in subsequent renewals of leases. Leases issued before 1962 had had an initial term of 21 years. These royalty rates were competitive, everything being taken into account, with those applying in other oil producing areas outside Canada.

Saskatchewan and British Columbia, the only other provinces which proved to have significant petroleum potential in this period (although Manitoba had early hopes), have also been concerned with maximizing the growth of the industry and the provincial revenues to be derived from it as owners of the mineral rights. To a considerable extent, they found the patterns set for them by Alberta, patterns from which they could not depart too far without diminishing the competitive attractiveness of their potential resources to the oil searchers and investors. In one respect they have had an advantage over Alberta. With smaller total production located closer to the major markets, they have been able to take the first slice of the available market outlet, leaving the larger Alberta production to adjust to what was left. Thus, they have largely avoided prorationing to market demand and have controlled production only to obtain best recovery.

From time to time policies of more purely local significance did emerge. The government of BC, for instance, exerted effective pressure on the industry to ensure construction of the pipeline to move BC Peace River crude to markets via Kamloops rather than by what would have been a more economical trunk line connection at Edmonton. The motive was to ensure that British Columbia crude stayed within provincial control, at least until it moved into export markets.

At a later date, British Columbia pressed those members of the industry with local refineries to provide a British Columbia outlet for certain provincial crude oils which were less desirable in quality and could be run locally only after investment in special equipment. This pressure, which was effective, was seemingly only insurance because the crudes in question were in strong demand by other refineries already equipped to use them and were being fully absorbed by refineries in the Puget Sound area. Steps such as these have negative effects over time on well head values and on exploration incentives, but their size in these two examples was probably so small as to be difficult to measure.

Beginning in 1972, the royalty picture changed drastically both for oil and gas production in all three producing provinces. The provincial authorities in each case have moved quickly to exact a much higher share of well head values for their own account and have, particularly in the case of natural gas, moved forcibly to raise well head values closer to what the market would bear, despite any contractual commitments which appeared to stand in the way. Royalty and other contractual provisions of existing leases tend to have been overridden equally. In the case of crude oil, the picture from the standpoint of the operators has been altered also by the federal government's 'voluntary' price freeze on crude entering into domestic sale and the 100 per cent tax applying to the price increments on crude entering into export sale.

The long term effects of these new approaches, or indeed the degree to which they may be a lasting pattern, cannot yet be foretold with confidence. What is certain, however, is that Alberta government practices during the preceding 2½ decades yielded provincial revenues of more than $3.5 billion while producing an active industry effort involving several hundred participants. Between them British Columbia and Saskatchewan received nearly another $1 billion in provincial revenue. In the same period, the industry, despite having achieved substantial production, did not break even on a cash flow basis. As an offset it had the future income possibilities of proved and prospective reserves to show for its continuing investment in exploration and development effort.

The exploration effort induced by geological prospects, market outlooks, and government policies led to substantial discoveries of crude oil during the '50's. Production multiplied by 15 times between 1948, the year after the initial major discovery, and 1957, when it reached a temporary peak, partly created by export sales temporarily made possible by the Suez crisis. For the next dozen years produceability exceeded market outlet substantially and a concern of government, particularly of the federal government, was to find ways to expand outlet. The Borden Commission and the public hearings associated with it led to the National Oil Policy initiated in 1961. The policy had two main thrusts: reserving a substantial part of the domestic market for Western Canadian crude oil and pushing the growth of exports of crude oil to the United States as quickly as Washington could find politically acceptable in light of its own struggle to limit external dependence. The National Oil Policy line in Canada ran roughly from Brockville north to Ottawa, keeping the Ottawa Valley generally in the import crude oil area to the east. West of the line the Canadian requirement was to be met entirely from Canadian crude oil, although there was always some leakage into the major Ontario markets, particularly of refined products. In the decade ending with 1972, Canadian crude oil production grew at a rate of 9 per cent compounded annually, reflecting growth within the protected domestic market of about 4 per cent per year and growth in sales to the United States of 15 per cent per year. By 1972 production slightly exceeded Canadian domestic demand. Exports absorbed more than half of this production, while imports of lower priced oil from Venezuela and the Eastern Hemisphere met the requirements of the area from Montreal east.

How well did the National Oil Policy serve Canada's interest? Without it, Western Canadian crude oil would either have been largely backed out of the important Ontario refining market or would have met import competition in that market at the expense of lower well head values. This would have resulted in well head values below those obtainable by sales to United States refineries, but because of United States policy restrictions, would not, one can guess, have had much if any effect on enlarging the steadily escalating informal annual quotas made available by United States policy.

In one perspective, the National Oil Policy can be seen as an arrangement for taking advantage of the available United States market at the cost of slightly higher prices for the consumers west of the NOP line.[3] It is clear that there was a positive contribution from the situation for the current account portion of the balance of payments. It is equally clear that, compared to a policy of greater self sufficiency which would have required the movement of Western Canadian crude oil farther into Eastern Canadian markets, there was a saving in real terms in transportation costs and investment. Although the merits of a further interference with free market forces by pushing the National Oil Policy line further east and constructing a pipeline to Montreal were debated fiercely, prior to late 1973 the economic and political costs of the step always seemed too great compared to the uncertain value of added supply security. The combination of Arab oil embargoes and production restraints with multiplying prices tended to alter perspectives on the issue.

The National Oil Policy undoubtedly provided some stimulus to the industry's exploration effort. Survey activity and exploratory drilling were sustained at consistently high levels throughout the decade. Exploration expenditures, including those for natural gas, which was finding rapidly expanding markets throughout this period as well, held up in Alberta and British Columbia and began to rise significantly in the frontier areas of the Northwest Territories after 1967 and in the offshore areas after 1968. Proved reserves of crude oil grew steadily throughout the decade until 1969, when they peaked and began to decline. This reflected the increasing difficulty of making significant new discoveries in the relatively well explored southern part of the Western Basin, a stage reached before the even more costly efforts to probe the possibilities of the frontier areas had yet begun to prove their promise.

It is often assumed that governments have a clearer picture of long term needs and can be better relied upon to take steps consistent with them than can private industry guided by market forces. More often than not this is an erroneous assumption. The history of Alberta's policies on tar sands development during this period may be taken as a case in point. Although the Alberta government undoubtedly recognized the long term importance of the tar sands, during these years it saw any early development of them as likely to result in undesired displacement of market outlet for conventional crude oil. It may, too, have been influenced by the fact that in then current terms the revenue possibilities for the government as mineral owner looked relatively less attractive from the tar sands than from conventional production. Whatever its motives and assessment, Alberta insisted that any tar sands projects beyond the first one must as a first condition develop new market outlets additional to those which would otherwise be available for Alberta conventional crude. By this and other means, including direct refusal of permits to competent applicants, the Alberta government delayed a second and properly scaled tar sands plant by at least five years. Now that it is evident that tar sands production cannot come in fast enough to offset the early stages of the impending decline in Western Canadian crude oil produceability which we face within the next two years, one must conclude that this was a faulty judgment. It is now clear, too, that, in light of drastically altered price prospects, the province as mineral owner need not be unenthusiastic about its own revenue potential from the tar sands.

During the past two years much has altered. Stimulated in part, no doubt, by the suddenly successful efforts of the members of Opec (Organization of Petroleum Exporting Countries), governments of the three western provinces have taken drastic steps to raise their take as mineral owners from both petroleum and natural gas production. In the face of rapidly rising world prices, the federal government has attempted to arrest the impact on Canadian consumers while ensuring that United States customers for Canadian crude pay all that the traffic will bear. In the process, there has been a series of confrontations between the federal government and the provincial governments, focussed partly upon the effects of the federal government's price control actions on limiting revenues from crude oil and partly on the sharing between the two levels of government of the very large increases in revenue resulting from multiplied prices.

From the standpoint of members of the industry, the net effect has not been encouraging. After taxes levied at 100 per cent on the export prices increases dictated by the federal government and drastically higher royalties extracted in a variety of ways from both oil and natural gas production, producers in Canada find that relatively little of the very large recent increases in world prices for energy trickles down into their own net revenues. Recently, too, they have been facing the possibility, based on the federal government proposal to consider royalties paid as still being part of taxable profits, that they might even find themselves in a negative cash flow and profit position on some of their production. More important than the immediate effects on the attractiveness of current production are the prospects in terms of prices and profits for the higher cost oil and gas of the future—the tar sands, Alberta's heavy crude of the Cold Lake type, and the still unproved Arctic and offshore possibilities. Nor can the apparent willingness of government to change the rules drastically and unexpectedly, to find ways around contractual or legislative commitments and arrangements, or even to force contracts to be reopened when there is no provision for doing so, be neglected when long range, high risk ventures[4] are being considered.

There are other elements of disincentive or uncertainty which tend to inhibit long term commitments at this time. Even the strongest member of an industry is unlikely to welcome the government as a competitor, if only because of the handicap of having to match a competitor who need not pass the ordinary tests of performance in the market place to secure his capital. Today in the Canadian petroleum scene, governments are appearing as competitors, self-invited partners, and monopoly purchasers and sellers with unilateral power to fix prices and terms.

Regulatory processes also have become both more costly and more threatening. At a time, for instance, when huge investments in exploration and development have already been made in the Arctic areas, and when early construction of transportation facilities is required if new supplies are to reach the market on time, the processes for getting approval of a pipeline from the Arctic look like delaying it for further indefinite periods, or even killing it altogether. Even at this late date, the policy terms on which a permit might be granted are highly uncertain, with difficult decisions still to be reached on such diverse questions as the environmental tests to be met, the recognition of the interests of the native peoples to be given, and the price constraints and market limitations to be imposed.

In the circumstances, it is not altogether surprising that drilling rigs and crews have been leaving Canada for the United States and the Eastern Hemisphere, while geologists and geophysicists have been walking the street in Calgary. Such actions are not the result of industry pique or of some concerted attempt to read governments a lesson. They are, rather, the reflection of a multitude of individual investor assessments of future prospects. Once well under way on a broad scale, such actions are not easy to reverse, especially when they are prompted by such a complex of causes of uncertainty.

Canada's need now in the petroleum field, both crude oil and natural gas, is for more effort, not less, for speeding up critical projects which have long lead times, not delaying them. Already it is clear that we face shortly the beginnings of a long decline in the produceability of our currently discovered reserves of conventional crude oil. Large as the contribution which the tar sands can make over time should be, that contribution will lag behind the early need and will require huge and sustained effort and resources to keep pace thereafter with the decline in conventional crude oil production from present sources. By the end of this decade natural gas production, too, will need support from the Mackenzie Delta or other new sources to keep pace with domestic demand growth while meeting present market commitments. In fact, this point has already been reached for British Columbia production.

In the whole of the energy supply field, long lead times, large investments, and a 20-year or longer life to recover investment and to make a return are characteristic. Inevitably, that means substantial economic risks, intensified at a time of high cost money and relatively unpredictable escalation in costs. For the oil and gas explorer, the economic risk is always great because of the uncertainty inherent in geologic and geophysical appraisals. Such risks, though, are a normal part of the business and can be given due weight in investment and operating decisions. Conclusions will often be wrong, as evidenced by the fact that only a relatively few operators have succeeded in a profits sense over the past 27 years of discovery and development of oil and gas in Western Canada. Most will find it even more difficult to deal with circumstances where there are, in addition, high political risks, as has come to be the case during the recent past.

Canada can ill afford the consequences. This is not to suggest that governments in Canada, whether as mineral owners, taxing authorities, or regulatory authorities, should neglect or drop some of their current concerns in the field of petroleum. Rather they should act always with a responsible concern for creating and maintaining adequate incentives, and sufficient certainty and confidence, to induce and permit the numerous and diverse members of the industry to maximize the contribution oil and gas development can make to the Canadian economy.

Notes

*Ritchie, R. S., "Public Policies Affecting Petroleum Development in Canada," *Canadian Public Policy*, 1:1, Winter, 1975 (reproduced by permission of author and publisher).

[1]Prorationing to market demand is the practice of limiting production to available market outlet, with allowable production for individual wells being set in some equitable relation to the total. Under Alberta practice, market outlet is indicated by monthly purchaser nominations. Within the total, individual well allowables have usually been set in some relation to efficient recovery limits. These allowables are designed to protect against one owner's portion of a reservoir being drained by wells of neighbours.

[2]Production allowables are the individual well production maxima set by the prorationing authorities.

[3]As a measure of this cost, it can be noted that refiners in Montreal during the '60's had an advantage of something less than 50 cents per barrel most of the time in their laid down cost of imported crude oil versus the cost to Toronto area refiners of Western Canada crude. This differential would have been cut roughly in half if the cost of moving imported crude oils into the Toronto area were taken into the calculation and perhaps nearly eliminated if certain quality considerations were allowed for. At the consumer level in gasoline and furnace fuel prices, the differential ranged normally from 1–2 cents per gallon. It should be noted, too, that some of the natural gas available in

Ontario was due to exploration and production of crude oil stimulated by the availability of the Ontario market.

[4]Exploration in the present state of knowledge is inherently high risk because geophysical and geological techniques can do no more than indicate the possibility of commercial reserves. Only extensive drilling guided by seismic and other exploration work can usually determine whether oil or gas exists in minimum suitable amounts and conditions to justify production, gathering, and transportation facilities. In the Canadian experience there are many examples of millions and in some cases hundreds of millions of dollars being spent with final negative results. A good recent example is a series of offshore wells drilled off the West coast. There are other examples in the Arctic frontier areas and the verdict is not yet in on much of the formidably expensive exploration and drilling activity which has been going on in the East coast offshore areas.

Section 3

Government Control of Business

Introduction

The logic of a free market, private enterprise economy does not easily accommodate the idea that business enterprises require regulation and control by government. This does not mean that such enterprises would be "uncontrolled" in such a system, for the market economy contains a potentially very effective but concealed method of control—competition. It is the force of competition that is supposed to ensure that business firms operate in the best interests of society. But what if, for some reason, competition does not exist? It would then seem to follow that government would be called upon either to do something to restore and preserve competition or to devise and substitute some other form of control for it. The readings in this section are intended to show that in Canada competition *is* impaired and that here, as in other countries with British traditions, government has made some effort to strengthen this mechanism of control through what, in this country, is rather quaintly called "anticombines" legislation. At the same time, however, government in Canada has also adopted a number of other methods to control business. These include several kinds of regulation, various forms of public ownership and, increasingly it would seem, some form of more or less open "negotiation" among interested parties.

Part 1
Competition Policies

Introduction

How competitive is business in Canada? This is not a simple question to answer, partly because there may be uncertainty about what we mean by "competitive" and partly because it is difficult to generalize about the conditions under which the great variety of business enterprises in a modern industrial economy operate.

When the economist uses the term competitive, he has in mind the concept of "perfect competition" or some tolerable approximation to it: he is thinking in terms of a situation in which individual sellers or buyers are unable to exercise any perceptible control over market supply or price for the commodity concerned. This condition will be expected to obtain when there are enough independent sellers or buyers in the market to ensure that no one seller or buyer accounts for a noticeable part of the total supply of the goods or services in question. To the extent that this condition is not fulfilled, the economist recognizes some element of "monopoly" in the market. This could include the extreme of pure monopoly where a single seller or buyer (a monopsonist) accounts for the total amount of the goods or services supplied or demanded in the market. Within the two extremes of perfect competition and pure monopoly, sellers and buyers have some degree of power over total output and the price established in the market. How effectively this power can be exercised depends upon the size of the individual seller's or buyer's contribution to total market supply or demand.

Thus, firms that account for most of the sales of a commodity are likely to have considerable market power. This is why economists studying the organization of industry are interested in measuring the "degree of concentration" of sellers (or buyers) in an industry or market; that is, the proportion of output or sales accounted for by some proportion of the firms in the industry.

Surprisingly little statistical evidence concerning the degree of concentration in Canadian industry has yet been accumulated. But what there is, combined with more general observation, indicates a considerable variation in the degree of concentration from one industry to another. Agriculture and some of the service industries provide good examples of extremely low concentration, with a great many producing units supplying the total output of the industry. Such an "atomistic" market structure confers little, if any, market power on individual firms, leading to a situation approximating the ideal of perfect competition. The public utilities industries (including transportation, communications, electric power, gas and water) and the financial industries (notably banking and insurance) are all highly concentrated, with a small percentage of the firms accounting for a high percentage of the total output. Other industries present a more complicated picture. Manufacturing, the only type of industry intensively studied with regard to structure, is an example of such a complex situation. Some of the evidence, with an analysis of it, is presented in Reading 22. In the following selection, Professor Kierans comments on the implications of the high levels of concentration in Canadian industry for our understanding of the general nature and characteristics of our political economic system as a whole.

The approach to the problems created by the weakness of competition most clearly compatible with the free market ideal is, of course, the application of antimonopoly laws and the breaking up of concentrations of economic power. The history of Canadian policies in this regard is set out in Reading 24. As the latter part of the item indicates, this whole matter is currently under review and, at time of writing, a new set of anticombines laws is being developed. It is not likely, however, that these will be much more extensive in their scope or drastic in their impact on particular large business enterprises than they have been in the past. Our main justification for suggesting this is simply that there appear to be very strong arguments against a policy of waging an all-out war against monopoly in this country. Many Canadians, including most businessmen and even some academic economists, not only believe that competition is not a good thing in itself, but also that monopoly has definite advantages! In particular it is frequently contended that large concentrations of economic power are necessary to ensure technological progress, and that the objective of dynamic economic efficiency is important enough to more than offset any short-run costs which may be imposed on consumers by large producers. This argument may be thought to have a particular significance in a country heavily dependent on foreign trade, but possessing only a small and fragmented domestic market. The traditional case for big business is succinctly set out in the brief presented by Bell Canada Limited to the Royal Commission on the Concentration of Corporate Power in Canada, reproduced here as Reading 25.

22 Concentration in the Manufacturing Industries in Canada *

Canada, Department of Consumer and Corporate Affairs

Introduction

This Report contains the results of a statistical inquiry into levels of concentration in Canadian manufacturing industries. It is intended to be of immediate assistance in the formulation and evaluation of industrial and commercial policies, especially those relating to competition. In addition, the appendices have been designed partly to provide the considerable detail often required by academic economists who wish to explore the causes and effects of existing levels of concentration.

Basically, measures of concentration of economic activity involve the ranking by size of the relevant economic units, such as companies or factories, in order to find out to what extent the activity is concentrated in the hands of the few largest units. One of the earliest and most renowned of such measures was by A. A. Berle and G. C. Means,[1] who reported on the position that had been occupied by the largest two hundred corporations in the United States some forty years ago. Not long afterwards, the Royal Commission on Price Spreads[2] found that the hundred largest companies in Canada had some 65 per cent of the total capital of all companies. Concentration measures of that kind provide a general indication of the degree to which private economic power is concentrated. When first published they caused considerable concern because they were sharply at variance with the stereotypes of a competitive economy which were then prevalent in the minds of economists as well as members of the public at large.

Those early measures of concentration helped to underline the need for a vast amount of empirical research to supplement the work of economic theorists. There has now evolved, especially in the United States, the field of economics known as industrial organization, whose purpose is to analyse the structure and organization of economic activity and their effects upon the performance of the economy. Moreover, with easy access to electronic computers, the capability of analysing data has increased rapidly.

The present Report, while containing some broad measures of concentration in Canada's business sector as a whole, focuses mainly upon the details of concentration in each of 159 separate manufacturing industries for the year 1965. For each manufacturing industry treated, measures of concentration are presented on two distinct bases. One base is the manufacturing establishment, which approximates the technological unit of production. The other base is the manufacturing enterprise which is defined as all manufacturing establishments in an industry under common control. For example, in a given industry, the Report shows what percentage of total industry shipments were accounted for by the four largest establishments and by the four largest enterprises. The two figures will be the same if each of the four largest enterprises operated only one establishment in that industry; otherwise, enterprise concentration will be higher than establishment concentration. Detailed results shown in the appendices have been aggregated and summarized in various ways in the text.

The only comprehensive statistics of concentration in Canadian manufacturing industries previously available were for the year 1948, found in the classic study of Gideon Rosenbluth published in 1957 under the auspices of the National Bureau of Economic Research.[3] Concentration statistics for United States manufacturing industries were first published before World War II. They are now published on a regular basis and have proven to be an extremely productive tool for policy makers and students of industrial organization.

A virtue of having concentration data at the level of individual industries is that each industry tends to be associated with a particular market or group of markets. Whereas general measures of the kind introduced by Berle and Means provide an indication of the overall distribution of private economic power, concentration data on an industry-by-industry basis provide an indication of competitive conditions in the many separate markets within the economy of a country. Where an industry consists of a number of firms such that no single one or single small group can exert a dominant influence on pricing, then the structural basis for a reasonably competitive market mechanism exists. On the other hand, where a small group of firms, such as the largest four of the largest eight in the industry, account for a dominant share of output, then the possibility of serious restrictions on the competitive process must be taken into account. Of course, no single structural test is conclusive in this regard. In particular instances such factors as foreign trade, the existence of substitute products from other industries, and the relations among the dominant firms would have to be considered as well. Nevertheless, concentration measures do provide an extremely useful indicator of the degree of competition in the economy.

Research into the causes and effects of high concentration can be done by using statistics of industry concentration in conjunction with the other data. The importance of internal company growth relative to external growth by mergers as contributors to concentration can be explored. Studies have been done in the United States and elsewhere on the relation of concentration to profit levels, price-cost margins, advertising expenditures and other factors.[4] It is hoped that the present report will stimulate research into the causes and effects of concentration in Canadian manufacturing industries.

Summary of Findings

GENERAL LEVELS OF CONCENTRATION

The business life of Canada in 1965 was shared by nearly 170,000 active corporations in addition to many thousands of farmers and individual small business proprietors. Thousands of corporations each with assets valued at less than $5 million accounted for the greater part of corporate economic activity in agriculture, personal and business services, wholesale and retail trade and construction.

On the other hand, relatively small numbers of large corporations play a highly strategic role in the business life of Canada. In 1965 the 174 largest corporations had 50 per cent of total corporate assets. Ninety-four largest non-financial corporations had 38 per cent of the assets of all non-financial corporations. Seventeen corporations in the utilities sector, most of them under some form of public control, had 72.7 per cent of the assets in that sector. Sixteen mining corporations accounted for 37.2 per cent of the assets in that sector. Eighty banks, insurance companies and other financial corporations had 61.7 per cent of the assets in that sector, and the fifty largest manufacturing corporations had 40 per cent of the assets in that sector.

Special tabulations were made to show the sizes of the largest 4, 8, 12, 20, 50 and 100 manufacturing enterprises in 1965. The largest four operated 117 manufacturing establishments in 29 industries and accounted for over 5 per cent of all manufacturing shipments. The largest hundred operated 1,263 establishments in 114 industries and accounted for 42 per cent of total manufacturing shipments. There were 453 enterprises which operated establishments in two or more industries. They operated 2,530 establishments and accounted for about half of the total manufacturing shipments. The remainder was accounted for by nearly 30,000 enterprises each of which operated in only one industry.

LEVELS OF ENTERPRISE CONCENTRATION IN INDIVIDUAL MANUFACTURING INDUSTRIES

Details of concentration in 159 manufacturing industries accounting for about 94 per cent of total value added by manufacturing were obtained. The remaining industries were rejected because of the heterogeneity of their products. Of the 159 industries for which data were obtained, five were excluded from the analytical tables, again because of product heterogeneity. The remaining 154 industries, which were subjected to careful analysis, accounted for about 88 per cent of total value added by manufacturing.

Levels of concentration were measured in several different ways, each method having particular advantages. Industries were first examined in terms of the number of largest enterprises in each which accounted for 80 per cent of the industry's shipments. Sixty manufacturing industries accounting for 37 per cent of total manufacturing shipments in the sample were found to be highly concentrated in that eight or fewer enterprises accounted for 80 per cent of shipments. At the other extreme, 57 industries accounting for 42 per cent of shipments in the sample had fairly low or low concentration in that over twenty enterprises in each industry were required to account for 80 per cent of shipments. When employment was substituted for shipments, it was found that levels of concentration, while still high, were appreciably lower than when measured by shipments.

Concentration was also measured in terms of the percentage of shipments in each industry accounted for by the largest 4, 8, 12, 20 and 50 enterprises. A total of 39 industries accounting for 30 per cent of the total shipments in the sample were characterized as highly concentrated oligopolies in that the largest four enterprises in each industry accounted for 75 per cent or more of shipments. Another 38 industries accounting for 19 per cent of the shipments in the sample were moderately concentrated oligopolies in that the largest four enterprises in each accounted for between 50 and 75 per cent of industry shipments.

LEVELS OF ESTABLISHMENT AND ENTERPRISE CONCENTRATION

Whereas the enterprise is the level at which major economic decisions are made, the establishment approximates to the technical unit of production.

The manufacturing industries in the sample were found to be less concentrated in terms of establishments than in terms of enterprises. Establishment concentration was high in 38 industries accounting for 22 per cent of the total shipments in the sample in that fewer than eight establishments in each accounted for 80 per cent of shipments. In comparison, sixty industries accounting for 37 per cent of the shipments in the sample had high enterprise concentration. A clear relation was found to exist between levels of industry concentration and the divergence between enterprise and establishment concentration. The higher the level of concentration the greater was the divergence between enterprise and establishment concentration.

An analysis was made of the characteristics of the largest enterprises in each industry. Leading enterprises and their establishments were both found to vary in size directly with the level of concentration in their industries. Moreover, the difference in absolute size between leading enterprises and leading etablishments was greater in the highly concentrated industries. However, it was found that in relative rather than absolute terms, the difference between the sizes of leading enterprises and leading establishments did not vary with the levels of industry concentration. Thus, leading enterprises tend each to have more than one establishment regardless of the level of concentration of their industry. A further analysis indicated that the large enterprises tended to have the large establishments.

Finally, an analysis was made of the extent to which enterprises with different size rankings in their respective industries tend to be multi-establishment operations. It was found that the tendency towards multi-establishment operation was greatest among the four largest enterprises in each industry, followed by the top eight. Enterprises which ranked twelfth or smaller were nearly always single-establishment operations.

In summary, there is a close relationship in Canada between high concentration and the fact that the largest enterprises in most industries tend to have two or more establishments each.

REGIONAL CONCENTRATION

Up to this point in the Report, no allowance was made for the fact that some industries consist of establishments serving a local or regional rather than a national market. Enterprises in such industries are usually faced with a smaller number of actual competitors than statistics on a national basis would indicate. It was found that 34 industries accounting for 36 per cent of total shipments in the sample had marked regional characteristics. Some measures of concentration on a regional basis were obtained for the 34 industries, but problems of confidentiality were such that reasonably comprehensive regional data could only be obtained for 18 of them. It was found that levels of concentration in the 18 industries, as shown by the regional data, were much higher than had been indicated by the national data. Using a weighted average of the regional data for each of the 18 industries, the largest four enterprises in seven of them accounted for 50 per cent or more of the shipments of their respective industries. Using the national concentration measures, only two of the same 18 industries showed as high levels of concentration.

TRENDS IN CONCENTRATION

Canadian statistical evidence respecting historical trends in levels of industrial concentration is scanty. Such evidence as there is indicates that in 1965 the general level of concentration in manufacturing industries was higher than in 1948 or in 1958. Taking the non-financial corporate sector as a whole, concentration appears to have declined somewhat between 1958 and 1965.

Comparisons at the level of individual manufacturing industries were made of concentration measures for 1948 by Gideon Rosenbluth and those for 1965 in the present Report. The statistics of only forty industries were found to be comparable. The levels of enterprise concentration in that sample had increased significantly between 1948 and 1965. In the former year, industries in which 12 or fewer enterprises accounted for 80 per cent of industry shipments made up 32.4 per cent of the sample by value added; in 1965 such industries made up 41.2 per cent of the sample. When looked at in terms of manufacturing establishment, no clear trend in levels of concentration was evident.

The assets of the 54 largest manufacturing corporations in 1958 were compared with those of the fifty largest corporations in 1965. The former had 38 per cent of the total assets of all manufacturing corporations in 1958, whereas the latter had 40.1 per cent of the assets of all manufacturing corporations in 1965.

However, taking all non-financial corporations, the largest 94 in 1958 had 40.6 per cent of the assets of all non-financial corporations, whereas the largest 94 in 1965 had 37.6 per cent. The indicated decline in concentration appears to have been related to the growth of sectors of low concentration such as services and to the decline of the position of the railways relative to that of other utilities.

COMPARISON OF LEVELS OF CONCENTRATION IN MANUFACTURING IN CANADA AND THE UNITED STATES

Comparisons with studies done in the United States showed that levels of concentration in Canadian manufacturing industries were considerably higher than those in the United States. The fifty largest United States manufacturing companies accounted for 25 per cent of value added by manufacture in 1963, whereas the fifty largest manufacturing enterprises in Canada accounted for 36 per cent of value added by manufacture in 1965. The figures for the hundred largest were 33 per cent of value added in the United States and 46 per cent of value added in Canada.

At the level of individual manufacturing industries, it was found that Canadian industry classifications tended to be considerably broader than those of the United States. In many cases two or more United States industries had to be combined for purposes of comparison with one Canadian industry. Altogether, 116 industries or groups of industries were compared. On the Canadian side, 123 manufacturing industries were included and on the American side 231 industries were included. They accounted for 68 per cent of total United States manufacturing shipments and 77 per cent of total Canadian manufacturing shipments. The results showed that Canadian manufacturing industries in 1965 were much more concentrated than their United States counterparts in 1963. Of the 116 industry groupings in the sample, 98 were significantly more highly concentrated in Canada than in the United States.

Finally, tests were made to determine the differences in indicated levels of concentration resulting from the use of the Canadian and United States systems of industry classification. Levels of concentration in 231 United States manufacturing industries were compared with levels of concentration in the same industries when combined into 116 industry groups comparable to the Canadian industry classifications. When concentration in each of 231 American industries was measured separately, 11 of them accounting for 15.17 per cent of the shipments in the sample were in the highly concentrated range. When the same industries were combined into 116 industry groups comparable to Canadian classifications, only 3 of the groups emerged in the highly concentrated range.

Thus, it appears that the level of manufacturing concentration in Canada would be far higher than as shown in this Report if the American system of industry classification could have been used. It is, however, beyond the scope of this Report to decide which classification provides the best basis for a concentration study. The Canadian classifications clearly err in the direction of being too broad and of leading to understatements of concentration. However, some critics have contended that the American classifications err in the other direction.

Notes

*Canada, Department of Consumer and Corporate Affairs, *Concentration in the Manufacturing Industries of Canada* (Ottawa: Queen's Printer, 1971), pp. 1-6 (reproduced by permission of Information Canada).

[1]Berle, A. A. and Means, G. C., *The Modern Corporation and Private Property*, Harcourt, Brace & World, Inc., N.Y. (Rev. Edn., 1967).

[2]*Royal Commission on Price Spreads*, Report, Ottawa (1937).

[3]Rosenbluth, Gideon, *Concentration in Canadian Manufacturing Industries*, NBER, Princeton (1957).

[4]For example:

Bain, Joe S. "Relation of Profit Rate to Industry Concentration: American Manufacturing, 1936-1940," *Quarterly Journal of Economics*, vol. LXV (August 1951), pp. 293-324.

Weisz, L. W. "Average Concentration Ratios and Industrial Performance," *Journal of Industrial Economics*, vol. XI (July 1963), pp. 237-254.

Miller, R. A. "Marginal Concentration Ratios and Industrial Profit Rates: Some Empirical Results of Oligopoly Behavior," *The Southern Economic Journal*, vol. LXXXIV (October 1967), pp. 259-267.

Collins, N. R. and Preston, L. E., *Concentration and Price-Cost Margins in Manufacturing Industries*, Berkeley: University of California Press (1968).

23 The Structure of the Canadian Corporate Economy*

E. Kierans

There is not much difficulty in attempting to understand the structure of the Canadian corporate economy. Each corporation is required to file an annual return with the Minister of National Revenue. These returns are generally prepared by accredited chartered or general accountants and conform to accepted principles of accounting and auditing practice. Thus a mass of unstructured financial information—balance sheets, operating statements, source and application of funds schedules, etc.,—is accumulated, standardized and published in a form suitable for tax, financial, and general economic analysis. Given the virtually absolute coverage of the corporate sector, the facts and data needed for a complete picture of the economy are there. We know where we are. The important question of how we got there remains, and this is a task for the economic historian.

This is the way it is. The latest reports by Statistics Canada cover the 1971 operations of 231,536 corporations, divided for analytical purposes into 37 major industry groups. The number is large enough to satisfy any theorist or econometrician, but the significance changes immediately when it is noted that 291 firms (one-eighth of one per cent of the total) controlled 58% of the assets ($159 billion of $275 billion), produced 30% of the goods and services ($48 billion of $162 billion sales), and collected 39% of total profits in the corporate sector ($4.5 billion of $11.6 billion). It is difficult to escape the conclusion that Canada is the example par excellence of corporate concentration and oligopoly dominance of price and output decisions.

This interdependence is clearly evident in the resource sector. There were 3,740 corporations in the mining sector at the end of 1971. Of that number, 34 firms (less than one per cent) controlled 55% of the assets ($9.5 billion of $17.4 billion), sold 61% of Canada's mineral and mining output ($3.8 billion of $6.2 billion), and earned 73% of the profits before income taxes ($693 million of $952 million). More specifically, if the metal mining group is separated from the rest of the resource sector, the 14 largest firms are found to control 73% of the assets, 71% of the sales and received 72% of the profits earned in exploiting Canada's metal mines. This is concentration of economic power with a vengeance.

Nor does Canada's manufacturing sector display the characteristics of a competitive capitalism. In the 21 major industry groups of Canadian secondary industry in 1971, there were 21,998 incorporated firms. Eighty-three of these firms (three-eighths of one per cent) controlled 45.6% of the assets ($22.9 billion of $50.1 billion), 37.5% of the output of goods and services ($22.5 billion of $59.9 billion) and made 43.2% of the profit before income taxes ($1.6 billion of $3.7 billion).

The primary metals industry is one of the 21 major groups within Canada's manufacturing sector. A total of 365 incorporated firms are engaged in the converting and processing of our natural resources. Eight of these firms dominated the group, controlling 81% of total assets ($3.8 billion of $4.7 billion). The same eight firms produced 69% of the output ($2.4 billion of $3.5 billion) and made 80% of the profits before income taxes ($247 million of $309 million). Clearly, these eight firms are not adjusting their price and output policies independently of each other as economic theory would suggest. Again we have the picture of oligopoly capitalism and price leadership.

The facts about the concentration of corporate power in Canada are generally known and understood in the community. Recent spectacular merger moves by Inco, Noranda, Power Corporation, etc., have increased public concern and misgivings about the policies that permit this wave of take-overs. It is only when the political fallout threatens the government's credibility that the Prime Minister announces the creation of a Royal Commission on Corporate Concentration, charged with the task of reporting upon and making recommendations concerning "(a) the nature and role of major concentrations of economic power in Canada; (b) the economic and social implications for the public interest of such concentrations; and (c) whether safeguards exist or may be required to protect the public interest in the presence of such concentrations."

The most glaring deficiency in the terms of reference has been the exclusion of an examination of the federal economic policies which have provided the major impetus to corporate concentration in this country. Perhaps such a reference would not have been acceptable to the chairman of the Royal Commission, for as the single most powerful economic adviser to successive governments since the Second World War he would, in effect, have been asked to judge his own policies, biases, and prejudices. While I would not suggest that Mr. Robert Bryce could not have second thoughts, his commitment to size ("bigger is better") has been too long and too deeply ingrained for him to undergo an intellectual conversion at this time.

Consider again our two volumes of statistics tracing out the shape and structure of the Canadian economy. If economic policy were truly committed to encouraging a competitive environment, one would expect a neutral corporate income tax system or, if not, a system favouring the growth of new, small and medium-sized firms. In fact, the reverse has been true since the corporate income tax became a substantial tool of policy during and after the Second World War. Of all categories in the manufacturing sector, the 83 firms with assets in excess of $100 million paid the lowest effective rate of corporate income tax in 1971, 30.8%. The next lowest rate was paid by firms with assets of more than $25 million but less than $100 million; the effective rate for the

197 firms in this category was 35.6%. The remaining 21,718 firms, i.e. with assets less than $25 million, paid an effective rate of 45.3% on their profits. As far as tax concessions are concerned, "them that has, gets."

Similarly, in the resource sector. The largest 106 firms, with assets over $25 million, provided $68 million for current income taxes in 1971 on profits of $961.8 million for an effective corporate rate of 7.1%. Two hundred firms, with assets between $5 million and $25 million, paid $26.8 million in taxes on profits of $70.1 million in the same year for an effective rate of 38.2%.

The enormous difference in effective rates stems from the nature of tax exemptions and privileges. In all instances, capital cost allowances, depletion, investment credits, exploration and developments, etc., favour the large and profitable firms. This has been the bias in the Canadian tax structure since the Second World War as government policy-makers have equated efficiency with size and discriminated against the employment of labour by favouring capital investment via tax concessions and subsidies.

Similarly, in manufacturing. The 83 largest firms were able to defer the payment of $1.3 billion in taxes out of a total deferral of $1.9 billion for the 21,998 corporations engaged in manufacturing at the end of 1971.

Incredible as it may seem, the pace of concentration did not satisfy the Canadian government. Impressed with the Herman Kahn theme that the multinational corporation would dominate the global economy of the nineteen-eighties, the Honourable E. J. Benson included in his Tax Reform(?) Legislation of 1971 measures that would ensure that the big would get bigger and fewer. Canadian corporations will be allowed a full deduction for interest paid on money borrowed to buy shares in other corporations. In order that there be no misunderstanding about the government's intent, the Minister of Finance went on to explain, "This deduction for interest provides a substantial incentive for Canadian corporations to invest in other corporations and permits them to compete on an even footing with foreign corporations. Assuming a tax rate of 50 per cent, the cost of borrowing money for share purchases will be cut in half."

Observe what is going on here. Clearly the government is addressing the oligopoly firm, i.e. the firm which has sufficient control of its market to ensure, by adjusting price and output, a continuing flow of profits over 10-15-20 years. Borrowing large sums for takeover purposes means annual interest charges for many years. Small firms, medium-sized firms with cyclical profit levels, farmers in the competitive sector need not apply. Nor is the interest-deductible privilege an advantage to firms that do not make profits.

Again we must pay attention to what the government is saying.

The federal government is not telling the large and profitable firms to invest their profits in more productive capacity or even to distribute the profits to shareholders. It is telling Inco, Noranda, Power Corporation, Abitibi, and the rest, to use their existing profits to buy each other out. If they do this, the government will give back the taxes due on profits spent for this purpose, thus financing half the costs of mergers and takeovers. It is quite fascinating to be a member of a cabinet that can put forward this type of tax privilege while affirming stoutly its belief in competition and anti-combines legislation.

Two assertions can be made about Canada's economic structure in the 1970's. In the first place, virtually every sector of the economy is dominated by less than a handful of huge corporations and, secondly, the single most important cause of this concentration of economic power has been and is federal economic policy.

A little reflection, apart from the data and statistics, would suggest that this must be so. The government of Canada has never believed in free trade or in competition. Despite all protestations, politicians want action now, growth in economic activity and employment. An economic structure composed of large numbers of firms busily competing away one another's profits may be advantageous to the consumer but does not throw up the surpluses that can be taxed or reinvested in new capacity and technology. Nature must be made to grow by leaps and bounds, cement and steel, skyscrapers and SSTs. That is the stuff and, to get it, governments go with the few and the large, with concessions and exemptions to force the pace of change.

Governments do not work against—they work with the vested, the established, the giants in place. The two sectors have exactly the same interest, increase the pace of economic activity and the growth of assets. The distribution of that rising product must permit increasing levels of retained earnings and savings out of high incomes to keep the show going. The problems of farmers who might employ an additional hired hand or small business with little surplus to reinvest are of no interest to ministers and their deputies craving policies with high visibility and little else to recommend them.

Politicians and bureaucrats can then point to a rising GNP and corporate chairmen can announce an increase in assets to their shareholders. Only the people are confused as they see little evidence of this increased wealth translated into a better standard of living for them and a more equitable distribution of what the nation does turn out.

With this community of interest between a powerful public sector and a rich and dominating industrial core, it becomes easier to understand the formation of new service corporations such as Reisman and Grandy Ltd. Two of the most powerful bureaucrats, a deputy minister of finance and a deputy minister of industry, trade and commerce laden with honours for their public service and the most generous pension arrangements granted by an unwitting public, take an early retirement, settle in on the tenth floor of the newest Ottawa skyscraper and prepare to guide the oligopolies that can afford them through the labyrinth of the federal bureaucracy and the potential pitfalls of Canada's latest Royal Commission, the inquiry into corporate concentration.

The level of concentration that presently exists in Canada is a direct consequence of government policy. Despite the lip service paid to laissez-faire capitalism, competition and the virtues of individual enterprise and initiative, no Canadian government has ever believed in, to the extent of practising, these principles. They could not afford to wait for the slow procession of natural, diversified and balanced growth. Politicians operate in the short run, and ad hocery is the response of men in a hurry. Re-election makes opportunists of us all.

Professor Naylor shows us how it was in the beginning of our history as a nation. Then, as now, the public and the private sectors were completely intertwined. The political framework was there—a new sovereign nation from sea to sea. It had to be given economic strength and depth, and instantly. Thus, the business of creating this nation fell into the hands of the few—in business. As Professor Naylor describes for us in language that bites, the directions of our growth were imposed upon us by the interests and well-being of particular, mainly commercial, groups. They built themselves into the very structure of the state and the economy could only move forward on their terms. Thus tariffs, capital inflows, subsidies, tax concessions and licences to exploit and export the nation's wealth. Just as the government found that it could achieve its aim of growth by fostering the corporations, so the corporations found in the government the means of ensuring their own development, privileges, and continuing dominance.

Notes

*Kierans, E., "Foreword" to T. Naylor, *The History of Canadian Business 1867-1914* (Toronto: James Lorimer & Co., 1975, reproduced by permission of author and publisher).

24 Legislative History of the Combines Investigation Act *

Canada, Department of Consumer and Corporate Affairs

The history of this legislation may be divided into seven periods: 1889-1910; 1910-1919; 1919-1923; 1923-1935; 1935-1951; 1951-1960; 1960 to the present date.

The report of the MacQuarrie Committee, which was appointed to study the legislation and make recommendations, was made in March 1952 and it contained the following historical survey.

"(1) 1889-1910

Canadian combines legislation had its origin in the report of a select committee of the House of Commons appointed in 1888 to inquire into the existence of combinations and trusts in Canada and their effect upon the Canadian economy. The Committee found that combinations inimical to the public interest existed in respect of a number of widely used commodities and services and recommended that legislative action be taken to curb such combinations. In 1889 an Act was passed, the parent of the present section 498 of the Criminal Code, making it a misdemeanour to conspire, combine, agree or arrange unlawfully,

(a) to unduly limit the facilities for transporting, producing, manufacturing, supplying, storing or dealing in any article or commodity which may be a subject of trade or commerce; or—
(b) To restrain or injure trade or commerce in relation to any such article or commodity; or—
(c) To unduly prevent, limit, or lessen the manufacture or production of any such article or commodity, or to unreasonably enhance the price thereof; or—
(d) To unduly prevent or lessen competition in the production, manufacture, purchase, barter, sale, transportation or supply of any such article or commodity, or in the price of insurance upon person or property.

In the general codification of the criminal law in 1892 the Act of 1889 became a section of the Criminal Code and the offence was made an indictable one. The awkward usage involved by employing the term "unlawfully" as well as 'unduly' and 'unreasonably' to describe the offence led to early difficulties of interpretation, and after various legislative amendments, the word "unlawfully" was eliminated from the section in 1900 and the wording settled in the form it has retained to the present time. (1952)

In its improved wording the section provided the basis for six prosecutions in the next ten years, four of these resulting in convictions. In addition the courts found agreements brought before them in a number of civil suits to be illegal as contrary to the section and refused the parties to the agreement any rights under them. In most of these instances, however, no criminal prosecution followed. Experience showed increasingly that, in combines cases, the problem of securing evidence was a peculiarly difficult one. In one instance, in this period, it was found necessary to resort to the appointment of a Parliamentary Committee to assemble the facts. It was a task normally beyond the resources of private individuals or the ordinary machinery of criminal investigation.

(2) 1910-1919

The Combines Investigation Act of 1910 sought to supply, for this weakness, special machinery of investigation. Any six persons could apply to a judge for an order directing that an investigation into an alleged combine be held.

A combine was defined by the Act as (a) 'any contract, agreement, arrangement or combination which has, or is designed to have, the effect of increasing or fixing the price or rental of any article of trade or commerce or the cost of the storage or transportation thereof, or of restricting the competition in or of controlling the production, manufacture, transportation, storage, sale or supply thereof to the detriment of consumers or producers of such article of trade or commerce', including (b) 'the acquisition, leasing, or otherwise taking over, or obtaining by any person to the end aforesaid of any control over or interest in the business, or any portion of the business of any other person' and (c) 'includes what is known as a trust, monopoly, or merger'.

If, after hearing, the judge found the situation to warrant an inquiry he could issue an order to that effect. The Minister of Labour was then to appoint a board of three commissioners, one selected by the applicants, one by the parties against whom the application was made, and the third, the chairman, who was to be a judge, nominated by the other two members. A board had power to compel the attendance of witnesses, examine them under oath, require the production of documents and general incidental powers to carry out a full inquiry.

A board had wide powers of report; it could make 'such findings and recommendations as, in the opinion of the board, are in accordance with the merits and requirements of the case'. Reports were to be transmitted to the Minister at the conclusion of an inquiry and to be published in the Canada Gazette.

Any person who was found by the board, after inquiry, to have done any of the enumerated acts being the same as those mentioned in section 498 of the Criminal Code, and who did not cease his activities within ten days after the publication of a report to this effect, made himself, under the Act, liable to a per diem penalty up to one thousand dollars for each day he continued to offend.

The Act of 1910 also carried forward a provision (which had first found place in Canadian legislation in 1897) for the use of tariff action to combat monopolistic practices. The Customs Tariff Act of 1897 had given authority for the government to have an investigation held by a judge into the existence of a trust or combination that unduly enhanced prices or promoted the advantage of manufacturers or dealers at the expense of consumers. If such a trust or combination were found to exist, the duty on the commodity or commodities affected could be lowered or removed by executive action. By the Act of 1910 this action could be taken when a board or a court had found such a combination existed. Furthermore an additional remedy was provided where a board reported that the owner or holder of a patent had made use of the exclusive rights under it to do any of the enumerated acts being the same as those mentioned in section 498 of the Criminal Code. In such cases the Minister of Justice could institute appropriate proceedings in the Exchequer Court to have the patent revoked.

The expectation was that, through its provision for public investigation and report, the Act would, in considerable measure, deter harmful activities without resort to prosecution; and that this failing, and prosecution becoming necessary, the new procedures for the discovery and marshalling of facts would facilitate the process of prosecution. In fact, the machinery of the Act was only used once before the country was swallowed up in the concerns of the First Great War. The legislation revealed two prime weaknesses. The first was that private citizens, six in number for each application, were reluctant to shoulder the considerable responsibility, by way of expense and publicity, of initiating investigations. Secondly, there was no individual or body to provide continuity in the administration of the legislation. A board was constituted on an ad hoc basis. Upon completion of the investigation and the submission of a report the board ceased to function. There was consequently no machinery to determine whether the recommendations of the report were being carried out or not.

(3) 1919-1923

The rapid rise in the cost of living which was an immediate economic aftermath of the First Great War led to the appointment of a special committee of the House of Commons in 1919. The committee recommended the setting up of a permanent board to administer legislation dealing with trade combinations and monopolies as well as with profiteering and hoarding.

The consequent legislation set up a permanent board—the Board of Commerce—consisting of three commissioners. The Board was charged with the administration of the Combines and Fair Prices Act. Under this Act the function of the Board was two-fold. The first was the investigation and restraining of combinations, monopolies, trusts and mergers constituting a combine and the second, control over the withholding of and the enhancement of prices of, commodities.

Under the First Part of the Act, the Board could begin an inquiry either upon its own initiative or upon a formal application made to it by one person. It had extensive powers of investigation and at the conclusion of its proceedings, could make orders requiring persons to cease and desist from any practices found to be contrary to the Act. The Act defined combine as one which, in the opinion of the Board, operated or was likely to operate to the detriment or against the interest of the public and was deemed to include:

'(a) mergers, trusts and monopolies, so called, and,

(b) the relation resulting from the purchase, lease or other acquisition by any person of any control over or interest in the whole or part of the business of any other person, and,

(c) any actual or tacit contract, agreement, arrangement or combination which has or is designed to have the effect of (1) limiting facilities for transporting, producing, manufacturing, supplying, storing or dealing; or (2) preventing, limiting or lessening manufacture or production; or (3) fixing a common price, or a resale price, or a common rental, or a common cost of storage or transportation, or enhancing the price, rental or cost of article, rental, storage or transportation; or (4) preventing or lessening competition in, or substantially controlling, within any particular district, or generally, production, manufacture, purchase, barter, sale, transportation, insurance or supply; or (5) otherwise restraining of injuring commerce.'

A person who failed to obey an order of the Board was guilty of an indictable offence and the Board might remit a case to the Attorney-General of a province for prosecution.

The Act also carried forward the tariff and patent provisions that had been included in the Combines Investigation Act of 1910.

The Act in its Second Part prohibited hoarding and profiteering. The Board was empowered and directed to inquire into and to restrain and prohibit any breach or non-observance of the Act, the making of unfair profits, and all such practices with respect to the holding or disposition of the necessaries of life, as, in the opinion of the Board, were calculated to enhance their cost or price.

It is to be observed that the legislation overcame two of the principal defects of the Act of 1910, namely the absence of a continuing enforcement authority and the initiation of investigations only on the application of interested private individuals.

The Board entered upon an active life which, however, was cut short when its powers were called in question in a constitutional reference to the courts in 1920. After an equal division of judicial opinion in the Supreme Court of Canada, the Judicial Committee of the Privy Council in 1921, on appeal, held that because of the administrative features of direct control contained in it, the legislation was beyond the competence of the Dominion to enact and it thereupon ceased to operate.

(4) 1923-1935

The Combines Investigation Act of 1923 followed. The comprehensive definition of "combine" of the legislation of 1919 was largely retained but no administrative power to order the cessation of activities was provided for. A Permanent Registrar was to administer the Act; to him, either upon formal application of six persons, or upon ministerial direction, or whenever he himself had reason to believe that a combine existed or was being formed, was committed the power to hold a preliminary inquiry. If after the preliminary inquiry the Registrar concluded or the Minister decided that a formal investigation was necessary, such investigation was conducted by the Registrar or by a commissioner appointed ad hoc.

At the conclusion of the formal investigation a report was transmitted to the Minister and in the case of a commissioner's report had to be made public within fifteen days of its receipt by the Minister except in those cases where the commissioner had recommended that its publication be withheld, in which event the Minister might exercise his discretion as to publication of the report either in whole or in part.

The Act made it a criminal offence to be a party or privy to or knowingly to assist in the formation or operation of a combine. A person found guilty of an offence was liable to a penalty not exceeding $10,000 or two years imprisonment, in the case of individuals, and a penalty not exceeding $25,000 in the case of corporations.

The earlier provisions relating to executive action in respect of tariffs and judicial revocation of patent rights were continued in the new legislation.

The legislation of 1923 after a number of investigations had been held under it in turn came under challenge on constitutional grounds. On a reference as to the validity both of the Combines Investigation Act and section 498 of the Criminal Code, the Judicial Committee of the Privy Council in 1931 held, affirming a judgment to the same effect by the Supreme Court of Canada, the enactments to be within the powers of the Federal Parliament as being legislation in relation to criminal law.

(5) 1935-1951

In 1935, consequent upon a review of combines legislation as part of a larger inquiry into price spreads and trade practices generally, the Dominion Trade and Industry Commission Act of that year created a three-man commission (the members of the existing Tariff Board constituted, under the Act, the commission) to which the administration of the Combines Investigation Act, including the power to initiate and conduct investigations, was transferred.

The existing provisions for investigation and report accordingly continued; but the new Act also empowered the Commission if it found, as the result of an investigation under the Combines Investigation Act, that wasteful or demoralizing competition existed in an industry, and that agreements among persons in the industry to modify competition would not unduly restrain trade or operate against the public interest, to recommend approval of such agreements to the Governor in Council. It could also recommend approval where, in its opinion, existing agreements prevented wasteful or demoralizing competition and did not operate against the public interest. The Governor in Council, if of opinion that the conclusions of the Commission were well founded, could approve the agreements and make regulations requiring the Commission to keep a check on the effect of the agreements.

The Commission had the power to require any persons engaged in the industry subject to an approved agreement to furnish full information relating to the operations of the industry, and, on its own motion and in its absolute discretion, could recommend to the Governor in Council that approval of an agreement should be withdrawn.

Approval of an agreement was a bar to prosecution under the Combines Investigation Act or sections 498 or 498A of the Criminal Code except in cases where the Commission gave its consent to such a prosecution.

The Commission could also investigate complaints of unfair trade practices and forward the complaint and any evidence in support thereof to the Attorney-General of Canada with a recommendation for prosecution if it appeared that any federal law prohibiting unfair trade practices had been violated. For the purposes of prosecution, a Director of Public Prosecutions, appointed under the Act, had the conduct of federal prosecutions and could assist provincial authorities when they instituted proceedings in trade practice cases, besides being available to assist the Commission with investigations into complaints.

The Commission could in addition hold trade practice conferences attended by persons engaged in a particular industry for the purpose of considering the trade practices in that industry and determining which were unfair or undesirable in the interest of the industry and of the public. Such conferences could be called by the Commission on the direction of the Governor in Council, at the request of representative persons engaged in the industry, or on its own motion. The Commission could make public the general opinion of the conference or of the Commission as to any trade practice considered to be unfair or undesirable.

The Commission was authorized to co-operate with boards of trade and chambers of commerce in connection with any commercial arbitration. On the direction of the Governor in Council it could conduct general economic studies.

A constitutional reference to the Supreme Court instituted shortly after the Act was passed established that the authority conferred on the Commission by section 14 of the Act to approve agreements limiting competition was beyond federal legislative power. The investigatory provisions were untouched by the decision. Though in form the Board continued to have legal existence until 1949 and from 1937 to 1946 shared jurisdiction over combines with the

Commissioner under the Combines Investigation Act, in point of fact the Board did not exercise any functions in respect of the Combines Investigation Act. Since 1946 both legally and in fact the Commissioner has been alone in his position as officer in charge of the Act.

The principal change made by the legislation of 1937 was to restore the administration of the Combines Investigation Act to a single official. The office of the Registrar, which had existed since 1923, was abolished and that of a Commissioner substituted. The machinery for the appointment of special, or ad hoc, commissioners was retained. The provision requiring the publication of reports now included the reports of the permanent Commissioner and he normally conducted most of the investigations under the Act. This was a reversal of the former practice. After 1937 the role of the special commissioner was merely to supplement the staff of the Commission when an immediate investigation was desirable and the Commissioner was already engaged in other duties."

As the Economic Council of Canada pointed out in its *Interim Report on Competition Policy* in July 1967, the 1923 Act:

"did in fact appear to include most, if not all, services in the definition of a Combine, but because most prosecutions during this period were based on the section of the Criminal Code prohibiting combinations rather than on the Combines Investigation Act, the position with regard to services was never clarified by the courts. In the process of amending the Act in 1935, the Bennett government originally introduced a bill which contained the same definition of a combine as did the 1923 Act. Following an unrecorded discussion by the Senate Banking and Commerce Committee, however, the Senate returned to the House, and the House eventually accepted an amended bill which restricted the scope of the Act to activities pertaining to articles and the price of insurance."

This report summarized the history of the legislation in the succeeding period, as shown in the excerpt which follows:

"The MacQuarrie Report and the Amendments of 1951-52

A controversy involving publicity and the suspension of anticombines activity during the Second World War, when production, the allocation of resources, and the setting of prices were subject to direct control, led to the establishment of the MacQuarrie Committee to review the legislation. In December 1948, the Combines Commissioner, Mr. G. A. McGregor, forwarded to the Minister of Justice the results of his inquiry into the flour-milling industry. In it, Mr. McGregor concluded that the leading milling companies had maintained price-fixing agreements since at least 1936, that these agreements were maintained in force during the war, and that the firms colluded in bidding for government contracts. Despite the requirements of the Act, the Report was still unpublished in October 1949. Mr. McGregor resigned on October 29, calling, in his letter of resignation, for 'an even stronger statute than the Act in its present form, and a clear statement of government policy with respect to its enforcement'. Tabled in the House of Commons on November 7, the flour-milling report raised, among other things, the issue of an industry being condemned for carrying out policies sanctioned by the Wartime Prices and Trade Board during the war and tacitly allowed by the government in the subsequent period of decontrol.

Faced with a barrage of criticism for its handling of the matter, the Government in 1950 appointed the MacQuarrie Committee to study the purposes and methods of the Combines Investigation Act and related Canadian statutes as well as those of other countries. The Committee was instructed to recommend any amendments desirable to make the Combines Investigation Act 'a more effective instrument for the encouraging and safeguarding of our free economy'.

After hearing representations from interested parties and conducting studies of its own, the Committee issued its Report in two parts. In response to the Government's specific request for opinions on resale price maintenance, an Interim Report, dated October 1951, dealt exclusively with this matter. The Committee assessed this practice against two standards: the desirability of a free economy and the need for economic efficiency. It concluded that resale price maintenance on the growing scale then practised was not justified. The Committee recommended that it should be made an offence for a manufacturer or other supplier:

1. To recommend or prescribe minimum resale prices for his product;
2. To refuse to sell, to withdraw a franchise or to take any other form of action as a means of enforcing minimum resale prices.

In connection with its examination of resale price maintenance, the Committee looked also at 'loss-leader' selling. The latter practice, though condemned as monopolistic and not conducive to the general welfare of the public, was not viewed as presenting any immediate danger in the then current period of inflation and relative scarcity.

The Interim Report was considered by Parliament in December 1951, and an amendment to the Combines Investigation Act was passed which made it an offence to fix minimum resale prices, although suggested resale prices were still allowed.

The final Report of the Committee was issued in March 1952. Despite strong statements about the need for public policies in support of competition to be "adaptable to complex and rapidly changing problems", the Committee refrained from recommending any substantial change in the concept or direction of the combines law. One impediment to change was the constitutional problem. The Committee stated that publicity and criminal prosecution had been the principal means used against monopolies, 'mainly because the legislation has been based on the federal power over criminal law and has been upheld by the courts on this ground'. Recognition was given to 'another view' to the effect that the federal power over trade and commerce would give Parliament complete jurisdiction in monopoly situations, at least those involving international and interprovincial trade. But, because neither of these views has been sanctioned by judicial decision, the Committee preferred to leave the question of extending the scope of the legislation to some future time. As the Report stated: 'Our recommendations are directed to the strengthening and improving of the procedures, organization and remedies laid down in the Act rather than to revolutionizing them.'

The chief recommendation of the MacQuarrie Committee was in regard to administration. The Committee proposed that there be a separation of function between investigation and research on the one hand and appraisal and report on the other. The Committee had received representations from the business community that the existing Commissioner was placed in the position of both prosecutor and judge. To effect a separation, the Committee recommended that the duties of the Commissioner be divided and assigned to two separate agencies: an agency for investigation and research, and a board for appraisal and report. The amendments to the Combines Investigation Act introduced in 1952 provided for a Director of Investigation and Research and for a Restrictive Trade Practices Commission consisting of not more than three members appointed by Governor in Council. The Director could initiate inquiries, but the powers needed to pursue an inquiry effectively—seizure of documents, oral examination of witnesses, and orders for written returns—could only be exercised after authorization by a member of the Commission. The Commission was to hear and appraise all evidence presented to it by the investigation and research agency as well as such other evidence as was necessary to ensure that persons under investigation had full opportunity to be heard.

The Committee recommended that the board report to the Minister, that the public report be retained for its deterrent effect, and that the scope of the Report be widened. The Committee was also concerned about the various areas of government policy which impinged on competition policy:

> Numerous other aspects of the Federal Government policy may greatly contribute to strengthen or weaken monopoly power. Money lending, currency management, negotiation of international trade agreements, import and export controls, public works, taxation, technological research may all directly or indirectly affect the interests of particular business groups. The way our legislation on banking, insurance companies and corporations is framed and administered may also greatly affect the monopolistic picture of our industry.

To effect the desired co-ordination of government policy, the Committee recommended, first, that administrative procedures be designed to ensure close liaison between the proposed board and other government departments whose activities might affect the competitive structure of the economy, and secondly, that the board should be empowered to recommend any legislative or administrative change within the competence of Parliament if 'such change could be used as an effective remedy to correct an undesirable monopolistic situation or practice'. Although no administrative procedures to ensure a greater degree of liaison were in fact established, the legislation of 1952 did direct that the report of the Restrictive Trade Practices Commission 'review the evidence and material, appraise the effect on the public interest of arrangements and practices disclosed in the evidence and contain recommendations as to the application of remedies provided in this Act or other remedies'.

With regard to offences, the Committee proposed no new prohibitions to strengthen the merger or monopoly provisions in the Act or to curb discriminatory or injurious monopolistic practices. In the body of the Report, discriminatory practices were defined to include quantitative price discrimination (via unjustified quantity discounts) and spatial forms of price discrimination such as freight equalization and freight allowance, and zoning of basing-point price systems: Other more injurious practices were said to be 'derogatory and harassing practices, price wars, "loss leaders", threats and spreading of false information'. The Government followed the advice of the Committee and, in the legislation of 1952, left the sections dealing with offences virtually unchanged, except that the provision relating to price discrimination was amended so as to prohibit only the systematic practice of price discrimination rather than any single act. The Committee did suggest that the Minister refer the loss-leader practice for review by the proposed new investigation and research agency and by the new board, but the subsequent study by these bodies led to no recommendations for changes in the Act.

The legislation of 1952 also incorporated the Committee's principal recommendation regarding remedies: that existing statutory limits on fines should be abolished and that the fine in each case should be at the discretion of the court. The Committee also suggested further use of supplementary judicial remedies such as the judicial restraining order. Accordingly, a provision was inserted in the Act authorizing the court to issue an order prohibiting the repetition or continuation of an offence. In a conviction under the merger, trust or monopoly clause, the court was empowered to order dissolution of the merger or monopoly 'in such manner as the court directs'.

The Committee's recommendation that research into monopolistic situations and practices should become 'one of the most important assignments of the investigation and research agency' led to the introduction of a new section in the Act. Section 42 provided that the Director of Investigation and Research, on his own initiative, or on direction from the Minister, or at the instance of the Commission, should carry out an investigation of monopolistic situations or restraint of trade in relation to any commodity that might be the subject of trade or commerce. Such a 'general inquiry' would be dealt with in the same manner as an inquiry involving a possible infraction of the law. In line with the suggestion of the Committee, the publication of the results of such a general inquiry should await subsequent review of the evidence by the Commission which should then forward the report to the Minister for publication. Since 1952, five such reports have been published, relating to: loss-leader selling; discriminatory pricing practices in the grocery trade; automobile insurance; drugs; and tires, batteries and accessories sold through service stations.

The 1960 Amendments

Only in 1960, when further amendments were introduced into the combines law, did the Government follow the MacQuarrie Committee's recommendation that the Criminal Code provision relating to combinations be brought into the Combines Investigation Act. In this process, the definition of 'combine' was dropped, the word 'trust' was eliminated, and separate provisions were enacted defining mergers and monopolies and making them offences only where they were likely to be, or to operate, 'to the detriment or against the interest of the public'.

In addition, Parliament attached certain provisions to the combination or conspiracy section of the Combines Investigation Act. In a rather unusual turn of phrase, one of the new provisions directed that 'the court shall not convict the accused if the conspiracy, combination, agreement or arrangement relates only to one or more' of certain matters, including exchange of statistics, defining of trade terms, co-operation in research and development, or restriction of advertising, or some other unobjectionable activity. Nevertheless, by a second new provision, Parliament made it plain that such an agreement must not be used as a device for breaching the fundamental prohibition of combinations or conspiracies.

A further new provision related to export agreements. Parliament provided that 'the court shall not convict the accused if the conspiracy, combination, agreement or arrangement relates only to the export of articles from Canada'. A qualification was added, however, to the effect that the provision does not apply if the agreement reduces the volume of exports of an article, works to the specific detriment of Canadian exporters or would-be exporters, or lessens competition unduly in the domestic market.

The section banning resale price maintenance was also amended. The law passed in 1952 included a provision making it an offence for a supplier to refuse to sell to a dealer who would not maintain the supplier's prices. In 1960, Parliament provided a group of defences for suppliers charged with refusing to sell. Henceforth no inference unfavourable to the accused could be drawn if he satisfied the court that 'he and any one upon whose report he depended had reasonable cause to believe and did believe' that the buyer was using the goods as loss leaders, was making a practice of misleading advertising in regard to such articles, or was not providing the level of servicing that his customers might reasonably expect. While Parliament in this amendment obviously viewed these practices with disfavour, it did not go so far as to prohibit them directly.

Parliament did, however, insert in the Act a provision to outlaw misrepresentation of the ordinary price of an article ('misleading price advertising'). Another new prohibition banned discriminatory promotional allowances. This latter provision had the twofold purpose of preventing discrimination in distribution and of limiting promotional expenditures.

Also in 1960, the prohibition of price discrimination on a territorial basis was strengthened by making it illegal for a seller to engage in a policy of selling articles in any area at lower prices than he exacted elsewhere in Canada if the effect or tendency or design was to substantially lessen competition or eliminate a competitor.

A change was also introduced in the procedure for prosecutions under the Act. Although proceedings in any case under the Act could continue to be launched in any superior court of criminal jurisdiction, they could henceforth also be instituted by the Attorney General of Canada in the Exchequer Court of Canada provided that all the accused consented to this. (An exception to this procedure was made for misleading price advertising, which offence was made punishable on summary conviction.) The new procedure had the advantage of by-passing intermediate appeal and of moving cautiously in the direction of a single, specialized court to hear competition policy cases.

In addition, in 1960 the scope of the injunction provision was extended to grant the courts power to dissolve an offending merger or monopoly without the necessity of first obtaining a conviction." (pp. 56-63)

At the end of 1965 the Minister responsible for the administration of the Combines Investigation Act became the President of the Privy Council, in place of the Minister of Justice, in whom it had been vested since 1946. Then in June, 1966 the Government Organization Act was proclaimed, setting up the Department of the Registrar General and making its Minister responsible for legislation on combines, mergers, monopolies and restraint of trade. The annual report under the Combines Investigation Act for 1967, summarized events as follows:

"On July 22, 1966 the President of the Privy Council announced that the Government has requested the Economic Council of Canada to undertake a study of certain important aspects of the responsibilities of the Registrar General of Canada and his department under the Government Organization Act, 1966 which at the time was awaiting proclamation.

The terms of reference are as follows:

'... in the light of the Government's long-term economic objectives, to study and advise regarding:

(a) the interests of the consumer particularly as they relate to the functions of the Department of the Registrar General;
(b) combines, mergers, monopolies and restraint of trade;
(c) patents, trade marks, copyrights and registered industrial designs.'

The Minister recalled that on May 24, 1966 on second reading of the Government Organization Bill, the Prime Minister informed the House of the Government's intention to ask the Economic Council of Canada to look at the field of consumer affairs along with some of the other functions now to be undertaken by the Registrar General of Canada under the new legislation with a view to providing advice as to the course of action that seems best suited to meeting the needs of the Canadian people and the Canadian economy in the consumer field.

The Minister stated that the Government has decided that as part of this study, the whole question of combines, mergers, monopolies and restraint of trade should be referred to the Economic Council for a fundamental review in the light of current and prospective needs of the Canadian economy; and furthermore, that another aspect of the work of the new department, namely, patents, trade marks, copyrights and registered industrial designs, should also be included in the fundamental economic study to be undertaken by the Council.

The Economic Council will be free to make interim reports on such particular aspects of the study as the Council deems appropriate to enable the Government to consider taking initial steps consistent with the general review.

With particular reference to proposals for amendments to the Combines Investigation Act that have been the subject of discussion in Parliament and the press, and of submissions by individuals and groups, the Minister stated that it is most important that this legislation should not be amended piecemeal. Any amendments to the legislation ought to be in keeping with its fundamental philosophy and in furtherance of it. When consideration is being given to reviewing the general structure and philosophy of the Act, it would be very unwise to enact immediate temporary and piecemeal amendments to correct particular situations. At a time when a general review is in contemplation, such particular measures ought to be taken up and considered in the context of the whole review and any revision that may take place in the light of the findings and recommendations of the Economic Council."

(Director's 1967 report, pp. 8-9)

On December 21, 1967, the name of the Department was changed to the Department of Consumer and Corporate Affairs, and its Minister continued to have responsibility for combines, mergers, monopolies and restraint of trade. Accordingly it was to this Minister that the task fell of considering and implementing reports of the Economic Council on consumer affairs and competition policy. The first of these reports was published in 1967 and following one of its recommendations, section 306 of the Criminal Code was repealed and re-enacted as section 33D of the Combines Investigation Act by The Criminal Law Amendment Act 1968-69. This new section, dealing with false and misleading advertising was proclaimed in force on July 31, 1969.

The second such report was the Interim Report on Competition Policy, July 1969. It was summarized in the Council's press release of August 7, 1969, which is quoted below:

"The Economic Council of Canada today recommended a revised approach to anticombines or competition policy, based on a mixture of criminal and civil law and with the single clear objective of furthering the interest of the Canadian consumer in an efficiently working economy.

The Council's proposals would extend the scope of competition policy to all commercial activities including services such as doctors and lawyers, professional sports, and other business and personal services. Also included would be the activities of banks and the 'unregulated activities of "regulated industries"'...

Two basic sets of recommendations are made:

1. Retained in the criminal law—but clarified where necessary, well publicized, vigorously enforced, and backed up by fines 'large enough to hurt' as well as by imprisonment—would be prohibitions on five practices judged by the Council to be 'rarely if ever productive of any substantial public benefit':

—collusion between competitors to fix prices (including bid-rigging on tenders);

—collusion between competitors to allocate markets (the Council noted that this prohibition might have to be qualified so as to allow such practices as drug stores arranging among themselves for certain stores to open on Sundays);

—collusion between competitors to prevent the entry into markets of new competitors or the expansion of existing competition;

—resale price maintenance (for example, cases in which a supplier of a product tries to force a retailer to sell it at a specified price or minimum price); and

—untrue, deceptive or misleading advertising.

2. Other criminal offences now in the Combines Investigation Act—such as its 'all but inoperative' provisions on mergers and monopolies—would be replaced by new proposals to create an independent Competitive Practices Tribunal that would operate in a civil law area in deciding on the basis of

economic analysis whether certain mergers and other business practices (including some not effectively covered by the present Combines Investigation Act) were in the public interest in the sense that they promoted economic efficiency, higher real incomes and consumer welfare.

The tribunal, with a high calibre membership and staff experienced in economics as well as business and law, would have the power to break up particular mergers or halt harmful business practices by issuing interim and final injunctions. It could also recommend that the government apply other remedies, including the withdrawal of tariff protection, licences to import duty-free or—as a last resort in extreme cases of dominance or monopoly—the application of direct regulations.

In addition to the power of general inquiry, the tribunal would also have the authority to 'register', and thus exempt from the ordinary application of competition policy, intercompany agreements to improve the competitive position of Canadian goods in export markets or—provided such agreements were found to be in the public interest, with savings likely to be passed on to consumers—agreements to specialize in certain products and thus achieve longer production runs and lower unit costs.

In proposing the creation of a civil tribunal, the Economic Council has assumed that it would prove constitutionally possible for the federal government to establish such a body, perhaps under the federal power to regulate trade and commerce. The Council comments:

> There can be no certainty concerning this matter until the courts have had an opportunity to pronounce upon it, but on the basis of highly competent advice, we are sufficiently persuaded both of the need for civil legislation and of the improved prospects for obtaining it that we are prepared to make this assumption.

In this connection, the Council drew special attention in an Appendix to its report to the high degree of economic interdependence that has developed between different areas in the country's complex, modern economic system.

The Council emphasized that it was *not* advocating exclusive federal occupancy of the field of competition policy in Canada. A provincial role would be 'a most welcome development'. But the federal presence is 'clearly indispensable' because a large part of Canadian economic activity crosses provincial and international boundaries and would be impossible to subject effectively to any provincial competition policy.

No specific provision is made in the Council's recommendations for dealing with monopoly and dominant-firm situations as such. Thus there would be no specific barrier to achievement of market dominance or monopoly through internal company expansion or superior efficiency. But if it was achieved through mergers or 'exclusionary' trade practices it would be open to examination and the imposition or recommendation of remedies by the tribunal. Also, the tribunal's assessment of particular mergers and trade practices would be affected by whether a monopoly or dominant firm was involved. And the tribunal would have a power of general inquiry to examine any existing monopoly or other undesirable situation and recommend to the government how it could be reduced or ended.

Too little recent information and analysis is available on international cartels and the operations of large international companies to make firm statements or proposals, the Council said, although it added that there is information suggesting the persistence of noteworthy international cartels. It suggested that the Department of Consumer and Corporate Affairs try to discover as much as possible about the effects on Canada of existing international cartels.

Large international corporations (many of them based in the United States) have potentials for both good and ill, the Council noted. One projection prepared for the Council is that by the latter 1980's the total output of the non-Communist world may be about equally divided between international corporations, other U.S. industry, and industry in all other countries combined. 'This would indeed seem to imply great market power, and if serious abuses of that power took place, this could well be the circumstance that called into being a supranational agency in the field of competition policy', the Council said.

Touchstone of the Council's whole approach to competition policy is the goal of economic efficiency. Such a single objective, clearly stated, would be new to Canadian competition policy. In part at least, existing policies reflect other considerations entertained by legislators in the past such as the desire to redistribute income and diffuse economic power, sympathy for the plight of small business, suspicion of big business, and concern for the fairness of competitive behaviour. The Council believes that a competition policy concentrated solely on the efficiency objective is likely to be applied more consistently and effectively. Such a policy may well also make some contribution towards the redistribution of income and the diffusion of economic power; but the contribution is likely to be a small one, and there exist more powerful policy instruments, such as tax and transfer payment policies, for attaining such goals to the extent that they are thought to be desirable.

The significance of the economic-efficiency objective for competition policy is indicated in this statement by the Council:

> . . . it may be explained by way of example that a competition policy that assigned equal importance to maximizing economic efficiency and diffusing economic power would be likely on occasion to run into a conflict of goals. It is a stern reality of a competitive market system that from time to time some competitors go to the wall. If this occurs mainly because of predatory or exclusionary tactics practised by other competitors, there may well be a good case for competition policy to intervene. But if the squeezing out of competitors appears to be part of a process likely to produce increased

efficiency and lower costs and prices (if, for instance, a number of small corner stores are being forced out of business by the entry of new, low-cost mass distributors) then a dilemma is faced. The economic efficiency goal might well suggest letting the process work itself out; the goal of diffusing economic power would call for intervention. By recommending that efficiency be the sole objective of competition policy, we are in effect saying that no individual competitor, corporate or otherwise, has an inherent right to stay in business.

The Council's proposal to extend competition policy to services—and indeed its whole approach—is based on this view:

In the first place, we have taken the view that the general set of competition policy should be one that aims at the achievement of efficient resource use in the Canadian economy. Second, we believe that some form of social control should be exerted over all commercial activities, and that over the greater part of the Canadian economy, efficient resource use will be more readily brought about through policies that maximize the opportunities for the free play of competitive market forces. The use of other forms of social control, namely, government regulation and government ownership, should be brought to bear only on those activities where monopolistic tendencies have all but eliminated competitive market responses, or where the protection of the consumer interest in matters such as health, safety, fraud, disclosure and standardization, among others, requires the implementation of explicit government regulations.

The present Combines Investigation Act is limited largely to goods-producing and goods-distributing activities. In effect it covers industries that account for about half of Canada's total output—forestry, fishing, mining, manufacturing, construction, retailing and wholesaling, insurance, and hotels and restaurants.

Industries largely exempt from the Act are in two groups. In one are agriculture and those industries in which certain activities of interest for competition policy are directly regulated—transportation companies, radio and TV broadcasting, telephones, and power and gas utilities. In the other are banks and other financial institutions together with real estate, personal services (including the medical and legal professions), business management services, and others.

Exclusion of certain services from competition policy is an anomaly, the Council said. Service industries now employ over half the Canadian labour force. Of all 22 nations in the Organization for Economic Co-operation and Development (OECD), only Canada and Ireland confine their competition policy to the goods industries.

'There is, in our view, enough evidence pointing to the existence in the service sector of anti-competitive practices detrimental to the public interest to lead to the conclusion that the continued exemption of parts of this sector from competition policy cannot be justified,' the Council said.

In recommending that its proposed competition policy apply to 'all commercial activities', including the 'unregulated activities of "regulated industries" ', the Council noted that some industries (for example, the telecommunications industry) are regulated only in certain parts of their operations.

Similarly, the banks and other financial institutions are subject to many kinds of legislation and control, but in most cases these are aimed at stability and solvency rather than competition. The Council's recommendations would make it possible, where considerations of monetary policy do not intervene, to 'strike down practices in the financial area that are inimical to the public interest in competition and efficiency'.

Dealing with the professions, the Council suggested that the past reluctance to extend the anticombines legislation to service industries 'may have stemmed partly from an unwillingness to interfere with the time-honoured custom of allowing professional bodies to fix their own fees and control entry into their professions'.

However, emergence of Medicare and other developments had drawn public attention to free-setting and other practices of professional bodies, and 'it has become highly appropriate to consider anew why these practices should not be subject to some suitably structured system of checks and balances'.

The Council said there is a need for such a system, but it could take the form of competition policy, collective bargaining (in cases where there was an adequate 'countervailing power' across the bargaining table), or direct regulation—or some combination of these.

In connection with fee-setting, the Council said one solution might be to allow the professions to 'suggest' rates but to make any attempt to enforce these rates subject to the ban on price-fixing. 'Many professions do not now enforce their tariffs; in those that do, there is some reason to believe that many individual members would welcome the freedom to charge below the suggested scale.'

The Council's basic recommendation in this area:

'As a general rule, arrangements for determining the remuneration of self-employed professional and other groups should be subject to competition policy. Where, however, a group prefers a collective-bargaining or public-regulatory arrangement, and where conditions are such that this arrangement constitutes an adequate check-and-balance system, it would be in order to grant an exemption from competition policy in respect of those matters specifically covered by the alternative arrangement.'

As for licensing, the Council said it is obviously in the public interest to have quality standards in such professions as medicine and law closely watched, and the members of those professions are best able to do the job.

'But there is also a public interest in ensuring that the power to regulate the quality of professional services is not used in an unduly restrictive way, and that the size of likely future needs for professional services be kept in mind. This aspect of the public interest is all the more relevant in an age when a large proportion of the cost of professional training is a charge on the general taxpayer.'

For this purpose the Council recommended that lay members should be appointed to the governing bodies of self-governing professions 'to represent consumers' interests and to check any tendency towards the exercise of power in the interests of the profession rather than that of the public'."

Immediately after the release of the report of the Economic Council of Canada, intensive work was undertaken in the Department of Consumer and Corporate Affairs to produce a bill that would adopt its recommendations and also represent a complete modern competition policy. In June 1971, this work was introduced for first reading by the then Minister, Hon. Ron Basford, as Bill C-256, the Competition Act. The bill was introduced with a volume of explanatory notes, press briefings and a request to all interested parties to make known their views, and a series of speeches and seminars was inaugurated. The Minister made it clear that he did not intend to proceed with the legislation during the session but wished it to become the subject of a public debate with a view to perfecting the drafting. He also indicated that there would be examination by Parliamentary Committees which he thought would hold hearings and receive representations from all interested parties. A broad summary of the proposed legislation follows.

Bill C-256 set up a series of criminal prohibitions with respect to restrictive practices made illegal *per se* because they are judged to be seldom, if ever, productive of any substantial public benefit. It proposed the establishment of a Competitive Practices Tribunal which would have power to examine and adjudicate upon mergers, specialization and export agreements, and specified trade practices brought before it by the enforcement authorities and interested parties. This Tribunal would deal with those aspects of trade restrictions deemed to be capable of operating either to the detriment or in the interest of the public, depending upon the surrounding facts. It would be required to follow statutory criteria in making its determinations. The basic philosophy of these criteria, as recommended by the Economic Council of Canada is that normally competition will maximize the efficiency of the economy. Where competition has to be sacrificed to bring about a scale of production large enough to ensure efficiency, then the measures required ought to be carefully examined to ensure that the public interest is well served.

The Bill provided for appointment of an official known as the Commissoner who would be charged with responsibility for commencing investigations, of representing the public interest before the Tribunal, and other statutory duties.

Whereas the Combines Investigation Act is generally confined to commodities, Bill C-256 covered services as well, but with a variety of exemptions where valid legislation regulating professions and industries is in effect.

PER SE OFFENCES: Section 16 listed ten types of agreements or arrangements subject to outright criminal prohibition; price fixing; allocation of markets; lessening or limiting production or supply; lessening or limiting quality, grades or kinds of products; lessening or limiting facilities for production or distribution; lessening or limiting channels of distribution; preventing market entry or expansion; causing withdrawal from a market; and boycotts against buyers or sellers. The intent of section 16 was to state, with more certainty than does the current Combines Investigation Act, the law relating to restrictive agreements.

In addition to these prohibited agreements, sections 17 to 26 inclusive prohibited: wilful monopolization; resale price maintenance; agreements unduly limiting opportunities for professional or amateur athletes; misleading advertising; referral selling; bait and switch selling; and selling at higher than an advertised price. In addition they established conditions for: pyramid selling; the use in advertising of performance and related tests, testimonials, games, lotteries and promotions.

The removal of the undueness test from section 16 on illegal agreements (which in the Combines Investigation Act determines whether or not a restrictive agreement is illegal) was intended to meet public criticism that the Combines Investigation Act was uncertain. In lieu thereof, the Bill specified numerous exemptions from section 16 for such things as registered specialization and export agreements, industries regulated by public bodies, arrangements between related companies, and so forth.

COMPETITIVE PRACTICES TRIBUNAL: The Bill provided for a Competitive Practices Tribunal with seven members knowledgeable in economics, business, law and public affairs. Its main functions would have been: to review and approve applications for registered export and specialization agreements, and accept registration of franchise agreements; to maintain a register of foreign and domestic mergers, and approve or prohibit such mergers as are challenged according to criteria in the Act; to consider and prohibit certain interlocking directorates; to hear evidence concerning price discrimination, promotional allowances, tied sales, directed selling, exclusive dealing or reciprocal buying, and make orders respecting such trade practices as provided in the Act; to hold hearings (on its own initiative or when requested by the Minister) into any matter within its jurisdiction and subsequently to publish guidance rules for the information of parties concerned giving the Tribunal's views on the matter examined; to conduct general enquiries, when requested by the Minister, into any matter relevant to the policy and objectives of the Act; to give advance rulings on what its position would be concerning a merger or proposed merger, or any other matter within its jurisdiction, at proceedings initiated before the Tribinal by the parties involved or the Commissioner. Such advance rulings would be binding on the Tribunal; to ensure that foreign laws, decrees or government directives will not operate in Canada contrary to Canadian competition policy.

The sections dealing with registered agreements would have required the Tribunal to register a specialization or export agreement which has been filed, unless challenged by the Commissioner, or unless the Tribunal considered that the public interest demands a hearing. It would approve the registration after a hearing unless it decided that the agreement was not in the public interest, as determined by the criteria specified in the Act.

Under the merger provisions a registration would have provided notice that a merger had taken place or was planned. If the merger were challenged by the Commissioner the Tribunal must hold hearings and make a decision, otherwise there would be no hearing. Only mergers involving companies with gross assets or gross annual revenue of $5 million or more, and those mergers where effective control of a Canadian company is acquired by foreign-controlled interests, would have been registered with the Tribunal.

The price discrimination section, among other things, would have outlawed "volume discounts".

SERVICES: The Bill would have brought services under the Act and included them in all relevant contexts. However, there were certain exemptions in respect of certain services. Specific exemptions were contained in section 89 for collective bargaining activities authorized under federal or provincial labour laws. Section 92 exempted "regulated industries" from the outright prohibitions of the Act, and from the provisions governing restrictive trade practices to the extent that the activities of the industry were expressly required to be supervised and regulated on a continuing basis by a public body charged with protecting the public interest. Section 92(2) provided a similar exemption to members of a group which is declared in a federal or provincial statute to be a profession or trade for the purposes of this Act, and which is regulated by a body expressly charged with supervising and regulating it in the public interest.

Exemptions were provided to general insurance companies and investment dealers in recognition of circumstances peculiar to these two industries. General insurance companies would have been allowed to agree on certain specified matters, and would have been allowed the advantage of a broader definition of "joint ventures" to allow agreements among companies to share a particular insurance risk designated as a special class of risk by the Tribunal, and to allow the formation of risk-sharing pools. Investment dealers would have been exempted from the general prohibitions to permit the continued use of syndicates to give broad distribution to securities and to permit orderly marketing during the initial selling phase.

Notes

*Canada, Department of Consumer and Corporate Affairs, *Proposals for a New Competition Policy for Canada: First Stage* (Bill C-227, November 1973, Second edition), pp. 1A-45A (reproduced by permission of Information Canada).

25 Submission to the Royal Commission on Corporate Concentration *

Bell Canada

I. Introduction

Bell Canada welcomes the opportunity to submit this brief to the Royal Commission on Corporate Concentration for a number of reasons. As a large privately owned company operating in a regulated sector of the Canadian economy, we would like to increase public awareness of the outstanding contribution of Bell Canada in particular, and regulated utilities in general, to Canada's social and economic progress. We also recognize that the onerous task given the Commission calls for responsive, considered and in-depth dialogue between the Commission and the business community. Finally, we wish to contribute to a process which could ultimately bring about important recommendations affecting the viability, size and nature of the telecommunications industry in Canada.

This brief is a response to the broad terms of reference of the Commission, viz:

> to inquire into, report on, and make recommendations concerning:
> (a) the nature and role of major concentrations of corporate power in Canada;
> (b) the economic and social implications for the public interest of such concentrations; and
> (c) whether safeguards exist or may be required to protect the public interest in the presence of such concentrations.

II. Nature and Role of Bell Canada

Among the primary determinants of the level of economic and social development of a country are its systems of transportation and communication. It is almost axiomatic that the more extensive the availability of the services and the more modern and efficient they are, the greater will be the potential for growth, for the creation of new jobs and for individual freedom of choice in the national social structure.

First established as a legal entity by a Special Act of the Parliament of Canada in 1880, Bell Canada initially supplied most of Canada with telephone service. Since 1909 the operations in Alberta, Manitoba and Saskatchewan have been in the hands of the respective provincial governments. Bell's telephone affiliates provide most of the telecommunications services in New Brunswick, Prince Edward Island, Nova Scotia and Newfoundland. Today, Bell Canada provides voice, visual, computer communications, radio and television transmission and other telecommunications services and facilities in Ontario, Quebec and in a large part of the remote Northwest Territories.

Bell Canada employs about 45,000 people—25,000 women and 20,000 men. The Company is the largest private employer of women in Canada.

Bell has more shareholders than any other Canadian corporation—about one-quarter of a million—and almost two-thirds of them are individuals holding less than a hundred shares each.

The Company is served by 20 directors—18 men and two women—drawn from the business and academic communities.

Throughout its 95-year history, Bell Canada has initiated projects which represent important economic and social achievements. The most important of these is the achievement of universal, low cost service on demand for the public. Another major development was the introduction, in 1958, of Direct Distance Dialing (DDD), which has since been expanded to serve even the smallest and most remote communities. Another milestone, in the same year, was the opening of the 3,900-mile Trans-Canada Microwave System—the longest such system in the world—built without a cent of government subsidy. This system made it possible to beam communications from the Atlantic to the Pacific coasts, and provided nationwide TV network capability in Canada for the first time. This Canadian network ranks in significance with our transcontinental rail system.

Bell Canada's leadership role has been strong and positive in the Trans-Canada Telephone System (TCTS), the association of major telephone companies representing each province and cooperating to provide the national telecommunications network.

By virtue of service agreements with Bell Canada, most of the principal telephone companies in Canada obtain advice and assistance on both technical and operating matters for a modest annual fee. This has had a great impact on achieving the best service standards throughout the country.

Bell Canada, in conjunction with the other members of TCTS, has been instrumental in introducing a stream of new services. In response to customer demand, service offerings such as VUcom—a series of visual display computer terminals; Dataroute—the world's first nationwide commercial digital data system; and Datapac—a universally available data network, were introduced. These, added to the basic network, add a major dimension to electronic communications opportunities for Canadian industry and institutions.

We believe that this stream of innovations is important not only for the results it has produced in Canada in terms of the quality and scope of low-cost universal telecommunications services but as an illustration of how corporate independence and maturity evolve. It is obvious that the benefits of these developments have been achieved through national corporate cooperation directed toward public interest goals and not as the result of legislative action.

The progress and growth of Bell Canada has been dependent to a large extent on the skills of its employee body. Bell Canada offers an abundance of employment opportunities to some 45,000 people—operators, installers, managers, computer programmers, engineers, accountants, salesmen, statisticians, economists, doctors, lawyers, service representatives, clerical staff and others. Paralleling the growth in the expertise of our employees has been an increased reliance on "home grown" technology. In past years there was heavy dependence on the technical, managerial and financial resources of the American Telephone and Telegraph Company in the United States. Bell Canada's current evolution to independent Canadian status has been based on decisions made years ago and implemented and developed over time.

Telecommunications is a capital-intensive business. Our capital outlays today are approaching a staggering one billion dollars a year. The large infusion of capital needed to satisfy the rising demand for our services is one of the reasons why Bell Canada has for years been able to achieve an average 6% annual total factor productivity gain, a performance unmatched in Canadian industry.

In the Fifth Annual Review, the Economic Council of Canada, commenting on the importance of productivity, said:

> a high rate of productivity growth is essential in the long run for increasing the standard of living of Canadians and more generally for consistently and simultaneously achieving all of our economic and social goals.

Bell Canada is making every effort to contribute toward the achievement of these objectives. It has grown in response to public demand for more high quality low cost service. It has been innovative and progressive in its management and use of new technologies to provide more and better service at ever decreasing real costs. Through such growth and innovation Bell Canada has made a significant contribution to the nation's economic and social welfare.

Bell Canada operates under a number of constraints which, when combined, negate any potential misuse of size, and, at times come close to negating its ability to do its job as well as it could and should be done. As a "natural monopoly" we operate in an economic environment where it is expected that in return for what might purport to be monopolistic powers, we are subject to public regulation. Regulation is expected to take the place of normal competition in a non-regulated economy. As a regulated business we are, nevertheless, competing in a free market for capital, employees, services and material. The only thing that is not obtained in a competitive atmosphere is the price for our services. Our prices are regulated but our costs are not.

Bell files tariffs with the Canadian Transport Commission (CTC) and obtains the Commission's approval for all its rates and charges. The CTC is required by law to ensure that all tolls shall be just and reasonable and shall always, under substantially similar circumstances and conditions, be charged equally to all persons. By charter, Bell has an obligation to provide service on request in its operating territory.

In addition to price constraints, Bell must receive approval from the CTC regarding the amount, terms and conditions for the issue, sale or other disposition of any part of the Company's capital stock. As well as providing monthly reports of financial and operating results, the Company must also submit to the Commission for approval all contracts, agreements and arrangements between the Company and other telecommunications carriers.

In the case of an application for a general rate increase, which may take many months to process, all facets of the Company's financial and operating results are probed in great depth both by the regulatory commission and by the intervenors at public hearings. This has been done six times since 1968 alone. Bell Canada has been the most investigated and examined company in Canada—far more so than any Crown corporation.

The last five years have seen a number of substantial social and economic changes. Consumer advocates, environmentalists, equal opportunity groups have all been very vocal, but not always with an appropriate sense of the necessary social balance between rights and responsibilities. Crusaders for clean air and water, truth in lending, in advertising and in packaging have focused attention on aspects of the quality of life, sometimes constructively, and at other times less so.

At the same time governments are playing a larger and larger role in our daily life. Federal, provincial and municipal enactments have in many cases seriously impeded the best and most efficient operation of corporations, while offering no offsetting social benefits. Lack of control of government spending has contributed to an inflation which has become the most disturbing aspect of the Canadian economy, while the role of corporate profits, as an essential ingredient for achievement of productivity advances and the achievement of social goals, has had inadequate recognition on all sides.

Because corporations have the ability to attract and retain highly competent people and to compete in international markets, it is in the public interest not only to have large corporations in Canada but also to ensure that they be financially successful. Increased recognition of the role of profits in the creation of a strong and stable economy in Canada is badly needed.

III. Bell-Northern Relationship

(a) HISTORY AND EVOLUTION

From the very beginning of the telephone industry, the need for reliable sources of equipment, built to telephone company specifications was apparent. Northern Electric Company, Limited has manufactured the bulk of Bell Canada's requirements over the years and today produces a wide range of products: telephones, business communications systems, switching equipment, wire and cable, high performance transmission systems and equipment for communications satellites. The dynamics of private enterprise and the vertical integration of research and development, manufacturing and operations have been instrumental in providing Canadians with a high quality, widely available, low-cost telecommunications system that is unsurpassed anywhere.

Although Northern Electric designs primarily for the North American network, it is a multinational company with 33 plants in five countries. Northern Telecom Inc. is the U.S. member of the family and is the first telecommunications company to be successful in penetrating the American market with Canadian designed telecommunications products. Northern's largest operation, however, is in Canada where its 24 plants in eight provinces provide for the bulk of the needs of Bell Canada and other telephone companies, except those of British Columbia Telephone Company, which buys mostly from Automatic Electric, an affiliated company.

Western Electric, the manufacturing arm of A.T. & T. in the United States, had a substantial minority ownership position in Northern Electric at its inception, and Northern's early growth and development was based largely on technology, processes and designs which originated in Western Electric. In the 1960's, when Bell Canada purchased the last of the Northern shares owned by Western Electric, Northern was already preparing to operate without the assistance of American technology which had proved valuable in the past.

The transition from dependence to independence was not achieved without difficulty and at substantial costs. Northern's earnings were not adequate at that time to finance its operations and they had to be supported by injections of new equity by Bell Canada and by debt financing. It was apparent that major changes in direction and performance were necessary if Northern were to survive in the Canadian market. It had to invest heavily in research and development to produce proprietary products which would protect its Canadian markets from foreign competitors. It had to modernize and streamline its operations, and, above all, it had to expand its market base internationally to support the heavy R & D and start-up costs of major new products.

The necessary changes have been made, and action has been taken to ensure a wide distribution of Northern shares in order to enable the company to grow profitably and to compete in world markets, rather than to be merely an inhouse supplier to Bell Canada.

Recent developments with respect to world-wide marketability of a full line of proprietary telecommunications products are very encouraging. Less encouraging is the current wage-price spiral in Canada and trends in Canadian production costs which raise grave doubts not only about Northern's ability to export from Canada to international markets, but also about its ability to retain its market share in Canada against lower-cost production from the U.S., Japan and Europe.

The inevitable consequences of Canadian telephone companies being dependent on foreign suppliers would be a loss of Canadian influence on design, a lower grade of service and fewer jobs for Canadians.

Without the parallel evolution of Bell Canada and Northern Electric to their present strength and capability through having taken full advantage of

American know-how, it is by no means certain that Canadians would own either of these companies.

Bell Canada has taken an active part in the management of Northern and in approval of its policies. Six directors of Bell are also directors of Northern Electric.

The impressive average annual 6% total factor productivity improvements achieved by Bell Canada in the last decade stem in large part from the integrated planning, jointly with its major supplier, Northern Electric, and its principal R & D source, Bell-Northern Research, of the telephone network, to ensure technological compatibility, adequacy and lowest possible cost of all elements. The accomplishment of this integrated planning better than others have done is the key to Bell Canada's position as one of the leading telecommunications companies of the world; to Northern Electric's ability to penetrate world market; and to BNR's success in attracting and retaining outstanding scientific and technical personnel.

This integration of research, development, manufacturing and operations, within a group of affiliated companies, permits a total-systems approach to telecommunications service; facilitates and speeds innovation; expedites meeting the demand for telecommunications equipment; improves quality control; and provides significant cost savings.

Notwithstanding the advantages of industry integration, there is a need for viable, smaller manufacturers in the telecommunications field. It is becoming increasingly evident that even the very largest manufacturing firms cannot hope to provide for all the needs of the telecommunications industry. Northern makes extensive use of the services of some 5,000 subcontractors in Canada and has contributed assistance to many of these firms to help them provide Canadian replacements for products previously imported.

(b) BELL-NORTHERN RESEARCH

The corporate ties between Bell Canada and Northern Electric were further strengthened when the decision was taken to increase substantially the research and development capability which had been operating as a division of Northern.

In 1970, Bell-Northern Research was established as a separate corporate entity, jointly owned by Bell Canada and Northern but with an independent presence in the deployment of skills and the arranging of priorities. Building on the base of skills and know-how acquired from the Bell Telephone Laboratories in the U.S., Bell-Northern has created the largest industrial engineering and research facility in Canada with a staff of 1,700 engineers and technicians. It has gradually changed the product-design situation from a position of virtual dependence on foreign sources of research to a position of leadership and substantial self-sufficiency.

As with other science-based industries, the impact of telecommunications technology on other technical activities is significant. Much of the technology developed at BNR is available for exploitation by others and has thus had a stimulating effect on the overall economy. It is the professional reputation of an organization such as BNR which attracts and retains skilled scientists in Canada.

BNR is the centre of technical leadership for Bell Canada and Northern Electric. It is funded by Bell and Northern for projects covering the full spectrum of telecommunications which are considered essential to provide the designs and products which will maintain a leadership position in the telecommunications field.

The ability of Bell Canada and Northern to fund R & D expenditures is entirely dependent on their financial strength. Inability to provide the funds necessary to support a strong research capability would inevitably cause deterioration to the telecommunications network in Canada with resulting higher costs for poorer service. It would also erode Northern's ability to compete in the development of internationally marketable products.

It is obvious that the success achieved to date in the integration of Bell, Northern and Bell-Northern Research is related to ownership and intercorporate coordination based on common goals and objectives. Where such conditions do not exist, as in most of Europe, for example, the opposite results are clearly evident. Service is poorer and its cost to the user is far higher than in Canada.

Bell Canada believes that it has been demonstrated beyond doubt that the most economic way of providing the best possible telecommunications service at the lowest possible cost, consistent with fair treatment for the employees and for the investors, is through the close correlation of research, manufacturing and operations.

This was recognized by the Economic Council of Canada in their Fifth Annual Review in commenting on the importance of research to economic growth and improved living standards:

> R & D by itself may add nothing to economic growth. It is the innovation process—beginning when management decides to move R & D into engineering, design and all the succeeding stages—which brings new products, processes and services into use, and which contributes to growth.

BNR could not exist without an innovative Bell Canada and an aggressive, international Northern Electric.

(c) IMPORTANCE OF INTERNATIONAL MARKETS

Northern Electric must be aggressive if it is to compete effectively with major multinational telecommunications corporations, not only in the domestic market, but in markets throughout the world.

A glance at the stature of Northern Electric in comparison with the foreign giants reveals that Northern, though it may appear a large corporation within Canada, is relatively small in the international arena.

The development of the Canadian telecommunications manufacturing industry is to some extent restricted by the relatively small size of the domestic market. Its hope for greatest expansion is through the establishment of production in other countries. In addition to helping to maintain a strong, viable, domestic industry, the broader scope enlarges the opportunities to innovate in competition in world markets.

The ability to function in the national environment alone, therefore, is not good enough. The need for more rapid growth is compelling, if the very large research and start-up costs necessary to keep up with the rapid rate of technological change in telecommunications are to be met, and if we are to beat international competitors with better new products and lower prices. We need a much larger sales base to support these very high costs of using new technology profitably and to extend the benefits to Canadian telephone companies and their customers.

Without expansion of markets, the prices charged by Canadian manufacturers of equipment to Canadian carriers will eventually be increased. The price increases would lead to a loss of exports, increased imports, an adverse effect on the balance of payments and a decline in the share of the domestic market available to Canadian manufacturers. This trend, once established, would be exceedingly difficult to reverse.

International competition is not for weaklings, nor is it played for small stakes. The Canadian telecommunications industry has the skills, the products, the resources and the determination to succeed against American, Japanese and European competitors, if Canadian governmental policies do not present unnecessary obstacles.

The importance to Bell Canada, as well as to the entire nation, of Northern Electric's initiatives cannot be under-estimated.

First, the public need, in Canada and throughout the world, for modern telecommunications is based on fundamental human demands which provide a massive and expanding market.

Secondly, twentieth-century technology offers tremendous opportunities to satisfy this public need and demand by providing new and better products which have a huge potential for improving national productivity performance and for satisfying individual and social wants.

Thirdly, maintaining a strong and viable telecommunications manufacturing industry in Canadian hands depends on our success in foreign markets.

Fourthly, with Canada's rapidly growing labour force, the high technology presence in the electronic and telecommunications industry takes on great importance for young Canadians seeking challenging careers.

Fifthly, the integration of research, manufacturing and operations through joint-ownership arrangements is the basic reason why telecommunications in North America far outstrip the rest of the world in the scope and quality of service and in the low cost to the user.

IV. The Case for Large Corporations

No review of the concentration of economic power can avoid an examination of large, potentially powerful corporations. In the case of Bell Canada, size and excessive power are far from being synonymous.

Size, as typically defined by assets or sales, generally implies firms which have developed significant economies of scale. Due in part to its size, Bell Canada is able to reduce its average unit costs as compared to a non-integrated organization. Technological developments in transmission systems, coupled with an increased volume of traffic, have made it possible to achieve large economies of scale which have permitted substantial reductions in long distance costs. These economies of scale are especially valuable in Canada where, as a nation relying on exports, we must encourage those techniques which contribute towards the creation of the most efficient possible infrastructure of which modern telecommunications is a vital and essential part.

Size creates opportunities for people. Not only are employees' needs met in the areas of working conditions, safety and benefits but, more importantly, in the variety of career opportunities within the business. While size in government does tend to encourage numbing bureaucracy, in private enterprise the drive for profits creates aggressive management and soon weeds out redundant work. In contrast to other sectors, there are no political appointments in Bell Canada, and tenure has long been replaced by modern appraisal techniques.

Bell Canada is responsive to the needs of the communities it serves and supports programs that help to improve the quality of community life.

Each year the Company and its employees contribute to the success of hundreds of diverse activities, ranging from large annual united appeal drives, to the provision of financial support for universities and sports trophies for community competitions.

This year the Company is giving about $950,000 to a variety of non-profit organizations dedicated to community betterment. Of this total about 45 per cent will go to health, welfare, united appeals and hospitals; 25 per cent to education; and 30 per cent to civic, cultural and other organizations.

Bell is a large company because it has a big job to do in providing telecommunications for Ontario and Quebec; in providing leadership commensurate with the importance of its territory in Canadian telecommunications; and in offering a market for Canadian suppliers who are capable of producing satisfactory, reliable products at a reasonable price.

The statistical evidence as to the adequacy of the profits being generated by large firms is at best mixed. In fact, if corporate financial statements are recast in current dollars, the evidence of serious erosion of their financial strength is more clearly visible. Bell Canada is earning currently a rate of return on common equity significantly below the cost of new debt capital. It is difficult to equate this fact with any notion about abuse of corporate power;

rather it suggests that regulation has not worked effectively under conditions of high inflation.

Bell must share power with the regulator, customers, unions, investors and suppliers.

At Bell we have some five million customers, each of whom expects, and in most cases receives, service on demand. We bargain with employees on an ongoing basis, primarily with the Canadian Telephone Employees Association and the Communications Union Canada which represents 28,000 and 8,000 employees respectively. We deal regularly on a contractual basis with about 40,000 suppliers.

In addition to these "watch dogs" over the abuse of power, there are definite legal constraints on the actions and judgements of the Board of Directors. Then too, the media exercise a meaningful role by ensuring that the corporate behaviour of Bell Canada is made visible and conspicuous to the general public. All of these groups form a real and effective constraint on any potential abuse by Bell Canada of its corporate power.

V. Areas of Concern

It is a fact of life that Bell Canada provides first class telecommunications service to the people of Canada at very reasonable cost. It is equally certain that a highly efficient communications system is crucial in satisfying the economic and social needs of the nation. Bell Canada is ready and willing not only to maintain but to improve on its record. It is with this over-riding objective in mind that we bring the following important considerations to the Commission's attention:

1. The terms of reference of the Commission are so broad that recommendations flowing from the various issues under study could have a substantial effect in shaping legislation as well as public perceptions of the corporate sector.

   Private corporations, during the past several years, have had to contend with their share of emotional outbursts from those who tend to equate corporate concentration with the abuse of power and who refuse to recognize the crucial role of profits in the free enterprise system. They have also had to contend with a legislative onslaught of increasing extent and intensity.

   Bell Canada respectfully submits that the mandate of this Commission provides an ideal opportunity to reverse these trends and to underscore the importance of profits; and in so doing help to create a favourable climate which will allow efficient and socially conscious corporations, both large and small, to contribute further to national economic growth.
2. Excessive legislative restrictions on the operations of the private corporate sector could have grave consequences not only on the ability of corporations to finance but on the entire capital market and the economy

as a whole. Certainly, in Bell Canada's case, investors have clearly demonstrated that they abhor risk and uncertainty. Furthermore, at a time when Canada is searching for ways to increase new capital formation, particularly for the public utilities whose ability to finance essential services has been seriously eroded by runaway inflation, regulatory lag and soaring energy costs, any disruption of the capital markets will have adverse implications for national economic well-being.

3. An in-depth analysis of corporate concentration in Canada should include the impact of both domestic and international competition on the effective power of any alleged corporate concentration. In addition, the growing influence and power of government and labour unions over the past decade should be examined. Corporate power cannot be examined in perspective unless labour power and government power are subjected to the same criteria of assessment.

4. In Bell Canada, we acknowledge the increased interest on the part of the federal and provincial governments in telecommunications policy matters. At the same time, we underscore the need to preserve our right to manage the business, to plan ahead, and to operate within general legislative guidelines and regulatory constraints, but without undue interference by governmental authorities.

We firmly believe that the responsibility for the planning and implementation of programs, for designing pricing structure, for the introduction of new technology, for establishing corporate structure, for raising capital and for entering into business agreements must continue to be the responsibility of management, subject only to the level of regulation necessary to protect the public interest and to ensure the attainment of the objectives prescribed in legislation. This does not preclude regular, extensive discussions with the regulators on goals, objectives, problems and their resolution, and other areas of mutual interest and concern.

Bell Canada holds to the view that the role of government is to define policy by legislation; the role of the regulatory authority is to regulate within the guidelines of the statutes; and the role of management is to manage the industry.

5. Bell Canada believes that, wherever practicable, competition should be fostered by government policy, so that the Canadian public can benefit from the socially perceived benefits of competition. On the other hand, it should be recognized that, in any modern society, certain services are most economically provided on a regulated monopoly basis.

There may well be further opportunities to increase the scope of competition in telecommunications. Bell Canada believes that these should be thoroughly explored, so that the monopoly aspects are confined to those areas where they are essential for best results.

6. The multiplicity of new legislation and the resulting administrative

directions, together with all the complexities of regulation, combine to absorb a tremendous amount of management time. Not only does this represent a significant cost to the business, but even more serious is the loss of this talent and time, because it is not being applied to the basic purposes of the corporation.

Federal, provincial and municipal enactments have in many cases seriously impeded the best and most efficient operation of corporations, and especially the large ones. This is in contrast to the situation in other countries where active government support is provided to such corporations. The growing nature of this problem and its implications for the productivity and competitiveness of Canadian enterprise should not be ignored in the Commission's recommendations.

7. We believe it essential that there be a complete exchange of information between governments and industry, supplemented by consultation to ensure thorough understanding of any proposed legislation affecting the telecommunications industry.

VI. Conclusion

Bell Canada submits that our country simply cannot afford experiments that affect or constrain the vital telecommunications system—the nerve system of our economy and of our society—without a thorough evaluation of the consequences.

We must have the freedom to change the organization structure so that we can carry out our responsibilities to our shareholders, to our employees and to our customers.

If short-term actions taken in the name of the public interest make long-range plans and large capital commitments neither feasible nor attractive, then great damage is done. Such a development would be contrary to the public interest at the best and disastrous at the worst.

In announcing the Royal Commission to study implications of major concentrations of corporate power, the Prime Minister said: "In a growing economy it is natural that participating corporations will grow in size, strength and capability and this is also desirable". We, at Bell, agree and seriously propose that the Commission find and recommend that the most grave long-run risk facing Canada is that the productive capacity and power of its privately owned industry will be inadequate to meet the demands placed on it.

Bell Canada is meeting the public's communications needs. It is providing dependable and efficient service and it is doing so at reasonable prices. We submit that real disadvantages to the public would accrue from the introduction of additional surveillance or legislative constraints.

Notes

*Submission by Bell Canada to the Royal Commission on Corporate Concentration (reproduced by permission of Bell Canada).

Part 2
Regulation

Introduction

Government regulation of business may take many different forms, ranging from the formal and highly centralized kind of control exercised over public utilities by national regulatory boards and commissions to the relatively simple kinds of legislation which set minimum standards of performance to which certain business are expected to conform.

The first reading in this part is intended to illustrate the latter type of regulation; how various laws impinge upon and influence the behaviour of firms operating in the retail trade. This industry is chosen because it is a relatively competitive industry; at least in the sense that at the point of contact between the consumer and the seller, a considerable number of firms are represented in the market place. But even in a case such as this, we apparently cannot rely on the forces of competition to ensure that the consumer will get as much for his money as is economically possible. Instead, a vast range of specific restrictions and requirements of various kinds are imposed on firms operating in such industries. The overriding reason for this appears to be a concern to protect the buyer against unscrupulous sellers. The growing "consumers' movements" in North America appears to have relatively little confidence in the possibility of using competition to protect consumers' interests and, perhaps realistically, seems to emphasize the need for regulation by government department or other bodies. If this is so it is an important indication of the trend away from the liberal ideal of a self-regulating market economy and toward the type of bureaucratically managed economy which is discussed in Section 4 of this book. Here, however, we are mainly concerned with the more narrowly defined economic implications of substituting regulation for competition and these centre around the question of "economic welfare."

The satisfaction of consumer wants is widely held to be the ultimate purpose of all economic activity. Consequently, all policies that affect the use made of our available resources will have some effect on the consumer's welfare. Indeed, as we saw in Section 1, it may be argued that the economic case for preferring a free market, private enterprise system of economic organization is that this system will prove superior to the known alternatives as a device for ensuring that our resources of all kinds will be used to produce the things consumers most want, in the desired relative quantities and with optimum efficiency. And, as we saw earlier in this Section, the principal guarantee of such performance is the force of competition. It is competition that, in the theoretical argument for this system, ensures that the interests of consumers, not producers, will be served. It is competition that is supposed to ensure the "sovereignty" of the consumer. But when markets are imperfect and cannot perform "satisfactorily," or when we believe that we can or should improve upon the market's performance, we substitute policies of regulation and public decision-making for them.

Our great problem here, however, is to find some way of determining whether these policies do in fact lead to welfare-maximizing use of our scarce resources. Do consumer protection policies lead to the "correct" quantities and qualities of goods and services being offered for sale or do they unduly restrict the output of certain commodities and cause prices to be higher than they otherwise would be? Economic analysis cannot provide a direct answer to this question. Some indications might be found by comparing prices and outputs in competitive markets with those in regulated ones, or by using econometric models to simulate the performance of an ideal market. In practice, however, such efforts are unlikely to produce unambiguous conclusions which all the parties concerned would accept as correct.

How difficult it is to determine the correct levels of output, quality of service and price for particular industries is well demonstrated by our experience with public utility regulation. Reading 27 sets out a case study of one of this country's largest and most important public regulatory agencies, the Canadian Transport Commission, which is responsible for establishing price and output policies for a large number of both privately and publicly owned firms in the transportation industry. As this study shows, the determination of what is correct in such situations is ultimately a political rather than an economic activity. The question faced by such agencies is not whether their judgements are correct in terms of technical economic efficiency criteria, but whether they are acceptable to the various interest groups concerned. These two considerations are not necessarily unrelated: one way of obtaining acceptance for a particular price or output decision is to support it with expert, technical analysis. Such analysis, however, is expensive to buy and expensive to communicate; a fact which gives large, well-organized firms or other organizations an advantage in any kind of decision-making process which relies on representations from interested parties.

26 Public Policy Towards Retailing: Canada *

Robert G. Wyckham and Max D. Stewart

Introduction

Retail decision-making in Canada is affected in almost every instance by government legislation, regulation, and control. Public policy at the federal, provincial, and municipal levels influences retail structure and strategy. At the federal level legislation controlling price discrimination has the effect of regulating the potential power of the retailer to obtain price concessions from his suppliers. Indirectly, federal excise taxes and tariffs modify the array of products available to the retailer for sale. The availability of federal funds for capital loans to retailers has the potential to change the retail structure in the competition of large against small, specialist against generalist, and independent against chain. At the provincial level, consumer protection legislation forces the retailer to disclose certain information about his credit programs to consumers. Provincial labor legislation causes the retail manager to design his staffing to conform with the law and still maintain effective utilization of personnel. At the municipal level, zoning laws dictate where the retailer may locate, and what size and shape his buildings may take. Store hours and days of opening may also be regulated by the local community through its elected representatives.

Canadian retailers may even be affected by foreign governments in making decisions about their operations in this country. American anti-trust legislation can influence merger decisions of U.S. subsidiaries in Canada; U.K. regulations on balance of payments can influence investment by British retail subsidiaries operating in Canada. Present tendencies suggest more direct federal influence on foreign-owned enterprises doing business in Canada. Whatever new policies might develop in this area will have little effect on the total retail scene that is predominantly Canadian-owned.

The system of Canadian government, as enacted under the British North America Act of 1867,[1] is comprised of a federal government and a number of provincial governments (presently ten). To the federal government are entrusted matters essential to the development, unity, and permanence of the country. These include the regulation of trade and commerce, taxation, postal service, currency, banking, weights and measures, interest rates, bankruptcy, and criminal law (within which are contained laws relating to monopoly and unfair trade practices), all of which affect the retail decision maker. The provincial governments are responsible for a specific set of local matters including direct taxation, property and civil rights, provincial incorporation of companies, licensing of retail concerns, and control of municipalities. Provincial governments delegate certain of their powers and duties to the municipal governments, for example, local taxation, licensing and regulation of retailers, inspection of the sale of natural products, and land zoning.

In view of the widespread effects of public policy on retailing, it is surprising to find a dearth of published material on this subject in Canada. Reading the accounts of the development of retailing in Canada, both by historians and participants, one is struck by the almost total lack of any indication that public policy had anything to do with assisting, retarding, or maintaining retail trade. It is also surprising to see how little attention governments have paid to retailing, with the exception of regulation. The report of the Royal Commission on Canada's Economic Prospects in 1958 allocated three out of 509 pages to retailing and wholesaling. When the economy of an area turns down, the government gives its attention to aiding farmers and manufacturers, but not retailers. And yet, retailing is a major facet of the Canadian economy. It is estimated that 52 percent of the consumer's dollar represents the costs of marketing activities and that retailing accounts for 53 percent of the costs of marketing. In 1961 approximately 12 percent of Canada's labor force was engaged in retailing.

Among the myriad of government departments and regulatory agencies, retail corporate bodies, and retailing associations, only a few appear to stand out in the public policy interface between the regulator and the regulated. On the government side the major structure is the Department of Consumer and Corporate Affairs. The Retail Merchants Association and the Retail Council of Canada are the two most important retailing associations.

DEPARTMENT OF CONSUMER AND CORPORATE AFFAIRS

Under various legislative responsibilities assigned to it by the British North America Act, the government of Canada carries on policies and activities that concern consumer affairs and hence affect retailing. Until recently, federal activities that influenced the retailing field were scattered across at least a dozen different departments.[2] The prospects for coordination were slight; the likelihood that both consumers and businessmen would be confused and find difficult the obtaining of needed information was great.

Significant milestones in that regard were passed in 1966 and 1967. First, the establishment of the Department of Registrar General marked a beginning of a continuing process of bringing together a number of heretofore uncoordinated activities, namely administering the following:

Bankruptcy Act,
Canada Corporation Act,
Combines Investigation Act,
Copyright Act,
Industrial Design and Union Label Act,
Patent Act, and
Trade Mark Act.

Second, a Department of Consumer and Corporate Affairs was established in 1967, following closely upon the recommendation of the Economic Council of Canada. Except where assigned by law to another department, the duties, powers, and functions of the Minister of Consumer and Corporate Affairs extend to all matters relating to consumer affairs; standards of identity and performance in relation to consumer goods; legal weights and measures; and the areas previously under the Registrar General. All matters are of course confined to areas of federal jurisdiction. The Act calls for coordination of relevant programs of the government of Canada; cooperation with provincial agencies and other interested parties; improved consumer information and necessary inspection services for the protection of the Canadian consumer. The minister is also expected to initiate appropriate consumer programs.

In addition to the duties of the Registrar General of Canada, as indicated above, the powers, duties, and functions of other statutes that affect consumers and retailing have been transferred to the Minister of Consumer and Corporate Affairs. These include several transferred from the Department of Trade and Commerce:

Electrical and Photometric Units Act,
Electricity Inspection Act,
Gas Inspection Act,
National Trade Mark and True Labelling Act,
Precious Metals Marking Act, and
Weights and Measures Act.

The department also participates together with other departments in the administration of the following statutes:

Canada Agricultural Products Standards Act,
Canada Dairy Products Act,
Fish Inspection Act,
Food and Drugs Act, and
Maple Products Industry Act.

They embrace quite extensive regulations prescribing in detail contents, grades, standards, and labels.

Two recently enacted statutes, Hazardous Products Act (June, 1969) and Textile Labelling Act (March 1970),[3] providing similar kinds of regulations, are administered by the Department of Consumer and Corporate Affairs. The Minister of National Health and Welfare is also concerned with some aspects of hazardous products regulations.

It seems reasonable to suggest that the establishment of the Department of Consumer and Corporate Affairs and the assignment to it of a general coordinating function represents a significant shift in emphasis. Matters affecting consumers, and hence directly or indirectly the retail industry, have been made a major responsibility of a single cabinet minister. To the older attitude of "let the buyer beware" has been added something of the philosophy of "let the seller take care." That subtle but discernible change in public policy is illustrated by the opening in April 1968 of Box 99, Ottawa, to provide a medium of communication with consumers. Since its inception, there has been a steady and growing flow of complaints and inquiries from the public. In addition to aiding consumers in their quest for satisfactory retail products, Box 99 is a source of useful information to the department as to current problem areas.

Structure

ORGANIZATION OF RETAILERS

There are two major organizations to which Canadian retailers belong. The largest, with a membership of 10,000, is the Retail Merchants Association which is composed mainly of small independent retailers (although Woodwards, a major west coast department store chain, is a member of the British Columbia division). This organization was originally conceived of as a pressure group to further the interests of independent retailers. Over the seventy-five-year history of the organization, it has been involved in attempts to curb trading stamps, arrest the growth of chains, eliminate phoney closing-out sales, stop price wars through resale price maintenance, and limit store opening hours. The second group is the Retail Council of Canada, whose membership includes the major retailers of the nation. This national organization is a well-financed and politically strong pressure group. The Retail Council participates in the financing of research of general interest to its members.

FIRM STRUCTURE AND CONTROL

Public policy influences retail firm structure in terms of the types of legal organization available, the amount and character of integration (vertical and horizontal) allowed, and the degree of exclusiveness of distribution permitted.

Retailing in Canada may be carried on as a proprietorship, a partnership, a private corporation,[4] a public corporation, or a cooperative. Numerically, the most popular of the legal forms for retailers is the proprietorship. In 1961, 71.5 percent of all retail stores were proprietorships and they did 30.9 percent of total retail sales. Partnerships accounted for 8.8 percent of total stores and 6.8 percent of total sales in 1961. Both the proportion of total stores and total sales for proprietorships and partnerships have been declining over the years. Corporations, both private and public, made the largest percentage of retail sales, 57.9 percent in 1961, and the proportion is growing, with only 18.2 percent of the number of stores. The cooperative is the least popular form of structure with .8 percent of total stores and 1.3 percent of total retail sales in 1961.[5]

The corporate form of ownership appears to be directly related to ease of growth, and hence size (because of limited liability, access to professional skills, and ease of raising capital) and so to a growing dominance of the retail sector. Only 2.9 percent of all stores had sales over one-half million dollars in 1961 and yet they made 41.5 percent of retail sales.[6]

The battle between the independent retailer and the chains is of long standing in Canada. The Hudson's Bay Company is said to have been the first chain-type retail operation in Canada, establishing a series of trading posts across the nation after 1670.[7] It was not until the decade of the 1920s, however, that chains became a major factor in the retail field with 7 percent of total sales.[8] No anti-chain store legislation was enacted to deter their growth (although provincial minimum loss acts were implemented without success and some municipalities placed higher taxes and licensing fees on chains) so that by the mid-1960s about 20 percent of all retail sales were carried out by chains. (This proportion does not include department stores, who tend to operate as chains, and have 8.6 percent of retail sales.) Public policy, which did not hinder the chain growth, also allowed the development of combinations of wholesalers and independent retailers to compete with chains. Individual chains grew by internal expansion and by purchasing competitors (Eatons took over Spencers in 1948; Hudson's Bay bought out Morgans in 1960). It does not appear that the anti-combines laws have slowed this development, although considerable political heat was generated in the past.[9]

Integration. Vertical integration by retailers began with the larger operators (Eatons, Simpsons) taking over the functions of the powerful wholesaler-importers in the 1870s. Eatons integrated into production in the late 1880s[10] and set up an independent wholesale business in 1892.[11] Although vertical integration was a topic of interest to the Royal Commission on price spreads in 1935, there is no evidence of subsequent anti-trust activity. In the 1960s, vertical integration was common in grocery, drug, department, gasoline, shoe, clothing, and drug retailing.

Horizontal integration of diverse types of stores is less common. When this has been done it generally has been accomplished through a holding company structure; for example, the Weston group of companies includes firms retailing bakery goods, groceries, and drugs. No attempt has been made by anti-combines authorities to limit this development.

Exclusive distribution is not illegal under federal law. Manufacturers, distributors, and retailers are permitted to establish exclusive distribution arrangements with territorial protection.

Foreign Ownership. Of 25,869 corporations in the retail trade in 1967, there were 4,544 reporting under the Corporations and Labour Unions Return Act; of these, 259 had 50 percent or more of their voting shares held by non-residents.[12]

A superficial examination of department store ownership indicates that the large majority of control is held in Canada.[13] The discount store sector appears to have a large measure of ownership outside of Canada, principally in the United States. Of the major chain grocery merchants, only two seem to be owned outside the country. The two largest chains of variety stores are wholly owned U.S. subsidiaries.

Increasing pressure from various quarters has resulted in some changes in the foreign ownership-management situation.[14] The Hudson's Bay Company, which has had its headquarters in London, England for 300 years, has moved its offices to Winnipeg. Principal reasons for the move were said to be weaknesses related to foreign exchange and taxation risks. The company hopes to increase the number of Canadian shareholders.

GOVERNMENT SUPPORT FOR SMALL RETAILING

The federal government has had a direct influence on retail size and structure through making capital loans available. For a number of years the Retail Merchants' Association and other retail organizations agitated for a capital loan fund to assist independent retailers.[15] Presently small business loans are available to retailers at chartered banks at advantageous rates under the Small Business Loans Act. The federally-operated Industrial Development Bank will also make capital loans to retailers.

GOVERNMENT-OWNED RETAILING

The government controls the sale of alcoholic beverages in all provinces. In most provinces beer, wine, and liquor are sold in government-operated stores. These products are not available to other retailers in the Maritimes. In the western provinces, packaged beer may also be purchased in beer parlors. Beer may be sold in stores operated at breweries in Alberta, Ontario, and Manitoba. Ontario allows wine manufacturers to sell their products in company-owned outlets. Only Quebec permits the sale of beer in non-chain grocery stores. Government control of the retail sale of alcoholic beverages includes product availability, package shapes and sizes, prices, and all phases of promotion.

Prior to World War II some provincial governments were involved in the sale of electric and gas appliances through state-owned utilities. This gave them some measure of influence with respect to the availability, pricing, and promotion of these products. It would appear that this practice terminated with the war. Some public utilities are indirectly involved in the retailing of appliances through services to appliance retailers. For example, the British Columbia Hydro offers a sales training program to appliance salesmen and collects and distributes to retailers statistics on the sale of various products.

Managerial Strategies

The retail manager is regulated in the development and execution of operating strategy by public policy. In this section the most important government influences concerning product control, pricing, promotion, personnel, location, store opening, firm structure, consumer protection, and credit will be considered.

PRODUCT CONTROL

Governmental control over products and product availability takes a number of forms. There is public regulation of the characteristics of goods available for sale in terms of quality and in terms of particular specifications for factor inputs or product performance. There is regulation as to channels of distribution and pricing of natural products (through government-sanctioned monopolies such as marketing boards) and direct control over the sale of alcoholic beverages and indirect control over such products as drugs and tobacco. There is also legislation governing the sale of products deemed dangerous, as, for example, fire arms.

The federal government influences the array of products available to the retailer by its policies relating to imports and the development of "infant" or "necessary" industries. Through the use of tariffs and import regulations and via the price mechanism certain classes and types of products from various sources are made more or less difficult for the retailer to obtain and sell. In some cases the import duty policies reflect the government's concern for encouraging the growth of particular industries or skills in the domestic market.

Resale price maintenance sections of the Combines Investigation Act give the government of Canada additional control over the availability of products at retail. Suppliers may not refuse to supply a retailer with products for the purpose of enforcing a price maintenance policy (although there are loss-leader exceptions). However, this does not outlaw selective or exclusive dealership arrangements, provided this is not done in collusion with other suppliers and provided the seller is not a monopolist. "The Eddy Match Company was convicted on this basis, and Canadian Industries Ltd. was 'persuaded' to ease their distribution policy in the Ammunition case."[16]

Products Under Special Controls. Product availability and product characteristics are also controlled by a number of federal statutes including:

Agricultural Product Standards Act,
Dairy Products Act,
Fish Inspection Act,
Food and Drugs Act,
Maple Products Industry Act,
Hazardous Product Act, and the
Textile Labelling Act.

Each of these seven statutes provides, in varying degree, for analysis, inspection, search, seizure, and forfeiture as well as direct penalties for violation. There are some items that are banned; that is, they cannot legally be advertised, sold, or imported. "Regulated" products can be advertised, sold, and imported only if the contents, packaging, and labelling comply with the detailed requirements of the law. Because these regulations are under continuing enforcement, review, and revision, the most up-to-date provisions are controlling. Although they do concern more directly importation and manufacture, a good many of the rules affect retailing of the products involved.

The National Department of Health and Welfare has been conducting a research and information program on tobacco products. By comparing the tar and nicotine content of various brands and communicating this data along with medical information on the dangers of smoking, the government has influenced the amount of tobacco products sold and the mix of these products.

The tendency toward more activity regarding product liability makes at least a brief reference to two recent judgments worthwhile. In a case arising from an eye injury to a shopper from an exploding soft drink bottle on a store shelf, the Supreme Court of Ontario gave judgment against the manufacturer (bottler), but dismissed the action against the retailers.[17] The Court held, however, that because the injured party was justified in bringing the retailer to court, he will be entitled to add to his claim against Coca-Cola Ltd. the amount he was required to pay the retailer as reimbursement of trial costs. In a case concerning a car that proved faulty, the British Columbia Supreme Court found against a car dealer in favor of the buyer.[18] The Court held that the car was so faulty as to mean a fundamental breach of contract, thereby denying the seller any protection from an exempting clause, which limited the vendor's liability.

Provincial legislation with respect to "natural products" specifies grade standards, stipulates inspection of quality and for disease, requires certain processes such as pasteurization, sets conditions of sale such as package sizes for dairy products, makes rules for marking and branding. Physical conditions under which natural products may be processed and stored, and the setting up and regulating of marketing boards to distribute natural products are also governed by provincial laws. Marketing boards have been set up for natural products under the National Products Marketing Act and provincial legislation. By controlling supply, setting quotas and prices, and regulating the flow of these products to the retail level, they constrain the retailer's decision-making role. Most provinces have had legislation banning the sale of margarine, but its sale is now allowed under certain conditions. Imitation dairy products are specifically outlawed in some provinces. In most cases the provincial legislation relating to natural products makes the retailer as well as the producer or processor liable for penalties.

Control of the sale of drugs at the provincial level takes the form of regulating who may operate a pharmacy and offer drugs for sale. In addition, an act on drug substitution is in force in Alberta and is in the development stages in British Columbia. This legislation allows the pharmacist to substitute a generic product, with the same chemical properties, if a physician prescribes a brand-name drug and does not prohibit substitution. Control by the provinces of tobacco distribution is carried out through licensing of sellers and a minimum age for purchasers.

Fireworks are also regulated at the provincial level. They are banned in some provinces and in some communities where the Municipal Act gives to the cities the right to control this product. In other provinces and cities the sale of fireworks is limited to particular times of the year (British Columbia) or to sale for public display only (New Brunswick). Federal legislation on the sale of firearms requires that retailers of guns keep records of each transaction. Most provinces have laws allowing only persons of a certain age to buy or possess firearms.

PRICING

For the most part public policy influences on pricing come at the federal level, but there are also some important provincial controls.

Federal Regulations. The Combines Investigation Act (Section 33A) makes certain pricing practices indictable offences.[19] First, it is illegal for a business to grant "any discount, rebate, allowance, price concession or other advantage" to one purchaser that is not made available to competitors of that purchaser "in respect of a sale of articles of like quality and quantity." Although this is a restraint to some extent on a retailer attempting to obtain a special concession from his suppliers, it would seem to pose no problem regarding his own selling prices. It is unlikely that final consumers would be held to be "competitors" in terms of the Act. Secondly, it is illegal to follow a policy of selling at lower prices in one part of Canada than in another, where that policy has the effect or tendency of substantially lessening competition. Although this seems to dictate to some degree a one-price policy, it is not a rigidly universal requirement across the entire nation. There is no mention of the possibility of varying costs being associated with the same price in different areas. Thirdly, a policy of "unreasonable low" prices is illegal. It is uncertain how effective that provision might be in cases of alleged loss-leaders.

Section 34 makes it an offence for any manufacturer or supplier to attempt to induce any other person to resell at a specified price or not below a specified minimum. That is, there must be no effort made toward resale price maintenance and refusal to supply because of a customer declining to resell at a specified price is illegal. There are saving clauses (sub-section 5) to the effect that a dealer may refuse to sell to a person who makes a practice of using the articles as loss-leaders (not for the purpose of making a profit thereon) or who fails to provide the level of servicing that might reasonably be expected. The combination of the ban on resale price maintenance and the saving clauses create considerable uncertainty with respect to specific application of the law.

Provincial Regulations. Provincial laws, taxes, and policies affect pricing in a number of ways. Legislation to curb below-cost selling, credit disclosure sections of consumer protection acts, and closing-out sales laws all play a role in retail price decisions. The prices of all goods at retail are adjusted by retail sales taxes. Special provincial taxes on such items as tobacco and gasoline have a direct influence on the prices of these products. All provinces directly control the prices of beer, wine, and liquor.

As a response to chain-store pricing, a number of provinces enacted minimum loss acts or below-cost selling acts (Manitoba, British Columbia). These were designed to assist the independent grocery retailer to counteract the low price and loss leader activities of chain supermarkets. These laws have been generally ineffective because "if the retailer accused proves that the total price charged for the combination (of grocery products) is not less than the aggregate of the prices at which each of such grocery product might lawfully be sold, the sale is not deemed to be a violation."[20] The Commodities Retail Sales Act of British Columbia gives the right to wholesalers and producers to set retail prices. Both minimum loss acts and provincial resale price maintenance laws appear to overlap federal legislation. If this is so it is likely that Dominion jurisdiction would prevail and the provincial law would be inoperative.[21]

Consumer protection legislation has an influence on pricing in a special way. Prior to the establishment of these laws retailers could present a product for sale and advertise it in such a way as to make the price appear lower than it was. This is now much more difficult to achieve. The fire sale, liquidator's sale type of promotion also presented opportunities for the retailer to price goods so that they seemed like bargains. Licensing and inspection appear to have curbed this practice.

Retail sales taxes are levied in nine of the ten provinces. The tax rates range from a low of 5 percent in British Columbia, Manitoba, Saskatchewan, and Ontario (Alberta has no sales tax), to a high of 8 percent in Quebec (a portion of which is a municipal tax) and New Brunswick, with the remainder of the provinces at 7 percent.[22] Some products are exempted (children's clothing and furniture, educational supplies) from the tax in some provinces. It is difficult to ascertain the influence of this tax on retail prices of individual commodities, although it has been noted that some prices have been designed so that the price plus the tax result in an even dollar figure. Because the tax is added on to the advertised price, it is unlikely to have had any influence on the setting of so-called psychological prices. It is obvious that such taxes, by cutting the level of real disposable income, have an effect on total retail sales.

It seems clear that provincial authorities have set special taxes on tobacco and gasoline believing that the demand for these products is relatively price inelastic in an upward direction. Taxes on these commodities have risen steadily over the years. In most provinces the tax on cigarettes (not including retail sales tax) amounts to about 18 percent of the retail price. Taxes on tobacco products may have a significant influence on the sales and profits of retailers specializing in this commodity. About one-third of the price of gasoline is made up of provincial taxes. Whether more retail gas sales would be made at lower prices is debatable.

PROMOTION

Public policy set at all levels of government influences retail decisions about various aspects of promotion. Under this title we will consider mass media advertising, store signs, mail and telephone order catalogues, and closing-out sales.

Federal proscription of deceptive advertising is provided in the Combines Investigation Act. One Section, 33C, makes misleading representation as to the price at which like articles "have been, are, or will be, ordinarily sold," an offence punishable on summary conviction.[23] Section 33D, brought into the Combines Investigation Act in 1969, makes it an offence punishable on summary conviction to publish statements regarding the performance of a product without a prior adequate and proper test. More severe penalties are provided in the case of other forms of misleading representation. An increasing number of cases against retail concerns are being brought to trial, which is consistent with statements of the Minister of Consumer and Corporate Affairs that the limits of legislative provisions will be tested in court. It seems clear that revisions of the law are likely to be introduced where protection against misleading advertising would otherwise prove ineffective.

Municipalities govern the distribution and posting of bills, placards, and circulars. Retailers using this form of advertising are constrained in using this device by licensing fees (Halifax), and by regulations as to the content of the advertisement, the location of its posting, and the process of distribution to potential customers.

Municipal procedures governing store signs vary from city to city. In Fredericton, the City Council decides on each application for a retail sign on its merits, but no general rules are in force. In Montreal the sign by-law is almost forty pages in length. Among other types of signs it regulates those on the buildings and vehicles of retailers. It covers the size (area), placing, location, over-street projection, and illumination of all signs.

Although other factors were vastly more important in the success of mail-order catalogues in the promotion of goods in Canada, public policy has played a role. "The government's need for cash for tax purposes put cash in circulation; banks sprouted branches, miles of toll-free road were built, improvements in parcel post, post office and bank drafts, and railway express meant a bright future for a cash only mail order business."[24] Without favorable mail rates (Eatons paid the postage on large orders to rural areas beginning in the 1880s),[25] the distribution of catalogues and the delivery of goods to customers would have been seriously hampered. Federal regulations on misleading advertising may have helped to protect the consumer and encourage confidence in catalogues, although as part of the Criminal Code they were rarely enforced. Despite the attempts by local retailers to have municipal laws enacted to ban the hated catalogues, millions are distributed each year. Government regulation as it applies to over-the-counter sales also controls sales by catalogue.

A retail promotional device of considerable influence that is now closely controlled at the provincial and municipal level is the closing-out sale. Strong pressure by retail groups was brought to bear on this problem in the mid-1950s, to curb abuses in the use of this type of sale. Municipal ordinances and provincial regulations set out standards and fees for licensing of sales ranging from going-out-of-business to creditor's sales. Rules cover the condition of the goods for sale and forbid the sale of goods brought in especially for this type of sale.

TRADING STAMPS

Trading stamps have had a varied life in Canada. At the turn of the twentieth century, a number of stamp systems flourished. Federal legislation in 1905 was designed to wipe out these schemes, but allowed "manufacturers' coupons to be used in exchange for gifts."[26] Amendment of the Criminal Code of Canada in 1954 led to a vigorous revival of the use of trading stamps by retailers. Stamp companies quickly spread their programs across the country. Provincial and municipal legislation in some areas have tended to retard the use of this promotional device. For example, in British Columbia, trading stamps must have a redeemable value of at least ten cents before they can be issued. Legislation in Alberta and Saskatchewan prohibits the use of stamps, while in Manitoba the Municipal Act gives the right to regulate the use of stamps to the municipalities. In the late 1960s major grocery retailers began to drop the use of stamps (because of rising costs, consumer disinterest, political pressure, opposition in the trade) until only a few stamp companies still operate. There is no stamp activity west of the Saskatchewan border and little in Manitoba and Ontario. Trading stamps still flourish in the major centers of Quebec and the Maritimes.[27] Steinberg's subsidiary, Pinkys Stamps Ltd., provides stamps for distribution through the company's supermarkets and department stores in Quebec. Recent activity by the Department of Consumer and Corporate Affairs serves to indicate that new legislation governing trading stamps may be put forward. At present, it appears that stamps are legal if they are redeemed:

1. by the vendor, or
2. in goods that are at least partly his property,
3. in the premises where the goods are purchased, and if
4. each stamp shows legibly on its face the address of the store and the merchantable value of the stamp, and finally,
5. if the stamps may be redeemed on demand at any time, no matter how small the number of stamps presented for redemption.[28]

LABELING

Government regulation of labeling is found at both the federal and provincial levels. Under Section 33D of the Combines Investigation Act, Canada has a measure of control over labels that might be seen as misleading advertising.

A number of acts administered by the national Department of Consumer and Corporate Affairs relating to natural products, textiles, and hazardous products contain provisions governing labels. The Food and Drug Act requires that food labels contain the brand name, the common name, a declaration of the net contents of the package in terms of weight or measure, a list of the ingredients, a list of preservatives, food coloring or artificial flavoring, and the name and address of the manufacturer. Drug label requirements are similar to the above, with the addition of the dosage for patent drugs and directions for use.

It is interesting to note the part played by retailers in the establishment of credible labeling. Apparently, before the turn of the present century, retailers replaced manufacturers' labels with more prestigious marks, attached false labels such as "imported" and "pure wool." Large retailers like Eatons refused to follow this practice and influenced others to stop.[29] Today many retailers operate laboratories that analyze the quality and characteristics of products from suppliers, thus ensuring more accurate labeling.

The language on labels is under provincial jurisdiction. For example, Ontario requires that all food products sold in the province contain labels printed in English. Quebec has recently extended its French labeling requirements on food packages.

PERSONNEL[30]

The personnel strategies of retailers are affected by public policy at all levels. Three main types of legislation are important: laws allowing unions and union activity, labor standard laws, and workmen's compensation laws. In addition, government expenditures on education influence retail staffing. Originally all union and labor standards law was enacted at the federal level. At present, federal legislation in these areas covers only employees of federally-chartered companies in such activities as banking and communication. Provincial laws cover all other employees. Since 1949 all provinces have had schemes of collective liability and compulsory insurance for workmen's compensation.[31]

The federal Trades Union Act of 1872 allowed the growth and development of unionism in Canada. Under the conditions of this act unions per se were not illegal and union activity was not viewed as restraint of trade. A 1925 Privy Council decision held that the provincial governments, as well as the federal parliament, had the authority to enact labor relations laws. However, it was not until after the second world war that most provinces became active in labor legislation.

Unionism in the retail trades is not extensive, with less than 10 percent of employees members.[32] Union membership among employees of the major department stores is very low. The ability of unions to influence retail management, however, is great because key trades such as butchers, plumbers, and truck drivers are unionized. The largest unions of sales personnel are the

Retail Clerks International Association with 21,000 members and the Retail, Wholesale and Department Store Union with about 20,000 members.[33]

The right to make laws concerning labor standards is vested in both the federal and the provincial governments. Legislation in this area includes: minimum wages, equal pay (for both sexes), hours of work, weekly rest-days, annual vacations with pay, public holidays, fair employment practices, notice of termination of employment, and workmen's compensation.[34] A number of provinces (Ontario, Quebec, Newfoundland) have different minimum wages by age and by sex, which seems to fly in the face of their equal pay and fair employment provisions. The lower minimum wage for women is obviously favorable to retails. Legislation that retailers claim discriminates against them concerns daily guarantee of hours. For example, in British Columbia an employer who calls in an employee must pay that person for a minimum of four hours. Retailers argue that this makes it much more expensive to effectively allocate staff to the various peak load hours.

Government expenditures on education have an effect on the employment and training practices of retailers. The general upgrading of the education standards of citizens means a better pool of potential candidates for retailers to hire and also results in a more sophisticated consumer who demands more capable retail employees. The offering of retailing and marketing courses in high schools, institutes of technology, community colleges and universities influences career choices as well as prepares students for positions in retailing.

LOCATION

Retail policy decisions on location become more complex with each new piece of zoning legislation and each new planning commission. General observation would lead one to believe that public planning has led to a rationalization of retail location. There appears to be less strip development on city streets and rural highways and an increasing trend to shopping centers (both neighborhood and regional, suburban and downtown). Whether this discriminates against the independent in favor of the chain is open to question. The daily press is a ready source of evidence that the processes provided for in municipal zoning laws have added a political characteristic to the economic and technical aspects of the location decision. Parking regulations affect retail location decisions in terms of influence on customer traffic generation and the economics of providing off-street parking in relation to available selling space. Location decisions are also influenced by differing business taxes, business licenses, and building and fire regulations in various communities.

Municipal zoning rules and the regulatory bodies designed to administer them are set up by the community under the authority of the provincial municipal acts and, in some cases, community planning acts (Saskatchewan). Regional or metropolitan planning is carried on in a number of areas

(Toronto, Winnipeg, Vancouver) in an attempt to coordinate land use in communities that are physically together, but politically separate. The purpose of planning legislation and regulation is to ensure appropriate land use "to conserve adequate open spaces for light and air; to reduce fire hazard; to prevent undue concentration of population; to avoid congestion on the streets and to promote the health, safety and general welfare of the inhabitants..."[35] That the interpretation of what is favorable to general welfare is controversial can be seen from the briefs presented to zoning boards by retail groups, real estate developers, and citizens' organizations.

Zoning takes two general forms. The first is control over land use, that is, the specific purpose for which a particular piece of land may be used (residential, commercial). The second is regulation of the characteristics of the building to be constructed on the property (placement on land, height, size, and shape of building, type of facade, off-street parking, and loading space). Regulation of the characteristics of structures in some municipalities extends to aesthetics in terms of building design, materials, and landscaping. Land-use zoning usually does not distinguish between retailing and other forms of enterprise, with the exceptions of service stations and shopping centers (for example, the Oakridge property in Vancouver, sold by the Canadian Pacific Railway in 1955, could only be developed as a shopping center as part of the Comprehensive Development District).[36] Zoning laws may be used to control the level of competition of particular types of retailing within a community.

Business taxes, business licenses, and building and fire regulations are an interactive set from the point of view of the retail manager. In order to obtain and retain a license to do business within a municipality the retailer must conform to all the by-laws of the community, which means paying the business tax and maintaining his property in accordance with the building codes. Some municipalities require one license to operate a retail establishment (Winnipeg); others require a series of licenses based on the types of commodities sold or service performed (Montreal). Business taxes vary from city to city in terms of amount and the method of calculating the amount. Businesses in cities in Nova Scotia pay not more than $200 per year, while the maximum in Quebec is $5,000. The maximum in British Columbia runs from $200 to $1,500 depending on the size of the community. Most tax calculation systems are based on the appraised annual rental value of the property occupied. In Vancouver the business tax is 8 percent of the rental value, but in Winnipeg the tax rate rises from 6 percent to 20 percent of the rental value, depending on the amount of the assessment and the type of business.

HOURS OF RETAIL OPERATION

Hours of store opening are governed by the municipal governments in all provinces except Quebec, where province-wide rules apply. Retail practice in hours of operation varies from strict adherence to municipal regulation (West Vancouver) to flagrant disobedience with fines considered a cost of doing business (Toronto), to no regulation of opening hours (Edmonton, Fredericton). The first attempt to influence retail hours appears to have come from Canada's largest retailer, Eatons. In Toronto in 1881, Timothy Eaton began a campaign to restrict his hours of opening and gain adherence from his competitors.[37] It is interesting to note that in recent years, this same company has been in the forefront of efforts to expand store hours in various centers across the nation.

In most municipalities a wide variety of retailers are not governed by store hours, or at least not by the strict rules covering other merchandisers. These include retailers whose principal business is in the sale of tobacco, newspapers, books, drugs, confectionary, fresh fruit and flowers, bread, milk, gasoline, and automobiles.

There is a general trend to the extension of store hours with evening openings on Thursdays and Fridays. A growing battle appears to be developing between the small retailer and the department stores and chains, with the latter groups agitating for longer hours. Most communities have extended hours in the pre-Christmas period.

The majority of cities regulate the days of opening or the number of days of operation per week. One day closed in seven is the general rule. For the most part, retailers must close on officially designated holidays. An exception to this is Edmonton, where the holiday closing by-law was repealed in 1969. In Quebec the days of opening of commercial establishments is governed by a provincial statute.

Exceptions to the hours and days of opening are special shopping areas like Yorkville in Toronto and Gastown in Vancouver, where extended hours and Sunday openings are the rule. The retailers in these unique districts deal mainly in antiques, works of art, and handicrafts.

CREDIT

Public policy on consumer credit has influenced retailing. The growth and speed of growth of retail sales (and hence retail structures) has been affected by Canadian government policy on consumer credit. This can be seen in such things as the changing of the Bank Act in 1954 to permit chartered banks to make personal loans and the moral suasion and manipulation of the interest rate by the Bank of Canada in 1969 to cut down on the flow of consumer credit.

CONSUMER PROTECTION

During the 1960s provincial legislation was enacted to give the consumer relief from a number of retail sales practices that were believed to be detrimental to public welfare. Generally these laws covered: cost of credit disclosure, advertising of credit provisions, proportionate rebates for early repayment, relief from unfair collection practices, "cooling-off" periods on itinerant sales, and relief from harsh contracts. Provincial consumer bureaus have also been set up to give advice and information to consumers and to investigate complaints.

For the retailer, these laws have affected his charge account and other credit-granting procedures in that the methods of reporting interest charges to customers have had to be changed. In some cases advertising practices have had to be adjusted to disclose the actual price of the goods, the amount of downpayment, the amount and number of installments, and the cost of credit expressed in dollars and as an annual percentage rate.

A federal bill, still to be approved by Parliament, amending the Bills of Exchange Act, will attempt to provide the consumer with protection when the retailer sells the purchaser's promissory note to a third party. Under present law, when a dealer sells finance paper to a third party, the consumer effectively has no legal right of recourse and is obliged to pay the debt whether the vendor lives up to delivery or service agreements.

MISCELLANEOUS RETAIL STRATEGIES

Two types of retailing strategies and the public policy influences on them will be considered here: door-to-door selling and automatic vending. In most provinces there are two pieces of provincial legislation governing direct selling. First there are provincial laws (or enabling legislation to allow municipalities to pass by-laws) licensing and controlling the activities of transient traders, that is, persons without residence in the community, and residents who sell from vehicles rather than fixed places of business. Special by-laws are in force in some cities (Halifax) covering the sale of subscriptions for books and magazines. License fees in force in many communities appear to be designed to limit the sale of goods by direct means. Door-to-door sellers are also regulated under consumer protection legislation (see above) by allowing purchasers to cancel contracts within a certain period, requiring delivery of a true copy of any sales contract, and limiting the rights of repossession by the seller.

Cities regulate automatic merchandising or vending machines through licensing, restrictions as to placement (only on private property—Vancouver), and control of characteristics of vending machinery (food vending, fuel oil vending—Montreal). It may be expected that additional legislation will be enacted as automatic vending grows in amount (.39 percent of total retail sales in 1965),[38] and as more and different types of products are sold by machines.

CONCLUSION

Although retail structures and managerial strategies of retailers in Canada are influenced by a vast number of public policies, there does not seem to be an overall public policy for retailing in the country. No coordinated policy of legislation and regulation is evident among federal, provincial, and municipal authorities. In fact it might be argued that governments have tended to ignore distribution institutions. Legislation and publicity have tended to be oriented toward protection of consumers, regulation of products, and control of manufacturers. It appears as if the fact that much of this legislation becomes operative at the retail level has not been of great concern to the law makers.

Perhaps the organizations representing retail owners and employees have played a part in the lack of a retailing policy for Canada. There does not seem to be a continuing visibility of retailing organizations. It is only at crisis points, when new laws are about to be enacted or regulations changed, that the merchants' organizations and the employees' unions attempt to make their influence felt.

It is important to note that Canada has taken a more passive role than other countries in the control of the growth of retail institutions. This is in line with the lack of rigorous anti-combines regulation applied to all corporations. No doubt in the future changes will occur, specifically with regard to vertical integration and foreign ownership.

Pricing and promotion are two strategic areas where there is a trend toward more public policy activity. The pricing of some sensitive products such as drugs, the revelation of large margins in some instances, and accusations of higher prices in lower socioeconomic neighborhoods, has made pricing a political football. Because retail advertising is all pervasive in the community, there has been a tendency for governmental authorities to attack misleading promotion violations at the retail level. No doubt these tendencies will continue.

Notes

*Wyckham, R. G., and M. D. Stewart, "Canada," in J. J. Boddewyn and S. C. Hollander, *Public Policy Toward Retailing: An International Symposium* (Lexington, Mass.: Lexington Books, D. C. Heath and Co., 1972, reproduced by permission of the author and the publisher).

[1]30 Victoria, Chapter 3 (UK).

[2]Economic Council of Canada, *Interim Report on Consumer Affairs and the Department of Registrar General*, July 1967, 13.

[3]Canada, *Office Consolidation of the Criminal Code* (Ottawa: Queen's Printer, 1963), 33.

[4]The private corporation has been a favorite type of legal structure for Canadian business. The main advantage is that a private company is not required to publicly disclose information on its affairs. Canada's largest retailer, Eatons, with sales variously estimated around one billion dollars, is a private company. In recent years, there has been growing pressure for change in the laws on public disclosures of information from private corporations. A 1970 federal law requires all federally incorporated private companies to publish certain financial statements annually.

[5]M. S. Moyer and G. Snyder, *Trends in Canadian Marketing*, Dominion Bureau of Statistics (Ottawa: Queen's Printer, 1967), pp. 85 and 87. It is likely that the small amount of sales generated by cooperatives has dampened the enthusiasm of those who would like the law to treat cooperatives as corporations for tax purposes.

[6]Ibid., pp. 90, 91.

[7]Clifford Henry Cheasley, *The Chain Store Movement in Canada* (Orillia, Ontario: Packet-Times Press Ltd. [undated]), p. 57.

[8]Moyer and Snyder, op. cit., p. 126.
[9]See for example the *Report of The Royal Commission on Price Spreads* (Ottawa: King's Printer, 1935).
[10]Mary-Etta Macpherson, *Shopkeepers to a Nation: The Eatons* (Toronto: McClelland and Stewart, Ltd., 1963), p. 26.
[11]William Stephenson, *The Store that Timothy Built* (Toronto: McClelland and Stewart, 1969), p. 43.
[12]Dominion Bureau of Statistics, *Corporations and Labour Unions Return Act, Annual Report for 1967*, Part 1, Corporations, (9802-503) December 1969, Table 130.
[13]Only very tentative conclusions can be obtained because the data only shows the percentage ownership of the major holding company by country of residence. Canada, *Inter-Corporate Ownership, 1967*, Dominion Bureau of Statistics (Ottawa: Queen's Printer, 1969).
[14]See for example, Melville H. Watkins, *Foreign Ownership and the Structure of Canadian Industry*, Report of the Task Force on the Structure of Canadian Industry (Ottawa: Queen's Printer, 1968).
[15]*Financial Post*, January 16, 1954. Report on a brief by the Retail Merchants' Association of Canada.
[16]Bruce Mallen, "The Combines Investigation Act: Canada's Major Marketing Statute," *M.S.U. Business Topics*, (Spring 1970), 72.
[17]*William Hart* v. *Dominion Stores Ltd. and Coca-Cola Ltd.* (1968) 1 O.R. 775.
[18]*Thomas G. Lightburn* v. *Ritchie Mercury Sales* in Canadian Sales and Credit Law Guide, par. 21-020, 1969, CCH Canadian Limited.
[19]An indictable offence roughly corresponds to a felonious offense as used in the United Kingdom and the United States.
[20]British Columbia, Commodities Minimum Loss Act, 572.
[21]Personal communication with Mr. Joseph Christian Stark and Company, Vancouver, British Columbia.
[22]John F. Due, *Provincial Sales Taxes*, Canadian Tax Papers #37 (Toronto: Canadian Tax Foundation, 1964), p. 1.
[23]*Combines Investigation Act*, Revised Statutes of Canada, 1952, c. 314, as amended, 1960, c. 45, Section 33C, s.s (1). A summary conviction offense roughly corresponds to a misdemeanour as used in the United Kingdom and the United States.
[24]Stephenson, op. cit., p. 47.
[25]Ibid., pp. 44-45.
[26]*Trading Stamps: The Social, Economic and Legal Aspects of Stamp Schemes in Canada and Why They Should be Eliminated* (Toronto: Retail Merchants Association of Canada, 1961), p. 20.
[27]Personal communication from D. W. Rolling, General Manager, Retail Merchants Association of Canada, August 6, 1970.
[28]*Trading Stamps*, op. cit., p. 23.
[29]Stephenson, op. cit., p. 15.
[30]Thanks are due to Professor Robert Rogow, Simon Fraser University, for his wise counsel on this section.
[31]Canada, *Workmen's Compensation in Canada*, Legislation Branch, Canada Department of Labor (Ottawa: Queen's Printer, 1969), p. 3.
[32]*Incomplete Agenda—The Unorganized* (Montreal: Industrial Relations Center, McGill University, 1968), p. 6.
[33]Canada, *Labor Organizations in Canada*, Economics and Research Branch, Canada Department of Labor (Ottawa: Queen's Printer, 1968), p. 111.
[34]Canada, *Labor Standards in Canada*, Canada Department of Labor (Ottawa: Queen's Printer, 1965).
[35]City of Regina, Zoning Bylaw Number 4306, 1.
[36]Douglas E. Harker, *The City and the Store* (Vancouver: Woodward Stores Ltd., 1958), no paging.
[37]Macpherson, op. cit., p. 22.
[38]Moyer and Snyder, op. cit., p. 203.

27 The Administration of Transport Policy: the Regulatory Problems *

K. W. Studnicki-Gizbert

Introduction

The subject of economic regulation in general and transport regulation in particular has been receiving considerable attention both in the professional literature and in political discussions. It is not the purpose of this paper to provide an overview of these discussions or a critical description of the existing regulatory structure as it exists at present in Canada. Given the vastness of the field and the limitations imposed by the format of this paper (as well as by the capacity of its author), the present discussion will concentrate on a few key issues set within a broad framework of 'positive'[1] policy analysis.

Approaches to Transport Regulation

Intervention of governments in the transport sector is almost universal. Economic regulation is an instrument—but not the only one—of state intervention. It is logical, therefore, to consider the usefulness and limitations of regulation within a broader context of the aims of government intervention. The over-all aims of government intervention are not always explicitly stated and are often difficult to formalize in an operationally meaningful manner. To a very large extent policy formulation, development, and change are continuous processes in which both the weights given to conflicting objectives and the way in which different policy instruments are used are adjusted.[2] This does not mean, however, that the policy development process does not generate a coherent approach or a broad 'band of policies' and general objectives even if the exact tradeoffs between conflicting goals are inherently imprecise. As long as this inherent lack of precision in 'policy objectives' and 'objective function' is understood, it is useful to employ the term 'policy objectives' as an expositional device.

In order to clarify the differences between various approaches to government intervention the following classifying device is employed.[3]

From the point of view of policy objectives, a distinction is made between objectives *exogenous* to the transport industry (e.g. regional development, industrial development, interregional or intergroup income distribution) and objectives *endogenous* to transport (i.e. the improvement of the functioning of the transport system per se). This classification broadly corresponds to the distinction drawn by the [MacPherson] royal commission on transportation between 'transport policies' and 'policies using transport as a policy instrument.' It can be argued that it is also reflected by the use of the terms 'adequacy' and 'public interest'; writers on the subject of regulation and government intervention assume industrial efficiency (i.e. endogenous objectives) as the policy objective and allocative efficiency rules as the guide. In this way the basic policy prescriptions are derivable from the normative analysis of economic efficiency, i.e. from welfare economics. This approach has also been adopted by the MacPherson commission and is the foundation of both the commission's recommendations and the concept of 'efficiency' in the declaratory section of the National Transportation Act.

From the point of view of approaches to transport policy and regulation, a distinction is made between a *neutral* or *corrective* approach, aimed at the improvement of allocative efficiency of the existing system, which essentially would simulate the working of perfect competition (in the technical sense of the term) thus ipso facto correcting market distortions, effects of monopolistic behaviour, etc. and an *active* or *promotional* approach aimed at the change of industry's structure or pattern and/or rate of development.

The majority opinion with respect to the underlying economic assumptions is that an economically efficient (i.e. competitive or competition-simulating) pricing system and proper compensation schemes for publicly imposed obligations would result in an optimal working of the system.

The Postulate of Efficiency

The term 'efficient' has a definite meaning in economic analysis. An efficient system of resource allocation implies the satisfaction of a set of strictly defined conditions.[4] It is demonstrable that the existence of 'perfect competition' (in the strict, technical meaning of the term) will result in the optimum, or the most efficient, allocation of resources, but this is not true if, instead of perfect or 'pure' competition, the feasible market form is 'duopolistic' or 'monopolistic' competition. It is possible to accept regulation of monopoly, of oligopoly, or of monopolistic competition aimed at simulating the results of perfect competition as a reasonable alternative way of achieving the most efficient ('optimal') resource allocation. This view has been expressed by a number of economists; for instance, Meyer et al. state:

> regulation is essentially a substitute for competition in the protection of public interest and it has developed historically in public service industries in which competition has demonstrated its inadequacy. Theoretical constructs, explicit or implicit, of the competitive outcome, therefore, have been retained as the standards for regulatory action. The substitution of the regulatory process for competition thus has involved no change in the ultimate objectives, only in the means of achieving these objectives.[5]

In discussing the efficiency criterion within the framework of welfare analysis, the simplifying assumptions of the theory must always be kept in mind; thus the optimum system of allocation described by elegant equations is by its very nature a highly stylized one and can only reflect imperfectly the complex reality. This is not to be construed as a critical statement. Serious welfare economists have made their simplifying assumptions fully explicit, and their writings abound with warnings against uncritical application of optimization rules, warnings often disregarded in applied studies. The problem that concerns us here is the extent to which special characteristics of transport industries (characteristics, incidentally, that transport shares with many other activities) affect the interpretation of efficiency rules.

The two characteristics singled out for this discussion are: the importance of 'service availability'; (this is related to the perishability or 'non-storability' of service); and the jointness of transport outputs. These two characteristics, or rather sets of characteristics, are responsible for conceptual difficulties in defining transportation output and consequently for much confusion in the discussion of policy issue.

Let us start with a very simple observation. A user of transport service is purchasing transportation of goods (or persons) from Here to There; the carrier supplies the capacity not only from Here to There but also from There to Here. There is no necessary relationship between the capacity provided by the carrier and utilized by the purchaser of transport services; or, rather, the capacity provided by the carrier must always be greater than, or in the limiting case equal to, capacity utilized. The capacity units are technologically determined and fixed by investment actions of the carrier (i.e. the carrier invests in certain sizes of vehicles and this size, or carrying capacity, is fixed within a certain range). Secondly, the capacity cannot be stored; unused capacity on a trip 'perishes' after the trip is commenced. Obviously, except in the rarest case, the system will produce excess capacity; statistically speaking, 'available ton-miles' almost always will exceed 'ton-miles carried.'

From the user's point of view transport is an input which, together with other inputs, is employed in the production or consumption activity; some of these inputs are directly related to transport service availability (e.g. maintenance of stocks, own time spent in waiting for a transport service, etc.). The objective of the user is to minimize not just transport costs but also the costs of all inputs, which usually implies a demand for excess capacity.[6] This can be restated as follows: the price of a transport service is really a composite of two (or more) elements: the price for actual carriage and a premium for service availability.[7] Similarly, the costs of providing transport services can be decomposed into costs of actual carriage plus costs of providing additional capacity to assure a certain level of service.

The efficiency of a transport system is thus related both to costs of carriage and to conditions of availability. Since the provision of availability is associated with costs, a demand-responsive transport system must not produce more service availability (or excess capacity) than the transport user demands (and is willing to pay for), and also it must provide at least the degree of service availability the user requires (and is willing to pay for).

The tricky part is the 'at least' condition. Where high density of traffic exists and where consequently the frequency of service is high, the proportion of the necessary excess capacity to total capacity tends to be lower, and thus a higher service availability can exist as a lower cost. The users of transport services on high-density routes therefore gain in two ways: bigger equipment and better facilities utilization bring down the costs of carriage; and more frequent schedules and greater choice of alternatives increase the service availability. (All that is true up to the point where high traffic volumes result in congestion costs.)

Once the factors of availability and external economies (or benefits) of traffic density are included, the analysis of efficiency criteria becomes more difficult.[8] Certainly, the exclusive concentration on rates-cost problems without due allowance for service availability and thus excess capacity is not admissible. The problem of costing excess capacity, which has plagued transport regulators for many years, arises from the phenomenon of directional imbalance and the difficulty of distinguishing between 'planned excess capacity' (which is a necessary element of any transport system) and 'unwanted surplus capacity.' This is a problem of direct relevance to the efficiency criterion: if one expects a cost-based rates scheme as a proxy for the strict application of the marginal costs efficiency criterion of welfare economists, then the estimate of necessary excess capacity is needed to cost the operation of the system, and this implies the determination of the 'necessary excess capacity.'

Another set of problems arises when parts of the necessary excess capacity are marketed at 'promotional' low rates (e.g. back-haul rates and off-peak rates: deferred delivery or space available rates). These problems have been extensively analysed by economists in the context of peak-off peak pricing policies;[9] the extension and application of this analysis to transport problems still remains to be done. The results of such analytical work should bring about further refinement of efficiency rules and provide an adequate framework for the assessment of the legislative prescriptions regarding the determination of compensatory rates.

The generation of external benefits and costs is an important aspect of transport activities. In general terms the problem of externalities has been extensively treated in both theoretical and applied literature. It arises if the net social or economic benefits exceed (or fall short of) those paid for through market transactions. Thus the welfare of the society would be advanced if the activity in question was extended (or curtailed) beyond the level maintainable by direct payments for services; this would require a subsidy in the case of positive difference between social and private (i.e. paid by market transactions) benefits and a specific tax when such a difference is negative. A considerable degree of sophistication has been achieved by theoretical economists working in this area; however, in order to make this analysis applicable to transport administration or regulatory actions, operationally meaningful ways of identifying and quantifying the externalities and an efficient set of rules for determining incentives and penalties will have to be developed.

The Structure of Regulated Industries

In the discussion of the efficiency postulate, two sets of problems should be considered: those related to the functioning of the transport system as it exists with the objective of maximizing its efficiency and protecting the user from monopolistic exploitation, instability, or inadequate provision of services; and the improvement and development of transport services to realize the potential of innovations and to accommodate traffic growth. In other words, the distinction is made between the efficiency of the existing structure and the efficient development or evolution of the industry. Implicit in the MacPherson royal commission recommendations, as well as in most discussions in economic literature, is that an efficient pricing system (which subsumes proper and neutral compensation payments for loss services provided in the public interest, and the absence or elimination of monopolistic elements) should assure the optimization both of the present system and of its future development. The validity of this assertion depends on rather strong assumptions. We do not know enough about the structure of Canadian transport industries, about the complex interrelationships between different parts of the system, or about the long-term conditions of the supply of labour, capital, and other inputs to judge definitively whether efficient development and desired structural changes will necessarily emerge from the efficient performance of the existing system. A strong case can be made that it will not. If so, then transport policy requires the existence of promotional or developmental instruments in addition to corrective ones; secondly, the corrective instrument should be used not only in a responsive way (to correct the perceived cases of malfunctioning of the system) but also in an active manner, i.e. to seek structural change and attempt to identify and correct the fundamental causes rather than deal only with specific cases which are the subject of complaint. It appears realistic to expect that more fundamental corrective actions would require a mix of regulatory and developmental or promotional actions.

The Postulate of Equity

The concepts of 'equity' and 'public interest' are basic to public discussion of the public utilities—including transport—behaviour, and often provide the rationale for government intervention. Yet they are extremely difficult to define. The concept of equity can be assigned two sets of meanings: as an outcome and as a process. Equity as an outcome is related to the distribution of income, or wealth, or some other desirable attributes (e.g. opportunities for employment without emigration). It is related to the welfare of underprivileged or poor groups or areas, economic or social underdevelopment, minimum or equitable standards of accessibility, delivery of services, quality of life, etc. 'Equal treatment of equals,' 'removal of undue burdens' or 'obstacles to development,' 'equality of opportunity' are some of the phrases used, which in turn lead to further problems of defining 'equality,' 'undue burdens,' 'equal opportunities,' etc.

In the more egalitarian sense, 'equal treatment of equals,' and its corollary, 'unequal treatment of unequals,' implies equalization of benefits received rather than a benefits / cost ratio or net benefits. The neutrality approach implies that the benefits per dollar spent (either privately by the users or by the public purse) should be equalized; the equalization-of-benefits approach requires that the benefits accruing to the different classes of users of the system should be equal, even if it implies that more dollars are to be spent in one situation than in another to achieve the same benefits. This extreme formulation would imply equality as a goal.

A more moderate approach is the 'difference principle,' which states that if the results of a policy or the results of the working of the system would benefit economically strong sectors of the society (or well developed regions) this is acceptable only if, at the same time, through the same process, or because of the compensatory problems, the position of the less advantageous sectors were also improved so that the difference between stronger and weaker sectors would not be increased but preferably diminished.[10] The advocates of this approach assert that due to historical developments including past investments certain areas have gained significant advantages over others less fortunate in the past. Without government intervention, new investments and migration would flow to the areas favoured in the past; due to the existence of economies of traffic density, a higher level of development would be also associated with lower transport costs, which in turn would favour further growth. Thus a strict neutrality would in fact favour more advanced areas. Therefore, equalization of opportunities would require assistance to the areas or locations neglected in the past, but such assistance would be restricted to the catching-up period.

The other way to look at this problem is this: both relative incomes and employment-creating capacities[11] of different regions are related to the rate of industrialization. One of the key factors in industrial location is the agglomerative factor, i.e. industry tends to go where industrial process is advanced. This factor relates to the past industrial development and past development of infrastructure. In order to equalize the opportunities, the development of infrastructure and improvement of access (more facilities, cheaper and better services) should be concentrated in the areas of past industrial underdevelopment.

The egalitarian approach to equity definition would also imply, in the transport policy area, the adoption of common accessibility standards (for example, all communities of a certain size and located within a certain distance from the centres of their main community of interest would be assured the same frequency of passenger services) and equalization of the burden of the freight rates with respect to similar transport costs for similar products. In brief, it would imply non-neutral policies to counteract the existence of distance and benefits of traffic density (or scale economies).

In a more neutral sense, equal treatment of equals implies the absence of discrimination, e.g. equality of rates under the same cost conditions (given equivalent distances, volume of traffic, and handling characteristics, rates per unit-distance should be equal) regardless of whether competitive conditions exist or not. It should be noted that in the absence of joint and common costs perfect competition would assure such a situation. However, an important characteristic of transport industries is the existence of joint and common costs, the allocation of which requires the existence of additional, arbitrary rules. Transport enterprises seeking the optimum utilization of their capacities —even if their objective is service maximization subject to cost recovery rather than the highest profits—would, under conditions of different demand elasticities and the existence of joint and common costs, introduce price differentiation, which may in public eyes appear as price discrimination. For example, if a directional traffic imbalance exists a lower promotional rate may be justified to improve two-way utilization of capacity; yet a difference in rates for the same distance creates an impression of rate discrimination. Service or system extensions also may provide some awkward cases. An airline providing an essential service to remote areas, for instance, may be able to improve its fleet utilization by extending its operations, on an added-costs basis, to a highly competitive leisure market. This extension would be beneficial to the airline and its users by improving the system's financial stability; yet again, the visible effect is a higher unit rate for an essential service than in a rich, inessential market. If 'equal treatment of equals' is interpreted to mean an equalization of the cost/price relationship throughout the system, requiring proportionate allocation of joint or common costs without reference to demand conditions, such a rule could only be introduced at the social cost of inefficient use of resources. Furthermore, if equal treatment of equals as applied to transport pricing is defined as a condition where transport tariffs should result in *at least* no change in distributional effects against disadvantaged (higher-cost) regions, areas, or communities or a given improvement in their position, an economically efficient tariff is unacceptable, and a degree of subsidy or cross-subsidization is required.

However, to what degree and at what cost a given distribution of income or employment opportunities is to be achieved, is not an economic or administrative decision but a political one. In a democratic state it is the government and not an administrative or regulatory agency which can translate the political or socioethical principles into operational rules. Equity-as-outcome and the related 'adequacy'[12] criteria are therefore not capable of being enforced by regulators without political determination of to what extent, at what costs, and at whose expense (taxpayers-at-large through subsidies or other users through cross-subsidization) they are to be applied.

Equity-as-process is a different concept and has different implications. This approach stems from four observations: 1/equity does not imply equality, but is usually considered as implying a better, or more equal, distribution of economic advantages. Therefore, at each point of development a consensus must be reached, implicitly or explicitly, on the level of differences in advantages that is socially or nationally acceptable. 2/ The outcomes of policies and the net balances are difficult, if not impossible, to predict in advance; acceptable processes to move to a hopefully better position can, however, be designed. 3/ People are concerned with the equitability or fairness of the process;[13] meaningful participation and strict observance of the rules are preferable to the actions of the benevolent authority. 4/ The rule of law should govern policy in economic affairs as well as in all other spheres.[14]

Current Debates on Regulatory Issues

In previous sections, some of the basic problems of regulating transport industry were sketched. The conclusions which can be drawn from that discussion are as follows. First, even on purely economic grounds it is difficult to establish operationally satisfactory regulatory criteria. Second, the introduction of equity considerations generates situations of conflict between rules derived from apparently reasonable postulates. Third, given the conflicts between efficiency and equity considerations, a regulatory system cannot produce satisfactory results in terms of any one set of criteria. Of course if policy guidelines were to be explicitly stated for the regulators, then the effectiveness of the regulations and regulators would be judged by a simple criterion: whether the system produces the results asked for by the policy-makers.

The present debates over the usefulness and performance of the regulatory system concentrate on the issue of costs and benefits of economic regulation largely considered from the point of view of economic and administrative efficiency. Given such terms of reference, the result leads to an almost universal condemnation of the regulatory system. The main points are these: 1/ regulation distorts interindustry competition;[15] 2/ regulation distorts the allocation of resources within the regulated industry;[16] 3/ regulation raises prices to transport users; 4/ regulation protects inefficiency and hampers innovation;[17] 5/ regulation is inherently associated with administrative delays and high costs to the interests concerned (which at least to some extent is an inescapable effect of the search for 'process equity');[18] 6/ regulation adversely affects competitive incentives; 7/ regulators become overidentified with the regulated firms.

The focus of the current discussion of transport regulation in Canada is somewhat different. This is not surprising. Even before the passing of the National Transportation Act the Canadian regulatory system tended to be more relaxed than in the United States and many European countries; no conscious interference with intermodal competition has been attempted. Considerable restrictions on intramodal competition have existed, especially in air transport, bus route services, and, in some provinces, trucking industries.

The lack of interference with interindustry competition is generally accepted by both the shippers and the carriers.[19] As far as the intraindustry competition is concerned the regulated (or protected) firms have reacted favourably. The traumatic effects of attempting to create parallel and competitive railway systems in the past, and the special role of national carriers, rightly or wrongly tended to produce acceptance of a basically non-competitive situation within the air[20] and bus industries.

The regulatory system in Canada is attacked, however, on different grounds. 1/ The regulatory system is not responsive to the cases where public interest requires more equitable interregional rates and where transport should be used as an instrument of regional development. 2/ The regulatory system is ineffective during an inflationary period, allowing the carriers easily to pass increased costs to the users. 3/ The carriers (especially the railways) criticize, although politely and *sotto voce*, the regulatory/political system for not allowing the rates to catch up with inflation thus creating a long-run capital shortage gap. 4/ The regulatory system suffers from serious illogicalities in provincial and federal allocations of responsibilities.

These two listings remind one of Solow's distinction between big-thinkers and little-thinkers:[21]

> The world can be divided into big-thinkers and little-thinkers. The difference is illustrated by the old story of the couple who had achieved an agreeable division of labour. She made the unimportant decisions: what job he should take, where they should live, how to bring up the children. He made the important decisions: what to do about Jerusalem, whether China should be admitted to the United Nations, how to deal with crime in the streets. Economists are determined little-thinkers . . . Little-thinking can easily degenerate into mini-thinking or even into hardly thinking at all. Even if it does not, too singleminded a focus on how the parts of the machine work may lead to a careful failure ever to ask whether the machine itself is pointed in the right direction.

It may appear that Canadians, like Solow's economists, prefer little-thinking on the subject of regulation. This very well may be so, except that in the process we have identified an important link between regulation and national planning, especially regional planning. Given the paucity of planning instruments available to the Canadian government, regulation of key industries—transport, energy, etc.—may become crucial.

Conclusions

The key questions that reappear implicitly or explicitly in the Canadian debate on regulatory policies and transport policies are the following.

1. Should economic criteria dominate transport policies? The MacPherson commission implicitly answered 'yes'; but current criticism, especially from the western provinces, questions the validity of this approach.
2. Should transport be used as an instrument of regional, social and industrial policy? The answer partially depends on the establishment of a better factual base for assessing transport effectiveness in this role. The majority of current economic research work indicates a degree of scepticism,[22] but a large part of public opinion takes the opposite view. The subject could, and should, be researched further.[23] The decision, however, is a political one.
3. Can reasonable criteria for judging the non-economic effects of transport performance be developed? That is, can equity concepts be made operational? Serious work in this field has been rather recent and general, and will have to resolve all the problems of an integrated, interdisciplinary approach.
4. Only if we are reasonably clear in the general framework can the issue of how much and what type of regulatory structure be more definitely settled? Yet time will not stop, and the regulatory work and adjustments to regulatory structure decisions must go on. Thus, preliminary rules must be developed and/or applied. A possible set of such working rules could be 1/ reliance on competition where the industry structure is sound and where competition exists; 2/ positive adjustment action that is related to, but goes beyond, regulatory work should be taken where structural problems exist; 3/ a workable integration of policy instruments, including regulation, would appear a step in the right direction; 4/ however, the importance of equity in the process of regulation and control should be preserved.
5. What should be the mix of federal-provincial initiatives? Should we attempt to integrate and co-ordinate these initiatives, or should we try for a sharper delineation of spheres of activity? This issue is the core issue of Canadian federalism; it is likely that the answers to these questions will change over time. The current trend appears to favour general co-ordination within a semi-informal or makeshift framework. It is impossible, however, to extrapolate current political trends too much forward. A more specific question is this: if federal-provincial policies are integrated or co-ordinated on a selective basis, should the transport area be one where co-ordination and collaboration are fruitful? Or even more specifically: which aspects of transport policies need to be pursued on a co-operative basis?

Notes

*Studnicki-Gizbert, K. W., "The administration of transport policy: the regulatory problems," *Canadian Public Administration*, 18:4, Winter, 1975 (reproduced by permission of author and publisher). The author is executive director of research, Canadian Transport Commission, and a fellow of McLaughlin College, York University. This paper is presented by him in the latter capacity and the views expressed are not related to his work for the commission.

[1]The term 'positive' is used in its technical sense, i.e. the analysis of the actual, as opposed to the 'ideal,' working of the system. It may be noted, in passing, that most important contributions to economic policy analysis have adopted the alternative route, i.e. a 'normative' (how should it be) or 'rational action' approach using the results of the normative analysis as standards for judging efficiency of the existing arrangements.

[2]For an elaboration of this point of view and the discussion of the difference between normative ('objectives-analysis-solutions') and 'behavioural-organizational' approaches see K. W. STUDNICKI-GIZBERT 'Transport policy: objectives and policy instruments,' in STUDNICKI-GIZBERT, ed., *Issues in Canadian Transport Policy*, Toronto, Macmillan of Canada, 1974, pp. 361-407.

[3]A more exhaustive discussion of this classification scheme is contained in K. W. STUDNICKI-GIZBERT, 'Regulatory policy options in transport,' Transportation Research Forum *Papers*, 1971, pp. 1-30.

[4]George W. Wilson's statement is adequate as a brief preliminary definition: 'An optimum system refers to an optimum allocation of resources both within and without the transport industry. What we want is the appropriate amount of resources devoted to transportation in toto and the appropriate amount devoted to each particular mode of transport' (GEORGE W. WILSON, *Essays on Some Unsettled Questions On the Economics of Transportation*, Bloomington, Indiana University Press, 1962, p. 8). This also implies efficient allocation within transport modes. For a rigorous discussion of optimum allocation criteria see I. M. D. LITTLE, *A Critique of Welfare Economics*, Oxford, Oxford University Press, 1967. J. DE V. GRAFF, *Theoretical Welfare Economics*, Cambridge, Cambridge University Press, 1957, and E. J. MISHAN, *Welfare Economics*, New York, Random House, 1964. (Mishan's survey article included in this volume provides also a review of literature.)

[5]J. R. MEYER, M. J. PECK, J. STENASON, C. ZWICK, *The Economics of Competition in the Transport Industries*, Cambridge, Mass., Harvard University Press, 1959, p. 1. Strictly speaking this assertion is correct only if no external effects (external benefits or costs) exist and if a number of other special conditions are held.

[6]For example, in many airline operations, where no major directional imbalance exists, *average* load factors of 60 to 65 per cent are considered necessary to assure a high level of service availability.

[7]This formulation was proposed by MAURICE ALLAIS, 'La théorie économique et la tarification optimum de l'usage des infrastructures de transport,' *La jaune et la rouge*, Numéro special de 1964 ('Les transports').

[8]'Economies of traffic densities' bring in problems, similar to those of 'cost-decreasing industries,' which have challenged some of the best economists.

[9]The most important contributions are: M. BOITEUX, 'Peak load pricing,' in J. R. NELSON, ed., *Marginal Cost Pricing in Practice*, Englewood Cliffs, Prentice-Hall, 1964; P. O. STEINER, 'Peak loads and efficient pricing,' *Quarterly Journal of Economics*, Vol. 71, 1957; J. M. BUCHANAN, 'Peak loads and efficient pricing, comment,' *ibid.*, 80, 1968; A. GABOR, 'Further comment,' *ibid.*

[10]Important recent contributions to the egalitarian view of social justice are contained in JOHN RAWLS, *A Theory of Justice*, Cambridge, Harvard University Press, 1971. For extensive reviews see DANIEL BELL, 'Meritocracy and equality,' *The Public Interest*, 29, Fall 1972; L. THUROW, 'Toward a definition of economic justice,' *ibid.* 31, Spring 1973; R. A. POSNER and L. C. THUROW, 'On economic justice: an exchange,' *ibid.* No. 33, Fall 1973. For the classic critique of the egalitarian position see F. A. HAYEK, *The Constitution of Liberty* (esp. chaps. 6 and 7), Chicago, University of Chicago Press, 1960.

[11]These are two different problems. In parts of Atlantic Canada we have both low rela-

tive incomes and low employment-creating capacity; in parts of western Canada (wheat belt) incomes are high, though unstable, but the employment capacity low.

[12]The term 'adequate' is used in the preamble to the *National Transportation Act.* It automatically raises the question Adequate for what? Presumably for the achievement of social, political, and other (non-economic) since they are subsumed in the term 'efficient' goals. This is clearly a matter of setting political or socioethical standards.

[13]The importance of process is well stated by Heclo: 'Watergate was a reminder that we must judge public organizations not only by what they do, but by how they do it—and the reminder was particularly timely after some years during which concern for outputs had almost totally eclipsed concern over the standards governing the production of those outputs. A profusion of program analysts, policy studies, management languages, and techniques attested to a widespread opinion that institutions were to be judged as more or less effective machines for producing desired policy results: "by their fruits ye shall know them" was the going criterion. But this is no longer the case. If the so-called post-Watergate morality means anything, it is that the imbalance between output concerns and process concerns is being rectified.' H. HECLO, 'OMB and the presidency—the problem of "neutral competence," ' *The Public Interest*, 38, Winter 1975, pp. 80-1.

[14]This implies that all 'the decisions are derived from general rules and not from particular preferences which guide the government of the moment or from any opinion as to how particular people ought to be situated. The coercive powers of the government still serve general and timeless purposes, not specific ends,' F. A. HAYEK, *The Constitution of Liberty*, p. 226.

[15]American authors assert that controlling rate competition makes traffic allocation between industries inefficient and probably affects adversely the railways in their ability to compete effectively with the truckers. European writers assert the inefficiency imposed on road transport in the interest of protecting the railways. For a comprehensive discussion of the US regulatory scene, see ALFRED E. KAHN, *The Economics of Regulation*, Vols. 1 and 2, New York, John Wiley and Sons, 1971. A good review of the regulatory problems and a thoughtful case for de-regulation is contained in R. E. POSNER, 'National monopoly and its regulation,' *Stanford Law Review*, 21, 1969, pp. 548-643.

[16]This relates to the situation where, because of the rate regulation, the regulated firm will employ a different (i.e. inefficient) mix of factors of production in order to increase the rate base, etc. Cf. E. E. BAILEY, *Economic Theory of Regulatory Constraint*, Lexington, D.C. Heath, 1973.

[17]Cf. P. W. MACAVOY and J. SLOSS, *Regulation of Transport Innovation: The ICC and Unit Coal Trains to the East Coast*, New York, Random House, 1967.

[18]This problem has been examined by the Ash commission (UNITED STATES, THE PRESIDENT'S ADVISORY COUNCIL ON EXECUTIVE ORGANIZATION, *A New Regulatory Framework: Report on Selected Independent Regulatory Agencies*, Washington DC, US Government Printing Office, 1971). For a recent article containing a proposal for a change in the regulatory process without abandoning regulation in transport, see W. B. SAUNDERS, 'Should we have deregulation or reregulation?' *Traffic World*, 27 Jan., pp. 64-8; 10 Feb. 1975, pp. 64-8.

[19]The trucking industry in Canada has tended to be in favour of truck-rail competition with minimum interference. The industry has been advocating certain provisions to regulate such competition, namely, a prohibition of predatory rate practices (i.e. rates below variable costs); some restriction on agreed charges (especially the condition which ties the shipper to the railway for all of its traffic); and some protection for piggyback traffic.

[20]Restricted, partial competition on a few routes, notably the transcontinental route, has had strong public support.

[21]ROBERT M. SOLOW, 'The New Industrial State or Son of Affluence,' *The Public Interest*, 9, 1967, p. 100.

[22]See, for example, M. R. STRASZHEIM, 'Researching the role of transportation in regional development,' *Land Economics*, 58, 1972, pp. 212-19, and the literature quoted.

[23]For a discussion of some of the analytical issues raised see J. HEADS, *The Economic Basis for Transport Subsidies*, CTC Research Paper, ESAB, 75-4, 1975.

Part 3
Ownership

Introduction

Public ownership of business has sometimes been seen as another alternative to competitive private enterprise. At a very simple level, the argument has often been advanced that if we must have monopoly, we are better off with a government-owned monopoly than with a private one. And, just as regulation has sometimes been seen as a preferred alternative to competition in some circumstances, so has public ownership sometimes been advanced as being preferable to private ownership. In Canada this has been particularly common not so much because of any ideological commitment of Canadians to public enterprise, but for purely practical reasons. These include, in the case of our public utilities, the problems of serving a geographically dispersed but relatively small number of users and, in the case of our financial and communications industries, the objectives of achieving national development, unity and independence despite the close proximity to the south of the economically and politically most powerful nation in the world.

For these and other reasons, public ownership has been relatively prevalent in Canada and, consequently, one familiar aspect of government-business relations here has been the coexistence of both government-owned and privately owned firms, even in the same industries. This raises a number of interesting issues. One of these has to do with the possibility that publicly owned firms may serve as a means of "regulating" their privately owned competitors. Another has to do with the question of relative efficiency. Can publicly owned firms operate as efficiently as private firms? Should they attempt to be profitable? A broad range of such issues is confronted by Eric Kierans in Reading 28, another extract from his Report on Natural Resources Policy in Manitoba.

A new feature of the Canadian approach to public ownership is the blurring of the traditional distinctions between public and private ownership. This is evidenced by the promotion of various forms of government "partnership" with private firms—occurring at both the provincial and federal levels—as governments not only continue the kinds of subsidy and other assistance programs discussed in Section 2, but now begin to participate as part owners of particular business enterprises. A particularly wide-ranging venture in this regard is the Canada Development Corporation, whose purposes and activities are described by its Chairman, H. A. Hampson in Reading 29.

28 The Recommendations *

E. Kierans

A new resource policy is not something that can be imposed overnight, short of expropriation. Its implementation involves the whole community, both those who would benefit from it and those who would be hurt by losing the privileges and advantages of the status quo. In the eyes of the latter, present policies have all the virtues of absolute truth, confirmed by history and resting on such foundations as the sanctity of private property and freedom of enterprise. Any change in policy will be interpreted as an attack on these values that can only reduce growth, efficiency and stability. They would refuse to concede that change might be directed at privilege and position that reflected the political power of prevailing groups rather than fundamental judgments and values as when Pitt, the father of the income tax, was forced to list ecclesiastical stipends and income from mines and quarries at the head of the table of exemptions and to apply the tax to income from effort, the wages of industrial workers, while freeing accretions to wealth and the income therefrom. Simple historical precedents have taken on all the force and coloring of dogma.

If present policies are not dogma but merely reflect the particular ideology of an earlier period, then this has to be communicated to a public much influenced by tradition and itself fearful of change. That is the task and challenge of politics and of policy-makers, to create a sense of community and to persuade a people to support new policies and programs. The urgency and rightness of such policies must be communicated. They cannot be imposed from on high by those who claim to have seen the light. Communication is education, the process by which people learn, are persuaded and will support new directions.

First of all, a policy decision to develop the natural resources of Manitoba by crown corporations implies no attack on property rights. The people already own the resources so there is no expropriation of private tenure rights. Public ownership, like private, is a privilege that imposes the responsibility of ensuring that what is owned is used to the best advantage. If present policies yield returns that are less than optimal then the stewards are at fault and better policies must be introduced. Professor Pigou set down this principle in his Economics of Welfare, "It is the clear duty of Government, which is the trustee for unborn generations as well as for its present citizens, to watch over, and if need be, by legislative enactment, to defend, the exhaustible natural resources of the country from rash and reckless spoliation." Rational use demands efficient development of resources both now and in the future.

We have shown with statistics gathered from the books of the corporations themselves that the returns are not optimal from a social point of view; they are, in fact, negligible both for Canada as a whole and Manitoba in particular. Governments have been willing to sacrifice not only the present but the future stream of revenue flows from their resources. In return for the direct costs, wages principally, being spent within the province they have given up not only the normal profits on the capital employed, which they could have easily found within themselves, but also the rents and surpluses that come from owning scarce resources in a period of rapidly increasing industrialization and population growth. By assigning the rights to exploit scarce resources for periods of 21 to 63 years, they have delivered to agents and intermediaries the increasing volume of returns in the future as the substance of Manitoba is depleted by accelerating demand. We have no less an authority for this rising demand than Mr. Wingate himself, the Chairman of International Nickel of Canada Ltd. when he reported to his shareholders on Feb. 17, 1972 that "Longer term, we continue to have a strong conviction that nickel consumption, and therefore nickel sales, will rise more rapidly than the growth of the world's economies. We expect this consumption (825 million pounds in 1971) to double in the decade ahead and to approach a 2,000,000,000-pound annual level in the early 1980's. Existing and definable new markets for nickel-containing materials—many of which are discussed in the report—are involved in this conviction."

Output of metal ores by the big 3 reached $295 million in Manitoba in 1970. Profits before taxes were $86 million while wages and salaries were $60 million. The Government of Manitoba, when it concluded its arrangements with the three large corporations, thought only in short-run terms. The additional employment and payroll was the pay-off. The profits and the rents, the real value of the resources, were given away for two generations. It is not only the $86 million in 1970 (it was $50 million in 1968) that is at issue but the increasing amounts in each succeeding year. What will they be in 1980? 1990? 2000?

A mining-only policy, begun in 1960, might easily have achieved sales of $200 million by 1970. It would have required relatively small initial injections of capital with subsequent expansion from internal flows. (The net worth of the entire metal mining industry in Canada exceeded $4 billion in 1969. The amount of funds contributed by investors initially amounted to $904 million.) In 1970, the crown corporations could have shown profits of $100 million (mining being more profitable than refining) controlled by Manitoba and available for investment in other sectors of the economy, not in eastern head offices or exploration in Guatemala. And these profits would be annual flows not borrowing on capital markets. It is true that the payroll would be less, perhaps $22 million instead of $60 million, but the annual investment flows would have financed much more employment and productivity in the other sectors. A developing nation will always remain a developing nation when the capital generated flows out and this is an accurate description of Manitoba's present policy.

Does a crown corporation policy interfere with freedom of entry and enterprise? Again, the answer is no. Enclosure of Manitoba's resources is coming anyway if it is not already here. The only question is how enclosure will be imposed, by political decision or by commercial cartel control. We have seen that 9 integrated firms have double the assets of 177 mining companies. The number of metal mining firms in Canada has declined from 849 in 1965 to 218 in 1970. By forcing the pace of exploration in Canada, the federal government accelerates the trend towards concentration. Present legislation continues the expensing of exploration and development costs against current income and will go much further in permitting a charge against profits of $4 for every $3 actually spent. This is over-motivation with a vengeance. The new entrant is eliminated for he has no income against which to charge the expense and must consider all outlays as capital investment, a hopeless disadvantage against the established firm. The small or medium firm does not have the profits against which to charge large expenditures on exploration and, therefore, loses ground to its large competitors. On the other hand, the industry leaders have every reason to engage in exploration even when their own reserves are more than sufficient for 30, 40 or 50 years of production. They must control both markets, the supply of resources and the demand for them, if they are to maintain their monopoly position. If new reserves are found, wherever, it is important that they control them to forestall the competition of new entrants. Otherwise, their own future and their ability to administer prices and restrict output is jeopardized.

Access to Manitoba resources is not free. One can hardly speak of free entry where only the rich firms can enter. Government policy, then, should recognize the effects of enclosure of provincial wealth by the resource based giants. Private enclosure means quite simply that the encashment of the resources, turning them into wealth and capital, is controlled not by the crown but by the intermediaries. The value in excess of the costs of transformation accrues to the private sector. In 1868, the resources were taken from the private sector, Hudson's Bay, and transferred to the federal government. In 1930, they were handed over to the provincial government. In 1973, they have been for all effective purposes and gains, repossessed by the private corporations.

If the government of Manitoba decides to maintain the status quo, with some marginal increases in taxes, then it should frankly say to the people of Manitoba that it is unable, helpless, to challenge the power and control of the corporations. In effect, the political authority admits that it cannot restrain or contain commercial interests. A government can always say that every other nation accords these benefits to international investment. But this is excusing not reasoning. Perhaps the other provinces and nations bribe investment because Manitoba does and they are just waiting for leadership. That leadership will eventually be provided by some nation but until it is the public will be denied the value of their own possessions.

On the other hand, if the government of Manitoba decides to implement a new policy on resources, it should spell out clearly its motives and objectives. A decision to develop resources by the means of crown corporations involves no attack on property rights since the resources are already publicly owned. Enclosure by the government will apply only to the few large corporations who have already effectively denied access to the numerous, the small and the new firms. That enclosure has denied a reasonable share of the returns from the sale of resources to the people who own them. This surely must be the reason for and objective of new policies, namely the desire of the government to ensure a more equitable distribution of the provincial wealth.

Nor does a new resource policy mean an attack on profits or the profit motive. The members of the Carter Commission had a healthy respect for the profit motive and for the role that profits played in attracting sufficient flows of savings and investment funds to promote growth and development in the Canadian economy. They simply felt that the definition of income should be more broadly based to include receipts and revenues that escaped taxation such as capital gains. More particularly, they believed that many of the exemptions granted to the resource sector exceeded the incentives needed to attract capital and, in fact, contributed to excess investment in the resource industry and a misallocation of the scarce capital available to Canadians. It is doubtful that there would be the present demand for a reexamination of resource policies if the Carter recommendations had been implemented. Perhaps the furious assault of the mining and petroleum associations on the report will turn out to have been a strategic mistake, after all.

A new resource policy, then, is not an attack on profits which are a legitimate return to people who have invested their money in commercial ventures rather than in banks or government bonds. There is a price that must be paid for savings in order to attract them into investment just as there is a price for work. But we are attacking what I will call for the moment, super-profits or super-returns. In a competitive market economy most super-returns tend to disappear. For example, when computers were first introduced there was a shortage of skilled operators and programmers. Until training programs increased the supply of technicians, corporations had the choice of paying the wages demanded or closing down their computer facilities. Similarly a monopolist can limit his output by charging high prices until new competitors appear, drive down the price and reduce profits to a normal level. When there is an adequate supply of housing, landlords can only charge normal rents. If governments decide to fight inflation by raising interest rates and cutting back on new housing starts, then landlords will be able to charge super-rents.

Super-returns are due to scarcity, either induced or natural. They represent a return in profits, wages or rents in excess of what would be required, under normal market conditions, to call forth the required supply of such factors of production. All such super-returns are called economic rent by economists, i.e., the excess part of the payment for land or labor or capital that can be demanded under conditions of scarcity. When the scarcity is eliminated by competition or increased supply, the economic rent, super-returns, will disappear without reducing the supply of the factors of production. The economic rents that can be eliminated in this way are called quasi-rents, meaning that they resemble the excessive returns to natural or established monopolies but are temporary.

We are concerned here, however, with excessive returns, economic rents, that are not temporary but can be expected to increase over time. Non-renewable resources actually decline with use. There may be undiscovered resources or increases in knowledge and technology that will eventually produce substitutes. For a relevant planning period, the supply is fixed, is depleting and is generally controlled by a few large producers. Economic rent, then, is likely to continue indefinitely under present policies. In Manitoba's case, these rents will not accrue to the owners but to their appointed agents.

A new resource policy then, is not an attack on profits, either normal profits on capital invested in mining or the less than normal profits that prevail in the smelting and refining sector. It is an attack on the super-profits, the economic rents that flow from the leased control of natural resources. These rents should flow to the government of Manitoba in simple affirmation of the principle of property ownership. Such a policy in no way interferes with the legitimacy of the principles of private property, individual enterprise or the profit motive. Such a policy acknowledges the economic necessity of enclosure of public resources already recognized politically and constitutionally, so that the distribution of the returns from the natural wealth shall be shared by all and not be used to further giantism or monopoly.

Resource development is the transformation of natural wealth into liquid form. Seeking to keep that surplus, the economic rent from exhaustible resources, at home is surely a legitimate and necessary objective of government policy. Such a policy may or may not lessen a province's dependence on foreign capital markets but it would surely save a province from the humiliation of having to borrow back at interest the capital that got away.

The reasons for separating the exploration and development functions and confining these roles to separate crown corporations are based on the different objectives that must guide the activities of each.

The objectives of a provincial exploration corporation are clear and easily defined—taking inventory of the province's wealth and valuing the ore reserves presently held by the private sector under lease. Since the province has perfect tenure over its own lands, the corporation can proceed at an aggressive but orderly pace. The public, either as consumer or taxpayer, is presently paying for the frantic and disorderly pace of exploration by the private sector, anxious about their security of tenure and nervous about discoveries by competitors that could damage their own market position. This wasteful and costly duplication, spurred on by federal incentives, leads to a dissipation of economic rent and, by locking up ores in the hands of those already possessing proven reserves for decades to come, eliminates competition and enables a few large corporations to maintain control of world markets. A provincial corporation, having no such costly anti-social aims and limited to its own borders, can balance the costs of failures with the benefits of success and so arrive at a proper valuation of the people's estate.

A development corporation has but one objective, to mine and mill at the lowest possible cost. The government and people will judge it solely on its cost of sales and the severity with which it regulates its overhead costs. The objective is the conversion of natural resources into a surplus available for capital formation to meet the priorities of the province. There is no depletion of existing wealth if there is conversion into other assets and if that converted wealth remains in Manitoba. As each new ore body is ready for production, I would recommend separate crown companies so that competition in performance could develop between companies and be judged by government and the public. Just as the private sector aims at maximizing profit, so will the operating mines strive to maximize the amount of new capital or surplus available to the government each year for reinvestment in housing, agriculture, secondary industry and services according to the priorities of overall government planning.

Policy decisions should be the responsibility of the premier and cabinet as a whole, not a particular ministry, since economic development is the most vital concern of government. Only the cabinet can make the decisions that will dictate the rate of output as they compare the value of more present production with the returns to output in the future of steadily diminishing supplies and rising demand for resources. Individual departments and crown corporations have, like the private corporations, their own growth at heart which may not always coincide with balanced provincial growth. Only the full cabinet can take the hard decision which may expand or reduce the rate of exploration for it is obviously senseless to invest scarce resources in more rapid rates of exploration if present reserves are large and new discoveries would not be exploited for decades to come. The private sector must commit enormous funds to such investment to protect its position and the consumer pays the carrying costs of idle investments. The province, secure within its own boundaries, can afford to invest in exploration as the need approaches and thus shorten the period, and investment outlays and interest charges, between discovery and recovery. It is this that makes the crown corporation a more efficient form of organization for carrying out the conversion of resources into new capital formation. The crown corporations, both exploration and development, should be responsible to the government and full cabinet through the appropriate committee.

Crown corporations, like private corporations, have their failures. Unlike the private sector, where the heavy losses of an RCA in computers, a Lockheed or a Penn-Central are quickly absorbed and disappear from view, the failures of crown corporations remain in the public eye. But crown corporations have their many successes in hydro, telephone systems, transportation and public services. Government planning of resource exploitation has overwhelming advantages over the existing concentration of raw materials in a few powerful hands. The worth of the resources, when known and valued by exploration, become a fixed factor, a natural monopoly owned by the public whose best interests can only be served by internalizing costs and planning output to achieve the maximum values over time. Planned output alone can avoid the excess capacity and investment, e.g., the potash industry, that drains economic rent away through waste and inefficiency.

We are not advocating crown corporations for the refining sector, but for the mining and milling operations only. Refining is a processing and manufacturing activity that should be left to the private sector. The crown mining corporation will carry the natural ores to the primary metal stages only. It is here that we find all the economic rent from conversion. The product is basic, homogeneous and undifferentiated. The market is the smelting and refining industries throughout the world which do not have mining divisions, e.g., Japan, and are reluctant to buy from their competitors, the international companies such as Inco, Anaconda, etc., which own their own mines. There is no market risk for the demand for primary metals is steadily rising against a dwindling supply and the high cost of private exploration, restricted output and the carrying charges of excess reserves.

Nor are there production risks for the operations are basic, the technology is in the public domain and there are competitive suppliers of the mining, milling and engineering equipment and services. The high costs of investment in research and development are avoided and left to the refiners developing new end uses for the basic ores that will keep their capital intensive refineries operating. The cyclical risks occur in the refining sector, accounted for mainly by excess capacity and overinvestment that lead to oversupply, price declines and losses on the capital invested.

Nor is capital the barrier that current mythology suggests. We have shown how little is needed, well within the capacity of economies far less developed and progressive than Manitoba, and how quickly one successful operation leads to two and two to four until economic policy and planning calls a halt. Even so, that little can be furnished by production loans and financing against future delivery. A most recent example is the money furnished to Imperial Oil by two midwest utilities for exploration in the Mackenzie delta against future delivery of gas on an, if and when, available basis.

There is no need to give up ownership, the right to the economic rents, for one day and certainly not for 21 years or forever. Renewing a lease to attract a smelter on these terms is to accept a price that is too high, too impossibly high. In the same way, a resource poor industrial nation will take the profits of participation if it can negotiate them but it is the resources that are needed, not the share in mining profits, to keep its economy going.

Integrating a resource policy into an overall economic plan means that a province should use the value of its exhaustible resources to finance the sectors of its economy that promise continuing economic activity, employment and development in the future. When the economic rents are given up for indefinite periods for the sole benefit of attracting smelting and refining activity, all other possible uses of the capital are foregone and an industry is created that is isolated from and unrelated to the main forces in the economy. These sectors remain weak and underfinanced as the economic surpluses from mining move out of the province. By retaining these surpluses in Manitoba, through the medium of crown corporations operating in the exploration and mining sectors, the natural wealth of Manitoba can be retained and used to reinforce the entire provincial economy.

Access to the natural resources of Manitoba by crown corporations only is the economic and commercial equivalent of their existing ownership by the public. There is nothing new or radical in such a policy. The government would simply be seeking the replacement by equivalent values of depleting wealth. Open access is the denial of the rights inherent in public ownership by assigning the wealth appropriated by discovery to the private sector, for a fraction of its value. Nor is there any prospect of the government acquiring the equivalent value of its wealth from the corporate sector under existing tax and institutional arrangements. The only practical alternative is a vigorous do-it-yourself program. The continuation of present policies will simply confirm the de facto enclosure already imposed by three or four large corporations.

Notes

*Kierans, E., *Report on Natural Resources Policy in Manitoba* (Prepared for the Secretariat for the Planning and Priorities Committee of Cabinet, Government of Manitoba, February, 1973, reproduced by permission of author and publisher).

29 The Canada Development Corporation *

H. A. Hampson

The Corporation's origins go back to the mid-1950s and Walter Gordon's Royal Commission on Canada's Economic Prospects which, among other things, examined the question of non-resident ownership and control of the Canadian economy. Mr. Gordon's subsequent writing and speeches suggested that the Corporation would be particularly concerned with pre-empting takeovers, and acting as a Canadian buyer of last resort. This approach then worked its way into the platforms of some of the political parties and emerged virtually unchanged in Mr. Gordon's Budget Speech of 1963, the famous Budget which featured the 30% takeover tax. As someone aptly put it, that tax was the guillotine and the CDC was the basket to be used to catch the dismembered heads! With the withdrawal of substantial parts of that Budget, the CDC dropped out of sight for a while, perhaps in part because shortly afterwards the Government found it necessary to seek exemption from the American interest equalization tax in order to ensure an undiminished flow of foreign capital into Canada! Obviously, against this background of balance of payments uncertainty, the time was not propitious to attempt to revive or replace the stillborn infant.

In the next few years, the underlying position changed considerably. The question of foreign investment in Canada receded somewhat from prominence for a variety of reasons as emphasis was put on other and more central strands of social and economic policy. Moreover, a number of specific measures were taken to deal with foreign ownership and control problems in selected areas of the economy, such as banking, life insurance, and the media of communication. Then, too, a number of published studies of foreign investment showed that the very real gains it brought to the Canadian economy in terms of employment and marketing and technical know-how did not involve as high a price in supposed lack of exports, research and purchasing in Canada as had been alleged. During this interval as well, there was a strong tendency for foreign-owned corporations to promote Canadian management to top positions, to elect more Canadian directors and to become more conscious of being good corporate citizens.

While all this was going on, a very fundamental change in Canada's trade and balance of payments was taking place; the growth of our exports substantially outpaced that of our imports because of the growth of demand for our natural resources, the improved competitive position and attitudes of our secondary manufacturing industries, and special factors such as the Automotive Pact. Our current account moved into overall surplus in 1970 and 1971, and the capacity of Canadian savings and financial markets to finance more of Canada's requirements expanded dramatically.

This is not to say that the foreign ownership and control issue is not significant in real terms in particular industries and areas, or that the issue lacks emotional appeal in certain areas of the country, perhaps most of all in Metropolitan Toronto. The recent upsurge of discussion in the press is testimony to that, as is the interest with which the Government's forthcoming pronouncement on the subject is awaited. However, as a background factor influencing the shaping of the CDC as it now is, the foreign investment issue was very much less significant than it had been some years earlier. Indeed it appears to me—and I should emphasize here that I had no "insider" role during this entire period—that the CDC began to be seen at the end of the 1960s primarily in terms of filling such gaps as existed in the Canadian capital market for large-scale developmental projects. Put in another way, it began to be thought of as a positive force to create and back Canadian investment projects, rather than as a mechanism reacting to foreign acquisitions.

Although the idea of the CDC appeared in Government Throne Speeches in a number of years in the late 1960s, it did not—because of other legislative priorities—reappear as a proposed piece of legislation until early 1971 when the present Bill was laid before Parliament and was adopted with minor amendments in June of that year. You will see from my later remarks that the child has become very different from that originally conceived in that it was no longer a special kind of mutual fund charged with being an instrument of Government policy to pre-empt foreign takeovers.

What emerged was, in fact, a rather unique Special Act Corporation charged with the following objects under Section 6 of its Legislation:

- (a) to assist in the creation or development of businesses, resources, properties, and industries of Canada;
- (b) to expand, widen, and develop opportunities for Canadians to participate in the economic development of Canada through the application of their skills and capital;
- (c) to invest in the shares or securities of any corporation owning property or carrying on business related to the economic interests of Canada; and
- (d) to invest in ventures or enterprises, including the acquisition of property, likely to benefit Canada;

and these activities "shall be carried out in anticipation of profit and in the best interests of the shareholders as a whole".

Section 2 of the Act summarizes these objectives by saying that the Corporation "will help develop and maintain *strong* Canadian-controlled and managed corporations in the *private* sector of the economy and will give Canadians greater opportunities to invest and participate in the economic development of Canada". Our Directors have, therefore, determined that we should not invest in enterprises which would continue to be controlled by any level of Government or Government agency. So do not look for us to invest in projects like that of James Bay in northern Quebec. And do not expect us to prop up weak or declining companies; we were not established to buy losses or to watch our underlying investments stagger from layoff to layoff, a consequence which seems inevitably to follow this sort of "bail-out" philosophy.

We are in fact very different from any other development corporation that I know of, either in Canada or abroad. And we do not intend to fritter away the advantages of our uniqueness by making the same mistakes as those other corporations. How are we different? I believe that our distinctiveness lies in four features: our independence from Government interference, our mandate to conduct our operations in anticipation of profit, our potential size, and the fact that a mechanism exists for Government participation in the Corporation to be scaled down by the Directors to not more than 10% at any time.

Envisaging the day when 90% of the shareholdings will be in the private sector, the authors of the Canada Development Corporation legislation provided that it not be a Crown Corporation, not require approvals of the Governor-in-Council in any aspect of the conduct of its affairs (although, of course, the Minister of Finance must receive the approval of the Governor-in-Council before he invests any of the taxpayers' money in shares or debt of the Corporation), and not report to Parliament. Parliament, however, having set out the objects and capitalization of the Company, must affirm any changes in those objects or capitalization approved by the Directors and shareholders, a necessary and logical protection against the theoretical possibility that the intent of the Legislation could be turned on its head; and a provision in effect like that applying to other specially-incorporated Canadian companies such as the chartered banks.

Section 11 of the Act provides that, unless otherwise determined by a directors' by-law sanctioned by at least two-thirds of the shareholders, the affairs of the Company shall be managed by its Board of Directors, consisting of not less than eighteen nor more than twenty-one persons. The Government made clear to these Directors upon their original appointment that it expected the affairs of the Corporation to be managed in a timely, flexible and creative way through an independent Board without interference from Government. The previous Minister of Finance also said publicly on a number of occasions that he meant the Board to be independent, expressing the hope that if they were ever directed to make investments with which they disagreed they would forthwith resign—with all the difficult political consequences for the Government which that would entail.

We are fortunate in having a strong Board of outstanding Canadians who have earned a high reputation for themselves, not only for their successful careers but for the calibre of their integrity and community service. You might note with interest that we have no lawyers, accountants, bankers, or stockbrokers on our Board, not because they would not qualify on the foregoing grounds, but because their services are always available through the normal market channels, and since it was thought desirable to obtain directors with the widest possible experience in industry. These Directors are responsible to the shareholders as in any normal corporation, the only distinction being that all Directors must be Canadian citizens and that four-fifths of the Directors can remove another Director from office, a feature presumably designed to enable the Board to deal with someone who has developed personal traits of such an embarrassing nature as to jeopardize the reputation or integrity of the Corporation!

It has been alleged in some quarters that a potential conflict of interest exists because of the business interests, directorships, or offices held by members of the CDC Board. Directors who are full-time officers of the CDC—the President, Mr. Marshall Crowe, and myself—are relinquishing all outside directorships, but it does not seem reasonable to expect other board members to give up their source of livelihood to serve as CDC Directors, particularly as the fees they earn from doing so would only serve to get them about halfway up to the poverty line! Surely, no reasonable person would expect a corporation in the multi-billion-dollar size range to be run by those who have neither employment in this country's industrial life nor experience that fits them for the job. In the unlikely event that a conflict of interest arose (and this could only be through a firm with which a director is in some way associated looking at the same investment proposition as the CDC, since we certainly will not be buying into our directors' enterprises), the director concerned would follow the normal practice of declaring his interest, removing himself from the room and taking no part in the Corporation's deliberations on the subject. I can assure you that our Board of Directors is so keen to ensure that the Corporation be successful and enjoy the highest of reputations that they are leaning over backwards to avoid even the remotest suspicion of problems in this area.

Our Directors do not regard our second unique mandate, to operate in anticipation of profit, as merely a piece of window dressing. We are not aiming at a nominal rate of return, or vague hopes of profit at some indeterminate future time. The projects in which we will invest will have to offer a competitive return commensurate with the risks entailed, which will normally be higher than those accepted by other financial institutions. This approach is very much in line with the philosophy publicly expressed by Mr. Benson. What sets us apart from others is that we are exclusively devoted to making equity investments of a developmental nature, and can therefore take a somewhat longer time-horizon than other institutions which are constrained by shareholder expectations or the nature of their liabilities to the public.

Some have suggested that this emphasis on profits will conflict with the object of developing Canadian enterprises in the long run, but we do not believe that this is the case: a sound, economic foundation is not built on losing enterprises; and one does not have to look outside the boundaries of Canada to see what happens to employment trends or the standard of living of whole communities when this is tried. Moreover, if the Government has some social, political, or welfare reason for putting money into a losing enterprise, it always has the option to do so through special subsidies or grants: that is a political judgment which should be made, not by the CDC, but by those charged with political office.

The opposite criticism of our profit mandate is sometimes made, namely that if we stress a competitive return on our investments, we will be in conflict with the existing private sector—in short, that everything that ought to get done on economic grounds will get done anyway and the CDC is therefore redundant. Our Directors do not share this view and believe that we have a role to play which complements, rather than conflicts with, the existing institutions.

First, the CDC and its shareholders will be able to take a somewhat longer view than the shareholders of other financial institutions since longer-range development is to be our principal business. Second, there is no large institution specializing in higher-risk equity investments of a developmental nature, although there are many corporations which devote a proportion of their resources to this activity in their own particular field. We believe that the nature of the skills which we build up, the outlook and the temperament of our management, and the potentially large and diversified size of our operations will permit us to undertake this sort of activity with less risk, and better returns, to our shareholders than many other institutions. Third, there is an implicit assumption in this argument against CDC that our present financial market system is operating with absolute perfection, and this is clearly not the case. We have a very flexible financial system in which innovations take place constantly, and the fact that this particular innovation came from the Government sector does not necessarily mean that it is less valid than those arising elsewhere in the system. Finally, we can observe that the competition to finance worthwhile major projects is not always intense; the fact that the Government had to participate in the Panarctic venture to make it viable is one case in point. The large inflow of foreign investment into some segments of our economy provides further evidence that there should be room for the CDC, although I would be the first to agree that a large part of this inflow has stemmed also from gaps in Canada's managerial, marketing or technical skills. Yet these skills tend to develop when there is a market need for them, and a source of financing to turn that market need into practical reality, a role which we believe the CDC can play to some extent.

The third area in which the CDC is unique is in its potential size. Our authorized capital consists of 200,000,000 common shares, of which 2,500,000 were initially subscribed for by the federal government at a price of $10.00 per share. Even if one assumes that the shares will not appreciate in value in the years ahead—and we expect significant appreciation—the sale of all our authorized common shares would bring in $2 billion. In addition, there is $1 billion of authorized preferred share capital—which would be issued in convertible, participating or other forms—as well as a capacity to leverage this equity capital through borrowing to whatever extent the Directors deem prudent. If this borrowing ultimately reached $1 billion, we would be looking at a $4 billion corporation in the years ahead—plus capital appreciation. This is a very sizeable sum even for today's inflationary age, and obviously we will only reach this size if we are successful in persuading the public that investment in our securities is a sensible and profitable way for them to employ their savings.

This in turn will depend on the success of our investments. The average size of these will be large, because we intend to concentrate on enterprises which are significant for Canada and which can compete in the growing international market. Obviously, these investments must also have unusual growth prospects to compensate for the risks involved. While not setting ironclad standards at this stage, we would want the profitability of our companies to grow at about double the anticipated annual growth rate of GNP in current dollars, which is of the order of 8%. These investments will not be selected out of regional considerations, but there should be opportunities to invest in each of the principal regions of Canada; indeed, of the dozen serious projects which have so far been identified from the veritable flood which has poured in since the doors opened, there is a surprising degree of regional balance.

We will not be attracted to a proposition simply because it offers an opportunity to "buy back" a company currently in foreign hands or because we are a "buyer of last resort" in the mind of the would-be vendor. Such propositions will be treated exactly like any other opportunity; if they meet our standards, we shall invest—but we shall not buy them simply because somebody is waving the threat of selling to non-residents at us. Incidentally, foreign takeovers have been a minor part of foreign investment in Canada since the war, with the total unlikely to have exceeded $1.5 billion, less than 1/20th of the present total outstanding. There is a good case to be made—despite the probable disappearance of Canada's current account surplus in 1972—that the share of foreign capital in Canada's industry generally is peaking out as Canadians increase their investment in equities. In any event, our role is to use our limited resources to best advantage, which will normally entail investing either in new ventures or in significant expansions of existing ones rather than merely transferring ownership of existing enterprises—which may be for sale precisely because they have lost their growth characteristics.

Even though our resources are potentially large, they are clearly not large enough to do everything. Put in another way, we must try to develop our own mini-industrial strategy and avoid the pitfalls, common to conglomerates and governments alike, of scattering resources too thinly in too many directions and thus losing both effectiveness and control. Rather, our mandate is to reinforce strength in selected areas, and to identify unusual growth opportunities where a unique Canadian competence can be developed or encouraged.

Initially, our Directors have identified six areas in which we should concentrate our efforts: these are oil and gas; health care; the petrochemical-related industries; mining; pipelines and related northern transportation; and venture capital. Each of these areas offers excellent growth prospects and permits us to expand the investment opportunities open to Canadians. By participating in the venture capital industry, either through forming a new enterprise or by making an investment in one or more existing enterprises, we can help to play a creative role in the financing of smaller, high technology business without getting directly involved in the specialized business of vetting and monitoring many smaller enterprises. Indeed, our legislation directs us not to make investments which involve less than $1 million, and in practice they would be even larger; otherwise, we would ultimately hold an enormous portfolio requiring a vast bureaucratic apparatus to supervise. There would be no faster way to kill the positive and imaginative attitudes which we hope will characterize the Corporation.

Generally speaking, we hope to make our investments in each of the fields mentioned through "vehicle" companies which would have their own skilled staffs and specialized operating management. This will enable us to keep a small, flexible and creative central staff—making good use of qualified consultants where required—to direct the general policy of the vehicle companies, to maintain appropriate financial controls over them, and to ensure that they remain innovative and growth-oriented. This structure should also be useful in bringing about mergers where larger scale and more specialization will genuinely enhance the competitive strength of Canadian industry.

Initially, we aim to have a sufficient shareholding in each enterprise—either alone or together with major and reputable partners—to achieve effective control of those enterprises. This does not mean that we must always have 51% or that there will not be times when we shall aim at 100%; the numbers are not so important as the ability to have a positive and constructive influence on the policy and operations of the underlying companies. The CDC is quite prepared to undertake joint ventures with others in the private sector, including non-resident-controlled companies, but not when control will lie with foreign interests.

The CDC, then, might be described as aiming to operate midway between the styles of a multi-division operating company and a merchant banker. There is no desire to interfere in the day-to-day operations of underlying companies (indeed, CDC would hopefully make investments only when good management was in place or obtainable). CDC's prime concern would be working out the basic strategy of those companies in concert with management, but always being prepared—if management proved weak or inadequate—to replace it. This is, or should be, the position that any normal major shareholder takes—as contrasted to a lender's approach, which would clearly not be appropriate to the CDC since it will not invest in debt securities.

Section 39 of the Act authorizes the government to sell to the CDC its interests in Polymer Corporation, Panarctic, Northern Transportation, and Eldorado at a fair and reasonable price; however, there is no obligation on the part of the CDC to acquire any or all of the corporations. Some observers have come to the erroneous conclusion that this section was put in the bill to make the CDC's earnings look good in the early years of its operation. This is certainly not the case; in fact Eldorado and Northern Transportation have both lost money in recent years. It is virtually certain that we will not acquire Eldorado in view of the weak demand for uranium, its high mining costs in relation to today's prices, and its heavy stockpile. The decision on Northern Transportation is still open, and will depend upon the outcome of our studies of its future profit potential.

Panarctic, of course, does not have any profits, either, since it is an exploration and development company; indeed, it will require significant infusions of new capital for some years. Polymer's profits have shrunk dramatically in recent years because of the conditions in the synthetic rubber industry. This company earned a very modest amount of money in 1971, although it expects to earn more in 1972 and succeeding years as its diversification programme begins to bear fruit. However, to achieve these improved earnings it will require substantial infusions of new equity in the next 12-24 months.

Nevertheless, we take a positive view of the prospects of both Panarctic and Polymer and have come to the conclusion that both these companies could fit into our own strategy. Incidentally, at this stage in their development, continued direct government ownership could involve delays and uncertainties in reaching the important business decisions they must make. In the case of Panarctic, the Department of Indian Affairs and Northern Development has conflicts of interest since it is responsible for the balanced development of the North, for protection of both the rights of the native people and the ecology, and for the granting of permits to all oil and gas companies, while at the same time being a shareholder in the largest company operating in the Arctic Islands.

In any event, our Directors have determined that we should be prepared to make a bid at fair and reasonable values for both Polymer and Panarctic. Even though these two companies would in effect be going only from one pocket of the government to another at this stage, through the issue of more CDC shares to the government—with the actual value realized by the government dependent upon the value of the CDC's shares when they are first offered to the public—both sides are putting great stress on arriving at a market price, a price at which a willing buyer and a willing seller would normally meet. This is not easy to do since neither company has a history of stable earnings and there are no other companies with which a comparison could easily be made. Nevertheless, both sides wish to be realistic, the government for obvious reasons, and we because we do not wish to be regarded as "marks" who have paid too high a price under the influence of government or as weaklings requiring some sort of favour from government in order to survive. In any case, it is encouraging and constructive development that Parliament can envisage companies moving out from under government ownership, since too often in the past there appears to have been a rule that when a government gets into something it should never let go of it.

This brings me to the fourth and final unique feature of the CDC's legislation, namely the provision in Section 36. 1(b), which gives the Company the sole discretion to redeem for cancellation at net asset value any number of common shares held by the government—or agents of the government—in excess of 10% of the total. This feature has been very much overlooked in discussions of the CDC; it represents a genuine attempt by the federal government to regard itself as the minority partner of a joint venture with individual Canadians to promote the growth of strong, domestically-controlled corporations in the private sector. For too long Canadian business and governments, or governments and private citizens, have adopted an adversary position towards each other, a position of mutual distrust—well-merited in some cases—instead of working together toward a common goal—the economic, social and political betterment of our country. We must all hope that the intended spirit of cooperation between government and private citizens as shareholders in the CDC will lead to a new attitude which will spread far beyond the boundaries of that organization. If for no other reason than this, the role of the government in the CDC, including its willingness to sell the Crown Corporations at realistic market prices, should be followed with a close and intense interest by you and all Canadians.

How quickly government's percentage ownership of CDC will decline depends upon the timing and acceptability of public issues of CDC securities, whether those be common shares, convertible preferred, debt with warrants, or some combination of the above. It is the Directors' intention to make such an issue as soon as possible after a reasonable portfolio of investments has been built up and is making satisfactory progress. The aim is to make the shares available to the widest possible range of Canadians, whether by way of warrants or in some other fashion, so that they may have an opportunity of investing at what is relatively a "ground-floor" stage. Although the risk will be somewhat higher at this earlier phase of development, and this fact will be emphasized in any offering, we believe that each potential shareholder should have the possibility of making his or her own decision as to whether or not to buy them. The Canadian public may also be offered a chance to participate directly in some of our underlying investments from time to time, particularly when we sell holdings which have matured and become acceptable to more conservative investors, in order to free our resources for more aggressive investments.

Before any public offering of the shares, CDC's operations will be financed by share purchases by the federal government, which has publicly indicated that it will subscribe $100 million in the first year of the Corporation's life, followed by $75 million in each of the next two years; there is also provision for a loan of $100 million from the government. The shares may prove to be of unusual interest to Canadians, not only because of the nature of the Corporation's activities, but because the Corporation has the power to purchase its own shares for cancellation (Section 23 of the Act) by a specific resolution of its Board. This feature, together with the issue of appropriate warrants—perhaps on a revolving basis—should help to avoid the discounts which commonly characterize closed-end investment companies. Otherwise, our share characteristics are similar to those of any other company, although only Canadian citizens or residents of Canada may purchase voting shares and no person may hold more than 3% of the total. This latter restraint is rather academic, and is aimed at preventing the Corporation being taken over by a single private group.

Summing up briefly, then, the CDC is a unique cooperative venture launched by government but designed to be run by independent directors for the benefit of all the shareholders, 90% of whom will ultimately be Canadian private citizens. It is large enough to have a worthwhile influence—both directly and as a catalyst—in helping to get profitable and constructive things done by Canadians—things that would not otherwise get done, or get done so fast. It aims to work in a close and creative, yet competitive, spirit with other private sector corporations to accelerate our country's progress. And its philosophy is to take a constructive view of the potential that lies ahead; to shape the future rather than recapture the past.

Notes

*Speech delivered by H. Hampson, Chairman, Canada Development Corporation, to The Empire Club in Toronto, Ontario, February 17, 1972 (reproduced by permission).

Part 4
Negotiation

Introduction

We noted earlier in the introduction to the preceding part that there are no generally available objective criteria of performance from which public regulatory agencies, or the managers of publicly-owned firms, can derive guidelines for particular businesses to follow. Instead, the determination of correct behaviour in such circumstances must be accomplished through the use of some kind of political decision-making process. Given our liberal-democratic form of government, it might well be expected that the performance criteria for controlled firms would be determined through the usual legislative and administrative procedures by which we arrive at all the other kinds of decisions which cannot be determined either spontaneously or by the use of "scientific" methods.

In principle, this would mean that Parliament would be the body responsible for determining price and output decisions, but in practice, as we have seen in earlier parts of this section, most of this responsibility has been delegated to various kinds of regulatory boards and commissions. The creation of crown corporations and joint publicly and privately owned hybrid enterprises has also served as a way of taking the day-to-day control of business out of Parliament. These kinds of arrangements have come to be accepted as a normal part of our political decision-making system. In recent years, however, there is some indication that other channels are being opened up through which governments and businesses can interact. These are largely informal or *ad hoc* procedures whereby consultation is carried on between governments, business enterprises and other interests. Some of these arise as an apparently inevitable consequence of the activities of regulatory boards and commissions. Others, however, seem to reflect the creation of broader interest groups whose purposes are to represent the interests of whole industries, or particular groups in the community, who are affected by public policy decisions. While there is nothing new about individuals and interest groups trying to influence public policy, such activity appears to be increasingly conspicuous and, possibly, more highly organized. If this is so, we may expect to see business and government interaction become a process more of "negotiation" than of "command" as these groups claim recognition and establish their legitimacy.

Reading 30 provides a case study of government–business interaction involving the oil industry and the federal government during the early period of the "energy crisis." Berry traces (a) the various channels through which the industry pursued its objective of re-establishing its position as a major participant in the process whereby Canadian petroleum policy is determined (it had previously been overridden by the course of events) and (b) the government's response to the industry's initiatives. Some further evidence of the importance of even more broadly organized economic groups in determining public economic policy is supplied by the account of the Canadian "Prices and Incomes Commission," which sought to negotiate and operate a voluntary wage and price restraint system in 1969-70. The focus of its efforts, as described in Reading 31, was on achieving agreement among representatives of three interested parties: management, labour and government. The implications of subsequent developments in the area of anti-inflation control programs are considered in Section 4.

30 The Oil Lobby and the Energy Crisis *

Glyn R. Berry

The assertion that a particular group is 'powerful' or 'influential' in its dealings with government is difficult to sustain empirically because such concepts as power and influence are not easily operationalized.[1] Nevertheless, some indirect economic and historical indicators of the oil industry's power are available, although two initial assumptions must be made: that economic wealth correlates with political power and that the continuation over time of policy outputs beneficial to an industry is reflective of its influence in governmental policy-making.

In economic terms the petroleum industry does indeed occupy an important place in the Canadian economy. Oil and natural gas accounted, in 1970, for 6 per cent of Canadian exports, 4 per cent of imports, and 30 per cent of direct foreign investment in the Canadian economy at that time.[2] In 1974, of the one hundred manufacturing, utility, and resource enterprises with the highest stock value in Canada, no less than twenty were oil-producing companies.[3]

Historically, the oil industry has borne few grievances towards Canadian government policy.[4] After some early technical problems, production of oil in Alberta rapidly expanded. The incorporation bill for the interprovincial pipeline moved through Parliament quickly in 1949, and the pipeline's completion in 1950, followed by its extension to Sarnia by 1953, gave the producing companies a greatly expanded market for Alberta oil. The industry grew rapidly during the fifties, the most serious threat being from American import policies—in particular, the initial unwillingness of the US Federal Power Commission in 1954 to allow imports of Canadian natural gas and the American imposition of oil import quotas in 1959.

The latter episode, together with the development of a world-wide oversupply of oil, threatened the industry's growing prosperity. This serious problem was solved, in 1961, with the introduction of the National Oil Policy, which ensured the industry a protected market and pledged the Canadian government to seek, together with the industry, an increase in exports to the United States. Within the framework of this policy, the petroleum companies continued to prosper throughout the sixties.

Given, however, that the industry constitutes an influential pressure group, how can we measure a reduction in its influence? This, essentially, is a comparative exercise. Before the first whispers of the approaching energy shortage were heard late in 1972, the industry enjoyed close consultation with both federal and provincial governments in which all three parties were agreed on the basic objectives of the National Oil Policy. The main object of concern to the industry, apart from American import policy, was the level of provincial royalties.

The following incident from 1972[5] is indicative of the type of relationship that existed between the oil industry and government prior to the energy crisis. As the case in point exhibited an uncommonly severe level of disagreement and a great deal of concomitant publicity, it is particularly instructive for purposes of this analysis.

At the end of April 1972, William Dickie, Alberta's minister of mines and mineral resources, presented a position paper to the provincial Legislature proposing to introduce a new 'mineral tax' on recoverable reserves.[6] Emphasizing that the provincial government would welcome alternative proposals from interested parties, he commented 'that the matter is of such significance that the petroleum industry and public organizations and groups generally should have an opportunity—to the extent practicable—to respond to this Tentative Plan before a firm government position has been established.[7] Three months of constant negotiations ensued between industry representatives and the Alberta government. Mr. Lougheed and his cabinet were the targets of an intensive letter campaign, while the industry press, although more restrained than at the height of the energy crisis, sustained a constant barrage of criticism. The result was essentially a compromise. Incentives were improved, and the companies, as they had requested, were allowed to choose between a higher acreage tax and a renegotiation of royalty contracts. The higher rate established for the latter, the government assured, would be fixed for five years. *Oilweek* welcomed the decision as a 'considerable softening of the government's posture' and interpreted the result as a victory for the industry.[8] The resolution of this particular engagement, therefore, demonstrates, in practice, the ingredients of what I have chosen to call 'influence'—consultation in policy-making, focused concentration of political pressure, and, ultimately, influence on policy. The episode thus provides a crude measure against which we may compare federal government-industry relations during the energy crisis.

The lobby's problem is particularly acute when issues become 'politicized.' The issues themselves may not change, but because of a transformation in the political and economic environment, they grow publicly more salient. Consequently, while defending the status quo normally provides an easier task than attempting to change it, there may be times when, due to a massive environmental shift (as with the energy crisis), the very raison d'être of the status quo is itself placed in doubt.

The Actors in the Crisis

It is difficult to isolate and define the 'oil lobby' in terms that clearly distinguish it from other groups. Several factors complicate this task. The oil companies are active not only in all aspects of the oil industry but also in

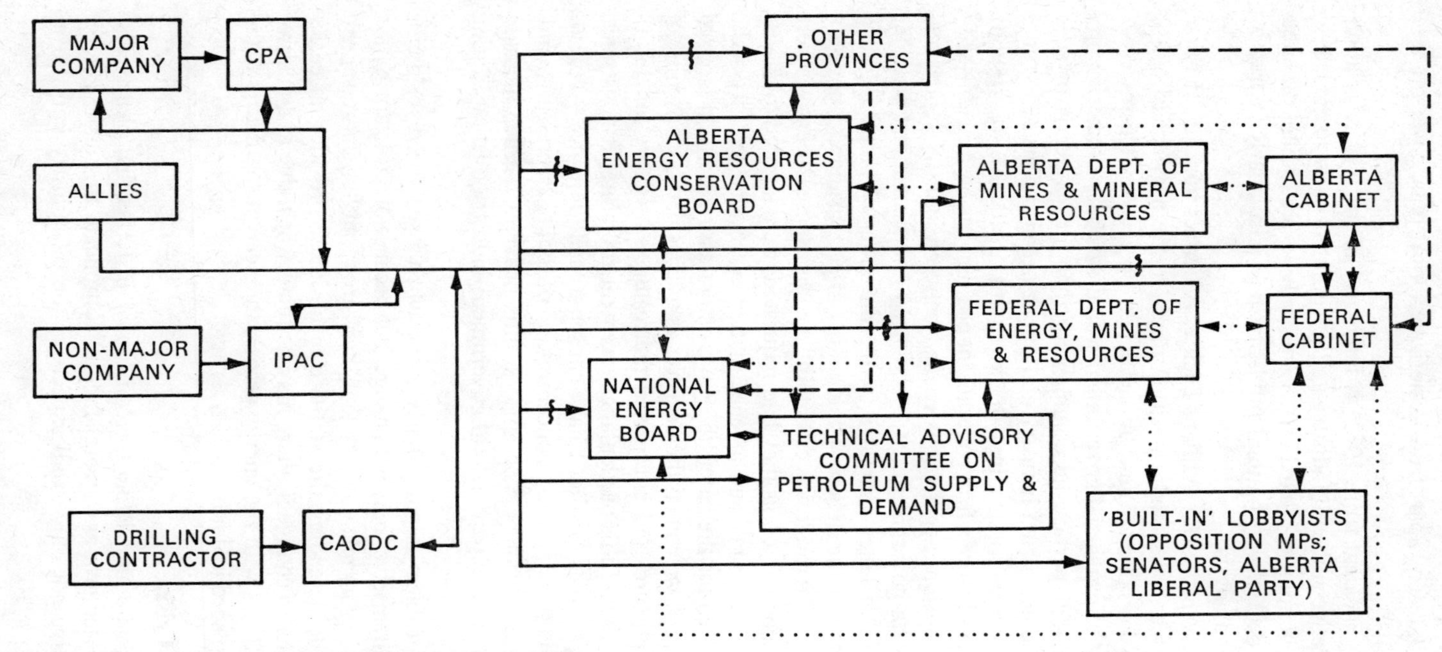

KEY CPA —Canadian Petroleum Association

IPAC —Independent Petroleum Association of Canada

CAODC—Canadian Association of Oilwell Drilling Contractors

Greater likelihood of resistance from other groups or provinces

Interest group: government contacts

Intergovernmental contacts

Intragovernmental contacts

Fig. 1: Major formal links in the influence net during the energy crisis.

the various branches of the petrochemical industry. On the other hand, many other commercial enterprises have a direct interest in the fortunes of the petroleum industry—steel companies, banks, and drilling contractors, for example.

To examine the activities of the vast range of groups through which the industry's views are expressed is not only beyond the resources of a single researcher but is probably unnecessary. Many of these groups are primarily technical in their interests, while the major companies are often members of several energy-oriented associations. The organizations selected for study in this article are those that, without doubt, have been the most persistent and vocal.

The 'oil lobby' will be considered to comprise three organizations: the Canadian Petroleum Association (CPA), the Independent Petroleum Association of Canada (IPAC), and the Canadian Association of Oilwell Drilling Contractors (CAODC).

The Canadian oil industry is dominated by the huge international oil companies,[9] a fact that pervades any discussion of the Canadian industry in particular. The latter, in essence, is a smaller version of the international gargantua, and its structure and behaviour reflect this. Consequently, observations on the nature of the international companies are in large part applicable to their Canadian junior partners. The activities of the former are fully integrated, involving control of all significant operations in the industry, from exploration to retail marketing. The companies have also formed de facto cartels, through tacitly accepted codes of 'orderly behaviour.'[10]

The Canadian Petroleum Association is a 'peak' organization to which the major and larger companies belong. Ably led, from April 1973 to April 1974, by its president, John Poyen, the CPA operates a total of twenty-two committees that are constantly gathering data on all aspects of the industry. It must be emphasized, however, that the major companies, particularly such giants as Shell, Gulf, and Imperial, are powerful pressure groups in their own right. Their influence is exerted, therefore, not only through the CPA, but independently of it.

The IPAC, on the other hand, is the main voice of the 210 small- and middle-sized companies, many Canadian-owned, that form its membership. Although it has differed with the CPA on a number of issues such as tax legislation and has refused to amalgamate with the more powerful body, the IPAC has been acting very much in concert with the CPA during the past year.

Like the IPAC, the CAODC is the main spokesman for its members. Totally dependent on the continued prosperity and expansion of the oil industry for their own economic security, the drilling contractors have no choice but to support the main industry; if the major companies decide to cut back on exploration, for either political or economic reasons, the drilling contractors must bear the brunt. The organized presence of the drilling contractors also constitutes an additional string to the lobby's bow, for they comprise the only section of the oil industry predominantly owned by Canadians.

The lobby attempts to make its influence felt in many quarters. At the federal level, for example, three agencies directly control the oil and natural gas industry: the National Energy Board, the Resource Management and Conservation Branch of the Department of Energy, Mines, and Resources, and the Northern Resources and Environment Branch of the Department of Indian Affairs and Northern Development (DIAND).[11] Other federal departments are less involved with the industry but are nevertheless concerned with some aspects of its activities. To illustrate the extent and concentration of this involvement, a simple count was made of the number of articles published in *Oilweek* during a three-month period that specifically mentioned federal departments by name. From July to September 1972, shortly before the first hints of shortages appeared, the names of seven federal departments or agencies appeared in more than one article (see Table 1).

Table 1

Number of *Oilweek* Articles Referring to Federal Departments and Agencies, July-September 1972

Department	*Number of articles*	*Examples of departmental interest*
Energy, Mines and Resources	13	Natural gas export policy, pipeline financing, resource inventory, intergovernmental co-operation
National Energy Board	8	Export regulation, pipeline approval
DIAND	5	Native claims, frontier resources, arctic pollution
Environment	5	Pipeline and refinery construction standards
National Research Council	2	Research into oil spill booms
Industry, Trade, and Commerce	2	Sarnia petrochemical project
Transport	2	Pollution at marine oil terminals, tanker safety

That the industry's main concern was with provincial regulation is illustrated by the fact that from July to September 1972 the Alberta Energy Resources Conservation Board was mentioned in no less than thirty-three *Oilweek* articles. The Board's main responsibility is to determine whether surpluses of oil and natural gas in Alberta permit requested production levels. The remaining provincial references of significance were to the Alberta and Saskatchewan Departments of Mines and Mineral Resources (six and five articles respectively). In the majority of articles referring to government in general rather than to a specific department or agency, Alberta was usually the object of attention. During the energy crisis, however, the industry became more concerned with government activity, and with the actions of the federal government in particular. From October to December 1973, the AERCB was mentioned in forty-six *Oilweek* articles, the departments of Mines and Mineral Resources of Alberta and Saskatchewan in eleven and three respectively, the NEB in thirty-nine, and the federal Department of Energy, Mines, and Resources in twenty-eight. Most of these references were to individual ministers rather than to departments as collective government agencies. During the crisis period, as before, the industry continued to enjoy a close relationship with the Alberta government, and this will be discussed further. It should be noted also that during the crisis the Alberta Department of Federal and Intergovernmental Relations, under Donald Getty, played a major role in federal-provincial negotiations.[12]

The federal Department of Energy, Mines, and Resources and the cabinet have been under particularly heavy fire, not only from the oil producers but also from opposition MPS, particularly Alberta Conservatives. Also at the federal level, the National Energy Board, which among other things sets quotas for exports, was from its inception extremely deferential to the approaches of major exporters.[13] There is reason, however, to doubt that this is any longer the case. Because of rising demands for consumer protection and the determination of the federal cabinet to respond to these demands, the NEB, now performing in the political limelight, must tread carefully in order to avoid accusations of pandering to particular interests. Finally, the other provinces are intimately involved in the energy problem as articulators of their own demands. A simplified model of interest-group/government interaction during the continuing crisis is presented in Figure 1, two-way arrows representing main 'feedback' flows.[14] We may now consider the targets chosen and the tactics adopted by the industry in the fight to decide the future of Canadian energy policy. This must begin with an analysis of a vital component of group influence—the possession of expertise.

The Monopoly to Expertise

The federal government is heavily dependent upon the petroleum companies for the technical information required for policy-making. Given the international nature of the industry and the immense cost and difficulty of sustaining an efficient, reliable, data-collection system, this is not surprising. During an interview with the Ottawa editor of *Oilweek*, Donald Macdonald, federal minister of energy, mines, and resources, pinpointed the information problem: 'I don't know exactly where the truth lies. One of the difficulties facing the Canadian government is that it is virtually dependent on the major international companies for its sources of information. They argue this [increasing oil costs] is a turn of events they have been unable to control. I've no real information to cross check this.'[15] Mr. Macdonald explained that one reason for establishing a national petroleum company was to develop an alternative, Canadian-oriented source of expertise.

Such expertise is easily employed for the production of distorted and highly selective information. Alan Plotnick, for example, has observed that during the hearings before the Borden commission, the independent companies and the major producers, each of which had different opinions on expansion into the Montreal market, presented economic projections supporting their own preferences.[16]

Because technical data can so easily be used to support different proposals, it is interesting to note Mr. Macdonald's suggestion, in a television interview in July 1973, that federal-provincial political consensus, rather than technical studies, might become the prime determinant of future Canadian energy policy. He considered existing data to be too unreliable to serve as a firm foundation for federal initiative in the energy field. Mr. Macdonald's reference to the unreliability of data is less significant than the political overtones of his statements. While the companies do enjoy a virtual monopoly of *technical* expertise that the political authorities fully acknowledge, the extensive political and constitutional ramifications of the energy problem have found them lacking the *political* sophistication that would ensure them a greater voice in federal energy policy.[17]

Choosing the Target

In seeking to influence governmental decision-making directly, the Canadian pressure group is faced initially with a choice of several points of access. The cabinet, members of Parliament, political parties, civil servants, advisory committees, and regulatory agencies may all be approached or utilized in different situations. In serious circumstances even the general public may be the focus of interest-group efforts. The choice of the appropriate target depends upon the nature of the group's concern: the formulation, negation, amendment, or implementation of policy in political or technical issue-areas. In the words of Robert Presthus: 'interest groups seek that point in the political structure where the authority and expertise required to reconcile an issue reside... When legislation is being formulated, the cabinet, caucus, other groups, and the public are the logical foci of attention; once it has been accepted in principle, the committees and back-benchers become sensible targets. Following its passage, attention shifts to those charged with its implementation, typically the bureaucracy and its regulatory agencies.'[18] The interest group's challenge is to select the correct channel at the opportune time. Consequently, pressure will often be exerted on those officials most sympathetic to the group's cause and, if possible, when and where opposing forces are at their weakest. However, during the energy crisis the oil industry encountered serious problems in locating such weak points.

Cabinet Briefs

Briefs may be presented to either provincial or federal governments. Imperial Oil, for example, submitting a brief to the British Columbia government in April 1973 on the latter's proposed Energy Act, argued strenuously against government regulation in the industry.[19] In particular, Imperial was concerned about the sweeping powers of the proposed BC Energy Commission. The company suggested, as an alternative, that the industry and the provincial government should meet and identify specific industry activities of concern to the government. These activities, Imperial suggested, could then be circumscribed by means of voluntary guidelines.

In the context of the energy crisis, however, such briefs, which tend to be general rather than specific in nature, have played no significant role in the petroleum industry's opposition to federal policy. While business leaders have been consulted by the cabinet, and specifically by Mr. Macdonald, their efforts generally seem to have been ineffective. The reasons for this will be explored later.

Advisory Committees

The industry will often attempt to influence policy advisory groups. Frank Mair, for example, manager of the administrative services section of Hudson's Bay Oil and Gas Company, has called for oil interests to confer with the tax policy group, which operates under the direction of Maxwell Cohen in the Department of Finance.[20] Mair suggested that in this way oil companies could gain greater tax write-offs for capital investment and exploration.

Of particular significance, in the context of the energy crisis, is the Technical Advisory Committee on Petroleum Supply and Demand. The committee was formed, after a meeting between Mr. Macdonald and the heads of importing and refining companies, on 19 October 1973. Mr. Macdonald described its function: 'The mandate given the Committee is as follows: firstly, to review and report on the short-term outlook for petroleum supply and demand in Canada, regionally as well as nationally. Secondly, to advise government as necessary regarding feasible measures for the improvement of the supply balance. Thirdly, meetings in Ottawa or elsewhere at the request of the minister.'[21] The committee includes senior officials from those companies canvassed for nominations and is chaired by a member of the National Energy Board. It should be noted, however, that the committee's range of responsibilities—focusing primarily on eastern Canadian supplies—is very narrow. It is not closely concerned with the export tax, energy self-sufficiency, or other more sensitive aspects of energy policy.

The House of Commons

On 15 November 1973, representatives of the Independent Petroleum Association of Canada met with all Conservative members of Parliament, and later with those Liberals and New Democrats who responded positively to the association's invitation. The association's general manager explained: 'Only by making the facts concerning Canada's energy supply and development perfectly clear to politicians of all political persuasions can we expect to overcome the present impossible situation.'[22]

It is interesting to observe that the NDP has not been entirely neglected. Because the party held the balance of power during the last Parliament it was widely considered to exert a very significant influence on government policy. It is not the purpose of this paper to test the veracity of this assumption, but the industry does seem to have shared the general view. *Oilweek*, for example, interpreted the creation of a National Petroleum Company as the ultimate surrender of a power-conscious minority government to the New Democrats.[23] Given such a perception of the NDP as a powerful force in the making of policy decisions, it is not surprising that some attempt was made to provide the party with the industry's views.

On 7 December 1973, for example, a special NDP caucus was addressed in Edmonton by John Porter, president of the CAODC, who appealed to NDP concerns by noting that the drilling business is 95 per cent Canadian-owned and that a reduction in drilling could cause job losses in a highly paid, labour-intensive industry.[24] The caucus also was addressed by Mr. K. F. Heddon, president of Great Canadian Oil Sands Ltd.

Many Conservative MPS, particularly from Alberta, have firmly supported the western oil interests. Harvie André (Calgary Centre) and Peter Bawden (Calgary South) have both been active in this regard. Mr. Bawden, in particular, in the Standing Committee on National Resources and Public Works, has proved remarkably vocal and superbly equipped with technical information.[25] Early in January 1974, in the National Resources Committee, Mr. Bawden proposed an amendment to the Energy Supplies Emergency Bill.[26] The amendment would have left existing contractual arrangements for natural gas exports immune from any implementation of emergency-regulation powers. Thus, it would effectively have emasculated the bill as it applied to natural gas. The amendment was rejected in division, with only the Conservative members of the committee voting in support. Messrs. André and Bawden have been strongly supported on the committee by the two other Calgary-area MPS, Eldon Woolliams (Calgary North) and Stanley Schumacher (Palliser). All have propagated the industry's view (which happens to have been in large part, it should be remembered, also the view of the government of Alberta). Furthermore, it appears that the federal Conservative party's Alberta caucus holds periodic meetings with Premier Lougheed's cabinet.[27] Questions of mutual interest are normally discussed, and these meetings offer an additional avenue through which provincial views are reinforced at the federal level.

The lack of government representation in the west must be seen as a factor limiting the utility of the standing committee as an instrument of the industry's aspirations. Nevertheless, the Liberal party can still offer a platform for the articulation of western viewpoints. At the Liberal party convention in September 1973, Alberta delegates maintained that their province should receive most of the income realized from the recently imposed export tax. Although the convention endorsed the introduction of the tax and the concept of lower fuel prices for Canadians, the government conceded that these prices should be tied, to some extent, to those in the international market and that Alberta should receive a 'large part' of the export-tax benefits. Particularly interesting to note was the individual chosen by the Alberta Liberal contingent to seek out a compromise with Mr. Macdonald—Alastair Ross, a past president of the Independent Petroleum Association of Canada.[28]

The Senate

Because of the Senate's ability to modify legislation, it too is the target of interest-group efforts,[29] particularly as its members are not bound by 'conflict-of-interest' rules.[30] As of October 1973, the Senate had ninety-one sitting members (eleven seats were vacant) who shared some 220 corporate directorships.[31] Of these, 130 were held by the twenty-two members of the Senate Banking, Trade, and Commerce Committee.

On the personal level, Senator J. J. Greene, former energy minister, is a member of the board of Petrofina Canada Ltd.; Senator Harry Hays is a director of Home Oil; and Senator Earl Hastings is a petroleum landman. In April 1974, Senator Ernest Manning, former premier of Alberta, gave an address to the Canadian Petroleum Association in which he strongly attacked increasing government intervention in the industry.[32] Perhaps the most ubiquitous of all, however, is Senator John J. Connolly, who is legal counsellor to Gulf Canada Ltd. and has been described as 'Gulf's man in Ottawa.'[33] Jerry McAfee, the president of Gulf, has admitted that Senator Connolly 'occasionally opens doors for us and provides the proper atmosphere.'[34]

In general, however, the Senate has been able to exert little influence on issues of major national importance. While its Banking and Commerce Committee, of which Senator Connolly is a prominent member, may obtain significant amendments to relatively non-controversial legislation, during the energy crisis the Senate has played no significant role.

The Professional Lobbyists at Ottawa

Oil firms have had to concentrate increasingly on establishing their presence in Ottawa. For the most part, this is because much frontier exploration is now carried on in federally administered areas, both in the north and around the coast. More recently, Ottawa's escalating interest in the export business has brought the industry into more direct contact with the federal government. The result is the existence of 'a nebulous oil lobby that has been established in Ottawa for a great number of years and is starting now to reach a form of second growth.[35] Typical of this lobby are such leading officials as Charles Pratt, head of the CPA's Ottawa office, who feeds questions to opposition members and provides the press with the companies' point of view.

The range of active lobbyists is not limited, however, to the representatives of the CPA and the IPAC, both of which maintain visible profiles in the capital. To their presence one must add representatives of the major companies, public-relations firms, lawyers, visiting executives, and other industrial 'umbrella' organizations such as the CMA and the Chamber of Commerce.

In view of the public concern now a feature of energy problems, it is interesting to note the appearance, in Ottawa, of full-time public-relations representatives of the major oil companies. One such example is Edna Scott, 'public-affairs advisor' of Imperial Oil, whose admitted function is to serve as a two-way information link between the government and the company she represents. Shell Canada already maintains an unofficial 'listening post' in its Ottawa divisional sales office but has been planning, in addition, to establish a governmental-affairs branch in its public-affairs division in order to strengthen its links with civil servants and politicians. Such innovations are, however, essentially long-term in their objectives, seeking to establish a more favourable political climate for the industry rather than to neutralize immediate threats to company interests.

The efforts in Ottawa of the CPA and the IPAC are complemented, in considerable part, by those of John Lindblad, the Ottawa representative of the Province of Alberta. He maintains close contact with federal civil servants whose activities impinge upon the oil industry and also devotes extensive attention to press relations.

The National Energy Board

John McDougall has pointed out that, while in earlier years few NEB personnel had even remote ties with the oil and gas industries, this has recently changed, as several senior positions have been filled by men with industry background.[36] Indicative of this trend was the appointment of Neil J. Stewart, associate vice-chairman of the National Energy Board, to the chairmanship of the federal Energy Supplies Allocation Board established in January 1974.[37] Before being appointed to the NEB in 1971, he had been employed by Standard Oil from 1953 to 1969, and then by its Canadian offshoot, Amoco, as treasurer and vice-president of administration and finance (1969-71).

In the late fall of 1973 Marshall Crowe succeeded Dr. Robert Howland as the new chairman of the NEB. He acknowledged, in a newspaper interview, the Board's enhanced concern with all aspects of the petroleum industry, and shortly after his appointment visited Calgary to confer with industry associations, the Alberta Energy Resources Conservation Board, and Alberta government representatives. He declared that he would not work towards more government ownership in the petroleum industry.[38]

There is no doubt, however, that the politically volatile nature of the energy issue has combined with the direction of government policy to sharply decrease the independence of the Board and its utility as a pressure-group target. It has ceased to be the powerful de facto policy-making body that public and parliamentary indifference permitted it to become during the last decade.[39] As the crisis developed, and once-technical issues became defined in political terms, the Board's activities fell under the penetrating glare of public scrutiny. If it had once been the industry's Trojan horse, the Board could no longer be so—it had become too visible.

Panel Discussions and Conferences

Oil company representatives regularly attend panel discussions or conferences dealing with energy questions. A few examples will serve to illustrate this point. At an arctic resources conference held in March 1973 under the auspices of the Canadian Arctic Resources Committee, Ronald Ritchie, a vice-president of Imperial Oil, strongly defended the existing oil leasing system.[40] In May 1973, the Canadian Bar Association sponsored a seminar at Dartmouth, Nova Scotia, on the subject of offshore oil and gas resources. Arne Nielson, president of Mobil Oil Canada Ltd., used the occasion to argue strongly against any politically motivated change in existing royalty rates.[41] When a panel session on oil exports was sponsored in August 1973 by the Ontario News Association of the provincial Progressive Conservative party, Mr. Poyen of the CPA was in attendance to ensure that the industry's viewpoint was heard.

Prior to the federal-provincial energy conference that met in Ottawa in January 1974, most of the major companies, as well as the industry associations, sought accreditation as observers. Their aim, at the very least, was to be available to the press, and John Poyen, president of the CPA, made frequent and prolonged television appearances while the conference was in session.

It remains doubtful that these types of meetings have been of much assistance to the industry in accomplishing its essentially defensive political objectives. The aim has often been simply to offer a balance to anti-industry arguments or to express the views of the oil companies on matters unrelated to the 'core' issues of the energy crisis.

Informal Social Contacts

Apparent governmental responsiveness to interest-group demands may be due simply to ideological congruence between governmental and interest group elites—that 'confraternity of power'[42] characterized by common educational backgrounds and similar social habits. This ideological affinity between elites is illustrated most conspicuously when civil servants and political leaders glide with ease in and out of the corporate aristocracy (an ambidexterity no less characteristic of many businessmen). Such informal social contacts between industry and government personnel are difficult to record comprehensively and certainly offer no direct evidence that they furnish useful opportunities to influence policy. One can assume with some justification, however, that they are maintained for very good reasons other than the force of personal attraction. A short paragraph in the *Globe and Mail* in November 1973 offered an interesting insight: 'Last Friday . . . an aide to Mr. Macdonald, an aide to NDP leader David Lewis, the Alberta government's man in Ottawa and an official of the Independent Petroleum Association stood cheek by jowl talking shop in Ottawa's National Press Club.'[43]

Although it may be hypothesized that many Alberta Conservatives and Liberals enjoy informal contacts with oil-industry executives, this is difficult to demonstrate. Nevertheless, Table 2 offers some indication that the political and industrial elites of the 'oil capital' enjoy similar social facilities. In such 'exclusive' Calgary clubs as the Glencoe and the Ranchmen's, it may be postulated, more than passing acquaintanceships develop. Such links clearly influence the prevailing environment within which policy is developed. However, during the hectic months of late 1973 when Ottawa and Alberta fought a war of words and principles, it is doubtful that significant decisions had their genesis in the select clubs of Calgary, Edmonton, or Ottawa.

The Industry and the Oil-producing Provinces

Because some 80 per cent of domestically produced Canadian oil originates in Alberta,[44] the actions of Peter Lougheed's Progressive Conservative government occupy a key place in any analysis of the political ramifications of the energy crisis. Thus, this section will concentrate upon the relations of the Alberta government with Ottawa and the industry, although we must remember that Alberta was not a lone recalcitrant locked in a bitter conflict with the rest of the country. The position of the Saskatchewan and Newfoundland governments, although not as crucial to the course of events that unfolded, were essentially the same as that of Alberta.

There were indications soon after the provincial election that brought Mr. Lougheed and his party to power in September 1971 that the premier himself was sympathetic to industry interests. In a penetrating psychological and political profile of Mr. Lougheed, Walter Stewart noted that the Alberta premier 'worries constantly because oil exploration, nearly all of it American, is falling off in Alberta. He hopes to establish incentives to speed it up again. Two members of Lougheed's crucial Communications Committee during the [provincial] election, Brock Hammond and Lorne Frame, are public relations officers with large US-owned firms (Gulf and Mobil, respectively).'[45]

On a broad range of questions, the industry and the Alberta provincial government have found themselves on common ground, particularly in the face of the federal challenge. In the spring of 1973 the chairman of the CPA, W. B. Dingle, expressed the view that the Lougheed government had become increasingly sympathetic to the companies' case during its relatively short tenure.[46] On the issue of exports and gas pricing, he noted, the province and industry positions were virtually identical. He regretted that

Table 2

The Social Interface

Name	*Position*	*Calgary Chamber of Commerce*	*Calgary Petroleum Club*	*Glencoe Club*	*Calgary Golf and Country Club*	*Ranch-men's Club*
POLITICAL						
Douglas Harkness	Former federal MP(PC) Calgary Centre		x			x
Patrick Mahoney	Former federal MP(Lib) Calgary South	x		x	x	x
Peter Bawden	Federal MP(PC) Calgary South		x		x	x
Eldon Woolliams	Federal MP(PC) Calgary North	x	x			
Peter Lougheed	Premier of Alberta			x	x	x
INDUSTRIAL						
Gibson Kelly	Board CHMN and chief executive officer of Pacific Petroleum Ltd.		x		x	x
D. Carlton Jones	President and director of Hudson's Bay Oil and Gas Co.		x		x	
Arne Nielson	President and general manager of Mobil Oil Canada Ltd.		x	x		
John Poyen	President of Total Petroleum Ltd. and director of CPA (1973-4)		x	x	x	x
Lyman Rasmussen	President and director of Pacific Petroleum Ltd.	x	x	x	x	x
John Rudolf	President and director of Bluemount Resources Ltd.		x			x

Biographical data taken from *The Canadian Who's Who 1970-72*; *National Reference Book 1971-72*; *Who's Who in Canada 1973-74*; data on Mr. Harkness's successor, Mr. André, was unavailable.

no such common bond of understanding existed with the federal government.

In the first week of December 1973, Alberta established a Petroleum Marketing Commission to take over the exclusive rights to buy, sell, and tax most of the crude oil produced in the province. This was part of the provincial counteroffensive against Ottawa on the issue of resource control. Ironically, for there was no serious outcry from the industry, the companies probably viewed this development as of benefit to them, given their harmony of interests with the provincial government. A generous and sympathetic provincial regulatory agency, it is reasonable to assume, was preferable to a predatory federal one. The Alberta minister of mines and minerals, William Dickie, demonstrated this close industry-government collaboration in the province. He noted that new royalty schedules would not be introduced for the time being, as the government and the companies were still discussing a mutually acceptable formula for a floating-royalty system. Mr Lougheed, meanwhile, openly shared the industry's annoyance that the voluntary freeze on prices would be extended beyond 31 January.

Although the Alberta government has had occasional differences with the companies on such economic matters as royalty rates, such conflicts have generally been solved with relatively little friction. However, in an episode reminiscent of the earlier royalty conflict in 1972, the petroleum industry was critical of Alberta's new natural gas royalty rates announced on 31 January 1974. The province declared its intention to raise the price of gas, set prices for its fuels, and develop mechanisms for diverting 'windfall' profits to the provincial treasury. Again, Alberta was using the jurisdictional weapon in its contest with Ottawa. The only way to defeat federal regulation was to institute provincial regulation, and the industry was caught in the middle of a federal-provincial conflict. Company spokesmen were concerned about the freedom of the Alberta government to vary the royalty rates at will and appealed to the government to review its decision. Several prominent voices, including those of the CPA and the IPAC, were raised against Premier Lougheed's more stringent measures.

Soon after the decision, oilmen expressing their concern met with Mr. Dickie, who had stated that the new royalty rates were non-negotiable and that only minor changes could be expected. The IPAC condemned the royalty decision as yet another blow in a federal-provincial squabble that was constantly undermining industrial morale. John Poyen reminded Mr. Lougheed that he needed industry support in his battle with Ottawa: 'Already he [Mr. Lougheed] is alone in the national arena and the Premier should try to retain his original home supporters in light of the remaining unresolved national energy issues.'[47]

Such pressure seems to have succeeded. Only four days later the provincial government revised the new royalty schedule, claiming that a 'mistake' had been made. The new schedule, instituting a sliding scale pegged to field prices, was considerably more palatable to the producers. The CPA expressed satisfaction and 'relief' at the result of its discussions with Mr. Dickie.[48] This incident offers a remarkable insight into the symbiotic relationship between the petroleum industry and the province of Alberta during the crisis. While they may have had their differences on the distribution of additional oil revenues, the province and the industry have been firmly united in desiring to divert the bulk of these revenues from Ottawa.

The NDP government of Saskatchewan has been equally determined to defend its jurisdiction against what it has considered unwarranted federal encroachment. Mr. Blakeney, in a television interview in December 1973, said that he supported the concept of an export tax, particularly because it was intended to keep windfall profits out of the industry's hands.[49] However, the premier maintained that all the proceeds of the tax should be returned to the producing provinces. Saskatchewan's new royalty legislation, the premier explained, was directed, like the federal export levy, at restricting company profits and would therefore make the export surcharge obsolete as applied to Saskatchewan. His main concern was to ensure that any windfall profits would be received by the provincial treasury. Defending, in principle, Saskatchewan's right to a world price for its oil,[50] Mr. Blakeney stated his willingness, nevertheless, to accept a lower Canadian price in return for concessions on freight rates, industrial development, and farm income stabilization.[51] In an interview with a Halifax reporter, Mr. Blakeney stressed that provincial payments to any oil price equalization fund should be levied on the basis of over-all ability to pay and not based on provincial revenue from oil in particular.[52]

On 18 December 1973, Bill C-42, the Oil and Gas Conservation Stabilization and Development Act, was passed by the Saskatchewan Legislature. The Act gave the government a broad range of authority, including the power to set wholesale prices in the province, to impose a new royalty surcharge, to increase the acreage tax on undeveloped holdings, and to limit production for conservation purposes. The new surcharge was to be equal to the difference between Saskatchewan's frozen wellhead price and the price in the Chicago market. Premier Blakeney told the Legislative Assembly that the act was intended to protect Saskatchewan consumers, extract the maximum benefit from higher oil prices, and, significantly, to prevent windfall profits accruing to the petroleum companies.[53] The provincial government was given the power to acquire title to most of the freehold oil and gas leases held in the province. In essence, Mr. Blakeney's objective was to intercept the federal export tax and hence strengthen his hand for the January federal-provincial conference. In achieving this, however, he encountered widespread industry opposition to his government's extensive measures.

The manager of the Canadian Petroleum Association, Mr. Hans Maciej, commented that the Saskatchewan government 'looks determined to kill the private industry in the province.'[54] His sentiments were echoed by other officials of the CPA and CAODC. The president of Imperial Oil was also critical of the provincial government for depriving the industry of a reasonable return and for taking excessive power into its own hands.[55] Shortly before the federal-provincial energy conference in January, Mr. Blakeney insisted that the new provincial surcharge would be introduced on 1 February 1974 even if Ottawa continued to impose its export level.[56] Five companies warned that they might cancel or reduce their February orders because Saskatchewan oil would become too expensive. The Saskatchewan government, unlike that of Alberta, decided to retain the entire price increase permitted by the federal-provincial agreement. Implying a satisfaction with Alberta's position on this decision, a CPA spokesman noted that 'it was hoped that at least part of the [April 1] increase might be passed on to the producer. This was the case in all other provinces but Saskatchewan, which retained the whole of the increase by way of a royalty surcharge.'[57] Only one of the 'other provinces' is, of course, a significant oil producer—Alberta.

The Saskatchewan government has on occasion been severely critical of the industry, accusing it of reluctance to search for new oil after making healthy profits from established reserves. In March 1974, for example, Elwood Crowley, Saskatchewan's minister of mines and mineral resources, told reporters in Regina that one reason for the reduction of exploration in the province was that oil companies were attempting to force the government into changing its resource policy.[58] The creation of Saskoil, the provincially owned petroleum corporation, was largely a response to declining exploration in the province. Thus, Saskatchewan's tactics have been double-edged, directed at the industry as well as at Ottawa.

This difference in orientation towards the industry constitutes the most important respect in which the actions of the Saskatchewan government during the period under review differed from those of Alberta. When Alberta introduced its new oil royalty rates in October 1973, Mr. Lougheed apologized to the industry, explaining that his first responsibility was to safeguard provincial jurisdiction. Consultation with the industry on implementing the new system was promised, and *Oilweek* praised Mr. Lougheed's move as 'another piece of one-upmanship over his federal counterparts.'[59] The response of the industry to Saskatchewan's royalty legislation was more critical because the provincial government was much less receptive to the industry's demands for a greater return on investment. Alberta's primary objective was to preserve provincial control of the most important industry in the province and enhance its prosperity—hence, the provincial government opposed the export levy introduced in September. The Saskatchewan government, however, was more interested in obtaining windfall profits for the provincial treasury and in bargaining with its more limited petroleum resources, if necessary at the industry's expense, for federal concessions in other areas. Mr. Blakeney was careful to emphasize, during a tour of eastern Canada in January 1974, that his government's aims were different from those of Alberta.[60] He stated that Saskatchewan's objective, as a less prosperous province, was the implementation of a national development policy to achieve equity within confederation.

However, in wishing to obtain the best possible returns for their resources, jealously safeguarding their constitutional prerogatives, desiring all the proceeds from the export tax, and demanding economic concessions to the west in other areas, Saskatchewan and Alberta shared the same ground.

Interest-group Allies

The other larger industrial corporations do not seem, from the sources examined, to have been very vocal in their support for the oil industry's position. Admittedly, they have not supported the federal government either, although a long-standing aversion to government interference in private industry would explain this. Nevertheless, the apparent aloofness of other industrial concerns seems surprising. Their relative indifference may well have stemmed from a pragmatic realization that their own competitive positions, particularly in the export market, would have been adversely affected by exponentially increasing fuel costs. The Ontario government's support for the federal stand was perhaps indicative of this.

However, the industry belatedly acquired a firm ally in the Canadian Chamber of Commerce, which attacked the policy of oil self-sufficiency in its annual brief to the cabinet. It echoed the petroleum companies in warning of exploration cutbacks and possible American retaliation and calling for domestic oil prices to reflect the long-term world price. The Chamber appealed, in the 'national interest of all Canadians,' for greater co-operation between government and industry in the formulation of energy policy and sought to ensure sufficient incentives for exploration and development.[61]

It would seem, however, despite occasional expressions of support such as that described above, that the industry's most important ally during the crisis has been the Alberta government. Other industrial voices concerned, no doubt, with their own serious problems (including fuel prices), have generally been silent. The industry, in alliance with Alberta, has had to fight its own battle.

Provinces Against the Industry

On 3 April 1973, William Davis, premier of Ontario, gave an address before the Canadian Petroleum Association. He proposed a national energy conference, called for a coherent national energy policy, and stressed that energy costs must be reasonable and allowed to escalate only slowly for the sake of continued industrial prosperity. The audience received Mr. Davis's remarks 'politely but unenthusiastically'—a distinct contrast to the 'thunderous ovation' given to Peter Lougheed only a week earlier when he had defended Alberta's claim to greater returns on natural gas sales.[62]

In announcing his $3.8 billion energy plan on 7 June 1973, Mr. Davis called for a re-evaluation of existing national energy policies, including export practices, and suggested that price regulation of petroleum products be seriously considered. Mr. G. W. Cameron, general manager of the IPAC, quickly responded with firm support for the Alberta position.[63] He accused Mr. Davis of being motivated by political considerations and expressed his agreement with Alberta's constitutional stand.

While Ontario has been vocal in support of federal measures, other provinces have also supported, to varying degrees, such actions as the export tax and the price freeze. The Manitoba government, for example, has taken the view that the industry should now be considered a public utility and be strictly controlled as such. The British Columbia government has also given some support to federal policies. In July 1973, for example, Leo Nimsick, the province's minister of mines and petroleum resources, declared strong support for the concept of a national petroleum company, while at the First Ministers' Conference in January 1974, Premier Barrett demanded that no further oil exports be authorized and that excess profits be heavily taxed.

For the Maritime provinces, which have always encountered severe problems in attracting industry, higher fuel prices can only threaten further economic hardship (unless, of course, offshore oil can be produced in significant commercial quantities). In an address to the Halifax Board of Trade in January 1974,[64] and a few days later at the First Ministers' Conference,[65] Premier Gerald Regan of Nova Scotia argued that large domestic price increases in Canadian crude were unjustified. Incentives could be offered in other ways, he suggested, through lower royalties or improved tax benefits. His sympathies have been echoed by Richard Hatfield of New Brunswick who has constantly expressed concern for the impact of the energy crisis on industrial prosperity in his province.

The industry has experienced less hostility from the Quebec government. Other than insisting on a subsidy programme, Quebec seems to have taken a somewhat ambivalent stand, perhaps because of the apparent incompatibility of Quebec consumer interests with the principle of provincial autonomy.

The industry has, however, received indirect support from Newfoundland, whose Conservative government, led by Frank Moores, has taken a strong provincial rights stand on the ownership and marketing of natural resources. No doubt anticipating large returns for his province from offshore oil and gas, Mr. Moores has consistently supported the right of Saskatchewan and Alberta to maximize their returns from oil production. For the industry, his has been a lone voice of comfort from the east.

The attitudes of the other provinces, therefore, have generally exacerbated the problems faced by the companies in making themselves heard in a serious and complex political and constitutional conflict. The industry has been unable, given the highly visible and politicized nature of the confrontation, to intervene on either side without incurring charges of irresponsibility. The foreign-based nature of the industry has only compounded this problem. Thus, company representatives have continued, heeded little by Ottawa, to stress economic arguments in support of their case, leaving to the Alberta government the more vital and ultimately decisive task of political and constitutional advocacy. The industry has had no choice but to accept a champion.

Interest Groups Against the Industry

On 9 January 1973, Imperial Oil raised its price of western oil by 20¢ per barrel. One day later, Gulf, BP Canada, Sun Oil, Great Canadian Oil Sands, and other companies brought in an identical rise in hot pursuit of the price 'leader.' This was attacked as arrogant and irresponsible by several organizations, including the Ontario Retail Gasoline and Automotive Service Association, representing fifteen hundred service-station operators in the main consuming province. The increases were described by the association's manager as 'an incredible insult to the motoring public.'[66]

Gasoline dealers have long exhibited frustration over the stranglehold enjoyed by the major companies in retail pricing. This frustration came to a head in May 1973 when the large companies, exporting gasoline to the United States in order to circumvent crude oil export quotas, indicated that some Canadian independent retailers would have to accept lower supplies at higher prices. The serious implications were first demonstrated when Capital City Gas and Fuels Ltd., operating twenty-four outlets in the Ottawa Valley, was threatened with closure.

At the end of May it became clear that many independent retailers would be forced to restrict planned expansion or possibly to close their outlets altogether. The independents' discount-selling practices, which had formerly allowed them to compete with branded products, were ceasing to be economically viable. 'The major oil companies,' noted a spokesman for Premium Oil, a large Toronto retailer, 'are increasing their number of discount bars while they keep putting up our prices and then undercutting us.'[67] Early in June 1973, the Ontario Retail Gasoline and Automotive Service Association issued a list of possible covert objectives the industry could have been pursuing in deliberately manipulating the energy crisis.[68]

Other purchasers of energy supplies have also attacked high fuel prices. Bruce Wilson, for example, president of Union Gas Ltd. of Chatham, Ontario, attacked Ottawa, the Alberta government, and the oil industry for their roles in the crisis. At a seminar at the University of Toronto he questioned the notion that Canadians should pay world prices for oil and gas and called for greater government involvement in resource development if American shortages were not to bring higher prices for Canadian consumers.[69]

More recently, in a brief to the federal cabinet, the Canadian Labour Congress has called for the construction of an oil pipeline to the Atlantic provinces, the taxing of all excess company profits, and increased processing, in Canada, of oil-derived products before further exports were permitted.[70]

Such interest-group opposition to the oil companies' claims, particularly from the retailers, has been vocal and well reported in the media. It has probably helped to counter the support that the industry has received from other, more sympathetic, commercial interests. However, because of the very fundamental political, constitutional, and economic problems generated by the energy crisis, these relatively marginal group activities, whether supportive of or contrary to oil company interests, have been symptomatic rather than causal in nature. They have not significantly altered the over-all configuration of power.

The Tone of Debate

As frustration with the federal government grew in the fall of 1973 the industry began to issue grave warnings, some of which closely approached overt threats. Both the IPAC and the CPA have, for example, repeatedly cautioned that increasingly heavy taxes on exports will erode investor confidence and reduce exploration in Alberta. Calgary itself, John Poyen of the CPA warned, would experience a 'gradual exodus of personnel from the city.'[71] Although presented as predictions, the line between prediction and threat in such remarks is difficult to draw.

The industry's often vituperative response to federal policies was an indication of its sense of impotence as the energy crisis unfolded. G. A. Van Wielingen, president of Sulpetro of Canada Ltd., wrote a personal letter to Mr. Macdonald in which the government was accused, among other things, of being 'discriminatory,' 'autocratic,' 'dictatorial,' and 'provocative'—words hardly chosen to extract sympathy from the energy minister. Mr. Van Wielingen's grim warning that 'retaliatory steps are now essential,' reflected the acute anger prevalent throughout the industry.[72] 'What has happened' *Oilweek* queried 'to the period of consultation and opinion seeking which was to follow the publication of the green paper on energy last June?'[73]

These vocal reactions are not mentioned in order to reflect disparagingly on the industry representatives quoted. Whether or not one agrees with Ottawa's responses to the energy crisis, one should appreciate that the lack of consultation[74] was considered by the industry to be totally unjustified. Years of consultation had preceded the introduction of the National Oil Policy in 1961, and, as we have seen, even such a heated disagreement as that which developed over the new Alberta reserves tax proposal in 1972 was solved through consultation and compromise. The federal government may indeed have been justified in its sudden imposition of the export surcharge—that is not the concern of this analysis—but one may also understand the industry's frustration at its exclusion from the decision-making process. Such angry outbursts were, however, an indication that 'quiet diplomacy' had failed to accomplish the industry's objectives. The tone of its public attacks on the government, therefore, was a symptom of the industry's weakness, not of its strength, a sign that other less public vehicles of expression were inadequate in a highly politicized situation.

The confusion and concern evidenced by the industry has been exacerbated by the federal-provincial dispute. *Oilweek* dolefully editorialized that 'the confrontation between Ottawa and Edmonton serves only to double the industry's turmoil and should be resolved without delay.'[75]

The Political Problems of the Industry

Hartshorn has pinpointed a number of potential disadvantages facing oil companies in the second half of the twentieth century.[76] First, the tax exemptions they obtain, combined with the immense wealth, make them a tempting target for government revenue-seekers: 'Wherever so rich an industry does business, local treasuries are usually anxious to find a formula that entitles them to a cut of the cake.'[77] Second, the industry's control of a vital strategic and commercial commodity exposes it to regulatory interference in the event of a supply crisis. Third, its identification in many countries, not only with large corporations but also with foreign ownership, leads to extensive public distrust. Fourth, as oil is an exhaustible resource, those who extract it must meet an increasing resistance from conservationist forces. These factors make the attainment of public 'legitimacy' very difficult for the major companies and have helped to generate a trend toward national integrated resource policies.

In the Canadian context these weaknesses have, until recently, been potential and untested. However, in the throes of crisis (whether 'contrived' or not), they have surfaced with force. They have been compounded by a long-standing tendency in Canada, more so than in the United States, towards extensive government involvement in commercial operations occupying a key place in the national economy and performing crucial and pervasive service functions. Thus, railways, telephone services, and power facilities are carefully regulated, and the oil industry has now partially joined them. Three interrelated aspects of the energy crisis have been primarily instrumental in creating this situation. The first, the constitutional nature of the conflict, has been referred to throughout the text. The others, still to be considered, are the rise of consumer concern and the speed of events.

Consumer Concern

As the price of what has become a basic commodity began to climb rapidly and as gasoline shortages loomed, the concern of consumers mounted. A few indicators serve to illustrate this concern. From 1 January to 31 March 1973 the *Globe and Mail* featured eight editorials concerned with oil and natural gas supply problems. The corresponding figure for the next three-month period, April-June, was four. From July to September, however, fifteen editorials appeared concerned with the crisis, and this increased to twenty-five during the last three months of the year. During the same successive periods, *Time Canada,* in its Canadian section, devoted 0, 20, 92, and 276 column inches to the energy crisis. In December 1973, an opinion poll[78] revealed that 63 per cent of those questioned supported the export surcharge, with only 16 per cent opposed, and 54 per cent considered that restrictions should be placed on all exports of oil and natural gas. Only 29 per cent were prepared to accept a gradual rise in prices, with 50 per cent opposed. A later poll, published in February 1974,[79] showed 75 per cent of those interviewed supporting the price freeze and the same proportion in favour of the pipeline extension to Montreal. Only 15 per cent disapproved of the freeze and 7 per cent of the pipeline extension. It should be added that the 75 per cent support registered for these two measures was the largest consensus on any issue recorded by the *Gallup Poll* from December 1973 to the time of writing.[80] In another poll issued in February, in which respondents were asked to name the most important problem facing the provincial government, the most frequently mentioned (21 per cent) was the energy crisis.[81] This increased concern with energy problems during the fall and winter of 1973 was reflected also in the House of Commons (see Table 3).

Admittedly, one cannot demonstrate empirically that this widespread, largely unarticulated concern affected the attitudes and actions of the federal government. Nevertheless, an elected government must eventually seek a mandate in order to remain in power. On an issue as vital as the price and supply of oil, in which Canada is theoretically self-sufficient, it would have been politically foolhardy for the government, particularly a minority government, to have allowed prices to rise to American levels when regulatory

Table 3
Oral Parliamentary Questions Concerned with the Energy Crisis, July-December 1973

Month	*Days of sitting*	*Number of MP's asking oral questions*	*Number of questions asked*
July	19	4	8
September *	16	19	47
October	13	26	89
November	21	39	193
December	13	61	143

*Includes 30 and 31 August; House recessed in August.

measures were available to prevent this. Nor is political survival the only objective of any Canadian government—politicians are citizens too, and are likely to share many of the attitudes found among the public at large. As Jerome Laulicht has observed, 'Politicians' decisions are influenced by their own attitudes but . . . these attitudes do not develop in a social vacuum.'[82]

The existence of a minority Liberal government, therefore, dependent upon the support of the NDP (never noted for its sympathy with the large corporations), facing mounting pressure from the oil-consuming provinces, and aware of widespread public apprehension, made stringent measures a virtual certainty. The oil industry has not been helped, in this already difficult situation, by its registering of record profits in 1973 or by widespread suspicions that the entire crisis was contrived by the companies for their own financial benefit.

The fear of consumer pressures explains the industry's reluctant acceptance of the price 'freeze.' Although the 'freeze' was only 'requested,' the possibility of mandatory controls hung, like the Sword of Damocles, over the industry's head. Company spokesmen fumed that it was a discriminatory and, in the long run, counterproductive measure, as the United States' experience with controls had allegedly demonstrated. Yet the industry's indifferent public image reduced, even further, its power to deny the government's request. As one oilman explained, 'the voluntary price freeze imposed by prime minister Trudeau could not, in all conscience, have been turned down by the industry which still bears the image of profiteering and monopoly formed in the public's mind way back in the days of the Standard Oil breakup.'[83]

The Speed of Events

A major problem for the industry has been the speed with which events have moved. Previously, government policy-making vis-à-vis energy had been a slow, deliberative process in which consultation with the industry was of paramount importance. This was no longer the case in 1973.

In mid-February 1973 when, at the urging of the National Energy Board, the federal government decided to impose export controls, western producers were caught by surprise. The threat of a domestic shortage, caused by large exports to the oil-deficient United States, was clearly paramount in the government's thinking. Having sustained this setback, however, the industry quickly rallied to press for the highest possible export quotas, guaranteed long-term growth for the export market, and generally, for the most flexible controls possible. At this stage of the crisis, most companies, including Imperial Oil, admitted that as yet there was little threat to existing operations. The events of September 1973 gave the industry its first traumatic shock.

The introduction of the price freeze was called a 'petroleum bombshell,' by *Oilweek*'s Ottawa correspondent.[84] Mr. Macdonald anticipated hostile reaction from the industry, but consumer interests, he maintained, would have to be given first priority. Only three days later the government imposed the export surcharge. Industry representatives, according to the *Globe and Mail*, were 'stunned' and described the measure as 'arbitrary,' 'arrogant,' and 'insulting.'[85] The IPAC declared its anger at the absence of advance notification and consultation. John Poyen expressed a similar viewpoint, condemning the measure as totally arbitrary.

More surprising federal moves came on 6 December, when Mr. Trudeau announced the proposal for a national petroleum company, an extension of the voluntary domestic price freeze, a pipeline extension to Montreal, and a continuation of the export tax. The proposal for a national petroleum company and the decision to extend the freeze were enthusiastically welcomed by the NDP and must be viewed, in part, as the price for their continued support of the government. Peter Bawden, oilman and Conservative MP for Calgary South, predicted the death of free enterprise in the petroleum industry. The industry itself saw the NDP as the villain of the piece and Mr. Trudeau as more interested in political power than economic rationality. The government, in responding to political pressures, had subdued the industry by simply ignoring it.

Repairing the Damage: the Public-relations Problem

A *Globe and Mail* interview with W. B. Dingle, who assumed the chairmanship of the CPA in March 1973, revealed his deep concern with the industry's public image and the debilitating effect this might have on the companies' political strength.[86] His aim was to institute a public information campaign which, with the aid of statistically simplified data on the state of the industry, would seek to convey one basic idea—that what was good for the oil companies was good for Canada. He promised a more overtly 'political' role for the association. No longer, he noted, were energy problems to be the sole preserve of a few individuals from industry and government.

The oil companies do indeed seem to be orienting themselves to the necessity of cultivating a more positive public image. In the summer of 1973, the IPAC began mailing copies of *Oilweek* to MPs and all MLAs as part of an effort to improve the industry's image among politicians and the general public. There is more expression of industry opinion through the media, and some companies have used advertising to improve their public standing and present their views.[87] Some companies, including Gulf and Imperial, have introduced short courses in media techniques for their executives, and Shell Canada has appointed Joe Mariash, a well known former television commentator, as the head of its media and information services department.[88]

Also, in 1973 Shell Canada and Gulf Oil for the first time released for public consumption detailed reports on their activities and their profits, justifying the latter on the basis of capital invested. Leading board members of Gulf also appeared before representatives of the press to explain the report.

'This was' *Oilweek* editorialized 'an excellent start for a beleaguered industry to upgrade its public image.'[89]

Conclusion

Such developments as those described above have been essentially reactive in nature, and from the industry's point of view much damage has already been done. Its new public relations orientation is aimed primarily at the long-term improvement, from the industry's perspective, of the environment within which policy is made. This new approach demonstrates that the oil companies, although they have lost a major battle, are rallying once again to defend their interests, but within a new set of rules that has emerged since September 1973. As *Oilweek* editorialized: 'The first ninety days of 1974 will be written in the annals of the Canadian petroleum industry as the birth of a completely new set of rules and regulations under which the business of finding, producing and marketing hydrocarbons will have to be conducted.'[90] The same editorial noted that the industry was no longer virtually its own master, subject only to the laws of supply and demand in the international market. The companies were now operating under a complex set of price controls, subsidies, and export regulations to which they have never been accustomed in the past.[91]

The energy crisis has presented the Canadian oil industry with an unprecedented situation. When decision-making on energy matters was relatively non-controversial, the companies' targets of influence—MPs, regulatory agencies, federal ministers, etc.—seem to have been benevolently responsive, or so the history of government policy would seem to indicate. Consultation with the industry on energy matters was an accepted element in the decision-making process. Both federal and provincial governments, as well as the oil companies themselves, desired a viable Canadian oil industry and the maximum possible increase in exports to the United States. Few groups were arrayed in opposition to the industry, and the public, for the most part, neither knew nor cared about energy problems.

With the advent of the energy crisis, however, all this changed. When the problem of rapidily rising fuel prices was injected into an already inflationary situation, public consternation grew and the majority of provincial governments, as well as some organized groups, pressed for federal action. When the federal government responded, the multifarious efforts of the oil companies were insufficient, in the new crisis situation, to preserve their former degree of autonomy, and the emergence of fundamental constitutional issues left the industry clinging to redundant technical arguments. The companies were forced to stand by as spectators while the short-term future of Canadian energy policy emerged from the federal-provincial bargaining process. Their position has been weakened further by the power possessed by the NDP during a period of minority government.

The industry still had its supporters in both the Commons and the Senate and retained a strong home base in Alberta. It gained representation on the Technical Advisory Committee on Petroleum Supply and Demand, was ensured ample representation at a wide range of conferences and other public forums and reinforced its presence at Ottawa. Some of its representatives were even willing to attempt to influence the New Democrats, so often perceived as the industry's bête noire. Company representatives also attacked publicly, and often bitterly, the government's handling of the crisis. Yet all this industry effort has been largely exerted on the fringes of a complex scenario. In the main arena, the federal and provincial cabinets have staked out their positions before manoeuvring privately into a generally acceptable compromise on a problem of crisis proportions. The very nature of this process and its immense implications for the future of confederation have left the industry excluded from the main locus of decision-making. Even the National Energy Board, once so deferential to the industry, must now consider the political ramifications of its decisions.

When energy issues could be defined in the narrow terms preferable to the oil industry, it enjoyed impressive power. But in 1973 new issues grew with the crisis, as it exploded into many areas—provincial autonomy, foreign policy, foreign ownership, consumer protection, and regional disparities. As such great issues swirled about it, the oil industry, a weakened monolith, was only a partisan spectator of the battle that decided the short-term future of Canadian energy policy. It could advise, encourage, cajole, or even gently push its champion in Edmonton, but it could not itself seize the weapon and fight the tortuous duel with Ottawa. It will now adopt more public methods of lobbying, but its pressure tactics will be formulated within a new set of rules governing its relations with government. The oil industry seems to have reluctantly accepted the greater role that government will play in its affairs. It will now seek to ensure that the intervention will be as consultative and non-coercive as possible.

Notes

*Berry, G. R., "The oil lobby and the energy crisis," *Canadian Public Administration*, 17:4, Winter, 1974 (reproduced by permission of author and publisher).

[1]For the purposes of this paper, 'power' and 'influence' are both defined as the ability of an interest group to obtain regulatory and policy outputs favourable to its interests as those interests are defined by the group.

[2]*An Energy Policy for Canada—Phase 1*, 1, 1973, p. 21.

[3]FINANCIAL TIMES OF CANADA, *Economic Forecast and Top Hundred: The Most Active Canadian Stocks*, 1974, p. 24.

[4]This brief survey of the industry's main problems since 1945 is taken from a short history of the Canadian oil industry, published in *Oilweek*, 31 Dec. 1973 – 7 Jan. 1974. It is interesting to note that this brief survey, written from an industry standpoint, focused on no specific complaints towards past federal policy except for references to increased regulation in general and tardiness in oil sands development in particular.

[5]The course of this interesting episode was traced in *Oilweek*, 1 May – 7 Aug. 1972.

[6]PROVINCE OF ALBERTA, *Hansard*, No. 35, 24 April 1972, pp. 17-25.
[7]Ibid., p. 20.
[8]*Oilweek*, 7 Aug. 1972. ,
[9]The five largest oil corporations, all foreign-controlled, operating in Canada—Imperial Oil, Texaco, Mobil, Gulf, and Shell—accounted for 40 per cent of total Canadian production in 1971 (*An Energy Policy for Canada*, p. 250).
[10]For more detailed analyses of the international oil industry see R. ENGLER, *The Politics of Oil*, New York, Macmillan, 1961, and J. E. HARTSHORN, *Oil Companies and Governments, London,* Faber and Faber, 1962.
[11]*An Energy Policy for Canada*, p. 266.
[12]Assented to in June 1972, the statute establishing the department declared that the new minister would be responsible for the co-ordination of Alberta's relations with other governments and the review of those relations and that he would he 'a party to the negotiation of all proposed intergovernmental agreements.' He was to sign all such agreements involving the province (see PROVINCE OF ALBERTA, *Statutes*, 1972, pp. 130-2).
[13]See JOHN N. MCDOUGALL, 'Regulation versus Politics: The National Energy Board and the Mackenzie Valley Pipeline,' in W. ANDREW AXLINE et al., eds., *Continental Community: Independence and Integration in North America*, Toronto, McClelland and Stewart, 1974.
[14]The model may be misleading in one particularly significant respect—in the spatial distance separating the industry from the Alberta cabinet. This would indeed be a serious fault were the model intended to represent the *nature* of the relationships that were significant during the crisis. Nothing so ambitious is intended. The purpose is only to provide the reader, at a glance, with a 'cast of characters,' together with its formal composition and structure, without which an understanding of the plot would be impossible.
[15]*Oilweek*, 21 Jan. 1974.
[16]PLOTNICK, *Petroleum*, p. 47.
[17]*Oilweek*, 21 Jan. 1974.
[18]ROBERT PRESTHUS, *Elite Accommodation in Canadian Politics*, Toronto, Macmillan, 1973, p. 147.
[19]*Globe and Mail*, 13 April 1973.
[20]*Oilweek*, 3 Dec. 1973.
[21]HOUSE OF COMMONS STANDING COMMITTEE ON NATIONAL RESOURCES AND PUBLIC WORKS, *Proceedings*, 10 Dec. 1973, p. 40.
[22]*Oilweek*, 12 Nov. 1973.
[23]Ibid., 10 Dec. 1973.
[24]*Globe and Mail*, 8 Dec. 1972.
[25]See, for example, HOUSE OF COMMONS STANDING COMMITTEE ON NATIONAL RESOURCES AND PUBLIC WORKS, *Proceedings*, 27 March 1973, pp. 25-6, and 28 March 1973, pp. 10-12.
[26]Ibid., 3 Jan. 1974, pp. 58-60.
[27]Confidential source.
[28]More recently, it should be added, the Alberta Liberal party elected as its new leader Nick Taylor, president of Lochiel Exploration Ltd., an international oil and gas exploration company. His opponent for the leadership was John Borger, a petroleum and environmental consultant (see *Globe and Mail*, 4 April 1974).
[29]See COLIN CAMPBELL, SJ, 'Canadian Senators as Appointees to a National Legislature: Group Consultants, The Lobby from Within, and Social Reformers,' a paper presented to the Annual Meeting of the Canadian Political Science Association, Montreal, 3 June 1972.
[30]See, for example, the comments of Jack Horner, HOUSE OF COMMONS, *Debates*, 26 Jan. 1973, pp. 710-11.
[31]*Halifax Mail-Star*, 9 Oct. 1973.
[32]*Globe and Mail*, 11 April 1974.
[33]Ibid., 10 Nov. 1973.
[34]Ibid., 10 Nov. 1973.
[35]Ibid., 9 Nov. 1973.
[36]JOHN N. MCDOUGALL, 'Oil and Gas in Canadian Energy Policy.'

[37]*Globe and Mail*, 19 Jan. 1974.
[38]Ibid., 29 Nov. 1973.
[39]JOHN N. MCDOUGALL, 'Regulation versus Politics.'
[40]*Globe and Mail*, 23 March 1973.
[41]Ibid., 29 May 1973.
[42]JOHN PORTER, *The Vertical Mosaic: An Analysis of Social Class and Power in Canada*, Toronto, University of Toronto Press, 1965, p. 522.
[43]*Globe and Mail*, 9 Nov. 1973.
[44]In 1970, Ontario produced 3,000 barrels of oil per day (b/d); Manitoba, 16,000 b/d; British Columbia, The Yukon, and the Northwest Territories, 77,000 b/d; Saskatchewan, 249,000 b/d; and Alberta, 1,131,000 b/d (*An Energy Policy for Canada*, p. 39).
[45]WALTER STEWART, 'The Upwardly Mobile Mr. Lougheed,' *Maclean's Magazine*, 85, Jan. 1973, p. 51.
[46]*Globe and Mail*, 5 April 1973.
[47]Ibid., 2 Feb. 1974.
[48]Ibid., 6 Feb. 1974.
[49]Ibid., 12 Dec. 1973.
[50]It should be noted that on the issue of oil pricing the Saskatchewan government's position was in conflict with that of the federal NDP. In a January press statement, a federal NDP spokesman admitted to such differences of opinion, commenting that 'the party is no monolith' (*Globe and Mail*, 22 Jan. 1974).
[51]*Globe and Mail*, 22 Jan. 1974.
[52]*Halifax Mail-Star*, 11 Jan. 1974.
[53]LEGISLATIVE ASSEMBLY OF SASKATCHEWAN, *Debates and Proceedings*, 20 Dec. 1973, p. 526.
[54]*Globe and Mail*, 12 Dec. 1973.
[55]Ibid., 22 Dec. 1973.
[56]Ibid., 22 Jan. 1974.
[57]Ibid., 19 April 1974.
[58]Ibid., 15 March 1974.
[59]*Oilweek*, 8 Oct. 1973.
[60]*Globe and Mail*, 22 Jan. 1974.
[61]Ibid., 19 Feb. 1974.
[62]Ibid., 4 April 1973.
[63]Ibid., 8 June 1973.
[64]Ibid., 12 Jan. 1974.
[65]*Halifax Mail-Star*, 23 Jan. 1974.
[66]*Globe and Mail*, 11 Jan. 1973.
[67]Ibid., 30 May, 1973.
[68]Ibid., 11 June 1973.
[69]Ibid., 21 Nov. 1973.
[70]Ibid., 18 March 1974.
[71]Ibid., 3 Nov. 1973.
[72]*Oilweek*, 1 Oct. 1973.
[73]Ibid., 10 Dec. 1973.
[74]For example, in responding to a parliamentary question from Eldon Woolliams (HOUSE OF COMMONS, *Debates*, 17 Sept. 1973, p. 6620), Mr. Macdonald stated that he had first discussed the imposition of the 40¢ export surcharge with Mr. William Dickie on the day it was introduced. Mr. Macdonald explained that his prompt action was necessitated by the NEB's decision, the previous day, not to permit October exports of crude oil at the existing price level. Alberta provincial ministers expressed little satisfaction with Mr. Macdonald's statement.
[75]*Oilweek*, 12 Nov. 1973.
[76]HARTSHORN, *Oil Companies and Governments*.
[77]Ibid., p. 194.
[78]CANADIAN INSTITUTE OF PUBLIC OPINION, *The Gallup Poll*, released 8 Dec. 1973. Regrettably, the author was unable to obtain any earlier copies of the *Gallup Poll* for 1973.

[79]Ibid., 13 Feb. 1974.
[80]Other issues upon which opinions were elicited during this period included American influence in Canada, foreign investment, Canada-US relations, inflation, trade union rights, campaign financing, wiretapping, housing, euthanasia, and the need for a federal election.
[81]*Gallup Poll*, 22 Feb. 1974.
[82]JEROME LAULICHT, 'Public Opinion and Foreign Policy Decisions,' *Journal of Peace Research*, 2, 1965, p. 147.
[83]*Oilweek*, 5 Nov. 1973.
[84]Ibid., 10 Sept. 1973.
[85]*Globe and Mail*, 14 Sept. 1973.
[86]Ibid., 5 April 1973.
[87]See, for example, the four-page advertisement placed by Imperial Oil in *Time Canada*, 3 Dec. 1973, in which the company's views on pricing and exports were persuasively presented to the public.
[88]*Globe and Mail*, 4 July 1974.
[89]*Oilweek*, 4 March 1974, p. 3.
[90]Ibid., 1 April 1974.
[91]See the comments of Robert Fowler, Chairman of BP Canada, in the annual BP Canada shareholders' meeting (*Oilweek*, 29 April 1974).

31 Can Incomes Policy Help? *

Canada, Prices and Incomes Commission

. . . Although incomes policies come in all shapes and sizes, their common feature is an attempt to check the pace of inflation directly by influencing decisions to raise prices, wage rates, other costs and profit margins. The means invoked range all the way from attempts at persuasion to agreed arrangements supported by informal government pressures to mandatory controls backed by legal sanctions. Such programs may be very comprehensive in scope or highly selective; they may involve a total freeze of prices and compensation levels or mild restraints on increases; they may be temporary or conducted within a framework of continuing institutional arrangements.

If the root of the inflation-unemployment dilemma lay in the ability of powerful unions and corporations to keep pushing up costs and prices indefinitely, regardless of demand conditions, there would seem to be a strong case for permanent wage and price controls. It is sometimes thought that such a belief provides the only possible basis for giving serious consideration to controls.

This is not our view. The Commission's analysis of the causes of recent Canadian inflation identified a number of areas in which changes in the degree or use of monopoly power had had significant effects, but in general we did not find this view of the nature of the basic problem convincing.

We do see serious difficulties, however, in trying to extricate the economy from a major inflationary outbreak originally generated by an overshoot of demand but persisting stubbornly because of widely held inflationary expectations and response lags. To be successful, an attempt to rely on demand restraint alone to restore reasonable price stability in such circumstances may well require the acceptance of abnormally high unemployment over an extended period.

It is in a situation of this kind that our analysis suggests a potentially useful role for a temporary program of controls. In conjunction with demand policies aimed at creating and maintaining a more stable demand environment, temporary resort to controls would seem to offer a means of bringing cost and price increases more promptly and reliably into line with the change in demand conditions, thereby speeding up the process of adjustment and reducing the transitional loss of jobs and output in bringing inflation under control. Even so, the process is unlikely to be quick or easy, and the results will not be lasting unless inflationary expectations can be changed.

Two essential conditions must be satisfied for a temporary control program of this kind to work effectively and then to be phased out with minimum risk of a renewed outbreak of inflation. First, the public must be convinced that such measures are necessary and that there exists on the part of governments a strong determination to make them operate as effectively and equitably as possible. Second, governments must be prepared to demonstrate a resolve and ability to maintain relatively stable prices and costs over a sufficiently long time span, embracing not only the control period but also its aftermath, to convince the public that inflationary expectations and patterns of behavior are no longer justified.

Unless demand is maintained at levels consistent with these objectives, then either the control system will prove unworkable or its removal will lead to renewed inflation. Given the uncertainties and lags in the response of market demand to changes in demand management, this will not be easy to do. European experience suggests, however, that if the control system breaks down or wages and prices rise rapidly following the end of the program, it will become difficult or impossible to enlist support for the use of incomes policy in the future.

It is our view, therefore, that temporary price and income controls should only be used as part of a longer-run policy aimed at maintaining underlying demand conditions both during and after the control period consistent with the target rates of increase in average price and income levels.

We begin by describing in very broad terms the essential characteristics of a full-fledged control system. After examining how difficult it is likely to be to accomplish significant and lasting results even with this most powerful form of restraint program, we turn to the suggestions which have been made for more limited and looser types of incomes policy.

The control program undertaken in the United States during the last year illustrates the general nature of such a system. The underlying rationale for this program appeared in the Economic Report of the President transmitted to the Congress in January 1972:

> The basic premise of the price-wage control system is that the inflation of 1970 and 1971 was the result of expectations, contracts, and patterns of behavior built up during the earlier period, beginning in 1965, when there was an inflationary excess of demand. Since there is no longer an excess of demand, the rate of inflation will subside permanently when this residue of the previous excess is removed. The purpose of the control system is to give the country a period of enforced stability in which expectations, contracts, and behavior will become adapted to the fact that rapid inflation is no longer the prospective condition of American life. When that happens controls can be eliminated.

Given the extent to which the U.S. program has been modified since its inception, any detailed description can quickly become dated. The general nature of the system can, however, be sketched out in the following terms. One central feature is a general 5½ per cent limit on wage and salary increases applicable to all employees on a uniform basis, with certain exceptions provided largely at the discretion of the control authority. There are those who argue that such a uniform limit is too rigid and that flexibility should be permitted to allow for differential rates of productivity growth among industries. There are two reasons for rejecting this approach. First, it conflicts with the basic economic mechanism through which productivity gains tend to be diffused throughout the whole economy rather than being reflected in lasting divergences in relative wage levels between industries with high rates of productivity increase and industries with low ones. Second, it would encounter strong resistance from those employees who justifiably felt that they had been unfairly treated.

While wage and salary control systems which have lacked a uniform rule have encountered serious difficulties, most control schemes provide for certain exceptions. In particular, decisions have to be taken about how to treat future increases already included in existing long-term contracts. Similarly, various special cases have to be dealt with, such as those where employers cannot obtain enough workers at existing wage rates. Thus, certain exceptions are essential, but some programs have been rendered ineffective through the multiplication of provisions for handling special cases.

The parallel price control system adopted by the United States is one of various possible schemes which could be used as part of an overall program. Price control systems of this kind impose limits on the extent to which prices can be raised by requiring that such increases do not raise profit margins. Under the system in force in the United States, a firm cannot increase prices unless it can show that cost increases will lower its margin of profit below the level prevailing at the outset of the program *and* below the level of the base period, i.e., the highest average margin realized in any two of the firm's last three fiscal years. In short, firms must satisfy a double test in order to raise prices. They are allowed to do so only to the extent necessary to maintain the lower of their profit margin immediately prior to controls or their margin in the base period. On the other hand, firms which do not increase prices have their profit margins subjected to control only under special circumstances.

Most control schemes, including that in force in the United States, contain provisions for limiting increases in rents, professional fees, and other kinds of prices and incomes. For example, the American system of rent control sets a limit of 2½ per cent for annual increases in rents over a wide range of residential housing accommodation, and provides that additional increases can be made only if required to meet tax increases or, within limits, to compensate for new major capital improvements. Special arrangements have been made to limit increases in medical fees and other health costs, some interest rates, dividends, and the fees and charges of state and local governments.

The U.S. price and income control system has much in common with programs of the same general character which have been introduced in other countries. Indeed, the kind of price and income restraint program which the Prices and Incomes Commission was discussing with management, labor and government representatives in 1969 was, with certain exceptions, broadly similar in its general approach. The discussions were broken off well before any agreement had been reached even in principle—let alone on details—but all the main elements of such a plan were actively examined, including an upper limit on wage and salary increases, a limit on price increases, control over rents, ways of limiting increases in other incomes, and means of ensuring compliance. When it became necessary to proceed with a much more limited program in early 1970, the National Conference on Price Stability adopted price restraint criteria which required firms to ensure that the revenue gains derived from price increases were limited to amounts clearly less than the increases in costs that the firms were experiencing.

There was, of course, a striking difference between the situation in which the U.S. control program was launched and the conditions under which a similar initiative was attempted in Canada. In the United States not only had efforts to deal with inflation through reliance on demand policy alone proved very discouraging, but the country was faced with an international financial crisis as well. Moreover, the fact that the Congress had earlier passed enabling legislation for the imposition of controls made it possible for the President to act with the full force of the law from the outset. Once a temporary freeze had been imposed it was then possible for the government to initiate concrete and pointed discussions with the major interest groups on the shape of the controls to follow the freeze.

Rightly or wrongly there were very few people in responsible positions in Canada in 1969 who thought that conditions had reached the stage where legislation providing for a mandatory price and wage control system would be justified. On the other hand, those who took part in exploratory discussions of the so-called "voluntary" program in 1969 had few illusions that any effective system of restraint could be devised without the need for substantial backing by governments, whether by way of regulations, fiscal devices or more informal methods of persuasion.

The decision to go ahead on a more limited basis with a price restraint program led to some positive results, including a modest contribution to the very striking price performance of 1970. It was recognized from the outset, however, that unless an effective way could be found for limiting wage and salary increases, any moderation of the rise in the price level was likely to be limited and temporary. A proposed upper limit of six per cent for annual wage and salary increases, with provision for exceptions, was put forward unilaterally in June 1970. This suggestion was strongly opposed by employee groups and did not gain the degree of general support from the public and governments which was necessary if it were to have much impact. After the formal restraint program terminated at the end of 1970, a common view was that although the six per cent upper limit may have had some positive effect in reducing wage and salary increases any such effect had been quite small.

In retrospect it seems clear that the attempt to arrive at an agreed restraint program acceptable to the major interest groups prior to any legislation for this purpose placed a heavy responsibility on the participants in the discussions. This was particularly the case with the union representatives. As subsequent events in the United States have shown, even when legislation is available to be used if necessary, it is very difficult to develop a control system which is both effective and broadly acceptable to employee groups. In an environment in which supporting governmental action would have had to be forthcoming from a number of governments, and when the absence of any experience with incomes policy left doubts about the effectiveness of commitments from business, the problem was doubly difficult for union members. Under other more favorable conditions, and with the practical experience gained both in Canada and the United States in conducting an incomes policy, the prospects for a measure of cooperation among private groups in fashioning an effective control system may be considerably more promising. It goes without saying, of course, that a recognition of the seriousness of the problem on the part of provincial governments, together with their active support for the measures required to deal with it, would make a major contribution to the chances of success of such a program.

It remains true that the Government of Canada has principal responsibility for the management of the economy, and on May 21, 1971, the Acting Prime Minister, The Honourable Mitchell Sharp, gave the following answer to a question on whether the federal government had the constitutional power to act: "It is our view, and this is why we have been looking at the possible options for enforcing mandatory price and wage controls if it becomes necessary, that under the circumstances then existing we would have that authority." (Hansard p. 6031)

It might be asked why opposition to price and income restraint programs has been so strong in North America and elsewhere. Programs of this kind are designed to curb inflation with less severe and prolonged adverse effects on employment and output than would be possible if reliance were placed on demand management alone. For the community as a whole there are important economic benefits to be had. Why then so much opposition?

One source of resistance is from those who fear that their real income gains will not be as large as they might have been otherwise. For some, this concern is justified. For many others it is not, since they stand to gain from lower living costs what they gave up in money income increases. When reinforced by mutual suspicion that others in the community are in a position to "beat the system", however, fears of this kind make it easy for opponents of controls to build a case that the coverage or effectiveness of any particular restraint program is inadequate.

Opposition based on justified or unjustified fears of adverse effects on individual real incomes finds ready support among those who raise objections on grounds of principle.

The first and most general of these objections is that a control program would infringe on individual, social and political freedom. The Commission shares the natural reaction of most people in a liberal democratic society to bureaucratic interference with individual freedom and the use of coercion to make behavior conform to imposed norms. This needs to be taken into account as one of the costs of any temporary program of controls.

A second source of opposition is based on the ideas and interests which have gathered over the last three or four decades around the institutions of free collective bargaining. Any direct interference in this process has the appearance of crude intervention in a complex and delicate network of relations with resulting adverse social and economic effects. It is not surprising that many of those with special knowledge and experience in this area resist any general form of price and income restraint with great vigor, and it is only when the view becomes widespread that the alternatives may be worse that some at least are prepared to accept a substantial interference with the free collective bargaining process.

Finally, there are those who have a strong belief in the virtues of private enterprise. This is partly the reaction of members of a particular economic group to being subjected to governmental interference in their affairs and partly a concern about the economic costs involved. Study of economic theory and analysis of the operation of a wide variety of economies over an extended period leave many with the view that there was much merit in Adam Smith's injunction of two centuries ago:

> The statesman, who should attempt to direct private people in what manner they ought to employ their capitals, would not only load himself with a most unnecessary attention, but assume an authority which could safely be trusted, not only to no single person, but to no council or senate whatever, and which would nowhere be so dangerous as in the hands of a man who had folly and presumption enough to fancy himself fit to exercise it.

Anyone with sympathy for this point of view would have the gravest reservations about a system of controls which had an air of permanence about it. It is less clear that a temporary program which builds on existing market conditions and merely sets limits on the degree of short-run response to market forces is open to so heavy a charge. There are bound to be economic costs arising from some distortion of market processes, the burdens of compliance and in some cases the blunting of incentives. In a temporary program, however, such costs may be fairly low and must be weighed against the alternative costs of continuing inflation and unemployment.

Nevertheless, the use of controls is undoubtedly open to many objections both on ideological and practical grounds. Thus it is not surprising that many people find it hard to accept the possibility that controls may, nevertheless, be the least undesirable of the alternatives open to us.

Since a number of other studies of the problem have avoided being driven to this conclusion, it may be helpful to examine the general position taken in one of them, the recent Report of the Senate Committee on National Finance, entitled *Growth, Employment and Price Stability*. There is much in this Report which parallels the Commission's findings, including the Senate Committee's view that expectations and lags provide most of the explanation for our recent difficulties. How is it then that the Committee was able to reach such a negative conclusion on the use of controls, which in its view should be limited to a situation in which the United States continued to employ "more and more stringent wage and price controls over an extended period of time"?

As already stated, one way of resolving the unemployment-inflation dilemma temporarily is to opt for inflation. Although the Senate Committee was prepared to accept as a target an annual rate of increase in the Consumer Price Index of two to three per cent—a rate somewhat higher than the traditional objective—and although its analysis suggests that some significant long-run gains in employment can be had from continuing inflation, taken as a whole its Report rejects an inflationary solution.

A second alternative considered by the Committee was to accept a less ambitious view than that widely held by the public concerning the level of unemployment which can be maintained without inflation. The Committee adopted this position. While arguing that the Economic Council's objective of a three per cent national unemployment rate was a valid goal for the longer term, the Committee recommended an unemployment rate of four to 4½ per cent as an interim target more appropriate to the present situation of the Canadian economy. This recognition of the need for greater realism about the level of unemployment consistent with economic stability helps to explain how the Committee was able to conclude that resort to controls might be escaped.

It is in connection with the Committee's discussion of the possible contribution of supply policies and demand management that difficult questions arise. Its Report expresses various criticisms of the way in which these policies have been used in the past and makes a number of suggestions for improvement. No doubt debate will continue on how these policies can be made more effective, and opinions will differ on the extent to which the Committee's suggestions are either feasible or would in fact contribute to this end. Whatever the outcome of that debate, a practical question arises as to how enough progress is to be made along such lines in the near future to deal with our emerging problems. It is, of course, part of the Committee's position that the war against inflation is a long one, but it does not explain how the immediate battles are to be fought while longer-term strategies are being worked out and progressively implemented.

When the Prices and Incomes Commission appeared before the Senate Committee, a question was asked about what was to be done if both unemployment and controls were unacceptable methods of controlling inflation.

The reply was as follows: "The public of this country are going to have to understand how narrow the choices are and how difficult the problem is." It is our view that the Committee's negative conclusion on the use of controls resulted from a failure to recognize how narrow the choices may have become.

If such a policy is attempted, is it important that it be applied only at a time and in a way which offers a high probability of success? The answer to this appears to be yes. Those who have played a role in the application of prices and incomes policies in other countries sometimes argue that while their attempts may not have been successful, it is possible to learn from one's mistakes and do better next time. This assumes, however, that the public will not respond to repeated failure by rejecting incomes policies entirely.

This possibility does not arise in the case of demand management. Like it or not, governments must tax, spend and manage the supply of money, and therefore cannot avoid having demand policies even if the actions taken are based on inflexible, self-imposed rules. Having an incomes policy, however, is a matter of choice. A case can be made, therefore, that on a longer view it would be self-defeating to put together another prices and incomes restraint program unless it has a high probability of success.

This suggests the need for caution in following suggestions for more limited forms of intervention in prices and incomes decisions. At one stage in the spring of 1970 the Commission went some distance in exploring the possibility of using tax disincentives as a means of limiting increases in money incomes, since the prospects for obtaining effective enforcement of guidelines in this area by other techniques remained in doubt. Means were studied whereby increases beyond stipulated percentages both in annual rates of employment income and in personal incomes derived from other sources would be subject to a graduated special withholding tax refundable only at some future date. The larger the increase in money income beyond this percentage, the larger the amount of this income currently withheld as refundable tax.

If a workable and effective tax device along these lines could have been devised, it offered the hope that the desired scaling down of the size of increases in wages, salaries and other money incomes could be achieved without detailed intervention in the collective bargaining process or in other aspects of income determination. In the end, however, the conclusion was reached that it was extremely difficult to devise a system along these lines which was sufficiently equitable, administratively workable and reasonably certain to produce the desired effects on private behavior.

Other proposals have been made which are much more limited in scope. It is sometimes suggested that particular cases of large and unjustified increases in prices or income levels should be selected for public attention, but it is not clear what standard should be applied to reach decisions on such cases. Similarly, it is not made clear how it would be possible, even if there were such a standard, to defend its use in passing judgment on some cases while ignoring a host of others. Finally, the question arises whether the glare of publicity is really, as some still appear to feel, a sufficiently strong weapon to serve as an effective deterrent in matters of this kind.

The Commission has always held the view that the place of "voluntarism" in a price and income restraint program should be largely restricted to agreement on the criteria to be followed, and that when it comes to applying criteria a means of enforcement is required. When, however, it became apparent that the price restraint program agreed to in February 1970 was unlikely to survive without some action being taken on wages and salaries, and when it became clear that for a variety of reasons it was not possible to use the tax system to provide an enforcement mechanism, resort was had to a unilaterally announced upper limit of six per cent for annual wage and salary increases and efforts were made to enlist the support of governments and the public. The limited success we had in obtaining support rendered this effort largely ineffective but incidentally provided a practical demonstration of what it is like to try to apply criteria unsupported by any effective means of enforcement.[1]

Repeated attempts to apply an incomes policy without sanctions are unlikely to accomplish much, and indeed may well be counter-productive if they bring the whole policy approach into disrepute. In short, while there may be some case for further experimentation with more limited forms of incomes policy, this is an area where half measures may be worse than no measures at all.

It may be that before long the march of events will bring Canadians to the view that serious consideration should be given to a temporary program of controls. With this in mind, it has been the Commission's view that a group should be retained within the government to continue work on these issues. On April 27, 1972, the Prime Minister announced the establishment of such a group to carry on the work of contingency planning, to complete the publication of the Commission's studies and to continue research on the role of prices and incomes policy in dealing with inflation.

This completes our summary of the analysis we have made of recent Canadian inflation and of the broad policy choices open to us. Our analysis of the causes and processes of inflation is more optimistic than some. On the other hand, our appraisal of the range of available policy alternatives does not lead to optimistic conclusions. A healthy sense of realism need not, however, lead either to fatalism or cynicism. In spite of the events of recent years, a return to something like the degree of price stability experienced in Canada in the past is still within our reach, and we have more chance than most countries to make some headway against the strong inflationary currents being felt all over the world today. The first step is to reach a measure of consensus on the nature of the problem and on the policy choices open to us.

Notes

*Canada, Prices and Incomes Commission, *Summary Report: Inflation, Unemployment and Incomes Policy* (Ottawa: Queen's Printer, June, 1972, reproduced by permission of Information Canada).

[1]Having been exposed to this demonstration, those who still advocate the use of incomes policy without any sanctions are not unlike the Scottish fisherman who asked his friend Jock to throw over the anchor to stop their boat from drifting on the rocks. "But Angus," said Jock, "don't you remember? The rope is broken." "Aye," said Angus, "but throw it over anyway. It may slow us down a bit."

Section 4

The Changing Role of Government and the Drift Toward Corporatism

Introduction

Preceding sections of this book have demonstrated the complexities of government involvement in the marketplace and the pervasiveness of various forms of state intervention in the Canadian economy. For better or for worse, and for a wide variety of reasons, Canadian governments have initiated innumerable policies designed to affect business. There have been policies pursued to promote business activity, to promote competition, to encourage growth, stabilization or income redistribution and to protect the consumer. Most of these policies have been *ad hoc*, being particular responses to particular problems. There seems to be no single, accepted "general theory" put forward to explain or to justify the apparently commanding presence of the state in our economic life.

In this Section, many fundamental questions remain to be considered. How "free" is free enterprise in Canada? Does competitive market capitalism remain the norm or the exception in our economic arrangements? It is a truism that the national policy created the Canadian economy and that the national policy involved deliberate action by the state to promote railways, to assist immigration and settlement and to protect the emergent national market by the erection of the protective tariff. But what sort of economy did the national policy create? If it was a "capitalist" economy, surely it was a highly "political economy." How are we to explain the growing politicization of our structure of enterprise since the fruition of the national policy, and how are we to interpret the vast and still increasing role of the state in our contemporary economic life?

The growing symbiosis of government and business is reviewed in Thomas Hockin's recent book, *Government in Canada* (1976). In his excellent chapter on "The Growth of Government" Hockin observes that the various public programs of industrial aid may reflect important pressures along a two-way street: not only the familiar pressure of business on the major political parties and on government, but also an erosion of some degree of business autonomy by the state. The power of business in the society and the reality of free enterprise may be undermined in various ways. They may be diminished by the gradual elimination of the small private entrepreneur by giant corporations, by "the straitjacket knitted by foreign ownership," or by the growth of "government-sponsored, government-encouraged, patterning of business activity." For these reasons, Hockin argues that the actuality of the rugged entrepreneur is becoming increasingly rare in Canada. Exhortations concerning the merits of private enterprise are seen as less useful than demands for government assistance to business. "The history of established Canadian firms," he suggests, "confirms the success of qualities other than risk-taking. Yet business retains the image of the rugged entrepreneur, not because it fully accepts it, but because it has not yet found an image with which to replace it."

If it is evident that business and government in Canada are increasingly interrelated, and if the relationship between them is more symbiotic than antagonistic, the question we must pursue is, why? Several answers may be suggested.

A primary and simplistic response might be, why not? Perhaps businessmen actually prefer, expect and demand a public-private symbiosis and deliberately choose to be hand-in-glove with the state in order to escape the rigours of market competition. Perhaps, as Michael Bliss's work mentioned in Section 1 indicates, business traditionally has demonstrated a flight from competition and simply persists in that pattern. Possibly the clamorous commercial rhetoric on the merits of competition is just that, rhetoric.

A second hypothesis is associated with the work of Harold Innis and the staples interpretation of our history. In essence it is that Canada has never experienced a period of pure laissez-faire. Unlike Britain and the United States, we have no background or tradition of unadulterated liberal capitalism. Instead, our earliest experience with economic development was characterized by the relative absence of competition and the important presence of the state, whether in the creation of the monopolistic fur trade or in the heavy public expenditures on canals and the early railroads. Never having known laissez-faire, Canadians are simply not accustomed to the classical model of free markets.

In a similar vein, Herschel Hardin's book *A Nation Unaware* (1974), urges the view that American concepts of pure market liberalism are essentially foreign and irrelevant to Canada. Hardin offers the proposition that this country has always had a genius for economic enterprise, but that genius has been mainly related to public rather than private enterprise. A closely related point was made earlier by S. D. Clark in *The Developing Canadian Community*. Clark's analysis reveals Canadian economic development as essentially bureaucratic-elitist, in contrast to the American experience of development through individualist enterprise. Writing on "The Limitations of Capitalist Enterprise in Canadian Society," Clark observes that "Canada has been what the late H. A. Innis called a 'hard frontier.' The exploitation of her resources has required large accumulations of capital, corporate forms of business enterprise, and state support. . . . The effect has been to weaken the development within Canadian society of capitalist, urban, middle-class social values and forms of social structure." In another brilliant essay in the same book, and again elaborating on Innis, Professor Clark emphasizes that even geography conspired against the emergence of individualistic enterprise in Canada. "Geography, which favoured individual enterprise and limited political interference in the conduct of economic, social and religious affairs over a large part of the continent, favoured on this part of the continent large-scale bureaucratic forms of organization and wide spread intervention by the state." To put the point most starkly, individualistic capitalism is not familiar, normal or indigenous to the history of the Canadian economy.

Third, the inextricable interweaving of the state and commercial enterprise may be the result of our national instinct toward defensiveness. Fearful of the loss of the British market after Britain embarked on free trade, embarrassed about living in the shadow of the American industrial giant and, more recently, intimidated by the threat of U.S. multinational corporations, the Canadian business community (like the rest of the community) has often appeared highly defensive. We tend to worry constantly about our nation's survival. In a book titled *Survival*, which examines our national culture as seen through literature, Margaret Atwood argues that Canadians are obsessively preoccupied with how to survive. We see ourselves as a marginal nation, a nation which may fail and dissolve; we see ourselves as "victims." Atwood suggests that if Moby Dick had been written by a Canadian, the tale would be told not from the perspective of Captain Ahab, but of the whale.

Similarly, Abe Rotstein, who sees Canada as "The Precarious Homestead," wrote a decade ago that "what haunts our public life and gives rise to the reticence and conservatism [of our politics] is the silent spectre of the nation's *precarious* situation." From a different (liberal) ideological perspective the historian Ramsay Cook, in *The Maple Leaf Forever*, talks of Canada as "a small, fragile country," a "precarious nation." It may well be that this perception of Canada as a threatened, timid nation, possessing a "let's circle the wagons" mentality, has bred into the Canadian people a profoundly cautious inclination to risk-avoidance, an innate defensiveness. The defensive nature of our public postures, in turn, may reinforce the tendency of our businessmen to seek aid and solace from the state.

A fourth hypothesis might be advanced to explain our growing interrelatedness of business and government in terms of the raw fact of size in the industrial system, the sheer size and complexity of the scale of enterprise. In years gone by, says the American sociologist Daniel Bell:

> one's achievement was an individual fact—as a doctor, lawyer, professor, businessman; in the reality of today, one's achievement, status, and prestige are rooted in particular *collectivities* (the corporation, being attached to a 'name' hospital, teaching in a prestigious university, membership in a big law firm), and the individual's role is necessarily submerged in the achievement of the collectivity. Within each collectivity and profession, the proliferation of tasks calls for narrower and narrower specialization, and this proliferation requires larger collectivities. . . .

Larger collectivities, Bell argues, become increasingly intertwined and enmeshed with each other and with the biggest collectivity of all, the state, which buys or subsidizes more and more of the goods and services which the various collectivities produce. And so the line between the private and public sectors of the economy, between private property and public property, becomes blurred. Or, as J. K. Galbraith would put it, we see the rise of "The New Industrial State," in which governments and large corporations become partners rather than rivals, increasingly interlocked rather than standing apart.

A fifth and more traditional explanation of the private-public symbiosis may be put in terms of the Louis Hartz–Gad Horowitz thesis that Canada, unlike the United States, contains a nonliberal element, a Tory fragment or a strong Tory touch, emanating from our British origins and our nonrevolutionary past. In his well known article on "Conservatism, Liberalism and Socialism in Canada" (*Canadian Journal of Economics and Political Science*, May, 1966), Horowitz reminds us that Canada's original English Tory settlers, like the precapitalist or semifeudal early settlers of Quebec, brought with them a conception of society which was corporate and hierarchic rather than liberal-individualistic. They tended to see society as an organism in which the whole was greater than the sum of its several parts, and saw the state as an ordinary and essential means of shaping and protecting the community or the nation, particularly the national economy. In this view the community, as represented by the state, takes precedence over the individual: it is therefore assumed that the state should play a decisive role creating and guiding the economic life of a new transcontinental nation. There can be little doubt that, through the influence of the groups such as the Family Compact and through individuals such as Sir John A. Macdonald, the Tory view of the primacy of community and the paternal role of the state runs very deep in the Canadian experience with economic development. Unlike the founding charter of the American republic, which stresses the individualist-liberal goals of "life, liberty and the pursuit of happiness," our Tory-touched B.N.A. Act emphasizes the Canadian goals of "Peace, Order and Good Government."

Alternatively, a Marxist view of economic development in Canada suggests that the capitalist class controlled and very effectively used the power and the credit of the state to support and finance the aspirations of the dominant haute-bourgeoisie. The state was manipulated by the capitalist class to establish monopolies and franchises which could only enhance the wealth of St. James Street and Bay Street. Marxists see the state as a tool used by the dominant commercial groups. From this perspective, the capitalist interests were not inhibited or shaped by the state, but the state was controlled by the capitalist interests to provide the underpinning of a system which would expand private wealth. Although the state is regarded as the subservient instrument of a particular class, Marxists concur that state intervention has been the rule rather than the exception in the Canadian economy.

Thus, from whatever perspective we view the phenomenon, there is broad agreement on the result: Canada does not have and never has had an "orthodox" capitalist system based on free markets and free enterprise. As Alexander Brady has remarked, "the role of the state in the economic life of Canada is really the modern history of Canada."

How, then, are we to interpret the nature of the state and the nature of the political economy within which we live? There have been many attempts to affix a generic name or label to the particular variety of capitalism that characterizes our economy. Professor Brady, for example, employs the term "collectivism" to describe the intermingling of public and private economic initiatives we have witnessed. Kenneth McNaught, in his Pelican *History of Canada*, prefers the term "neo-mercantilist." Many economists simply dismiss the question by asserting that ours is a "post-Keynesian" capitalist economy, and do not trouble to examine ideological issues any further. Probably the most general and familiar appellation is that of the "mixed economy," one combining both private and public enterprise, both market and non-market forms of economic control, in some unspecified combination. Whatever our political and economic culture is, it is different from that of the United States, and hence it departs from the American norms of liberal-capitalism.

Our own view is that the Canadian economy has always displayed certain characteristics which might best be described as "corporatist," and that the most suggestive interpretative concept to apply to Canadian economic experience is corporatism.

Probably the first writer to apply the term corporatism to Canadian economic experience was Robert Presthus. In a book titled *Elite Accommodation in Canadian Politics* (1973), Presthus examined the similarities and close interrelationships between elite groups. His analysis suggests an even more intimate system of elite accommodation than that described a decade ago in John Porter's *Vertical Mosaic*. In fact, Presthus implies, Canadians may have failed to comprehend the unusual nature of their own political culture. Preoccupied by traditional debates as to whether the Canadian economy is more or less free enterprise, or more or less collectivist, we have failed to recognize the possibility that the essence of our political economy may be something quite unrelated to either of these liberal-democratic concepts.

In Chapter II of his remarkable book, Presthus describes corporatism as "a conception of society in which government delegates many of its functions to private groups, which in turn provide guidance regarding the social and economic legislation required in the modern national state." Corporatism, he observes, reflects an essentially *organic* view of society, in which the aspirations of the nation or the collective community "are seen as prior to those of any discrete individual or group, including the state." Much of the motivation toward corporatism springs from the hope of discovering some method of overcoming the profound antagonisms and schisms between social classes, particularly between capital and labour. Corporatists seek a solution to the class struggle by bringing various private groups directly into the governing process as partners or agents of the state.

In the minds of many Canadian scholars, corporatism is a foreign doctrine associated with the political extremism of naked fascism, but this is a misleading oversimplification at best. Fascism is a variant of corporatism, but the latter concept has many facets and variations. Although there is a strong element of paternalism or authoritarianism in the concept, we are not suggesting that corporatism in Canada is fascist: nor are we referring merely to the dominant position of commercial corporations in the economy as described by Galbraith, or by Charles Reich in his book *The Greening of America.* We are concerned with a more general and inclusive political ideology with longer antecedents.

Textbooks and dictionaries of politics usually define corporatism as a conception of society—seeing the community as composed of economic or functional groups rather than amalgams of atomistic individuals—having its origins in the Christian or conservative reaction against the excessive individualism of the French Revolution and the mechanistic-individualistic modes of thought associated with the Industrial Revolution.

The roots of corporatism run very deep in British political thought. Chapter I of Samuel Beer's *British Politics in the Collectivist Age* reminds us that both the Old Tory and Old Whig views of society were corporatist. They saw the state and society as organic. Just as R. H. Tawney in *Religion and the Rise of Capitalism* described Tudor and Stuart social policy as maintaining "an ordered and graded society in which each class performed its allotted function," so too Beer describes precapitalist British political formulations as "corporate and hierarchic. They were the fixed and corporate communities of an organic state. . . ." In Old Whig as in Old Tory thought, says Beer, "the corporatist was inseparable from the hierarchic ideal." When we recall that the liberal paradigm emphasizes the primacy of competitive *individuals*, and the Marxist paradigm proceeds from assumptions of economic *classes* and the class struggle, we may more clearly recognize the sharp contrast of a conservative-Tory paradigm which regards the *community* as an organic whole, with the claims of community seen as prior to those of individuals or classes. In this sense, corporatism is by no means "foreign" to Canada, but readily identifiable with the strong Tory touch which persists in our political heritage from Britain.

What we are asserting, then, is that nonliberal organic corporatism may be a pervasive fact of the Canadian political economy. Our political system's organization of power is not merely elitist, but corporatist. Elites interact and attempt to accommodate each other. The various elites often appear to clash, or pretend to clash, but usually maintain a realistic willingness to balance or harmonize their diverse interests and to preserve the interests of the community through collaboration with the state. When our elites perceive that they are threatened by external enemies, free trade, foreign competition, foreign investment, class divisions or inflation, the orthodox Canadian response is an organic corporatist response: to seek the cooperative interaction of various groups; to eschew market norms of liberal competition; to rally around the concept of a unique Canadian community.

Therefore, here in Section 4 we attempt to illustrate the increasingly pronounced drift toward corporatism in Canada.

Reading 32, excerpted from the *Newsletter* of the Bank Canadian National, illustrates how the representatives of even major financial institutions have accepted as "given" the "jointly managed economy." Whatever our economic system is, it is far from the orthodox capitalist norm of private decision-making about private property. It is rather, as the *Newsletter* puts it, a system in which private enterprise and government "share the initiative in making important economic decisions."

Mackenzie King, the most influential Canadian Liberal of this century, baffled many liberals when he published *Industry and Humanity* in 1918, from which we take Reading 33. King argued that "A community interest, where it is real, and widely diffused, must prove a stimulus to all the parties to Industry. Labour, Capital, Management and the Community can have no finer incentive than that of working together toward the one end, the well-being of the Community." Professor R. Whitaker, in reviewing the 1973 reissue of King's tract (*Canadian Journal of Political Science*, March, 1974), correctly perceived that *Industry and Humanity* was a prophecy of things to come, "the corporatist state in which capital, organized labour, and the 'community' are all represented in the interior processes of political decision-making, and are thus collectively responsible for these decisions." Whitaker notes that *Industry and Humanity*, "with its rejection of individualistic laissez-faire and its emphasis on the corporate or group organization of the economy and the political system—indeed the virtual fusion of economic structures with political forms—demonstrates how deep the corporatist roots run in the political traditions of Canadians." Professor Whitaker, with Presthus, has a strong claim to membership in the vanguard of those who recognized early the importance of corporatism in Canadian political thought.

In Quebec in the 1930's and 1940's, a strain of corporatism flourished, with the implicit sanction of the Catholic Church, as a means of containing class strife and solidifying the beleaguered nationalist impulses of French Canada. Pierre Elliott Trudeau was quick to recognize and denounce the nationalist and introverted tendencies of French Catholic corporatism, and to substitute liberalism, in the Introduction to his book, *The Asbestos Strike* (1956). The counterpoint of these two views is illustrated in Readings 34 and 35. In retrospect it seems fair to suggest that Quebec's strong corporatist strain, far from being an aberration in Canadian political thought, was well in tune with other theory and practice in Canada, emphasizing the primacy of community, but merely as a narrower linguistic community than liberals or English Canadians could contemplate. There can be no doubt, however, that the corporatist strain is indigenous to Quebec. Possibly the prevalent

Québecois view of the political economy of Canada is less atypical, or closer to the mainstream, than is generally acknowledged.

Reading 37 by Michael Trebilcock underlines how ubiquitous the principle of state regulation of the economy is in Canada, and how the interests of the regulators and the regulated are frequently intermingled. We have become so accustomed to the presence of public regulatory agencies that we seldom notice their influence or their considerable departure from the norms of liberal capitalism.

Many socialist writers have pondered the Canadian penchant for state activity in collaboration with private interests. (See, in particular, T. Lloyd, "State Capitalism," in LaPierre and McLeod, *Essays on the Left*, 1971.) The socialist paradigm is by no means dominant and yet the state effectively intervenes in the market, not to foster equality, but to assist private ownership. This is the essence of corporatism, even though its name is not invoked.

Karl Jaffary, an NDP supporter and a former alderman in Toronto, ponders why the presence of Big Government in Canada has yielded such unsatisfactory results. After reviewing the changing role of government, he observes that people want and need more government services, but notes also the growing popular distrust of state activity which is often "incompetent." The communitarian ideal (essential to corporatism) is stressed by Jaffary with the contemporary urban twist that communities should be as small, autonomous and decentralized as possible. Although Jaffary is a socialist and not a corporatist, his thoughtful essay serves to highlight the quest for community which has always been an underlying theme of corporatism and a counterpoint to market liberalism. In some ways, the search for an "Ethic of Community," as George Grant styles it, may relate the socialist left to the assumptions of Old Tories and "Red Tories," and unite these diverse views in an opposition to liberal individualism.

Many students will find food for thought in "The Theology of Free Enterprise," Chapter 5 of P. C. Newman's *The Canadian Establishment*, Vol. I, and in Wallace Clement's *The Corporate Elite*, particularly in the concluding chapter. Clement notes the ubiquitous presence of the state in fostering economic enterprise, and notes that "public capital is used to promote private gains." Here again, perhaps inadvertently, we see the implicit essence of corporatism as the exercise of public power and public decision-making to support private property and the *status quo*, and to avoid class strife.

Robert Stanfield in Reading 38, speaking from a "Red Tory" stance, not only modifies George Hogan's view of Conservatism in Canada, but insists upon the primacy of the national community over business enterprise, in a way which reinforces the claims of the organically conceived society over individualistic entrepreneurs. For Stanfield, as for any genuine Tory, Canada comes first, and business interests (while important) must be subservient to the common good.

Carolyn Tuohy, who studies the politics of professions, examines physicians and health policy to demonstrate that doctors reacted to the political economy of public medicare, not always as rugged individualist entrepreneurs or as monopolists, but often as corporate partners with the state, seeking "corporate accommodation" through bargaining and *de facto* partnership.

Michael Barkway brings out the fact of increasing "consultation" and negotiation, rather than confrontation, between business and government as the political norm, a norm which is more consistent with corporatism than with market capitalism.

We want to emphasize that the characteristic strategy of the corporate state is to avoid as much as possible adversarial confrontation between business and government. Private ownership is left undisturbed. The strategy is for government to establish an "incomes policy" for society while calling for increased partnership or collaboration between the state and all major economic groups. Instead of confrontation, corporatism seeks to substitute the principle of social harmony or unity through negotiation and cooperative interaction between business, labour and the state.

Recently it has become fashionable for politicians as well as businessmen to call for wage restraints. The creation of the Canada Labour Relations Council in 1975, which includes representatives of labour, management and government, was clearly patterned on a tripartite quasi-corporatist model. In a speech delivered on September 19, 1975, Labour Minister John Munro expressed the long-run hope that the new Council "could ultimately lead to the establishment of a rational tripartite incomes policy for Canada."

This representative model, of course, is no novelty. It is familiar to any observer of the Economic Council of Canada which was established in 1963. R. W. Phidd, in his article "The Economic Council of Canada, 1963-1974" (*Canadian Public Administration*, Vol. 18, No. 3, 1975), which is too lengthy for inclusion here, draws attention to the way in which the Economic Council has always combined representatives of management, labour and government. Phidd notes that the planning work of the Council reflects "new trends in governmental management." Its representative structure, he observes, is tripartite, "intended to associate business and trade unions more closely with government."

It is noteworthy too that in the contemporary scene we also hear more frequent appeals by businessmen for greater collaboration between the state and commercial enterprise. For example, Mr. Peter Gordon, president of Steel Company of Canada, was quoted in *The Financial Post* (March 22, 1975) as favouring public-private joint ventures in the field of energy development. State investment with business in Panarctic Oils Ltd. and in the Syncrude tarsands project reflected "healthy signs of cooperation in the national interest," said Gordon. He also urged that "it is in the national interest for government and business to get closer together to solve the problems at hand."

Obviously, the most dramatic recent thrust of the state into the economy, whether in Britain, the United States or in Canada, has been the creation of programs of wage and price controls. A more significant departure from free capitalist markets can scarcely be imagined. Although the fundamental tenet of the market system is individual decision-making about private property, on October 14, 1975, Canadians were faced with a radically different system, one in which an agency of the state determines "acceptable" levels of wages and prices and the basic allocation of the slices of the national economic pie. The only word which characterizes this new system adequately is corporatism. How ironic that Trudeau, having opposed corporatism in Quebec under Duplessis, should become a principal architect of contemporary Canadian corporatism.

Reading 42 is taken from the White Paper on Wage and Price Controls, October 1975. The implementation of this policy appears to have obtained surprisingly widespread public support, but it has also sparked much bitter criticism, as Reading 43 will attest. Richard Rohmer speaks bluntly of there being a "new economic system in place in this country," a system of rigorous economic controls under which "free enterprise in Canada was buried alive."

Rohmer is not alone in his belief that something very fundamental changed on Thanksgiving Day, 1975. John Diefenbaker, for example, conveniently ignoring the fact that his party had been the first to champion controls during the 1974 election, thundered that wage and price fixing by the state constituted a basic threat to individual liberty. NDP leader Ed Broadbent spoke of "the death of collective bargaining as we know it." John Bullock, President of the Canadian Federation of Independent Businessmen, published a newspaper advertisement (Oct. 30, 1975) urging support of wage and price controls in the short run: "We must all support the Government in its attempt to beat inflation or it will beat us and bring in a permanent dictatorship with controls, either right or left." Journalist Anthony Westell brooded (Toronto *Star*, 17 Oct., 1975) that "if the free market is unacceptable and the mixed economy has become unworkable, what remains but government control?" Westell expressed the fear that controls might become "a permanent fixture."

Similarly, the former Dean of Administrative Studies at York University, William Dimma, noted (Toronto *Star*, 28 Oct., 1975) that "Sadly, we live in a world in which the market is more deified than observed. . . . Most of the major decisions which affect our economic destiny are churned out by the ponderous interaction of various sorts of large bodies jostling each other for position." Dimma underlined the "total incompatibility between permanent controls and our economic system. . . . The greatest single problem faced by western democracies is the lack of an incomes policy which . . . evokes consensus, but is also compatible with both democracy and some reasonable version of free enterprise."

Can such compatibility be achieved? Our view is a pessimistic one. Rolling back the powers of government or reversing the growth of state power over the economy has never proven an easy task. It is possible that the implicitly corporatist policy of wage and price controls will succeed in overcoming inflation. It is possible that such controls may prove temporary rather than permanent. It is also conceivable that the growing authority of the state over our economic life may be diminished, and that we will turn back toward closer approximations of a free enterprise market society. However, the lessons of Canadian economic history and our own analysis lead us to conclusions of extreme skepticism. As we witness the drift, or rush, toward corporatism, we have grave doubts about the prospects of individual liberty in a democratic society: as A. J. Liebling once observed, "A man is not free if he can't see where he is going."

Looking ahead, Professor D. V. Smiley's essay, Reading 41, suggests alternative scenarios for future policy implementation. He indicates why he finds our corporatist hypothesis less than compelling. The final selection in this Section is Prime Minister Trudeau's reflections on the economy, taken from his speech of 19 January, 1976.

We recognize that excessive emphasis on ideology, whether liberal, Marxist or corporatist, can produce knee-jerk substitutes for real thought. Ideological concepts such as corporatism should be used, not to answer questions, but to ask new questions: their utility lies in prompting the re-examination of material in the search for new meanings. The contention here is not that the concept of corporatism provides the only, or necessarily complete, framework within which to analyse Canadian economic reality. We do contend that corporatism may be inherent in our past and more prominent in our future. However, in attempting to describe corporatism, we do not wish to advocate it. Normative advocacy we leave to others.

In summary, we see the essence of corporatism (which may take many forms) as private ownership plus state control. Where we diverge from most orthodox economic analysis is in placing less emphasis on competitive markets and more emphasis on the state as the prime economic decision-maker. Where we differ from orthodox liberal political science is that, in the particular field of economic policy, we do not see Parliament or even the cabinet as the effective repository of supreme power in practice. Most of the pervasive, important bread-and-butter decisions of public economic policy are taken, we would hypothesize, not by the cabinet, but by senior bureaucrats and by the numerous regulatory agencies of the state.

Our analysis leads us to agree with Trebilcock's critique of liberal mythology. It is *not* true that most of our economy is "competitive" rather than regulated. It is *not* true that most regulatory bodies deal with technicalities rather than with the fundamentals of pricing and resource allocation. It is *not* true that most producers hate and resent being regulated: rather, those so regulated become positive and powerful forces, virtual partners in the regulatory process. Functional or co-opted producer groups have thus become closely associated with the state as collaborators.

Orthodox liberal economics and orthodox liberal political science were not designed to explain this process. The challenge now is to devise a new conceptual framework to help us understand the working of the system we now see emerging. To this end we believe that the "corporatist" paradigm may, whether we like it or not, come closer than any other to describing the realities of the developing Canadian economy.

32 The System *

Bank Canadian National

The usual image of society which most people have today is that of a dog-eat-dog world where everyone must struggle to earn a living by selling whatever individual "product" he or she may have—manual or skilled labour, specialized talents or ideas.

Everyone can easily see that each is part of a system upon which all must depend. How does this system work? How is it organized? What is its purpose? Everyone must know the answers to these questions in order to understand the system better.

Knowledge of the system's internal structure and organization and what it does are important if it is ever wished to modify it. Its advantages and disadvantages must be weighed against each other, its good qualities and its faults, before undue criticisms are raised. Before comparing it with other existing or proposed systems around the world, varying local conditions and factors must be studied closely.

The system has been described in various ways as the free market economy, the law of supply and demand, or the free enterprise system. No one brief phrase can fully define just what the system is and how it works. The best way to start is by examining its three major characteristics:—

1. Free enterprise, or the freedom of individuals to negotiate and conclude agreements of every kind.
2. Private ownership of property.
3. The predominant role of government.

All three levels of government play such substantial roles in the system that it should be defined as a *jointly managed economy*. In other words, one where private enterprise and government, or the state, share the initiative in making important economic decisions.

The subject is so complex that it is impossible to cover all the ground at one time. This Newsletter, then, will concentrate mainly on the multiple ways in which the laws of supply and demand accomplish those fundamental tasks which prevent the entire economic system from falling into utter chaos.

So that what is to be said later will be more easily understood, let's take a look at the two primary objectives of the economic organization of society as a whole.

I—Full use of resources

In the first place, a well organized economy must provide employment for all those who wish to work, and are able to. Furthermore, the work done by all these individuals must be properly coordinated. But that isn't such a simple task as it may appear. In Canada, for instance, there are millions of workers doing thousands of different jobs. Every morning, the same complicated mechanism is set in motion. These millions head for their individual jobs and perform them, most completely unaware that what each is doing somehow meshes into the system as a whole like so many cogs in a gigantic clock.

The first function of our economic system, then, is basically the *allocation of resources.* The country's entire resources of men and women, financial capital, industrial machinery and tools, mineral wealth, must be marshalled and shared among all sectors of the economy, according to the needs of each. Ideally, this should be done in such a way that the economic system can produce to full capacity, providing the maximum return in consumer goods and services of every kind.

The sum total of all these goods and services produced each year is called the Gross National Product (GNP). A country's GNP is an important indicator of its economic health.

II—Sharing the wealth

A well organized economy should also provide for the needs of every member of society. Money generated by the production of all these things must be distributed in the form of salaries, wages, rents, profits and other types of income so that each person receives a fair share according to his contributions and his needs.

The pay cheque or envelope is the sole source of income for the great majority of people and the laws of supply and demand in large part determine the wage levels for each type of occupation. More and more, wage rates and other working conditions are being set by collective bargaining, but even here the economic laws cannot be ignored.

Retired people and old age pensioners receive incomes from the state. This money comes from society as a whole in the form of taxes which are then redistributed, as in the case also of family allowances and unemployment insurance benefits. Many people receive income in the form of interest on money which they have loaned out or as dividends on investments and rents on their properties. Only a very few inherit any substantial amount.

All this helps to explain why individual incomes vary so widely and why allocation of resources and sharing of the wealth produced must go hand in hand.

Disregarding union activity on the one hand and government intervention on the other, it can be fairly said that all economic activity is ruled by the laws of the marketplace. Supply and demand at one and the same time determine how human and material resources are to be used in production and what money is to be paid to the owners of these resources.

The fundamental problem of economic life, therefore, is to ensure maximum production by allocating available resources, while ensuring equitable sharing of the wealth produced.

In one way or another, the freely operating market system tries to solve this problem, although it often must rely upon government intervention as noted previously to fill in the gaps and correct its failures. Thus, it is important to understand more about why a pricing system is needed and the many ways in which these two primary objectives can be achieved.

How Values Are Set

Whenever a consumer makes a purchase this is, in effect, a vote of confidence and preference for the product in question. The businessman, naturally, will only supply products which are in demand. Demand can be stimulated by advertising, but the product will be made available only as long as consumers are willing to pay the market price.

In a competitive economy, where many firms are battling one another to capture the consumers' dollars, demand fluctuates constantly. Prices thus reflect changing market conditions. They are first of all coefficients of value or of choice. They express consumer preferences and indicate the relative value which the market places on competing goods or services, taking into account variations in quality.

As a result, these freely set prices make it possible to know the trading relationship set up between various articles (as in primitive times barter ratios were set up between cows, sheep, salt, etc.).

Information System

Prices thus provide guidelines for production by signalling changing market conditions. If nickel mine workers go out on strike, nickel prices will rise sharply as a result of the sudden or threatened scarcity of that metal. Stock market prices around the world will immediately reflect the new situation. Some readjustments will be made, following the lead given by prices in spreading the news of scarcities or surpluses of goods on the market as a whole.

Publication of prices in newspapers and catalogues, as well as the stock market quotations which indicate the relative financial health of product manufacturers and service suppliers, allow business experts to compare prices on different markets and from various suppliers, so that resources can be deployed and used efficiently.

Each business enterprise keeps a watchful eye on the prices of products and resources which it uses, because profits depend upon them. Prices to the businessman are like the dials on an instrument panel. If the readings are too high or too low, decisions must be taken to reallocate resources and reset production schedules.

This would not be possible if prices were fixed. In a world where production activities are so widely scattered and competitive, day-by-day prices make it possible to coordinate the actions of a great many individuals and business firms. In that light, it must be admitted that the supply and demand system of establishing prices is the most efficient information system available today.

Prices as a Stimulus

Along with setting up relative values for products and spreading information to that effect, prices can also be an important stimulus to essential economic activities. Many people who would be unwilling to work at the North Pole for their present wages might jump at the chance if they were offered double the money. The "prices" paid for different kinds of work vary widely, thus ensuring an active and diversified work force so essential to the proper functioning of the entire economic system. If there were but one identical rate of pay for all occupations, the whole structure would collapse. There would be no incentive for anyone to try to climb higher in the system.

Among other things, this economic stimulus establishes a basis for allocating millions of workers to the millions of jobs to be filled. In some places, such as the army or certain institutions, duties are allotted in an autocratic or bureaucratic fashion. Even if you have a talent for music, you must work in the kitchen. So, everyone is a loser: the one who does the cooking and those who must eat it!

A good economic organization must allow everyone to use his special talents or abilities. Stating this as a vital role of the present system does not deny the fact that unemployment rates are now unacceptably high, not that thousands of workers are far too poorly paid. The system has its failings, certainly, but it cannot be judged entirely on those. Its potential is too great.

Rationing the Resources

Possibly the most important role played by prices is to signal scarcities, the keystone of all economic science and activities. Allocation and use of limited resources is a key economic problem in the face of the innumerable and constantly growing demands which must be met on all sides. Businesses and governments must figure out budgets with a sharp pencil, often postpone or abandon certain projects.

The supply of goods is also limited in comparison with the needs to be supplied. The essential role of prices is to limit the demand to match the available supply. Prices force consumers to restrain their desires: in other words, to ration the demand. Only those who are ready, or able, to pay the price will have their needs satisfied.

Similarly, when money is scarce, interest rates rise, thus discouraging would-be borrowers. Money will only be loaned for priority projects. In a free market economy, priority is given to those who have the ability to pay. Granted, this is like the law of the jungle, but that's the way the system works.

Prices thus play a very important social role. Take as an example the prices charged for municipal parking lots, parking meters and garages. Even if the revenues from these were less than administrative costs, the city must maintain them. The aim is not to fill the city coffers, but rather to control street congestion by offering parking to those who really need it and are willing to pay the price. If all parking were free, the jamups and confusion would be unimaginable.

The same rule applies even in the case of public facilities such as municipal swimming pools. Entrance fees charged, while not covering all the costs involved, help to keep the crowd within more or less reasonable bounds.

In yet another respect, prices also help to prevent rare resources from being wasted. People are most inclined to squander those natural resources or wastefully use products which are abundant and relatively low in price. Paper is one glaring example in Canada, as compared with less fortunate countries.

The armed forces use a very different rationing method. Each man receives an equal and arbitrarily set ration. He does not eat what he wants, but what he gets. The military rationing system does not take account of individual desires. Someone in authority makes the decisions for all. The supply and demand pricing system, on the other hand, gives each individual the right to buy what he really wants and likes, always provided he has the money to pay for it.

Dividing the Spoils

The individual worker's wages represent just one small cost to the employer, yet they are his major or even sole source of income. This dual aspect of the labour pricing system is the source of permanent conflict within the system. The employer wants to keep his costs as low as possible; the employee wants the highest possible income. Since these two objectives are completely incompatible, labour-management tension is inevitable.

Each worker and each owner of some particular resource is paid the going market price for his labour or services, for the things he sells or money he lends. The sum total of all these prices for all kinds of real or monetary products and tangible or intangible services determines how much money there is to be distributed.

Unfortunately, the distribution is made very unequally from one income group to the next. But the system is based upon this inequality, as explained earlier, since the method of allotting incomes according to the work done is the main stimulus to greater productivity, efficiency and ambition.

Some governments are now trying to rectify some of the most glaring aspects of this inequality in what we call a "wealthy" society. The various types of transfer payments are attempts to fill in the gaps in the system, somehow or other, because by itself the system tends to be blind, impersonal and often inhuman.

It is extremely difficult to survive on the fringe of the system. Every individual depends upon it, but the system has no need for anybody. Nobody is irreplaceable, and everyone's activities are limited by immutable rules. One government succeeds another, but all look and act much alike.

Only very recently have we seen some really significant social policies; the work of courageous men who are truly statesmen capable of favourably influencing the orderly evolution of the system. But much remains to be done to correct the failings of the system and the roles played by governments.

Conclusion

Through those five major roles of evaluation, information, stimulation, rationing and distribution of wealth, prices serve to coordinate all economic activity in our system.

Similar functions are performed in various ways in other forms of organized societies. But they have been described here as they work within the framework of a free enterprise economy where most institutions are geared to the orderly functioning of the laws of supply and demand.

Nevertheless, due to some of the system's failings and major defects, the state has had to intervene in various areas of economic life today:—

1. Government has assumed responsibility for several services judged essential for the collective safety or well-being of the population as a whole: national defence, education, public health, parks and autoroutes.
2. The free enterprise system is restricted in its operations by rules of many kinds: building codes and zoning regulations, farm products price supports and industrial subsidies, permits and licences of all kinds.
3. Left to itself, the system is unable to generate sufficient incomes for all classes of people. Government tries to bridge this gap by redistributing incomes in various ways and at various levels. This is done by transfer payment plans such as unemployment insurance, family allowances, social welfare assistance and the like. We can agree or disagree with some aspects of these measures, as we wish, but the only way they could now be eliminated would be by changing the entire system.
4. Finally, and more fundamentally, governments can control economic activities by using the well-stocked arsenal of monetary policies and taxing powers at their disposal. This is too involved a question to be treated in a few lines. But one thing is certain: the state has the power to influence not only the growth of certain industries but also the general pace of economic activity and price levels in general.

Notes

*Bank Canadian National, *Monthly Newsletter*, 3:2, February, 1972 (reproduced by permission of publisher).

33 Government in Industry: the Principle of Joint Control *

Wm. L. Mackenzie King

Whilst it is unlikely that Socialism in the form of the omnipotent and ever-present State, or Industrial Unionism controlling Industry in conjunction with a democratized State, will ever permanently succeed the present order, it is altogether probable that Collectivist ideals, and in particular what they represent of the community idea and improvement in the status of Labor, will vastly expand their influence in the years to come. This is but continuing a natural evolution which experience has wholly justified. A belief in the wisdom and justice of a measure of State interference succeeded the older conception of *laissez-faire*, which looked to unrestricted competition as the ideal in matters of industrial organization. Regulation, especially as respects a minimum of social well-being, is more and more the accepted order of to-day.

What would appear as most likely to happen is that managers, investors, and workers alike will be obliged to yield an increasing measure of interest and control to the Community. The function of Government in Industry will cease to be monopolized by any one or two or three of the parties, and will be shared by all, in ever-increasing measure of equality. Whilst Industry may continue chiefly a matter of individual enterprise, kindred enterprises will more and more coalesce and expand. The status of the wage-earner in the control of Industry will gradually rise toward equality with that of the investor. Labor's voice will become correspondingly important and authoritative.

Any development which tends to equalize Control between all the parties is promoting Partnership in Industry. Simultaneously, it is helping to evolve genuine Industrial Democracy. If one stops to analyze what Control signifies, it will be seen that, in a very real sense, all Control is in the nature of Ownership. To own a thing is to have the right to control it. Ownership apart from control is a negative kind of possession; control with or without ownership is a positive one. Public Ownership and Public Employment do not of themselves bring about any unity of the interests of the worker with those of the public body which employs him. Some direct interest in the results, and some special representation of the workers actually employed are essential, even in a public enterprise, if individual effort and individual freedom are to be maintained.

The ideal of Joint-Control of Industry, as respects both individual enterprises and Industry as a whole, would doubtless be control by Labor, Capital, Management, and the Community, equally represented on what would be the equivalent of industrial directorates, and enjoying an equal voice in round table conference. By such directorates, policies would be framed and agreements reached as the result of discussions in which thought of the common interests of the several partners in Industry would be uppermost, just as, in a Cabinet, expression is given to the common interests of a nation.

The form of industrial organization, and even the immediate ownership of the instruments of production, are wholly secondary to Control. If the contributing factors to production, Labor, Capital, Management, and the Community, were to constitute a Directorate of Partners, what any one or all actually owned of the instruments of production would be unimportant as compared with the degree of control which each exercised over the workings of Industry and its results.

Few men have done more to preserve popular liberties and to advance constitutional government than the illustrious stateman John Pym. He was returned in 1614 to the House of Commons at Westminster by men who represented the determined spirit of the nation against the unscrupulous and arbitrary behaviour of James I. He was imprisoned by James for joining with other members in protecting the privileges of the House against the King's disregard of Parliament. He eloquently supported the Petition of Right in protest against the concession of *sovereign power* to Charles II. In the Long Parliament he denounced unsparingly the arbitrary proceedings of the Government. It was he who characterized the Earl of Stafford as 'the greatest enemy to the liberties of his country, and the greatest promoter of tyranny that any age had produced,' and who, when the Commons decided on Stafford's impeachment, carried the message to the bar of the Lords. It was he also who exposed in Parliament the design of Charles to bring up the army to overawe the deliberations of the Commons. He declined to lessen his independence by accepting, at the instance of the Crown, the Chancellorship of the Exchequer. Because of this refusal, he was named by royal message one of the five members in an impeachment which helped to provoke the Civil War. Of this impeachment, Macaulay has said: 'It is difficult to find in the whole history of England such an instance of tyranny, perfidy, and folly.'

Speaking of the principles which underlie all free government, Pym said: 'That form of government is best which doth actuate and dispose every part and member of the State to the common good.'

No more splendid maxim of Government has ever been devised. Were Pym's words so transposed as to be made applicable to Industry, the maxim would read: *That form of Government in Industry is best which doth actuate and dispose every part and member to the common good.*

Labor, Capital, Management, and the Community: these are the parts and members of Industry. They are the partners in Industry, partners in individual enterprises, partners in Industry as a whole. Self-government in Industry worked out on some basis of adequate representation of all the partners should prove as nearly perfect as any form of Industrial Government it is possible to conceive.

There is an important distinction between a Directorate and a Management, and it is in the form of a Directorate, not as a Management, that a more equitable distribution of the control of Industry among all its contributing factors is to be desired. The function of a Directorate is to create and lay down policies, and to find ways and means of providing what is necessary to carry them out. The function of Management is to see that the policies determined upon are executed in accordance with the spirit by which they are actuated. Once the right relationship of a Directorate to a Management is grasped, the possibilities of Industrial Directorates become more apparent, and the whole problem of Government in Industry is relieved of many of its embarrassing features.

The method of conducting political Government in free communities helps to make clear the essential difference between the functions of a Directorate and a Management. Government in the State is divided between bodies which make the laws, and bodies which execute them. In other words, there are two main functions in Government: the one legislative, the other executive. In the British Isles, and throughout the self-governing Dominions of the British Commonwealth, the central law-making body is styled Parliament; in America it is spoken of as Congress. Parliament and Congress through legislation define what may or may not be done by men in their relations as citizens. They do not attempt, however, to carry out their own policies, or to execute the laws they enact. The work of Executive Administration is left to salaried officers, composed, in the countries mentioned, of the Head of the Nation and his Cabinet, the Civil Service, and the Judiciary. Within the limits prescribed by law, the authority of the Executive in all its branches is supreme. Without permitting wide discretionary authority to the individuals chosen to administer and execute the laws, and without reserving to them ample power to give, and to compel obedience to orders, it would be impossible for the business of Government in the State to be carried on.

Because Management exercises what is essentially an executive function, it does not follow that Management may not also be a part, and, for that matter, the most important part, of the Directorate which shapes policy. Though differing in many particulars, both the British and the American constitutions afford conspicuous examples of the exercise of this dual function by the Executive. Under the workings of both, the National Executive sees to the effective enforcement of policy and laws. Under both, however, the Executive, in the exercise of its control, is itself controlled by the will of the people as a whole.

If Government in Industry were to undergo a transition similar to that effected in the evolution of Government in the State, Management need not be robbed of any of its necessary measures of control. Its function in Industry would continue to correspond with that of the Executive in the State. As in the case of the State, the distinction in Industry between legislative and executive powers would become more and more clearly marked. The executive would be rendered more and more responsible to the body which has to do with the shaping of policies. In the case of Industry, this body would be the Directorate representative of Labor, Capital, Management, and the Community, with Management advising, and often dictating to, the other constituent elements, just as under the British constitution, the Prime Minister and his Cabinet, and under the American constitution, the President and his Cabinet, notwithstanding that their primary function is executive, advise, and, within bounds, dictate to Parliament and Congress respectively.

If in the course of industrial evolution something resembling the system of Representative and Responsible Government in the State is to be effected in Industry, the evolution is certain to be gradual and wholly intermittent. It will come in industries individually before it extends to Industry collectively. It will find expression now in this individual enterprise and trade, now in that; here in one group of allied trades and industries, there in another and wholly different group; and the men who help to promote a peaceful development are the men whom History will honor.

The application of principles underlying Partnership, on which all the rest is founded, need not await the day of equal representation of the four partners on Industrial Directorates. A frank recognition of the fact that there are four parties to Industry, instead of one, or two, or three, and that each is entitled to a voice with respect to conditions affecting itself; and an equally frank acceptance of the principle of round table conference through representation, as the best of methods of arriving at a common policy, are all that is necessary to start the machinery of Government in Industry in the right direction. Necessary adjustments will readily disclose themselves, and perfecting processes can be worked out as time and occasion permit.

Nor in the effort to further Self-government in Industry, is it necessary to fashion all developments in one and the same mould. It will serve our day and generation if, in the making of necessary adjustments, we were true to the broad conception of Industry as a joint venture in which there are the four partners, each interested in the joint product, and each concerned in rendering a much needed social service. Progress hitherto has been impeded through a false emphasis, by one or other of the parties, upon a sole right of control; and by a forgetting that Industry is something more than a revenue producing process; that it is a form of the highest social service as well.

The day of ultimate achievement may be far off, but the ideal, if it does nothing more than enlarge our range of vision, serves a useful purpose. It is sufficient, for the present, to comprehend that *a Constitution is in the process of making*. The expression in words of the Constitution Industry has already won will do much to promote the development of harmonious and just relations between the parties to Industry.

The Magna Charta, the Petition of Right, and the Bill of Rights, constitute, in the words of Lord Chatham, 'the Bible of the English Constitution.' Taswell-Langmead has pointed out[1] that in each of these documents, whether it be of the thirteenth or of the seventeenth century, is observable the common characteristic of professing to introduce nothing new. Each professed to assert rights and liberties which were already old, and sought to redress grievances which were for the most part innovations upon the ancient liberties of the people. Is the time not now at hand when, out of rights universally recognized and liberties generally conceded, *an Industrial Constitution* can be framed which will serve to all the parties to Industry as a bulwark of freedom in the period of transition through which even now we are passing, and in distant years to come? After all, have we, perhaps, not reached the stage in the evolution of government in Industry where we can apply to those highest in authority the dignified utterances of Sir Edward Coke? 'Was it ever known that general words were a sufficient satisfaction for general grievances? The King's answer is very gracious; but what is the law of the realm? that is the question. I put no diffidence in His Majesty; but the King must speak by record, and in particulars, and not in general. *Let us put up a Petition of Right*; not that I distrust the King, but that I cannot take his trust, save in a parliamentary way.'

Notes

*Mackenzie King, W. L., *Industry and Humanity* (first published 1918. New edition reprinted by the University of Toronto Press, 1973), pp. 268-273 (reproduced by permission of University of Toronto Press, © University of Toronto Press 1973).

[1]*English Constitutional History*, p. 79.

34 Principles of Corporate Organisation *

J. B. Desrosiers

. . . Every human society, in order to respond to the physical, intellectual, and moral needs of those who comprise it, needs a leader who imposes on each person a respect for the rights of others and directs everyone toward the common good; since, as St. Thomas said, commenting on Aristotle,

> If it is natural for man to live in populous society, there must be among men someone who governs them. Where there is a multitude of men, each one seeking his own advantage, dislocation is not long in coming, as long as there is no one to preoccupy himself with what is good for the multitude.

To assure the wellbeing of each and every person, the supreme leader of civil society cannot directly govern each of the individuals who comprise it, since civil society is not simply an agglomeration of individuals; it is a living reality, a synthesis of differentiated organs. . . .

In the social whole, as in the human "whole", each part must fulfill its proper functions, and the influence of the head cannot be transmitted directly. It would be ridiculous to imagine a human body in which each of the organs wanted to bypass the parts that tie it to the centre, in which for example the fingers ignored the influence of the hand in trying to directly obey the head. . . .

The Church . . . is asking that professional societies be founded, i.e. that workers and employers of a single profession or sector be grouped together. Since all men who engage in a single profession, be they employers or simple labourers, have something in common, they are naturally inclined to unite to protect this profession that they have chosen as an honourable means of earning a living against the unworthy and incompetent.

. . . . The Church asks that in these corporations useless distinctions between different categories of workers not be made; that they not be grouped according to the place that they occupy in the labour market, since such a distinction necessarily produces a division between employers and employees. It wants employers and workers in each branch of human activity grouped together and wants equal rights given to one and all.

That does not mean that there must be no authority in these corporations. On the contrary, according to Christian social philosophy, in every human society there must be an authority which all obey. There must be at the head of each corporation a superior council elected by the members of the profession, by all the employers and workers of whatever trade they may be.

The supreme authority of the country or of the province will give to this superior council of each corporation the power to make laws and survey their application. Thus the superior council of each corporation will enter into the hierarchy of power; it will become an organ of government. . . . [But] the members of the superior councils must not be named by the government, they must be elected by the various syndicates or regional groups of the profession. . . . That does not mean that the government will have nothing to do with the corporations. It must oversee them, seeing above all that members of the superior committees do nothing contrary to the statutes of their corporation and nothing contrary to the common welfare. . . .

[In addition] there must necessarily be an *intercorporate organization* above the corporation, and delegates of different corporations (for example, of all the corporations in the Province of Quebec) must meet from time to time to study and promote the overall interests and to make general regulations, without which corporate organization would become an instrument of disorder. If individual egoism is possible, it is also unfortunately possible to have corporate egoism. Without a solid intercorporate organization, the employers and employees of a single industry (for example construction, shoemaking, etc.) could well agree to maintain selling prices that are altogether disproportionate to the cost of living and detrimental to the common good.

Notes

*Desrosiers, J. B., "Principes et description de l'organisation corporative," *L'Action Nationale*, 9, premier semestre, 1938, pp. 143-9 (reproduced by permission of publisher). Translated by David Rayside.

35 The Nature of the Occupational Corporation *

Richard Arès

The occupational [or functional] corporation is a legally constituted body, grouping all the members of the same occupation under a single authority, having the power to act with a view to the common good and to impose its decisions on all those concerned.

The corporation is at one and the same time a social body and a public body:

(A) Social body—not to be confused with the state or with private associations. It has its own regulative power. . . . It constitutes a real society, an autonomous organism . . . intermediate between the family and the state.

(B) Public body—an institution recognized by the state and on which authority is conferred over the ensemble of the occupation. The corporation brings together all those who work at the same occupation. By that it differs from the union which groups only part of those concerned and which is free and independent. The authority of the corporation gives it the capacity to act with the common good in mind and to impose its decisions on all those who fall under its jurisdiction.

THE NECESSITY AND ADVANTAGE OF THE CORPORATION

(A) To order the economy. An ordered economy is an economy which respects the hierarchy of values, an economy at the service of man, of the human person, of all human persons. . . .

(B) To restore social peace. . . . Society is plunged into a violent and unstable state, because it is founded on classes that are always in conflict and inclined toward hate and war. The remedy? Substitute for these classes "well organized bodies . . . which group men according to the different branches of social activity to which they are attached" [Quadragesimo Anno]. The corporation is a natural society; social peace is therefore impossible as long as these organs are not properly constituted and harmoniously regulated.

Notes

Arès, R., *Plans d'étude sur la Restauration Sociale* (Montreal: L'Ecole Social Populaire, 1941), pp. 57-8 (reproduced by permission of publisher). Translated by David Rayside.

36 Corporatism in Quebec *

Pierre Elliott Trudeau

Corporatism is without a doubt the most important reform to delight our social thinkers. The greatest variety of men, in the most different circumstances, and for the most opposed ends, proclaimed the gospel of corporatism. Their voices were as one, and they preached their futile homilies with unflagging enthusiasm. Nothing more starkly revealed the monolithic nature of our ideology.

From year to year, in connection with everything and nothing, lecturers at the Semaines sociales (Symposiums on Social Issues) found ways to apologize for corporatism. They included Mgr. Paquet and the future Mgr. Desranleau (1921), Jean Bruchési (1936), and Maximilien Caron (three times from 1938 to 1942). Caron relied upon such disparate authorities as Cardinal Villeneuve ("Corporatism all the way!") and the prime minister of the province ("Anything that brings us closer to corporatism is a step forward."). At the Semaine sociale of 1942, Gérard Picard was still speaking of trade unionism as a means of achieving a corporative organization of society.

The contributors to *L'action nationale* also went through a phase of hard-line corporatism. In November 1937, Roger Duhamel expressed the opinion that nationalism would emerge victorious from a national and Catholic trade union movement, which could reach full maturity within a corporative framework. The next year, a long inquiry into corporatism began. In the course of it, the greatest variety of learned doctors found themselves in agreement with one another: Abbé J. B. Desrosiers (in a Semaine sociale held at Jean-de-Brébeuf College, November 1937, he also recommended that family allowances be obtained through corporatism); François Hertel (who advocated a corporatist version of personalism; he still adhered to this doctrine in 1945, in his *Nous ferons l'avenir* [We Will Make the Future]); F. A. Angers (who held that unions must develop towards corporatism). We should also add the names of other zealots who participated in this inquiry: Hermas Bastien, Gérard Filion, Esdras Minville. Father Lévesque was also part of the group: he recommended joint action by the adherents of the cooperative movement and the supporters of corporatism.

Father Arès devised a corporatist catechism, and in his trade union catechism, he emphasized (Question 45) that the trade union movement is a first step towards corporatism. Victor Barbeau made a remarkable inquiry into our economic hardships; he concluded it with a statement in favour of an economic and political order based on corporations. In the same year, the Jeunesses patriotes (Young Patriots) published a book on separatism, *Le séparatisme*, by Dostaler O'Leary. O'Leary called for "the establishment of a corporative regime in the Free French Canadian State." The Bloc universitaire (University Coalition), at its Duchesnay convention of 1939, passed a resolution that "each of our Schools of Social Sciences should make a special effort to interest all students . . . in corporatism."

We could add to the list indefinitely, but the nature of our philosophic idealism is clear enough. Several decades of social thought are summed up almost in a word: corporatism. Since the word had crossed the lips of the Pope, and since the English were hardly enthusiastic about corporatism, we were glad to regard it as a universal panacea. Everybody was happy to recommend this miraculous remedy, which had the advantage of *not requiring any critical reflection.* Nobody felt that he had to search for an approach to social issues in tune with the course of history. Anyone who endorsed the fashionable prejudice was granted the title of Catholic and national sociologist.

I do not intend to deal here with the question of whether or not corporatism has some contribution to make to a political theory based on the idea of progress. Objective political economy and sociology have certainly not yet shown how a legal superstructure, which makes no essential changes in capitalist institutions, could reconcile the opposed interests of capital and labour, except in limited areas and for limited periods of time. Social and economic tendencies to monopoly, inherent in these reconciliations, would very likely create conflicts of interest (cartel against cartel, cartel against the consumers, etc.). These conflicts could be resolved only by oligarchy, eliminated only by dictatorship. It would therefore be most dangerous to attempt corporate organization, except among people whose democratic development was so far advanced that one could be utterly certain that special interests (the concern of the corporations) would be subordinate to the general interest (the concern of the State).

Now, most of our thinkers saw corporatism in a completely different light: they regarded it as a means to tame the *democratic* thrust of the trade union movement. They tolerated unions only because they believed that they would soon be contained by corporations. Our brand of corporatism was actually devised for an "elite," who saw it as a means to discipline popular movements and to maintain its authority over the masses organized in this fashion. The people were not at all taken in by this. When we finally made an objective inquiry into the results of nearly half a century of theoretical corporatism, we realized that defeat was total: "There is not one organization whose administrative structure corresponds exactly to the ideal type described by the militants."

The Book of Ecclesiastes still offers the finest comment on our social ideas in general in the half century before the asbestos strike: *Mataiotès mataiotètôn, ta panta mataiotès.*

Notes

*Trudeau, P. E., *The Asbestos Strike*, translated by James Boake (Toronto: James Lorimer & Co., new edition, 1974), pp. 24-6 (reproduced by permission of author and publisher).

37 Winners and Losers in the Modern Regulatory State *

Michael J. Trebilcock

The Consumer Interest in the Regulatory Process: Recent Policy Responses

Three myths surrounding the present nature of public regulation widely persist. The first is that our economy is largely unregulated and is disciplined mainly by competitive forces. In fact, in Canada, there are over 100 Federal regulatory agencies and in most provinces more than 50 regulatory agencies.[1] This does not include, of course, government Departments directly administering regulatory statutes or subsidy programmes. Agencies and Departments regulate everything from telephone, rail, and air-line rates, foreign investment, capital markets, broadcasting licences, product tariffs, agricultural produce prices, food, drug and safety standards to the licensing of various classes or merchants, from insurance agents to door-to-door salesmen. Few areas of our lives are untouched by public regulation.

The second myth is that most regulation involves technical questions of little interest or relevance to the average citizen. Nothing could be further from the truth. While many regulatory decisions may involve initially an analysis of technically complex facts, once these facts have been ascertained the ultimate decision to be made will often be of an immensely important political and social character, for example, highways versus public transport, energy resources versus the environment, foreign investment versus economic sovereignty.[2]

The third myth is that most major forms of regulation are forced on unwilling producers by hostile non-producer groups. In fact, the contrary is the truth. Most of the extensively regulated industries, at least, prefer being regulated to competing and actively seek and sustain accommodating regulatory regimes. As Stigler remarks,[3] "as a rule, regulation is acquired by the industry and is designed and operated primarily for its benefit."[4] The sheltered life of a regulated protectorate is likely to be more comfortable than life in a vigorously competitive market-place. As Stigler elsewhere remarks:[5]

> Competition, like other therapeutic forms of hardship, is by wide and age-long consent, highly beneficial to society when imposed upon—other people. Every industry that can afford a spokesman has emphasized both its devotion to the general principle and the over-riding need for reducing competition within its own markets because this is the one area in which competition works poorly.

Regulatory issues have massive impacts on many more interests than those of the regulatees, and the case for these other interests being represented in this form of regulatory decision-making is, on the face of it, undeniable. The consequences of a failure to be represented and heard are stated as follows by a former Canadian Minister of Consumer and Corporate Affairs, the Hon. John Turner:

> I've looked at a lot of regulatory agencies, and the longer I'm around here, the more I believe that every one of these tends, in a period of time, to reflect the interests of the industry it is supposed to be regulating.[6]

The failure of government in the past to recognize that merely setting up regulatory agencies to protect the public interest is not in itself enough is vividly described by Rod Sykes, Mayor of Calgary, in Winnipeg, October 12th, 1973:

> In those cases where protest has been organized within the neighbourhood, there is no funding to enable the residents to oppose the experts, the high-priced engineers, and the real estate dealers. The government, in effect, has all the power on its side. It sets up a public hearing format and says, now look, here you are, a fair deal, a public hearing. We're going to hear from both sides and deliver our verdict on the merits. That is exactly what Roman Emperors used to say to Christians when they invited them into the lion's den. One lion, one Christian, and may the best lion win.[7]

The same phenomenon has been the subject of longer and more intense concern in the U.S. As Roger C. Cramton, formerly Chairman of the U.S. Administrative Conference, recently stated:

> The cardinal fact . . . is that governmental agencies rarely respond to interests that are not represented in their proceedings. And they are exposed, with rare and somewhat insignificant exceptions, only to the view of those who have a sufficient economic stake in a proceeding or succession of proceedings to warrant the substantial expense of having lawyers and expert witnesses to make a case for them. Non-economic interests or those economic interests that are diffuse in character tend to be inadequately represented . . .[8]

The problem of the "empty consumer's chair"[9] in regulatory proceedings has now begun to elicit a variety of government responses, as governments have come to recognize that, as the creators of these agencies, they carry the primary responsibility for ensuring that their functions are effectively discharged.

The Canadian Response: CAC's Advocacy Programme

During the tenure of the Hon. Basford as Minister of Consumer and Corporate Affairs, the Canadian Consumer Council, a citizens' advisory agency to government, was asked in 1971 to commission independent research over a four year period into the status of the consumer interest in proceedings of independent regulatory agencies, decision by agricultural marketing boards, the conduct of the self-governing professions, and the operations of Crown corporations. The first two stages of this research have been completed and the last are now proceeding under the aegis of the new Consumer Research Council.

In June, 1973 the Hon. Herb Gray, then Minister of Consumer and Corporate Affairs, announced that as an interim experiment the Government was making a special unconditional grant of $100,000 to the Consumers Association of Canada (CAC) to enable it to intensify and expand its advocacy activities. Of this sum, $35,000 was allocated by CAC to formal advocacy activities before regulatory agencies. Early in 1974, the Federal Government announced that it was extending the experiment a further year with a grant of $116,000, all of this money to be used in regulatory proceedings, appeals therefrom and test cases in the courts. For 1975-76, the grant was increased to $215,000 to permit more fundamental policy research on the regulated industries to be undertaken. With these grants, CAC has set up an advocacy unit in its Ottawa office, staffed by two lawyers, three secretaries and assisted by outside technical experts and counsel on retainer paid for out of the balance of the grant. Most of the activities of the programme have been directed at the regulatory arena.

While it is not the purpose of this article to explore the finer intricacies of public utility regulation and related regulatory issues, it may be useful to survey quickly the principal initiatives of the programme since it was implemented in September, 1973.

The first regulatory initiative by CAC's advocacy programme was taken in late 1973 following an application by Ontario Hydro (a Crown corporation) to the National Energy Board for a licence to export hydro-electric power to the United States. The particular proposal envisaged the importation of coal from Appalachia in the U.S. for firing coal-burning generators located in Ontario near major metropolitan centres and the exportation of the power so produced back to the U.S. (the U.S. was to get the power, Ontario the pollution). Ontario Hydro estimated that the net gain to Hydro from this proposal was of the order of $6 to $8 million annually. CAC and Pollution Probe, an environmental group, jointly intervened in the hearing before the NEB, objecting that the estimated net economic worth of the proposal failed to take into account substantial social costs in the form of environmental degradation which witnesses for the intervenors estimated at $8.5 million per annum, and which Ontario Hydro was, in effect, attempting to disregard by imposing on the public at large. Ontario Hydro submitted no serious evidence on this issue. The NEB, in the result, found that these estimates of environmental costs were too speculative and granted the licence application. The decision was later confirmed by the federal Cabinet. CAC and Pollution Probe then sought leave to appeal to the Federal Court of Appeal, asserting that the NEB had failed to follow its own regulations and previous decisions in not requiring Ontario Hydro to carry the burden of satisfying the Board on the environmental impact of its proposal, and asserting further that the Board's submission of its decision to the Cabinet for confirmation before making it public allowed persons to participate in its decision who had not heard the evidence and were not members of the Board. Leave to appeal was refused by the Court.

On the face of it, the outcome of the case represented an unqualified loss for CAC. However, in this kind of advocacy, wins and losses are not so easily calculated. For example, both Ontario Hydro and the NEB have subsequently hired social cost analysts to assist in future applications, and in similar cases that have since come before the Board much more rigorous requirements as to environmental impact considerations have been imposed. Moreover, the considerable media publicity that attended the case may have contributed something to a heightened public consciousness about social costs —a consciousness needed, for example, to prompt decisions like that of the federal government to set up the Berger Commission to assess the impact of the Mackenzie Valley pipeline on the Northern environment and native peoples.[10] More to the point, in an Ontario Hydro rate case in 1975 before the Ontario Energy Board, Ontario Hydro announced that, as a result of the earlier hearing before the NEB, they had added a small charge to the price of exported power to cover social costs.

Early in 1974, the Bell Canada "B" rate application hearings before the Canadian Transport Commission commenced. The telephone rate increase sought would have given Bell an additional $51.8 million during 1974, had it been granted on January 1 of that year. The hearing lasted 47 days. Bell spent nearly $1 million on its case (all tax deductible and included in its rates). The outcome of the case was disappointing for CAC, which devoted a great deal of its time and limited resources to it. All but $4 million dollars of the requested increase was granted. The $4 million reduction did, on the other hand, occur in areas where CAC had placed some emphasis—the proposed across-the-board increases in charges for pay telephones, which were denied in institutions with a predominance of low-income consumers. Other issues which were argued with less success focussed on whether cross-subsidization of business subscribers by residential subscribers was involved; definition of the quality of service to be received for a given tariff; whether the company's huge construction programme really was needed (or might involve an element of rate base padding) and really would benefit consumers (as opposed to other classes of service user); whether Bell could be intelligently regulated when many of its most profitable activities had been spun off to unregulated subsidiaries, such as Northern Electric, enabling Bell to argue, in relation to its regulated activities, perpetual pending financial doom; and whether some part of Bell's monopoly could be deregulated and exposed to market forces, for example, the provision of terminal equipment.

Again, however, it is difficult to make a long-term assessment of this kind of intervention by CAC. The hearings attracted considerable media publicity. Bell rate cases have long been matters of major public contention in Canada, and perhaps partly in response to a continuing climate of public concern at ever more frequent rate increases and partly, no doubt, as an attempt to rationalization, the federal government, shortly after this case, announced its intention to transfer all telecommunications regulation to the Canadian Radio and Television Commission, one of the most socially responsive federal regulatory agencies.[11] . . . .

[There follows a detailed examination of CAC activities relating to air and rail transportation, and the oil and energy industries (eds.).]

Outside the regulatory area, CAC, in 1974, commissioned a substantial, independent research paper from Professor Neil Williams of Osgoode Hall Law School on the law relating to consumer class actions in Canada, together with proposals for reform and a Model *Consumer Class Actions Act*. Now completed, the report has received wide currency within federal and provincial governments across Canada and is under active consideration by several who have reform of their class action rules under review.[12]

How should we evaluate the aggregate impact of this flurry of specialized advocacy on behalf of the consumer? Have consumerism's political disabilities been effectively denied?

An Interim Stock-Taking

I. SHORT-RUN LESSONS

In the immediate context, the need for sustained, systematic consumer advocacy before regulatory agencies is unanswerable. Sensitizing regulators to interest other than those of the regulatees is not a short-term exercise and is not a matter that can be allowed to depend on fortuitous, sporadic interventions by the odd concerned citizen or group of citizens. Appropriate institutional forms need to be devised to ensure a consistent consumer presence.

The essentially political nature of the regulatory process must be recognized both by regulators and legislators. The argument that regulatory agencies should be "independent" of the political process misconceives their function. Because of the immensely important economic and social decisions that agencies make, strong emphasis must be placed by governments in searching out high calibre personnel for appointment to the boards and staff of these agencies. The tendency to retread retired political warriors and reward party bagmen by appointing them to positions on agencies, and the added tendency to appoint personnel with backgrounds, directly or indirectly, related to the regulated industries, on the grounds that they alone possess the requisite expertise, discounts the need to find appointees of high intellectual calibre with a wide range of social sensitivities.

A substantial increase in the quantity and quality of research as opposed to administrative resources available to an agency is needed if agencies are to become less dependent on industry data and analyses. Regulators also have to be educated to understand the fundamental difference between highly concentrated and thinly spread interest groups. In connection with the previous political analysis of interest groups, regulators must be made to realize that to take the view that consumers should not be concerned about a $52 million telephone rate increase because it only costs them 20 or 30 cents more each month (although, obviously, it costs them in aggregate $52m) is subversive of the need ever to take the consumer interest into account in public decision-making. Without that recognition, consumers will systematically be "nickelled" and "dimed" into economic oblivion, dying the death of a thousand near-invisible cuts.

Low-intensity groups embarking on this form of advocacy need to recognize the importance of advocating their cause not only in relevant regulatory forums but also before the public, by proper utilization of the relatively costless media. By "widening the scope of the conflict" an appropriate climate of public concern in the regulatory outcome can be created which forces the regulators to address the matters about which the public is concerned. This involves advocacy skills which traditional professional training does not provide for public interest advocates. These have to be consciously learned. Also, new strategic criteria for assessing "wins" and "losses" have to be learned as alternatives to the way the traditional practising lawyer makes such an assessment in a case-to-case setting.

There is a powerful case for establishing a set of minimum procedural standards for guiding the conduct of regulatory proceedings. For example, there should be consistent rules applying to most agencies governing the amount and nature of notice to other parties; the right to a hearing on the merits; who carries the onus of proof; the right to issue interrogatories to, and cross-examine, parties and obtain relevant information from them; the right to standing both before an agency and before the courts on an appeal from an agency's decision; and the right of non-business intervenors to a free transcript. Also, agencies should be given a discretion at the outset of a hearing to award the costs of an intervention, out of the projected rate increase, or public funds in non-rate cases, to serious low-intensity, non-subsidized intervenors. This will help keep the process as open as possible. Either an omnibus Act, similar in concept to the Ontario *Statutory Powers Procedures Act*[13] or the U.S. *Administrative Procedure Act*[14] but emphasizing ease of access as much as due process, or at least amendment of individual regulatory statutes with a view to the same end, is badly needed.[15]

In addition, the much larger question of the right of public access to government information, whether within regulatory agencies or elsewhere within the government urgently calls for a response. The continuing refusal of the Foreign Investment Review Agency, under the *Foreign Investment Review Act*,[16] to make public more than derisory reasons for its decisions is a contemporary example of this need. With government expenditures now comprising 40% of Canada's GNP, increasingly consumers are consuming, and paying for, public rather than private goods. Government has been very willing to impose packaging, labelling and other informational requirements on the private sector but has been much more reticent in imposing similar requirements on itself so that the public can more effectively evaluate the worth of government programmes which they as taxpayers are paying for. Legislation similar to the U.S. *Freedom of Information Act*[17] should be developed and enacted in each legislative jurisdiction as a matter of the highest priority.[18] If these matters are attended to, the attaching of sweeping special powers to a Consumer Advocacy programme, as envisaged in the U.S. proposals, becomes less necessary and smacks of a special status for one interest group, which is hard to justify. Consistent with the previous political analysis, most of the foregoing suggestions involve ways of reducing information and participation costs (i.e. opportunity costs) to the public.

The teaching of Administrative Law in the law schools also needs to adjust to the real dynamics, and problems, of the regulatory process. Judicial review and the prerogative writs—favourite preoccupations of administrative lawyers—are mostly irrelevant to the issues raised by the activities of major regulatory agencies today.

It is important from the point of view of political legitimacy that any consumer advocate programme, even though state subsidized, be under citizen control so that broad priorities and positions reflect the views of those on whose behalf they are presented. Without this, such a programme is likely to degenerate into a highly paternalistic, elitist, personal power play, in which an oblivious constituency is illegitimately co-opted to provide professional advocates with the appearance of a populist platform. The absence of this safeguard appears to be a major weakness in the U.S. proposals. The sentiments expressed by Peter Newman, in an editorial in *Maclean's* magazine of April, 1974, need to be nurtured:

> Many of the really important decisions that will fundamentally affect and transform our future are being made not by parliament but by regulatory agencies . . . If [they] are to take the public interest seriously into account, [they] must provide a mechanism for hearing directly from the people. That will require the funding of third party interventions which represent no vested interests. . . .
>
> Politicians and particularly bureaucrats get feeling edgy and threatened whenever they're faced by real people with live opinions. They shouldn't be. They are being threatened only with enlightenment.

II. LONG-RUN PROBLEMS

While we have been focussing our attention on CAC's experience in the regulatory arena, the long-run issues raised by it are not confined to the regulatory arena but relate to the political process at large, and are not restricted to the consumer movement but relate to the role of any large, latent, interest group in the political process. Some serious long-run problems are exemplified by CAC's experience in the regulatory arena.

Being funded by the party in power by executive grant, CAC's advocacy programme faces the danger of compromising its independence through concern over funding continuity. This has not proved to be a problem to date, but as the programme becomes more effective, as government departments find their regulatory policies called into public question, and as other, entrenched, interest groups begin to find life less comfortable than formerly, it is reasonable to assume that this danger will not always be hypothetical. This problem would not seem insuperable and would seem to require a legislative framework for the programme that carries insulating elements designed to ensure its independence from party politics in matters of priorities, policies, personnel and budget. At least, then, changes would be effected through parliamentary, and thus public, debate.

The question of the constituency for whom consumer advocates speak poses more fundamental problems. Just as disproportionately few citizens will find it worthwhile to join a consumer organization offering mostly collective goods, so also will most of those who do join find that it is unlikely to be worthwhile to participate extensively in collective goods decision-making. Thus, in CAC, only a handful of members find it worth the effort even to vote for membership of the association's small Board of Directors, let alone involve themselves further in the formulation of the association's policies. This might have been predicted from Olson's analysis and is confirmed by Kariel,[19] who stresses the essentially oligarchical character of large, latent, interest groups.

Compounding this factor, in the case of CAC's advocacy programme, is the fact that every taxpaying citizen in the country has, in effect, been coerced into membership of the association, with all the massive role conflicts that this entails. Was CAC speaking for the president of Bell Telephone and the presidents and shareholders of the airlines and railways (all contributors to its programme) in its recent interventions? Who was it in fact speaking for, and with what mandate? Where all members of all interest groups are coerced into becoming members of one oligarchically controlled interest group, theories of pluralism and interest group liberalism start to look a little shaky.[20]

Even if the constituency issue can somehow be resolved, pluralist concepts of interest group liberalism themselves are coming under increasing question as operational philosophies for intelligent government of modern mixed economies. Critics of pluralist philosophies point out that the open-ended delegations of power by legislatures to regulatory agencies which have become typical are antithetical to rational planning of societal priorities and policies. Lowi asserts bluntly: "Interest group liberalism renders government impotent. Liberal governments cannot plan."[21] Substituted both for the allocative function of a competitive marketplace and that of central planning is interest group bargaining through an almost infinite number of largely autonomous regulatory agencies under no compulsion to act in concert in furtherance of more general collective policy goals. Thus, *participation, organization, structure* and *process* become ends in themselves. Let students, women, workers, the poor ethnic groups, consumers, etc. *organize*, and all problems (if any are agreed upon) will go away. The rationality and overall coherence of substantive outputs become subordinate to these new means-ends.

A further objection sometimes urged against a pluralist approach is that it is impossible to ensure participation by all affected interest groups, present and future, in public decision-making processes affecting them. As Charles Reich writes:

> The very concept of balancing is in one sense a contradiction of the concept of planning. Fashioning values and goals out of existing interests prevents any really long-range policy making or planning from ever being done. It equates policy-making with satisfying the majority or the most powerful interest, although the country might benefit more from policies which favour weaker or minority interests, or interests not yet in existence. It tends to place emphasis on those interests which have a commercial or pecuniary value as against intangible interests such as scenery or recreation. The most fundamental infirmity of the present concept of the public interest as a guide for planning is that it defeats planning by responding only to immediate pressures.[22]

To bring all affected, extant groups into the political process would involve massive state support.[23] This might create in turn several new problems, albeit of a lesser kind, such as the emergence of groups looking only for new, paid occupations (a new kind of unemployment insurance), and the further paralysis of regulatory proceedings as participants multiply. In the case of future interest groups (for example, the interest of people as yet unborn in present decisions affecting their environment), it is difficult to see any solution.

In addition to these pragmatic problems, there is the more fundamental question of the ideological stake which supporters of the doctrine of pluralism (particularly those who gain substantially from it) have in perpetuating the pluralist philosophy and not admitting or encouraging groups who will expose the philosophy to fundamental challenge. As Wolff writes:

> Pluralism is not explicitly a philosophy of privilege or injustice—it is a philosophy of equality and justice whose *concrete application* supports inequality by ignoring the existence of certain legitimate social groups. This ideological function of pluralism helps to explain one of the peculiarities of American politics. There is a very sharp distinction in the public domain between legitimate interests and those which are absolutely beyond the pale. If a group or interest is within the framework of acceptability, then it can be sure of winning some measure of what it seeks, for the process of national politics is distributive and compromising. On the other hand, if an interest falls *outside* the circle of the acceptable, it receives no attention whatsoever and its proponents are treated as crackpots, extremists, or foreign agents.[24]

In other words, "plural" has a tendency to become strictly limited. The implication of this restricted interpretation of pluralism for citizens' advocacy programmes is that apart from problems of internal group dynamics which tend in the same direction, continued state support of such programmes over the long term appears likely to be contingent on broad acceptance by the groups concerned of the parameters of the regulatory *status quo*. Funding for established groups is also likely to be used as an excuse for not supporting other groups who wish to challenge political and regulatory policies in very fundamental or radical ways. Public participation in the regulatory process is likely to be seen as lending new legitimacy to, and thus reinforcing and perpetuating, what may be inherently illegitimate or irrational processes. Strategically, in terms of an interest group's public posture, it may be very difficult simultaneously to opt in and opt out. The danger of co-optation by the *status quo* is a critically serious one. Its costs will be more fully explored below in the discussion of the rationale of regulation.

One final objection to subscribing to a doctrine of pluralism that is sometimes urged is that the doctrine implies a fundamentally uncivilized view of society. Collectivists such as Wolff see it as involving a form of government by guerilla warfare. Wolff writes:

> We must give up the image of society as a battleground of competing groups and formulate an ideal society more exalted than the mere acceptance of opposed interests and diverse customs. There is need for a new philosophy of community.[25]

The dilemma raised by this view is that even if we wish to move to a more collectivist approach to decisions about resource allocations, how does one interest group detach itself from the adversary ethic without making itself highly vulnerable to the depredations of other groups? How do we reach for "Consciousness III" without becoming Uncle Toms? On the other hand, if the solution lies in a spontaneous shift in community-wide values, does this leave us waiting, perhaps forlornly, for the Apocalypse?

The possibility, through participation in the regulatory process, of being co-opted into accepting and endorsing its essential forms carries serious potential costs. First, it involves the consumer movement acquiescing in the incoherence and decisional dysfunctions produced by the random outputs of the fragmented, proliferating regulatory regimes of the modern state.[26] A related cost is acquiescence in the increasing paralysis of the total apparatus, in terms of its ability to respond quickly, rationally, and decisively, to rapidly changing social challenges and crises.[27] The inability of government in Canada to evolve coherent national or even regional policies in such key sectors as energy, food, transportation and housing, exemplifies these costs of the modern regulatory state.

Another cost goes to conventional considerations of economic efficiency raised by the fact of regulation itself. A growing group of commentators from

Ralph Nader,[28] on the one hand, to Lewis Engman, the Nixon-appointed Chairman of the Federal Trade Commission, on the other, are now urging massive de-regulation of the economy and an attempt to restore vigorously competitive markets, wherever possible. At least in such a market, a consumer has to decide that it is worth his while to incur the transaction costs entailed in participating in a transaction before his interests can be affected. In other words, he will have to be privy to most market decisions which affect his economic interests as a consumer, unlike most regulatory decisions which affect those interests. In Canada, prime sectors for substantial de-regulation and enforced competition might include transportation, communications, banking, agriculture, and the professions. As a society, we can no longer operate effectively the elaborate, intricately interwoven regulatory infrastructure that we have developed. Daniel Patrick Moynihan made this point simply but poignantly in a speech to a NATO meeting in 1970: "... modern government must learn to respond to technologically induced difficulties with something of the same economy of talent that technology has devised. We cannot go on devising government arrangements that only extraordinary men can make work. Most of the work of the world had to be done by men of average endowment, energy, and social vision."

Where competitive markets are not possible, increasingly we must accept the stark alternative of much more direct, explicit, unashamed, central planning. A major political advantage of greater use of central planning instruments is that interest group inter-action is more focussed, more circumscribed, and more visible, and outcomes are subject to more political accountability.[29] Effective central planning entails, at a minimum, much greater use than at present of central regulatory instruments, such as tax, tariff, and competition policies. However, as the experience with competition policy and tax reform in this country has shown, a bold range of additional steps must be contemplated if the ideal of a more coherent, widely responsive central planning process is to be seriously pursued. An agenda for future research might focus on issues such as the following: Where regulatory agencies are found indispensable, would much more detailed, frequent, legislated policy directions to the agencies be desirable and feasible?[30] Should the central government, or, where appropriate, regional government, have the power to overrule the decisions of major agencies on the basis of published reasons open to parliamentary and public debate? Should all major agencies and Crown corporations be accountable, through a Cabinet Minister, to Parliament? Should much greater research support from general revenues be provided to opposition parties (also large, latent, interest groups), individual M.P.s and Parliamentary Committees, in the hope that the central political process might then exercise a more effective, direct, oversight role in relation to agencies, Crown corporations, and government subsidy programmes? Should the heads of these agencies and programmes be personally and regularly accountable to

Parliament in Parliamentary Committee debates on estimates? Should traditional Anglo-Canadian concepts of civil service tenure be preserved, or should there be a much greater ability in the central political authority to hire (from anywhere) and fire (at any time) regulators, Deputy Ministers, Assistant Deputy Ministers and other senior civil servants influential in policy formation to prevent dissonance and foot-dragging in the command structure?[31] Another line of inquiry which bears exploration is whether regulatory officials (and thus, indirectly, government) should in some contexts, for example food, drug, product safety, securities regulation, and welfare entitlements, be held civilly liable for negligence to aggrieved citizens, thus attaching private costs to those who make bad public decisions and creating additional incentives for a more responsive regulatory environment?[32] Effective central planning may also entail a much more effective oversight function by the Courts in relation to legislative and regulatory activity. For example, within the interstices of the law left open to judicial interpretation (e.g. "inter-provincial trade and commerce") should the courts more consciously promote substantive rationality of economic outputs, and retreat less into legal formalism?[33] In the case of the Federal Court of Appeal and the Supreme Court of Canada, is there a case for appointing to the Court two or three luminous non-legal intellects, with a pervasive sense of the larger social and economic fabric in which particular issues arise, and not merely the limited technical considerations raised by those issues? Should litigants be more actively encouraged to address issues of policy rationality in their submissions? Should Brandeis briefs be invited from interest groups indirectly affected by the outcome of major judicial decisions? Should legislation limit or proscribe corporate campaign contributions and provide for the funding of election campaigns out of public funds, so that the participation rate of high-intensity and low-intensity groups in the political process is more equal? What rights of access should the public be given to government information? What additional forms of assistance should be given to citizens to facilitate participation in legislative and regulatory decision-making? The potential impact of something as seemingly trivial as the broadcasting and televising of parts of the Parliamentary process, so that information costs to the public about public decision-making are reduced, also requires assessment.

The costs of over-regulation and under-government have been eloquently articulated in a recent speech by Lewis Engman:

> Though most government regulation was enacted under the guise of protecting the consumer from abuse, much of today's regulatory machinery does little more than shelter producers from the normal competitive consequences of lassitude and inefficiency. . . . The consumer for whatever presumed abuse he is being spared is paying plenty in the form of government sanctioned price fixing.[34]

Engman proceeds to give a number of examples from the regulated industries of state-sanctioned monopoly profits, and estimates that in the transportation field alone hidden regulatory subsidies may cost consumers in excess of $16 billion a year ($80 per annum per man, woman and child in the U.S.).[35] He continues:

> To me, the most distressing development is the pervasive and well-accepted dishonesty that pervades the government's approach to regulation. The existing crazy quilt of anti-consumer subsidies embodied in the intricately woven fabric of federal and state statutes and regulations is pernicious because: (1) the subsidies are deliberately hidden from public view; (2) the government had irresponsibly lost track of the actual cost of these subsidies;[36] (3) in most, if not all cases, we have adopted the least efficient form of subsidy with the purpose of hiding the subsidy from the public and obfuscating its true cost. . . .[37]
>
> From time to time, proposals have been made to provide direct cash subsidies in lieu of the patchwork of regulatory subsidies that now pervade our economy. Opponents rise indignantly to object that hardworking individuals and business do not want handouts. Well, a rose by any other name .... Our airlines, our truckers, our railroads, our electronics media and countless others are on the dole. We get irate about welfare fraud. But, our complex systems of hidden regulatory subsidies make welfare fraud look like petty larceny... The fact of the matter is that most regulated industries have become federal protectorates, living in the cozy world of cost-plus, safely protected from the ugly spectres of competition, efficiency and innovation.

Engman concludes that unless the whole regulatory apparatus can be radically rationalized, "our regulators will continue to stumble around in an increasingly expensive game of blind man's buff".

His remarks are equally applicable to the Canadian regulatory scene. Apart from the regulated industries, which in many cases are effectively administering their own markets with the complicity of the State, other occupations have won the right from the State explicitly to administer their own markets. For example, in Schedule I to the Quebec *Professional Code*,[38] thirty-eight different professions are listed, including social workers, agronomists, denturologists, industrial relations counsellors, vocational guidance counsellors, and town planners, all of whom are given some degree of monopoly power by the State. The medical profession has, of course, been given a State-sanctioned right to administer its own market with the helpful adjunct of being able to make its own subventions out of public revenues. Proving that State-sanctioned monopolies are contagiously attractive, most parts of the agricultural sector, drawing expressly on the precedent of "professional" marketing boards, have either received or are demanding the right to create producer-controlled agricultural marketing boards with comprehensive supply management powers. Add to this the emergence of international supply and price management cartels in oil, sugar, coffee and other staples, beyond the reach, of course, of domestic anti-trust laws, and the economic order in the world seems bent on a retreat from nineteenth century laissez-faire capitalism to thirteenth century feudalism, back from contract to status. Business (with government) has now emerged as the chief subverter of the competitive economy which it claims to remember so fondly.

It is submitted that the general form of the antidote to be urged by consumerism that emerges from the foregoing analysis is this: *As a first priority*, we should preserve or re-activate vigorously competitive markets wherever possible and not succumb to producer pleas to substitute accommodating regulatory regimes. *As a second best solution*, in the event of demonstrated and significant market failure, or in the event of undesirable social outputs from admittedly competitive markets, we should invoke central planning instruments such as competition, tariff and tax policies or legislated direct subsidies, through a more publicly accountable central political process. On the level of more specific and limited legislative programmes that significant market imperfections might elicit, a substantial consumer consensus might be found for stronger laws sanctioning misleading advertising and sales practices so as to reduce the amount of misinformation given to consumers, disclosure requirements (e.g. true interest rates, informative labelling, unit pricing), public product and service grading, public price comparisons, and business complaints rating services, whenever the potential benefits to consumers from possessing this information exceed the costs of providing it. Expanded consumer education programmes, and, very importantly, vastly improved access to private law enforcement mechanisms might also attract similar consumer support. These programmes would focus on the complementary concepts of feeding better information into the market-place and elevating the importance of private law enforcement mechanisms over criminal and administrative enforcement mechanisms, thus seeking to squeeze as much non-competitive slack as possible out of the market. These twin approaches would try to ensure that consumers have instruments placed at their disposal which make them the principal agents in their own protection, and reduce their dependence on public regulatory responses. *Only as a third best solution*, where delegation of regulatory authority is unavoidable, should delegated regulatory agencies be utilized, provided, however, that they are much more publicly accessible and politically accountable than at present. In some situations, of course, a mix of all three approaches may be dictated but even here we should not lose sight of where, presumptively, the relative policy emphases should lie.

III. CONCLUSION

This article has sought to identify some of the larger issues in the modern regulatory state that consumerism must constantly confront, if in Heilbroner's words, it is to claim a role as one of "the sentries of society."[39] For consumerism, in the last analysis, is about the fundamentals of our economic system. To eschew this role can only mean that consumerism will become part of the flotsam and jetsam of the modern regulatory state, adrift in a fathomless sea of regulatory dross, carried wherever the dictates of the tides and winds of the moment decree.

To come full circle to the opening political analysis of this article, two specific challenges now face modern consumerism. First, recognizing the diffusion of the consumer interest . . . , can the consumer movement overcome the organizational, and thus political, disabilities that afflict large, latent interest groups? Secondly, as the consumer movement seeks to mobilize substantial political support, is it at the same time possible for it to play the role of a fearless and far-sighted social critic by forging a broad-based coalition of citizens around a set of collective goals that embrace new and relevant concepts of economic justice? Or will the consumer interest always be too fragmented to allow of such a coalition? Does Dr. Stigler's prognosis express an eternal verity? As the analysis in this article has sought to show, these are daunting challenges, but to leave them unanswered may be also to have abdicated on many other seemingly more pressing questions about the future of our existing economic order.

Notes

*Trebilcock, M. J., "Winners and Losers in the Modern Regulatory State: Must the Consumer Always Lose?" Osgoode Hall Law Journal, December, 1975 (reproduced by permission of author and publisher). Abridged.

[1]See Inventory of Provincial and Federal Regulatory Agencies prepared by the Canadian Consumer Council, 1971.

[2]Cf. Charles Reich, *The Law of the Planned Society*, 75 Yale L. J. (1966).

[3]*The Theory of Economic Regulation*, Bell J. of Econ. and Mgmt. Science v. 2 (1971) at p. 3.

[4]For a critique of Stigler's thesis, in terms of its ability to explain the emergence of regulation in all its contexts, see Posner, *Theories of Economic Regulation*, Bell J. of Econ. and Mgmt. Science v. 5 (1974) 335.

[5]Stigler & Cohen, *Can Regulatory Agencies Protect the Consumer?* (American Enterprise Institute, 1971) at p. 9.

[6]Cited by Sack & Sack, *Citizens' Advocates and Poverty Lawyers*, Canadian Forum, May 1972, p. 37. See also the comments of Robert Andras, now Minister of Manpower and Immigration (formerly Minister of Consumer and Corporate Affairs):

> It is a commonly observed phenomenon that sooner or later a regulating body tends to identify with the interests of those it is regulating, unless there is strong pressure either internally or externally to resist this tendency.
>
> (Address to 25th Annual Meeting of C.A.C. 1972.)

[7]Canadian Council on Urban & Regional Research, Urban Research Bulletin v. 5, no. 3 (Nov. 1973), at p. 3.

[8]*The Why, Where & How of Broadened Public Participation in the Administrative Process*, 60 Georgetown L.J. 525 at p. 529 (1972); see also William O. Douglas, *Go East, Young Man* (Random House, 1974) at pp. 216, 217; see generally Bernstein, *Regulating Business By Independent Commission* (Princeton, 1955).

[9]See Congressman Benjamin S. Rosenthal in Hearings, Subcommittee on Executive Reorganization and Government Research of the U.S. Senate Committee on Government Operations, on S. 1177 and H.R. 10835, 92nd Cong., 1st sess. Nov., 1971.

[10]Order-in-Council, 1974-641, March 21, 1974, pursuant to s. 19 of the *Territorial Lands Act* R.S.C. 1970.

[11]See Bill C-5 October 2, 1974.

[12]"Consumer Class Actions in Canada—Some Proposals For Reform"(1975) 13 Os-

goode Hall L.J. 1.
[13]1971, S.O., c. 47.
[14]5 U.S.C. para. 551.
[15]See generally, Cramton, *The Why, Where and How of Broadened Public Participation in the Administrative Process* 60 Georgetown L.J. 525 (1972); Lazarus and Olek, *The Regulators and the People* 57 Virginia L. Rev. 1069 (1971); Gellhorn, *Public Participation in Administrative Proceedings,* 81 Yale L.J. 359 (1971).
[16]C. 46, S.C., 1973-74.
[17]5 U.S.C. para. 552.
[18]For rudimentary discussions of the U.S. *Administrative Procedure Act* and *Freedom of Information Act,* see Schwartz and Wade, *Legal Control of Government* (Clarendon Press 1972) pp. 108ff, 77ff, 329ff, and 339ff. For a more detailed discussion of those two Acts, see generally Davis, *Administrative Law Text,* 3rd ed. (West, 1972).
[19]*Op. cit.*, chap. 14.
[20]The problem is, in fact, much more pervasive than this. Business lobby groups may deduct their lobbying expenses from income for tax purposes and thus, in effect, transfer some of the cost of their lobbying activities to the general body of taxpayers, who are not voluntarily part of their constituency. The financial figures involved in this form of coercion dwarf the government's grant to C.A.C. but collectively call into question the rationality of the whole theory of interest group pluralism when groups can no longer be clearly identified and delineated. As a matter of interest, should not every citizen who expends time and money in pursuing any collective good be able to claim the expenses as a tax deduction, if business can? Alternatively, should nobody be able to claim them? (cf. Bond in *Issues in Canadian Economics*, ed. Officer and Smith (McGraw-Hill Ryerson, 1974) at p. 98. On a similar point should not every consumer with a justified individual complaint against business be able to recover "aggravation" damage (transaction and opportunity costs) in pursuing the complaint to equalize business's ability to treat such costs on its side as costs of doing business? (cf. *Jarvis v. Swan Tours* [1973] 1 All E.R. 71 (C.A.).

For an argument favouring coerced support of collective goods decision-making to solve the free-rider problem, see Rawls, *A Theory of Justice* (Belknap Press, 1971) at p. 267.
[21]*Op. cit.*, p. 288; see also Kariel, *op. cit.*; Presthus, *op. cit.* n. 3 at p. 348.
[22]*Op cit.* at 1239.
[23]The conscious creation by the State of necessary new countervailing power groups is explicitly urged by a number of commentators: see e.g. Galbraith, *American Capitalism: The Concept of Countervailing Power* (Hamish Hamilton, 1952) chap. X; Kariel, *op. cit.*, p. 272.
[24]*The Poverty of Liberalism* (Beacon Press, 1968) at p. 154; cf. Presthus, *op. cit.* n. 3 at p. 349.
[25]*Op. cit.*, at p. 161.
[26]A current example of this kind of incoherence is that, despite the declared goal of the Federal Government of national self-sufficiency in oil, the unco-ordinated attempts of the Federal Government, Provincial Governments and assorted Energy Boards and Commissions to tax and otherwise regulate the oil industry may produce exactly the opposite result.

A further example of regulatory confusion is the history of the 45-foot height limit by-law regulating development in downtown Toronto passed two years ago by the Toronto City Council and evolved and implemented through endless Council Committees. In its application, random exceptions were increasingly made and in late 1974, it was overturned by the Ontario Municipal Board from whose decision the City appealed unsuccessfully to the Provincial Cabinet—in the meantime total confusion as to who is running Toronto, how, and towards what goals. Another interesting insight from this case is that in two municipal elections, a substantial percentage of citizens had felt it worthwhile to incur the information and opportunity costs entailed in voting in a "control development" council. In the lengthy hearings on the by-law before the OMB, a non-elected body of technocrats (who described the Council's decision as "political"—what else should it have been?), only 36 developers and the City Council itself found it rational to incur the much higher costs of participating. No citizens seriously participated. The outcome was predictable (whatever its merits).

[27]A current example of this paralysis is the housing sector. While the federal government has made large sums of money available in an attempt to alleviate the acute shortage of low-income housing, various municipalities have refused the funding on the ground that the restricted property tax base given them by senior levels of government does not enable them to raise the revenues to service lower priced housing. The federal government, provincial governments and municipalities seem incapable of co-ordinating all the pieces of a compatible policy capable of decisively addressing the housing crisis.

[28]See Green, Nader, Winter debates, *op. cit.*

[29]See Lowi, *op. cit.*; Kariel, *op. cit.*; Heilbroner, *op. cit.*; Myrdal, *Beyond the Welfare State* (Yale, 1960) in which the importance of *participatory* central planning is especially emphasized.

[30]Cf. Lowi, *op. cit.* Chap. 10; Bernstein, *op. cit.* at 284-286.

[31]As to arguments for the need for appropriate lines of political accountability for regulatory decision-makers, see Bernstein, *op. cit.*, Chap 5; *Report on Selected Independent Regulatory Agencies* by the President's Advisory Council on Executive Organization (the Ash Council), U.S., January 1971, pp. 14 *et seq*; Kariel, *op. cit.*, Chap. 15; Lowi, *op. cit.*, Chap. 10.

[32]Cf. Tullock, *Public Decisions as Public Goods* 79 J. Pol. Ec. 913 (1971).

[33]As to the difficulties faced by courts making rational decisions in this area without the relevant economic data before them, see the observations of Laskin, J. in *A.G. for Manitoba v. Manitoba Egg & Poultry Association* (1971) 19 D.L.R. (3d) 169 at pp. 181, 182.

[34]Speech to Fall Conference of the Financial Analysts Federation, Detroit, October 7, 1974.

[35]Canadians are estimated to spend one dollar in five on transportation costs, how much on subsidies nobody knows.

[36]A typical Canadian example of this kind of "dysfunction" is the current prosecution (the second in recent years) of sugar refiners for price-fixing by the Department of Consumer and Corporate Affairs, while the Department of Finance insists on maintaining a customs tariff on imported, refined sugar.

[37]A recent, notable example of this last point in Canada is egg marketing boards, where, in the alleged interest of the marginal farmer, a producer-determined subsidy is levied on all consumers of eggs indiscriminately, whether they can afford it or not (i.e. a regressive tax), and distributed to all producers indiscriminately, whether they need it or not. This produces bizarre wealth redistribution effects, and is also inconsistent with the federal government's declared intention of bringing down food prices by increasing supply rather than through controls, as witness the destruction in the summer of 28 million eggs by the central egg marketing agency (CEMA). If an income transfer to marginal family farmers is thought socially desirable, why not a direct, selective transfer through the progressive income tax system? If the problem is also fluctuating farm incomes, why not better tax averaging provisions?

Another example is airlines regulation where in order to receive a profitable route, an airline has to agree to fly some unprofitable routes. This creates irrational cross-subsidy effects between passengers on high-traffic routes and those on low-traffic routes. Why not let all regional, national and international carriers compete on all routes as they please and if some are abandoned as uneconomic, let the government let out to competitive tender the right to fly these routes in return for a direct cash subsidy paid out of general revenues? We would have more competition, and in the case of subsidized routes, we would know, and decide, who is to pay what to whom (cf. address by J. W. Pickersgill to the Air Transport Association of Canada, Vancouver, Oct. 30, 1974).

[38]Bill 250, July 6, 1973, S.Q.

[39]*Op. cit.*

38 The Conservative Tradition *

Robert Stanfield

First I would like to make a few comments on the role of political parties such as ours in Canada. Not only is it unnecessary for political parties to disagree about everything, but some acceptance of common ground among the major parties is essential to an effective and stable democracy. For example, it is important to stability that all major parties agree on such matters as parliamentary responsible government and major aspects of our constitution.

In our parliamentary tradition, which is substantially the British tradition, parties have a unifying role to play. For example, the British Conservative party has always tried to appeal to Britons in all walks of life because it felt that it represented Britons in all walks of life.

Towards Harmony

There are, of course, times when stands must be taken which will seriously divide the country. However, a truly national political party has a continuing role to try to pull things together, achieve a consensus, resolve conflicts, strengthen the fabric of society and work towards a feeling of harmony in the country. Success in this role is, I suggest, essential if a party is to maintain a strong position in this country. This role of a national political party, and success in this role, are particularly important in countries as vast and diverse as Canada and the United States.

It is partly because of this that I do not favor the Manning thesis which urges polarization of political viewpoints in this country. In Canada, a party such as ours has a harmonizing role to play, both horizontally in terms of resolving conflicts between regions, and vertically in terms of resolving conflicts between Canadians in different walks of life. It is not a matter of a national party being all things to all people—this would never work. But a national party should appeal to all parts of the country and to Canadians in all walks of life, if it is to serve this essential role, and if it is to remain strong.

Turning now to the consideration of the Conservative Party as such, I would not wish to exaggerate the concern of British Conservatives through the years with principles of theory. After all, they were practising politicians for the most part, pragmatists dealing with problems, and of course, politicians seeking success. There are, however, some threads we can follow through the years. . . .

Precious Order

British Conservative thinkers traditionally stressed the importance of order, not merely "law and order," but social order. This does not mean that they were opposed to freedom for the individual; far from it. They believe that a decent civilized life requires a framework of order.

Conservatives did not take that kind of order for granted. It seemed to them quite rare in the world and therefore quite precious. This is still the case. Conservatives attached importance to the economy and to enterprise and to property, but private enterprise was not the central principle of traditional British Conservatism. Indeed, the supreme importance of private enterprise and the undesirability of government initiative and interference was Liberal 19th century doctrine. It was inherited from Adam Smith and was given its boldest political statement by such Liberals as Cobden and Bright. It was they who preached the doctrine of the unseen hand with practically no reservation.

The Conservative concept of order encouraged Conservative governments to impose restrictions on private enterprise where this was considered desirable. We all studied William Wilberforce and his factory legislation when we were in school. These were logical measures for Conservatives to adopt; to protect the weak against the excesses of private enterprise and greed. That is good traditional Conservatism, fully consistent with traditional Conservative principles. It is also good Conservatism not to push regulation too far—to undermine self-reliance.

Because of the central importance Conservatives attached to the concepts of order they naturally favored strong and effective government, but on the other hand they saw a limited or restricted role for government for several reasons.

Because a highly centralized government is quite susceptible to arbitrary exercise of power and also to attack and revolution, Conservatives instinctively favored a decentralization of power. National government had to be able to act in the national interest, but there had to be countervailing centres of power and influence. In the past, these might consist of the church, the landed gentry or some other institution. Today in Canada, the provinces, trade unions, farm organizations, trade associations and the press would serve as examples.

Another reason why Conservatives traditionally saw a limited role for government was because Conservatives were far from being Utopians.

They certainly saw the world as a very imperfect place, capable of only limited improvement, and man as an imperfect being. They saw evil as an on-going force that would always be present in changing form. It would therefore not have surprised Edmund Burke that economic growth, and government policies associated with it, have created problems almost as severe as those that economic growth and government policies were supposed to overcome.

A third reason for Conservatives taking a limited view of the role of government was that men such as Edmund Burke regarded man's intelligence as quite limited. Burke was very much impressed by how little man understood what was going on around him.

Burke questioned whether any one generation really had the intelligence to understand fully the reasons for existing institutions or to pass judgment on those institutions which were the product of the ages. Burke pushed this idea much too far, but Conservatives have traditionally recognized how limited human intelligence really is, and consequently have recognized that success in planning the lives of other people of the life of the nation is likely to be limited. Neither government nor its bureaucracy are as wise as they are apt to believe. Humility is a valuable strain in Conservatism, provided it does not become an excuse for resisting change, accepting injustice or supporting vested interests.

There is another important strain to traditional Conservatism. Conservatism is national in scope and purpose. This implies a strong feeling for the country, its institutions and its symbols; but also a feeling for all the country and for all the people in the country. The Conservative party serves the whole country and all the people, not simply part of the country and certain categories of people.

I suggest that it is in the Conservative tradition to expand the concept of order and give it a fully contemporary meaning. The concept of order always included some concept of security for the unfortunate, although the actual program may have been quite inadequate by our present day standards.

The concept of order certainly includes the preservation of our environment. And the concept of order, linked to Conservative concern for the country as a whole, certainly includes concern about poverty.

For a Conservative in the Conservative tradition which I have described, there is much more to national life than simply increasing the size of the gross national product. A Conservative naturally regards a healthy economy as of great importance, but increasing the size of the gross national product is not in itself a sufficient goal for a civilized nation according to a Conservative.

A healthy economy is obviously important, but a Conservative will be concerned about the effects of economic growth—what this does to our environment, what kind of living conditions it creates, what is its effect on the countryside, what is its effect on our cities; whether all parts of the nation benefit or only some parts of the nation, and whether a greater feeling of justice and fairness and self-fulfilment results from this growth, thereby strengthening the social order and improving the quality of national life.

At any given time our party is likely to contain those whose natural bent is reform and those whose natural bent is to stand pat or even to try to turn the clock back a bit. I think it is fair to say that Conservative statesmen we respect most were innovators. They did not change Conservative principles, but within those principles they faced and met the challenges of their time.

Big Stick

Traditional Liberalism started with the individual, emphasizing liberty of the individual and calling for a minimum of government interference with the individual. Conservatives, on the other hand, emphasized the nation, society, stability and order.

In this century, Liberals have resorted to the use of government more and more. Today big government and Liberalism are synonymous in Canada.

The Conservative tradition of government has been to interfere only where necessary . . . to achieve social and national objectives. Conservatives favor incentives, where appropriate, rather than the big stick.

Of course, it has always been and remains important to Conservatives to encourage individual self-reliance; and certainly red tape and regulation have today gone too far, especially in the case of small business. Self-reliance and enterprise should be encouraged, but Conservatism does not place private enterprise in a central position around which everything else revolves.

Conservatism recognized the responsibility of government to restrain or influence individual action where this was in the interests of society.

I would not suggest that Conservatives have tried or would try to build a radically different society from that which they have known. But to reform and adapt existing institutions to meet changing conditions, and to work towards a more just and therefore a truly more stable society—this I suggest is in the best Conservative tradition. Resistance to changes and the support of privilege has been a part of the behavior of Conservatives from time to time, but neither is nor ought to be Conservative principle.

The emphasis on the nation as a whole, on order, in the Conservative tradition that I have described, was surely seldom more relevant than it is today, with inflation raging and life becoming more and more a matter of every man for himself and the devil take the hindmost. We see increasing stresses and strains in our society, wildcat strikes, increasing distrust and mounting tension and violence.

This is a period when true Conservative principles of order and stability should be most appealing. Principles of conservation and preservation are also high in the minds of many Canadians today, and a Conservative can very legitimately—and on sound historical ground—associate with these. Again I emphasize that these kinds of bedrock principles are national in scope and reflect an overriding concern for society at large.

Stability Goal

Enterprise and initiative are obviously important, but will emphasis upon individual rights solve the great problems of the day? I mean the maintenance of acceptable stability—which includes price stability, acceptable employment, and an acceptable distribution of income. Would we achieve these goals today by a simple reliance on the free market, if we could achieve a free market?

It would certainly be appropriate for a Conservative to suggest that we must achieve some kind of order if we are to avoid chaos; an order which is stable, but not static; an order therefore which is reasonably acceptable and which among other things provides a framework in which enterprise can flourish. That would be in the Conservative tradition.

Notes

*"Memorandum to the Conservative Caucus," printed in the Toronto *Star*, 30 November, 1974 (reproduced by permission of the author).

39 The Role of the State in a Technological Society *

Karl D. Jaffary

I have been asked to discuss the role of the state in Canadian society over the next twenty years. Since any such discussion must be highly personal, it is appropriate to state my background and my bias. I am a lawyer, the son of an academic social worker, and a municipal politician representing an economically depressed area in the City of Toronto. My political approach to the world has been moulded very significantly by my membership in the New Democratic Party of which I am presently a federal vice-president. I have never been exposed to even the most rudimentary course in political science and, therefore, hesitate to say that my point of view is a socialist one. Within the New Democratic Party it is now not merely respectable to be a socialist, it has become a *sine qua non* for acceptability by one's colleagues, and the only thing that saves some of us from the fearsome charge of being a liberal is that there is no general agreement within the Party about who is sufficiently wise to be able to distinguish socialists from everybody else. My views have been affected by my association with many less than perfect socialists, by the black anarchism that runs rampant through the down-town ward I represent, and by the legalistic style I was taught at a very large corporate legal firm.

My first position, and until a few years ago my only one, is that an urban industrial society demands ever-increasing interventions by the state. Even at the most localized level of government, the complexity and concentration of modern life demands an increase in the level of even the most traditional government services. We are faced with the task of creating an almost completely unnatural environment. Water, earth, and air must all be, if not man-made, at least man-controlled. Urbanization and the consequent centralizing of large numbers of people go hand in hand with greater government participation in everyday life. That seems to me to be a very basic proposition on which I would expect to find general agreement. Taxes will go up and government services will increase. It is not really a question of whether or not this is a good thing or a bad thing—it seems to me to be an inevitable thing that we all recognize.

This increase in the role of the state at other levels of government will, in my opinion, revolve around two pivots—education and the economy. Automation and technical change mean unemployment for the under-educated and unskilled, and employment for the specialized and technically qualified. We still believe that work is good for people, and in our present society this is demonstrably true. It may be changing, but it has not changed yet. Somehow, we have to provide some employment for everyone in the society. The unemployed generally do not enjoy their predicament. Unemployment frequently produces cancerous rot in a family's life. James Lorimer, a York University economist, has documented this very clearly in his book *Working People* (Toronto, James Lewis and Samuel, 1971). It is rare to find an unemployed able-bodied person whose life-style we find attractive. The only examples I can think of are a few old reprobates and some young people. Most of today's youth think of work as being necessary to provide the 'necessities' of a 'satisfactory' life, even though they may experiment with kinds of work that do not produce much cash, like community organizing or organic farming. Some people involve themselves in the arts, and if they are any good they are clearly working; if they are not, they seem to be performing an occupational therapy kind of work substitute.

In any event, these social changes involve the state very deeply. On the educational front we expect the state to produce people who can do the sorts of jobs that the increasingly complex society demands, and at the same time to so educate people that they will be able to play a useful part in society even when they are not doing economically productive work. We attempt to educate people so that they will be artists, politicians, and athletes, and also to educate them to be critics, audiences, and voters. This dichotomy in the aims of education puts an almost impossible strain on educators. How can you inculcate in one person a desire to work hard at being an entrepreneurial executive (even though he will die of a heart attack at forty-five), and in another a desire to work only for his own pleasure—when both are present together in the same classroom? And, yet, those seem to be two kinds of people we need. Since society needs these kinds of people it will continue to demand that the educational system produce them.

Manipulation of the economy, the other main task of government, is the problem of somehow keeping the whole system going and changing at a rate that is reflective of the educational system and the other social changes that are going on. Sudden widespread unemployment, or ill-conceived government make-work projects, can disrupt the economy and play havoc with the society. Look at the combination of the Opportunities for Youth Program and the federal program to encourage kids to hitchhike—both programs designed to keep young people out of the labour market. The government will have constantly to experiment with various features of the social and economic system. It will have to fiddle with fiscal and monetary policy. By providing funds for development and by controlling plant closings and encouraging plant openings, government will inject itself into commerce and industry. It will buy agricultural produce or pay farmers not to produce. It will provide the economy with research and back-up services. It will provide mortgage loans in measured quantities to encourage or discourage the building trades. It will provide student aid and will make grants to assist artists. It will impose and withdraw selective taxes and it will continue to introduce more and more programs like medicare, unemployment insurance, the Canada Assistance Plan, guaranteed annual incomes, and everything else that lets it control the number of jobs available, the kind of work offered, and the standard of living of those who do not get the jobs. Government involvement in the economy and in education will surely be the focus and role of the state in the seventies and eighties.

Now that sums up the way I was brought up: the 'first position' I said I was going to put; the argument that increasing complexity and concentration demands an increased role for the state. However, I find great hostility to an increased role for the state on every side. I find tendencies in our society which I can only describe as anarchistic. I find more and more people wanting the state to go largely out of business. And I find their arguments very persuasive.

The problem is two-fold. In the first place, the state is frequently incompetent. In the second place, when it is competent and does what it wants to do, it succeeds in manipulating people's lives to an extent that they find highly offensive. Let me deal first with competence, and I will start with examples from municipal government.

People want transportation services, and the recent expressway fight in Toronto simply proved to thousands that the municipal government was not providing those services competently. The Spadina Expressway would have been as good an expressway as could have been built along the route it followed, but the horrors it would have created made it very clear to a great many people that the need for that expressway was far less than the need for increased public transit facilities. That recognition got people looking at the long-range plans and convinced them that the plans for increased public transit facilities were inadequate. There was no way to change all the planning to get transit facilities without stopping Spadina. Reasonable and responsible consideration of the whole matter seemed to be forthcoming from everywhere but the municipal government. That government subjected the citizenry to verbal abuse, tried to hide its plans and its data whenever it could, and generally exposed its clay feet. The government was incompetent, or the impasse would not have developed.

For another example, I turn to Opportunities for Youth. There were some good projects and there were some terrible ones and the distinction seems quite unplanned. Random selection of projects would surely have produced equally good results. I have trouble thinking of any other federal spending of the order of $25 millions that has so quickly been considered by the public at large to be a complete administrative disaster. It is keeping kids out of the labour force, but what can possibly be said about its project selection process? The story about an Opportunities for Youth grant that let draft-age Americans grow marijuana may not be true, but it is a great story and it typifies Opportunities for Youth in the public mind. Most projects were defensible, but the program as a whole certainly appeared to be incompetently administered.

An older and more traditionally run federal program is Unemployment Insurance. Incompetence of the same order was found there in mid-1971, and only time will tell whether amendments to the Act will cure the situation. In 1971 the Toronto UIC offices were located in distant suburbs and the unemployed were encouraged to make claims by mail and to enquire by phone. The phones were constantly busy. When someone claiming benefits got through, someone else took the information and said he would call back. The claimant waited by the phone for hours or days, and when the UIC staff called, they rarely had any conclusive information. Claims and cheques were processed by a computer in Belleville, over a hundred miles out of the city, so staff in the city often did not know what was happening. Many people waited months to receive benefits. In the meantime, they often had to apply for welfare in order to live, and that took more forms and more waiting at home for a visit. Finally, when the unemployment insurance cheque came, the Welfare Department wanted to be paid back its money. The recipient, who was generally broke and in debt, watched a cheque payable to his order vanish into the bowels of another government department.

Anyone who finally got his unemployment insurance looked at the size of the cheque and realized it really was not insurance at all; it was just welfare. Unemployment insurance generally paid less than welfare, but it was a very special kind of welfare for which the poor were specially taxed to the extent of 50 per cent of the benefit. It was second-rate welfare for which the poor were taxed, which they often could not get when they needed it, and which they could not get proper answers about when it was not paid. Now, that is a high order of incompetence and the recipients knew it. They do not blame any particular employee of the scheme, nor any particular politician, and neither do I. We all accept that the UIC consists of intelligent people doing their best. But, it developed, perhaps by accident, into another government fraud on the public. I understand that the new Act will provide slightly higher benefits with part of the cost being borne by the middle class. I doubt whether the level of service will improve, or whether the public attitude to the scheme will change.

I do not wish to labour the point of government incompetence. I could discuss the benefit levels of workmen's compensation, the provincial welfare regulations, passenger-rail transportation in Canada, and a host of other programs. I wish to state that I do not believe that everything governmental is incompetent, nor do I say that government is *more* incompetent than industry. Dealing with Eatons is much the same as dealing with the Unemployment Insurance Commission, but there is rarely the same urgency. Income taxes seem to be collected with admirable efficiency. I hear no complaints about our city's water services and the difficulties about garbage collection and snow removal can, I believe, be related to scale. I will deal with them later. My points are, firstly, that some government services are run with inefficiency that can only be called incompetence, and secondly, that the areas where government performs worst are those into which I already have said that governments are likely to expand—the economy and education. Thirdly, the government's handling of these two factors makes people less willing to let governments do more.

Besides incompetence in the delivery of services, people are faced by the very harsh effects of government action when it does succeed in doing what it wants to do. The federal government has the power to create unemployment, and when it decides to use its power, it certainly does create unemployment. Quite naturally this action on the government's part creates feelings of antagonism.

The Province of Ontario created the Ontario Housing Corporation to provide public housing, and while most of its tenants are better housed than they otherwise would be, and while OHC tries to be a good landlord, tenants miss the freedom of choice that goes with being a private tenant. You cannot move out and live somewhere else if you are an OHC tenant—at least not without going back into the economic housing market—and many OHC tenants can no longer face that market. Yet there is only one public housing agency, and when it turns somebody down, he is really turned down. The presence of an agency that does part of the job removes the pressure for effective government action in the whole field, and both the government and the public realize that.

Simply put, the government is doing a lot of things which affect a lot of people who are not universally happy about the effects. The worst part of it is that the bad effects often seem to be merely accidental by-products of something that the government is doing and with which the affected person has no real quarrel. People are less ready to trust the government with power than they would have been if the past performance had been better.

I hope that this analysis sets the stage. We have many compelling reasons for increasing the power and the role of the state; we have various feelings throughout the country suggesting that governments are incompetent, or will hurt people by their actions and ought, therefore, to restrain themselves. What ought the state to do?

At this point I think I must touch on two fundamental questions. First, what ought the function of the state to be? Second, what is the society of the next twenty years likely to be? I think the state's job is to do whatever it must to let the existing society continue to function smoothly; to help it to change in ways of which people approve; and to try to prevent it from changing in ways of which people disapprove. The problem is that the society itself is changing very rapidly. Government must assess and deal with that changing organism, and must give recognition to any number of ills in the society which the public wants cured by government action. In other words, the state must preserve the society and improve it, while recognizing that society has a life of its own beyond the state, and is changing itself at a rapid pace. What to preserve? What changes to encourage? I think people in general would like to see poverty eliminated, but they do not wish a reduced living standard themselves and they do not want to see a large part of the population living unproductive and useless lives on welfare as it is now understood. People have a very strong desire to control their own lives, and I believe they want the possibility of collective controls where they cannot have individual ones. Thus, people want to be able to choose their kind of work, their place of work, their living space, where and how they will travel and what sort of food and clothes they will buy, and what they will read and see on TV. They want choices since that is what gives them control. Most of the excitement about the Americanization of Canada is about the loss of Canadian control. Some of the feelings are directed at the government's loss of control over the economy and international affairs, but much involves choice and control at the personal level. In Ontario we have a problem with foreign control of magazine and book distribution and it worries people because it affects the choices of books they will be able to buy at the newsstand. People want the government to act in that situation to ensure that Canadian viewpoints will be among the viewpoints that Canadians can choose to read.

As the society changes we expect government to take note, assess what is happening, and move to reinforce or to discourage the changes. We see crimes of violence on the increase in US cities and we want government to watch that situation and not let it happen here. Some of us call for more police, some call for a wide range of social programs, and some call for both. Whatever the solution, it is clear that people want the government to prevent society from changing in that direction.

We see a widespread desire on the part of teenagers to play a more responsible role in society. We expect governments to act to reinforce that desire by at least lowering the age of majority and perhaps by doing other things. I think people may really want to see a competent Opportunities for Youth Program.

We see changing attitudes to education. Some people think that the schools are too permissive, that self-discipline is built on external discipline, that unstructured schools do not provide this, and so they withdraw their children and start their own schools. Others think that the schools are merely elaborate propaganda machines designed to create conforming members of a society of which they disapprove, that undue stress is placed on the transmission of information and cultural values, and that inadequate emphasis is placed on the development of human relationships between peers, and so they withdraw their children and start their own schools. This situation demands action by various levels of government, and some action is taken. Local school boards try running a variety of different kinds of schools and giving people a choice about which school they will attend. Provincial departments are urged to give tax money to the alternative schools.

As society changes, as it is always changing, government is required to react to the change. It gets into trouble when it fails to do so (i.e., the expressway transportation problem), or when it cannot decide or the public cannot decide whether a change in the society is a good or a bad thing, or when it cannot assess what the change really is. That last situation, the situation where there is no agreement what constitutes the change, leads me to the other question I posed, 'What will the society of the next twenty years be?' The really profound social changes are least likely to produce agreement.

It seems to me that despite the good fun of crystal ball gazing, governments do not in fact ever try to reach conclusions about what society will be like in the future. They may speculate, but they do not base any legislation or any spending on that sort of speculation. That is probably wise of governments. Governments deal only with immediate things, the things the public insists that it needs immediately. I believe I must give an example of this because it is easy to fall into the trap of saying that nothing can be done until we know the future, or can at least make assumptions about the future. Those assumptions may be necessary for transportation and sewage planning, but they cannot and should not be made about the really profound changes our society is undergoing. And, of course, the profound changes will inevitably throw out all our necessary assumptions about physical planning. We planned expressways, spent hundreds of millions on them, and then learned of a swing of popular support towards transit. We zoned and planned and built sewers for high-density apartments, and then we encountered a move to save and restore the small, older houses we expected to see demolished.

When the government is able to sense that these changes are occurring, it is sometimes able to change the plans and redirect the spending. Unfortunately, only a responsive, strong political system can fight back the momentum that a bureaucracy creates. The Spadina situation in Toronto indicates a weak political system.

The most significant force in the society today is the change that is occurring in the basic social unit, the family. For fifty years or more families have been getting smaller and infant mortality has been dropping. Family planning has become widespread in at least the upper and middle classes. More jobs have been becoming available to women. The result has been great changes in a social organism that has been evolving for hundreds of thousands of years. Anyone who has read the popular biology of Desmond Morris or Konrad Lorenz has been struck by the similarities between the family life of aggressive carnivores, like wolves, and human beings. When even the basic social unit, the family, is undergoing profound change, the state cannot know what trends to support and what to reject. It cannot visualize the society that the public wants to see in twenty years' time. We would be in danger if the state were to try to set the mould for the future.

That is a very good thing. If government ever gets to the place where it really believes in its own twenty-year plans, where it aggravates violent upheaval in the social system in order to produce results it believes to be desirable, then all of the beneficial safeguards of a democracy will be lost. The collective consciousness of the public knows what is good for it better than the government can ever know, and has found very useful ways of making its opinion felt by politicians.

The 'Waffle' group in my political party started out with the charge that a New Democratic Party government would not create a socialist society any more than a Liberal or a Conservative government would. I believe that to be true and to be highly desirable. Government should not impose social systems on people; they should encourage people to build the social system they want. The Waffle group then went on to say that the only way to elect a government that would legislate socialism would be to turn the people into socialists. I agree with that, too, except that I have a fear of the belief that legislation can create a society, socialist or otherwise. I think a society creates legislation to serve itself. People do not plan their lives in terms of political or economic ideology, but in terms of choice and control. They use ideology to give themselves choice and control. The Waffle, having recognized the need to change people's outlook, has devoted itself to playing politics within the New Democratic Party. Yet the fight is not within the NDP or within the legislature. The composition of the legislature is a mere periodic measuring of the changing feelings of the public against the changing ideologies and personalities of the political parties. An election is not the real fight for social change; it is a social reaction. The fight is on the street. It is a fight to broaden the horizons of choice so that the society will be able to strengthen and renew itself.

Perhaps we must take comfort in the blindness of the state. Perhaps it must be a slow, stupid leviathan, moved only by the immediate political hunger for votes, prevented always from trying to deal with distant and theoretical problems, like the shape of society in 1991. The government will pass equal pay for equal work legislation, and perhaps will grant maternity leaves, and those favouring the change will notice the action while few others will. The government will seek votes and the process of change will be speeded. If society decides collectively that it does not like the direction of change, it will tell the government so. Political evolution works if one assumes public support for changes to be evolutionary mutations and assumes increased votes to be the test of survival. Perhaps we should expect nothing better than political evolution.

I therefore conclude that, over the next twenty years, there will be an *increasing* demand for government services and a *decreasing* popularity of government power and service delivery, *unless* things like the movement of kids back to farms become a trend that decreases population concentration, and *unless* widespread use of birth control results in a great reduction in births, and *unless* the machinery of state education succeeds far better than heretofore in producing better citizens who do not complain about the state manipulating their lives. I further conclude that all of the qualifications I put on increased services and decreased popularity are not proper considerations for government policy. Governments should deal with the present problem of service versus popularity to the extent that shrewd political judgment dictates, the collective will of the society as politically expressed being the one reliable survival instinct that society has created. The only way of dealing with the present service versus popularity problem is by decentralizing, and so broadening, the horizons of choice to the public. People have choice when they have control. People want control over what touches them, and they object to government action which affects them and which they do not control. I believe that people will accept collective control where personal control is impossible, but only where their role in that collectivity is as strong as it can be. We decentralize so that collective choice can be exercised here and there without endangering or committing the whole society by radical change.

Horizons are broadened by education and by community organization. I gather that the continued delivery of health services is as great a concern in Saskatchewan as in Ontario, yet I know of no teaching going on about that subject in educational establishments below the university level. The people in Riverdale and in Regent Park, two Toronto 'slum' areas, have learned a great deal about the alternative of the community health centre run by a community board and employing doctors, by meeting and talking about it. The differences between corner stores and supermarket chains are known to everyone, but the choice only becomes real when people organize a cooperative food store. Organizations of welfare recipients exchange opinions and information and finally learn of alternatives to the welfare system. They devise a better one than previously existed.

The City of Toronto proper has a population of close to three-quarters of a million people and its council is at the most localized level of government. That location of power is too distant for some matters. If people on a short residential street serving only those who live there are asked whether they favour a street widening, they can decide that question. The widening will take some trees but perhaps provide a safer environment for children. At present, council decides, after harangues about safety and ecology, with both sides quoting the same ambiguous staff opinions. The people who ought to decide that question are those who live on the street. Let them. If they had a local government that really represented them on questions like that they would also have a local government with about the right quantity of clout to push their community health centre projects along.

Now the examples of the street and the health service are very small—some might say insignificant—examples, of the decentralization of decision-making power. There are, of course, big, impressive examples that involve the federal and provincial governments and that appear to make constitutional reform impossible. Why ought those few souls in the province of Prince Edward Island (population 107,000) set the policy of welfare assistance for themselves when the two million people in Metropolitan Toronto cannot do the same thing? Why cannot the really neighbourhood aspects of government be conducted by the neighbourhood? Why must each government function be performed by a tier of government just beyond the reach of effective political pressure? I believe that to be the situation we have at present, and I believe its basic cause to be the desire of both politicians and civil servants to avoid political issues. I think that is a dangerous situation. I believe that a further cause has been the enormous revenues taxed in by the federal, and to some extent provincial, governments and the practice of those governments of retaining their taxing powers and giving more or less conditional grants to the levels of government actually delivering the service. The result has been to make local government a mere retail store for the more remote federal and provincial government, administering programs devised in a vacuum by those with no responsibility for their implementation. These governments are unresponsive to change, are unable to deal with local conditions, and are able to go on delivering such woefully inadequate programs as unemployment insurance year after year, with no real pressure for change being brought upon them.

I have no quarrel with the federal government's function of correcting regional disparity and international disparity through equalization payments and foreign aid. However, I think the federal government should stop doing most of what it is doing and should stop collecting the taxes that pay for most of the things it now does. If the people of Ontario want to live in a backward province without adequate medicare, let them. I am satisfied that the people of Ontario can devise social assistance programs that meet their needs, and can raise the tax revenues for those programs without the intervention of the federal government.

If Toronto, Vancouver and Moosemin, Saskatchewan, all adopt different priorities and find different ways of spending money, surely that is a decision for the citizens of those municipalities. Why must they be tied to National Housing Act allocations, or the federal government's rather narrow view of what makes a good sewer system?

There are both provincial and federal aspects to the problem of regional disparity. Toronto is an imperial capital, drawing wealth from Northern Ontario. Toronto must be taxed to provide benefits to the north. That is a proper provincial function, and it is different from the enactment of a welfare act that gives the same housing allowance to people in Toronto and in North Bay.

My main quarrel is not with federal centralization, it is with the tendency of every government to centralize and to draw to itself programs that ought to be devised, administered, and paid for by some more local level. We need another level of government, at the neighbourhood, and we can do without at least one of the levels of government we now have. My only problem is deciding whether the municipal, the regional, the provincial, or the federal government could be most advantageously abolished. I have heard good arguments for each, but tend personally to favour the federal. It sometimes seems to me that federal problems might better be handled by treaties between provinces with a central secretariat. After all, that is what the federal-provincial conference system is really giving us, with the House of Commons and prime minister being retained for their symbolic value. It also seems clear to me that virtually every federal intervention into our city is destructive. We are glad to take federal money, but we observe that it is only our own people's money being paid back, generally on terms that are quite unsatisfactory. CMHC controls our growth more than does our own official plan, but we cannot affect CMHC policy. Perhaps the suggestion that we eliminate the federal government is premature, and may even seem facetious, even though the elimination would create better cities. In any event, we need real local government. We need it because there is no other way in which the government can become politically responsive. In no other way can it become an organ of the society rather than a manipulator of the society.

We will achieve real local governments and a real distribution of powers between different governments primarily by funding community organizers. Organized communities will demand controls with sufficient political effect to force the leviathan of the state into action. It will change a little here and a little there, and structures will change. The state will not wither away, nor will it be overthrown by violence or ignored in irrelevance. It will be so transformed that government operates according to a scale that emphasizes the problems of its inhabitants and recognizes the necessity of constantly renewing our commitment to democracy. It will become the servant of those who elected it, and when it does we will all see the necessity and value of delivering all power to the people.

Notes

*Jaffary, K. D., "The role of the state in a technological society," *Canadian Public Administration*, 15:3, Autumn, 1972 (reproduced by permission of author and publisher). This paper was read at the twenty-third annual conference of the Institute of Public Administration of Canada, Regina, 1971.

40 Pluralism and Corporatism in Ontario Medical Politics *

Carolyn J. Tuohy

Bentley may have overstated the case with his assertion that group behaviour constitutes the entirety of political life and hence comprises the entire scope of political scientific inquiry;[1] nonetheless it is undeniable that the relationships between politically active groups and the formal institutions of the state form much of the stuff of politics and of political science. Anglo-American political culture offers us essentially two ways of thinking about the phenomena of group-state relationships. These different perspectives, which one might call those of "pluralism" and "corporatism", suggest to the political scientist two sets of questions appropriate to the study of group-state relationships; while to the political decision-makers they prescribe different norms of legitimate behaviour.[2]

"Pluralism" and "corporatism", that is, function as models of group-state relationships in two senses. In the first place, they represent different sets of values, different notions of what such relationships ought to be and what conditions they ought to promote. They function as *normative* models, then, representing different ideological perspectives on what constitutes legitimate group-state interaction. In the second place, pluralist and corporatist models function as *ideal-typical* models to guide empirical enquiry. That is, they represent abstractions from the reality of group-state relationships; they represent sets of characteristics, derived from the observation of concrete systems, which suggest rather different lines of enquiry and foci of attention in the investigation of group-state relationships.

The Pluralist Approach

Neither of the terms we have chosen to characterize these two perspectives is well-defined. The term "pluralism" in particular has been used to describe a wide range of non-totalitarian systems; but it has come to be most clearly associated with a liberal democratic normative model of group-state relationships, and with an ideal-typical analytic model which Robert Dahl has labelled "polyarchy".[3]

Pluralism, as a normative model, places great emphasis upon the protection of individual interests, influence, and liberty in the context of the large-scale organizations which characterize modern industrial states. Groups are legitimate participants in the political process, in this perspective, only to the extent to which they foster (or at least do not threaten) these individualistic values. And in their concern with individualistic values, the pluralists focus very much upon the *processes* of public policy-making, and especially upon the importance of competition. As a normative model, pluralism provides no absolute concept of the public interest; the public interest is that to which men would agree if they could freely choose. The pursuit of the public interest in any given situation, then, is a matter of following certain "rules of the game" which maximize the probability that all affected interests will be heard and that individuals are free to register their preferences and to have these preferences equally weighted in the formulation of policy.

The ideal-typical pluralist model purports to describe what a fully "pluralist" system would look like in reality, and hence to allow political scientists to determine the degree of pluralism in a given system. It is, in a sense, an abstraction by political scientists from their observations of systems dominated by pluralist ideology; but the abstraction itself has been very much shaped by that ideology. In the pluralist, or "polyarchal" ideal-type, public policy results from a process of group competition within a set of institutional conditions, including the existence of alternative sources of information, freedom of expression and association, competition among political leaders (in governmental and non-governmental organizations) for votes and other support, and institutions for making government policy depend upon votes or other expressions of preference.[4] "Groups" in this model are voluntary associations of individuals formed for the purpose of pressing their claims upon government and upon other groups in society, or for the purpose of exercising some self-regulatory functions and hence reducing the extent to which state power presses directly upon the individual. They may, that is, be analysed as "pressure groups", as "private governments", or as both. In either case the pluralist model directs the analyst's attention to the form, intensity, scope, and effectiveness of group activity, and to the internal policy-making processes of these groups, usually measured against some standard of liberal democracy.

The Corporatist Approach

The "corporatist" model of group-state relationships is most fully developed as a normative model; the analytic ideal type has received less attention by political scientists. Its value premises are very different from those of pluralism. It assumes the paramouncy, not of individual, but of collective interests and goals. Groups have an intrinsic legitimacy as functional parts of the social organism (the body "politic"), and not, as in pluralist theory, merely an instrumental legitimacy as protectors of the prior values of individual liberty and interest against the autocratic exercise of state power. The relationships of these corporate groups to each other are grounded in a comprehensive framework of social values prescribing their functional responsibilities, their social obligations, and, to a large extent, the "just" rewards attached to the fulfillment of these responsibilities and obligations. There is, then, in the corporatist model, a notion of a transcendental public interest, ideologically or theologically prescribed. It is a substantive value framework which defines the social "place" of each group, and it contrasts with the procedural consensus of the pluralist model—the agreement on the "rules of the game" within which groups contend for the prizes of the polity. The process of public policy formation in the corporatist model ought to be characterized not by group competition in the political arena, but by a form of institutional accommodation wherein groups, each within its own sphere, prescribe and enforce rules within the context of a prevailing structure of social values.

What would a fully "corporatist" state look like in behavioural terms? Can we abstract from the reality of group-state relationships where corporatist ideologies prevail to define an ideal-typical analytic model? Eckstein and Presthus have noted that the existence of corporatist ideologies in Britain and Canada respectively have meant that groups, being more legitimate in the eyes of political decision-makers, are less likely to engage in overt, highly visible "lobbying" and public relations activity than are their counterparts in the United States.[5] Group-state relations are more likely to be characterized by an on-going collaboration among the political executive, the public bureaucracy, and various functional groups, in which government either delegates its rule-making functions in a particular sphere to corporate groups, or at least makes its policies dependent upon the agreement of the affected group or groups. If the concepts of "pressure groups" and "private governments" belong to the pluralist framework, the concepts of "syndicates" and "guilds" are more appropriate to the corporatist model.

There is less concern in the corporatist than in the pluralist model with the internal democracy of groups. A number of scholars have noted that Anglo-American versions of corporatism have been associated in practice with what Presthus has called "deferential patterns of authority"[6] and what Eckstein has called the "Old Tory" theory of authority, "the tendency . . . to delegate inordinately wide powers to leaders and spokesmen, to ratify decisions of leaders almost as a matter of form".[7] This elitist aspect of corporatism might well be attributed to its conception of groups as organic entities. Accordingly, the leadership of a group might be held to represent its membership, not because it holds a democratic mandate, but because the leadership intrinsically represents the traditional, occupational, and other values associated with the group. On this argument, a physician might be said to represent the medical viewpoint not because he has been democratically elected or instructed by his peers, but because he *is* a physician, because he shares a professional tradition and a common set of experiences with his peers.

To summarize, pluralism presents us with a model of political activity in which public policy is formed through the interaction of voluntary associations which compete with each other for society's resources in the context of an underlying consensus regarding the rules which ought to govern group competition. The state is theoretically sovereign; but in practice its power is checked by the countervailing power of private associations. Groups and the state maintain a continual suspicion of each other; each is legitimate to the others only to the extent that it can claim to hold a democratic mandate from its constituents. The political activity of groups tends to centre upon the mustering of political resources to increase their respective bargaining power —the forging of alliances, the winning of public support, the marshalling of information, etc.

Corporatism, on the other hand, presents us with a model of accommodation among functionally interdependent groups, each of which is largely sovereign within its own sphere so long as it acts in accordance with prevailing concepts of distributive justice and social obligation. Membership in groups is for the most part prescribed, and members are bound together by ties of tradition, occupation, and obligation. Since the distribution of resources is largely determined by the prevailing value framework, groups do not compete with each other or with the institutions of the state; rather they relate to each other as "collaborators in the task of social control".[8] Group activity tends to take the form of boardroom negotiation, rather than competition in the public arena. Finally, the corporatist model directs the attention of students of and participants in the political process to the *outcomes* of the public policy process, as measured against some standard of social justice, rather than to the process itself.

The Case of Medical Politics in Ontario

To what extent are these two models relevant to the understanding of group-state relationships in Canada? In a political culture which bears strains of both normative perspectives,[9] we should not be surprised to find that both pluralist and corporatist ideal-types capture certain dimensions of political activity in the Canadian system.

The relevance of both models is perhaps nowhere more evident than in the case of the relationships between the medical profession and the state. The medical profession is not a political monolith: the political activity of certain of its institutions resembles the pluralist model, while others engage in a form of corporate accommodation with the state.

Let us turn, after this lengthy introduction, to the case under consideration here: the relationships between the medical profession and the government of Ontario in the period following the introduction of government medical care insurance. We shall be concerned to distinguish between the activity of the voluntary association of the profession, the Ontario Medical Association,[10] and the activity of what we shall call the "core" institutions of medicine—the licensing and regulatory body (the College of Physicians and Surgeons), and the medical schools. The latter are "core institutions" in the sense that it is they who prescribe the rules governing the acquisition and exercise of medical skill, the College through its state-delegated authority to determine the qualifications necessary for licensure and to regulate the practice activity of licensed physicians, and the medical schools through their control of the medical curriculum.

The governing bodies of both the OMA and the College are, in varying degrees, elected by their respective memberships, but there are important differences. The governing Council of the College has the following composition: from twelve to sixteen physicians elected on a geographic basis by the membership; one representative of each of the five medical faculties in Ontario; and from four to six "lay" representatives appointed by the Lieutenant-Governor-in-Council.[11] The lay public is also represented on the College's Registration, Complaints, Discipline and Executive Committees. The internal political structure of the OMA allows for a much wider range of membership participation but not for lay involvement. Its governing body is a General Council of 320 members elected by the membership on a regional basis. Its Board of Directors is composed of 24 members, 18 elected by the constituent district associations, 5 by the General Council at its annual meeting, and one appointed by the five medical schools in rotation.[12] The OMA also maintains an elaborate committee network.

Before considering the external political activity of these bodies, let us consider the governmental policy initiatives by which they have recently been challenged.

The Policy Initiatives: An Overview[13]

Under conditions of national medical care insurance, faced on the one hand with the pressure to control costs, and on the other with the phenomenon of an escalating rate of increase in the volume of claims upon its insurance plan, the government which wishes to maintain a given level of coverage has three options. In the first place it may negotiate with the suppliers of medical services in an attempt to reduce or at least to avoid further increase in their price per unit of service. In the second place, it may either directly or through professional channels exercise regulatory power over the volume of medical services provided. Finally, it may seek to effect, through both legislative and organizational change (including change in the payment mechanism) a reallocation of some "medical" functions to less highly trained and less expensive personnel.

The pursuit of the first two options challenges the economic discretion of physicians over the price and volume of their services. The pursuit of the third involves as well a confrontation with the institutions through which the scope and the standards of medical practice have traditionally been defined and maintained: the licensing body and the medical schools.

The government of Ontario has taken up the first of these options: it is experimenting with the second; but its efforts regarding the third have been largely symbolic. (1) It has structured its payment mechanism in such a way that the overwhelming majority of physicians have found it economically rational to accept a fixed fee per service as the basis of their remuneration. Having established the fixed fee principle, the government has proceeded to negotiate the level of these fees with the Ontario Medical Association, through the mechanism of a Joint Committee on Physicians' Compensation. (2) The province's experimentation with the second option has involved the establishment in the College of Physicians and Surgeons of a Medical Review Committee to investigate the practices of physicians whose billings are disproportionately large within their particular specialties. It has sought to limit the number of *physicians* as well as the volume of services provided by individual physicians, through the development, in collaboration with the College, of restrictions upon the licensing of physician immigrants to Ontario. (3) With regard to the third option, policy is at a very early stage of development. Recently enacted Health Disciplines legislation[14] falls short of establishing a legislative context for the rationalization of the allocation of functions among health care personnel; but it does establish a procedural consistency among the government bodies of the health disciplines, and it creates a Health Disciplines Board empowered to review and make recommendations upon the decisions of these bodies in individual cases. Regarding the establishment of an *organizational* context for the rational allocation of functions, policy initiatives have been even more tentative. The provincial Ministry of Health has written contracts with a limited number of community clinics, providing for the development of capitation payment mechanism which might facilitate such changes. As of this writing, however, the province has announced that it will enter into no new contracts pending the development of a mechanism for evaluating the performance of these clinics. The legislative context for a re-allocation of function is at an equally rudimentary stage of development.

Of symbolic importance also is the fact that the pursuit of each of these options has involved the formal introduction of "lay" participants (that is, persons associated neither with a health discipline nor with a governmental body) into the structures of policy-making. The discussions of the Joint Committee on Physicians' Compensation are presided over by a neutral chairman. Two of the eight members of the Medical Review Committee are "laymen" chosen and appointed by the Minister of Health. The membership of the Health Disciplines Board is entirely drawn from outside the ranks of the health disciplines and of government.

In Ontario, then, the three options enumerated here have been treated more or less as constituting a sequence of policy development. Government has challenged first the physician's discretion over the *price* of his services; it has begun to challenge his discretion over the *volume* of his service. But it has not fundamentally challenged the power of the profession over the allocation of functions among health care personnel.

The Response of the Ontario Medical Association

In the face of these challenges, the Ontario Medical Association has consistently defended the interest of individual physicians in preserving their ability to exercise entrepreneurial discretion. It has conducted this defense with scrupulous regard to the maintenance of a policy mandate from its membership, and through the use of a wide range of "pressure groups" tactics, including fairly extensive public relations activity.

The OMA's first line of defence was to seek to preserve the individual physician's discretion over the prices charged in particular cases against governmental attempts to establish a fixed schedule of fees as the basis of medical remuneration and to negotiate that schedule with the profession. Policy statements adopted at OMA general meetings reflect this position.

Until 1973, the public stance of the Ontario Medical Association was one of consistent opposition to the negotiation of its fee schedule with government. It has maintained, moreover, that this fee schedule is not to be interpreted as binding upon medical practitioners but rather is to be seen as a guide to appropriate charges, allowing each physician discretion in "negotiating an individual fee with an individual patient".[15] To preserve both the profession's prerogative in determining its fee schedule and the individual physician's discretion in particular cases, the OMA has consistently encouraged its members to "opt-out" of government insurance plans: that is, to submit their bills to their patients, who are then responsible for payment of the bills and for collection of the insurance benefit. Furthermore, it has repeatedly called upon the government agency to develop a mechanism to enable the physician to identify those of his patients whose health insurance premiums are subsidized by the government plan (that is, persons or families with incomes below a certain level), in order that these persons not be charged in excess of the government benefit.[16]

In short, the OMA's initial reactions to the existence of government health insurance was designed to preserve what one must assume were its traditional approaches to pricing; it sought, a) the preservation of a context in which physicians could charge differential prices for the same service, and b) information which would enable the physician to charge according to the patient's ability to pay.[17]

It is difficult to estimate the extent to which these official positions of the OMA in the early post-medicare period reflected the mix of opinion within the profession as a whole. We do know that, from the inception of the OHSIP program in 1969, the overwhelming majority of fee-for-service physicians chose, contrary to OMA advice, to submit at least some of their bills to the government plan; but we do not know how many also submitted bills to their patients. After all, the plan allowed them to decide in individual cases whether to submit bills to their patients (for an amount negotiated with the patient), to the government plan (for the amount of the government benefit—a fixed percentage of the OMA fee for each service) or to both.

In 1971, government mounted the first of its challenges to the practice of price discrimination. The so-called "practice-streaming" rule adopted by the government plan in 1971 required physicians to deal either exclusively with the plan or exclusively with their patients.

The OMA's official response to the legislative package which included the "practice-streaming" rule (and more controversial initiatives to be discussed shortly) was angry and vociferous. Advertising in every daily paper in Ontario on July 7, 1971, it reprinted a sympathetic editorial from a Toronto newspaper, and urged the public:

> If you really care, let the politicians of all parties know that you want your personal medical services to remain a confidential matter between you and your doctor. And that politicians and civil servants have no place in the consulting rooms . . . or on doctors' backs.

At its general meeting in May 1971, the Association adopted a resolution urging upon its members to "opt out" of the government plan, and to submit all accounts to patients.[18]

The vast majority of Ontario physicians appear, in their individual practice situations, to have interpreted their entrepreneurial interests differently than did the OMA. Nearly 90 per cent of the fee-for-service practitioners in Ontario chose to deal exclusively with the government plan, thus foregoing the opportunity to vary their prices, but gaining a rationalized payment system guaranteeing payment of all accounts (at 90 per cent of the OMA schedule).

The decisions of nearly 90 per cent of Ontario physicians to accept a fixed rate of remuneration could not be ignored, and OMA policy soon came to reflect this reality. In 1973, the OMA was brought to agree to the negotiation of its fee schedule with government, through the mechanism of a Joint Committee on Physicians' Compensation. The 1974 fee schedule increase was negotiated through this body, which is appointed by and advisory to the OMA and the provincial government, and which continued to meet weekly, despite a revision of its role on the part of the OMA, until October 1975, when it suspended negotiations pending the publication of federal anti-inflation guidelines regarding professional fees.

The OMA's recent revision of the role of the Joint Committee, moreover, would appear to make it a vehicle of consultation rather than negotiation.[19] At its general meeting in February, 1975, the OMA Council re-asserted its own prerogative of unilaterally determining the fee schedule which would form the basis of charges to patients. The role of the Joint Committee, in this view, would be the development of a "schedule of benefits" to form the basis of OHIP payments to physicians. The Council reiterated its appeal to physicians to opt out of the government plan to recover the difference between the two schedules. It might be argued conversely by government that while it *consults* with the profession regarding its "schedule of benefits", it is under no obligation to win OMA consent to that schedule.

While the vast majority of physicians are remunerated on the basis of a fixed schedule of fees determined by government in consultation with the profession, and hence have lost their individual discretion over price, they can exercise their entrepreneurial discretion in another way: by adjusting their workloads and the various factor inputs of their practices.[20] They may come to accept the limitation of their entrepreneurial discretion over price (particularly if the alternative rationalizes a cumbersome collection procedure), but any governmental threat to the individual physician's discretion over the volume of his services or the organization of his practice can be expected to meet with a second wave of resistance.

As the provincial government has proceeded to take up its second option, the regulatory control of physicians' billable service volumes, it has indeed encountered such resistance. It has also, however, encountered a willingness on the part of a small but significant segment of the profession to engage in a strategic collaboration with government. While the large majority of physicians have accommodated to a fixed price structure by exercising and defending their entrepreneurial discretion, even this mode of response may be becoming increasingly obsolete as a result of a growing accommodation between the core institutions of medicine—the regulatory college and the medical schools—and government. These core institutions have been experimenting with the establishment of upper limits on physicians' incomes and service volumes, and with a variety of clinic forms and mechanisms of remuneration which threaten the previously sacrosanct area of the physician's discretion over his own workload. They have entered into this collaboration in order to retain intact what they consider to be essential to professionalism: the power to define and to regulate the content and the standards of medical practice. In the process, however, they are in danger of suffering the fate of all "collaborators". The ranks of the profession may identify them with the enemy; they may cease to be part of "us" in the eyes of the majority of the profession, and may rather become part of "them". We now turn to a consideration of these developments.

Corporate Accommodation and the Core Institutions

The most visible expression of this accommodation in the eyes of the profession as a whole may well be the Medical Review Committee of the College of Physicians and Surgeons. In establishing this body, government has exercised the second of our enumerated options: the exercise of indirect regulatory control over billable service volumes. In agreeing to its establishment, the College has in essence agreed to the principle of regulating the productivity of individual physicians, as long as the regulatory process is administered by a professional body. The Review Committee functions as part of an audit procedure in which "aberrant accounts" (accounts of physicians billing the government plan in excess of the acceptable range for their specialties) are identified by the plan's computer and referred to the Committee for investigation. As originally conceived, the review committee was to have been located within the Ministry of Health. Under pressure from the OMA and the College (we noted above the OMA's angry reaction to the entire 1971 legislative package, including the "practice-streaming" requirement), the legislation was changed before passage to establish a strange hybrid mechanism more appropriate to the medical commitment to collegiality: it provided for the appointment by the Minister of a committee of not more than seven members (five of whom were to be physicians) from a list submitted by the College, and established this committee as a committee of the College. It is responsible, however, not to the Council of the College, but to the Minister of Health.

In the first year of the Committee's operation (1972-73), the government plan simply referred to it the accounts of all physicians billing in excess of $10,000 per month for three consecutive months. In May, 1973, dissatisfied with the crudeness of this measure, the Committee announced that physicians with high levels of servicing would henceforth be identified on the basis of formulae (the "quality service payment formulae") relating dollar volumes to maximum weekly service volumes which, in the judgement of professional committees, were compatible with the maintenance of acceptable levels of quality. The College has emphasized that the development of this procedure arose from its recognition that "there is a limit to the number of services which an individual physician can perform at an acceptable standard of practice beyond which the quality of the services both individually and collectively will decline"[21] and not from a desire to limit the incomes of physicians; and that in any event, identification of a physician's accounts by the "formula screen" does not imply "over-servicing" on the part of the physician but simply calls for a judgement of his peers, on less strictly quantitative grounds, as to whether his servicing levels are appropriate. The mechanism has incorporated the medical commitments to quality of care and to collegial authority, and has been defended on that basis; but the potential effect, of course, is to establish income ceilings varying across specialties. Although these formulae are not refined instruments, and although they will be revised and ultimately supplanted, the decision to develop them is significant. It marks the first time the College has moved beyond the enforcement of the principle of "a just fee for a service rendered", to place restraints upon the physician's productivity.

The economic discretion of the individual physician is being limited not only with the development of the OHIP-College monitoring mechanism, but also with the increasing scale of organization of the delivery of health care services. The number of physicians who carry out most of their practice in hospital and other institutional settings is steadily increasing, and for many of them this setting implies a form of remuneration which limits their entrepreneurial discretion.[22]

One of the most significant departures from pure fee-for-service remuneration has occurred in the case of the clinical departments of medical schools, as the result of complex budgetary arrangements between the medical faculties and government agencies. Although the mechanisms of remuneration defy general description, varying as they do across departments, all imply some form of limitation upon the economic discretion of full-time clinical teachers. The budgets of the clinical departments derive from the public treasury through three channels: the university budget, teaching and research funds granted by the provincial and federal health departments, and fees paid to individual staff members under the health insurance plan. The practice has been for the clinical departments to curb the economic discretion of their staffs through a variety of "pooled income", income ceiling, and salaried arrangements, which allow some of the income foregone by individuals to remain with the clinical department as discretionary funds.

The core institutions of medicine, then, have moved slowly in the direction of limiting the economic discretion of their members. On its part, government has refrained from any fundamental challenge to professional self-regulatory institutions. Despite the creation of two new structures for the oversight of professional self-regulatory bodies, the challenge has been more symbolic than real. The Health Disciplines Board, which is to hear appeals from the decisions of governing bodies of the five "senior" health professions, is a creature considerably weaker than the Board originally proposed by the province. The power to overturn regulations of a college council remains with the Cabinet, not the Board as originally proposed; the legislation merely makes more explicit the Minister's power of review of delegated legislation.[23] The Hospital Appeal Board, created in 1971 to hear appeals from physicians denied hospital privileges by hospital boards of governors and their associated medical staffs, is not located within the College of Physicians and Surgeons as the College originally proposed, but its membership is drawn almost entirely from the hospital sector. In each of these cases government has reminded the profession that its regulatory activities are subject to review. Significantly, however, it has not challenged the *policies* of the self-regulatory bodies; it has rather chosen to establish mechanisms of appeal from their decisions on a case-by-case basis.

The desire to limit the total volume of medical service provided in the province has led government to seek, through professional channels, to limit not only the entrepreneurial discretion of individual physicians, but the total number of physicians, at least in "over-serviced" or adequately serviced areas. The mechanism whereby they have sought to accomplish this involves limiting the discretion of immigrant physicians over the location of their practice. The College, with the approval and encouragement of the provincial government, passed a regulation under the new Health Disciplines Legislation establishing as a condition of licensure either Canadian citizenship or an employment visa granted by Canadian immigration authorities. Under arrangement between the provincial and federal authorities, such a visa will be issued to a prospective immigrant physician only if he contracts with the Ontario Ministry of Health to practise in an "under-serviced" area for three years. The development of this policy represents a remarkable coincidence of governmental and professional goals, remarkable in that as late as 1971, the Ontario government was holding to its policy "certification and licensure should not be restricted because of such factors as age, sex, nationality, citizenship, or length of residence in Ontario".[24] However, the government appears to have recognized that, at least under conditions of an administered fee schedule, an increase in the supply of physicians leads not to a decrease in the price of their services, but only to an increase in the total volume of payments to physicians. At least in the short run, then, it appears to have chosen to collaborate with the College in restricting the number of immigrant physicians, rather than to bring about a confrontation with the OMA over the issue of fee-for-service payment.

Government's pursuit of its second option, then, has brought it into increased contact with a set of institutions—the College and the medical schools—with whom it has traditionally had a pattern of relationships quite different from its relationship with the OMA. The relationships between the state and these "core institutions" of medicine are much closer to the corporatist model. They are, for example, much less publicly visible. If one medium of public visibility is press coverage, the number and prominence of column-inches devoted to OMA activity and OMA-government confrontation as opposed to those devoted to College activities and relationships with government indicate a much higher OMA "profile".[25]

Furthermore, there appears to be much less concern with the maintenance of a democratic mandate with the councils of the College and the medical schools. Committees and officials, once appointed, operate with a great deal of discretion, and without the need for continual referral to a "general assembly" of delegates for approval which characterizes policy formulation in the OMA. Indeed, the elections to and deliberations of the College council appear to have little salience in the minds of the majority of physicians;[26] and a recent study by the present author suggests that, by a ratio of 7 to 1, Ontario physicians see the OMA rather than the College as the appropriate channel through which to seek to influence government policy toward the profession.[27]

Finally, the sharp distinction from government which appropriately characterizes the OMA's political stance cannot be made in the case of the College and the medical schools—they are essentially public institutions, although with strong traditions of autonomy. The medical schools draw their budgets largely from the provincial treasury; the College exercises regulatory power delegated by the state; and its governing Council and committees include a number of governmental appointees.

In effect, in delegating broad authority to the College and the medical schools to prescribe the rules governing the acquisition and exercise of medical skill, the state has recognized the profession's corporate property rights in medical skill. Let us consider briefly the nature of these property rights.[28] They are essentially *corporate* in nature: the individual's right to use and to derive revenue from the use of medical skill is defined by his relationship to the professional group. They are *exclusive*, or "private": the corporate body of the profession may exclude from as well as admit to the group of those authorized to exercise medical skill. And they are *conditional* upon the fulfilment of social obligations: in authorizing professional groups to control entry to their ranks and to police the behaviour of their members, the state charges the groups with the maintenance of standards of competence and ethics in the public interest. In the past, however, the conditional nature of medical property rights has been mitigated by the fact that the social responsibilities of the profession have been defined largely by the profession itself in the form of the standards of ethics and technical competence which it prescribes and enforces upon its members.

In attempting to restrict the volume of medical service provided, government has not challenged the professions' corporate property rights: the regulations affecting service volumes and the licensing of immigrant physicians have been made through the College structure. But it has broadened the notion of the *social obligations* attendant to these property rights to include a financial responsibility to control of aggregate impact of the exercise of those rights on the pool of society's resources. It is a mode of state action very close to the corporate model.

Future Developments

The continued success of this mode of action in achieving governmental policy objectives, however, is threatened by at least three factors: the lack of cohesion in the medical profession; the incompatibility of governmental and professional goals as government moves to pursue its third option of organizational change; and the broad problem of the lack of the comprehensive framework of social values ultimately essential to corporatist modes of decision-making. Let us consider each of these problems in turn.

DIVISIONS WITHIN THE PROFESSION

The reactions of the Ontario Medical Association to the limitations on physicians' services volumes suggest that there is a developing schism between that body and the College.[29] Although initially mollified by the location of the Medical Review Committee in the College rather than the Ministry of Health, the OMA's reaction to the activities of the Committee has been one of growing dissatisfaction. Its initial response to the Committee's "quality service payment formulae" in May, 1973 was one of guarded approval. The establishment of maximum weekly service volumes was endorsed by the OMA General Council only with the proviso that these limits not be considered as arbitrary payment ceilings, but rather as constituting a device to identify individual physicians who would retain the right to attempt to justify their high volumes of service to the Review Committee.[30] One year later, it had become apparent that the Review Committee was not routinely allowing physicians a personal hearing before recommending that their payments be reduced; and the attitude of OMA Council delegates at their annual meeting was considerably more hostile. The Canadian Medical Association Journal reported the following rather convoluted comment as capturing the essence of this attitude:

> Use of college letterhead [by the Medical Review Committee] has either led people into believing that the MRC is a committee of the College—which it is not—or we are rapidly coming to the point where the minister of health and his department, committees appointed by the government—like the MRC —and the college are really regarded as arms of the same institution—the provincial government. Perhaps it's time we recognized that the college is "they" and no longer "us."[30]

CONFLICT OVER THE ALLOCATION OF FUNCTIONS

If the direction of government policy in attempting to limit the volume of medical services has run counter to the entrepreneurial interests of individual physicians as represented by the OMA, the probable future direction of government policy may challenge not only these interests but also the traditional understanding between the College and the government regarding the nature of the corporate property rights vested in the College. The challenge to entrepreneurial discretion will intensify as government proceeds with the development of alternatives to fee-for-service remuneration. But more fundamentally, the pressure to control costs will eventually force government to reconsider the extent to which it has delegated rule-making authority to the profession. Government will be brought to mitigate, through either regulatory or budgetary mechanisms, professional control over service volumes. And it will ultimately be brought to challenge professional control over the definition of the content and the standards of medical care. In determining what constitutes an acceptable standard of medical care and what component of this care must be provided by or under the supervision of expensively trained medical personnel, the core institutions of medicine determine to a large extent the parameters within which resource allocation decisions in the health field must be made. Government must seek to modify these professionally-determined policy parameters, and to effect a re-allocation of certain allegedly "medical" functions to new and existing less expensive alternatives to the physician. There are limited indications that this issue is assuming some importance on the political agenda in Ontario.[32] In pursuing this policy option, government will no doubt seek to work, as in the past, through the existing corporate structures of the health professions and occupations. As it has done in other cases of inter-professional "property disputes",[33] it will undoubtedly attempt to refrain from legislative action until the groups involved have reached an accommodation.

The Health Disciplines legislation, it will be remembered, does not empower the lay Health Disciplines Board to resolve disputes among professional colleges with respect to their scopes of practice. Furthermore, the legislation allows for the Colleges of Physicians and Surgeons, Dental Surgeons, and Optometry to "authorize persons other than [their] members to perform specified acts in the practice of [their respective disciplines] under the supervision or direction of a member".[34] The grant of power is much more sweeping in the case of medicine than in the case of the other two professions. The jurisdiction of the latter is restricted to the practice of dentistry and optometry as specifically defined in the legislation; the jurisdiction of the medical College is restricted by no such legislative definition of its scope of practice. An allegedly medical act may be removed from exclusive medical control by including it in the statutory definition of the scope of practice of another health profession; and the Ontario government has shown itself willing, if reluctant, to take such action when the development of consensus appears impossible, as in the case of the long-standing and apparently irreconcilable dispute between physicians and optometrists regarding the right to administer drugs to the eyes.[35] But in general, at least as a short-term measure pending the development of a consensus among the affected groups, government has preferred to delegate to the medical profession the authority to determine which acts are "medical" and which of these may be "delegated" to non-medical personnel.

This attempt to effect through professional channels a re-allocation of functions which is consistent with prevailing notions of competence and fairness, however, seems almost certain to fail, and the reasons for its likely failure extend beyond the nature of professional-state relationships to the nature of social values in our "technological society".

THE LACK OF A COHERENT FRAMEWORK

If corporatist group-state relationships are to function effectively, they must be grounded in a substantive consensus regarding the appropriate responsibilities and rewards of various functional groups in society. Governments now appear, in the health field and elsewhere, to be attempting to engage in "corporatist" modes of decision-making *in the absence* of such a consensus. In earlier, organic corporatist societies (as distinct from the state-imposed pseudo-corporatism associated with fascist Italy and Germany), the prevailing social wisdom regarding the allocation of rights, responsibilities, and rewards was "given", either as a theology or as an ideology arising out of the functional interdependencies of groups in the context of a relatively stable technology. But surely one of the outstanding characteristics of the present era is the overwhelming pace of technological change. The functional relationships among groups cannot remain stable in the context of such change; and with the disruption of those relationships, the web of social values which at once develops from and supports those relationships is disrupted as well. As the development of medical technology creates new and highly specialized technical functions, and new and specialized aids to the performance of existing functions, the appropriate allocation of the responsibilities and the rewards for the performance of these functions is far from clear or "given". The lack of consensus within the health field is evident in the nascent disputes between the College of Physicians and Surgeons and the College of Nurses regarding the section of the Health Disciplines legislation granting the former the power to authorize the delegation of "medical" functions under supervision, and more full-blown disputes between the medical College and the College of Optometry, and between the professional Colleges of medicine and dentistry and "professionalizing" groups such as chiropodists and denture therapists. When the problem of assigning responsibilities and rewards for the maintenance of health is extended beyond the health occupations to include the responsibilities of industry for the operation of programs of occupational and environmental health, and the responsibilities of individuals to modify their life-styles, the lack of consensus is even more evident.

Conclusion

The health field represents, in microcosm, the problems faced by Canadian governments in attempting to draw upon Canada's corporatist traditions in solving current and future problems of conflict resolution and resource allocation. Functional groups, even traditional professional groups like medicine, are not cohesive, and subgroups dissatisfied with the actions of their corporate spokesmen may seek to pursue their ends through the competitive pluralist politics which are also legitimated in Canadian political culture. Faced with the lack of cohesiveness within functional groups, and the lack of an organically-based substantive consensus on social values, governments may move in either of two directions, neither encouraging for the health of the political system. On the one hand, they may pursue the incrementalist strategies associated with pluralist politics, resorting to *ad hoc* measures of marginal change in response to short-term political and economic pressures, testing group response at each step. On the other hand, they may move toward an artificial pseudo-corporatism on the fascist model, in which the structure and powers of corporate groups, and the value framework within which their accommodation occurs, is defined by the state.

Whatever the differences between the pure corporatist normative and ideal-typical models and the reality of modern Canadian political life, the apparent "re-discovery" of Canadian corporatism by her political scientists may improve the quality of political scientific inquiry in this country. It reminds us that the pluralist models with which we were preoccupied in the 1960's are inadequate to the understanding of group-state relationships in Canada. And it reminds us of the importance of considering not only the structure and processes of policy-making, but also the substantive impact of the policies adopted, as assessed against some standard of distributive justice. The study of health politics, as of the politics of other issues, can only be improved by such reminders, though few of us are likely to be encouraged by our findings.

Notes

*Written especially for this book by Professor Tuohy.

[1]"When groups are adequately stated, everything is stated. When I say everything, I mean everything. The complete description will be the complete science." A. F. Bentley, *The Process of Government* (Bloomington, 1949), p. 208.

[2]We are ignoring here the third major approach to the understanding of group-state relationships—the class conflict model—as being outside the mainstream of Anglo-American political culture.

[3]For an elaboration of the polyarchical model, see R. A. Dahl and C. E. Lindblom, *Politics, Economics, and Welfare* (New York, 1953), pp. 272-323; R. A. Dahl, *A Preface to Democratic Theory* (Chicago, 1956), pp. 63-89; and R. A. Dahl, *Democracy in the United States: Promise and Performance* (New York, 1972) pp. 35-39.

[4]Dahl, *Democracy in the United States*. pp. 35-39.

[5]Harry Eckstein, *Pressure Group Politics* (Stanford, 1960) pp. 24-25; Robert Presthus, *Elite Accommodation in Canadian Politics* (Toronto, 1973), pp. 24-28.

[6]Presthus, *op. cit.*, pp. 28-37.

[7]Eckstein, *op. cit.*, pp. 24-25.

[8]The phrase is taken from Lane W. Lancaster, "Private Associations and Public Administration," *Social Forces*, Vol. XIII (December, 1934) p. 234; quoted in Corinne Lathrop Gilb, *Hidden Hierarchies: the Professions and Government* (New York, 1966). Gilb's work is an excellent discussion of mediaeval corporatist models and their relevance to the understanding of professional-state relationships in the contemporary United States.

[9]See, for example, Gad Horowitz, "Conservatism, Liberalism, and Socialism in Canada: an Interpretation," *Canadian Journal of Economics and Political Science*, Vol. XXXII, No. 2 (May, 1966) pp. 144-171; and the introduction to this section.

[10]The charter of the OMA, whose membership comprises over three-quarters of the physicians practising in Ontario, lists as its objectives the advancement of the character and honour of the profession, the raising of the standards of medical education, the promotion of the public health, the furtherance of unity and harmony among members, the provision of a connecting link between the local medical societies and the Canadian Medical Association, and assistance in the advancement of medical legislation for the good of the public and the profession.

[11]The Health Disciplines Act, Statutes of Ontario, 1974, Chapter 47, Section 48.

[12]J. W. Grove, *Organized Medicine in Ontario*, a study prepared for the Ontario Committee on the Healing Arts (Toronto, 1970) pp. 25-27.

[13]This discussion of policy initiatives is taken largely from Carolyn J. Tuohy, "Medical Politics after Medicare: the Ontario Case," *Canadian Public Policy* (Spring, 1976).

[14]S.O. 1974, chapter 47.

[15]The Ontario Medical Association, "Transactions of Council, January 14 and 15, 1965," reprinted in *Ontario Medical Review* (March, 1965), p. 217; ——— "Transactions of Council, May 12 and 15, 1969," reprinted in *Ontario Medical Review* (July, 1969),

p. 31; ——— "Transactions of Council, May 10 and 11, 1971," reprinted in *Ontario Medical Review* (July, 1971) p. 346.

[16]*Idem.*

[17]The OMA's defence of the practice of price discrimination could be seen, not as a defence of the entrepreneurial discretion of individual physicians, but rather as an attempt by a powerful and cohesive discriminating monopoly to defend a context in which it might enforce a collectively rational discriminatory price structure upon its members. Such an interpretation, however, is inconsistent with other OMA policy positions, as argued in Tuohy, *op. cit.*

[18]Ontario Medical Association, "Transactions of Council, May 10 and 11, 1971," reprinted in *Ontario Medical Review* (July, 1971) p. 346.

[19]The terms are Harry Eckstein's: "Negotiations take place when a governmental body makes a decision hinge upon the actual approval of organizations interested in it, giving the organizations a veto over the decision; consultations occur when the views of the organizations are solicited and taken into account but not considered in any sense to be decisive. . . . Negotiations, then, demand the concentration of authority on both sides, as well as the vesting of considerable discretionary authority in the negotiators." Eckstein, *op. cit.*, p. 23.

[20]For discussions of this entrepreneurial model of physicians' practice behaviour, see R. G. Evans, "Models, Markets, and Medical Care," in L. Officer and L. B. Smith, *Canadian Economic Problems and Policies* 2nd edition (Toronto, 1974); and Alan D. Wolfson, *The Supply of Physicians' Services in Ontario*, unpublished doctoral dissertation, Harvard University, 1975.

[21]The College of Physicians and Surgeons of Ontario, Medical Review Committee, *Bulletin* (May, 1973) p. 1.

[22]A Canadian Medical Association survey in 1967 showed that approximately 23 per cent of Canadian physicians spent more than half of their time in activities, including the direct care of patients, for which they received salaried remuneration; approximately 13 per cent spent more than 90 per cent of their time in such activities. See R. D. Fraser, *Selected Economic Aspects of the Health Care Sector in Ontario*, a study prepared for the Ontario Committee on the Healing Arts (Toronto, 1970), p. 243. In 1973, a study prepared for the Ontario Medical Association estimated that "between 25 and 30 per cent of Ontario physicians both in practice and in administration [were] on salary either in whole or in part," and predicted that the proportion of salaried physicians would increase. Ontario Medical Association, *Report of the special study regarding the medical profession in Ontario*, E. A. Pickering, project director. (Toronto, 1973), p. 119.

[23]The Health Disciplines legislation was first tabled in the legislature in draft form, as a set of proposals, to be revised in the course of committee hearings and deliberations. The legislation in final form necessitated a re-writing of each of the existing statutes governing the regulation of the individual health disciplines. In the negotiations involved in the re-writing and integration of this existing legislation as well as the draft legislation, the College of Physicians and Surgeons, with the other professional colleges, urged that the Health Disciplines Board be empowered only to make recommendations to Cabinet regarding the revision of regulations; and that in areas of conflict among professional colleges or between a college and the Board, the conflict be resolved at the Cabinet level. The attempt to preserve access to the Cabinet may well represent an attempt to preserve a traditional point of access which has proved effective. In a recent survey of Canadian interest groups, Robert Presthus found professional groups to be most effective in securing access at the Cabinet level. Presthus, *op. cit.*, p. 208. For the medical profession, of course, the point of Cabinet access has been the Minister of Health. Of Ontario's eleven Ministers of Health from 1925 to 1973, seven had been physicians; Ontario had had a medical Minister of Health for 36 of those 48 years.

[24]Government of Ontario, Minister of Health, *Guiding Principles for the Regulation and the Education of the Health Disciplines* (Toronto, January 21, 1971). Principle 12, p. 4. These *Principles* were developed following the report of the Committee on the Healing Arts, a government commission of inquiry whose appointment had been catalysed by,

among other issues, government's concern with possible discriminatory practices by professional colleges in the licensing of immigrant professionals.

[25]The College's public advocacy of policy positions is usually confined to statements in its annual report and briefs to governmental bodies. Although these statements receive some attention in the press, the coverage does not compare in visibility with that given to OMA general meetings and the periodic public statements of its officials, not to speak of its own public relations activity.

[26]See, for example, Malcolm Taylor, "The role of the medical profession in the formulation and execution of public policy," *Canadian Public Administration*, Vol. 3, No. 3 (September, 1960), p. 111.

[27]Carolyn J. Tuohy, *The Political Attitudes of Ontario Physicians: a Skill Group Perspective*, unpublished doctoral dissertation, Yale University, 1974.

[28]For a further discussion of professional property rights, see Carolynn J. Tuohy, "Private government property, and professionalism," *C.J.P.S.*, September 1976.

[29]This schism was presaged as early as 1967. As Horace Krever reports, "At a public hearing of the Ontario Committee on the Healing Arts in 1967, a spokesman for the Ontario Medical Association . . . took the position, in answer to a hypothetical question that it would be acceptable professional conduct for doctors collectively to withhold their services when they disagree with a statute enacted by the legislature establishing a new method of paying physicians. At a hearing attended by members of the [College] council, the registrar of the College said he would prepare a list of the offenders and send it to the College's Complaints Committee if such conduct should occur." Krever, "National Health Insurance and Problems of Quality," in S. Andreopoulos, ed., *National Health Insurance: Can We Learn From Canada?* (New York, 1975), p. 212-3.

[30]Ontario Medical Association, "Transactions of Council, May 14 and 15, 1973," reprinted in *Ontario Medical Review* (September, 1973), pp. 577-8.

[31]Quoted in D. A. Geekie, "OMA Council meeting shows concern with doctors' rights and review committee," *Canadian Medical Association Journal*, Vol. 110 (June 22, 1974), p. 1401.

[32]See, for example, the address of the Minister of Health to the 50th Annual Conference of the Registered Nurses Association in Ontario, in which he emphasized the importance of developing greater numbers of paramedical and allied health personnel to "allow us to be more precise in matching skills to patient needs and in doing so, make our health system more cost effective." See "Minister urges close matching of skills to need in health care," *The Globe and Mail* (Toronto, June 14, 1975).

[33]The Ontario Government, for example, has not enforced contentious legislation regarding the practice of architecture, whose interpretation is a matter of dispute between architects and engineers; and has delayed legislative change pending a resolution of the dispute. The premier has stated the government's official position as follows: "The two professions should be able to achieve a reasonable consensus among themselves. The dispute is not the responsibility of the provincial government." Quoted in Roger Worth, "Ontario architects don't like engineers' designs," *The Financial Post* (Toronto, April 19, 1975).

[34]Statutes of Ontario, 1974, Chapter 47, Sections 25(1), 50(k), 96(i).

[35]The Optometry Part of the Health Disciplines Act defines as within the practice of optometry the administration of such drugs as are prescribed by the regulations of the College of Optometry under the Act. S.O. 1974, Ch. 47, Sec. 91(f), 96(g).

41 For Private Enterprise, the Challenge of a New Role*

Michael Barkway

It is not news that business is worried about government encroachments. Of course it has always been. But the concern and the conflicts, actual and potential, have reached a new level—almost a new dimension—in these last few years.

The new sense of urgency among businessmen may have been sparked by the recent treatment of resource industries by both federal and provincial governments. They are still the loudest in their complaints.

It has certainly been fanned by the obvious ineffectiveness of governments in handling inflation and labor unrest.

But more fundamentally it results from the sheer accumulation of laws and regulations over the last 10 to 15 years.

A study done for the Law Reform Commission, quoted by J. W. Younger, general counsel for the Steel Co. of Canada Ltd., estimates that federal statutes have now created some 20,000 criminal or quasi-criminal offences. Provincial statutes account for another 20,000.

And, says Mr. Younger, "more such laws are being churned out at every session of Parliament and the legislatures."

The effect of legislation in the last 10 years, he says, has been "the progressive transfer of decision-making power and of economic resources from the private sector to the state."

The scores of businessmen with whom I have talked, in every kind and size of business and in most of the provinces, are trying to live with the results.

I heard certain themes repeated so often that I began to take them for granted:

The public doesn't understand business.

Governments are increasingly hostile to business.

The bureaucracies are inherently anti-business.

Officials exercise too much power.

The catalogue ranges all the way from the small businessmen's complaints about the ignorance and arrogance of minor officials to the top executives of large companies who told of threats by ministers or deputy ministers: "Do what we want, or else . . ."

The specific stories varied widely. But the pattern was much the same whether the target was the Liberals in Ottawa, the Tories in Toronto and Edmonton, or the NDP in Victoria and Regina.

It is true that in British Columbia and Saskatchewan, where elections are expected soon, there are plenty of fiery spirits determined to "throw out the socialist rascals."

Business leaders in Vancouver are trying to combine the anti-socialist vote behind William Bennett, son of the former premier, who is working to revive the Social Credit party. But even there I found a significant "silent minority" who are looking beyond politics and party labels.

The rambunctious NDP premier, Dave Barrett, talks (at least privately) in very pragmatic terms. He boasted to me of his support for small business.

"I was brought up in a small business family," he said. "My father had his own business, peddling bananas. He made a very good thing of it. I've got my own dreams, too. I'm not going to stay in politics forever."

In Saskatchewan the main victims of the NDP government's determination to control the resource industries are national or multinational companies with headquarters outside the province. Premier Blakeney and the NDP make the most of that. And the opposition leader, Liberal Dave Steuart, complained to me that the big companies had been "incredibly weak-kneed" about the really shocking things the NDP has done.

"The business people react too violently to the wrong things," he said.

When you compare these NDP governments with what Conservative governments are doing in Alberta and Ontario and what the Liberals are doing in Ottawa, you are left to wonder whether there is a significant difference of kind, or only of degree; whether the political labels hide a difference in principle, or only in presentation.

The question was raised repeatedly in my conversations. And the most frequent answer, by far, was that the old philosophical debate about free enterprise vs. socialism is dead.

The challenge now, said the large majority of businessmen, is to make the best of the new roles of government and business.

This is a new challenge for most senior executives. It involves coming to terms with the bureaucracy as much as, or more than, lobbying politicians. And the worst bureaucratic problem is in Ottawa, because it is so remote and because it is so big, and because it appears so inbred.

It ought to be much easier to maintain contact between the two worlds of business and government in Toronto, where at least they live side by side. But even there, both the businessmen and the politicians tend to be baffled by the cocksureness which the departmental hierarchies generate.

At the end of the line, it is the minor officials—tax collectors, inspectors and petty administrators—who impinge on the private citizens most infuriatingly. They are the little men and women who are given the power to bully, delay and frustrate.

But they, after all, are the creatures of the senior officials, the policy-makers or mandarins.

And the mandarins, in turn, are the creatures of the elected ministers; who, in their turn, depend on the legislatures and the voters.

If business is to have any real say in decision-making, it will have to be at all levels. The majority of those I talked with put major emphasis on consultation with senior officials and with ministers.

When I saw Darcy McKeough, the treasurer of Ontario, he was in the early stage of preparing the budget which he brought down last week; and he was engaged in an intensive round of meetings with several dozen different groups from outside government.

"The officials don't always like it," he said. "But it's good for them to know that their advice can be balanced against other people's views.

"For example," said Mr. McKeough, "if the government decides it has got to get a lot more revenue from the mining industry, I don't see any reason why we shouldn't sit down with them and work out the best way of doing it without hurting the industry."

A week later, I sat in the premier's office in Victoria; and Mr. Barrett told me that a delegation from the mining industry had visited him the previous day.

"We met in the cabinet room," he said. "After they had talked for a while, I said to them 'Don't just orate about the evils of socialism. We want $100 million from the mining industry. Go and sit down with the minister and work out the best way of raising it.' "

In the evolving pattern of government-business relations, there will be shocks and surprises on both sides.

Some of the most puzzled men in the country must be the directors of Canadian Cellulose Co. Ltd., owned by the B.C. government, and of Pacific Western Airlines, owned by the Alberta government.

I talked to members of both boards, which are made up entirely of solid and respected businessmen. In both cases their directive from the new owners is to run the business profitably. Both have been able to do so, and both report that they have not been interfered with—not, at least, so far. But the doubt remains. In the last resort, if things get tough, how long can governments keep their hands off? The taxpayers' money is at stake, whether they wanted to risk it or not.

Short of outright government ownership, another novelty is appearing in the form of joint ventures by government and private companies. Are Syncrude Canada Ltd. and PanArctic Oils Ltd. and the Alberta Energy Co. prototypes of a new pattern?

Views differ. In Vancouver a forest industry executive answered yes. He said: "With the astronomical capital expenditure involved in resource development, and with the virtual certainty that government will make—and change—all kinds of rules, private companies will refuse to start a big project *without* government participation."

In Calgary an oil executive also answered yes—at least in the case of PanArctic. "It's very useful to have the federal government as a partner," he said. "At least when they come to make regulations and set royalties, they will have a stake in the industry."

Petro-Canada, he said, is another story: "a monstrosity."

Government ownership, in whole or in part, raises the hackles of most businessmen. But it may not be such a big step from the now familiar incentives which all our governments have been providing to make industry do what they want.

Ottawa's DREE program still marches on, though it hardly gets a good word from anyone. Ontario's latest move passed almost unnoticed, though it promised a perpetual subsidy far beyond DREE's generosity. It has lured Texasgulf Inc. into building a smelting and refining plant at Timmins which would be quite uneconomic without the government's tax concession.

In Regina a spokesman for the NDP government told me: "We don't believe in all these incentives. We'd rather take the equity." And there is a simple logic in that, whether you like it or not.

It will not be easy to develop a way out of this tangle of government involvement, nor to break the web of bureaucratic controls which threaten to smother private initiative.

It will not be easy to preserve, or restore, the widely-dispersed responsibility for economic decisions which has always been regarded as a main bulwark of freedom.

It may be true, as so many businessmen told me, that business has been very slow to come out of its shell and take its proper role in this fast-changing society.

But all the people I talked to in my strictly unscientific survey left me with an encouraging sense that there's life in the old dog yet.

Notes

**Financial Times of Canada*, 14 April, 1975 (reproduced by permission of publisher).

42 Attack on Inflation *

Policy Statement tabled in the House of Commons by the Honourable Donald S. Macdonald Minister of Finance, October 14, 1975

Introduction

Canada is in the grip of serious inflation.

If this inflation continues or gets worse there is a grave danger that economic recovery will be stifled, unemployment increased and the nation subjected to mounting stresses and strains.

It has thus become absolutely essential to undertake a concerted national effort to bring inflation under control.

There are no simple or easy remedies for quickly resolving this critical problem. The inflationary process in Canada is so deeply entrenched that it can be brought under control only by a broad and comprehensive program of action on a national scale.

This paper outlines the measures being proposed by the federal government and the obligations that the provincial governments and Canadians generally are being asked to assume.

Our continuing commitment as a nation to the goal of achieving price stability must be seen as part and parcel of our continuing commitment to the goal of achieving high and stable levels of employment and real incomes.

The Problem Confronting Us

The problems that inflation creates were clearly spelled out in the budget of June 23, 1975:

> In its present cost-push form, inflation threatens to price our goods out of world markets and to lessen the capacity of our business firms to expand their operations. It disrupts financial markets and impairs rational planning by business and government. It undermines the effectiveness of the traditional instruments of demand management policy to keep the economy on course. When inflation reaches a certain point, the stimulation of spending may simply lead to higher prices rather than more goods and more jobs; in the longer run, it actually makes unemployment worse.
>
> Not only that, but inflation ultimately inflicts grievous damage to the fabric of society. It lowers the living standards of those on fixed incomes, including pensioners. It leaves people without reliable, understandable guideposts by which to arrange their economic affairs. It injects grave uncertainty into family budgets, housing, savings and provision for old age. It provokes deep frustration, social tension and mistrust of private and public institutions. Collective bargaining is embittered; industrial relations are damaged. We in Canada are already beginning to live some of these experiences.

Inflation is a dynamic process which feeds upon itself. In the absence of strong measures to bring it under control, the kind of severe and prolonged inflation we have been experiencing tends to generate expectations of further inflation and defensive responses to these expectations which, unfortunately, serve only to confirm them later on.

The risk has mounted that both the rate of inflation and the rate of unemployment will rise in the months and years ahead if no decisive action is taken. This is unacceptable to the government. The evidence of widespread and deep-seated concern in the country shows that it is unacceptable to all Canadians.

The severity of the problem is compounded by the need for further increases in the relative prices of some forms of energy, of some commodities, and perhaps of some classes of rents if necessary supplies of energy, commodities and rental housing are to be forthcoming. In addition, the steepness of the increase of average wages over the recent past means that those groups that have not had recent adjustment have tended to fall seriously behind. They will have to have some chance to catch up. Thus, we have to get the average rate of increase of prices and incomes down while allowing these particular increases in prices and incomes to occur.

Faced with this situation, the problem is not just to get over the worst of our current troubles, difficult as that is likely to prove. It is to reduce inflation in ways that do not store up further trouble for the future, and to find ways of improving the structure of our economy so that the same troubles do not recur.

The Government's Program for Attacking Inflation

The program that the government is setting in motion has four main elements:

1. *Fiscal and monetary policies* aimed at increasing total demand and production at a rate consistent with declining inflation.
2. *Government expenditure policies* aimed at limiting the growth of public expenditures and the rate of increase in public service employment.
3. *Structural policies* to deal with the special problems of energy, food and housing, to ensure a more efficient and competitive economy and to improve labour-management relations.
4. *A prices and incomes policy* which establishes guidelines for responsible social behaviour in determining prices and incomes of groups, together with machinery for administering these guidelines and ensuring compliance where necessary.

The government is convinced that the full participation of provincial governments and of the major interest groups in the community will be essential to the success of this program of action. As an integral part of the program, intensive consultations with the provinces and with representatives of business, labour and other interest groups are being arranged. The government is entering into these consultations anxious to hear the views and suggestions of others for improving the program.

Fiscal and Monetary Policies

The success of the government's whole program for achieving a progressive lowering of the rate of inflation, together with a sustained recovery of the growth of output and employment, will depend crucially on its success in keeping the over-all level of demand in the economy growing at a pace consistent with successively lower rates of price increase.

This is the central task of fiscal and monetary policy. The government has repeatedly emphasized its rejection of the use of severe monetary and fiscal restraint to stop inflation at heavy immediate cost in terms of unemployment and foregone output. It also rejects the notion that the guidelines will allow fiscal and monetary policy to be directed solely at the unemployment aspect of the current problem. Lowering the rate of inflation and reducing the level of unemployment must go hand in hand, and can only be gradual. It is essential for the success of any prices and incomes policy to avoid too rapid a rate of growth of demand and the development of excess pressure on resources. In a situation in which inflationary expectations are still unsettled, a monetary policy which permitted excessively rapid expansion of the money supply in an attempt to produce artificially low interest rates could not succeed. It would, in fact, be counterproductive. The government's clear determination not to accommodate continued high or increasing inflation must be embodied not only in prices and incomes policy, but also in the settings of fiscal and monetary policy.

The fiscal stance set in the June 23, 1975 budget, together with the announced intention of the Bank of Canada to allow the money supply to expand at a rate consistent with moderate real growth and a decline in the rate of inflation, constitutes an over-all demand management policy consistent with these objectives.

Government Expenditure Policies

In recent years, the federal government has introduced many new programs and expanded existing programs for the benefit of Canadians. Inevitably these steps have been reflected in rising expenditures. In particular, the federal government has endeavoured to offset the effects of inflation on those most vulnerable to it by amending much of its social welfare legislation so that payments of many benefits rise automatically with the cost of living. The federal budget has also borne a major portion of the cost of unemployment insurance.

The rising trend of increasing government expenditures has not been unique to the federal level of government.

Government Expenditures as a Per Cent of the Gross National Product
(exclusive of intergovernmental transfers)

	1965	*1970*	*1971*	*1972*	*1973*	*1974*
Total federal government	12.9	13.8	14.0	15.0	14.6	16.1
—excluding transfers to persons	8.7	9.1	9.0	9.0	8.8	9.9
Total provincial government	6.8	10.2	11.2	11.2	10.8	11.3
—excluding transfers to persons	5.0	7.1	7.9	8.1	7.8	8.3
Total local governments	8.1	9.4	9.1	8.8	8.3	8.3
Hospitals	2.1	2.8	2.9	2.8	2.7	2.8
Pension plans	—	.2	.2	.3	.3	.4
Total all governments	29.9	36.4	37.7	38.2	37.0	39.1

Source: Statistics Canada, "National Income and Expenditure Accounts".

This table shows that the expenditures of all governments have risen faster than the economy as a whole. But especially at the federal level, the growth has been most concentrated in transfers to persons, such as pensions, family allowances and unemployment benefits. Other kinds of federal expenditure maintained an almost constant 9 per cent relationship to the gross national product until 1974. Since then they have been rising largely because of the subsidy on imported oil.

A very large proportion of the federal government's expenditures are made under statutory programs, and other arrangements where there is little flexibility.

Some 56 per cent of the budgetary expenditures approved for the start of the fiscal year 1975-76 were for payments under statutory programs. These are detailed in the following table.

Statutory payments	($ Millions)
Old Age Security and Guaranteed Income Supplement	3,969
Interest on the public debt	3,575
Fiscal transfers to provinces	2,469
Family allowances	2,007
Hospital care	1,546
Unemployment insurance—government cost	890
Medicare	862
Canada Assistance Plan	701
Post-secondary education assistance	511
Military pensions	330
Railway subsidies—maintenance of branch lines	196
Payments to Quebec in lieu of conditional grants	156
Other statutory expenditures (crop insurance; guaranteed loans; forgiveness of winter works loans; salaries and pensions for judges, senators, and members of parliament; RCMP pensions; etc.)	664
Total	17,876

Contractual payments such as payments to the provinces under the manpower training program and certain CMHC housing and sewage programs, and fiscal transfers to the territories account for a further 3 per cent of expenditures.

Another 3 per cent is accounted for by formula payments, such as veterans pensions and aid to developing countries.

Another 9 per cent is accounted for by such essential support programs as consumer subsidies on petroleum products, programs relating to Indians and Eskimos, grants for regional economic expansion, and manufacturing milk subsidies to farmers.

The defence program accounts for another 8 per cent.

The operating deficits of the Crown corporations such as the CBC, Atomic Energy of Canada, etc., account for a further 2 per cent.

All other expenditures, including the construction of public buildings, the operation of the Post Office and airports, the RCMP, inspection services and all other costs of running the government account for only 19 per cent of expenditures.

Thus there is little scope for the government to reduce expenditures—or the growth in expenditures—without affecting one or more of the following:

—transfer payments which directly affect the welfare of individuals, equalization payments to provinces and other transfers paid to provinces as a one-half share of their major social programs;

—programs of essential support such as those designed to assist research and development, to help the development of our native peoples, to cushion the impact of rising international oil prices or to assist agriculture;

—the quality or quantity of service to the public.

The scope for such action has been further reduced by the cuts in expenditures and manpower already announced in the budget of June 23, 1975.

Nevertheless, the government will endeavour to avoid an increase in the total numbers employed in the public service of Canada, despite the unavoidable and desirable increases in the Post Office, the penitentiaries, the RCMP and elsewhere. All of these requirements arise out of the demands of the public for better service and protection.

Statistics Canada data on numbers on the payroll show that the rate of growth in public service employment in the period since 1969 has been somewhat higher at the provincial and local levels of government than at the federal level. For its part, the federal government has decided that the growth in the authorized level for the federal public service in 1976-77 will be held to 1.5 per cent over the level authorized in the 1975-76 Main Estimates.

This is in marked contrast to the average of about 7 per cent for the two years ending 1974-75 and the 4.1 per cent authorized for 1975-76. The equivalent of about one percentage point of the 1975-76 growth was taken away through the freezing of close to 3,000 man-years at the time of the June 23 budget.

Within the 1976-77 growth limit, it will be necessary to accommodate:

(a) additional personnel necessary in connection with the economic measures;
(b) additional personnel for police and penitentiaries; and
(c) some expansion in certain essential services.

This can only be done by first reducing the authorized man-years in all departments for 1976-77 below that originally authorized for 1975-76. In fact only those given additional resources for economic measures, for the maintenance of peace and order or for the provision of essential services will show any growth. The majority of the department will have fewer man-years in 1976-77 than in 1974-75.

The President of the Treasury Board will also issue directives prohibiting the normal replacement of office furniture, the use of first-class air travel and suspending the normal schedules for replacement of departmental automobiles. He will also require the re-imposition of the 10 per cent reduction in travel expenditures and expenditures on consultants.

Despite the limited scope for reductions in expenditures as outlined above, the federal government is determined to effect further economies wherever possible. It is also determined to participate with other governments in endeavouring to avoid increases in tax rates to limit borrowings—indeed to move to a position where both the burden of taxation and the need for borrowing can be reduced. The federal government shares the view that the trend of total spending by all governments in Canada should not rise more quickly than the trend of the gross national product.

Structural Policies

There are several structural problems which need to be addressed in a comprehensive anti-inflation program. The first relates to the need for substantial upward adjustment in particular areas of the price structure if adequate new supplies are to be forthcoming. The second relates to the need for more competition and flexibility in the economy. The third relates to the need to improve labour-management relations.

The situation in the energy field provides perhaps the clearest illustration of the difficult problems that must be overcome in finding and maintaining the right balance between a general policy of lowering the overall inflation rate and the need to permit an orderly upward adjustment of the relative prices of certain important products and services.

The underlying trends in world energy demand and supply have brought on an era of much higher relative prices for energy throughout the world.

Major structural shifts in patterns of production and consumption towards using less energy per unit of national activity are required everywhere. Major efforts are also required to develop and exploit energy supplies efficiently and to limit further increases in the real cost of energy in the future. Facing consumers and producers with higher relative prices for energy is the most important single policy available to promote more effective use and production of energy.

The government has recognized the damage which would be created by large abrupt increases in the price of energy. But the government has also recognized the necessity of allowing Canadian prices of oil and gas to rise at a measured pace toward world levels. The degree of urgency has been heightened by the somewhat disappointing reports on Canada's energy reserves which have appeared during the past year.

As was envisaged in the enactment of the Petroleum Administration Act, it will continue to be the policy of the government to permit the price of energy to rise in a series of orderly steps. But in present circumstances, it is even more important to find other ways of reducing the consumption of these scarce resources. Thus energy conservation programs will be intensified.

The future supply of housing also requires special policy attention within the program to fight inflation. There is clearly a need for more housing, both owner-occupied and rental housing, particularly for people of low and moderate incomes. To have a reasonable level of residential construction, there must be adequate incentives for builders to undertake new projects at prices, rents and carrying costs that people of low and moderate incomes can afford. Rent levels that make it unprofitable to build rental housing and mortgage rates that make home ownership expensive discourage an adequate supply of new housing. Special incentives in housing policy will be required in these circumstances, and the federal government will shortly be presenting and implementing further measures in this regard.

A particular source of increase in the price of housing has been the increase in the price of land. The fundamental answer to this problem is to increase the supply of serviced land for housing. Any attempt to control the price directly would be incompatible with this objective. Measures to deal with this problem, including action by the municipalities to speed up the approval of sub-divisions and the provision of services, will be discussed with the provinces.

Similarly, to ensure an adequate supply of food, farmers must be assured of a rate of return commensurate with the large investment of labour and capital essential to agricultural production. This return should come from the market place, but producers must be given some protection against large losses arising from highly variable and uncertain markets. They are especially vulnerable today as a result of higher and rising production costs. The government must, however, be particularly careful not to prevent increases in productivity or to impede desirable adjustments. It must also ensure that the food handling and processing sector is competitive and efficient.

Many non-food prices may have become unduly rigid as a result of government policies. The federal government intends to focus with some urgency on identifying ways in which supply bottlenecks and price rigidities in its own area of responsibility can be reduced.

The government also intends, in concert with provincial governments and with the advice of interested private groups, to identify and modify those broader aspects of government policies and programs which may have had the effect of keeping costs and prices above market levels to an extent which is clearly undesirable.

The process will take time; in the interval, the government will ask each of its departments or agencies to assess the probable impact of their policies and programs on both short-term and longer-term price trends.

Competition policy is being improved and strengthened. The government hopes that the House and Senate will soon finish work on Phase One of the revised Competition Act, and for its part plans to proceed with the introduction of Phase Two of the new competition policy—those sections dealing with monopoly and mergers—at an early date. Together with a more selective and vigorous enforcement policy, Canada's competition policy should help to ensure a more efficient economy working to the benefit of all.

The government intends to reassess the costs to the private sector of many government rules and regulations in the context of their benefits to society at large. The government further intends to continue reviewing the role of its regulatory agencies. It is important that these agencies, established to protect the public interest in matters such as the prices to be paid by the users of particular services, should conduct their affairs with an adequate appreciation of the broader problems the country faces in bringing inflation under control.

In the case of industrial relations and wage and salary determination, labour and management have for many years conducted their affairs relatively unfettered under a well-established system of collective bargaining, whereby each party strives to obtain the best deal possible for those it represents. In more settled economic circumstances the collective bargaining process has operated reasonably well. In the current inflationary climate, however, the number of friction points has increased.

The fragmentation of collective bargaining under the present system contributes little by way of keeping the broader interest in view. There are no fewer than 10,000 local unions in Canada representing some 2.5 million members, operating under various federal and provincial enactments. With each group striving to obtain what it considers to be its fair share of a limited pie and, given this degree of fragmentation, the potential for disruption is considerable. In the air industry alone, for example, there are no fewer than

70 bargaining units, each potentially able to close the industry down at any given time at great economic cost and inconvenience to the public.

The government is aware of the many critical problems that exist at present in the area of industrial relations, and in co-operation with the two groups directly involved—labour and management—it will seek practical solutions. The government has established the tripartite Canada Labour Relations Council to assist in this effort.

Prices and Incomes Policy

The government has concluded that the time has come to implement a prices and incomes policy in Canada with the following main characteristics:

1. Maximum emphasis on voluntary compliance with price and income guidelines.
2. The fullest possible degree of consultation both with the provincial governments, whose joint participation is being sought, and with business, labour and other groups.
3. Provision for statutory enforcement of guidelines in respect of key groups.
4. A determined effort to keep to a minimum the need for detailed regulation, reporting, and surveillance and thereby to keep to a minimum the size of the administrative staff involved.

A description of the principal features of the legislation, administrative machinery and guidelines is contained in the following two sections.

Legislation, Administration and Provincial Participation. The government intends to introduce legislation to provide authority to require specified groups to restrain prices and profit margins, compensation and dividends. While the emphasis of the government's approach towards these specific groups will be to seek voluntary compliance through consultation and negotiation, authority will be available to ensure that the public interest will prevail.

The specified groups subject to the legal enforcement of restraint under the legislation include the following:

(a) firms which employ more than 500 employees. For this purpose, firms are defined to include any group of corporations which would be treated as associated corporations under the Income Tax Act of Canada.
(b) firms, any or all of whose employees bargain in association with employees of other firms.
(c) firms in the construction industry which employ more than 20 employees.
(d) the federal government and all its emanations.
(e) participating provincial governments and their emanations including municipal institutions.

(f) employees of the entities referred to above.
(g) individuals or other firms that are carrying on a business that is a profession.

The legislation will also provide authority for the Governor-in-Council to add to the groups that are subject to the legislation. This power may be exercised only if the Anti-Inflation Board referred to below, upon being asked by the Governor-in-Council to consider the matter, determines that a group is of strategic importance to Canada and recommends that the group be added.

In order to clarify the guidelines, to monitor their observance and, where necessary, to begin the process of bringing certain organized groups or individuals under a system of restraint, the government will establish an Anti-Inflation Board, initially by Order-in-Council under the *Inquiries Act* and later in the proposed legislation. The terms of reference of the Board will be set out in the legislation and will involve:

—monitoring movements in prices, profits, compensation and dividends in relation to the guidelines;
—identifying actual or proposed movements that would contravene the guidelines in fact or in spirit;
—endeavouring through consultations and negotiations with the parties involved to modify actual or proposed increases to bring them within the limits and spirit of the guidelines or to reduce their inflationary effect;
—referring to an official with the authority of enforcement, to be called the Administrator in the proposed legislation, the actual or proposed movement of prices, profits, compensation and dividends if the consultations and negotiations do not lead to their modification; and
—promoting greater public understanding of the inflationary process by publishing reports, arranging public hearings and meetings, and by other means.

The Board, therefore, is designed to permit both flexibility and maximum co-operation. The Board will exercise all of the powers of a person appointed as a commissioner under Part I of the *Inquiries Act* and will, once the legislation is in force, have additional powers to obtain relevant information.

Where the Board or the responsible Minister determines that there are reasonable grounds for believing that an actual or proposed movement of prices, profits, compensation and dividends has contravened or is likely to contravene the guidelines, the Board or Minister may advise the Administrator to this effect. The Administrator, an official to be appointed by the Governor-in-Council, will attempt to establish whether the supplier or employer has contravened or is likely to contravene the guidelines. He will also attempt to determine whether there are circumstances that justify the supplier or employer in contravening the guidelines.

In those cases where the Administrator finds that the guidelines will be or have been contravened without good reason, the Act will empower the Administrator to order that:

—the person be enjoined from contravening or continuing to contravene the guidelines; and

—the person be required to pay to the government, or back to the buyer, as appropriate, the whole or any portion of excess payment or receipt, as the case may be, arising from that contravention of the guidelines.

Those persons against whom the Administrator has acted will, during a period of sixty days, have a right of appeal. The legislation will establish an Anti-Inflation Appeal Tribunal, consisting of a chairman and others to be appointed by the government. The Tribunal will dispose of appeals by either dismissing them or by allowing them in one of three ways. The order of the Administrator may be entirely rescinded, the order may be varied or the matter may be referred back to the Administrator for reconsideration. An appellant will be able to appeal the decision of the Appeal Tribunal to the Federal Court of Appeal. Further, the Cabinet within thirty days of an order by the Administrator, will be permitted under the terms of the legislation to rescind the order of the Administrator or instruct him to vary his order.

The federal government is obliging itself and all its crown corporations and agencies to follow the guidelines with respect to both prices and compensation. The federal government is inviting the provincial governments to participate in the program by adhering to the guidelines and submitting to the legislation in the same way as the federal government, both with regard to their own operations and the operations of provincial enterprises and agencies and municipalities. It is being proposed to the provinces that the Anti-Inflation Board would establish a distinct public sector panel to deal with prices and compensation in the public sector, and they would be invited to nominate some of the members of such a panel. Participating provinces would be expected to enact such legislation as may be required. Any province not prepared to participate would be asked to enact legislation essentially similar to the national regime.

In addition to participating in the program in these ways, the provincial governments are being asked to undertake responsibility for a program of rent control and to regulate professional fees in accordance with the guidelines. It is expected that federal-provincial consultative machinery will be established in these important areas of the program.

The Initial Guidelines

INTRODUCTION

This section sets out the broad guidelines which all Canadians are being asked to follow. The government fully anticipates that the great majority of Canadians will be prepared to conduct their affairs in accord with the guidelines.

It therefore expects that the powers of enforcement applicable to specified groups identified under the legislation will have to be used only rarely and in exceptional cases.

These guidelines are based on the principles proposed by the government in the consensus discussions of last winter, a description of which was tabled in the House of Commons by the Minister of Finance on May 8. These proposals have benefited greatly from the discussions with representatives of business, labour and the provincial governments.

In this policy statement the guidelines are referred to as "initial" guidelines. They have deliberately been so labelled in order to emphasize the willingness of the government to modify them in their technical aspects, in the light of considerations advanced in Parliament or Committees of Parliament, in the consultations with provinces, business and labour, by the Anti-Inflation Board or by other interested parties. In moving into an unfamiliar field of administration, it is inevitable that important considerations will have been overlooked. The government in addition wishes to have the flexibility to modify the guidelines as the program proceeds, the state of expectations in the economy returns to more normal levels and structural changes in the economy take place.

The guidelines will be effective October 14. For purpose of those specified groups subject to legal enforcement of restraint, the guidelines will be issued as regulations under the legislation. Those regulations will be deemed to be effective October 14.

Guidelines for Price and Profits

General Principle. The general principle is that increases in prices should be limited to amounts no more than required to cover net increases in costs. The precise form of the objective will be adapted to the different circumstances of different kinds of suppliers, but should lead to broadly equivalent behaviour when these differences are taken into account.

Firms Which Are Able to Allocate Costs to Individual Products. Firms which are able to allocate costs to individual products are expected to increase prices of these products by no more than increases in costs allocated to this product. Similarly firms are expected to reduce prices if costs decrease. If the firm can establish that the price in effect at the time of the announcement of the program was not typical, it may select another price which was in effect during the previous thirty days.

In this example, material costs rise by 6 per cent or 36 cents per unit of output. Wage rates rise 10 per cent, but the increase in output from 5,000 units to 5,200 units is obtained with the same labour force due to an increase of productivity. Thus labour costs per unit of output rise only 5.8 per cent or 69 cents. Taking labour and material costs together, the net increase in costs per unit is $1.05. Thus, the firm is entitled to increase its price by $1.05. Its profit per unit of output remains the same, but with larger volume total profits rise by 4 per cent. In relation to sales, however, the margin of profit declines from 10 per cent to 9.5 per cent.

	Prior to October 14, 1975		*After October 14, 1975*	
	Per unit	*Total*	*Per unit*	*Total*
Volume		5,000		5,200
Employment		5		5
Sales	$20.00	$100,000	$21.05	$109,472
Less costs:				
Materials	$ 6.00	$ 30,000	$ 6.36	$ 33,072
Labour	$12.00	$ 60,000	$12.69	$ 66,000
Total costs	$18.00	$ 90,000	$19.05	$ 99,072
Profit	$ 2.00	$ 10,000	$ 2.00	$ 10,400
Profit margin		10%		9.5%

In setting prices which will be in effect for some period of time ahead, firms may make increases in prices on the basis of forecasts of cost increases.

These forecasts, however, should be based on known changes, or changes which can be expected to occur within the period for which the firms normally set prices in advance and which can be foreseen with a reasonable degree of assurance.

To compute the increase in costs which may be passed on, it will be necessary to estimate the cost of a product on or near October 14, 1975. A similar estimate of the cost of the product in question must be made at the date the selling price is to be increased. The difference between the two cost estimates is the maximum amount by which prices should be changed.

Costs may vary considerably from day to day and many firms may not customarily compute their costs on a daily basis. Therefore the two required cost estimates should be made on a reasonable basis, and both should be consistent with the firm's usual accounting practices. Future cost increases that have been recognized in the October 14, 1975 selling price should be treated as if they had already occurred. They will therefore form part of the October 14 estimate of product cost.

Firms Which Are Unable to Allocate Costs to Individual Products. If a firm finds it impossible to allocate costs to individual products, it should price its products in such a way as to leave its percentage pre-tax net profit margin no higher than 95 per cent of its average percentage pre-tax net profit margin in the last five completed fiscal years. The Anti-Inflation Board will be prepared to provide information on appropriate net margins to firms which have not existed long enough to have a five-year average.

For the purposes of the percentage net profit margin guideline, profit will be defined as total operating *revenue* (computed in accordance with generally accepted accounting principles applied on a consistent basis) which can be reasonably regarded as having been earned in the normal course of business by the firm *minus* the *costs* allowable for the purpose of justifying price increases. The percentage net profit margin will be defined as profits divided by total operating revenue.

Definition of Costs. The definition of costs allowable for purposes of justifying an increase in any price is that portion of the unavoidable outlays and expenses of the supplier (computed in accordance with generally accepted accounting principles applied on a consistent basis) that can be reasonably regarded as having been made or incurred for the purpose of gaining revenue from the sale. The regulations will include a detailed list of items which should be excluded from allowable costs. Included in this list will be such items as losses resulting from occurrences which are not typical of the normal business activities of the supplier, capital losses incurred by the supplier, certain expenses which are incurred at the discretion of management, and the excess over the fair market value of goods purchased in non-arm's-length transactions.

Frequency of Price Changes. Firms are expected to refrain from increasing the price of any individual product more frequently than once every three months, except where this would impose severe hardships on the firm. Retailers and wholesalers will be exempt from this requirement.

Distribution Sector. In the distribution sector customary pricing policies are generally based on gross margins. Retail and wholesale firms should not increase markups on their various merchandise categories. Where the nature of the trade makes the application of this limitation impracticable, such firms should not exceed the percentage gross margin realized during the last complete fiscal year before October 14, 1975. The latter proposal would permit firms to follow their customary pricing practices and vary markups on particular products in line with market forces but restrict the gross profit margin expressed as a percentage of total sales. If a firm finds it necessary to follow the more general percentage gross profit margin rule, it should ensure that no one product line has an excessive increase in its markup.

Under the guidelines for the distribution sector, percentage net profit margins would not change significantly if operating costs rose at the same rate as material costs. If operating costs rose faster than the costs of goods sold, profit margins would be reduced. In some cases, operating costs may rise so quickly that absolute profits would fall. In such a situation firms would be justified in raising prices to restore the level of absolute profits to the level in the last complete fiscal year. If the cost of goods sold rose appreciably faster than operating costs, net profit margins would increase. In such cases, the firm should reduce markups in order to reduce its percentage net profit margin to the level in the last complete fiscal year.

Food Prices. Prices received by farmers and fishermen for their products are exempt from the guidelines. The operations of marketing boards will be discussed with the provincial governments to ensure that they are consistent with the guidelines.

The general obligations related to prices and profits would apply to processors and distributors of foodstuffs.

Exports. Firms supplying the international market will be expected to sell abroad at international market prices and to ensure that, in selling products or services to a person or firm with whom they do not deal at arm's length within the meaning of subsection 251(1) of the Income Tax Act, the product or service is sold at its fair market value. In general, firms also supplying the domestic market will be expected to ensure that the domestic market is fully satisfied in terms of quantity, at a price consistent with the general guidelines. If a firm can demonstrate that it is setting its domestic prices in accordance with the cost-pass-through rule, and that its overall net margin on all sales satisfies the percentage pre-tax net margin rule, it will be regarded as having followed the guidelines.

If, however, a firm can demonstrate to the Anti-Inflation Board the impracticality of or hardship entailed in following the general guidelines, the following arrangements are proposed. The firm would price its domestic sales in a way consistent with the guidelines, and would be subject to a special levy on the profits derived from its export sales. If a firm can demonstrate to the Anti-Inflation Board that it would be impractical or harmful to the national interest for it to price in the domestic market differently than in the international market, the firm will not be regarded as having failed to follow the guidelines if it prices all its products at international prices, but would be subject to the special levy on all its profits. Once firms have received permission to be treated in a particular way, they will continue to be treated that way for the whole of the program.

The nature and form of this special levy will be announced following consultations with interested parties.

Financial Institutions and Interest Rates. Banks and other financial institutions are expected to conform to the general principle: that is to say, increases in service charges and interest rates charged by these institutions should be justified by increases in the interest rates which they pay and increases in their operating and other expenses. It would not be feasible to control interest rates determined in financial markets given their nature and the importance of international capital flows to Canada. It should be stressed, however, that interest rates may be lower on average if the program is successful in establishing a widespread expectation that the rate of inflation will steadily decline. Insurance premiums should be increased only by the amounts required to cover net increases in the cost of claims and operating expenses.

Regulated Industries. Where industries are subject to regulation under existing statutes, as in transportation and communications, federal regulatory agencies are to use their powers over prices and the quality of service in order to ensure conformity with the program. The provincial governments are being asked to instruct their regulatory agencies to do likewise.

Construction Industry. Whenever possible the cost-pass-through principle will apply to firms in the construction industry. For example, a contractor continuing to build houses of a similar standard and quality to those which he has been building in the recent past should increase the price per square foot only by the amount required to cover increased costs. Where cost allocation is not possible, the percentage net profit margin rule will apply, but there will be consultations with the industry to adapt it to the special circumstances which may prevail. Construction, engineering and other firms bidding on individual contracts for custom designed structures, projects and products are requested to follow their customary tendering procedures. Monitoring will take place to ensure that competitive conditions are being maintained.

Rents. The provincial governments are being asked to undertake responsibility for implementing a program of rent control based upon the following principles: (a) increases up to a certain percentage would be permissible, (b) increases above this percentage must be justified on the basis of increased costs, (c) new structures where rents have not yet been established would be exempt from control for at least five years after completion of the building, in the event that rent control should be in effect for that length of time. This is to ensure an adequate incentive for construction of new rental accommodation.

Selection of Guidelines. The Anti-Inflation Board will have the right to advise firms which guidelines they should follow. Thus, the Board may represent to a firm that it can allocate costs to individual products and therefore should follow the cost-pass-through guideline rather than the percentage net profit margin guideline. It may advise a firm engaged in production as well as distribution that it should follow a single guideline or apply different guidelines to the different operations.

Exceptions. None of the guidelines requires a firm to price in a way which will perpetuate or create a loss in its overall operations.

A firm will be regarded as having acted in accordance with the program if its profit per unit of output or percentage net profit margin exceeded the guidelines as a result of unusual productivity gains resulting from the efforts of the firm, or of favourable cost developments which could not reasonably have been anticipated.

Guidelines for Incomes

Compensation: General Principles. There are four elements in the guidelines for wages and salaries and other forms of compensation. These are:

1. The basic protection factor.
2. Share in increases in national productivity.
3. Adjustment for past wage and salary experience.
4. Minimum and maximum dollar increases.

These guidelines set the upper limits to increases in compensation which should be paid. Employees and employers will be free to negotiate new collective agreements and employers to increase pay scales for non-unionized employees, but these upper limits should not be exceeded. Future increases provided for in contracts and agreements in force as of October 14, 1975 including cost-of-living adjustments, will be exempt from the guidelines. Where agreement has been reached by October 14, 1975 on compensation increases to be incorporated in new contracts, such increases will also be exempt from the guidelines. Special consideration will be given to those cases where contracts have expired and negotiations are underway, where the expired contract was signed prior to the beginning of 1974.

Existing contracts may not be reopened without the consent of the Anti-Inflation Board. Employers are not allowed to agree during the program to pay increases after the termination of the program for services rendered during the program.

The Basic Protection Factor. The basic protection factor provides a substantial degree of the protection that will be afforded to workers against price rises in the future. It will be supplemented, as the program proceeds, by the application of a retrospective provision that any excess of the cost of living increase over the increase provided for in the basic protection factor for that year may be included in the allowable compensation increase of the following year.

In order to give guidance to those who wish to conclude multi-year contracts as well as to those who wish to make agreements for one year only, the basic protection factor will consist of three numbers, applicable to the first, second and third years of the contract, agreement or award. The initial set of numbers comprising the basic protection factor will be 8 per cent for the first year of a new contract, 6 per cent for the second year and 4 per cent for the third year. These basic numbers may be changed from time to time, probably more often than once a year, as the program proceeds and the rate of inflation in the economy changes.

By way of amplification, it may be explained how this feature of the guidelines would operate in the second year of the program. Suppose that the cost of living index had risen by 9 per cent in the first year by comparison with the basic protection factor for that year of 8 per cent. Workers under two-year contracts would be allowed a 1 per cent increase to allow for the difference in the first year between the cost-of-living increase and the basic protection factor of that year, plus the 6 per cent basic protection factor provided in their two-year contract. Workers entering into new contracts at the conclusion of contracts negotiated under the guidelines would also be allowed the 1 per cent increase that provides the retrospective protection plus whatever is the current basic protection factor pertaining to the first year of new contracts.

If the consumer price index has increased by less than the basic protection factor, no adjustment need be made.

Share in Increases in National Productivity. In addition to the basic protection factor, the guidelines provide for a share in increases in national productivity. The standard amount provided for this in the initial period of the program is 2 per cent per annum. This compares with the average increase in productivity, defined as the real gross national product divided by the number of employed persons, of 2.08 per cent for the period 1954-74.

Adjustment for Past Wage and Salary Experience. A further element in the compensation guidelines is related to the past experience of each group. Some groups have fallen behind in the last two or three years because of the time at which their contracts were negotiated or for other reasons. It is essential that they should be provided with an opportunity to catch up. On the other hand, some groups have obtained relatively large increases in this period, and some element of adjustment for this situation is necessary if the program is to succeed.

The adjustment for past experience is to be calculated as follows. The average annual increase in a group's compensation in the last two years or over the life of the existing contract, whichever is the greater, is compared to the average annual increase in the consumer price index over the same period plus 2 per cent. If the group's increase was the same as the national benchmark, no adjustment is made. If its increase was 1 per cent smaller, then 1 per cent is added to the basic protection factor, plus the share in increased national productivity. If its increase was 2 per cent smaller, then 2 per cent is added. If its increase was 1 per cent larger, the 1 per cent is subtracted from the basic protection factor plus the share in increased national productivity. If its increase was 2 per cent larger, then 2 per cent is subtracted. This adjustment factor cannot exceed plus or minus 2 per cent.

Thus, groups that have fallen behind may not recover all their losses in the first year. Losses will be carried forward into the future so that groups which incurred substantial losses in the recent past may achieve above-average gains in subsequent years. On the other hand, no group is asked to accept less than the basic protection factor as a result of this guideline.

Allowable Increases in the Initial Period

Difference between group's average gain and the national benchmark	−4	−3	−2	−1	0	1	2	3	4
Basic protection factor	8	8	8	8	8	8	8	8	8
Share in national productivity	2	2	2	2	2	2	2	2	2
Past wage experience factor	2	2	2	1	0	−1	−2	−2	−2
Allowable increase	12	12	12	11	10	9	8	8	8

Minimum and Maximum Dollar Increases. The fourth element in the compensation guidelines places minimum and maximum dollar limits on permissible increases. At the lower end of the scale, increases of $600 may be paid in any event, and regardless of the size of the increases received in the past two years. The $600 figure represents a 12 per cent increase for those earning $5,000 a year, about the minimum wage. At the upper end of the scale, no group, no matter what the change in compensation over the last two years, should have an average increase for its members of more than $2,400. This represents 8 per cent, the initial basic protection factor, of a salary of

Allowable Increases by Income Level and Past Wage and Salary Experience

Difference between group's average gain in last two years and national benchmark	−4	−3	−2	−1	0	1	2	3	4
Income—$	*Percentage and dollar increases*								
5,000	12%	12%	12%	12%	12%	12%	12%	12%	12%
	600	600	600	600	600	600	600	600	600
7,000	12%	12%	12%	11%	10%	9%	8.6%	8.6%	8.6%
	840	840	840	770	700	630	600	600	600
10,000	12%	12%	12%	11%	10%	9%	8%	8%	8%
	1200	1200	1200	1100	1000	900	800	800	800
25,000	9.6%	9.6%	9.6%	9.6%	9.6%	9%	8%	8%	8%
	2400	2400	2400	2400	2400	2250	2000	2000	2000
50,000	4.8%	4.8%	4.8%	4.8%	4.8%	4.8%	4.8%	4.8%	4.8%
	2400	2400	2400	2400	2400	2400	2400	2400	2400

$30,000. The table above illustrates the effect of this guideline rule on different income groups. Someone earning $7,000 a year could get an increase of 8.6 per cent even if he had obtained large increases in recent years while someone earning $50,000 a year could get only a 4.8 per cent increase in any circumstance. The proportion of employees who will benefit from the minimum dollar provision will increase as the rate of inflation declines.

Groups Covered. The guidelines apply to "groups" defined either as bargaining units or as combinations of employees which employers have established for the unilateral determination and administration of pay. Although the principles apply to groups rather than individuals, some groups such as executive groups may be very small, and some in very particular circumstances may even have only one member. The $2,400 maximum rule means that the average increase to all executives in a certain category cannot exceed $2,400, but some executives may receive more than $2,400 providing others receive less.

Forms of Compensation Covered. All forms of compensation, including for example fringe benefits, bonuses and stock options, are to be included in compensation for the purposes of the guidelines. Where it is administratively impossible to include any of these elements in compensation for purposes of calculating the past wage experience factor, these elements may be excluded from that calculation.

Promotions and Reclassification. Increases in wages and salaries resulting from promotions from one established level to another are not covered by the guidelines. Employers should not, however, modify their existing promotion policies or their systems of job classification currently in force for the purpose of evading the guidelines. It should be pointed out that employers are obliged not only to limit the increases in pay scales for each category of employees in a group, but to avoid changing the proportion of employees in the various categories in a way which would result in an increase in average pay for the group in excess of the guidelines.

Piece Rates and Commissions. The guidelines are not intended to prevent individuals from increasing their earnings under existing piece work, commission or production pay plans. When changes are made in such plans the effect will be determined by assuming the same amounts and kinds of output achieved in the past. The effect of changes in the plan will be subject to the guidelines. No limit will be placed on increases in earnings, under the new or revised plan, resulting from greater output. Changes in premium rates, such as overtime, must be included as a form of compensation.

Cases Where Groups Cover Wide Ranges in Incomes. If a group has members some of whom would be eligible for the $600 minimum rule, and others who would not, members eligible for the $600 may be excluded in determining the average increase.

Exceptions. It is difficult to develop a set of rules covering wages which are wholly equitable and capable of allowing wages to continue to play their important role in the allocation of resources. There will, therefore, be exceptions to the above guidelines. If an employer can demonstrate that he cannot attract or hold workers at existing wages and that an increase above the guidelines is necessary, the employer will not be regarded as having breached the guidelines.

There may also be other grounds for exceptions, such as increases necessary to maintain long-established historical relationships between wages in closely related groups and other special cases of equity. Employers may also grant increases in compensation above the guidelines if such increases result from taking measures to improve the health or safety of the employees while at work, to eliminate restrictive work practices, to offset experience deficiencies in pension funds, or to eliminate sex discrimination in pay practices.

Professional Income. Increases in fees for professional services, such as the services of doctors, lawyers and accountants should be governed by the same general principles as apply to other prices and incomes. Specifically, professional fees should be increased only by the amounts required to cover the increased costs of providing the services and to improve the net income of the self-employed professional person by the same amount as would be available to the salaried professional person. Thus the $2,400 maximum increase would apply in the determination of professional fees. Professionals would, of course, have the right to increase their incomes by more than $2,400 if that increase reflected increases in workload. The basic fee schedule must not be increased, however, in a way which would allow the average professional working the same amount as in the base year to increase his income by more than the guidelines permit.

The provincial governments are being asked to use the guidelines as the basis for setting fee schedules in areas such as health where they have direct control, and to use their powers and influence to ensure that in other areas fee schedule changes are in conformity with the guidelines.

Dividends. The general principle will be that there will be no increases in the first year in the dollar level of dividends per share from the last completed fiscal year. Exemptions may be granted in such cases as where a firm could show that an increase was necessary in order to raise new equity capital or a firm could show that last year's dividend was clearly atypically low.

Conclusion

Canada today is confronted by major challenges and major opportunities. We are richly endowed with resources in a world that is becoming increasingly short of them. But we must meet the challenges that now face us if we are to realize fully the opportunities unfolding before the nation.

What is required is a broad national program and a concerted national effort to resolve the serious problems that have emerged out of rapid and far-reaching changes in economic conditions and circumstances at home and abroad over the past few years.

As a first essential, it is imperative that we take determined action as a nation to halt and reverse the spiral of costs and prices that jeopardizes the whole fabric of our economy and of our society. This will require the exercise of restraint by every sector and the pursuit of fiscal and monetary policies aimed at ensuring sustained and stable economic growth. Over the longer term, we must make our economic system more innovative, dynamic and efficient by reducing existing rigidities and intensifying competition. We must deal with major structural problems so as to ensure an adequate supply of energy, food and housing to meet our needs in the years ahead. And finally we must ensure that sufficient physical and financial resources will become available to complete the massive new capital investment that is required over the next decade and more, to increase substantially our productive capacity, employment and our real standard of living.

In all of these undertakings, governments at all levels can and must provide leadership and direction, but they cannot act alone. All sectors of the economy must actively cooperate together. This in turn requires the fullest possible discussion and consultation among us on how best to achieve our mutual goals.

The attack on inflation set out in this paper is designed to ensure that the recovery of our economy from its present recession leads to healthy and enduring growth of employment and real incomes. These basic objectives are shared by labour, by business, by governments and indeed by all Canadians. We all have a compelling interest to work together to foster and promote the national interest.

Notes

*Government of Canada, "Attack on Inflation: a program of national action," 14 October, 1975 (reproduced by permission of Information Canada).

43 Wage-Price Controls and the Road to Anarchy *

Richard Rohmer

Ten days have passed since the Thanksgiving pronouncement of the Prime Minister decreeing the imposition of a scheme of prices and incomes controls against a carefully selected set of workers and corporations within the Canadian nation.

In those 10 days the true philosophy of the Prime Minister has emerged, together with his lower-than-a-snake's-belly regard for democracy, Parliament, the workers of Canada, the fundamental rights of the citizens of this nation and equity and justice.

Are these words justified? Let's look at the evidence. Fifteen months ago, July 8, 1974, a federal election was held which returned Mr. Trudeau to power with a majority. The main issue of that campaign was whether prices and incomes controls should be imposed. The Conservative leader proposed controls. Mr. Trudeau was against them.

For the voter the issue was as clear cut as any in modern times. And for Mr. Trudeau nothing could have been simpler—there should be no prices and incomes controls.

The *Globe and Mail* of May 28, 1974, carried this report of a politicking foray into Metropolitan Toronto:

"He (Trudeau) said wage and price controls would not work in Canada because a third of what Canadians consume comes from overseas, and the prices of these goods cannot be frozen by Canada.

" 'The application of the controls the Conservatives are talking about leads to pretty terrifying results.' "

The controls the Conservatives were talking about were general and not discriminatory. If they could be called terrifying, then the selective scheme the Prime Minister has imposed against the expressed will of the voters can be called not only terrifying but also appalling, inequitable, unjust, unfair, authoritarian, indeed totalitarian, and a concerted attack on the productive people of this nation—the unionized workers and the professional people of Canada.

But there's more.

From a balmy day in Timmins, June 28, 1974, the following newspaper report emerged:

"TIMMINS (Staff)—Prime Minister Pierre Trudeau maintained his onslaught on Conservative price and income restraint policies before a large noon-hour crowd here yesterday.

"Mr. Trudeau said the proposed 90-day freeze, followed by up to two years of controls, would take vast numbers of bureaucrats to administer. Even then, it wouldn't work, he said.

" 'You can't freeze executive salaries and dividends because there are too many loopholes to squeeze through.'

"Mr. Trudeau said Conservative Leader Robert Stanfield had already said he would not freeze the prices of farm produce and fish. He could not freeze the prices of U.S. imports or Arab oil, and he admitted he would exempt housing prices.

" 'So what's he going to freeze?' Mr. Trudeau shouted. 'Your wages. He's going to freeze your wages.' "

The majority of people bought the Liberals' platform and promise that if elected they would not impose prices and income controls. . . .

Notwithstanding this democratic direction of the people the Prime Minister and his colleagues have imposed prices and incomes controls in Canada. They are dropping on selected union and professional workers, large corporations, and the construction industry a penalizing, restraining freeze, backed up by jail sentences and fines in a discriminatory infringement on civil rights and liberties never before attempted in this nation except in wartime.

In my opinion, the Prime Minister had a democratic obligation to the people of Canada to place his program of prices and incomes controls before the House when it convened on Oct. 14. Then he should have attended upon the Governor General to ask for dissolution of the House so the government could seek the approval of the voters in a general election.

What about the labor unions?

When the decree came down from the mount it trapped about 500,000 workers in mid-negotiation. However, one major exception was made for the 22,000 mail handlers and clerks who are now on strike, bringing the mail service in this country to a halt once again.

Hang on for a minute. There is news from the West. In Winnipeg the Prime Minister has lowered the boom. It isn't written into law anywhere but the Prime Minister will instruct Mr. Pepin, the newly appointed chairman of the Anti-Inflation Review Board (which makes him the second most powerful man in Canada—"by appointment," of course) how to deal with any striking unions, including the postal workers.

The newspaper report says this: "Winnipeg—Postal workers will gain nothing by strikes because any wage increase beyond the guidelines will be taxed away, Prime Minister Trudeau said yesterday.

" 'We'll just tax it out of your pockets afterwards, so there's not much point to strike.' "

This bald, naked demonstration of one man's newly assumed authoritarian, totalitarian powers must send shivers of apprehension along the spine of every freedom-loving Canadian, be he or she a labor union member, a professional person or any other individual who works for a living.

If the trade unions of this nation reject this discriminatory, authoritarian action of the Prime Minister—and I cannot see any choice for them but to do so—then I predict they will have no recourse but to take actions such as a general strike which will bring Canada to the brink of an abyss which I could never have believed possible—the abyss of anarchy.

With this ruthless decision made, why do Mr. Trudeau and Mr. Mackasey continue this stupid facade of letting the Canadian people and the entire economy suffer through a futile strike? Why not do the sensible thing in the interests of the public and the postal workers—take legislation into Parliament to end the strike immediately? This kind of action would be gentle in comparison to the steps the government has taken in the past 10 days.

What has caused the Prime Minister to invoke the demon "inflation" for the purpose of pointing at the labor unions and the manufacturing resource and service industries of this country and saying: "It's your fault! So we're going to get you!"?

In my view his arbitrary, selective, imposition of controls will serve to draw attention away from the real inflation culprit, no other than the Prime Minister himself, his cabinet colleagues and that cosy cadre of at least 450,790 civil servants (up from 378,617 in '70).

From a slight surplus of income against revenues in 1970 the federal government forecast in its June, 1975, budget a cash deficit for fiscal 1975-76 at $5.3 billion (the forecast in the November '74 budget was $3 billion). More recent private projections move toward a $7 billion deficit for this period.

Against this sordid background, which demonstrates a runaway growth of the bureaucracy and an apparently uncontrollable government spending syndrome (in combination these two factors are the biggest cause of inflation in Canada), what does the Prime Minister offer to do about federal spending? The answer is nothing.

And where is freedom and where is privacy now that Mr. Pepin, Mrs. Plumptre and their agents can, in the name of the omnipresent state, finger through every corporate file and every income tax return of every person who has the unacceptable quality of being a productive Canadian worker?

By what right has this government the power to control what you and I earn or what profits your firms can make when it refuses to control or cut back its own spending at this so-called time of crisis? It has none whatsoever in equity or justice. It does have the right in law because it has a majority in the House. But even that right is questionable because the Prime Minister and his colleagues obtained that majority by hoodwinking the people into voting for the Prime Minister, who stood for and represented to the people a policy of no prices and incomes controls.

And what about the length of time these controls are to be in effect? For six or 12 months? Until inflation is in hand, say back to 8 per cent from its current 11 per cent and controls are no longer needed?

No way. The government likes this new-fangled power so it's going to be three years come hell or high water.

And after that another three years? Or will we have the federal government as a permanent Orwellian Big Brother by 1984? My belief is this—as of Oct. 14, 1975, there is a new, government controlled economic system in place in this country. Free enterprise in Canada was buried alive on Thanksgiving Day.

And on that day the nation was placed on a path which leads directly to anarchy, to calamitous confrontations between government and the affected sectors of society, and to the deliberate dissolution of parliamentary democracy as we have known it.

At this time I fear for my nation.

Notes

*Toronto *Star*, 28 October, 1975 (reproduced by permission of the *Star*).

44 The Non-Economics of Anti-Inflation *

D. V. Smiley

In 1961 Frank Scott wrote of the increasing influence of fiscal and monetary policies as economic regulators and the effect of these developments in blurring the respective jurisdictions of the federal and provincial governments. He said, "The lawyers are moving out and the economists are moving in." It may well be that in the new regime promulgated by the federal government on October 14 the economists will in turn move out, although it is perhaps more accurate to say that what is in process of being displaced is the economist's way of looking at the world which has deeply influenced even those of us who have not been sanctified by professional training in the craft.

Perhaps the economists will not surrender easily. In the statement on anti-inflation policies issued by John Crispo, Douglas Hartle and their colleagues early in December 1975, the judgement, in my mind an accurate one, was made that the effective control of inflation made necessary a radical restructuring of power in Canadian society. Now an economist who discovers power after being employed in denying its existence—at least so far as matters within his professional purview are involved—throughout his adult life characteristically manifests a bemusement akin to that of an elderly virgin precipitously introduced to sex, neither of them in the immediate excitement aware that the newly-found phenomenon is of considerable complexity. However that may be, in its present difficulties the country will need all the help it can get—particularly perhaps from the economists who persist in the more usual kinds of economic analysis. We shall also need the social psychologists and the ethical philosophers. And because our situation poses questions of power and justice and the relation between them in very dramatic and urgent forms, the political scientists may come to have something useful to say too because their discipline in its origins was focused on these concerns.

To begin with justice. R. H. Tawney in his *Religion and the Rise of Capitalism*, in my view the most beautifully written book of social analysis in recent times, traced the process by which the ongoing march of liberal capitalism removed economic conduct from the judgements of religious morality. The Anti-Inflation Review Board is charged with nothing less than putting Humpty-Dumpty together again. It is devoutly to be hoped that someone in the bowels of the AIRB bureaucracy has been charged with urgency to distil and to put in operational form the conclusions of the mediaeval schoolmen about the just wage, the just price and usury—a project of infinitely more relevance to our current difficulties than the tendentious exercises in contriving "alternative futures" with which an increasing number of researchers on the Ottawa pay-roll busy themselves.

Even with all the assistance they can get, the task set for our new economic czars is clearly impossible. The prevailing distribution of income in Canada as in other western nations has been determined by a complex process involving skill, luck, inheritance, market power, access to political power, historical contingency and a broad consensus about equity whose most important element was agreement that those who have pleasant and satisfying occupations should be rewarded more than those who do not. It is impossible to defend this system of rewards by reference to any conceivable formulation of distributive justice or, alternatively, the functional necessity of inducing certain kinds of economic behaviour. But the AIRB is handed the responsibility both of evolving and applying *some* standard of justice and of perpetuating elements of the existing distribution which have been made by processes to which justice was irrelevant. Poor Pepin!

The Canadian community *has* evolved certain standards of economic justice, although these seem not directly applicable to our new circumstances. We have advanced on the income-maintenance front. Progress has been made in removing the financial barriers between citizens and certain public amenities defined as being within the social minimum. But in its most crucial element economic justice in Canada has come to be defined largely in terms of territorial considerations, in attempts to equalize the range and standard of public services and the available economic opportunities both among provinces and regions and within individual provinces. This kind of thrust is clearly compatible with perpetuating or even exaggerating inequalities within particular regions, provinces or smaller areas and at any rate has little direct relevance to the work of the new bureaucratic apparatus for inflation control.

Unless inflationary pressures in Canada are abated largely by influences arising from outside its borders, the new programs announced in mid-October 1975 will almost inevitably lead to a fundamental realignment of power in the national community. There are two alternatives here, which I shall designate as "plebiscitary" and "corporatist" respectively. A plebiscitary regime is one in which those who wield final and authoritative political power are exclusively sustained by and restrained by the wills of individual citizens without the mediation of either private groups or of governmental institutions less immediately responsive to citizen opinion. Corporatism involves the absorption of the major social and economic institutions of the national community into the apparatus of the state.

A plebiscitary scenario might go something like this. As the government and the AIRB under the pressure of time—and perhaps the demonstrated incapacity of their policies to restrain inflation—make an increasing number of inevitably arbitrary decisions about wages, prices and profits almost every important interest group in the economic sphere is aroused. Faced with such mounting opposition the Prime Minister causes an election to be called and makes this kind of appeal, "We are committed to controlling inflation. We went the voluntary route. We later enacted selective controls. We have asked Canadians in every way we know how to dampen their economic expectations. We know most Canadians want their national efforts to succeed but our policies have been and are being frustrated by those organized interests in the business, labour and agricultural sectors who are too greedy and too undisciplined to restrain their demands in the interests of the wider community. The basic issue of this election is who is to govern Canada—these special interests and their allies in the opposition parties or those whom by your votes you have elected. I pledge to all of you that if I and my party are returned we shall take whatever measures are necessary to banish once and for all this scourge of inflation." A Liberal victory in such an election would almost inevitably be followed by an increase in the comprehensiveness and ruthlessness of anti-inflation measures.

According to an excellent analysis by Wayne Cheveldayoff in the *Globe and Mail* of December 10, 1975, Mr. Trudeau and his colleagues prefer the corporatist alternative to the plebiscitary. One element of the new economic order as projected is to be industry-wide collective bargaining. But much more crucially, there are to be new institutions of "co-determination" by which a small number of representatives of government, business and labour from time to time come together to divide up the national income.

In the earlier days of the Trudeau regime Canada proceeded a considerable distance towards corporatism in fields other than the economic. For a period, the Department of the Secretary of State became the paymaster of the youth counter-culture. Grants flowed freely to ethnic organizations. The government activated and gave financial support to associations of the deprived such as Indians, residents of the inner city and poverty groups. With the honourable exception of the Canadian Civil Liberties Association, human rights associations came to exist largely on federal largesse. By way of new legislation related to campaign finance, the political parties themselves became drawn in to the state apparatus. Research has come to be largely funded by government and scholars are prodded and pushed into doing that kind of research that their political masters decide from time to time to be relevant. On the whole fortunately, the current financial austerity in Ottawa has resulted in some retreat from corporatism in these non-economic spheres and re-opened the possibilities of genuinely private varieties of associational life.

Corporatism in economic matters will require a much more radical restructuring of institutions and of power relations. It was the mistaken assumption of the exercise undertaken by the Prices and Incomes Commission in 1969 and 1970 that major economic decisions could be made by joint agreement among representatives of government, business and labour. This assumption is now being reviewed. But the distribution of power in the Canadian community is both inegalitarian *and* fragmented. In the context of government–business–labour relations the representative role of, say, a business leader might include one or more of these elements: (1) his personal influence within the business community, (2) his ability to commit his own corporation, (3) his ability to commit other corporations than his own, either on an industry-wide or an "estate-wide" (i.e. private industry-wide) basis. It is now this third component which is absent. Is it reasonable to expect that a body of manageable size could commit the investment and pricing policies of Canadian corporations, including of course those which are parts of multinational enterprises? Is it conceivable that the labour federations could commit their constituent unions and locals to behaviour inconsistent with the normal processes of collective bargaining? Can Ottawa commit the other levels of government?—although in this "estate" there are devices for securing compliance with national decisions more powerful than in the other two. According to the published record of the Prices and Incomes Commission, only the Canadian Bankers Association of all the national economic groups was able to make specific commitments on restraint; such others as the Retail Council of Canada, the Canadian Chamber of Commerce and the Canadian Manufacturers' Association could only suggest certain actions to their members. However, the CBA appears almost unique in Canada with a pattern of internal relations and of relations with government being set on corporatist lines in a period prior to the establishment of a Canadian central bank.

As in other aspects of Canadian life, the characteristic national institution in the economic sphere is a "congress", a "federation" or an "association." The nomenclature is significant. These organizations have varying capacities to articulate the common interests of their members and to press these interests on government and other elements of the community. But in their present forms they are clearly incapable of effecting important distributions *among* their constituent elements or of directing these elements towards action not in the latter's immediate interests. For example, one of the major macroeconomic decisions a Canadian Council of Government, Industry and Labour would need to take would be the distribution of the gains in per capita productivity among profits, wages, lower prices and taxes. Even if it were possible to make this global distribution is it conceivable that the national labour bodies could divide up this reward among their constituents, including most importantly those elements where high productivity gains occurred and other unions and locals of unions? Similar considerations would of course prevail among the other estates.

Canada in short is not Sweden or Holland, and the attainment of corporatism will require a radical restructuring of power which can be effected only by the ruthless action of Ottawa itself. Federalism, at least in the form we have come to know it, will clearly have to go. And even more crucially, the present capacity of business corporations and labour unions—and associations of these institutions—to press their own interests within the law will be superseded by their incorporation into the apparatus of the corporatist state.

In my scale of values, the plebiscitary alternative is by a wide measure preferable to corporatism. Inflation and measures to control inflation polarize the community, and because the incidence of both is complex, it is likely that there will be new cleavages which are impossible to manage without vastly increasing the proportion of coercion as against consent in the governing of Canadians. But with all this, plebiscitarianism leaves relatively autonomous institutions of political and economic power in place.

The context of the current anti-inflation policy cannot be understood without some reference to the personality and the characteristic ways of behaviour of Mr. Trudeau. Prior to deciding on a settled course of action the Prime Minister is a cautious and sometimes even a vacillating man. But once a commitment to action is made—as he demonstrated in his decision to contest the leadership of the Liberal party and his conduct in the October crisis—he proceeds with vigor and even ruthlessness. Mr. Trudeau is undoubtedly aware that prices and incomes policies in other western nations have been on the whole unsuccessful. His response appears to be that these failures have resulted from such policies having not been applied comprehensively or ruthlessly enough and he is determined that Canadian efforts will not suffer these deficiencies.

In his recent utterances on anti-inflation policies, the Prime Minister on occasion after occasion has asserted that Canadians must find a new set of values. Is Mr. Trudeau simply giving voice to the banal view that we have pushed our individual and group avariciousness too far? The Cheveldayoff article suggests that there is something more to it than that, that we are being prepared for corporatism. For myself, I become worried when politicians begin talking about values in any other way than enunciating the "motherhood" commitments of the community; Harold Macmillan showed much good sense when being questioned about values by responding that the person should go to see his archbishop rather than his prime minister, and a strong case can be made that in a free society the repository of the highest values will remain those without coercive power—the priests and professors and poets and playwrights. But to what values does the Prime Minister refer? More than a generation ago Sinclair Lewis asserted that if fascism came to the United States it would do so in the name of anti-fascism. The Canadian euphemism is to be "co-determination" or perhaps in more Orwellian language "Liberalism". A very few years ago Mr. Trudeau's spear-carriers in the intellectual and journalistic communities conferred on him an exaggerated reputation for philosophical acuteness on the basis of his reiteration of the trite but true proposition that a free society required autonomous sources of countervailing power. But where are the Trudeauvian "counterweights" in the new regime for which we are being ideologically conditioned?

Notes

*Smiley, D. V., "The Non-Economics of Anti-Inflation," *The Canadian Forum*, March, 1976 (reproduced by permission of author and publisher).

45 Reflections on the Economy *

Prime Minister P. E. Trudeau

The most pressing reality is inflation. The most urgent national need is for all of us to co-operate in making sure that our anti-inflation program works.

An essential part of the program is the search for ways to make the economy work better in the future, when the program is ended—ways which will prevent a serious recurrence of inflation, promote healthy growth, reduce unemployment, and reduce the need for imposed controls.

If we are seriously interested in adapting our economic system to our present and future needs, it would be helpful if we could agree on the nature of the system we have now. The free market system, in the true sense of that phrase, does not exist in Canada. I have said that we haven't been able to make even a modified free market system work in Canada to prevent the kinds of problems we are now experiencing; and that it will do no good to try to create a pure free market economy to solve our future problems, because that won't work either.

For that, much public comment has accused me of wanting to kill free enterprise and substitute a system of state control over all economic decisions. That is a phony issue, because in the year-end interview which stimulated this controversy, I made absolutely no mention of free enterprise. I spoke about the free market. There is a difference.

The fact is that for over 100 years, since the Government stimulated the building of the Canadian Pacific Railway by giving it Crown land, we have not had a free market economy in Canada, but a mixed economy—a mixture of private enterprise and public enterprise. It is precisely because it has been a mixture that we have had the prosperity we have enjoyed.

Until I heard the shrill comments made by some businessmen during the past few weeks, I had thought that the great depression of the nineteen thirties had destroyed forever the notion that a free market economy, if unassisted by governments, would produce by itself the ideal state of steady economic growth, stable prices and full employment.

The Depression convinced most people of the necessity of Government intervention on a broad front, in the interests of overall economic stability.

It was also recognized that governments had to intervene in the economy to redistribute income, for example, and to make sure that private industry acted in the public interest.

Every reasonable person now recognizes the duty of the federal Government to manage the country's economy in the interests of all its people and all its regions. That duty carries with it the consequent responsibility to intervene when necessary to stimulate employment, to redistribute income, to control inflation and pollution, to protect the consumer, to promote conservation, productivity, and an adequate supply of the things we need.

But, nonetheless, there remain very large sectors of the economy where the free market and consumer choice continue to flourish. A wide variety of choices are offered by, for example, the retail sales industry, the travel and service industries, the clothing industry, and by many thousands of small contractors and independent manufacturers.

And there is no desire on the part of the Government or the people of Canada to impose more regulation on the truly competitive sectors of the economy—on the small business sector, for example, where free enterprise is strong, where individual initiative, independence and risk-taking are present, where self-reliant men and women continue to build a better life for themselves and their communities by investing their time, their capital and their abilities in ways which add to the strength of Canada and its people.

The preservation and strengthening of the free market sector of our economy is absolutely central to the Liberal view of the Canada of the future. That is why we reject socialism, which seeks ever greater Government ownership and control of the production and marketing of goods; and that is also why we reject corporatism or statism, which seeks to have all important economic decisions made by a formal partnership of big business, big labor and big government.

That is also why, in the last session of Parliament, the Government introduced the Competition Act, which will protect the public interest by discouraging anti-competitive behavior; and why we created the Small Business Development Bank, which will give greater support and encouragement to the many thousands of small businessmen in Canada.

We have a mixed economy which, in the way it has evolved, has served us very well in the past, and is uniquely suited to Canadian beliefs and values. However, it is not serving us adequately right now, as the gravity of our problems clearly demonstrates. The economy is out of joint, and will get worse if we don't do something about it.

But the issue is not whether to throw out our present system and substitute something entirely different. The issue is whether we are prepared to adjust the system, through changes in legislation, institutions and attitudes, so that it will help us to meet the challenges of the present and the future.

The most obvious challenge is that the Canadian economy and the economies of the other free nations of the world are experiencing very serious rates of inflation and unemployment at the same time.

Some would have you believe that the federal Government has caused these problems all by itself by excessive increases in the money supply, excessive spending, and excessive interference in the marketplace. This, too, is a phony issue. If our policies alone were to blame, why is it that every industrialized country in the free world is in the same difficulty?

Why is it that, with a badly battered world economy, Canada is still performing better than most? It is estimated that our growth rate last year, although close to zero, was still among the top three of the 10 leading countries of the free world. This year it is estimated that our growth rate will be second only to that of the United States.

Canada's economic achievements clearly result from the combined efforts of the private and public sectors. When things go well, we both deserve to share the credit. When they don't, we both deserve to share the blame.

So let's stop wasting our time looking for villains. Let's get on with the job of finding better ways to build a better future.

The number one priority, obviously, is to find better ways to prevent the unacceptably high rates of inflation and unemployment which we now have.

In previous economic cycles, these problems usually surfaced alternately. When unemployment was the major problem, we were able to attack it by stimulating demand for goods and services, thereby stimulating production and creating more jobs.

When inflation then became the major problem, we were able to keep it within reasonable bounds by reducing demand. The goal, always elusive, but always thought attainable, was the creation of price and employment stability within the context of steady growth, through the use of conventional economic instruments.

Those conventional instruments aren't working as well as they used to. The Economic Council of Canada commented recently that "in view of the gravity of the problem, there is a need for other techniques to complement traditional policies."

The inadequacy of conventional techniques is the principal reason why the Government had to intervene in the economy so drastically in October with the imposition of income and price controls. The control period will not only help us to reduce the rate of inflation but will also give us the necessary time to reform our economic institutions, our attitudes and public policies. The nature of that reform is the subject of the debate in which we are now engaged.

The gravity of the problem is not defined by inflation and unemployment alone. There is also a need for structural and rather basic changes in the way we seek to ensure an adequate and reliable supply of the energy and food which are needed in increasing volume by ourselves and the people of other nations.

We need better ways to control pollution and urban congestion, to reduce the human and dollar cost of traffic accidents—better means of improving the lives of low-income families, improving labor-management relations, balancing the competing power of big business, big labor, and big government.

We have yet to achieve a proper balance between the public interest and the growing size and power of some corporations and some labor unions.

A very high priority for this country must be to find a way to settle labor-management disputes with justice, while at the same time avoiding the enormous loss of productivity which strikes are now causing.

The size of governments at all levels, and the impact of their size upon national productivity, cannot escape the spotlight of re-examination.

I believe all Canadians want their governments to have an adequate strength and power to protect the public interest; and that therefore the legislative and regulatory aspects of government activity might well have to increase in the future.

But I see no intrinsic reason why governments should stay forever in the business of providing some services which could be provided by the private sector.

In that context, the issue before us is to what extent we will be controlled by Government regulation, and to what extent we will be controlled by our own sense of responsibility. I think we all favor as little of the former and as much of the latter as is humanly possible.

Government, too, has to act more responsibly; and part of its responsibility is to learn to say "no" more often and more effectively, just as it is part of the responsibility of the citizen to restrain his demands for new grants or improved public services which the nation cannot afford.

If we want or need to spend more in one area of the economy, we'll have to spend less in others. Hindsight permits the judgment that governments over the past 20 years have not insisted strongly enough on such a trade-off—have not insisted that if people demand and receive benefits like higher pensions and medical insurance, for example, we must all pay the cost by accepting either a lower level of services in other areas or, alternatively, a slower rate of increase in our individual standard of living.

If we all prefer to act from free choice rather than coercion, to accept responsibility rather than endure Government regulation, then I would expect the unions and corporations, for example, to tell us how they propose to restore peace and stability to the collective bargaining process when the control period is over, and how they propose to start right now to work in that direction.

Some extreme free enterprisers have suggested that our best hope for the future lies in the creation of a true free market economy, a market system designed according to economists' models of perfect competition. I believe they are wrong.

Such a system would involve, for example, the breaking up of some of our giant corporations and unions. Do we really want that, even if we could?

Before you say "yes", ask yourself how Canada could be largely self-sufficient in steel, for example, if we didn't have some very large steel companies capable of amassing the enormous amount of capital needed for the job, the sophisticated technology, the managerial experience and skilled labor force.

We need some large corporations, because of their efficiency, because of their unique ability to do the jobs that need to be done, because of their ability to sustain and increase our export trade.

The problem is not the existence of monopolies or quasi-monopolies in certain sectors of our economy. The problem is how to ensure that their power is used in the public interest, and is directed toward the achievement of national goals.

I would ask the executives of corporations whether they are prepared to accept the social consequences of their decisions. When an industry causes pollution, for example, is it the industry's responsibility to clear it up, and prevent it from happening again? Or is that the Government's responsibility?

If the latter, how is it to be done without increasing Government spending and regulatory power, to both of which the private sector takes strong objection?

I would ask private industry whether it is prepared to act voluntarily to distribute economic opportunity more equitably across the nation, through decisions on plant location, and whether it is prepared to encourage energy conservation.

For example, will the automobile industry decide to produce cars which achieve better mileage per gallon of gas, or will the Government have to force that decision through greater control of the industry? The job must be done. Who will do it?

I would ask the trade union movement what steps it is prepared to take to ensure a better balance between wages and productivity, and thus help to reduce the rate of inflation.

There can be no debate about whether Canadian consumers should waste less food and energy. It must be done. How will it be done? Through individual responsible decisions, or through Government control?

What I am attempting to demonstrate is that Canada faces enormous challenges in the years ahead, and that our ability to meet these challenges will depend primarily on our willingness to adapt out attitudes and habits to the facts of life.

Our greatest hope lies not in new laws or greater use of the power of the state, but in ourselves, in the capacity of each of us to adopt different social and economic values in response to the new reality of our times.

The action has begun. We have introduced an anti-inflation program which will give us the time to make choices. We have a breathing space which will enable us to rethink our ways of doing things, while the income and price controls prevent us from further indulgence in self-damaging activity.

The Government, too, has a responsibility to use the next few years to help bring about, in discussion with Parliament and the people, the social and economic reforms which will enable Canada to emerge from the control period with a renewed sense of purpose and confidence.

The Government is continuing to define its specific policy options, in developing alternative ways of attacking such problems as industrial and regional growth, the price and supply of energy, labor-management relations, international economic relations, food policy, income distribution among individual Canadians and among regions of Canada, and the relationship between Government and the private sector.

In attacking these problems as Liberals, our strong preference is to find solutions which give people the incentive to decide freely to do what must be done—rather than solutions which impose penalties on those who act irresponsibly.

This is a time for wisdom, for self-discipline and co-operation. We have the opportunity to enjoy the most valuable gift of a free society, the right to make our own choices about our own future. This is also a time for hope.

I am full of confidence that a people whose forebears created this nation out of the wilderness, a people who have overcome the severe trials of a great depression and two world wars, a people who have united to build one of the world's great democracies, will unite once again to meet the present economic challenge in a manner worthy of those who will inherit from us this fortunate land.

Notes

*Extracts from notes for Prime Minister Pierre Trudeau's address 19 Jan. '76 to the Canadian Club in Ottawa. Some minor changes were made in delivery, but these did not alter the tone or general substance (reproduced by permission).